REMEDIES IN THE EMPLOYMENT TRIBUNAL

AUSTRALIA
LBC Information Services—Sydney

CANADA AND USA
Carswell—Toronto

NEW ZEALAND
Brooker's—Auckland

SINGAPORE AND MALAYSIA
Thomson Information (S.E. Asia)—Singapore

REMEDIES IN THE EMPLOYMENT TRIBUNAL

DAMAGES FOR DISCRIMINATION AND UNFAIR DISMISSAL

By

Norman Lamb

LONDON
SWEET & MAXWELL
1998

Published in 1998 by
Sweet & Maxwell Limited
100 Avenue Road
London NW3 3PF

Phototypeset by Selwood Systems Limited, Midsomer Norton

Printed and bound in Great Britain
by Butler and Tanner Ltd, Frome and London

No natural forests were destroyed
to make this product, only farmed
timber was used and re-planted.

ISBN 0421 594004

A CIP catalogue record for this book
is available from The British Library.

Acknowledgements

I would like to express my enormous appreciation to Rita Stewart for her contribution to this book. She had a remarkable ability for deciphering so much hand-written material very accurately. Her capacity to churn out the text at such a rate constantly amazed me. Her willingness to stick with it and keep to tight deadlines was extraordinary. Heartfelt thanks. Thanks also to my family: Mary and sons Archie and Ned; Mary for doing more work on the keyboard and Archie and Ned for their patience in foregoing shooting practice on the football pitch and much else because of my long absences in the University of East Anglia library. I must also record my appreciation to my partners at Steele & Co for enabling me to develop our employment unit and for then being prepared to allow me to write this book. Finally, thanks to Sally Brock at Steele & Co for all her invaluable background work.

Grateful acknowledgement is made to the following authors and publishers for their permission to quote from their works:

The Automobile Association: Vehicle running costs (1997). Reprinted by permission of the Automobile Association

The Institute of Chartered Accountants in England and Wales: Technical Release TR851 (November 1991), Technical Release TR830 (April 1991). Reprinted by permission of the Institute of Chartered Accountants in England and Wales

The Law Society Gazette: extracts from the Law Society Gazette dated 3 November 1993 and Nelson Jones table, dated 24 September 1998. Reprinted by permission of the Law Society Gazette

RAC Motoring Services: Vehicle running costs (1998). Reprinted by permission of RAC Motoring Services

Preface

I was asked to write this book after having chaired the Armed Forces Pregnancy Dismissal Group. This was a co-ordinating organisation for lawyers and other advisors pursuing claims against the Ministry of Defence on behalf of women who had been unlawfully discharged on becoming pregnant. Most of these claims were heard in the aftermath of the lifting of the lid on compensation for unlawful sex discrimination. For the first time tribunals were faced with substantial claims. Several well publicised awards totalling, in some cases, £200,000–£300,000 followed. Practitioners and tribunals were having to grapple with claims for compensation for loss suffered over several years.

The lifting of the lid on compensation necessarily resulted in a much sharper focus on the assessment of compensation. For example, it has become essential to understand how the principles of mitigation will be applied by tribunals in the employment context. Also, the possibility of substantial settlements and tribunal awards has meant that the tribunal practitioner also needs to have an understanding of tax law as it relates to termination and compensation payments. Although, at the time of going to press, compensation for unfair dismissal is still capped at £12,000, the Government's *Fairness at Work* White Paper has raised the spectre of that cap also being lifted.

Having learnt so much by handling the pregnancy dismissal claims, my aim in writing this book has been to provide a practical guide for the busy practitioner. The text is written particularly as an aid for anyone representing or assisting someone pursuing a claim to the tribunal. It takes the reader through all the stages of preparing a claim for compensation, stressing the importance of starting early in the gathering of information in order to maximise the sum recovered. Checklists are included to assist in gathering together essential documents and information.

There is also guidance to assist in determining how the loss of benefits will be compensated and what costs incurred can be recovered. There is then commentary on using the tribunal's powers to force your opponent to provide information and documents to assist in calculating loss accurately. Precedent schedules of loss are included. Then comes a section to assist in the settlement of a claim with guidance on the tax treatment of termination payments. Important source documents on tax and pension loss are included in appendices.

Guidance is also given on preparing for a remedy hearing in the tribunal. Then the text moves on to examine the powers of the tribunal in assessing compensation for first unfair dismissal, then unlawful discrimination, including a case digest on awards for injury to feelings, and then commentary on awards for claims which can be made in respect of rights during employment.

Dedicated chapters also consider compensation for pension loss, the law on mitigation and the powers of the tribunal to award costs. The tribunal's extended jurisdiction to hear contractual claims is also covered, including practical guidance on choosing between the tribunal and the county or high court as the venue to pursue such a claim. Finally, consideration is given to the likely impact of the proposals relating to compensation contained in the Government's *Fairness at Work* White Paper.

In a nutshell, the text seeks to provide comprehensive practical guidance to help ensure that full compensation is recovered and a commentary on the full range of remedies available in the tribunal. In terms of style, I have tried to include as much cross-referencing as possible, to guide the reader speedily around the text.

Norman Lamb
October 1998

Table of Contents

Appendices

Table of Cases

Table of Statutes

Table of Statutory Instruments

CHAPTER 1

Introduction

1–01 In any litigation, when representing the applicant or plaintiff, it is easy to fall into the trap of focusing primarily on proving liability without giving sufficient attention to the remedies available. This is, perhaps, particularly true in the Employment Tribunal where the statutory cap on compensation artificially suppressed awards of compensation for loss suffered in both unfair dismissal and discrimination cases. Equally, tribunals have in the past tended towards caution in making awards for compensation for injury to feelings in discrimination cases. See, for example, the case of *North West Thames Regional Health Authority v. Noone* [1988] I.R.L.R. 195. Here the Court of Appeal reduced the tribunal's award for injury to feelings from £5,000 to £3,000. Clearly the maximum compensation at that time of £7,500 affected the Court of Appeal's thinking: "I have to bear in mind the maximum compensation that could have been awarded, which might well have included matters other than injury to feelings, was £7,500" (Balcombe L.J.). However, the European Court then ruled that the cap on compensation in sex discrimination cases was unlawful (see *Marshall v. Southampton and South West Hampshire Area Health Authority (No.2)* [1993] I.R.L.R. 445 ECJ). Compensation had to be full and realistic in order to meet the requirements of the Equal Treatment Directive 76/207/EEC.

1–02 In order to ensure parity between the treatment of sex and race discrimination cases the statutory maximum was lifted for both types of discrimination. This has now been followed by the Disability Discrimination Act which provides for similarly uncapped compensation for someone found to have suffered unlawful discrimination. With the cap removed in discrimination cases there has come a renewed focus on the law of compensation because now the stakes can be so much higher. The litigation pursued by women unlawfully discharged from the armed forces because of pregnancy provided the first opportunities in the tribunal following the lifting of the cap to claim substantial awards of compensation for loss suffered. The claims received much publicity with a number of women receiving awards of over £200,000.

1–03 Now the Government proposes the removal of the statutory maximum for compensation for unfair dismissal (see "Fairness at Work" White Paper). Along with these developments, there has been a substantial growth in the number and range of rights employees enjoy in the workplace. Many of these rights are given teeth by allowing the employee to seek compensation in the tribunal for breach of such a right or if the employee suffers some sort of detriment at the hands of his employer. This book is designed as a practical guide for the advisor on the remedies available in the tribunal. It covers all the essential steps from first taking instructions, preparing a schedule of loss through to the stage at which remedy is determined by the tribunal.

1–04 In order to maximise the compensation which may be awarded it is essential to start the process of assessing loss and, in a discrimination case, building the case for compensation for injury to feelings, from the point at which you first take instructions. Checklists are provided to aid the busy practitioner together with examples of applications to the tribunal seeking orders for discovery, further and better particulars and interrogatories on issues relating to calculation of loss. Various important source materials are also included for ease of reference. The text includes important guidance on the law of mitigation, tax rules on termination payments, guidance on negotiating a settlement and compromise agreements.

CHAPTER 2
The Employment Tribunal's Jurisdiction

SCHEDULE OF COMPENSATION AWARDS AND REMEDIES

2–01   The powers of the employment tribunal derive from statute. The tribunal has jurisdiction to consider a vast number of claims and to order a wide variety of remedies. Set out overleaf is a schedule of the powers of the tribunal to award compensation together with cross references to commentary in the text on the powers available.

Compensation in the Industrial Tribunal
Checklist of Powers to award Compensation

Claim	Statutory Provision	Limits on Compensation	Where to find commentary
Unfair Dismissal	ss.111–134 ERA		
Basic Award	ss.118–122 and 227(1)(a) ERA	Maximum week's pay £220 Maximum basic award 30 × £220 = £6,600	Chapter 9
Minimum Basic Award (Special Cases) *See also T.U. dismissal	s.120 ERA	£2,900	Chapter 9
Compensatory Award	ss.118 and 123, 124 ERA	£12,000	Chapter 10
Additional Award	s.117 (3)(b) & s.117(5) & (6) s.117(4) and s.227(1)(b)	13–26 weeks' pay (£2,860–£15,720) 26–52 weeks' pay (£5,720–£11,440) (based on max week's pay of £220)	Chapter 8
Special Award	s.118(e) & s.125 ERA T.U. cases s.157–158 TULR(C)A	104 weeks pay or £14,500 whichever is greater (no limit on week's pay) Upper limit of £29,000 (or 156 weeks' pay or £21,800 whichever is greater)—if refusal to comply with re-employment—no maximum	Chapter 8
Reinstatement	ss.113 & 114 & s.116 ERA	No limit for loss up to reinstatement	Chapter 8
Re-engagement	ss.113, 115 & s.116 ERA	No limit for loss up to reinstatement	Chapter 8
Interest on late payment	Industrial Tribunals (Interest) Order 1990; SI 1990 No. 479	Currently calculated at 8%	Chapter 18

Claim	Statutory Provision	Limits on Compensation	Where to find commentary
Unfair Dismissal			
T.U. activities or membership	s.152–s.160 TULR(C)A		
Compensatory Award	s.124 ERA	£12,000	Chapter 10
Minimum Basic Award	s.156 TULR(C)A	Current minimum = £2,900	Chapter 9
Awards against Third Parties	s.160 TULR(C)A		
Application for Interim Relief	s.161–s.167 TULR(C)A and s.128–s.132 ERA		Chapter 12
Sex Discrimination			
Financial Loss	s.65 SDA & Equal Treatment Directive (ETD)	No limit	Chapter 13
Injury to feelings	s.66(4) SDA	No limit	Chapter 13
Interest	Industrial Tribunals (Interest on Awards in Discrimination Cases) Regs 1996, (SI 1996 No.2803)	Currently calculated at 8%	Chapter 13
Equal Pay	Equal Pay Act 1970	2 years arrears of pay or damages (but note challenge to this provision)	Chapter 13

Claim	Statutory Provision	Limits on Compensation	Where to find commentary
Race Discrimination			
Financial Loss	s.56 & 57 RRA	No limit	Chapter 13
Injury to feelings	s.57(4) RRA; s.56(5) RRA	No limit	Chapter 13
Interest	Industrial Tribunals (Interest on Awards in Discrimination Cases) Regs 1996, Reg 8	Currently calcuated at 8%	Chapter 13
Disability Discrimination			
Financial Loss	s.8 DDA Enforcement, remedies, procedure	No limit	Chapter 13
Injury to feelings	s.8(4) DDA	No limit	Chapter 13
Interest	s.8(6) + Tribunal (Interest on Awards in Discrimination Cases) Regs 1996	Currently calculated at 8%	Chapter 13

Claim	Statutory Provision	Limits on Compensation	Where to find commentary
Redundancy Payment	s.135 ERA Right to redundancy pay s.145 ERA Relevant date s.148–154 ERA Eligibilities by reason of lay-off or short-time s.155 ERA Qualifying period s.156 ERA Upper age limit s.157 ERA Exemption orders s.158 ERA Pension rights s.159 ERA Public offices s.160 ERA Overseas government employment s.161 ERA Domestic servants s.162 ERA Amount of redundancy payment s.163–s.164 ERA Reference to Tribunal claiming redundancy payment s.165 ERA Written statement of amount	Maximum week's pay £220 Maximum redundancy payment $= 30 \times £220 = £6,600$	Chapter 21

Claim	Statutory Provision	Limits on Compensation	Where to find commentary
Detriment in Employment			
Health and Safety cases	s.44 ERA; s.48 Complaint to tribunal s.49 ERA Remedies	No limit Financial loss and injury to feelings Just and equitable test having regard to infringement and loss	Chapter 22
Sunday working for shop and betting workers	s.45 ERA, s.48 Complaint to tribunal s.49 ERA Remedies		Chapter 22
Working Time Regulation cases	s.45A ERA, s.48 Complaint to tribunal s.49 ERA Remedies		Chapter 22
Trustees of occupational pension schemes	s.46 ERA, s.48 Complaint to tribunal s.49 Remedies		Chapter 22
Employee representatives	s.47 ERA, s.48 Complaint to tribunal s.49 ERA Remedies		Chapter 22
Action Short of Dismissal			
Trade Union membership or activities	s.146 TULR(C)A Rights s.146(5) Complaint to Tribunal s.147 Time limit s.148 Consideration of complaint s.149 Remedies s.150 Awards against third parties s.151 Interpretation	No limit Financial loss and injury to feelings Just and equitable test having regard to infringement and loss	Chapter 22
Claims to Secretary of State —sums due by employer	s.166–s.170 ERA		N/A

Claim	Statutory Provision	Limits on Compensation	Where to find commentary
Guarantee Payments	s.28 ERA Entitlement s.29–s.33 Supplementary s.34 Complaint to Tribunal	Amount of guarantee payment due Based on week's pay but shall not exceed £15.35 in respect of any day	Chapter 22
Protective Awards, Collective Redundancies Failure to properly consult or provide information	s.188 TULR(C)A Duty to consult etc s.189 TULR(C)A 92 Complaint to Tribunal s.190 Entitlement under protective award s.191 Termination of employment during protected period s.192 Complaint to Tribunal	Just and equitable test—having regard to seriousness of employer's default Up to 90 days pay if proposal for >100 employees redundant within 90 days If >20 but <100 employees in 90 day period—30 days pay Based on week's pay	Chapter 22
Transfer of Undertaking Failure to property consult, provide information	Reg 10 TUPE 1981 Duty to inform and consult Reg 11 TUPE 1981 Failure to inform and consult—complaint to Tribunal	<4 weeks pay—regard to seriousness of employer's default	Chapter 22
Right not to be unjustifiably disciplined by T.U.	s.64 TULR(C)A s.65 TULR(C)A Meaning of unjustifiably disciplined s.66 TULR(C)A Complaint to tribunal s.67 TULR(C)A Compensation s.67(7) TULR(C)A May be reduced—caused/contributed to by employee s.67(8) TULR(C)A Maximum awards	Just and equitable test 30 × max weeks pay (subject to £220 max) = £6,600 + £12,000 max compensatory award Min of £5,000 if claim heard by EAT (s.67(8))	N/A

Claim	Statutory Provision	Limits on Compensation	Where to find commentary
Time off for T.U. duties			
Officials Members of Trade Union Activities	s.168 TULR(C)A s.169 Payment for time off s.170 TULR(C)A s.171 Time limits s.172 Remedies	Just and equitable having regard to employer's default and loss sustained by employee	Chapter 22
Time off for T.U. activities	ss. 170–173 TULR(C)A	Just and equitable having regard to employer's default and loss sustained by employee	Chapter 22
Right not to be excluded or expelled from T.U.	s.174 TULR(C)A s.175 Time limit s.176(5) TULR(C)A Remedies s.176(5)Power to reduce compensation s.177 Interpretation	Just and equitable 30 × max weeks pay (subject to £220 max) = £6,600 + £12,000 Minimum £5,000 in EAT	N/A

Claim	Statutory Provision	Limits on Compensation	Where to find commentary
Refusal of employment on grounds related to union membership	s.137 TULR(C)A		Chapter 14
Refusal of service of employment agency on grounds related to union membership	s.138 TULR(C)A		
	s.139 TULR(C)A Time limit for above claims		
	s.140(1) TULR(C)A Remedies s.140(2) TULR(C)A s.140(3) TULR(C)A s.140(4) TULR(C)A	Just and equitable May include injury to feelings Possible increase if failure to comply Maximum £12,000	
	s.141 Complaint against employer and employment agency		
	s.142 Awards against third parties		
	s.143 Interpretation		
Time off work for public duties	s.50 ERA	Just and equitable with regard to employer's default and employee's loss	Chapter 22
Complaint to Tribunal	s.51 ERA		
Time off to look for work or arrange training	s.152 ERA		Chapter 22
Right to remuneration for time off under s.52	s.53 ERA s.54 ERA Complaint to tribunal	40% of week's pay (s.54(4) ERA)	Chapter 22

Claim	Statutory Provision	Limits on Compensation	Where to find commentary
Right to time off for ante-natal care	s.55 ERA		Chapter 22
Right to remuneration to time off under s.55	s.56 ERA s.57 ERA Complaint to tribunal	Remuneration due	
Right to time off for pension scheme trustees	s.58 ERA	If not paid for time off—the amount of remuneration due If denied time off—just and equitable having regard to employer's default and employee's loss	Chapter 22
Right to payment for time off for duties under s.58	s.59 ERA s.60 ERA Complaint to tribunal		
Right to time off for representatives of employee safety	Sched 1 and 2 to the Health and Safety (Consultation with Employees) Regulations 1996	If not paid for time off—the amount of remuneration due If denied time off—just and equitable having regard to employer's default and employee's loss	Chapter 22
Right to time off for union safety representatives	Reg 11(3) and Schedule to the Safety Representatives and Safety Committees Regulations 1977	If not paid for time off—the amount of remuneration due If denied time off—just and equitable having regard to employer's default and employee's loss	Chapter 22

Claim	Statutory Provision	Limits on Compensation	Where to find commentary
Employee Representatives	s.61 ERA	If not paid for time off—the amount of remuneration due If denied time off—just and equitable having regard to employer's default and employee's loss	Chapter 22
Right to remuneration for time off for duties under s.61	s.62 ERA s.63 ERA Complaint to tribunal		
Unlawful deductions from wages	s.13, s.14 ERA + s.23-s.26 ERA Enforcement	Amount of unlawful deduction	Chapter 22
Recovering of sums paid to employer	s.15, s.16 + s.23–s.26	Amount of unlawful payment made to employer	
Deductions and payments in retail employment	s.17, s.18, s.19, s.20, s.21, s.22, s.23	Amount of excess of limit of 10% of gross wages (final payment of wages—no such limit)	
Failure to give written reasons	s.92 and s.93 ERA	2 weeks pay	Chapter 22
Breach of contract arising or outstanding on termination of employment	Industrial Tribunal's Extension of Jurisdiction Orders 1994 s.3 Industrial Tribunals Act	Up to £25,000 for all contract claims under contract of employment	Chapter 25
Failure to provide Statement of employment particulars	s.1 ERA Right s.11 ERA Reference to tribunal s.12 ERA Determination of reference	Confirm particulars	Chapter 22
Failure to provide itemised pay statement	s.8 ERA Right s.11 ERA Reference to tribunal s.12 ERA Determination of reference	Repayment of unnotified deductions	Chapter 22

CHAPTER 3
Taking Instructions

3–01 When first taking instructions from a potential complainant in a tribunal claim it is important not just to focus on liability but to properly deal with remedies including compensation. Some steps may need to be taken straight away to properly protect the individual's position. Consider the following:

UNFAIR DISMISSAL CLAIMS: WHICH REMEDY TO PURSUE

3–02 If the complainant is claiming unfair dismissal he needs to decide whether to claim reinstatement or re-engagement on the Application to the Tribunal (ETI). Note that these remedies are not available with a discrimination claim (see paras 8–02 to 8–58 for commentary on reinstatement and re-engagement.) When completing the ETI, the complainant is asked whether he wishes to claim compensation or re-engagement or reinstatement. Such re-employment orders are not frequently made but, if this is the remedy the complainant seeks, he would be wise to claim it at this stage. Note that the complainant can change his mind at any time up to the remedy hearing and seek compensation instead. Note also the tribunal's powers to award extra compensation (additional or special awards see paras 8–39 to 8–61) where re-employment is unsuccessfully requested. Note in particular the rules with regard to the special award at paragraph 8–49. If re-employment has been requested then the special award will be ordered if no order for re-employment is made. See also the powers to reduce the special award (paras 8–60 to 8–61). Also note that inserting a request for re-employment on the ETI puts the employer on notice. This may make it more difficult for the employer to justify appointing a permanent replacement (which is one of the factors the tribunal takes into account in determining whether it is practicable for the employer to re-employ the complainant (see para. 8–12).

INTERIM RE-EMPLOYMENT ORDERS: AUTOMATIC UNFAIR DISMISSAL CASES

3–03 If, on taking instructions, it appears as if the individual may have been dismissed for one of a range of inadmissible reasons which could lead to a finding of automatic unfair dismissal then it is important to consider, straight away, whether he wants to apply for interim relief. This, if successful, has the effect of preventing the dismissal from taking full effect until the full claim is heard by the tribunal. It is possible to make an application for interim relief in the immediate aftermath of dismissal. Urgent action is required. The procedure to follow and the rules on the circumstances in which interim relief may be ordered are explained in Chapter 12.

HAS THE COMPLAINANT LODGED AN INTERNAL APPEAL?

Note the new provisions introduced by the Employment Rights (Dispute Resolution) Act 1998 providing for an increase in compensation if the employer has denied the dismissed employee the chance of using an internal appeals procedure and also giving tribunals the power to reduce compensation if the dismissed employee has himself failed to appeal having been informed of the right (see paras 3–18, 10–10 and 11–01).

IMPORTANCE OF EARLY PREPARATION: CAN A SETTLEMENT BE ACHIEVED?

3–04 There may be an opportunity to achieve a quick settlement. The employer may wish to avoid tribunal proceedings. Consider the following:

1. The employer may recognise or be advised that their position is weak. They may therefore prefer a speedy settlement avoiding costly proceedings and considerable management time. Always explore this.

2. Whatever advice the employer receives on liability, they will be advised that they are unlikely to recover costs from the complainant even if a claim is successfully defended. This consideration may encourage the employer to offer, at least, a "commercial" settlement—a payment which may amount to less than they will incur in defending the claim and which avoids the "cost" of management time. Such an offer, at an early stage, may need to be carefully considered by the complainant but it needs to be assessed in the light of full information about the potential compensation which may be awarded.

3. The complainant needs to assess the extent to which the employer may wish to avoid a tribunal hearing for other reasons. Could press coverage of the proceedings be a concern for the employer? Avoid pursuing claims or including irrelevant issues in an application to the tribunal simply to frighten the employer into settling but recognise that if aspects of the claim could be damaging to the employer, this might increase the prospects for an early settlement.

4. Because the assessment of compensation is a dynamic science and depends to some extent on the actions of the complainant following the event which has given rise to the claim, the complainant must understand the basic rules on remedies available from the start. Compensation, primarily, but not exclusively, depends on loss suffered by the complainant. If he gets new employment quickly, the loss may be very limited. In such circumstance the case for an early settlement may be strong.

5. Should an opportunity for early settlement present itself, the information must be available from which to prepare a full draft schedule of loss. The complainant's position may be considerably strengthened by demonstrating to the employer that proposals for settlement are based on a properly calculated schedule of loss rather than a figure which has been plucked out of thin air.

THE STEPS TO TAKE

3–05   The steps which should be taken at this stage are:

1.   Determining which compensation claims can be pursued.

2.   Information gathering.

3.   Advice to client on how compensation is calculated.

4.   Guidance on essential steps which should be taken by the client.

1. WHICH COMPENSATION CLAIMS CAN BE PURSUED

3–06   It is, of course, important to ensure that all possible claims are pursued in order to maximise properly compensation which can be recovered. A dismissed employee may have a number of different claims which could give rise to compensation awards. Set out below is a checklist of possible claims to consider when taking instructions from a dismissed employee.

1.   *Unfair dismissal.*

2.   *Discrimination: sex, race or disability.*
     Remember to check whether there are any discrimination claims not only in respect of the dismissal itself but also based on events prior to dismissal. Note the three-month time limit for bringing claims from the date of the discriminatory act but remember that "late" claims may be allowed if the tribunal considers that it would be just and equitable to do so (see s.68(6) RRA; s.76(5) SDA; DDA Schedule 3, paragraph 3(2)).

     In *MOD v. Mutton* [1996] I.C.R. 590, Mrs Mutton was unlawfully discharged by the MOD on grounds of pregnancy. However, she had previously decided to have an earlier pregnancy terminated in order to keep her job (the Ministry of Defence at that time had a rule that if a serving woman became pregnant she was automatically discharged. This policy was subsequently accepted as being unlawful because it was contrary to the Equal Treatment Directive.) She therefore pursued two claims: one for injury to feelings resulting from the termination of her first pregnancy and the second for the unlawful discharge which followed her second pregnancy (see also paras 13–63 and 13–122 to 13–125 for commentary on termination of pregnancy cases).

3.   *Possible claim for unlawful deductions from wages s.13 ERA*
     3–07   This includes non payment of wages (*Delaney v. Staples* [1991] 1 All E.R. 609, [1991] I.R.L.R. 112 CA and upheld in House of Lords [1992] 1 All E.R. 944, [1992] I.R.L.R. 191).

     Check whether there has been any non payment of wages.

     Wages include(s. 27 ERA):

     ●   holiday pay

- fees, bonuses, commission*
- Other emoluments from employment
- SSP   Statutory Sick Pay.
- SMP   Statutory Maternity Pay.
- Guarantee pay (s.28 ERA).
- Pay for time off for carrying out T.U. and other duties etc. (s.169 TULR(C) A and Part VI ERA) (see para. 22–35).
- Remuneration on suspension on medical grounds (s.64 ERA) (see paras 22–42 to 22–45).
- Remuneration on suspension on maternity grounds (s.68 ERA). (see paras 22–42 to 22–45).
- Sums payable following order for reinstatement or re-engagement (s.113 ERA). (see paras 8–17 to 8–31).
- Sums payable in pursuance of an order for continuation of contract of employment (s.130 ERA or s.164 TULR(C)A 92) (see para. 12–15.)
- Remuneration under protective award (s.189 ERA).
- Vouchers of fixed monetary value which can be exchanged for money, goods or services.

Excluded payments are:

- Payment by way of advance under a loan agreement or advance of wages.
- Payment of expenses relating to employment.
- Pension payments, allowances or gratuities relating to employment.
- Redundancy payments.
- Other payments made to worker which are unrelated to work.

Note that payments in lieu of notice are not wages for this purpose *Delaney v. Staples* [1992] 1 All E.R. 944 (see Chapter 25—claims for breach of contract).

3–08   Any deductions from any of the payments defined for these purposes as wages will also be recoverable unless they are authorised by the contract of employment, or required by statute (such as PAYE) or if the worker has previously agreed in writing to the deductions being made (see s.13 ERA) (but such an agreement must predate the event giving rise to the deduction—

---

* Commission which the employee was due to receive after the date of dismissal counts as wages provided the sums due and the date they became due were readily identifiable. *Blackstone Franks Investment Management Ltd v. Robertson, The Times*, November 12, 1996 EAT (see also para. 22–61).

The payments need not be payable under the contract of employment. Non payment of, for example, a discretionary commission may be an unlawful deduction. Such a payment amounts to wages for these purposes. This discretionary commission must be regarded as being payable in the reasonable contemplation of the parties (*Kent Management Services Ltd v. Butterfield* [1992] I.R.L.R. 394) (see also para. 22–60).

for example if the employer has loaned money to the employee which he then seeks to recover by way of deduction of the amount due from the final payment of wages this is only permitted if the written signed agreement predated the making of the loan (see *Discount Tobacco and Confectionery Ltd v. Williamson* [1993] I.R.L.R. 327 EAT, for further commentary on unlawful deductions from wages, see paras 22–58 to 22–67).

4. *Entitlement to a statutory redundancy payment (see Chapter 21) or a contractual enhanced redundancy payment*

5. *Possible wrongful dismissal claim.*
   Check whether the employee has received his statutory or contractual notice entitlement or compensation in lieu (see Chapter 25 for commentary on such claims). Note in particular the importance of ensuring that where the employee has been dismissed without notice or sufficient notice (and he is not guilty of gross misconduct) he must be compensated not only for pay due during the notice period but for all other benefits due under the contract for that period. For example, loss of company car, fuel card, accommodation, pension payments etc. (see paras 25–42 to 25–63).

6. *Other pre-existing claims at date of dismissal*
   For example, unlawful action short of dismissal (see paras 22–01 to 22–15). See also Chapter 22 for details of other rights during employment.

7. *Protective Award made or entitlement to a protective award?*
   In a redundancy situation, there may have been a failure to consult or provide information to elected representatives or a recognised trade union. In such circumstances employees made redundant may benefit from a protective award in accordance with s.189 TULR(C)A (see para. 21–28).

8. *Compensation for failure to consult or provide information in connection with transfer of undertakings*
   3–09 If there has been a transfer of an undertaking to which the Transfer of Undertakings (Protection of Employment) Regulations 1981 (S.I. 1981 No.1794) apply, there are duties to consult and provide information to a recognised trade union or other elected representatives of affected employees. Failure to comply with these requirements may give rise to a claim for compensation by the trade union, other elected representatives or the affected employees (see Regulations 10 and 11, Transfer of Undertakings (Protection of Employment) Regulations, 1981) (see para. 21–28).

9. *Compensation for failure to give written reasons for dismissal*
   If the dismissed employee had been employed for two years at the effective date of dismissal (s.92(6) ERA) and the employer has not given written reasons for the dismissal, the employee can request such reasons (s.92 ERA). (This includes circumstances where a fixed term contract expires without being renewed s.92(1)(c) ERA).
   So if, on taking instructions, it is clear that no written reasons have been given the complainant should be advised to request them in writing. You will either get the employer's assertion of the reasons for dismissal or, if he fails to respond adequately, a potential additional two weeks' pay (see Chapter 23).

2. INFORMATION GATHERING

3–10 If the complainant is pursuing a claim for unfair dismissal or is alleging that he has suffered discrimination, he can, of course, claim compensation for net financial loss suffered (see Chapters 8 to 11 for unfair dismissal compensation, and Chapters 13 and 14 for discrimination). The complainant must therefore be able to give the tribunal full detailed information from which financial loss can be calculated. It is useful to use a checklist to assist in ensuring that all the necessary information is obtained. This should only be used as an aide memoire. There may be other possible losses not covered by the checklist which must all be explored. Whether the complainant is claiming unfair dismissal or is pursuing a discrimination claim relating to the termination of employment (or the discriminatory failure to offer employment) a full and careful assessment of the net value of the complainant's remuneration package is essential. Note that the basis for calculating loss for the purposes of determining the compensatory award following a finding of unfair dismissal is set out in section 123 ERA (see Chapter 10).

3–11 The compensatory award "shall be such amount as the tribunal considers just and equitable in all the circumstances having regard to the *loss* sustained by the complainant in consequence of the dismissal in so far as that loss is attributable to action taken by the employer" s.123(1) ERA.

Loss is specifically stated to include

(a)   any expenses reasonably incurred by the complainant in consequence of the dismissal, and

(b)   loss of any benefit which he might reasonably be expected to have had but for the dismissal.

Therefore the four heads of loss coming within the compensatory award for unfair dismissal are:

(1)   Immediate loss of earnings, *i.e.* loss of earnings between dismissal and remedy hearing.

(2)   Future loss: for period following hearing.

(3)   Loss of statutory employment protection rights.

(4)   Loss of pension rights.

3–12 Compensation in discrimination cases is based on the measure of damages in tort (see para. 13–24). Exactly the same information with regard to the total net remuneration package is required as with an unfair dismissal claim. Note however that consideration also needs to be given at this stage to the possible claim for compensation for injury to feelings (see paras 13–96 to 13–183).

Remember that the tribunal's task will be to compensate the complainant for loss suffered during the period *following dismissal*. The essential question is: what would the complainant have received in pay/benefits, etc., had he *not* been dismissed? Therefore if overtime is unusually high for other staff for the period following dismissal (and not simply because the complainant has been dismissed and they are therefore short staffed) then this must be taken into account.

Similarly, pay increases which the complainant would have received but for the dismissal should be taken into account. If the tribunal concludes that a pay increase was possible, but not certain, the tribunal can assess the chance that this would have occurred and apply a percentage reduction to the value of that increased pay (*York Trailer Co. Ltd v. Sparkes* [1973] I.C.R. 518 NIRC) (see also para. 13–75 for commentary on use of the percentage chance approach in discrimination cases). The complainant may also have lost the chance of qualifying for "service pay"—an additional payment based on length of service.

Basic Award: unfair dismissal

3–13 In order to calculate the basic award in a unfair dismissal claim, full details of the contractual week's pay must be gathered. Whereas the compensatory award can compensate for financial loss, whether contractual or discretionary, and can include compensation for loss of "payments in kind", the basic award is limited to contractual remuneration (see Chapter 9 for commentary on the basic award and Chapter 24 for commentary on calculation of a week's pay).

Documentary Evidence

3–14 As part of the information gathering exercise make sure you obtain all relevant documentation detailing the complainant's entitlement to pay and benefits. Get copies of all relevant documents in the complainant's possession and identify all those documents which may exist but which the complainant does not have access to. (see Chapter 4 for commentary on obtaining necessary documents using the powers of the tribunal). Set out below is a checklist of relevant documents.

Checklist:

1. Wage slips (obtain as many as possible over last year to show fluctuations in pay, etc.).

2. Statement of main terms/contract of employment/offer letter.

3. Any additional employee handbook detailing benefits, bonuses, etc.

4. Correspondence/memos, etc., detailing payment of bonuses or relating to any other benefits.

5. Pension handbook and any other associated documents.

6. Car policy documents.

7. Any other documents detailing the employer's policy on payment of any benefits.

8. Records of overtime worked by complainant and by other comparable employees since complainant's dismissal (this is unlikely to be available from the complainant at this stage but may be important to obtain from the employer)

What pay and benefits did the complainant receive?

3–15 Set out below is a checklist for use in this information gathering exercise.

Checklist:

1. Salary / wage rate / details of annual pay review. (remember to check whether the complainant believes he would have received a pay increase had he not been dismissed)

2. Overtime rates.

3. Overtime worked over last 12 months.

4. Seasonal fluctuations in overtime available.

5. Profit related pay

6. Bonus entitlement and any entitlement to "service pay" based on length of service

   Contractual or discretionary?
   Basis of calculation of bonus.

7. Particularly if discretionary, how much bonus has been paid over the last 12 months?

8. *Other benefits*:
   Medical Insurance:

   for example, BUPA
   PPP
   Norwich Union

   Permanent Health Insurance
   Pension / Life Insurance

   If Final Salary Scheme, obtain details of:

   a) deferred pension entitlement
   b) employer's contributions to fund

   If Money Purchase Scheme, check employer contribution rate—see payslip.
   Legal Insurance
   Luncheon Vouchers
   Shares / Share Options / Profit Sharing

   Reward schemes
   Details of value
   Number of shares owned

   Tips from customers
   Telephone rental paid?
   Private telephone calls paid?
   Mobile phone
   Car

   Type
   c.c.
   Employer's mileage rates
   Registration
   Purchase price
   Private mileage paid?

Diesel / petrol

Subsidised benefits

Cheaper mortgage
Purchase of company product at discount
Travel vouchers
Travel paid by employer
Discount schemes
Membership of health club/social/sports club
Accommodation (free or subsidised)
Loans at no or low rates of interest
Meals
Expenses reimbursed: Do these reflect actual expenses incurred or is there a profit element? (See para. 3–36)

Any entitlement to enhanced redundancy payment under contract of employment (see *Lee v. IPC Business Press Ltd* [1984] I.C.R. 306 EAT—by being unfairly dismissed he had lost benefit of that enhanced payment.)

(See also case digest at paras 3–32 to 3–47 for benefits claimable). There may also be a regular practice of making enhanced payments on redundancy. Such payments may become a contractual entitlement by custom and practice. Even if they are discretionary, the loss of the expectation of such a payment may be taken into account in the assessment of compensation (see para. 3–41).

9.   Note information for basic award (Unfair dismissal):
Age
Salary/Wage
Other contractual bonuses/allowances
Start Date—taking into account any continuity of employment from former employer. For example if there has been a transfer of an undertaking (TUPE Regs). (See Chapter 9 for commentary on the basic award).

Other information to obtain from complainant

Payments on termination of employment

3–16 Check what, if any, payments have been made on termination of employment. It may be important to identify the nature of any such payment. Chapter 15 for commentary on treatment of such payments in assessing compensation.

Gathering evidence to resist attempts to reduce compensation

3–17 In the unfair dismissal context, consider the extent to which the complainant may be vulnerable to arguments from the employer that some sort of misconduct or other culpable behaviour by the complainant prior to dismissal (whether or not connected to the dismissal) should lead to the tribunal reducing compensation (see Chapter 11 for the tribunal's powers to reduce the compensatory award, paras 9–20 to 9–35 in respect of reduction of the basic award and paras 8–56 to 8–61 in respect of the special award).

In discrimination claims consider rules on possible percentage reductions to compensation (see paras 13–58 to 13–76) and gather evidence which may counter arguments for such reductions.

Internal Appeal

3–18 Check whether the complainant has pursued an internal appeal against dismissal. Note the new rules under the Employment Rights (Disputes Resolution) Act 1998 (applying to dismissals on or after January 1, 1999) providing for the reduction of compensation if an internal appeal procedure has been provided and the employee has been given written notification of it but has not used it. Consider whether to advise the complainant to appeal if he has not already done so. There are also powers to increase compensation by up to two weeks' pay if the employee has been denied the chance of pursuing the internal appeals procedure (see paras 10–10 and 11–01 for further commentary).

Check Outstanding Contractual Entitlement

3–19 Has the employer paid all outstanding contractual entitlements to date of dismissal such as:

- Accrued holiday pay (check contract of employment for entitlement on termination of employment)
- All bonuses/profit related pay etc. up to termination of employment
- Commission payments for the period prior to dismissal

(See paras 22–58 to 22–66 for commentary on remedy for unlawful deductions from wages).

In circumstances where the complainant has been dismissed without notice, unless the employer can establish that the complainant was guilty of gross misconduct he will be entitled to compensation for all contractual entitlements during notice period. If pursuing a claim for unfair dismissal or discrimination also consider claiming compensation for breach of contract. Such compensation cannot, for example, be reduced for contributory fault in the same way as the compensatory award can be. Remember compensation for the notice period includes not only net pay in lieu of notice but compensation for the net value of all other benefits. Note that unless the contract provides otherwise, holiday entitlement would have accrued during the notice period and the complainant can be compensated for this.

Example

An employee is entitled to 20 days holiday per year. He is entitled to contractual notice of one month. He is dismissed without notice. Had he received his contractual notice he would have accrued an additional 1.66 days holiday in that month. This should be included in a claim for breach of contract if it has not already been paid.

Assessing lost pay

3–20 Check the extent to which pay varies from week to week. The position may be straightforward where the employee has been on a fixed salary with no overtime payments and no anticipated pay increase. However, if the employee's pay was based on piece rates or fluctuated significantly for any other reason some sort of judgment needs to be made to assess the weekly loss recoverable for the purposes of the compensatory award in an unfair dismissal claim or a discrimination claim. In unfair dismissal cases, the tribunal will have to make this judgment according to what is "just and equitable in all circumstances" (s.123(I) ERA). A reasonable approach may be to calculate an average weekly wage over perhaps a 12 week period prior to dismissal.

Remember, however, that you are seeking to identify what the employee would have earned in the period following dismissal and if there is evidence that other comparable employees have been earning a particularly high sum during that period— for example seasonal work—then this should be taken into account in calculating the lost wages. Note also the special rules which apply in calculating a "week's pay" for the purposes of the basic award and various other remedies (see Chapter 24).

Check whether employee is receiving less than contractual entitlement at date of dismissal

3–21 If the employee is actually receiving less than they are contractually entitled to (for example the employer may have unilaterally cut the pay rate without the employee ever agreeing) then the calculation of loss should be based on the contractual entitlement (see *Kinzley v. Minories Finance Ltd* [1987] I.R.L.R. 490). If there is a dispute between the complainant and former employer as to what wage they were entitled to, this is something which the tribunal should investigate and make a finding in relation to when assessing the compensatory award for unfair dismissal or when assessing loss in a discrimination claim. Note also the possibility of pursuing a claim for unlawful deduction from wages (see paras 22–58 to 22–67).

Expenses incurred since dismissal attempting to find new work or in mitigating loss in any other way

3–22 Check what expenses may already have been incurred by the complainant in seeking to mitigate his loss either in searching for new employment or, alternatively, in trying to set up in business (see also paras 3–53 to 3–60 for further commentary on expenses recoverable and Chapter 19 for commentary on the duty to mitigate loss).

New Job

3–23 If the applicant has already found a new job you will need to carefully assess the value of the full remuneration package. Obtain full information of the remuneration package of any new job. Check all the benefits which go with that job just as when gathering information about the job from which the complainant has been dismissed. Subject to special rules relating to the notice period in respect of unfair dismissal claims (see paras 10–38 to 10–43), these new earnings will have to be set against loss suffered as a result of the dismissal. This may result in your reaching the view that it is not worth pursuing the claim if little or no loss has been suffered and the new job is likely to be permanent (see further commentary at paras 10–44 to 10–59). Equally, if the loss is limited it may be worth seeking an early settlement while costs are low on both sides. Even if a new job appears at first sight to leave limited loss when set against the remuneration package prior to dismissal other factors must be taken into account. Factors to consider in respect of the new job include the following:

New job may be temporary

3–24 Check whether any new job is likely to be temporary. If it is then loss following the ending of that job may be recoverable (see para. 10–52 for commentary).

Expenses in finding and taking up new job

Remember that it may be possible to recover removal expenses incurred in taking up employment elsewhere in the country (see commentary on expenses recoverable at para. 3–56).

Travel costs

The new job might involve significantly increased travel costs travelling from home to work. Full details of such costs must be obtained from the complainant in order to assess the extent of loss (see Appendix L: AA/RAC tables for guidance in calculation of such costs).

Promotion prospects

If the new job is at a lower rate of pay and there is a clear continuing loss, examine the prospects for pay increases and promotion. If the evidence is that the job is likely to continue at much the same rate of pay and that promotion is unlikely, then the tribunal may decide that loss is likely to continue for a considerable period of time. In a sense, the loss has been crystallised.

Unemployment: Period of Loss

3–25   If the complainant remains unemployed following dismissal, check on any factors which may affect the chances of finding new work:

- Local job market (see paras 10–26 and 10–44)

- Mobility—consider family circumstances (see para. 19–45)

- Health—has ill health been caused or contributed to by unfair dismissal or by discrimination, such as harassment? (see paras 10–34 to 10–36 and 19–57)

- Issues personal to the complainant and discrimination in the labour market (see paras 10–29 to 10–30 and 19–10 to 19–13)

- Child care responsibilities (see paras 10–30 and 19–12)

- Age (see paras 10–31 to 10–32)

This information will have to be regularly updated in the period up to the tribunal hearing.

Injury to Feelings (Additional Information for Discrimination Claim or Claims re Action Short of Dismissal)

3–26   If the complainant is pursuing a claim for sex, race or disability discrimination remember the potential entitlement to compensation for *injury to feelings* (see s.66(4) SDA 75; s.57(4) RRA 76; s.8(4) DDA 95) (see paras 13–96 to 13–183 for analysis of entitlement to compensation for injury to feelings and case digest). In claims for unfair dismissal, no compensation can be awarded for injured feelings associated with the manner of the dismissal. However, the behaviour of the employer with regard to the way in which the dismissal was effected, or by dismissing for a reason which cannot be substantiated, may have an effect on the complainant's prospects for getting new work and may therefore increase the financial loss and compensation awardable (see para. 10–10).

Information required from complainant in respect of injury to feelings

3–27 The complainant's statement should include evidence to support a claim for compensation for injury to feelings. The tribunal will exercise its discretion in determining the level of compensation under this head on the basis of the evidence before it. An award for injury to feelings is not automatically to be made wherever unlawful discrimination is proved or admitted. The injury itself must be proved, though the tribunal will not take much persuasion to conclude that anger, distress and affront caused by the act of discrimination has injured the complainant's feelings (see para. 13–100). Obtain full details of any distress suffered by the complainant as a result of the discriminatory act. Cover the following:

1. Complainant's reaction to discriminatory act—was there a reaction of any of the following: shock, anger, distress, affront, humiliation, ostracism, ridicule, contempt and insult?

2. How long that reaction has continued, whether it affected relationships; was sleeping affected; whether there was any medical reaction—if so obtain full details.

Consider obtaining a medical report. If reaction has been severe then a psychiatric report should be seriously considered. Consider using the Law Society's panel of expert witnesses. Remember that the medical expert who prepared the report may have to give evidence at the tribunal. Making arrangements to obtain a medical report early is very important. It may take a long time to get an appointment and then obtain a report. Also, the report is likely to be more effective if there has not been a long delay following the action complained of. However, if a medical reaction is continuing there may be a strong case for obtaining a follow-up report later on.

Loss of Congenial Employment/Career Prospects

3–28 It is established that compensation for injury to feelings can include compensation for loss of "congenial employment" (see *MOD v. Cannock and others* [1994] I.R.L.R. 509 EAT) (see paras 13–103 to 13–105). The complainant's statement should therefore include, where appropriate, evidence of how significant the loss of a career has been to the complainant.

Sexual harassment: complainant's attitudes

3–29 For a claim in respect of sexual harassment, evidence of the complainant's attitude to sexual matters may be relevant if it demonstrates the extent to which the complainant has been distressed by particular conduct. Examining the likely evidence against an complainant is equally important (*Snowball v. Gardner Merchant Ltd* [1987] I.R.L.R. 397) (see paras 13–109 to 13–110).

Aggravated Damages

3–30 An award for injury to feelings can include aggravated damages. There must have been "high-handed, malicious, insulting or oppressive" behaviour on the part of the employer (see paras 13–126 to 13–134). If there is evidence of this sort of conduct on the part of the employer then the complainant's statement should contain full details.

Other witnesses to support claim in respect of injury to feelings/aggravated damages

3–31 Reference has already been made to the possibility of obtaining medical evidence to support a claim for compensation for injury to feelings. Consider also whether other witnesses may be able to give supporting evidence to demonstrate the effect that the discriminatory behaviour had on the complainant: other employees, relatives, or friends. Judgments can later be made as to the strength and value of such evidence but the possibility of obtaining supporting statements should be considered.

CASE DIGEST COMMENTARY ON BENEFITS CLAIMABLE

3–32 Note: Although the cases below are all unfair dismissal claims, the heads of loss identified can clearly be claimed as part of a discrimination claim.

Accommodation

3–33 *J. Hedger v. Davy & Co. Ltd [1974] I.R.L.R. 138*
A value was attributed to the free accommodation owned by the employer and occupied by the complainant. In this case, he continued to have the benefit of the free accommodation following dismissal and the tribunal set the value of this against the financial loss suffered. Equally, if free or subsidised accommodation is lost on dismissal this increases the loss suffered by the complainant and can be taken into account.

W. Butler v. J. Wenden & Son [1972] I.R.L.R. 15
The tribunal took into account the value of the tied cottage which went with the job but was lost following dismissal. The industrial tribunal made its own judgment of the value of the farm cottage to the complainant.

Nohar v. Granitstone Ltd [1974] I.C.R. 273
The complainant had paid a "normal" rent to his employer for the house he occupied during his employment. He was awarded no compensation for the loss of this accommodation because it was not a benefit in the sense that it was rent-free or at a subsidised rent.

It may be worth putting evidence to the tribunal of the value of lost accommodation using a surveyor or estate agent. In *Denyer v. The Cowdray Estate* COIT 2071/80D the tribunal looked at the value of lost accommodation and at the cost of council house accommodation obtained following dismissal and determined an annual loss of £1,300.

In *Jackson v. Shavington Social Club* COIT 1072/65 Jackson was evicted by court order following dismissal from accommodation which went with the job. The court ordered her to pay rent at £18 per week until possession and ordered court costs of £42. After a finding that the employer had unfairly dismissed her, the tribunal decided that all payments ordered by the court in the possession action were recoverable as part of the compensatory award.

Car

3–34 The provision of a car for private use is a clear benefit, the loss of which should be compensated.

AA/RAC Tables

Tables published by the AA and RAC each year provide a basis for calculating the loss of this benefit (tables are reproduced at Appendix L). This method was used in *Shove v. Downs Surgical plc* [1984] I.R.L.R. 17 (a personal injury case) to assess the loss suffered in respect of a car, making an adjustment to the estimated running costs so that the plaintiff was only compensated in respect of private mileage.

In *Nohar v. Granitstone Ltd* [1974] I.C.R. 273 the complainant had the benefit of the use of a company car. Following his dismissal he purchased a replacement car which he later sold when he gained fresh employment with the benefits of a car. He suffered a loss of £118 through buying and selling the car and insuring and taxing it. It was reasonable for him to be compensated for this.

Inland Revenue Tables

Sheen, J. in *Shove v. Downs Surgical plc* [1984] I.R.L.R. 17 specifically rejected the use of Inland Revenue rates to assess the loss of a car. "In my judgment, the figures laid down in the Income Tax Acts do not afford any useful guide to the actual loss suffered." AA tables were, in fact, used in this case.

Costs of Hire

The cost of hiring a replacement car may provide a reasonable basis for assessing the value to attach to the loss of a car, particularly if one is looking at a short period, perhaps where the complainant has actually hired a car following the return of the employer's car, so that, for example, he can seek to mitigate his loss by travelling to job interviews—or actually travelling to a new job which does not have the benefit of a car as a contractual entitlement.

Tips

3–35   Tips received by the complainant from customers can be taken into account in the assessment of the compensatory award even where the employer has nothing to do with such payments and they are received direct from customers (loss of tips are equally recoverable in a discrimination claim). However, in assessing the loss, tax and National Insurance should be deducted from gross average tip receipts to achieve a net figure (see *Palmanor Ltd t/a Chaplins Night Club v. Cedron* [1978] I.R.L.R. 303).

(Note, however, that the same case makes clear that such payments should *not* be taken into account in the assessment of the week's pay for the purposes of the basic award. However, in *Nerva & Ors v. R L & G Ltd* [1996] I.R.L.R. 461, the Court of Appeal held that waiters tips will normally be counted as pay for the purposes of determining the basic award unless paid direct from the customer to the waiter. So, for example, if tips go into a pot and are then distributed equally to staff, this would count as pay (see also para. 24–41).

Expenses Paid by Employer

3–36   In *Tradewinds Airways Ltd v. Fletcher* [1981] I.R.L.R. 272 EAT, it was held that tax-free allowances paid to the employee which simply reimbursed him for expenses incurred in doing his job should not be regarded as a benefit for the purposes of calculating the compensatory award (there was no profit element involved from the point of view of the employee). However, the complainant can be compensated for a profit element of expenses (see *S & U Stores Ltd v. Wilkes* [1974] I.C.R. 645 NIRC, see also paras 24–45 to 24–46 in respect of calculation of the week's pay for the basic award). The taxation of such payments will indicate that they should be regarded as a benefit rather than simply a reimbursement of expenses incurred. Note that where a sum is described as "expenses" simply to avoid it being taxed then the whole contract might fall because of illegality (see para. 24–46).

Loss of holiday entitlement

3–37   On the basis that the compensatory award is designed to compensate the complainant for the financial loss, it is hard to see how the loss of holiday entitlement can be compensated as part of the award. However, in the case of *Tradewinds Airways Ltd v. Fletcher* [1981] I.R.L.R. 272, the EAT upheld an award by the tribunal of the sum of £240 for the loss of holiday leave. Nevertheless, the EAT's decision is based on facts peculiar to this case in that the employer had identified this as a potential head of loss.

In *Wilson v. Tote Bookmakers* COIT 15570/81 Mrs Wilson was unfairly dismissed. She had holiday already booked at the date of dismissal which she could not take because her new employer would not allow holiday to be taken for the first year of employment. The tribunal awarded compensation as part of the compensatory award for the loss of holiday pay in that first year of employment.

Loss of National Insurance Contributions

3–38   The loss of N.I. contributions can be compensated for in circumstances where the complainant's N.I. payments are not being met following dismissal. This may occur if, for any reason, the complainant is disqualified from entitlement to Jobseekers Allowance. If a complainant is awarded compensation for a period of future loss this will disqualify him from entitlement to benefits and therefore no payments of N.I. will be made on his behalf during this period (normally N.I. contributions are deducted from Jobseekers Allowance). In such cases it is possible that the tribunal may award compensation for the loss of these N.I. payments.

In *Allen v. Key Markets Ltd* COIT 1425/41, the tribunal awarded compensation for future loss totalling 52 weeks. During this period there would be no entitlement to benefits and therefore no payments of N.I. contributions. The tribunal considered this to be a sufficiently long period to warrant the award of £4.30 per week for the full 52 weeks to cover N.I. payments and to enable the complainant to make the payments himself.

Loss of Statutory Notice

3–39   In cases where the complainant had several years of service with the employer it may be possible to recover compensation for the loss of the entitlement to statutory notice protection.

In *Daley v. A.E. Dorsett (Almar Dolls) Ltd* [1981] I.R.L.R. 385, the EAT described this as "an intangible benefit, ... that of being entitled in the course of ... employment to a longer notice than might otherwise be the case". The EAT awarded a sum equivalent to half his *statutory* notice entitlement. The EAT indicated that in periods of high unemployment the value of a long notice entitlement may be greater.

3–40   Since then the waters have been muddied. In *Muffett Ltd v. Head* [1986] I.R.L.R. 488, the EAT held that entitlement to compensation for loss of service-related notice entitlement depends on the "double contingency that the dismissed employee will get a new job and that he will be dismissed from that job before building up entitlement to the same period of notice". This makes the judgment of the tribunal highly speculative and the chances of an award being made under this head unlikely.

However, in *Guinness (Arthur) Son & Co. (Great Britain) Ltd v. Green* [1989] I.C.R. 241, Garland J. decided that an award of four weeks' pay (in circumstances where the complainant had been employed for longer than 12 years) was appropriate. "It has, of course, become the practice in a proper case to award a sum calculated by multiplying net take-home remuneration by a fraction of the statutory maximum period of notice of 12 weeks. This represents compensation for the accrued right to receive 'long' notice. The convention is never to award a sum based on a multiple greater than 6 weeks."

Loss of Entitlement to Enhanced Redundancy Package

3–41 Section 123(3) EPA states that the loss (for the purposes of calculating the compensatory award) includes any loss of:

(a) "any entitlement or potential entitlement to a payment on account of dismissal by reason of redundancy (whether in pursuance of Part XI (statutory redundancy pay) or otherwise), or

(b) any expectation of such a payment", in so far as it exceeds the basic award.

So if the complainant was entitled, as a term of his contract, to an enhanced redundancy package (if made redundant) or if he had an expectation of an enhanced payment (where, for example, the employer generally paid an enhanced amount but was not contractually bound to do so, possibly under the terms of a collective agreement not incorporated into the contract of employment) then an unfair dismissal will have denied him his entitlement to that potential benefit. In *Lee v. IPC Business Ltd* [1984] I.C.R. 306, the EAT held that the employee should be compensated for this lost benefit. The level of compensation depends on how likely it was that a redundancy would have occurred. The case of *Lee* gives no guidance on how to calculate the value of the benefit in circumstances where there was no imminent risk of redundancy. One approach is to award a percentage of the enhanced payment based on the tribunal's assessment of the chance of a redundancy occurring in the future.

Low-cost Mortgages and Loans

3–42 If the employer provides low cost mortgages or loans as a perk of the job, the loss of such a benefit can be claimed as part of the compensatory award. Assessing the value of such a benefit may be difficult but evidence should be put to the tribunal of the difference between the cost of benefit charged to the employee and what he would have to pay on the open market.

In *UBAF Bank Ltd v. Davis* [1978] I.R.L.R. 442, Mr Davis enjoyed a cheap mortgage as a perk of his employment which, ultimately, he lost following his dismissal. He calculated that the annual difference between the amount he was paying for his mortgage during this employment and what he would have had to pay to a building society was £675. The tribunal awarded £2,000 in respect of loss of various benefits including the loss of the cheap mortgage. It is not clear to what extent the tribunal accepted Mr Davis' method of calculation but neither the tribunal nor the EAT rejected this approach.

Check whether, in fact, the actual benefit of the cheap mortgage continues after dismissal. If it does, then this may be a continuing benefit to set against other losses.

Loss of Anticipated Pay Increases

3–43   If it can be demonstrated that had the complainant not been dismissed he would have received a pay increase at some future date then the loss of this increased rate of pay can be reflected in the compensatory award or in compensation for loss in a discrimination claim. There may be a contractual right to a pay increase, for example, where pay rates are nationally negotiated and every employee has the right to any agreed increase or there may be a reasonable expectation of an increase.

In *York Trailer Co. Ltd v. Sparkes* [1973] I.R.L.R. 348, Mr Sparkes received, as part of his compensatory award, £300 to reflect the fact that there was an anticipated salary increase of that amount. The EAT accepted the principle of compensating Mr Sparkes for the loss of this increased salary but reduced the sum by £50 to reflect the fact that the expected salary increase was only a probability and not a certainty (see also Chapter 11).

In *Penprase v. Mander Bros Ltd* [1973] I.R.L.R. 167, Mr Penprase was three-and-a-half years from retirement date. He was awarded compensation for that full period. The compensatory award included a sum in respect of likely pay increases of £100 per year for the next three years. Taking into account, on a rough and ready basis, the fact that these sums would be subject to tax the tribunal added £300 for the three-and-a-half-year period in respect of lost salary increases.

Back Dated Pay Increase

3–44   A back-dated pay increase awarded after dismissal can also be taken into account in assessing loss—*Leske v. Rogers of Saltcoats (ES) Ltd* EAT 520/82.

Overtime Payments

3–45   Regular overtime payments which would have been received by the complainant had he not been dismissed can be included in the calculation of loss. This is so whether there was a contractual entitlement to overtime or if it can be shown that there was a reasonable expectation that the complainant would in fact have worked such overtime.

The likelihood of overtime needs to be more than speculative (see *Mullet v. Brush Electrical Machines Ltd* [1977] I.C.R. 829 EAT). The tribunal's task is always to look to see what would have happened if he had not been dismissed (see para. 4–03 for commentary on discovery of documentation and information about overtime worked since dismissal).

Share Option Schemes/Profit Sharing

3–46   If the employee has had the benefit of a profit sharing scheme or the option to buy shares in the Company then the loss of such benefits can be compensated.

In *O'Laoire v. Jackel International Ltd* [1991] I.R.L.R. 170, the Court of Appeal confirmed that the complainant could be awarded compensation for loss of stock options "if satisfied that [the complainant] would in fact have obtained the options if he had been made managing director" a position to which Mr O'Laoire had expected to be appointed had he not been dismissed. The tribunal was not limited to giving compensation for loss of a contractual right to stock options.

A contractual provision under which the rights to a stock option lapse on dismissal, may be not effective to deny compensation as part of a compensatory award or may fall foul of s.203 ERA (the restriction on the right to contract out of or limit to operation of this Act). Valuation of a lost stock option may need expert help. One straightforward method is to calculate the profit which would have been made had the stock been purchased and sold immediately (see paras 25–59 to 25–63 in respect of compensation for lost share options in a wrongful dismissal claim).

Assessing Value of Benefits

3–47   Assessing the value of benefits such as free medical insurance, private health care, free meals can be done by determining the open market cost of obtaining the benefit following dismissal and deducting anything the complainant had to pay for the benefit before dismissal. Tribunals will use their best judgment to decide the value of a particular benefit where it is difficult to assess its value. In *Casey v. Texas Homecare Ltd* EAT 632/87, the EAT used their judgment on the basis of the evidence available to determine the value to Mr Casey of a share option scheme at £1000. This took into account the chance that share prices could drop and that by recovering the award the complainant had received the benefit sooner than expected.

3. ADVICE TO CLIENT ON HOW COMPENSATION IS CALCULATED

3–48   It is, of course, important to advise a potential complainant at the start how compensation will be calculated and to give as much information as you can on the likely range of possible outcomes should the claimant get over the first hurdle of proving liability. For the complainant it is part of the essential advice required to assist him in deciding whether or not to pursue the claim. Set out below is a sample letter for an unfair dismissal case but ensure that the advice you give at this stage is tailored to the complainant's own potential claim. Inevitably, a letter of advice at this stage can only summarise the legal position.

Dear

Your claim for unfair dismissal (*amend if appropriate*)

I write further to our recent meeting and now comment as follows:

  1. Statement
      I enclose a copy of your statement which has been prepared from the information taken down during our meeting. Please check through this and make any amendments or alterations you feel are necessary. Please then sign and date the statement and return it to me. If there are a large number of amendments, I will arrange for these to be incorporated into the statement and a final copy sent to you for signature.

  2. Application to the Tribunal
      I have also prepared an application to the Tribunal and enclose this for your consideration and signature. As soon as I receive the signed application I will be in a position to submit this to the Tribunal and get your claim under way.

3. Time Limit

It is important when claiming unfair dismissal (*amend as appropriate*) to remember that your claim must be issued within three months of the date of dismissal (note that if there is also an additional cause of action predating the dismissal, such as a separate act of discrimination, the time limit for that matter will be calculated from the date of the discriminating action). The relevant date in your case is (*please complete*). It is therefore vital that you return any documents to us and respond to any queries as quickly as possible.

4. ACAS

In all cases of unfair dismissal and sex, race or disability discrimination, a copy of the application to the Tribunal will be forwarded to ACAS (Advisory, Conciliation and Arbitration Service). ACAS is an independent organisation whose services are impartial, confidential and free. Their task is to assist in setting tribunal claims.

5. Re-employment

You have the right to apply for reinstatement (getting your old job back with no loss of continuous service) or re-engagement to another suitable job (again with no loss of service). Such orders are not often made but if you do apply and the tribunal orders either reinstatement or re-engagement and the employer refuses to comply you may be entitled to additional compensation. The tribunal has to be satisfied that it is practicable to order re-employment of one form or another.

6. Possible Award of Compensation

In claims of unfair dismissal, if you do not pursue re-employment or are not successful in achieving re-employment, the compensation you can hope to receive, if you win, is made up of two elements. These are the basic award and the compensatory award.

7. Basic Award

This is calculated taking into account length of service, age at the date of dismissal and gross weekly contractual earnings up to a maximum of £220. It is calculated in a similar way to a redundancy payment (If the claim for unfair dismissal relates to redundancy, and a redundancy payment has already been received, a basic award will not generally be payable). In your case the maximum amount you could receive in respect of the basic award is (   ).

8. Compensatory Award

The purpose of the compensatory award is to compensate the employee for the financial loss suffered as a result of being dismissed, including expenses incurred and loss of benefits such as company car, pension, etc. This will include the loss of net wages up to the date of any hearing and may include loss of future earnings beyond the date of the hearing. In calculating net earnings, tax and national insurance will be deducted. Any net wages earned from a new job are deducted in order to calculate your loss.

We can also claim a sum of between £200–250 in respect of "loss of statutory rights". This is designed to provide some compensation for the fact that you will not have to work for a further two years in a new job to gain protection for unfair dismissal and redundancy. It is important to note that the compensatory award is capped at £12,000.

9. Mitigation of Loss
    As I explained, when claiming unfair dismissal, you have a duty to mitigate your loss, *i.e.* keep your loss to a minimum. This means that you must actively look for alternative employment and you must be able to prove this.

    It is therefore necessary for you to keep a careful note of all jobs you apply for and check the result of these applications. You should also make a note of how often you check through newspapers and visit the job centre. I enclose a form for you to complete (see para. 3–50). Please keep it up to date and when you require further copies you should send in completed sheets to me.

    You should also keep copies of all adverts, letters, application forms, etc. We can then show, without doubt, that you have been looking for work.

    Please let me have this information at regular intervals.

10. Expenses
    You should also keep a note of all expenses you incur in looking for alternative employment, as these can be claimed as part of your compensation. Included in this category are telephone calls, postage, mileage, etc. The key question to ask yourself is "Have I incurred this expense as a result of losing my job?" You should keep a record of these expenses on the enclosed schedule (see para. 3–52). Again, please keep it up to date. It is very important to have this evidence to give to the Tribunal.

    Once again, please let me have this information at regular intervals.

11. Recoupment
    If you have been in receipt of state benefits at any time during the conduct of your case, the recoupment provisions may apply. The recoupment provisions allow the DSS to claim back a sum in respect of benefits you have received, out of any compensation you have been awarded. It is important to note, however, that the recoupment provisions only apply if you are awarded compensation by the Tribunal and not if you receive compensation by way of a settlement between the parties. This is an important consideration when negotiating a settlement.

12. Reductions
    There are some circumstances in which both the basic award and the compensatory award can be reduced. We will advise you fully concerning this if applicable in your case.

13. Conclusion of Claim
    It is likely that your claim will take up to (insert reasonable estimate based on experience at your Regional Tribunal) months to complete, once your application has been issued with the Tribunal.

14. Contact
    If at any time during your claim you are contacted directly by the other side, you should advise them that you have legal representation and ask them to contact us to discuss any matters in relation to your claim.

    If you have any queries concerning any of the above matters, please do not hesitate to contact me.

    Yours sincerely

Note that for a discrimination claim, paras 5, 6, 7, 8, 11 and 12 are not relevant. Other references to unfair dismissal should be removed. The following may be included as a guide to compensation in discrimination cases (but note full commentary on the rules at Chapter 13).

If you are successful in your claim you are likely to receive compensation. The tribunal must make an award of compensation if it considers it "just and equitable" to do so. There is no specific limit to this compensation.

The aim of the compensation is to put you in the same position financially as you would have been in had the discrimination not occurred. This is often difficult to assess because it may be hard to judge how long it will take to find work at the same rate of pay/benefits etc. Your loss of net wages/benefits etc. has to be assessed. The tribunal has power to reduce the total loss you believe you may have suffered in certain circumstances and I will explain this further to you if it appears to be a possibility.

You should also note that state benefits you receive will be deducted from lost wages/salary in order to calculate your total net loss. If you are still unemployed at the date of the tribunal hearing or if net wages and benefits in a new job are lower than in your previous job then you can claim for continuing loss suffered.

Injury to feelings
If you are successful, you can also recover compensation for what is called "injury to feelings". This is to compensate you for distress, hurt, anxiety or perhaps a sense of depression or outrage suffered as a result of the employer's discriminatory act. Also taken into account may be the loss of a job or occupation you particularly enjoyed or found fulfilling. Awards are not fixed but depend on what the tribunal considers appropriate. The minimum is usually £500 but it can be significantly more than this.

Interest
We can also claim interest on the loss you suffer and on any award for injury to feelings. When we prepare a breakdown of your claim I will show you how this is done.

4. GUIDANCE ON ESSENTIAL STEPS WHICH SHOULD BE TAKEN BY THE CLIENT

Evidence of efforts to find work

3–49 Any loss suffered by the complainant will have to be proved at the tribunal. Evidence to support the claimed loss is also important for the purposes of negotiation. In claims for unfair dismissal and discrimination the duty of mitigation applies (see Chapter 19). In respect of unfair dismissal, the duty to mitigate is specifically referred to in the ERA. The compensatory award compensates the complainant for loss in consequence of the dismissal "in so far as that loss is attributable to the action taken by the employer" s.123(1) ERA. Section 123 (4) confirms that the tribunal applies the same rule concerning the duty of a person to mitigate his loss as applies to damages recoverable under the common law.

3–50 Essentially, the duty to mitigate is the principle that the complainant should only be compensated for unavoidable loss resulting from the unlawful act. Avoidable loss which cannot be attributed to the employer is not compensatable. So if the complainant sits at home allowing his loss to grow and makes no efforts to find other work he will suffer avoidable loss. This will not be compensated. It is the task, then, of the complainant and his representative to demonstrate that proper efforts have been made to mitigate his loss. At the start, the complainant should be advised of this and of the need to show mitigation of loss. Set out below is a simple schedule which can be given to the complainant at the start for him to keep a record of all efforts to find work. This will put the complainant in a strong position to show that he has made reasonable efforts to mitigate his loss.

Schedule of Efforts to Find Work				
Name:	Case No.			
Date	Action Taken e.g. Letter; Phone Call; Application; Job Centre; Interview	Name of Company or Firm	Reason for contact incl. type of position; wage/salary and hours	Comments/Result

Evidence of likely Future Loss

3–51 The complainant must always be advised that it may be important to provide evidence of likely future loss. If by the time the tribunal hearing takes place the complainant is still out of work, or in a job with an inferior remuneration package, the tribunal will have to assess likely future loss. Whilst this exercise is inevitably speculative the tribunal will not simply make assumptions about future loss without hearing any evidence. See *Adda International Ltd v. Curcio* [1976] I.R.L.R. 425 EAT— "There must be some evidence of future loss and the scale of future loss to enable the tribunal to make any award under this head. The tribunal must have something to bite on and if the applicant produces nothing for it to bite on he will have only himself to thank if he gets no compensation for loss of future earnings." (see further commentary at paras 10–21 to 10–63 (unfair dismissal) and 13–81 to 13–92 (discrimination)).

What evidence then might the complainant give to the tribunal?

- Evidence of jobs applied for

- Unemployment statistics for the area
  (see *Sandown Pier Ltd v. Moonan* EAT 399/93. The tribunal found that Mr Moonan, who was aged 50 at the date of dismissal, was likely to remain unemployed for the rest of his working life. Unemployment was running at 20 per cent in that area)

- Evidence from recruitment consultant or other professional with local labour market knowledge

- Medical Evidence

Evidence of expenses incurred

3–52   In calculating loss for the purposes of the compensatory award in an unfair dismissal claim, section 123(2)(a) ERA provides that "expenses reasonably incurred by the complainant in consequence of the dismissal" should be included. Similarly, expenses incurred as a result of discrimination are also recoverable. The same basic principles apply. First, it is important to identify what expenses might be recoverable. Secondly, the complainant must be able to prove that such expenses have been incurred. Maintaining an accurate and complete record of all expenses following dismissal is therefore very important. Set out below is a simple schedule for the complainant to use in recording expenses incurred.

Schedule of Expenses Incurred in Search for Work				
Name:	Case No.			
Date	Nature of Expense e.g. Letter, Phone Call, Photocopying, Stationery, Newspaper	Costs Incurred	Travel Details: If own transport— No. of miles, Type of Vehicle	If public transport—Type of Transport Fare

What expenses are recoverable?

3–53   Clearly recoverable are direct expenses incurred in seeking to mitigate loss, see *Leech v. Berger, Jensen & Nicholson Ltd* [1972] I.R.L.R. 58. Set out below is a checklist of potentially recoverable expenses. The tribunal has to be satisfied that they have been incurred "in consequence of the dismissal" s.123(2)(a) ERA (in the unfair dismissal context).

Checklist

Telephone calls to potential employers.

Letters and postage to potential employers.

Travel expenses to attend interviews.

Newspapers/magazines purchased to identify jobs advertised.

Course fees if course undertaken in order to mitigate loss.

Removal expenses to relocate in order to take up new work.

Removal expenses if evicted from property of former employer occupied in order to do the job.

Additional travelling expenses incurred in travelling to new job.

Expenses in setting up business.

Additional family expenses such as school fees if a direct result of dismissal.

CASE DIGEST

Legal Expenses in Selling House

3-54 In *United Freight Distribution Ltd v. McDougall* (218/94), McDougall, an assistant operations manager, was dismissed. After considering employment opportunities he decided to set up a business. He also brought unfair dismissal proceedings and included in his compensation claim the costs of setting up his business. One expense was £550 for legal fees incurred in selling his house. This was awarded by the tribunal and upheld by the EAT. The tribunal had regarded it as a reasonable expense associated with the setting up of the business.

Cost of a Loan

3-55 In the same case (*United Freight Distribution Ltd v. McDougall*), McDougall had also borrowed £2,500 from his father. He described it as a "relocation loan". This sum was awarded by the tribunal. The EAT sent the case back to the tribunal to reconsider the facts. It was not clear what McDougall had spent the money on. If the money was used to mitigate his loss by setting up the new business then this would be recoverable.

Removal Expenses

3-56 In *Daykin v. IHW Engineering Ltd* COIT 1440/117, following his dismissal, Mr Daykin was forced to sell his house and move to a council flat during his search for work. He was awarded removal expenses and conveyancing charges and estate agents commission.

In *Scottish Co-operative Wholesale Society Ltd v. E.C. Lloyd* [1973] I.R.L.R. 93, Mr Lloyd was awarded £20 to cover the cost of moving from tied accommodation, plus £390 increased liability for rent and rates (see also *Co-operative Wholesale Society Ltd v. Squirrell* [1974] I.T.R. 191—removal expenses of £800 awarded in circumstances where Mr Squirrell moved to a more populous area to improve his employment prospects).

Increased School Fees

3-57 In *Derrick v. The De Vilbiss Co. Ltd* COIT 1471/104, following dismissal, Derrick moved to take up a new job. He wanted to leave his daughter in her private school until she had completed her exams. She stayed on as a boarder. He successfully claimed £1800 additional school fees and expenses. The industrial tribunal was satisfied that it was a consequence of his dismissal that he either had to incur substantial travelling costs in commuting to work or pay extra boarding fees.

Expenses in Setting up Business

3–58 In *Gardiner-Hill v. Roland Berger Technics Ltd* [1982] I.R.L.R. 498, the EAT decided that it was reasonable in all the circumstances for Gardiner to seek to mitigate his loss by setting up his own business. Accordingly, he should be compensated for the £500 it cost to set up that business.

In *Sparkes v. E.T. Barwick Mills Ltd* COIT 611/68, Mr Sparkes set up in business as a commission agent. He was awarded two years' interest on capital which he borrowed to establish the business. He was also compensated for the down-payment on a car which he required for the business.

The tribunal, therefore, first has to be satisfied that setting up a business is a reasonable way to mitigate loss. Then the reasonable costs of setting up that business will be allowed (see also paras 10–64 to 10–67 and 19–51 to 19–52).

Course Fees

3–59 If the dismissed employee can demonstrate that a decision to retrain or pursue further qualifications was directly caused by the dismissal and that it was reasonable to take such steps in order to mitigate loss then expenses incurred in such retraining, etc., are recoverable. Note the test of causation set out in *Simrad Ltd v. Scott* [1997] I.R.L.R. 147 where it was held that a decision to give up a low paid job with no career prospects (some time after dismissal) and retrain as a nurse was not directly caused by the dismissal and therefore the increased loss resulting from that change of direction was not recoverable. For further commentary on these issues see paras 10–15 to 10–19 and 10–60 to 10–63.

Legal Expenses

3–60 Legal expenses incurred in pursuing a claim for unfair dismissal or discrimination are not recoverable as part of the loss suffered as a result of dismissal. The rules on the tribunal's powers to award costs are contained in the Employment Tribunals (Rules of Procedure) Regulations 1985 (S.I. 1985 No.16), Rule 12 (see Chapter 17). Such costs have never been recoverable as part of an award of compensation for unfair dismissal or for discrimination. See *Nohar v. Granitstone Ltd* [1974] I.C.R. 273 NIRC.

CHAPTER 4

Gathering Information in Support of Claim for Financial Loss or Re-employment: Using the Tribunal's Powers

4–01 This chapter provides guidance on how to go about gathering information needed in order to prepare a comprehensive schedule of loss. The guidance is relevant to both unfair dismissal and discrimination claims. In straightforward cases where the complainant received a wage which remained constant from week to week and where there were few, if any, other benefits or bonuses available, the complainant is likely to be able to provide all the necessary information for preparation of the schedule of loss. However, this is not always the case. A range of information sometimes needs to be obtained from the employer. This may be in the form of documents or answers to questions posed by the complainant. Set out below is some guidance on examples of such information.

Information on lost earnings and benefits

4–02 It is important to remember that the complainant in both unfair dismissal and discrimination cases is claiming compensation for financial loss suffered *since* the dismissal or other discriminatory act. Therefore, in a dismissal case, it is the wages and other benefits which the complainant would have received had he not been dismissed which you are seeking to quantify. Wages and benefits received prior to dismissal will provide a good starting point in quantifying that loss but that may well not be enough. There may, for example, have been a general wage increase since the dismissal. If it is likely that the complainant would have benefited from that, it must be taken into account in the assessment of loss. You may need to obtain information about that wage increase from the respondent.

Overtime worked by other employees

4–03 Likewise, if there is evidence that other employees, who continue to work for the respondent, have worked a lot of overtime since the complainant's dismissal, this again is likely to be highly relevant in the assessment of loss. It may, therefore, be appropriate to seek to obtain detailed schedules of overtime worked by other employees during comparable work since the date of the complainant's dismissal (It may, of course, be the case that the overtime worked has only been necessary because of the complainant's dismissal—because the respondent is short-staffed. In such circumstances, had the complainant not been dismissed, the overtime may not have been necessary and it cannot therefore be said that the complainant has lost the benefit of such overtime).

Value of Benefits

4–04   It is often necessary to get more information from the respondent to assist in valuing various fringe benefits such as pension, health insurance, share options, etc. Such information may not be provided sufficiently by documents such as the staff handbook.

Pension: Actuarial Evidence

4–05   The complainant may want to call actuarial evidence of the loss suffered in respect of pension entitlement (see Chapter 20). Information and documents may be required from the respondent in order for the actuary to calculate loss. Any actuarial reports prepared on behalf of either party should be disclosed long enough before the hearing to enable the other party to consider it and assess the analysis.

Alternative Employment

4–06   In unfair dismissal cases, it may be the case that the complainant asserts that he should have been offered alternative employment rather than being dismissed. This may be the case in a redundancy situation or where the complainant has been dismissed on grounds of incapacity. The complainant may argue, perhaps as a fall-back position, that he should at least have been offered some sort of alternative employment which may have a less attractive remuneration package. You may need to obtain information about the value of that package.

Information relevant to application for reinstatement or re-engagement

4–07   If the complainant is seeking reinstatement or re-engagement, it may be very useful to seek information from the respondent about availability of work, vacancies advertised and whether a permanent replacement has been appointed.

Disability Discrimination Cases

4–08   In disability discrimination cases involving a dismissal, the complainant may argue that the employer could have made some reasonable adjustment so as to enable him to continue in employment. (A similar argument may be used where the complainant claims he has suffered discrimination in not being appointed to a particular post). One such adjustment could be a reduction in working hours or the offer of another perhaps less onerous job. That job may be on lower pay. Again, information should be obtained from the respondent to assist in the process of quantifying loss on the basis of the complainant losing the chance to earn that reduced income.

Evidence in Support of Claim for Aggravated Damages

4–09   In discrimination cases, the complainant can pursue a claim for compensation for injury to feelings as well as for financial loss (see paras 13–96 to 13–183). Furthermore, the complainant may claim, particularly in harassment cases, that the respondent aggravated the injury to feelings by high-handed, oppressive behaviour, possibly over a considerable period of time (see paras 13–126 to 13–134). The complainant may know that documentary evidence exists, such as notes of meetings which took place or memoranda, which will assist in proving such high-handed, oppressive conduct. Discovery of those documents may therefore be of importance in recovering proper compensation.

Medical Reports

4–10   A complainant in a discrimination case may have obtained a medical report in support of his claim for compensation for injury to feelings. Also, it may have been agreed between the parties that the respondent could obtain their own medical report by arranging for the complainant to see a specialist. Orders for disclosure of such reports between the parties would clearly be appropriate. Normally, of course, the parties would agree beforehand the basis upon which the complainant would agree to co-operate in being examined by a specialist appointed by the respondent.

Discrimination Recruitment Cases

4–11   Where the complainant claims that he has suffered discrimination by not being appointed to a job, it is likely to be the case that information will be required from the respondent in order to assess the value of the remuneration package which the complainant would have received had he been appointed. In such cases the complainant is likely to have limited knowledge of the value of the package.

Information Requested by the Respondent

4–12   It may also be the case that the respondent wants information from the complainant in order to assess the likely scale of the complainant's loss or to challenge a schedule of loss prepared by the complainant. The respondent might want this information to assist in the task of deciding whether to settle or continue to defend the claim. In particular, the respondent may want to assess the quality of evidence which the complainant has gathered which demonstrates that he has properly attempted to mitigate his loss. This is likely to be particularly important in discrimination cases where the complainant may be claiming a substantial sum in respect of financial loss over a long period. In the Ministry of Defence pregnancy dismissal cases, the MOD sought detailed information from complainants relating to their efforts to mitigate loss in the period following compulsory discharge.

Obtaining Information from the Respondent

4–13   The first step is always to make a straightforward written request. This can be by way of a letter which sets out all the categories of information and documents you need for the purpose of assessing loss. Alternatively, a more formal document can be prepared. A deadline should be set for reply. Depending on the amount of information/ documents requested, 14 or 21 days is generally a reasonable period. Set out below is an example of such an application.

Dear Sirs

**Application for discovery and answers to interrogatories where
liability admitted: unfair dismissal**
Case No:

We comment as follows:

1.   Disclosure
We should be grateful if you would provide copies of the following documents:

(1) Full personnel file for the applicant
(2) Contract of Employment
(3) Company handbook
(4) All other documents detailing the company bonus scheme
(5) Pension handbook

2. Interrogatories

Please confirm that you agree that the applicant was entitled to the following benefits during his employment with you, providing your assessment of the value of each and every benefit listed:

(1) Bonus under the Company's Bonus Scheme
(2) Private Health Insurance
(3) Accident insurance
(4) Free lunch
(List any other benefits)

With regard to the applicant's final salary pension please confirm the following:

(1) Value of deferred pension
(2) Applicant's gross weekly pensionable pay
(3) Company' normal contribution to pension scheme as a percentage of payroll

We look forward to receiving the above documents and answers within the next 14 days, failing which we will apply to the Employment Tribunal for the appropriate orders.

Yours faithfully

In drafting this voluntary request, you need to consider the basis upon which later on you may be able to require the respondent to provide the information and documents you need. The following section provides commentary on the relevant tribunal powers.

Relevant Tribunal Powers

4–14   Where a respondent—or a complainant—fails to respond to a voluntary request for either discovery of documents or to answer questions in the form of interrogatories or by way of a request for further and better particulars, then the tribunal has power in some circumstances to require that party to respond. The tribunal's powers are contained in Schedule 1 to the Employment Tribunal (Constitution and Rules of Procedure) Regulations 1993.

Discovery and Inspection

4–15   Rule 4 (1)(b) of Schedule 1 to the 1993 Regulations provides that the tribunal may, on the application of a party made either by notice or at the hearing of the originating application, "require one party to grant to another such discovery or inspection (including the taking of copies) of documents as might be granted by the county court". The tribunal may also state when and where the inspection of documents is to take place and the time limit within which discovery is to take place. The discretion which the tribunal exercises under this rule clearly allows the tribunal to order inspection and/or discovery of documents which are relevant to quantum as well as those which relate to questions of liability.

4–16   In the MOD pregnancy dismissal case of *MOD v. Meredith* [1995] I.R.L.R. 539, the EAT considered an order made by the tribunal for discovery of documents relating to quantum. The MOD agreed to provide discovery of some of the classes of documents covered by the tribunal order but challenged the requirement to disclose other classes of document.

The tribunal chairman had ordered the production of documents for inspection but had made no provision for discovery by list. This meant that there was no opportunity for the MOD to claim privilege or public interest immunity in respect of any particular document within a class of documents which had to be available for inspection. In the EAT, Smith J. made clear that "in any case in which the possibility exists that such claims might be advanced, an order under Rule 4 should be made, as it is in the County Court under CCR Order 14, by providing first for discovery by list and then for production for inspection after an interval of several days".

Exercise of discretion to order discovery

4–17   Rule 4 in the 1993 Regulations provides that the tribunal may make such an order for discovery of documents as may be made by the County Court. The relevant provision in the County Court Rules is Order 14 rule 8. This rule states that if the court is satisfied that the discovery, disclosure, production or supply sought is not necessary, or not necessary at that stage of the action or matter, it may dismiss or adjourn the application. Furthermore, the court must refuse the application if and in so far as it is of the opinion that discovery, disclosure, production or supply, as the case may be, is not necessary either for disposing fairly of the action or matter or for saving costs.

Timing of Application

4–18   Note, therefore, that the tribunal may refuse an application for discovery if the tribunal thinks that it is not necessary at that stage of the action. Generally tribunals take the view that it is not necessary to order discovery of documents—or replies to interrogatories—relating to quantum before the question of liability has been resolved.

Nonetheless, this is a matter for the tribunal's discretion and, given that the emphasis in the tribunal is on settlement of claims where possible, there may be a good case for arguing in some circumstances that discovery of documents relating to quantum at an early stage may save costs and assist in the fair disposal of the action. It may be argued, for example, that efforts to explore settlement on a without prejudice basis cannot be made until the complainant can properly establish the extent of his loss and that this requires discovery. Whether such an argument would succeed is, however, open to considerable doubt.

The question as to whether the tribunal will order a complainant to disclose particulars relating to compensation to the respondent before the issue of liability has been determined was considered by the EAT in the case of Colonial Mutual Life Society v. Clinch [1981] I.C.R. 752. Browne-Wilkinson J. rejected the respondent's attempt to get information relating to the complainant's earnings since dismissal. They wanted this information so that they would be in a position to make a settlement offer. "We think it unnecessary and undesirable, for the purpose of the fairness of [a tribunal] hearing on compensation, that the particulars of compensation should be given at the stage before liability had been determined" (Browne-Wilkinson J).

The point was made that such information can normally be obtained via the ACAS officer assigned to the case. Browne-Wilkinson J also alluded to the fact that tribunals are intended to provide "a quick and simple procedure available to people without the benefit of legal advice". He also pointed to the fact that "normally the sums involved are comparatively small". What has changed since then is the lifting of the lid on compensation for discrimination cases. It may be that, as a result, the case has grown for tribunals to reconsider the exercise of their discretion on the basis that, in some cases, early discovery/interrogatories are necessary for the saving of costs.

Discovery necessary for fair disposal or for saving costs

4-19   First it is clear that for the tribunal to order discovery of a document it must be relevant to an issue in the case. The concept of relevance should be widely construed (see *Compagnie Financiere et Commerciale du Pacifique v. Peruvian Guano Co.* [1982] 11 Q.B. 55). However, it takes more than mere relevance. Discovery and inspection will only be ordered if it is necessary for the fair disposal of the case or for saving costs. The tribunal will not sanction a fishing expedition. Documents which provide information about the extent of financial loss suffered or which help to prove behaviour by the respondent in a discrimination claim which has had the effect of aggravating the complainant's injured feelings may certainly be not only relevant but also necessary for a fair disposal of the action or to save costs.

4-20   In the *Meredith* case, (see para. 4-16) the EAT overturned the tribunal chairman's order for discovery on the following basis. The order concerned documents relating to the state of mind of the MOD at the time of Mrs Meredith's dismissal. In particular she sought to demonstrate, as a result of obtaining discovery of documents, that the MOD knew that they were acting unlawfully. She argued that this would be relevant to the claim for aggravated damages. However, Miss Meredith certainly did not know, at the time of her discharge, that the policy of compulsory discharge on grounds of pregnancy was unlawful. It is therefore impossible, said the EAT, that her injured feelings could be "aggravated by any improper conduct or motive on the part of [the MOD] of which she was wholly unaware" (see paras 13–126 to 13–134 for commentary on aggravated damages). Smith J. in *Meredith* also made the point that discovery will not be ordered if it is oppressive.

Confidentiality

4-21   Note also that the confidentiality of a document is not, in itself, enough to prevent an order for discovery. This is unlikely to be an issue with most documents relating to quantum although an exception may be documents relevant to a claim for aggravated damages. In such a case the tribunal may decide to inspect the documents first to test for relevance and to decide whether any particular steps are necessary to protect confidentiality (see *Science Research Council v. Nasse* [1979] I.R.L.R. 465).

Voluntary Disclosure

4-22   Note that if a party decides to make voluntary disclosure of documents, that party cannot be unfairly selective. He must disclose other documents if necessary to prevent his opponent gaining a misleading or false impression of the true nature, purpose or effect of the voluntarily disclosed documents (*Birds Eye Walls Ltd v. Harrison* [1985] I.R.L.R. 47). For example, if some workers in similar employment to the dismissed complainant have done a substantial amount of overtime since the dismissal, it would not be acceptable to voluntarily disclose only those records of other employees who had done little or no overtime. That may underestimate the loss suffered by the complainant.

Interrogatories

4-23 For the first time, the 1993 Procedure Regulations introduced into the tribunal the power to require written answers to questions which clarify issues in the proceedings. The power is contained in Rule 4 (3), Schedule 1 to the 1993 Regulations. The tribunal may make such an order if an answer to the question may help to clarify any issue which is likely to arise. This clearly includes questions relating to loss. The tribunal also needs to be satisfied that an answer before the hearing would be likely to assist in the progress of the proceedings. The tribunal will set a deadline for providing answers.

4-24 In cases involving substantial loss it may be worth serving interrogatories with the draft schedule of loss with the aim of narrowing the areas of dispute between the parties. Questions such as the following may be relevant:

1. In respect of the draft schedule of loss, please state in relation to each head of loss whether the figure stated is accepted and, if not, why not, setting out your proposed figure, if any.

2. In respect of the potential loss of earnings, please state whether you accept the anticipated promotion which would have occurred during the period of loss and, if not, please state each and every reason why it is asserted that the complainant would not have been promoted, making reference to any documentary evidence on which you intend to rely at the hearing.

3. (In pregnancy dismissal cases) In respect of the deduction for child minding costs, please confirm whether you accept the sum deducted and, if not, why not and what you intend to rely on to challenge the figure provided.

4. In respect of the loss of other benefits in the Schedule of loss, please confirm whether you accept that the complainant was entitled to (for example):

   free health insurance;
   subsidised travel costs;
   subsidised accommodation, etc.

   Please confirm in respect of each benefit set out above details as to the value of each on a monthly or annual basis.

5. Is the figure for injury to feelings accepted? If not, please state each and every reason why it is alleged that a lower figure should be awarded.

Further and Better Particulars

4-25 In cases where the originating application sets out details of the loss claimed including, in discrimination cases, details of alleged injury to feelings and possibly assertions in support of a claim for aggravated damages, the respondent may seek further and better particulars of the grounds relied on by the complainant. This is provided for by rule 4(1)(a) of the 1993 Regulations. Likewise, the respondent's notice of appearance may set out a basis for resisting certain heads of loss. Again, the complainant may make application for further and better particulars of these grounds.

THE STEPS TO TAKE

4–26 As stated at paragraph 4–13, the first step in seeking discovery and inspection or getting replies to questions, or to provide further and better particulars, is to make a voluntary request of the other party giving perhaps fourteen or twenty one days to reply, depending on the amount of information or number of documents requested. If some, or all, of the information or documents requested have not been supplied within the time limit given then the next stage is to write to the tribunal asking for an order to be made requiring the respondent to provide discovery and inspection and to answer any questions or to reply to a request for further and better particulars which were put to the respondent by way of the voluntary request.

4–27 If the tribunal is satisfied that orders should be made—applying the law as described in paragraphs 4–14 to 4–25 then an order may be made and served on the respondent. Alternatively, the tribunal chairman may decide to hold a directions hearing. If the tribunal chairman makes an order as requested following a written request, the party upon whom the order imposes requirements may apply to the tribunal to vary or set aside the requirement, (Rule 4(5)). The application is made to the Secretary of the tribunal. If such an application is made a hearing will be fixed for the parties to make submissions.

Striking Out

4–28 Note that the tribunal has power under Rule 4(7) of the 1993 Regulations to strike out an originating application or a notice of appearance as the case may be or to debar the respondent from defending if an order in respect of discovery, interrogatories or further and better particulars has not been complied with. The tribunal must first, however, serve notice on the defaulting party giving him an opportunity to explain his failure and to state why the tribunal should not take that action against him.

Use of the Questionnaire Procedure in Discrimination Cases

4–29 In sex, race and disability discrimination cases, the complainant may serve a questionnaire on the respondent requesting information which will assist him in formulating and presenting his case in the most effective manner (as well as helping him to decide whether to issue proceedings) (see s.74 SDA, s.65 RRA and s.56 DDA). Such a questionnaire must be served either before the issue of proceedings or within 21 days of the issue of proceedings. Whilst the questionnaire procedure is primarily intended to identify information which is relevant to liability, it is perfectly legitimate to include within the questions, requests for information and documents to assist in assessing loss.

CHAPTER 5

Preparing the Schedule of Loss

5–01 Using the guidance set out in the previous chapters it should be possible to start the process of preparing a schedule of loss. Early preparation of the schedule of loss facilitates opportunities to negotiate a settlement and ensures that the starting point for any such negotiations is based on a certain amount of science (although inevitably a lot of assumptions will have to be made). You will have identified all the elements of the remuneration and benefits package.

In a discrimination claim, it will be necessary to decide what figure to include in the schedule of loss for injury to feelings and whether to include within that an amount in respect of aggravated damages (for full commentary on compensation for injury to feelings and aggravated damages see paras 13–96 to 13–134. See also the case digest on awards for injury to feelings and aggravated damages at paras 13–137 to 13–183. Remember also in discrimination claims to include a sum in respect of interest from the date of the discriminatory act (see paras 13–42 *et seq* for commentary on interest calculations).

5–02 Whether the schedule of loss is in respect of an unfair dismissal claim or a discrimination claim, the other essential issue to consider is the period of loss. Consider what evidence you have gathered which might support the period of loss you are claiming. See paras 3–10 to 3–48 (information gathering) and paras 3–51 and 10–20 (factors which may extend period of loss). Whilst tribunals are cautious about awarding compensation for future loss and in unfair dismissal cases will rarely award more than a year's future loss (see paras 10–21 to 10–23), it is important to include with the schedule compensation for the full period which you believe the complainant will suffer loss. However, gather together evidence to support this.

5–03 Guidance on the principles which the tribunal will apply in determining the period of loss is given at paras 10–20 to 10–63 in respect of unfair dismissal and paras 13–56 to 13–95 in respect of discrimination cases. Remember to include within the schedule compensation for any other claims included within the tribunal application, such as unlawful deduction from wages, compensation for failing to give written reasons for dismissal, etc. The complainant's schedule of loss will, of course, be aimed at maximising either the sum agreed in a settlement or the award made by the tribunal. However, both in preparing the schedule of loss and in any negotiations that follow it is important to understand the ways in which compensation may be reduced by the tribunal. Set out below is a checklist of matters which may affect total compensation awarded together with cross-references for further commentary.

Unfair Dismissal

Basic Award:

5–04 Power to reduce award for:

(i) Refusal to accept offer of reinstatement (see paras 9–21 to 9–22)

(ii)   Conduct of complainant (see paras 9–23 to 9–35)

(iii)   Payments made in respect of basic award (see paras 9–18 to 9–19)

Compensatory Award

(i)   Deduction of payments made by employer (see Chapter 15)

(ii)   Deduction of wages earned in mitigation (see Chapter 19)

(iii)   Deduction of benefits (see Chapter 16)

(iv)   Recoupment provisions (see paras 16–18 to 16–30)

(v)   Reductions for contributory fault (see paras 11–38 to 11–87)

(vi)   Reductions on a just and equitable basis (see paras 11–03 to 11–37)

(vii)   Order of deductions/reductions (see Chapter 15)

(viii)   Limit to period of loss because of a failure to mitigate (see Chapter 19)

(ix)   The effect of an intervening act, a *novus actus*, which breaks the "chain of causation" (see paras 10–15 to 10–19)

(x)   The rules on reduction to award where failure to pursue internal appeal or increase where internal appeal procedure has been denied by employer (see paras 10–10 and 11–01)

Discrimination

(i)   Deduction of payments made by employer (see Chapter 15)

(ii)   Deduction of wages earned in mitigation (see Chapter 19)

(iii)   Percentage chance approach (see paras 13–58 to 13–76)

(iv)   Order deductions/reductions (see Chapter 15)

(v)   Limit to period of loss because of failure to mitigate (see Chapter 19)

(vi)   The effect of an intervening act, a *novus actus*, which breaks the "chain of causation" (see para. 13–79)

(vii)   Reduction of benefits (see Chapter 16)

SCHEDULE OF LOSS

5–05 Set out below are examples of schedules of loss for unfair dismissal and discrimination together with checklists and cross-references to aid completion of the schedules.

Checklist for completion of draft schedule

Unfair Dismissal

Basic Award

(see Appendix P for ready reckoner to assist in calculation of the basic award)

_____ v _____

Schedule of Loss: unfair dismissal
Without prejudice
Hearing date:

Basic Award
Contractual weekly gross pay (subject to stat. Max of £220):
Age of complainant (at dismissal):
Service (full years):
No. of weeks pay due:

Basic Award =

Compensatory Award
1) Immediate net loss of earnings/benefits, etc. from (*date of dismissal*) to (*date of hearing*)
   (set out all lost fringe benefits and net value)

   Calculate net weekly loss of earnings/benefits
   Multiply by no. of weeks
   Sub-total =
   Deduct all earnings/benefits received (apart from during notice period) from (*date of dismissal*) to (*date of hearing*)

   Total immediate loss =
2) Future loss
   Determine current net weekly loss
   Deducting any current earnings/benefits
   Decide period of future loss claimed
   Multiply current weekly loss by no. of weeks future loss claimed.

   Future loss =

3) Loss of Pension benefits
   Determine immediate loss
   Determine future loss
   Determine loss of accrued pension rights (final salary schemes)

   Total pension loss =

4) Loss of statutory rights   £250

5) Expenses

Immediate expenses incurred
Future expenses likely to be incurred =

Total Compensatory Award =

Total Amount claimed for unfair dismissal =

Add any additional claims
Such as unlawful deduction from wages
Contractual claims
(avoid double recovery of same loss)

TOTAL AMOUNT CLAIMED =

  (i)   Check week's pay (see paras 9–01 to 9–15 and Chapter 24), age and length of service

  (ii) Apply statutory formula (see para. 9–05) use ready reckoner (see Appendices)

Other Claims

Have other claims been pursued which should be added to schedule of loss? (see paras 3–06 to 3–09)

Compensatory Award

  (i)   Check all pay and benefits including pension from previous employment and calculate net value (see para. 10–08 and checklist at para. 3–15) Remember you are seeking to recover loss for period *following* dismissal. Have you got all the information you need from the employer: overtime worked in that period, annual or other pay increases, bonus payments? (see Chapter 4).

  (ii) Assess total of all expenses incurred as a result of dismissal (see paras 3–52 to 3–60)

  (iii) Include sum for loss of statutory rights (see paras 3–48 and 10–14)

  (iv) Consider period of loss (immediate and future) to claim (see paras 10–20 to 10–66)

Discrimination Claim

Financial Loss

5–06   (i)   Same as set out in compensatory award but leave out claim for loss of statutory rights

Injury to Feelings

  (i)   Determine level of claim for injury to feelings (see paras 13–96 to 13–183)

  (ii) Should figure be enhanced by way of aggravated damages? (see paras 13–126 to 13–134).

Interest

    (i)   Separately calculate interest on financial claim and on injury to feelings (see paras 13–42 to 13–54)

Other claims to be included

(see paras 3–06 to 3–09)

————— v —————
Schedule of loss: discrimination claim
Without prejudice

Financial Loss

1) Immediate net loss of earnings/benefits, etc. from (*date of dismisssal*) to (*date of hearing*)
   (set out all lost fringe benefits and net value)
   Calculate net weekly loss of earnings/benefits
   Multiply by no. of weeks
   Sub-total =
   Deduct all earnings/benefits received from (*date of dismissal*) to (*date of hearing*)

   Total immediate loss =

2) Future loss
   Determine current net weekly loss
   Deducting any current earnings/benefits
   Decide period of future loss claimed
   Multiply current weekly loss by no. of weeks future loss claimed.

   Future loss =

3) Loss of Pension benefits
   Determine immediate loss
   Determine future loss
   Determine loss of accrued pension rights (final salary schemes)

   Total pension loss =

4) Expenses
   Immediate expenses incurred
   (list all expenses)
   Future expenses likely to be incurred =

   Total expenses =

Total financial loss =

Injury to feelings

Interest
Interest on immediate financial loss
Interest on injury to feelings

Total interest =

Total amount claimed for discriminatory dismissal =

Add any additional claims such as unfair dismissal basic award loss of statutory rights unlawful deduction from wages (avoid double recovery of same loss)

TOTAL AMOUNT CLAIMED =

5–07   Note the separate heads of loss identified in the schedules. For commentary on heads of loss see paras 10–12 to 10–13 in respect of unfair dismissal. A similar approach can be taken with a discrimination claim with the addition of injury to feelings/aggravated damages and interest (see Chapter 13). Include Discrimination schedule of loss.

Practical Tip:

It is generally the case that remedies will not be considered at the first hearing dealing with liability. If there is a finding of unfair dismissal or discrimination, it is common practice to agree to an adjournment to allow the parties an opportunity to negotiate a settlement avoiding the need for a further hearing and avoiding—so far as unfair dismissal claims are concerned—the recoupment provisions (see paras 16–18 to 16–30). By this stage there may be a substantial period of loss since the date of dismissal.

5–08   For the purposes of the first draft schedule of loss, immediate loss (loss since dismissal) may cover a much more limited period of time with all the rest of the compensation claimed being lumped into future loss. It is important to amend the draft schedule from time to time as immediate loss grows, the longer it is since the date of dismissal. Make sure it is marked as a draft and that you reserve the right to amend it. As time goes by more evidence may come to light which may justify a longer period of future loss, the complainant's circumstances may change—he may get a job or lose a temporary job (see para. 10–52 in respect of unfair dismissal). All these factors will need to be referred to in an amended schedule of loss.

CHAPTER 6
Negotiating a Settlement

6–01 There are often good reasons to attempt to negotiate a settlement before the claim is heard in the tribunal. Equally, once the tribunal makes a finding that there has been an unfair dismissal, or that there has been unlawful discrimination, there is a strong case for exploring the possibilities of settlement.

THE FACTORS WHICH HAVE TO BE TAKEN INTO ACCOUNT ARE AS FOLLOWS:

1. Uncertainty as to the outcome

6–02 It may be difficult to establish the chance of success on either liability or on the level of compensation which might be awarded. Part of the task of preparing a claim—or the defence against a claim—is an assessment of prospects. Inevitably, however, there is never certainty of success. In the assessment of compensation the tribunal has a broad discretion. See, for example, Chapter 11 for commentary on the powers of the tribunal to reduce compensation for unfair dismissal. In respect of discrimination cases, see paragraphs 13–58 to 13–76 for commentary on the power to apply a percentage reduction to compensation. From the point of view of both the complainant and employer, uncertainty as to how all these issues will be determined by the tribunal encourages compromise.

2. No Order for Costs

6–03 In most circumstances the tribunal makes no order for costs. The Employment Tribunal (Constitution and Rules of Procedure) Regulations 1993, Schedule 1 paragraph 12(1) provides as follows:

"Where, in the opinion of the tribunal, a party has in bringing or conducting the proceedings acted frivolously, vexatiously, abusively, disruptively or otherwise unreasonably, the tribunal may make—

a) an order containing an award against that party in respect of the costs incurred by another party" (see Chapter 17 for commentary on the powers of the tribunal to award costs).

Although the original wording (contained in the previous procedure rules), which stated that an award of costs is not normally to be made, has been removed, awards of costs are still the exception rather than the rule. This applies to unfair dismissal and discrimination claims as well as to other proceedings brought in the tribunal.

6–04 Note also that the means of the party are a relevant consideration in determining the amount of any order for costs made by the tribunal. So, for the respondent, even if, for example, he considers the claim to be frivolous or vexatious, an order for costs may not go far in covering costs incurred if the complainant has limited means. For this reason there is, again, an incentive for both parties to consider settlement. This is particularly so with unfair dismissal where the maximum award is restricted by the statutory cap on the compensatory award (currently £12,000) and the basic award is calculated using a statutory maximum weekly pay (currently £220) (see para. 9–08). So if the complainant is paying for representation the costs may assume a significant proportion of the total award made by the tribunal.

Warning as to Costs

6–05 Remember that if liability appears to be clear, the complainant's representative should always consider warning the respondent that if liability is not admitted then an application for costs will be made on the basis that the respondent would be acting unreasonably in the conduct of proceedings and that this would result in the complainant incurring extra cost.

Example: [redundancy dismissal]

"We have considered the Notice of Appearance filed by the respondent in this case. It is clear that the Notice does not set out any defence to the claim that the complainant has been unfairly dismissed. In particular, it is noted that there is no assertion that the respondent consulted with the complainant, or warned him, with regard to the redundancy situation. Further, the Notice of Appearance does not provide any basis for asserting that the complainant was fairly selected for redundancy.

"We therefore consider that the tribunal will find that the complainant has been unfairly dismissed. We invite you to admit liability so that we can discuss with you settlement of the complainant's claim for compensation. Further we put you on notice that if liability is not admitted and the claim has to proceed to a full tribunal hearing then we will make application to the tribunal for an order of costs on the basis of unreasonable conduct in these proceedings (see Industrial Tribunals (Constitution, etc.) Regulations 1993 Schedule 1 Rule 12(1))."

3.   The Effect of the Recoupment Regulations

6–06 If the complainant has been in receipt of Jobseekers Allowance or Income Support since the dismissal then a sum to cover the total amount of those benefits must be deducted by the employer from any award of compensation for unfair dismissal made by the tribunal before sending the balance to the Complainant (see paras 16–18 to 16–30 for commentary on the Recoupment Regulations). This rule, however, only applies to awards of the tribunal and not to sums paid under a settlement (it is possible that the regulations do apply if the full terms of settlement are recorded as an award of the tribunal).

Note that the Regulations apply to benefits paid prior to the award of the tribunal being made. Note also that the Regulations do not apply in relation to awards of compensation in discrimination cases.

6–07 Whilst the Regulations provide for the deduction of benefits received from the total award, it should also be noted that receipt of Jobseekers Allowance and Income Support is disregarded in the assessment of the compensatory award. The effect of the Regulations is to provide another strong incentive to consider settlement of unfair dismissal claims—both from the point of view of the respondent and the complainant. If, for example, the tribunal was to award £9,000 as the compensatory award and the complainant has, since dismissal, received £2,000 in benefits then the complainant will end up receiving £7,000. Without considering any other factors, it would be in the interest of both parties to settle the claim at £8,000: the respondent pays out £1,000 less than he would if the tribunal makes an award and the complainant receives £1,000 more than by way of an award.

4. The effect of an award of future loss on entitlement to benefits

6–08   Whilst the recoupment rules do not apply to awards in respect of future loss of earnings or other benefits, there is another strong reason for the complainant to consider settlement rather than waiting for the tribunal to make an award. If the tribunal makes an award which, for example, covers future loss of earnings for six months then the complainant will be disqualified from recovering benefits for that period. This applies to both unfair dismissal and discrimination cases. However, a global settlement reached between the parties will not affect entitlement to benefits in the future (see para. 16.04).

5. Avoiding damaging publicity

6–09   The parties may also be influenced by a desire to avoid adverse publicity which frequently results from a tribunal hearing. This may encourage either party to settle and should not be underestimated when considering, for example, by how much to discount a legitimate claim in order to achieve a settlement. The respondent may be concerned about publicity encouraging others to pursue claims or it may consider that evidence of fault on its part may damage its reputation.

6. Scope for agreeing references, confidentiality clauses, etc.

6–10   The tribunal is limited to the remedies provided by statute. A settlement, however, may be able to address the needs of the parties more effectively. An agreed reference may be very important for an unemployed complainant. The respondent, and sometimes the complainant, may want to include a confidentiality clause in a settlement. It may also be possible for the respondent to negotiate for a covenant of one sort or another restricting the complainant's future activities for a fixed period of time (see paras 6–45 to 6–46 for further commentary on the tax implications of payments made in return for such covenants).

7. Tax Issues

6–11   It may be possible to negotiate a deal which is more tax-efficient than an award of the tribunal. This might include circumstances where the parties agree to a payment being made into a pension scheme as part of the termination agreement. Such payments may be capable of being made gross without deductions of tax (see paras 6–37 to 6–74 for commentary on tax issues).

THE STEPS TO TAKE

6–12   To initiate negotiations for a settlement it is always wise to present to the respondent a full schedule of loss together with supporting justification for any assumptions made in the assessment of loss. This can then form the basis of discussion between the two parties (see Chapter 5 for guidance on drafting the schedule of loss). In particular, consider providing evidence to demonstrate that the complainant has made proper efforts to mitigate his loss (see paras 3–49 to 3–50 for guidance on gathering evidence to show efforts to mitigate loss). Clearly, a judgement has to be made as to how much to reveal to the respondent at this stage. The risk is that if the claim does not settle the respondent will be forewarned ready for cross-examination on this issue. However, if the evidence on mitigation is strong it may well facilitate settlement to reveal the strength of your hand.

6–13   If discussions are taking place prior to the tribunal determining liability, the respondent is likely to rely on his denial of liability as a basis for either resisting any discussions on settlement or making a modest offer as a "commercial payment" of a sum which is less than is likely to be incurred in legal costs to defend the claim. The respondent or his representative may also seek to challenge

1)   the heads of loss

2)   the period of loss claimed

In an unfair dismissal claim, the respondent may also argue that the tribunal is likely to reduce the award because of:

1)   Contributory fault (see paras 11–38 to 11–87);

2)   Other blameworthy conduct by the complainant (see paras 11–30 to 11–35);

3)   The likelihood that the complainant could have been fairly dismissed had a fair procedure been followed or because of some subsequent event, for example the closure of the factory where the complainant worked (see paras 11–04 to 11–29);

Likewise, with a discrimination claim the respondent may argue for some sort of percentage reduction to compensation. For example, in a claim alleging that the complainant has been dismissed because she was pregnant, the respondent may argue that had she not been dismissed she was unlikely to return from maternity leave. If the claim proceeds to a tribunal hearing and the tribunal accepts that the complainant may not have returned after maternity leave then a percentage reduction can be applied to the loss suffered (see paras 13–58 to 13–76 for further commentary).

6–14   Remember to submit the schedule of loss as a draft and make clear that further facts may emerge which may lead to an amendment of the schedule. Remember also to submit the schedule on a "without prejudice" basis. Consider stating at this stage that all further discussions on settlement will be on a "without prejudice" basis but also ensure that this is restated before each and every further discussion aimed at compromising the claim. There may, of course, in some circumstances be good reason for having open discussions but this has to be judged on a case by case basis.

ACHIEVING SETTLEMENT

6–15   It is in both parties interests that any settlement is binding and enforceable. The respondent will almost certainly want an agreement that settles all potential claims. From the complainant's point of view he must ensure that he understands what claims are being settled. It may well be wise, for example, to exclude from the agreement personal injury claims and claims in respect of accrued pension rights.

Options available to settle claims

6–16   Remember that the starting point is that agreements which prevent a person from bringing or continuing tribunal proceedings are void (see s.203 ERA and, with regard to discrimination claims, s.77(3) SDA, s.72(3) RRA, s.9(1) DDA and in relation to claims under TULR (C) A, s.288 (1) of that Act) (Contract claims brought in the tribunal by virtue of the Employment Tribunal Extension of Jurisdiction (England and Wales) Order 1994 (S.I. 1994 No.1623) are not subject to these rules and can be settled by agreement between the parties in accordance with the standard common law rules (offer and acceptance, consideration, an intention to create legal relations and the absence of duress, undue influence, misrepresentation or mistake)). There are, however, exceptions to the general rule that agreements preventing an employee bringing or continuing proceedings are void. The exceptions are as follows:

1. Compromise agreements;

2. ACAS settlements;

3. Agreements entered into during the tribunal hearing leading to a consent order.

6–17   There may be opportunities to achieve a settlement:

1. Before proceedings have been issued;

2. After the issue of proceedings but before the claim is heard by the tribunal;

3. After the tribunal has decided liability and the hearing has been adjourned specifically to give the parties the chance to reach a settlement.

At all these stages a binding agreement can only be achieved by way of one of the above exceptions. Note, however, that there is nothing to stop an employer reaching agreement with an employee (or ex-employee) in full and final settlement of all claims on the basis that a sum of money is payable to an employee provided that no proceedings are issued by the employee. The sum, or part of it, may be payable at some future date—perhaps after the expiration of the usual three month period for bringing claims, or it may have been paid on the basis that if tribunal proceedings are issued the sum will be repayable to the employer.

6–18   Such agreements do not prevent the employee bringing proceedings and are not void but the implications may be:

1. The sum paid may be repayable under the terms of the agreement (or if it has not yet been paid, the employer may be able to avoid paying it if the agreement so provides);

2. If the sum paid is not repayable under the agreement then it will be taken into account in assessing compensation (see Chapter 15);

3. In an unfair dismissal claim, the tribunal may conclude that it would not be just and equitable to award further compensation. In *Courage Take Home Trade Ltd. v. Keys* [1986] I.R.L.R. 427, the ex-employee accepted a sum in settlement of his claim for unfair dismissal but then continued with tribunal proceedings because the settlement had not been concluded under the auspices of ACAS (compromise agreements were not at that time available). The

tribunal concluded that it would not be just and equitable to award compensation in the circumstances. However, if the employer has put unreasonable pressure on an employee to enter such an agreement, for example by refusing to pay sums due under the contract of employment unless he signs up (such as pay in lieu of notice), then it is likely that the tribunal would consider it just and equitable to award further sums (subject to proof of loss by the complainant). Whether the tribunal considers that it would not be just and equitable to make an award of compensation in such circumstances will depend on the facts of each case.

Settlements Concluded Through ACAS

6–19 ACAS conciliation officers can be used to help conciliate a claim. If proceedings have not been issued then they will only assist if asked to do so by one of the parties (see s.18(3) Industrial Tribunals Act, 1996). Once one of the following claims has been issued ACAS will appoint an officer to be assigned to the case:

- Unfair dismissal;

- Sex, race and disability discrimination;

- Breach of equality claims under Equal Pay Act;

- Unlawful deduction from wages;

- Infringement of various rights under the Trade Union and Labour Relations (Consolidation) Act 1992;

- Claims relating to a wide range of rights during employment under the ERA;

- Breach of contract claims;

- Redundancy payment claims (see s.11 Employment Rights (Dispute Resolution) Act 1998;

- Working Time Regulation Claims (see Reg 33 Working Time Regulations 1988).

[For a full list of claims in relation to which a conciliation officer is under a duty to assist, see s.18 of the Industrial Tribunals Act, 1996.]

6–20 A Conciliation Officer will not rubber stamp an agreement already reached between the parties. He must have been involved to some extent in reaching a settlement. This was one of the conditions set out in a 1990 ACAS Practice Direction for ACAS agreeing to conclude a binding settlement. The other conditions were:

- the employee must have been dismissed or received notice terminating employment (or if ACAS is satisfied that the ex-employee believes he has been constructively dismissed), and

- the ex-employee's employment rights must have been infringed.

ACAS cannot, therefore, be used in circumstances where there has not yet been a dismissal but the parties wish to reach an agreement for the employee to leave on agreed terms. In such circumstances the employer and employee may consider the use of a compromise agreement to reach a binding settlement (see paras 6–30 to 6–36).

ACAS Involvement Once a Claim Has Been Issued

6–21 Note that Section 18(4) of the Industrial Tribunals Act, 1996 places an obligation on the ACAS officer to promote re-instatement or re-engagement where a complainant has complained to a tribunal that he has been unfairly dismissed. This duty does not apply if the complainant does not want to be re-employed or if re-employment is not practicable. In such circumstances the duty is to promote agreement as to a sum of compensation to be paid by the employer. In *Moore v. Duport Furniture Products Ltd and ACAS* [1982] I.R.L.R. 31 HL, the ACAS Conciliation Officer reached the conclusion that there was no prospect of the employer agreeing to re-employ the complainant. In such circumstances the House of Lords held that it would have been futile to seek to promote re-employment. The only duty, therefore, was to seek to promote a settlement of the complaint without it being determined by the tribunal. In this case Mr Moore signed a COT3 which settled his potential claim for unfair dismissal on the basis of a payment of £300 by the employer.

6–22 A conciliation officer has a duty to promote settlement if so requested by one of the parties or, in the absence of a request, if he believes that there is a reasonable prospect of success if he was to be involved (s.18(2) ITA 1996). This duty continues following a finding of liability where, for example, the hearing has been adjourned to give the parties an opportunity to settle compensation. Remember that the ACAS officer is independent, does not give a view on the merits of a particular claim and does not consider the evidence. The officer will discuss possible settlement with both sides. Information passed on from one side to the other during this process will not be admissible in evidence in the tribunal unless the person giving the information gives consent (s.18(7) ITA 1996). However, if the information or documents would be admissible, without having been communicated by the ACAS officer, then it can be put in evidence (see *M & W Grazebrook Ltd v. Wallens* [1973] I.R.L.R. 139). In this case, Sir John Donaldson confirmed that, without consent, "no evidence can be given of the content of oral statements made to a conciliation officer in connection with the performance of his functions ... or indeed that such statements were made". Documents, however, are in a special position. The admissibility of a document depends on "the general law in relation to privilege from disclosure. The privilege would extend to any document which was prepared solely for the purpose of communication to a conciliation officer whether in connection with his functions ... or, more generally, with a view to achieving a settlement". In this case, minutes of a management/shop stewards' meeting did not come within this privilege and had to be considered as if they had never been handed to a conciliation officer.

Concluding an Agreement Through ACAS

6–23 The agreement concluded with the assistance of ACAS is normally recorded on form COT 3. This is not an absolute requirement and an agreement may be binding even if nothing has been recorded in writing (see s.203 ERA; s.77(4) SDA; s.72(4) RRA; s.9(2) DDA; s.288(2); TULR(C)A). If the conciliation officer has acted under s.18 ITA 1996, and an agreement has been concluded either not to institute or not to continue proceedings, then it will be binding. However, to achieve certainty always ensure that the agreement is properly recorded on COT3.

6–24 The COT3 agreement can be used to settle all the various potential claims which the complainant might have. However, it must be clear and precise. If, for example, a complainant agrees to settle an unfair dismissal claim by way of a COT 3 agreement, and the wording of the agreement only refers to settlement of this claim, then, subject to the statutory time limits, he can then pursue any other claim. It is not enough to state that the agreement is in full and final settlement of all claims. The claims which the agreement aims to settle should all be set out. "It is of course helpful for parties to be able to 'wipe the slate clean' but the agreement must relate to those matters which are within their presumed contemplation at the time." Wood J. in *Livingstone v. Hepworth Refractories plc* [1992] I.R.L.R. 63. If claims under European Union law are also to be excluded then these must be dealt with as well (see *Livingstone v. Hepworth Refractories plc*).

Setting aside ACAS Agreements

6–25 Once an agreement has been concluded with the assistance of ACAS, tribunals will be reluctant to interfere. If there has been such duress that the action of the employee in entering the agreement amounts to an "involuntary act" then it may be over-turned. The question is: "Did the employee have no alternative but to acquiesce in the agreement?" (see *Hennessy v. Craigmyle & Co. Ltd. and ACAS* [1986] I.R.L.R. 300). In that case, the Court of Appeal found that the employee had an alternative course of action, namely to complain to a tribunal. "Highly unattractive though that option might have been, it was a real alternative." The Court of Appeal also pointed out that where an agreement had been reached after the employee received independent advice and assistance from a skilled conciliation officer, "it must make the possibility of economic duress more remote" (Sir John Donaldson).

6–26 Attempts to challenge agreements concluded with the assistance of ACAS are also unlikely to succeed unless you can show that the conciliation officer has acted in bad faith. In *Slack v. Greenham (Plant Hire) Ltd* [1983] I.R.L.R. 271 EAT, Mr Slack entered an agreement through ACAS on termination of employment. He subsequently discovered facts which made him consider that the dismissal was unfair. He also discovered that he could have claimed for loss of earnings in the tribunal. He issued a claim which was dismissed because of the ACAS agreement. The EAT upheld the decision to dismiss his claim. The ACAS officer has no duty to advise or inform an employee of his right to claim loss of earnings and does not have to follow a specific formula when seeking to conciliate. The ACAS officer's approach will depend on the circumstances of each case. However "if a conciliation officer were to act in bad faith or adopt unfair methods when promoting a settlement the agreement might be set aside and might not operate as a bar to proceedings" (Tudor Evans J.).

Agreement entered into by advisor without the consent of the party ostensibly represented

6–27 If an adviser has been held out as representing a party and having authority to act then if he enters an agreement through ACAS that party will be bound even if the adviser had, in fact, no authority. The only course of action available would be to pursue a claim against the adviser in negligence (see *Freeman v. Sovereign Chicken Ltd* [1991] I.R.L.R. 408). In this case the EAT held that the tribunal was right to conclude that the Citizens Advice Bureau had the ostensible authority of the complainant to reach agreement. The CAB adviser had held himself out as having the authority to negotiate and reach a settlement and, in the absence of any notice to the contrary, the other party was entitled to assume that the adviser did have such authority. The agreement was binding. This means that it is of crucial importance for the adviser to ensure that the party he represents fully understands the nature and terms of the agreement.

6–28 Set out below is an example of a schedule to the standard COT3 agreement.

Remember, though, that the terms of the agreement must be tailored to the circumstances of the particular case.

Example of Schedule to COT3 Agreement

Case No:

("the Applicant")

("the Respondent")

The Applicant and the Respondent have agreed the following terms in full and final settlement of all and any claims (with the exception of industrial injury [and accrued pension rights]) that the Applicant may have against the Respondent, [and the Respondent may have against the Applicant,] relating to his/her employment, the termination of his/her employment or any other matters whatsoever including but limited to any statutory claims for a redundancy payment or unfair dismissal against the Respondent under the provisions of the Employment Rights Act 1996, claims under the Sex Discrimination Act, 1975, the Race Relations Act, 1976 and the Disability Discrimination Act, 1995 or any other UK or European employment law provision:

1.　The Applicant hereby withdraws his claim of [unfair dismissal] before the Employment Tribunal under the above Case No.

2.　The Respondent will pay to the Applicant on the signing of the agreement:

　　(a)　compensation in lieu of [　] weeks notice entitlement which amounts to £[　]

　　(b)　a further *ex gratia* sum in compensation for termination of employment of £[　] without admission of liability

　　[(c)　the sum of £[　] in return for the Applicant's undertaking in clause 3 below relating to confidentiality] (see paras 6–45 to 6–46)

3.　The outcome of these proceedings and these terms of settlement shall remain confidential to the parties hereto, their Legal Advisers and ACAS.

Signed　　...

Signed　　...

Tax Implications

6–29　It is important to ensure that the tax implications of any sums paid under an ACAS agreement are fully understood. See paragraphs 6–37 to 6–74 for commentary on the key issues to consider.

Compromise Agreements

6–30　This relatively recent invention was designed to address circumstances in which an agreement concluded through ACAS is not available. As we have seen, ACAS officers will not "rubber stamp" an agreement already reached between the parties (see para. 6–20). Further, an ACAS agreement is not available unless the employee has already been dismissed or received notice of termination. It is not possible, therefore, to terminate employment on binding agreed terms using ACAS. Now, compromise agreements are widely used and can provide a reasonably simple, straightforward way of settling claims.

6–31   The relevant statutory provisions are for:

1.   Unfair Dismissal and other claims under the ERA: s.203(2)(f) ERA;

2.   Claims under the SDA and EPA: Section 77 (4)(aa) of the SDA—known as "compromise contracts";

3.   Claims under the RRA: Section 72 (4)(aa) of the RRA—also known as "compromise contracts";

4.   Claims under the DDA: Section 9 (2)(b) of the DDA, (not given any particular name!);

5.   Claims under the TULR(c)A: Section 288 (2A) of the TULR (C) A—known as "compromise agreements";

6.   Claims under Working Time Regulations 1988—known as "compromise agreements" (see Reg 35, Working Time Regulations 1998).

6–32   For an agreement under any of these provisions to be binding, strict conditions have to be met:

1.   The agreement must be in writing;

2.   The agreement must relate to a particular complaint (see below);

3.   The complainant must have received advice from a "relevant independent adviser". The range of independent advisers has been extended as a result of the Employment Rights (Dispute Resolution) Act 1998. Under this Act, a relevant independent adviser may be one of the following:

  (i)   Qualified lawyer (solicitor, barrister, or an authorised advocate or litigator who is not a solicitor or barrister);

  (ii)   Officers, officials, employees or members of an independent trade union. The person concerned must be authorised in writing by the trade union as being competent to give such advice and permitted to do so on behalf of the union;

  (iii)   An advice centre worker (either a volunteer or employee) with written certification from the advice centre, of competence to give the advice and confirming that he is authorised to give it on behalf of the centre. In this case, the advice must be free;

  (iv)   The Secretary of State may add other categories of adviser by Order.

  The adviser must not be acting for the employer or an associated employer, nor must he be connected with the employer. The advice must be with regard to the terms and effect of the proposed agreement and in particular its effect on the complainant's ability to pursue his rights before a tribunal;

4.   The adviser must be covered by a "contract of insurance, or an indemnity provided for members of a profession or professional body" (See Section 10 of the Employment Rights (Dispute Resolution) Act 1998 which has sorted

out unsatisfactory wording in the original provisions which appeared not to cover professional indemnity insurance which solicitors are required to have);

5. The agreement must identify the adviser.

6. The agreement must state that conditions regulating compromise agreements/contracts are satisfied.

(See ERA s.203(3); SDA s.77(4A); RRA s.72(4A); TULR(C)A s.288(2B); DDA s.9(3)).

The Agreement Must Relate to the Particular Complaint

6–33 It is no good stating that the compromise agreement is in full and final settlement of all claims. This does not meet the statutory requirements. For a particular claim to be compromised in this way it must be an issue between the parties (but this does not mean that tribunal proceedings must have been brought in respect of the complaint) and the agreement must specifically refer to the potential claim. Note that if a potential claim has been referred to in the compromise agreement but the claim has never been raised, prior to that, between the parties (for example in a letter before action or a tribunal application) it could later be argued by the complainant that this was not a "complaint" at the time the agreement was signed. However, if the complainant and his adviser have consented to the agreement making reference to such claims, it is difficult to imagine circumstances in which he could later contend that it was not an issue between the parties. If the agreement seeks to compromise claims under the various different statutory provisions referred to above (see para. 6–31) the agreement should make reference to the fact that it satisfies the requirements of all the relevant statutes (see para. 6–32).

Addressing Other Issues in the Compromise Agreement

6–34 It is common for a compromise agreement to deal with a number of other issues such as:

1. payment of legal costs—(see paras 6–53 to 6.55) for important tax provisions relating to legal costs;

2. payment of part of the agreed sum into a pension scheme which may be paid gross even if the total sum exceeds £30,000 (see para. 6–62);

3. The provision of an agreed reference (which would normally be appended to the agreement);

4. The return of the company property;

5. Indemnity in respect of tax liabilities;

6. Confidentiality—as to the terms of the agreement, or to the circumstances leading up to termination of employment and the signing of the agreement (see paras 6–45 to 6–46 for commentary on tax implications);

7. Other covenants relating to the activities of the employee following the signing of the agreement such as:

    (a) avoiding misuse of trade secrets and other confidential information;
    (b) prohibiting the employee from soliciting or dealing with customers of the employer;

(c) other non-competition covenants;

(d) prohibiting the employee from taking other staff with him.

(See paras 6–45 to 6–46 for commentary on tax implications.)

6–35 A proposal on the part of the employer to introduce some sort of restrictive covenant into a compromise agreement is likely to be an important issue in the negotiations relating to the size of the total payment. The covenant is likely to have some "value". The employer's motivation for including some restriction on the ex-employee's future activities is likely to be based on a concern as to the damage which that ex-employee might be able to do to the business—for example by taking customers away. If the ex-employee is going to agree to restrictions he is likely to want something in return.

Drafting a Compromise Agreement

6–36 It is important that the agreement is carefully drafted. From the employer's point of view he wants to ensure certainty (see para. 6–33 for commentary on the need to specify the particular claims you seek to compromise). Set out below is an example of a compromise agreement. Note, however, that it is vital that it is tailored carefully to address the particular needs of the parties. Further, the potential tax implications have to be carefully considered. This is particularly the case where the agreement provides for a substantial payment to the complainant.

Compromise Agreement

1. This Agreement is made the _____ day of _____ between _____ (the "Employee") and _____ of _____ (the "Employer").

2. The Employee was employed by the Employer and the terms set out in this Agreement have been agreed between the parties.

3. The Employee's employment by the Employer terminated on [_____] and the Employee will be paid his salary and accrued holiday pay to that date. Such payment is subject to normal deductions under PAYE.

4. This Agreement has effect for the purpose of compromising by means of full and final settlement any claim or potential claim which the Employee may have against the Employer arising out of his employment or the termination thereof [but excluding any claim in respect of accrued rights under the Employer's pension scheme] [or any claims for personal injury]. This includes all claims he may have at common law or under Statute against the Employer and including (but not by way of limitation) the following claims:

   (a) Any claim for pay in lieu of notice or damages for termination of employment without notice;

   (b) Any claim for holiday pay;

   (c) Any claim for outstanding pay, overtime, bonuses or commission;

   (d) any claim of unfair dismissal;

   (e) Any claim of sex discrimination or of victimisation under the Sex Discrimination Act 1975;

(f) Any claim of disability discrimination or of victimisation under the Disability Discrimination Act 1995;

(g) Any claim under the Employment Rights Act 1996 in respect of the unauthorised deduction from wages; or

(h) Any other complaint under the Employment Rights Act 1996 or the Trade Union and Labour Relation (Consolidation) Act 1992;

(i) Any claim for redundancy pay;

(j) Any claim under Regulation 30, Working Time Regulations, 1998.

5. The parties hereto believe the following statements to be true:

(a) That the Employee has received advice from a relevant independent adviser (within the meaning of the Employment Rights Act 1996) as to the terms and effect of this Agreement and in particular its effect on his ability to pursue his rights before an Employment Tribunal;

(b) The relevant independent adviser referred to in paragraph (a) was _____ of the firm of _____ ("the Adviser");

(c) There was in force when the Adviser gave the advice referred to in paragraph (a) a contract of insurance or an indemnity provided for members of a profession or professional body covering the risk of a claim by the Employee in respect of loss arising in consequence of the advice; and

(d) The Adviser by signing this Agreement warrants that the circumstances set out in paragraph (a), (b) and (c) are correct.

6. This agreement satisfies the conditions for regulating:

(a) Compromise agreements under section 203 of the Employment Rights Act 1996 including the provisions relating to unauthorised deductions from wages;

(b) Compromise contracts under Section 77 of the Sex Discrimination Act 1975;

(c) Compromise contracts under Section 72 of the Race Relations Act 1976;

(d) Agreements under Section 9 of the Disability Discrimination Act 1995;

(e) Compromise agreements under section 288 of the Trade Union and Labour Relations (Consolidation) Act 1992;

(f) Compromise agreements under Regulation 35, Working Time Regulations, 1988.

7. The Employer will pay to the Employee the sum of [   ] such sum to be paid within _____ days of the concluding of this Agreement. [It is understood by both parties that the first £30,000 of this sum is tax free and will be paid as such.]

8. The Employer will pay to the Employee the sum of [   ] as consideration for the undertakings made by him in paragraphs 12, 13 and 14 (see paras 6–45 to 6–46 for commentary on the tax implications of such payments).

9. The Employer will in addition pay to the Employee the sum of [   ] in payment of the Employee's legal costs directly resulting from the termination of his employment and advice received in respect thereof, such sum to be paid within _____ days of the receipt of a VAT invoice from his legal advisers, _____, will be paid and directly to them (see paras 6–53

to 6–55 for commentary on the tax treatment of legal costs).

10. Whereas:

   (i)   The Employee considers that he has suffered discrimination at the hands of the Employer on the ground of his mental health and that he has, as a result of the discrimination, suffered injury to feelings which has further damaged his mental health and that compensation or damages on account of such injury from the Employer would be recoverable by reason of the provisions of the Disability Discrimination Act 1995 ("the DDA");

   (ii)   It is reasonable to assume that at least [   ] might be recovered by the Employee on account of such compensation or damages.

   (iii)   The Employer agrees to pay forthwith to the Employee [   ] in return for the Employee giving up his right to claim such compensation or damages under the DDA or in a negligence claim (see paras 6–59 to 6–61 for commentary on the tax treatment of payments in respect of personal injury).

11. The Employer will, if so requested, provide a written reference in respect of the Employee only in the terms of the attached draft, and respond to any oral enquiries in the spirit of that agreed reference.

12. Neither the Employer nor the Employee will, directly or indirectly, disclose the terms of this settlement other than to their legal and financial advisers and to any state agencies as may lawfully require such information. Such disclosure may also be made by the Employee to his immediate family and by the Employer to those officers and members of staff who of necessity require that information for the proper performance of their duties.

13. The Employee will refrain from passing any adverse or derogatory comments concerning the Employer or its officers or employees and/or taking part in any conduct conducive or potentially conducive to the bringing of the Employer or its employees into disrepute and the Employer acknowledges a similar obligation in respect of the Employee.

14. The Employee will not use, divulge, or communicate to any person (other than those whose province it is to know the same or with the proper authority) any confidential information or trade secrets of the Employer (including in particular internal financial and similar information) which he may have received or retained while in the service of the Employer.

15. On the completion of this Agreement, the Employee will deliver to the Employer any property in his possession belonging to the Employer including in particular the keys to any properties of the Employer. The Employer will also return to the Employee any personal property of the Employee which it has in its possession.

Signed   ....

     The Employee

Signed   ....

For the Employer

Signed   ....

The Adviser

Tax Implications of Payments to the Employee

6–37   In any circumstances where payments are made, either on the termination of employment or in settlement of a claim following termination, it is important to understand the potential tax implications of such payments. This is essential both in negotiating a settlement in order to accurately measure the amount which will actually be received by the complainant and to ensure that any written agreement is framed correctly. Here is a checklist of issues to consider.

Checklist:

- Does payment fall within £30,000 exempt limit?
- Is the payment or part of it taxable for any of the following reasons:
  - Contract of employment provides for it.
  - Payment made in return for undertakings by ex-employee?
- Can payment of legal expenses be exempt from tax?
- Is any part of the payment, compensation for injury to feelings or personal injury?
- Should a tax indemnity be considered by either party?
- If a sum is taxable, who is responsible for making the payment, the employer or employee?
- Note rules on taxation of interest payments.
- Is payment made in circumstances where the employee is retiring taxable?
- Is any part of the payment in respect of statutory redundancy pay or an additional *ex gratia* redundancy payment taxable?
- Are there potential tax implications in relation to any non-cash benefits?

This section examines the tax rules relating to termination payments.

Payments arising from an entitlement under contract of employment and other emoluments from employment

6–38   Any payments due to an employee on or after termination of employment— whether or not as part of a termination agreement—which are provided for under the contract of employment or were payable in respect of employment will be taxable as emoluments from employment under section 19 ICTA (Emoluments are defined in s.131(1) ICTA: "emoluments shall include all salaries, fees, wages, perquisites and profits whatsoever"). Examples of such payments are:

1. Holiday pay due;

2. Arrears of salary or bonuses (whether contractual or discretionary);

3. Payments in lieu of notice (PILON) where the contract provides for the right to make a PILON.

Note that a PILON may be a contractual payment and therefore taxable under s.19 ICTA where a staff handbook or wage agreement provides for such a payment. Such a provision may be part of the contract of employment. Equally, it may have been verbally agreed and therefore part of the contract. Also, if the employer regularly makes a PILON instead of giving notice then it may be arguable that it becomes an implied term of contract.

6–39   If the contract simply reserves the right or discretion to make a PILON, the Revenue regard such a payment as being an entitlement and therefore taxable under s.19 ICTA (See Tax Bulletin, August 1996 Appendix K). Note that if the contract does not provide for a PILON then if the employer terminates the employee's employment without notice, he will be acting in breach of contract (unless he is dismissed for gross misconduct entitling the employer to dismiss summarily) and any payment in respect of the notice period will be properly characterised as compensation for wrongful dismissal (not an emolument from employment) and is therefore not taxable (subject to the £30,000 exempt limit—see paras 6–42 to 6–43). This analysis has been confirmed in *EMI Group Electronics Ltd. v. Coldicott (Inspector of Taxes)* High Court (Chancery Division) (1997) British Tax Cases 532 and IDS Brief 605 1998.

6–40   In circumstances where there is no contractual right to make a payment in lieu of notice, but on termination of employment the employer and employee *agree* that the contract is to be terminated without proper notice, it seems that the payment of a sum in lieu of notice is not an emolument and therefore is not taxable under s.19 ICTA. Instead it is taxable under s.148 ICTA 1988 and benefits from the £30,000 exemption (see Tax Bulletin, August 1996, Appendix K).

The description of payment is not conclusive

6–41   What matters is a proper analysis of the nature of the payment rather than what the parties choose to call it. If a payment is described as "compensation" but in fact is a payment provided for by the contract of employment then the Revenue will regard it as a taxable payment. In *Dale v. De Soissons* (1950) 2 All E.R. 460, the employee had a three-year contract which also allowed the company to terminate at the end of the first or second year. In such circumstances the employee was entitled under the contract to a lump sum payment "by way of compensation for loss of office". The contract was terminated by the company at the end of the first year with the employee receiving the lump sum payment. The Court of Appeal held that the payment was taxable as a contractual payment despite its description in the contract as "compensation for loss of office".

Other payments made on or after termination of employment

6–42   Payments made on or after termination of employment as compensation for the loss of employment are not "emoluments from employment" and are generally taxable under s.148 ICTA 1988 (see paras 6–38 to 6–40 for exceptions). s.148(1) ICTA provides that payments and other benefits received in connection with termination of employment or any change in the duties of or emoluments from a person's employment are chargeable to tax under this section if and to the extent that their amount exceeds £30,000. If such a payment is made at, or just after, termination the position is generally straightforward. Any balance over and above £30,000 is taxed as income and it is the responsibility of the employer to deduct tax at source (see para. 6–74 for commentary on the amount of tax the employer should deduct).

6–43   Where a termination settlement provides for benefits continuing after termination into future years—for example the provision of a car or a low or nil interest loan—Currently such benefits are treated as income in year in which the benefit is used or enjoyed (s.148(3) and (4) ICTA 1988). Equally a cash payment made in a subsequent year is treated as income received in that year. This is a change to the law introduced by the Finance Act, 1998. Note that a new Schedule 11 to the ICTA has been introduced by the Finance Act 1998 which provides further rules supplemental to s.148 ICTA.

Advance Clearance by Revenue

6–44   It is worth noting that the Revenue operates an informal system of advance clearance. If there is doubt as to the nature of a particular payment and the employer wants informal guidance as to whether the payment is likely to be taxable, a request for guidance can be put to the Revenue. However, informal guidance does not necessarily bind the Revenue. (See ICAEW Technical Release 1991 TR830) and text of letter at Appendix I). Further information about seeking advance clearance can be obtained from the local tax office. (See also para. 6–49 for commentary on advance clearance for redundancy payments).

Restrictive Covenants

6–45   As referred to at paragraph 6–34, the employer may wish to introduce into a compromise agreement, restrictions on the former employee's activities—usually to protect the company's customer base. Any payment made in return for such a covenant is taxable under a special provision in s.313 ICTA. The important drafting consideration is that if the compromise agreement contains such a covenant (unless it simply repeats what was already in the contract of employment) then any sums paid by the employer as consideration for those covenants should be kept separate from *ex gratia* compensation payments (which have the benefit of the £30,000 exemption, see paras 6–42 to 6–43. If no separation is made, the risk is that the Revenue can challenge sums which should properly be non taxable as *ex gratia* compensation payments.

6–46   There was concern prior to 1996 as to whether any payments made under a compromise agreement (or other termination agreement) in consideration for the employee giving up his right to pursue a claim in the tribunal might be taxable under s.313 ICTA. The Revenue clarified the position by way of a Statement of Practice SP3/96 (April 4, 1996) (see text at Appendix D). The Statement makes clear that payments made to compromise claims in a court or tribunal will be accepted as not subject to tax. The Statement also confirms that payments made in respect of restrictive undertakings are taxable under s.313 ICTA. Note that this could include an undertaking simply to maintain confidentiality as to the terms of the agreement or the circumstances leading up to termination of employment. Such an undertaking could be regarded as important by the employer. Therefore payments made in return for such an undertaking should again be kept separate from *ex gratia* compensation payments.

Redundancy Payments

6–47   The statutory redundancy payment is not taxable (s.579(1)ICTA) but is taken into account in assessing the sums coming within the £30,000 exemption under s.148 ICTA. For example, if there is a statutory redundancy payment of £4,400 and an *ex gratia* compensation payment of £28,000, the total payment is £32,400. £30,000 is tax-free. £2,400 is taxable (see also paras 6–42 to 6–43).

Contractual redundancy payments are also exempt from tax unless they exceed £30,000 in which case the balance over that sum is taxable. (This is an exception to the usual rule that contractual payments are taxable, see paras 6–38 to 6–40). This was confirmed by the House of Lords in *Mairs (HM Inspector of Taxes) v. Haughey* [1993] I.R.L.R. 551. Such payments are taxable under s.148 ICTA and benefit from the £30,000 exemption. A payment made to an employee as compensation for giving up a contingent entitlement to a contractual redundancy payment is treated in the same way.

6–48   Similarly, an *ex gratia* payment made as compensation for redundancy (without any contractual obligation to make the payment) is taxable under s.148 ICTA with a £30,000 exemption. The Inland Revenue has issued a Statement of Practice SP1/94 confirming and clarifying the *Mairs* decision (see text of Statement of Practice at Appendix A).

The Statement makes clear that if a payment is, in reality, a terminal bonus rather than a redundancy payment it will be taxable under s.19 ICTA as an emolument from employment (see para. 6–38). Examples given of such terminal bonuses are:

(a) payments made for meeting production targets,

(b) payments for doing extra work in the period leading up to redundancy;

(c) payments conditional on continued service for a period of time.

6–49   The distinction is drawn between genuine payments made to compensate for loss of employment through redundancy and payments made as a reward for services or for having been an employee. The latter category of payment is taxable as an emolument under s.19 ICTA. Specific reference is made to the opportunity for employers to submit proposed schemes of payments to an Inspector of Taxes for clearance. Full facts should be submitted in writing together with the "scheme document and the text of any intended letter to employees".

Ex Gratia Pension Schemes / Payments on retirement

6–50   *Ex gratia* lump sums paid on retirement are taxed under s.148 ICTA but do not benefit from the £30,000 exemption. They are therefore taxable in full unless the employer has submitted the relevant scheme to the Inland Revenue for approval as a special *ex gratia* pension scheme. If approval is given, lump sum payments under the scheme will be tax-free. Contractual schemes may also be given approval by the Revenue. (See Revenue Statement of Practice SP 13/91 at Appendix B, the Statement explains how the "approval" arrangement works). (See also text of Revenue Statement of Practice SP 2/81 "Contributions to Retirement Benefit Schemes on termination of employment" at Appendix 7) (see also Appendix J ICAEW Technical Release TR851 Nov 1991 on Taxation of ex-gratia payments which gives further guidance on Statement of Practice SP 13/91).

Is it a redundancy, other *ex gratia* payment, or retirement payment?

6–51   Where a worker is approaching retirement age it may be difficult to determine whether a payment made should properly be categorised as a redundancy payment or other *ex gratia* payment or a payment on early retirement. The closer to retirement age the more likely it is that the Revenue will regard the payment as being in respect of early retirement, particularly if there is evidence that the ex-employee is not seeking new employment (see correspondence between Law Society and Revenue and also between the Faculty of Taxes and the Revenue at Appendix C).

Non Cash Benefits

6–52   Any benefits given to an ex-employee on termination of employment such as allowing them to keep the company car or continuing a low or nil interest loan or mortgage will be taxable under s.148 ICTA and subject to the £30,000 exemption. The Revenue would assess the market value of a car. The Institute of Chartered Accountants has published the text of guidance from the Revenue with regard to the tax treatment of company cars as part of an *ex gratia* severance package. This confirms that the value of a car transferred to an ex-employee as part of a settlement is aggregated with any cash payment when applying the £30,000 exemption.

Legal Costs

6–53   Payments made to the ex employee in respect of legal costs incurred may be exempt from tax by virtue of a 1993 extra-statutory concession by the Inland Revenue (see Appendix E for text of concession). The starting point is that payments made by way of recovery of costs (either in a settlement or as a result of a court or tribunal decision) are assessable to income tax under s.148 ICTA. This means that provided the total payments made, including legal costs (but separate from emoluments taxable under s.19 ICTA: see para. 6–38) do not exceed £30,000, no tax is payable.

6–54   The concession specifies circumstances in which the Revenue will not charge tax on legal costs paid by the employer to the ex-employee (irrespective of the £30,000 exemption). For example, in circumstances where an ex-employee receives an *ex gratia* compensation payment of £30,000 and the employer further agrees to pay legal costs covered by the Concession of, say, £5,000 then those legal costs would not be subject to tax. For costs to be exempt they must be:

- paid direct to the former employee's solicitor;

- in full or partial settlement of the solicitor's account;

- costs must have been incurred by the employee only in connection with termination of employment;

- there must be a specific term of the settlement agreement providing for the payment.

If payment of costs results from a tribunal order rather than as part of a settlement the payment can be made direct to the employee.

6–55   The concession does not cover other professional fees, such as accountancy fees, unless such fees are a proper disbursement which a solicitor incurs in consulting other professionals in respect of a claim being pursued. See also Appendix F for the text of a letter from the Revenue to the Tax Faculty explaining the Concession. Note that the letter makes clear that the Concession does not cover expenses incurred in "negotiating the amount of compensation." It is supposed to relate to expenses incurred "when enforcement of claims through the courts has to be considered."

From the point of view of drafting a Compromise Agreement, if agreement has been reached for the employer to pay some or all of the ex-employee's legal expenses then care should be taken to ensure that clauses are carefully drafted so that those costs identified by the Concession—and not others—are paid without deduction of tax. See paragraph 6–36 for draft compromise agreement including a clause providing for payment of exempt legal fees.

Out-placement Counselling Fees

6–56   Sections 589A and 589B ICTA provide a specific statutory exemption from tax on outplacement counselling fees. If, therefore, part of a settlement provides for the employer to make such payments this should be clearly provided for in the Compromise Agreement. The payment can be either direct to the provider of the service or by way of reimbursement of fees paid by the ex-employee. "Allowable" travelling costs can also be paid free of tax. To be "allowable" they must be travelling expenses which would have been allowable if the counselling were a duty of employment and the employee was still employed by the same employer (s.589B(4) ICTA). For details of qualifying counselling services see s.589B(2) & (3) ICTA.

Payments made to employee during employment as part of a compromise agreement

6–57   There are many circumstances in which a claim is brought (or threatened) during employment which results in a compromise agreement to settle the claim. For example: discrimination claims, claims in respect of suffering a detriment or action short of dismissal related to health and safety duties or trade union membership or activities, breach of contract or unlawful deduction from wages (for further commentary on compensation for detriment/action short of dismissal see Chapter 22). Payments ordered by the tribunal in respect of financial loss during employment, such as where the employee has not been paid for time off work (see paras 22–24 to 22–46), are paid net of tax to the complainant so that he receives what he should have received.

6–58   If the sums paid as part of a settlement or an award are akin to general damages such as injury to feelings or compensation for action short of dismissal (other than in respect of financial loss) then the payments will not be taxable under s.19 ICTA. Where an employee agrees to a variation to his contract of employment and in return receives a lump sum payment as compensation then it is likely that the payment will be taxable (see *Bird v. Mortland; Bird v. Allen* [1982] B.T.C. 259). Two employees agreed to give up company cars in return for a lump sum payment. It was held that this payment was taxable. They received the lump sum because they were employees having perquisites which were to be withdrawn.

Payments in Respect of Personal Injury and Injury to Feelings

6–59   In a claim of unlawful sex, race or disability discrimination, compensation may be awarded for injury to feelings or for personal injury sustained as a result of the discrimination. An ex-employee may also pursue a claim in negligence in the County or High Court for damages for personal injury suffered. A compromise agreement settling such claims may include a specific sum in respect of personal injury or injury to feelings. Paragraph 3 of Schedule to the ICTA exempts from charge under s.148 ICTA "a payment or other benefit provided ... on account of injury to or disability of the employee." Such a payment is therefore payable free of tax even if total payments under s.148 (*i.e.* payments such as *ex gratia* compensation payments) exceed £30,000 (see paras 6–42 to 6–43 for commentary on Section 148 ICTA).

6–60   Injury is not defined specifically for the purposes of s.188(1)(a). It is defined for the purposes of another section dealing with tax treatment of interest on damages for personal injuries (s.329 ICTA). There it is defined as including "any disease and any impairment of a person's physical or mental condition" (s.329(4) ICTA). This provides useful guidance.

The Revenue's Statement of Practice 10/81 (see Appendix H for text) confirms that "disability" is taken to cover a continuing incapacity to perform the duties of an office or employment "arising out of the culmination of a process of deterioration of physical or mental health caused by chronic illness". Medical evidence should be available to satisfy the Revenue that a payment is in respect of an injury or disability (see *Horner v. Hastead* [1995] S.T.C. 766) (Inland Revenue Schedule E Manual, para. 2562 (as updated at September 1997)).

6–61   It is not clear how broad a definition of injury the Revenue will allow for the purposes of determining whether a payment made for "injury to feelings" comes within s.188(1)(a) and experience suggests that practice varies. Injury to feelings awards can be made for distress suffered as a result of a discriminatory act (see paras 13–96 to 13–183). The employer can always seek guidance from an Inspector (see para. 6–44) or hold back a sum sufficient to cover tax on the injury to feelings payment until the Revenue determines the issue. Subject to these issues, if the compromise agreement involves a substantial payment of compensation (in excess of the £30,000 exempt limit) including a payment for injured feelings or personal injury then it is worth providing separately for such a payment in the compromise agreement so that it might be accepted by the Revenue as exempt from tax. (See draft compromise agreement including such a clause at para. 6–36).

Payments Into Pension Scheme

6–62   The Revenue's Statement of Practice 2/81 (see Appendix G for text) provides for exemption from tax in respect of payments into retirement benefit schemes on termination of employment. The retirement benefits must be within the limits and in the form prescribed by the rules of the scheme. It is, therefore, important for an advisor to take instructions from the ex-employee to determine whether he wishes to explore the opportunities for taking advantage of this rule.

Interest Payments

6–63   Where a tribunal makes an award of compensation in respect of sex, race or disability discrimination it will award interest calculated in accordance with the Industrial Tribunals (Interest on Awards in Discrimination Cases) Regulations (S.I. 1996 No.2803) (see paras 13–42 to 13–54 for commentary). Interest is also payable in respect of late payment of an award of compensation (this applies to unfair dismissal as well as discrimination claims). Tax is payable on such interest payments under a separate provision. It may not, however, be payable where the interest is in respect of compensation for injury to feelings (s.329 ICTA) (see para. 6–66). Unlike emoluments or compensation in excess of £30,000, the employer does not deduct tax at source from payments of interest. Any tax payable is the responsibility of the recipient.

6–64   Interest is chargeable to tax by virtue of s.18 ICTA. There is no exempt element. Tax is charged on the full sum. An interest payment is assessable as income in the year payment is actually received—rather than the year in which the cause of the award (usually a dismissal) occurred. Individuals have to declare interest received on the tax return form for the year in which the interest is actually received. Interest due as part of a settlement is disregarded for the purposes of determining whether compensation payments exceed £30,000 thereby incurring tax liability on the excess over that sum. For example, if compensation for termination of employment totals £30,000 and on top of this there is interest payable of £2,000, that sum of £2,000 is not taken into account in determining tax liability under s.148 ICTA and therefore the compensation will be within the exempt limit. The interest payment of £2,000 is paid gross to the ex-employee who then accounts for it on his tax return and pays tax on it under the provisions of s.18 ICTA.

6–65 In some discrimination claims, the total compensation awarded (without any statutory limit) may be very high. A significant period of time may have elapsed since the discriminatory act. There may therefore be a substantial award of interest which will be taxable in the hands of the recipient. However, the important point to make in the context of compromise and other settlement agreements is that if the parties agree a global settlement—in which no element is identified as being in respect of interest then no liability will arise under s.18 ICTA 88.

Negotiations to achieve a settlement may, of course, take place either before or after liability has been determined by the tribunal. When liability has been found against the respondent the case may be adjourned to allow an opportunity for the parties to achieve a settlement. But there may still be substantial dispute as to the calculation of compensation and therefore the amount of interest due. There are likely to be competing schedules of loss each with different calculations of interest. However, if a compromise is achieved providing for payment of a global figure somewhere between the two competing positions, no calculation of interest can be made and a charge under s.18 ICTA does not apply. If the total sum paid to the complainant did not exceed £30,000 then no tax would be payable. If the total sum exceeded £30,000 then tax would be charged on the excess over £30,000 by virtue of s.148 ICTA.

Tax on Interest in Respect of Injury to Feelings Compensation

6–66 Section 329 ICTA provides that interest "shall not be regarded as income for any income tax purpose" if it is interest on "damages in respect of personal injuries". Personal injuries is stated to include "any disease and any impairment of a person's physical or mental condition", s.329 (4) ICTA. So just as some payments in respect of personal injuries or injury to feelings may be exempt from tax (see paras 6–59 to 6–61), the interest on such payments will also be exempt.

Grossing up and the Gourley Principle

6–67 Compensation for loss suffered both in unfair dismissal claims and in discrimination claims is based on net loss of both salary and the value of fringe benefits (after deduction of tax and national insurance). The complainant is therefore compensated for the loss which he has actually suffered (subject to any reductions to compensation—see Chapter 11 in respect of unfair dismissal claims and paras 13–58 to 13–76 in respect of discrimination claims).

The case of *British Transport Commission v. Gourley* [1956] A.C. 185 HL and [1955] All E.R. 796 is authority for the basic principle that a plaintiff who has lost his job should not receive more in respect of lost wages than he would have earned had he remained in work. Tax which he would have paid, had he remained in work, should be deducted.

6–68   As we have seen (see paras 6–42 to 6–43) for awards of compensation for lost earnings of up to £30,000 the complainant will pay no tax on the award. Therefore the *Gourley* principle demands that a sum equivalent to the tax he would have paid, had he remained at work, should be deducted. The problem is that if compensation for loss suffered is a sum greater than £30,000 then, under s.148 ITCA 1988, tax is payable on the amount over £30,000 which therefore means that without any adjustment the complainant would end up recovering less than the loss he has suffered. For example, X is awarded £40,000 compensation for net loss suffered. The first £30,000 is tax free but he is charged tax at 40 per cent on the excess £10,000 leaving him with £36,000 rather than £40,000. The sum of £40,000 was a net figure arrived at by deducting the tax and national insurance which the employee would have had to pay had he not been dismissed. A further reduction to £36,000 would mean that X would receive less compensation than his assessed loss.

6–69   Because of this potential unfairness a scheme has to be devised to ensure the employee recovers the full extent of his loss. (The issue is unlikely to arise in unfair dismissal cases because of the statutory maximum compensatory award but it can often arise in discrimination cases). The scheme for avoiding what would, in effect, be a double taxation of sums over the exempt element (currently £30,000) was first used in *Stewart v Glentaggart* [1963] S.L.T. 119 and approved in *Shove v Downs Surgical plc* [1984] I.R.L.R. 17. Sheen, J. described the approach. The correct principle was "to start by estimating the net amount which would have been received by the plaintiff after the deduction of tax from his gross income. That net amount would represent as realistically as possible his actual loss. Thereafter, in assessing the damages, the court should take into account the plaintiff's liability to tax upon the damages awarded so that the net amount received should, so far as possible, equal the net or actual loss suffered".

6–70   For example, it is calculated that a complainant in a discrimination claim has suffered a net loss of £55,000—a figure arrived at by deducting tax and national insurance from the gross lost wages and benefits for the period of loss. This is the amount which the complainant would have earned had he not been dismissed. £30,000 of this sum is exempt from tax under s.148 and s.188 ICTA. The balance of £25,000 will be subject to tax under s.148. To ensure that the complainant ends up with £55,000 in his hands, the sum of £25,000 has to be "grossed up". This involves identifying the sum which, after deduction of tax at 40 per cent, leaves a total of £25,000.

Taking account of tax liability when negotiating a settlement

6–71   It is essential when negotiating a settlement to take into account the tax liability on compensation in excess of £30,000 and to advise the complainant fully in this respect. For the purposes of negotiation it may be wise to prepare a schedule which simply shows gross loss over £30,000 (without any deduction of tax and national insurance on that element) so that the respondent understands clearly the total amount he will have to pay.

Addressing the question of tax liability where tribunal is making an award

6–72   If compensation is determined by the tribunal, then the tribunal may, with the assistance of schedules of loss from either or both of the parties, go through the process of grossing up compensation over £30,000 and arriving at a final figure for compensation. Alternatively, the tribunal may determine the total net loss which the complainant has suffered and which he should receive in his hands and then adjourn the hearing to allow the grossing up exercise to be carried out by the parties. The parties could then either arrange for an independent accountant acceptable to both parties to determine the grossed up compensation or seek to agree the tax liability with the Revenue. Another approach is for the parties to agree to a consent order confirming the amount of compensation which the complainant is to receive in his hands, with the respondent undertaking to pay the tax liability due on the basis of a grossing up exercise. The order would provide for liberty for either party to apply to the tribunal for a further hearing if there was default in carrying through this agreed approach.

National Insurance Liability

6–73 *Ex gratia* payments of compensation do not attract liability to pay national insurance. The DSS has stated that "if an employee seeks redress through the courts and payment is made as a result of, or to prevent, legal action, no National Insurance Contributions are due". If payment is in respect of a contractual entitlement then a N.I.C. would be payable in respect of that sum.

Duties of Employer in Respect of Tax

6–74 The employer making a payment to an employee on or after termination of employment must give particulars in writing of the payment to the Revenue in accordance with regulations made by virtue of paragraph 15 of schedule 11 to the ICTA. The employer is also under a duty to deduct tax due in respect of taxable payments made to an ex-employee. If the payment is actually made whilst the employee remains in employment or before the P45 is issued then the duty is to deduct the full amount of tax due (see Income Tax (Employment) Regulations 1973 (S.I. 1973 No.334 Regulation 13). If the payment is made following issue of the P45 the duty on the employer is to deduct basic rate tax on payments above the exempt limit of £30,000 (Regulation 16(1) of the 1973 Regulations). This may well underestimate the amount of tax actually due on the payment. The balance of tax due will be the responsibility of the ex-employee.

CHAPTER 7
Remedy Hearing: Preparation

7–01 Following a finding of liability, the tribunal may adjourn the case generally or fix a date for the remedy hearing which will be available in the event that the parties fail to settle. If no date has been fixed, the complainant should request a remedy hearing if it becomes clear that settlement negotiations are getting nowhere. In previous chapters, we have considered the information gathering exercise, the use of the tribunal's powers to obtain documents and answers to questions relating to loss from the respondent, and the preparation of the schedule of loss. We have also looked at the rules relating to the settlement of claims and the tax consequences of payments made to employees following termination of employment.

7–02 If the parties are unable to settle the claim, either before or after determination of liability, the tribunal will have to decide the remedy, on the assumption, of course, that there has been a finding in favour of the complainant on liability. It may, at this stage, be worth considering putting the respondent on a warning as to costs if the complainant is of the view that he is acting unreasonably and that this conduct will lead to costs being increased by having to attend a remedy hearing. The respondent cannot be criticised for properly disputing the calculation of loss but if he does nothing and fails to respond to the complainant's attempts at settlement the tribunal might conclude that he has acted unreasonably (see Chapter 17 for commentary on costs).

Bundle of Documents

7–03 Prior to the remedy hearing the complainant should ensure that a bundle of documents is produced to support the claim for compensation for loss. If possible, aim to get the bundle agreed with the respondent or his representatives. Six copies of the bundle should be taken to the tribunal if the remedy hearing is before a full tribunal panel. Where the claim is for compensation, the bundle should contain:

1. The schedule of loss.

2. All supporting documents including:

    (i) Employment contract or schedule of main terms.
    (ii) Employee handbook (if it exists).
    (iii) Pension rules/handbook.
    (iv) Any supplementary documents—such as rules on discretionary bonus scheme.
    (v) Documents showing increases in salary, if appropriate.
    (vi) Analysis of overtime work, if appropriate.
    (vii) AA/RAC tables if appropriate.
    (viii) Any other documentary evidence to support other claimed losses: removal expenses, value of property lost, etc.
    (ix) Schedule of all expenses incurred as result of dismissal with supporting documents, receipts, etc., if possible.

    (x)   Schedule of efforts to find new employment with supporting evidence (letters, job adverts, application forms).

   (xi)   Evidence of any earnings since date of dismissal including details of wage/salary package, entitlement to benefits, etc.

  (xii)   Evidence of any additional travel costs associated with new job.

 (xiii)   Medical report if obtained in support of claim for injury to feelings/ personal injury in a discrimination claim.

Anticipating the Employer's Arguments

7–04   As we shall see at Chapter 11, the tribunal has a wide discretion to reduce the compensatory award for unfair dismissal (and the basic award) in a number of ways. Likewise, note the tribunal's powers to reduce compensation for discrimination using the percentage chance approach (see paras 13–58 to 13–76). If without prejudice discussions have revealed that the employer is likely to argue for a reduction to the compensatory award then be prepared to address such arguments.

Statement of Evidence

7–05   It is likely to be necessary to call the complainant to give further evidence to support the schedule of loss. Consider preparing a fresh statement dealing solely with compensation issues and, possibly, dealing with likely arguments from the employer.

If you consider it imprudent to include rebuttal arguments—perhaps in connection with alleged misconduct discovered subsequent to the dismissal (see para. 11–30)—in the statement, at least get a full note of the evidence which can be called if necessary to deal with the issue.

It may be appropriate to consider calling other witnesses in support of a claim for injury to feelings in a discrimination claim. This may include a medical practitioner who has prepared a medical report or a work colleague, friend or relative who has witnessed distress suffered as a result of discrimination. Statements should be prepared for other such witnesses (the medical practitioner will simply go through the report he or she has prepared). The tribunal may order exchange of witness statements prior to the remedy hearing. If this has not occurred, six copies of all statements should be taken to the tribunal (if the remedy hearing is before a full tribunal panel).

Re-employment Cases

7–06   Note the rules relating to awards of costs against the respondent in circumstances where the complainant seeks re-employment following unfair dismissal and the respondent has failed to provide information about availability of the complainant's old job or other work and an adjournment is necessary as a result (see para. 17–14). A similar rule applies to claims relating to a refusal to allow a woman to return to work following maternity leave where the respondent fails to provide information about the job she had before maternity leave, thereby necessitating an adjournment (see para. 17.14).

Costs

7–07   Consider taking to the tribunal a clear breakdown of costs. This is also a wise move even for a hearing to consider liability. Cases frequently settle "at the door of the tribunal" and if you believe that there would be a strong basis for applying to the tribunal for costs, then use this in any negotiations which take place (see Chapter 17 for full commentary on rules relating to costs).

CHAPTER 8

Unfair Dismissal Remedies: Re-employment, Additional Award and Special Award

RE-EMPLOYMENT AND THE STEPS THE TRIBUNAL MUST TAKE

8–01   Once a tribunal has made a finding of unfair dismissal and the complainant seeks re-employment a potentially complex process is triggered to determine remedy.

Remedies Available

8–02   The remedies available following a finding of unfair dismissal are either:

(a)   Re-employment

(b)   Compensation

Re-employment can take the form of either reinstatement to the original job on entirely the same terms and conditions, or re-engagement in a role which is different in some respect to the previous employment. Re-employment is rarely ordered by the tribunal. The much more common remedy is compensation. The rules on assessment of compensation are considered at Chapters 9, 10 and 11. Nevertheless, the complainant may want to pursue re-employment of one sort or another and the tribunal is under a duty to consider such an application before it does anything else. The following section considers steps that the tribunal must take at the remedy hearing and describes the rules which apply to the two forms of re-employment. It goes on to explain the power to award additional compensation in circumstances where the respondent does not comply with an order for re-employment. Finally, the circumstances in which a "Special Award" may be made are considered.

THE REMEDY HEARING

Stage 1

8–03   The tribunal must explain re-instatement and re-engagement to the complainant and also explain the circumstances in which an order for either form of re-employment may be made (s.112(2)(a) ERA). The tribunal will then ask the complainant if he wants such an order to be made (s.112(2)(b) ERA). This is an important stage for the tribunal. Failure to follow this statutory procedure amounts to an error of law. The requirements are mandatory. (See Bristow, J. in *Pirelli General Cable Works Ltd v. Murray* [1979] I.R.L.R. 190—"This requirement, however unnecessary it might seem in cases where a 'complainant' is professionally represented, is mandatory ... While we sympathise with the desire of this tribunal ... to take a sensible short cut, the fact that they have done so results in a failure to comply with the mandatory requirements of the statute and is a plain error of law".)

8–04   However, such a failure will not result in the ultimate decision of the tribunal being overturned by the EAT on appeal unless it has caused injustice or unfairness to the complainant. The decision is therefore not void. However, "there is a well-established alternative which has been applied by the courts in a wide spectrum of cases in which there is a statutory obligation to give information, namely that the failure to do so renders the proceedings voidable if there is a possibility of prejudice or injustice having been suffered by the person to whom the information should have been given", Hoffman L.J. in *Cowley v. Manson Timber Ltd* 1995 I.R.L.R. 153 CA. In this case there was "no suggestion of any prejudice likely to have been suffered by the applicant. He was represented at the hearing; his complaint form said that what he wanted was financial compensation and there was no contrary suggestion from him or his representatives before the tribunal".

This reinforces the importance of the complainant claiming re-employment on the application to the tribunal (the ITI) if there is any prospect of him seeking such an order. It puts the tribunal on notice that it should properly go through this first stage to test the complainant's wishes rather than moving straight to consider financial compensation.

Stage 2: Decision of the Complainant

8–05   If the complainant does not want re-employment the tribunal will move straight to consideration of financial compensation (S112(4) ERA)—see Chapters 9, 10 and 11.

Stage 3: Re-employment

8–06   If the complainant seeks re-employment the tribunal must first consider *reinstatement* (s.116(1) ERA).

The Test

8–07   The tribunal has to consider the following in deciding whether to order reinstatement:

1.   The wishes of the complainant.

2.   Whether it is *practicable* for the employer to comply with such an order.

3.   Where the complainant caused or contributed to his dismissal, whether it would be just to order reinstatement (s.116(1) ERA).

There is nothing to stop the tribunal taking other material factors into account.

1.   Wishes of the Complainant

8–08   In stating that he wants to be the re-employed the complainant can express a preference for reinstatement or re-engagement. This can be stated on the ITI but the complainant can change his mind at any time up to the remedy hearing. In practice, the tribunal is unlikely to order reinstatement if the complainant has requested re-engagement.

2. Practicability

8–09 This is the key test. The tribunal may have to consider it again later if the respondent refuses to comply with an order for re-employment. The issue arises at that stage in determining whether there should be an additional award. (Note the circumstances in which a special award is made instead of an additional award, see para. 8–48. At this preliminary stage, the tribunal must take it into account in deciding whether to make an order for re-instatement. The same test of practicability applies when considering re-engagement (see paras 8.23 to 8–31).

The process at this stage involves the tribunal making a determination as to whether it is practicable for the respondent to reinstate the complainant, but that determination is a provisional one (see *Port of London Authority v. Payne* [1994] I.R.L.R. 9 CA). If the issue arises again at the later stage of deciding whether it was practicable for the respondent to have complied with the order for the reinstatement, this provisional determination will not limit the respondent in re-arguing his case. He can at that later stage not only raise both new issues and circumstances arising since the provisional determination but also revisit the same issues raised at the earlier stage in his efforts to convince the tribunal that it was not practicable to comply with the order.

8–10 In the *Port of London Authority* case, Neile L.J. stated that "the determination that is made [at this stage before making an order for re-employment] is a provisional determination or assessment. It is not a final determination in the sense that it creates an estoppel or limits an employer [at the stage which arises when the employer has failed to comply with an order for re-employment] so that he can only rely on facts which have occurred after the order".

What does "practicable" test mean?

8–11 The tribunal should not refuse to make an order for reinstatement on the basis that they did not consider it "expedient" to do so. In *Qualcast (Wolverhampton) Ltd. v. Ross* [1979] I.R.L.R. 99, Arnold J. said that expediency is "not, as it seems to us, a matter which is a proper deciding ground of a tribunal exercising the discretion as to reinstatement conferred by [what is now s.116 ERA]".

In *Rao v. Civil Aviation Authority* [1992] I.R.L.R. 203, Wood J. gave the following guidance with regard to the task of the tribunal at this stage. He referred to the use of the word "practicable". "It is not 'possible'; it is not 'capable'. At that stage [a tribunal] is not required to reach a conclusion on practicability—whether it is or is not practicable ... but the Act specifically requires that the [tribunal] shall take into account practicability for the employer to comply with the order. [A tribunal] must use its experience and common sense, looking at what has happened in the past and what can reasonably be anticipated in the future, always maintaining a fair balance, that which is, in all the circumstances, fair, just and reasonable between the parties."

Replacement Employee

8–12 As a general rule, the tribunal must not take into account the fact that the respondent has taken on a permanent replacement for the complainant in determining whether or not it is practicable for the respondent to re-employ the complainant (s.116(5) ERA). However a permanent replacement can be taken into account if the respondent can show:

1. that it was not practicable to arrange for the complainant's work to be done without engaging a permanent replacement or,

2. that he engaged the replacement employee after a reasonable lapse of time
    having heard nothing from the complainant to indicate that he wanted to be
    re-employed and that when he took on the replacement it was no longer
    reasonable for him to arrange for the complainant's work to be done other
    than by a permanent replacement (s.116(6) ERA).

So if a respondent replaces a dismissed employee and he cannot satisfy the tribunal
that it was not practicable to get the work done in any other way they could be forced
into having to dismiss the replacement in order to comply with an order for re-
employment. Inevitably, it will be easier for a small employer to show that the
complainant had to be replaced than it will be for a large organisation.

Examples of the application of the "practicability" test:

8–13   Set out below are a number of examples of where the tribunal has found
that re-employment is not practicable.

1. At the time that the tribunal considers re-employment there is insufficient
    work for the complainant to do and re-employment would lead to redun-
    dancy—not practicable (*Cold Drawn Tubes Ltd v. Middleton* [1992] I.R.L.R.
    160).

2. Look at the consequences of re-employment, for example on industrial
    relations—re-employment likely to cause industrial strife and unrest—not
    practicable (*B. Coleman and R. Stephenson v. Magnet Joinery Ltd* [1974]
    I.R.L.R. 343).

3. No work available together with lack of union support for application for
    re-instatement and growing resentment among other employees were factors
    to be taken into account—not practicable (*Meridian Ltd v. Gomersall* [1977]
    I.R.L.R. 425).

4. Complainant believed herself to be the victim of conspiracy by employers
    (she had made allegations against members of staff)—not likely to be a
    satisfactory employee—not practicable (*Nothman v. London Borough of
    Barnet (No.2)* [1980] I.R.L.R. 65 CA).

5. Genuine search for available work has failed to identify vacancies—not
    practicable (*Freemans plc v. Flynn* [1984] I.R.L.R. 486). However, a bare
    assertion that there are no vacancies is insufficient to establish that re-
    employment is impracticable (*Port of London Authority v. Payne* [1992]
    I.R.L.R. 447 AT 466 EAT.

6. The employee would be insufficiently employed having lost his driving
    licence, therefore could not do that part of his work which involved driving—
    not practicable (*Tayside Regional Council v. McIntosh* [1982] I.R.L.R. 272).

7. The parties would be in a close working relationship. "It is not realistic to
    make an order ... where the parties involved were in a close personal
    relationship to each other as they were in the present situation. It is one
    thing to make an order for reinstatement where the employee concerned
    works in a factory or other substantial organisation. It is another to do so
    in the case of a small employer with few staff. Where there must exist a
    close personal relationship, as is the case here, reinstatement can only be

appropriate in exceptional circumstances." Complainants had worked as cooks in the respondent's small hotel—not practicable (*obiter*) (*Enessy Co. S.A. v. Minoprio and Minoprio* [1978] I.R.L.R. 489).

8. Allegations of sexual indecency: insufficient investigation to justify dismissal but because of responsibility on council to safeguard children—not practicable (*ILEA v. Gravett* [1988] I.R.L.R. 497 EAT).

9. The employers had genuinely lost confidence in a senior manager. The EAT accepted that it would not be practicable to re-employ him whether or not the reasons for the loss of confidence were well founded—not practicable (*SMT Sales & Service Co. v. Irwin* EAT 485/79).

10. Mr Thompson suffered from a stress related illness. He was dismissed. Re-employment was ordered on the basis that the order be complied with when he was fit for full time employment. EAT held that the absence of a known date for return to work made the order invalid and also demonstrated that re-engagement was not practicable—not practicable (*British Tele-communications plc v. Thompson* EAT 884/95.

8–14 Set out below are examples of cases where the tribunal found that re-employment was practicable.

1. Mr Coady was dismissed on grounds of redundancy. However, the tribunal decided that he was not in fact redundant and that the respondent had simply wanted to replace him with someone that they considered to be better. Reinstatement was ordered. This was upheld by the EAT. The respondent had argued that reinstatement would cause overstaffing. This was, however, a result of the way the respondent had managed the business and the way they had dismissed Mr Coady—practicable to re-employ (*United States Navy v. Coady* EAT 275/94.

2. Mr Carpenter was made redundant. The company had engaged a "contract engineer" from an agency. In such circumstances, it was practicable to re-employ—practicable (*Carpenter v. ABB Industrial Systems Ltd* COIT 3088/179.

3. Mr Baldwin was dismissed for assaulting a work colleague. The tribunal found that he was a good employee and that this had been a one-off incident. The man assaulted by Mr Baldwin said that he could not work with him again. This, however, should not amount to a veto on re-employment—practicable (*Baldwin v. KLM Royal Dutch Airlines* COIT 3265/205.

4. In a reorganisation of a time-share operation, the accounts function was transferred from an individual resort to a central location. The Resort Manager had previously handled the accounts. His post was therefore redundant. He was not offered a new post of Resort Supervisor, which was instead given to his deputy. The tribunal considered he was "the obvious candidate for the job". Although the respondents referred the tribunal to complaints about the complainant from visitors to the resort, no disciplinary action had been taken. As to the appointment of a permanent replacement (see para. 8–12) the tribunal stated that they had had no evidence of the number of employees at the site or of the problems of re-engagement. "We have merely had a bland statement ... that it would result in over-manning

and a redundancy situation ... There has been no evidence to back up this statement".—practicable *Dickinson v. Wimpey Group Services Ltd* COIT 49893/96.

3. Complainant Caused or Contributed to his Dismissal

8–15 The third factor to be taken into account by the tribunal in deciding whether to make an order for re-employment is whether the complainant caused or contributed to his dismissal. This test is the same as that in s.123(6) ERA in determining whether there should be any reduction in the compensation award (*The Boots Company Ltd v. Lees-Collier* [1986] I.R.L.R. 485). If a tribunal would have concluded that there was no blameworthy conduct such as to justify a reduction in the compensatory award then contributory fault cannot be a factor to take into account in deciding whether to order re-employment (see commentary on reductions to compensatory award where complainant caused or contributed to his dismissal at paras 11–38 to 11–87).

8–16 In circumstances where a tribunal has found that the complainant has "caused or contributed" to his dismissal they then have to consider whether it would be just to re-employ him. Fault is, however, not an absolute bar to re-instatement. Where the tribunal is considering re-engagement there is more flexibility. It can take contributory fault into account in considering the terms of a possible re-engagement—for example by awarding less then the full back-pay between dismissal and re-engagement (see *Morganite Electrical Carbon Ltd v. Donne* [1987] I.R.L.R. 363).

What is Re-instatement?

8–17 An order for re-instatement requires the employer to treat the complainant "in all respects as if he had not been dismissed" (Section 114(1) ERA). The order itself must state:

(a)   any amount payable by the employer in respect of any benefit which the complainant might reasonably be expected to have had but for the dismissal (including arrears of pay) for the period between the date of termination of employment and the date of reinstatement;

(b)   any rights and privileges (including seniority and pension rights) which must be restored to the employee; and

(c)   the date by which the order must be complied with (s.114(2) ERA).

8–18 The rate of pay as at the date of dismissal is used to calculate back-pay rather than the rate at the date of re-instatement. See *Electronic Data Processing Ltd v. Wright* [1986] I.R.L.R. 8 where pay rates had gone down since dismissal. However, if the complainant's pay or other benefits would have improved had he not been dismissed then such improvement must be reflected in the order for re-instatement (s.114(3) ERA). It is, therefore, very important to gather evidence as to what the complainant would have earned during the period between dismissal and reinstatement had he not been dismissed (see paras 3–43 to 3–45 for commentary on the information gathering exercise with regard to increases in pay and overtime worked by other staff during that period. See also paras 4–02 to 4–03 and Chapter 4 generally for commentary on the use of the tribunal's powers to obtain information from the respondent).

8–19 In calculating the sum payable to the complainant in respect of back-pay the following shall be deducted:

- pay in lieu of notice;

- any *ex gratia* payment paid by the employer;

- remuneration from another job since dismissal;

- other benefits which the tribunal thinks appropriate (s.114(4) ERA).

Note that there is no statutory maximum to the amount ordered with reference to benefits received by the complainant during the period between dismissal and reinstatement. Note that normal recoupment provisions apply (see paras 16–18 to 16–30).

The calculation of the sum due involves the tribunal assessing benefits which the complainant "might reasonably be expected to have had but for the dismissal". The sum, therefore, is not limited to contractual pay over the relevant period but could include overtime payments if it is reasonable to assume he would have received them. (Note that similar wording is used in respect of the compensatory award for unfair dismissal (s.123(2)(b) ERA). It is well established that loss for the purposes of the compensatory award includes non contractual payments which the complainant would normally have received.)

No reductions for failure to mitigate

8–20 The tribunal is not permitted to reduce the amount payable on the basis that the complainant has failed to mitigate his loss. If, for example, the tribunal finds that had the complainant pursued her complaint more vigorously or expeditiously she might have been re-employed sooner, there is no basis for reducing the back-pay and benefits to her (see *City and Hackney H.A. v. Crisp* [1990] I.R.L.R. 47). The tribunal must also specify any rights and privileges (including seniority and pension rights) which must be restored to the employee and the date for compliance.

Holiday Entitlement

8–21 Note also that the employee would have accrued holiday entitlement during the period between dismissal and reinstatement. In order to treat the complainant "in all respects as if he had not been dismissed" such holiday entitlement should be honoured. It would be wise to ensure that this is confirmed and agreed by the respondent and that the tribunal is asked to include this in the order for reinstatement. Holiday entitlement is after all a "right or privilege which must be restored" (see s.114(2)(b) ERA, see also para. 8–17).

Sickness during period between dismissal and re-employment

8–22 If the employee has been unfit for work for part of the period between dismissal and re-employment then compensation for the lost pay during this period is based on what he would have received from his employer had he not been dismissed. If he would have received sick pay then the compensation will be based on the rate of sick pay to which he would have been entitled. (See *Foot v. MOD* COIT 1569/182 where for four months of the seven-month period between dismissal and reinstatement Mr Foot had been unfit to work. For this period he received compensation for sick pay he would have received.)

Re-engagement

8–23 If the tribunal decides not to reinstate, it then goes on to consider re-engagement (s.116(2) ERA). Here there is more flexibility. Re-engagement can be with the respondent or a successor of the respondent or with an associated employer (s.115(1) ERA). In the case of *Department of Health v. (1) Bruce and (2) Department of Social Security* EAT 4.12.92 (14/92), IDS 496, Ms Bruce was dismissed from her job at the DSS. This had, until not long before the dismissal, been part of the old DHSS. That department had been split into the DSS and the Department of Health (DH). The tribunal ordered re-engagement but the order was directed at the DH. The EAT held that the tribunal had been wrong to regard the Civil Service as an "inalienable whole" in deciding who was Ms Bruce's employer. The EAT did, however, uphold the order for re-engagement. They accepted that there was a special relationship between the two departments. They could be considered as one department.

8–24 Employment can be either comparable to that from which he was dismissed or other "suitable" employment. (s.115(1) ERA). The terms of employment should be, so far as is reasonably practicable, "as favourable" as those upon which he was employed before dismissal. The tribunal does have power to order re-engagement on less favourable terms in circumstances where the tribunal has found that the complainant was guilty of contributory fault in relation to the dismissal (s.116(3)(c) ERA). But the tribunal should not order re-engagement on substantially better terms than he would have enjoyed on re-instatement. Orders for re-engagement should be "realistic". In *Rank Xerox (UK) Ltd. v. Stryczek* [1995] I.R.L.R. 568, Mr Stryczek had been employed, before redundancy, on a salary of £16,779. The tribunal ordered re-engagement to a vacant, more senior post with a salary of £18,000 and a company car. The EAT held that this order was not one that the tribunal could make because the terms were significantly more favourable. Butler J., stated that "as a matter of interpretation it is not permissible for [a tribunal] to order re-engagement in respect of employment significantly more favourable than that which the employee might have obtained if reinstatement had been ordered ... Any other interpretation would, in our judgement, produce curious results which were not, we believe, intended by Parliament".

8–25 It has been suggested that, when ordering re-engagement, tribunals should aim to identify the nature of the proposed employment rather than specifying a particular job but there may be circumstances where there is only one specific and suitable vacancy in the firm, in which case the tribunal may properly identify that particular job (see *Rank Xerox (UK) Ltd v. Stryczek*). These comments were *obiter* and do not seem to accord with other EAT decisions referred to at paragraph 8–27 to 8–28 and with what is required to be stated in the order for re-engagement (see para. 8–26). In deciding whether to order re-engagement the tribunal must take into account:

1. the wishes of the complainant;

2. whether it is practicable for the employer to comply with an order for re-engagement;

3. if there has been contributory fault on the part of the complainant, whether it would be just to order re-engagement and, if so, on what terms (s.116(3) ERA).

Note that, just as when the tribunal is considering whether to make an order for reinstatement, these factors are taken into account. So again, only a provisional determination of the question of practicability is required at this stage (see paras 8–09 to 8–11). The same test of practicability applies to re-engagement as with re-instatement—(see commentary at 8–09 to 8–14). This includes the implications of the appointment of a permanent replacement (s.116(5 and 6) and para. 8–12).

Order for Re-engagement

8–26   The order for re-engagement must specify the terms on which it is to take place including

(a)   identity of employer;

(b)   nature of employment;

(c)   remuneration for the employment;

(d)   any amount payable by the employer in respect of the period between dismissal and re-engagement—arrears of pay and other benefits—such as overtime, commission, compensation for loss of vehicle, which the complainant "might reasonably be expected to have had but for the dismissal" (see also paras 8–17 to 8–22 for commentary in respect of the equivalent provision in relation to reinstatement);

(e)   any rights and privileges (including seniority and pension rights) which must be restored to the employee;

(f)   the date by which the order must be complied with (s.115(2) ERA).

8–27   In *Pirelli v. General Cable Works Ltd v. Murray* [1979] I.R.L.R. 190, the tribunal made an order for re-engagement on terms to be agreed between the parties. The EAT held that the tribunal had erred in not setting out the terms of its order for re-engagement.

The case of *Stena Houlder Ltd v. Keenan* EAT 13.12.93 (543/93) is another example of the tribunal failing to sufficiently specify the terms upon which re-engagement was to take place. The tribunal ordered that Mr Keenan be re-engaged on or before 19th June 1993 "in employment comparable to that from which he was dismissed or other suitable employment as agreed between the parties and on terms and conditions and remuneration also to be agreed". The order did not, therefore, state the nature of employment in which Mr Keenan would be re-engaged or the rate of remuneration. The EAT allowed the employer's appeal and sent the case back to the tribunal to reconsider the order.

8–28   It is not open to the tribunal to make an order directing an employer to make an offer of re-engagement. The tribunal in *Lilley Construction Ltd v. Dunn* [1984] I.R.L.R. 483 did just this. The employer made an offer in accordance with the order but Mr Dunn refused the offer. In obiter comments, Waite J. doubted whether there was a legal basis for making such "offer directions". "One ground of challenge might be that having legislated in considerable detail for forms of order on reinstatement and re-engagement, Parliament, had it intended tribunals to have power to achieve similar results by different forms of order, would have so stated in terms." Waite J. also made the point that "such cases could cause confusion in the minds of the parties and the tribunal".

Arrears of pay where re-engagement on inferior terms

8–29 As we have noted, in circumstances where the tribunal finds that the complainant was guilty of contributory fault, re-engagement may be on inferior terms compared to his previous remuneration. In such circumstances the arrears of pay and other benefits for the period between dismissal and re-engagement shall be calculated on the basis of the complainant's pay prior to dismissal. The calculation of arrears up to the date of re-engagement is therefore based on what the complainant would have earned but for the dismissal. This was the conclusion reached by the EAT in *Electronic Data Processing Ltd v. Wright* [1986] I.R.L.R. 8.

No statutory maximum compensation

8–30 Note that, just as with orders for reinstatement, there is no limit to the compensation for loss up to the date of re-employment.

Sums set off against compensation for loss

8–31 Note that the same rules apply as with orders for reinstatement (see para. 8–19). All sums received by the complainant by way of pay in lieu of notice, other *ex gratia* payments from the former employer, pay received from other work since dismissal and other benefits as the tribunal thinks appropriate in the circumstances are set off against loss of wages and benefits suffered between dismissal and re-engagement.

Complainant unreasonably prevents order from being complied with

Note that s.117(8) ERA provides that if the complainant unreasonably prevents an order for re-employment from being complied with, the tribunal can take this into account as a failure to mitigate (see para. 19–34).

Stage 4 Enforcement

8–32 The Tribunal has no power to force an employer to comply with an order for re-employment. The penalty for non compliance is financial. But first the respondent who refuses to comply with an order for re-employment has another chance to persuade the tribunal that it was not practicable to comply with the order.

Partial Non-Compliance (s.117(1) ERA)

8–33 The tribunal will make an award of compensation if an order for re-employment has been made and the complainant has been reinstated or re-engaged but the terms of the order have not been "fully complied with" s.117(1) ERA. That award of compensation is for such amount as the tribunal thinks fit having regard to the loss suffered as a result of partial non-compliance (s.117(2) ERA).

Note that there is no cap on such compensation. Section 124(3) provides that the normal limit on compensation (currently £12,000) may be exceeded "to the extent necessary to enable the award to fully reflect the amount specified as payable" for loss between dismissal and re-employment in the order for re-employment. The purpose of this provision is to ensure that the employer cannot gain an advantage by failing to fully comply with the order for re-employment. The loss since dismissal may exceed the statutory maximum of £12,000 and the full amount should be awarded.

8–34 An important issue is the distinction between a situation where an order for re-employment is not "fully complied with" and a situation where such an order is not complied with at all. If the tribunal has ordered re-instatement and the complainant is taken back on but on inferior terms, that is not re-instatement and the tribunal will treat it as failure to re-instate rather than a failure to fully comply (see *Artisan Press v. Srawley and Parker* [1986] I.R.L.R. 126). Popplewell J. stated that "if he [the complainant] is reinstated but on less favourable terms, he has not been reinstated in accordance with [s.114 ERA]. It is impossible to say that the terms of the order "are not fully complied with".

8–35 So what, then, can amount to a failure to "fully comply with" an order for re-instatement? Popplewell J. in *Artisan* identifies the ancillary matters now set out in s.114(2) ERA. Hence if, for example, the complainant is re-instated but does not receive the full amount of back-pay and cash benefits for the period between dismissal and re-instatement, then the tribunal will award compensation to make good that shortfall. The tribunal cannot make an additional award where there has been only partial non-compliance (see paras 8–39 to 8–46 for commentary on the additional award). A failure to fully comply with an order for re-engagement may involve a re-engagement on inferior terms to that ordered by the tribunal. This would still be a re-engagement and in compensating the complainant for loss suffered as a result of such partial non-compliance the tribunal would not be limited to the statutory maximum.

Total Non-Compliance (s.117(3) ERA)

8–36 If the employer fails to reinstate or re-engage in accordance with such an order the tribunal will then order compensation as follows:

1. Basic award (see Chapter 9)

2. Compensatory award (see Chapters 10 and 11. Note the power to exceed the statutory maximum compensatory award in such circumstances, see paras 10–03 to 10–05)

3. Additional award unless not practicable to comply with re-employment order (see paras 8–37 to 8–38) (but note the circumstances where a special award is made instead at paras 8–47 to 8–48).

Not practicable to comply with order for re-employment

8–37 The employer can avoid an additional award if he can satisfy the tribunal that it was not practicable to comply with the order (s.117(4) ERA). This is the second opportunity the employer has to argue this issue. The employer can raise the same issues again in support of his case together with new arguments which might have arisen since the order was made (*Freemans plc v. Flynn* [1984] I.R.L.R. 486). As explained at paragraphs 8–09 to 8–10, at the initial stage of the tribunal deciding whether or not to make an order for re-employment, the question of practicability is only a consideration—one of the factors for the tribunal to take into account. At this later stage, when the tribunal is deciding whether or not to make an additional award the burden of proof is on the employer to satisfy the tribunal that it was not practicable to comply with the order. At this stage the tribunal has to make a definite finding.

8–38 It will consider evidence of what has happened and what steps have been taken by the employer to comply and the results of those efforts since the making of the re-employment order. But, as already noted, the tribunal can also reconsider arguments previously advanced by the employer when making the original order for re-employment. Note also the rules which apply in circumstances where the employer has appointed a permanent replacement (see para. 8–12).

In *Port of London Authority v. Payne* [1994] I.R.L.R. 9, Neill L.J. considered the task facing the employer in showing that it was not practicable to re-employ the complainant. "The tribunal, though it should carefully scrutinise the reasons advanced by an employer, should give due weight to the commercial judgement of the management, unless of course the witnesses are disbelieved. The standard must not be set too high. The employer cannot be expected to explore every possible avenue which ingenuity might suggest. The employer does not have to show that reinstatement or re-engagement was impossible. It is a matter of what is practicable in the circumstances of the employer's business at the relevant time" (see paras 8–13 to 8–14 for further guidance on the application of the practicability test).

The Additional Award

8–39   So in cases where the tribunal has ordered a re-employment and the employer has failed to comply and the tribunal has gone on to conclude that it *was* practicable to comply with the order then (subject to the cases dealt with at paras 8–47 to 8–48 where a special award is made) the tribunal will make an additional award. Note that s.117(3) ERA makes it mandatory in such circumstances for the tribunal to make an additional award. The amount of the additional award depends on the nature of the dismissal. If the dismissal is an act of sex, race, or disability discrimination (with the meaning of the SDA, RRA and DDA) then the tribunal will award a higher additional award of between 26 and 52 weeks' pay (inclusive) (see Chapter 24 for commentary on calculation of a week's pay) s.117 (5)(a) ERA. Note that this higher award applies to dismissals which also amount to an act of disability discrimination as a result of an amendment introduced by s.14 Employment Rights (Dispute Resolution) Act, 1998. In any other case the additional award is between 13 and 26 weeks' pay, inclusive s.117(5)(b).

Maximum Week's Pay for Purposes of Additional Award

8–40   Note that section 227(1)(b) ERA provides that a weeks' pay for the purpose of calculating the additional award is subject to a statutory maximum—currently £220.00. This means that the range of additional awards is as follows:

1. Sex, race and disability discrimination cases (26–52 weeks) £5,720–11,440

2. Other cases (13–26 weeks) £2,860–5,720

Note that the maximum week's pay is reviewed annually. If the maximum sum changes, then the maximum which applies is the amount in force at the date fixed by the tribunal, by when an order for re-employment must be complied with. This rule is set out in the statutory instrument which brings into force the increased maximum weeks pay.

Calculation Date

8–41   The "calculation date" for the purposes of calculating the amount of the week's pay is the date the employer served notice of termination of employment or, if no notice was given, the effective date of termination (s.226(2) ERA).

Tribunal's discretion in determining amount of additional award

8–42   The tribunal has a discretion to set the additional award within these parameters but they must exercise that discretion judicially. In *Morganite Electrical Carbon Ltd v. Donne* [1987] I.R.L.R. 363 EAT, the tribunal had awarded the maximum additional award of 26 weeks' pay (it not being a case involving sex or race discrimination). The EAT held that the tribunal had failed to address their minds to the fact that the size of the additional award was a matter for their discretion and that in exercising that discretion they had to consider what factors ought properly to be taken into account. Although it was a wide discretion there had to be some sort of proper assessment and balance applied.

8–43   Factors which might be taken into account in assessing the appropriate amount of additional award are:

(a)   The conduct of the employer in refusing to comply with the order made (probably the most important factor). In *A.J. George v. Beecham Group* [1977] I.R.L.R. 43, the tribunal stated that it was entitled to mark its disapproval of the employer's decision not to comply. "We do indeed find it most regrettable that after mature reflection at a high level a national employer of this size and responsibility should feel unable to comply with a tribunal order in respect of a modest production line employee of this nature". An additional award of 20 weeks' pay was made.

See also *Motherwell Railway Club v. McQueen* [1989] I.C.R. 418 EAT. In this case re-employment was ordered. The employer refused to obey the order and the tribunal made an additional award of 20 weeks' pay. Although the employer did not know it at the time, the complainant was, in fact, medically unfit to take up re-employment. The employee had not, therefore, suffered any financial loss. However, the EAT held that the tribunal was entitled to make such an additional award because of the employer's blatant conduct in refusing to obey the order for re-employment.

(b)   The extent to which the compensatory award has met the actual loss suffered by the complainant (noting the effect of the statutory maximum award) (see *Morganite Electrical Carbon Ltd v. Donne* [1987] I.R.L.R. 363 EAT).

Note, however, that as a result of section 20 of the Trade Union Reform and Employment Rights Act 1993, s.124(4) ERA now enables a tribunal to exceed the statutory maximum so as to ensure that the aggregate of the compensatory and additional awards reflects the loss of wages and benefits between dismissal and the date ordered for re-employment (see paras 10–03 to 10–05 for further commentary).

8–44   Other factors may include consideration of the extent to which the complainant has attempted to mitigate loss. A failure to mitigate should not result in a quantifiable reduction to the additional award but can be taken into account as a general factor going to the merits of the case (see *Mabirizi v. National Hospital for Nervous Diseases* [1990] I.R.L.R. 133 EAT). The EAT in this case also accepted that the additional award could take into account the fact that the complainant had not received the award covering arrears of pay contained in the reinstatement order.

Costs

8–45 Note that if the Complainant has expressed a wish to be reinstated or re-
engaged which has been communicated to the respondent at least seven days before
the hearing and the hearing has had to be postponed or adjourned because the
respondent has failed "without a special reason, to adduce reasonable evidence as to
the availability of the job from which the applicant was dismissed . . . or of comparable
or suitable employment" then an award of wasted costs can be made against the
respondent (see Industrial Tribunals (Constitution and Rules of Procedure) Regulations
1993, Schedule 1 paragraph 12(5), see also para. 17–14).

Setting off *ex gratia* payments against the additional award

8–46 If an employer has made an *ex gratia* payment to the complainant on
termination of employment and the employer has made it clear that the payment "is
offered and accepted in satisfaction of, or in contribution towards any additional
award if such an award should in due course be made" then it seems as if the tribunal
can set such a payment off against the additional award. This was the obiter view of
Hull J. QC in *Darr v. LRC Products Ltd* [1993] I.R.L.R. 257 EAT. Hull J. also
suggested that an analysis of the facts of a particular case might give rise to the
implication that an *ex gratia* payment was made with this purpose in mind and that,
accordingly, a set off against the additional award could be made.

The Special Award

8–47 As explained at paragraph 8–36, in circumstances where there has been an
order for re-employment which the employer has not complied with and the tribunal
has found that it was practicable to have complied with the order, then in most cases
the tribunal is required to award not only the basic and compensatory award but also
an "additional award" (s.117(3)). There are some special cases where no additional
award is made but instead the tribunal must make a "special award".

8–48 Set out below are the categories of cases where a special award will be made
if the statutory criteria are met (see para. 8–49 to 8–50). These categories of case are
all automatic unfair dismissal cases where the employee has protection from the start
of his employment. Note, however, that not all cases of automatic unfair dismissal
qualify for the special award.

(a) The employee has been given, by his employer, health and safety responsibilities (Note that the Management of Health & Safety at Work Regulations
1992, Regulation 6 requires the employer to appoint competent persons to
assist promoting health and safety) and he is dismissed or selected for
redundancy for carrying out such activities (s.100(1)(a) ERA).

(b) The employee is a health and safety representative of workers or a member
of a safety committee under relevant legislation (Health and Safety at
Work, etc., Act 1977 s.2(4)–(7), provisions relating to appointment of safety
representatives by recognised Trade Unions and establishment of Safety
Committees at request of such safety reps (see also Safety Representatives
and Safety Committees Regulations 1977 (S.I. 1977 No.500) and elected
representatives of employee safety under the Health and Safety (Consultation
with Employees) Regulations 1996) (S.I. No 1513) or is acknowledged as a
representative or member of a safety committee by his employer and he is
dismissed or selected for redundancy for performing or proposing to perform

such functions s.100(1)(b). Note that being dismissed for taking part in elections to become a representative of employee safety (s.100(1)(ba)) does not, however, give rise to the possibility of a special award.

(c) The employee is a trustee of an occupational pension scheme (under Pension Schemes Act 1993 s.1) relating to his employment and he is dismissed or selected for redundancy for performing or proposing to perform functions of a trustee (s.102(1) ERA).

(d) The employee is an elected representative for the purposes of collective consultation in a redundancy situation (s.188 TULR(C)A) or for the purposes of consultation where there is a business transfer (Regulation 10 Transfer of Undertaking (Protection of Employment) Regulations 1981) or is a candidate in an election to become such an elected representative and was dismissed or selected for redundancy for performing (or proposing to perform) the functions or activities of such a representative or a candidate.

(e) The employee was, or proposed to become, a member of an independent trade union or had taken part, or proposed to take part, in the activities of an independent trade union or was not a member of any trade union or of a particular trade union or of one of a number of particular trade unions or had refused or proposed to refuse to become or remain a member and was dismissed or selected for redundancy for any of those reasons (ss.152 and 153 TULR(C)A).

(f) The employee is dismissed or selected for redundancy for refusing or proposing to refuse to comply with a requirement imposed by the employer (or which he proposed to impose) in contravention of the employer's obligations under the Working Time Regulations 1998 or for refusing (or proposing to refuse) to forego a right under those regulations or for failing to sign a workforce agreement (under those regulations) or to enter into, or agree to vary or extend, any other agreement with his employer provided for in those regulations or for being an elected representative (under those regulations) or a candidate to become such a representative and performing (or proposing to perform) any functions or activities as such a representative or candidate (s.101A ERA).

In what circumstances is the Special Award made?

8–49 The complainant must have requested an order for re-instatement or re-engagement (s.118(2)(a) ERA and s.157(1) TULR(C)A. Bear this in mind when completing the application to the tribunal (ITI). Although such a request can be made later, it is safest to make your intentions clear at this stage. In the case of *Ireland v. Northern Courier Services Ltd t/a Document Interlink* EAT 70/94, Mr Ireland died before remedy was decided by the tribunal. However, he had indicated on the ITI that he wanted reinstatement. The EAT held that his estate was entitled to the special award.

If, having applied for re-employment, the tribunal either makes no order for re-employment or makes such an order but the employer fails to re-employ in accordance with the order then if the dismissal falls within the categories set out above the tribunal will make a special award (s.118(2) ERA). Unlike the additional award, the special award is payable even where no order for re-employment is made provided it has been requested. Note, however, that where an order for re-employment is made but not complied with, and the tribunal is satisfied that it was practicable to comply with it, this can increase the amount of the special award—(see paras 8–51 to 8–52).

Exceptions

8–50   No special award will be made if the principal reason for the dismissal was redundancy and either

1. the complainant is not regarded as having been dismissed (ss.121 and 138 ERA) because his contract has been renewed or he has been re-engaged following an offer made before termination of employment (with renewal or re-engagement taking place immediately or within four weeks) (see s.138 for detailed provisions), or

2. the complainant received an offer to renew his contract or to be re-engaged before the end of his employment which he unreasonably refuses, provided the offer was on the same terms as his previous contract or it amounted to suitable alternative employment (s.141 ERA) or where such an offer of re-engagement has been accepted or his contract of employment has been renewed but during the trial period he unreasonably terminates the contract or unreasonably gives notice to terminate it (s.141 ERA).

Amount of Special Award

8–51   s.125 ERA and s.158 TULR(C)A
Subject to certain powers to make reductions, the special award is a fixed sum:

1. Where there has been no order made for re-employment the Special Award equals:

   104 weeks' pay (see para. 8–54 and Chapter 24 for commentary on "week's pay")

   £14,500, whichever is the greater with an upper limit of £29,000

   (s.125(1) ERA, s.158(1) TULR(C)A)

   Note: Sum can be increased by Secretary of State by order—reviewed annually. Normally takes effect of April 1 each year (see s.125(7) ERA and s.159(1)(b)).

2. If, following an order for re-employment, the complainant is not reinstated or re-engaged in accordance with the order and the tribunal concludes that it was practicable to have complied with the order, the special award increases to:

   156 weeks' pay

   or £21,800, whichever is the greater.

   s.125(2) ERA and s.158(2) TULR(C)A

   Note: There is no upper limit to the calculation of 156 weeks' pay.

   (See paras 8–09 to 8–14 for commentary on "practicability")

8–52   If an order for reinstatement is made and another job is offered (whether or not it is accepted) it will not amount to compliance with the order because the employee is not put back into the position he would have been in had there been no dismissal and therefore the special award is payable (see *Artisan Press Ltd v. Srawley & Parker* [1986] I.R.L.R. 126). Where the employer has engaged a permanent replacement, the tribunal must not take this into account in deciding whether it was practicable to comply with an order for re-employment (and therefore whether or not the complainant is entitled to the higher rate of special award) unless the employer can show that it was not practicable for him to arrange for the complainant's work to be done without engaging a permanent replacement, (s.125(6) ERA and s.158(6) TULR(C)A).

8–53 If an order for re-employment has been made but the employer satisfies the tribunal that it was not practicable to comply with the order, the special award will be calculated in the same way as if no order for re-employment had been made (see para. 8–51). If the order for re-employment is complied with by the employer no special award is payable. If the order for re-employment is partially but not fully complied with, compensation is payable under s.117(2) ERA but, again, no special award is payable (see paras 8–33 to 8–35 for commentary on partial compliance).

Weeks Pay

8–54 Unlike the basic award and the additional award (see 8–40), the special award is not subject to a statutory maximum. It is calculated in accordance with s.220–s.229 ERA (see Chapter 24). The calculation date for the purposes of calculating a week's pay is the date the employer served notice of termination or, if no notice was served, the effective date of termination (s.226(2) ERA and s.158(7) TULR(C)A). Gross pay rather than net pay should be used as the basic of the calculation of a "week's pay" (*Secretary of State for Employment v. John Woodrow & Son (Builders) Ltd* [1983] I.R.L.R. 11).

Employees Between Age of 64 and 65

8–55 Where the complainant is between the ages of 64 and 65 on the date of dismissal the special award is reduced in just the same way as the basic award is reduced (see s.125(3) ERA and s.158(3) TULR(C)A and s.119(4) and (5) ERA— calculation of the basic award). The sum is therefore reduced by one-twelfth of the amount otherwise payable for each month of service completed over the age of 60 (see para. 9–07 with regard to the basic award).

Other Reductions in Special Award

Conduct of the Complainant

8–56 The tribunal must reduce the special award in circumstances where it considers that the conduct of the complainant before dismissal (or if dismissal is on notice before service of such notice) was such as to make it just and equitable to make such a reduction (s.125(4) ERA and s.158(4) TULR(C)A). The extent of the reduction is within the tribunal's discretion and is unlikely to be overturned on appeal. In *Hollier v. Plysu Ltd* [1983] I.R.L.R. 260 CA, Stephenson L.J. stated that the task of the tribunal "is to take a broad common sense view of the situation". It would take a plain error of law or perversity to persuade the EAT to overthrow the tribunal's finding.

8–57 The conduct of the complainant need not have been the reason for the dismissal (Unlike Section 123(6) ERA relating to the compensatory award, this section does not refer to action by the complainant which caused or contributed to the dismissal). The wording of s.125(4) ERA mirrors the test for the reduction of the basic award based on conduct of the complainant. It may be conduct which only subsequently comes to light. The conduct has to be culpable or blameworthy but it is not limited to conduct amounting to a breach of contract or a tort. It could simply be conduct which is bloody-minded, perverse or foolish or unreasonable (depending on the extent of unreasonableness.) (For further commentary on conduct of complainant which may be taken into account see paras 9–23 to 9–25 and 11–38 to 11–67).

Trade Union membership/activity cases

8–58   In union membership/activity cases certain conduct must not be taken into account in determining whether to reduce the special award (or the compensatory or basic awards) (s.155 TULR(C)A). Guidance is set out below.

Conduct to be disregarded:

1.   Conduct or action amounting to a breach or a proposed breach of a requirement:

    (a)   to be or become a member of a trade union or of a particular trade union or one of a number of trade unions;
    (b)   to cease to be or refrain from becoming a member;
    (c)   not to take part in trade union activities.

2.   Conduct or action which amounts to a refusal or proposed refusal to comply with a requirement to make a payment in lieu of membership of the union or;

3.   Conduct or action which amounts to an objection to the operation of a scheme of deductions in lieu of membership.

8–59   In other words, the behaviour itself which led to the dismissal and which makes the dismissal automatically unfair cannot provide a basis for arguing for a reduction in the special award (or indeed for a reduction in the basic or compensatory award). However, the way in which the employee conducted himself, for example in resigning from the union without any discussion, may deserve criticism and can be taken into account by the tribunal in deciding whether to reduce the special award.

A distinction can be drawn between that which is done by the complainant—*e.g.* resigning from the union (which cannot be considered by the tribunal in determining whether to reduce the special award) and the way in which it is done—which can be taken into account. In *Transport & General Workers Union v. Howard* [1992] I.R.L.R. 170, Mrs Howard's resignation from the TGWU (which was the cause of the dismissal) was without any prior discussion and was, said the tribunal, "confrontational and, if not bloody-minded, was certainly unreasonable". Such conduct could, therefore, be taken into account so as to reduce the special award. (See paras 9–32 to 9–33 for further commentary in respect of reductions to the basic award).

Fault where dismissal unfair because of selective dismissal or re-employment of employees involved in collective industrial action

Commentary on the circumstances in which the compensatory award may be reduced where there is a finding of fault in such cases is at paragraphs 11–56 to 11–60. The same principles apply to the special award.

Complainant Unreasonably Prevents an Order for Re-instatement or Re-engagement from being complied with (s.125(5) (a)) ERA & s.158(5)(a) TULR(C)A

8–60 If the tribunal finds that the complainant has unreasonably prevented an order for either re-instatement or re-engagement from being complied with then the tribunal shall reduce the special award to the extent that it considers it just and equitable to do so based on that finding. Again the tribunal has to exercise its discretion.

Complainant unreasonably refuses to accept offer of reinstatement

8–61 Likewise, if the complainant unreasonably refuses an offer of reinstatement (made other than in compliance with an order for reinstatement) the tribunal shall similarly reduce the special award (s.125(5)(b) ERA, s.158(5)(b) TULR(C)). Note that a reduction to the special award will only be made if the offer was for reinstatement which would put the complainant back to the position he would have been in had he not been dismissed. No reduction to the special award can be made if the complainant refuses an offer of re-engagement. So the complainant who applies for re-instatement with his eye on the special award, and with no real intention of returning to his previous employer, may end up losing part or all of that special award. (See para. 9–21 to 9–22 for equivalent provision in respect of the basic award).

CHAPTER 9
Unfair Dismissal: Basic Award

9–01 Where the tribunal makes an award of compensation for unfair dismissal, the complainant is entitled to:

(a) Basic Award (s.118(1)(a) ERA)

(b) Compensatory Award (s.118(1)(b) ERA)

In some circumstances the complainant may also be entitled to a special award or an additional award (see paras 8–36 to 8–50). Note also the new power to make a supplementary award where the employer has denied the employee the chance to pursue an internal appeal (s.118(4) and s.127A(2) ERA) (see para. 10–10 for commentary). In this chapter we consider the rules relating to the calculation of the basic award and the powers of the tribunal to reduce it in some circumstances.

9–02 The basic award is different from the compensatory award in that it is capable of exact calculation. It depends on three factors relating to the complainant at date of termination:

1. Week's pay (see paras 9–08 to 9–09 and Chapter 24)

2. Age

3. Length of service (see para. 9–05).

9–03 The calculation is the same as for statutory redundancy pay, subject to the following:

1. With redundancy pay, only years over 18 years old count. For the basic award, all complete years count (subject to a maximum of 20 years)—see (para. 9–05).

2. If the complainant has been made redundant and he is not entitled to a redundancy payment because he has unreasonably refused or left suitable alternative employment (s.141 ERA) or his contract of employment has been renewed or he has been re-engaged (s.138 ERA), the basic award will be two weeks' pay (s.121 ERA).

3. If the dismissal or selection for redundancy was for

   (a) a Trade Union reason (ss.152(1) and 153 TULR(C)A);
   (b) certain Health and Safety reasons (s.100(1)(a) and s.100(1)(b) ERA);
   (c) the reason that the complainant was a trustee of an occupational pension scheme (s.102 ERA);
   (d) the reason that the complainant was an elected representative or a candidate for such post in a business transfer or collective redundancy situation (s.103 ERA);

(e) A reason related to rights, etc., under the Working Time Regulations, 1998 (s101A ERA).

9–04 In these cases the minimum award will be £2,900 (s.120 ERA and s.156 TULR(C)A). Note that this is the same category of cases in which a special award will be made where an application has been made for re-employment which is either not granted or is not complied with by the employer (see para. 8–48 for a fuller description of the category of cases qualifying for an enhanced basic award and a special award). This, however, may be subject to reduction (s.122 ERA—see paras 9–20 to 9–35). The Secretary of State may change the minimum basic award by Order (s.120(2) ERA, and s.159 TULR(C)A. If the calculation of basic award on the normal basis exceeds the minimum figure then the minimum figure is ignored and the normal calculation applies.

Calculation of Basic Award

9–05 The basis of the calculation of the basic award is set out in s.119 ERA. In order to calculate the basic award these steps must be followed:

1. determine number of complete years service counting back from the effective date of termination to the start of continuous employment up to a maximum of 20 years;

2. check age of applicant;

3. assess week's pay at the calculation date (subject to statutory maximum—see para. 9–08 and see para. 9–09 for calculation date);

4. multiply number of complete years of employment during which he was aged 41 or over by 1.5;

5. add this to the number of remaining complete years of employment by that age when he was not below the age of 22;

6. multiply any remaining complete years of employment by 0.5;

7. add together 4, 5 and 6. Multiply this figure by the week's pay at calculation date.

9–06 The "ready reckoner" set out at Appendix P can be used to determine the figure by which the week's pay is multiplied to determine the basic award. Note, however, the need to adjust the ready reckoner if there are years of employment below the age of 18.

Example (using same numbering)

(1) 10 years' service.

(2) Employee 46 years old.

(3) Week's pay—£200.

(4) 5 years over age of 41: $5 \times 1.5 = 7.5$.

(5) Add remaining number of years' service: $7.5 + 5 = 12.5$.

(6)   No further complete years of employment.

(7)   12.5 × 200 = £2,500   Basic Award.

Applicant Aged Over 64

9–07   If the effective date of termination is after the applicant's 64th birthday the basic award is reduced by one-twelfth for each whole month from 64th birthday to effective date of termination.

Example

The applicant's birthday is December 15. He is dismissed with effect from March 13. There are two complete months between his 64th birthday and date of dismissal. Therefore basic award reduced by two-twelfths. There is no entitlement to the basic award if the complainant is 65 or over on the effective date of termination.

Maximum Week's Pay

9–08   For the purpose of calculating the basic award, a week's pay is subject to a statutory maximum (s.227(1) ERA). At present this is fixed at £220.00. This sum applies where the "calculation date" is on or after April 1, 1998. The Secretary of State has power to change this limit (s.227 ERA) following the annual review he is obliged to carry out (s.208 ERA).

The maximum basic award is 20 × 1.5 × 220 = £6,600.

The Calculation Date

9–09   In order to determine the basic award it is necessary to establish the week's pay of the complainant at the "calculation date" (see para. 9–05). As noted at paragraph 9–08, this is subject to a statutory maximum which is currently £220.00. The calculation date for the purposes of the basic award is determined in accordance with s.226 ERA. The rules are as follows:

1.   Complainant receives no notice or gives no notice (in a constructive dismissal situation).

    Calculation date: the complainant's last day of employment (s.226(3) ERA).

2.   Complainant receives shorter notice than the statutory minimum notice required or gives shorter notice than the statutory notice which would have been required of the employer.

    Calculation date: the date the notice expires (s.226(3) ERA).

3.   Complainant receives statutory minimum notice or gives notice equal to the statutory minimum notice which would have been required of the employer.

    Calculation date: the date notice was given (s.226(6) ERA).

4.   Complainant receives more than the statutory minimum notice required or gives notice which is longer than the notice which would have been required of the employer.

    Calculation date: latest date notice could have been given by the employer which complies with the statutory minimum notice requirement and which would have terminated the contract on the date the actual notice expired (s.226(6) ERA).

Example:

The employee receives six weeks' notice. He has been employed for four years. The statutory minimum notice required is therefore four weeks. The calculation date is four weeks prior to the date actual notice expired.

5. Where the complainant is a woman who has been unfairly dismissed by virtue of the employer refusing to allow her to return after maternity leave (see s.96 ERA).

Calculation date: last day the woman worked under her contract of employment immediately before starting her maternity leave (s.226(3) ERA).

Effective Date of Termination

9–10   The effective date of termination is calculated in accordance with s.97 ERA. It can be significant in the calculation of the basic award because it can affect the number of complete years of employment which are brought into the assessment of the basic award. The different circumstances contemplated by s.97 ERA are considered below.

Employment terminated on notice by the employer

9–11   Effective Date of Termination (EDT) equals expiry of that notice (s.97(1)(a) ERA), *but* if statutory minimum notice would have been longer than the actual notice given then the date the statutory minimum notice would have expired is the EDT (s.97(2) ERA).

Employment terminated by employer without notice

9–12   Unless the employee was properly dismissed for gross misconduct, the EDT will be the date when statutory minimum notice would have expired. If properly summarily dismissed for gross misconduct the EDT will be the actual date of dismissal (s.97(2) ERA).

Employment terminated by employee

9–13   Where the tribunal finds the complainant has been constructively dismissed, the EDT equals the date when statutory minimum notice would have expired had the contract been terminated by the employer serving notice on the date notice was given by the employee (or if no notice was given by the employee, the date when the employee terminated the contract of employment) (s.97(4) ERA).

Expiry of a fixed term

9–14   Where a fixed term is not renewed the EDT is the date the contract expires (s.97(1)(c) ERA).

Refusal to allow woman to return to work after maternity leave

9–15   In such circumstances the EDT is the date the complainant gave for returning to work (which was refused by the employer (s.97(6) ERA)).

Basic Award in "Redundancy" Dismissals

9–16   Where the tribunal finds that the reason for the dismissal was "redundancy" and the employer has already paid the statutory redundancy payment or the tribunal awards a redundancy payment, then the statutory redundancy payment is set off against the basic award which in most cases will extinguish the basic award (see paras 9–02 to 9–04 for circumstances where basic award is calculated differently from the redundancy payment).

Dismissals described at a redundancy

9–17   Where, however, the employer has asserted that the reason for dismissal was redundancy but the tribunal finds that the real reason is something different then the basic award is payable even if the employer has paid a sum which was described, erroneously, as a redundancy payment (*Boorman v. Allmakes Ltd* [1995] I.R.L.R. 553 CA).

Employers frequently seek to disguise a dismissal for incompetence as a redundancy and then seek to soften the blow by making a "redundancy payment". If the dismissed employee subsequently achieves a finding of unfair dismissal, and the tribunal agrees that it was not by reason of redundancy, the employer may get no credit for the "redundancy" payment. The basic award will be awarded with no set off for the payment made by the employer. Such a payment, however, can be set off against the compensatory award (*Boorman v. Allmakes Ltd*). However, if, for example, the complainant's total loss equals £15,000 and he received a payment of £1,100 from his employer which was erroneously described as a redundancy payment (and the tribunal finds that the dismissal was unfair and was not on grounds of redundancy) then that payment can be set off against the total loss of £15,000. This brings the loss down to £13,900. The statutory maximum (£12,000) is then applied and the complainant is awarded £12,000. The employer has gained no benefit from having made the payment on termination of employment (see also Chapter 15 for further commentary on payments set off against compensation).

Payments made in respect of basic award

9–18   If the employer has made a payment to the complainant which has been specifically described as being in respect of his entitlement to a basic award then this sum is set off against the basic award. A payment by the employer to the complainant which is more vaguely described as compensation paid in settlement of the employee's claims for compensation may satisfy the tribunal that the intention of the parties was that it was payable in respect of both the compensatory and basic awards and that the payment can therefore be set off against the basic award (*Chelsea Football Club & Athletic Co. Ltd v. Heath* [1981] I.R.L.R. 73). Each case has to be looked at on its own merits to determine the intention behind the payment. Was it intended to refer to potential entitlement to the basic award? Slynn J. stated in this case that "in each individual case it is a question of construction as to whether the payment made is to be taken to have included any rights which the employee might have under the provisions of the statute. If the employer makes a general payment—particularly if it is made *ex gratia*—he will risk the argument that he has not paid something which is referable to the liability for the basic award should he be held to have been dismissed unfairly. But it seems to us that there can be cases in which a payment is made and which is, as a matter of construction or of fact, to be taken as including such rights as the employee may have under the statute, even if entitlement to the monies is initially denied by the employer."

9–19   In that case the chief executive of the football club had written to Mr Heath as follows:

> "I therefore have very much pleasure in enclosing the club's cheque for £7,500, being the *ex gratia* compensation that was agreed by the Board, as a result of the termination of your employment, to take effect from 30 November. I can confirm that that gross sum is not subject to tax."

The EAT accepted that this amounted to "an offer without prejudice to liability to pay compensation for such rights as Mr Heath might have in respect of his dismissal". Slynn J. took the view that the parties generally know, when they are negotiating an agreement, that if unfair dismissal is proved the employee will be entitled to a basic and compensatory award. Accordingly, they were satisfied that the intention was that the payment was made in respect of both basic and compensatory awards and could be set off against both.

Reductions to the Basic Award

9–20   The basic award can be reduced in the following circumstances:

Refusal to accept offer of re-instatement

9–21   If the tribunal finds the complainant *has already* refused an offer of full re-instatement and considers that such refusal was unreasonable, the tribunal shall reduce the basic award to such extent as it considers "just and equitable" (s.122(1) ERA). Note that no reduction is permitted on this basis unless the complainant has been offered actual re-instatement. An offer which falls short of that is no good. Guidance was given to tribunals by Mummery J. on how to determine whether to reduce the basic award on this basis and if so, by how much, in the case of *Parkes v. Barnham Patent Locks Ltd* EAT 207/96. The tribunal should ask a series of questions as follows:

1.   Has the employer made an offer of reinstatement?

2.   If the offer was accepted would the effect of it be to fully reinstate the complainant as if he had not been dismissed?

3.   If this is the case, did the complainant refuse the offer?

4.   If the offer was refused, did he act unreasonably in doing so?

5.   If the complainant had acted unreasonably, is it just and equitable to reduce the basic award and if so, by how much?

9–22   An invitation by an employer to the dismissed employee to come in to discuss the dismissal is not a basis for reducing the basic award. This happened in *McDonald v. Capital Coaches Ltd* EAT 140/94. Mr McDonald refused the invitation and brought unfair dismissal proceedings. The tribunal, after finding that the dismissal was unfair, reduced the basic award to nil because, they said, Mr McDonald had unreasonably refused an offer of reinstatement. The EAT overturned this reduction. A reduction is only appropriate if there has been an offer of actual reinstatement, capable of being accepted. The EAT did, however, uphold the tribunal's decision to reduce the compensatory award to nil on the basis that he had failed to mitigate his loss. The

EAT was satisfied that had Mr McDonald accepted the employer's invitation it was likely that this would have led to reinstatement (see paras 8–17 to 8–22 for commentary on reinstatement, see also Chapter 19 for commentary on limiting the compensatory award on the basis of a failure to mitigate loss).

Conduct of complainant

9–23 If the tribunal considers that the conduct of the complainant before the notice of termination was given, or if there was no notice, before dismissal, was culpable in some way and because of that it would be just and equitable to reduce or further reduce the basic award to any extent, the tribunal shall reduce or further reduce the basic award (s.122(2) ERA). Note that the conduct need not have contributed to the dismissal for the tribunal to effect a reduction. It could indeed be argued that any culpable conduct during employment may be taken into account. However, the more distant the alleged misconduct is from the date of dismissal the less likely it will be that it would be just and equitable to take it into account.

9–24 The employer may have been entirely unaware of the culpable conduct when dismissing the complainant. Nonetheless, if later discovered conduct leads the tribunal to decide that it would be just and equitable to reduce the basic award, the tribunal must reduce it to such an extent as it thinks fit. Note the distinction between this and the specific provision dealing with fault in relation to the compensatory award (see paras 11–38 to 11–87). Section 123(6) ERA specifically refers to conduct which caused or contributed to the dismissal as being a basis upon which the tribunal can reduce compensation. However, the catch-all provision of s.123(1) allows the tribunal to take later discovered conduct into account in determining the compensatory award because the award must be "just and equitable in all the circumstances" (see paras 11–03 to 11–37).

9–25 In determining whether to reduce the basic award because of the conduct of the complainant, no account should be taken of how the employer has dealt with other cases. In *Parker Foundry v. Slack* [1992] I.R.L.R. 11 CA two employees were caught fighting. One, whom the employer found to be the aggressor, was dismissed, the other one suspended. "The [tribunal] ... is not required or indeed entitled to take into account what happened to the other employee ... who was a participant in the fight".

Conduct must be "culpable or blameworthy"

9–26 It is clear that the complainant's conduct must have been culpable or blameworthy in some respect for the tribunal to reduce the basic award (the same principle applies to the compensatory award, see paras 11–42 to 11–67 for commentary).

> "If a man is blameless it can be neither just nor equitable to reduce his award for an unfair dismissal" Sir Hugh Griffiths in *Morrish v. Henlys (Folkestone) Ltd* [1973] I.R.L.R. 61.

In *Nelson v. BBC (No.2)* [1979] I.R.L.R. 346, Brandon L.J. stated that the conduct need not necessarily amount to a breach of contract or a tort. It includes conduct which is "perverse or foolish or ... bloody-minded ... or unreasonable in all the circumstances". However "it must depend on the degree of unreasonableness".

Can the percentage reduction in basic award be different from that in the compensatory award where the reduction is based on the conduct of the applicant?

9–27   Both the relevant provisions dealing with reductions to the compensatory award and the basic award are concerned with the conduct of the applicant, but the wording of the provisions is different. Section 123(1) ERA provides that the amount of the compensatory award shall be such amount as the tribunal considers just and equitable in all the circumstances having regard to the loss sustained by the complainant in consequence of the dismissal in so far as that loss is attributable to action taken by the employer. Section 123(6) ERA states that where the tribunal finds that the dismissal was to any extent caused or contributed to by any action of the complainant, it shall reduce the amount of the compensatory award by "such proportion as it considers just and equitable having regard to that finding". With regard to the basic award, s.122(2) ERA provides:

> "Where the tribunal considers that any conduct of the complainant before the dismissal ... was such that it would be just and equitable to reduce the amount of the basic award to any extent, the employment tribunal shall reduce ... that amount accordingly."

9–28   The tribunal may conclude that the percentage reduction in the basic award may be different from the reduction made to the compensatory award. "A judgment made [in respect of a reduction to the basic award] reflects factors that are materially different from those bearing upon a judgment made pursuant to [a possible reduction] to the compensatory award." (Holland J. in *Charles Robertson Ltd v. (1) White, (2) Hobbs* [1995] I.C.R. 349 EAT). In that case the tribunal reduced the compensatory award by 100 per cent because of contributory fault, but only reduced the basic award by 50 per cent under what is now s.122(2) ERA. The tribunal took the view that it would not be just and equitable to reduce the basic award by 100 per cent. The complainants had "lost an important right. The employers are a substantial employer, and it is a serious matter not to afford employees their rights before dismissal. To reflect the loss of that right, we consider that an appropriate amount, having regard to the total basic award, which was not large in any event, would be 50 per cent of the basic award in each case." The EAT upheld this decision (see also paras 11–38 to 11–87 in relation to contributory fault and the compensatory award).

9–29   In *Royal Society for Prevention of Cruelty to Animals v. Cruden* [1986] I.R.L.R. 83, it was, however, pointed out that in the majority of cases the approach in assessing reduction to the basic and compensatory awards would be the same. But this is not always so. The judgment in *RSPCA v. Cruden* contains the following analysis of the rules on reductions to the basic award because of the conduct of the complainant (s.122(2) ERA) and the rules on reductions to the compensatory award because of contributory fault (s.123(6) ERA). "Plainly both sub-sections involve the exercise of discretion, and the wording of each, while sufficiently different to admit of differentiation in cases where the tribunal finds on the facts that it is justified, is sufficiently similar to lead us to conclude that it is only exceptionally that such differentiation will be justified."

9–30   In *Rao v. Civil Aviation Authority* [1982] I.R.L.R. 203, Sir Thomas Bingham points out that in assessing possible reductions to the compensatory award the tribunal may have already determined that there should be a deduction under what is now s.123(1) ERA on the basis of a finding by the tribunal that the complainant would not have remained further employed in any event. "That can affect what is just and equitable under Sub-section (6) [contributory fault]". This two-stage process does not apply to the assessment of any reduction to the basic award and it may result in the reduction of the compensatory award on the grounds of the employee's contributory conduct not being the same as the reduction which it is just and equitable to make from the basic award on the basis of conduct of the employee.

9–31 Facts: Mr Rao was employed by the Civil Aviation Authority for several years as an Air Traffic Control Assistant. Dismissal was because of a serious absence record with some evidence to suggest malingering. Finding unfair dismissal the tribunal found that, but for the unfair dismissal, his employment would only have continued for about another three weeks by which time a medical report would have been received and considered. Thereafter there was only a 20 per cent chance of his employment continuing. This first finding could well have a significant bearing on whether to make a further reduction from the compensatory award for contributory fault under section 123(6).

Conduct to be disregarded in determining whether to reduce basic award

9–32 In trade union dismissals under ss.152 and 153 TULR(C)A any conduct which constitutes the act itself which led to the dismissal (for example "conduct" in refusing to resign from a Trade Union.) cannot amount to a basis for reducing the basic award (s.155 TULR(C)A). However, the way in which the complainant went about, for example, resigning from the union may be blameworthy and could lead to a reduction in the basic (and other awards). In *TGWU v. Howard* [1992] I.R.L.R. 170, the tribunal held that the reason for Miss Howard's dismissal from her job with the TGWU was that she had refused to remain a member of that union. This made it automatically unfair. The tribunal also found that "the applicant's conduct in resigning from the union without seeking prior discussion was confrontational and if not bloody-minded was certainly unreasonable". However, the tribunal held that the conduct of the complainant had to be disregarded.

The EAT disagreed. A distinction can be drawn between that which is done by the complainant and the way in which it is done. "If the conduct of an employee prior to dismissal deserves to be criticised, the power of reduction is there, but the immediate circumstances giving rise to the finding of the principal reason for dismissal are to be excluded" (Wood J.)

9–33 If before resigning from the union or refusing to join, as the case may be, the complainant has acted in a bloody-minded and unreasonable way; if his actions were confrontational; if he resigned from the union without any discussion, then this sort of conduct can be taken into account. This is culpable conduct (see also paras 8–58 to 8–59 in respect of reductions to special award in such circumstances). Equally the refusal itself to agree, for example, to make payments in lieu of union subscriptions (s.152(3)(a) TULR(C)A) or an objection to a scheme for deductions from salary for this purpose cannot be taken into account as "conduct" in considering a reduction to the basic award.

Contributory fault and redundancy dismissals

9–34 If the reason for dismissal was redundancy, the basic award, generally, cannot be reduced on the basis of the conduct of the complainant (s.122(3) ERA). However, if the selection for redundancy was because of certain health and safety reasons (s.100(1)(a) and (b) ERA) or because the employee was a trustee of an occupational pension scheme (s.102 ERA) or was an employee representative (s.103

ERA) or for the various Trade Union reasons (s.152 and 153 TULR(C)A), or for reasons under the Working Time Regulations (s.101A ERA) then the enhanced minimum amount of the basic award under s.120 can be reduced (see paras 9–02 to 9–04). If the normal calculation of the basic award (under s.119 ERA) comes to more than the minimum enhanced basic award then the additional amount over and above that minimum figure may not be reduced.

Fault where dismissal unfair because of selective dismissal or re-employment of employees involved in collective industrial action

9–35   The tribunal does not have jurisdiction to hear a complaint of unfair dismissal relating to a dismissal of an employee for taking part in a strike or other industrial action (or where the employer is conducting or instituting a lock-out). This is the case unless the employer does not dismiss other employees involved in the industrial action or selectively re-engages others involved (s.238 TULR(C)A). Where there is a finding of unfair dismissal in such circumstances, compensation including the basic award cannot be reduced on the basis of contributory fault simply because of participation in the strike or other industrial action. The tribunal cannot judge blameworthiness or otherwise of a particular employee's conduct without reference to the conduct of other employees concerned and the employer. However, individual blameworthy conduct additional to, or separate from, the mere act of participation in industrial action could, in principle, amount to contributory fault (*Crosville Wales Ltd v. Tracey & Others (No.2)* [1997] I.R.L.R. 691 HL). See also paras 11–57 to 11–60 for further commentary on this case).

CHAPTER 10

Unfair Dismissal:
The Compensatory Award

10–01 The Compensatory award shall be "such amount as the tribunal considers *just and equitable in all the circumstances* having regard to the *loss sustained by the complainant in consequence of the dismissal* in so far as that *loss is attributable to action taken by the employer*" (s.123(1) ERA). The various elements of the process of calculating the compensatory award will be considered below but, first, some preliminary considerations.

PRELIMINARY CONSIDERATIONS

Statutory Maximum

10–02 Section 124(1) ERA imposes a statutory maximum on the compensatory award. It is currently £12,000. The Secretary of State can increase this limit by order (s.124(2) ERA). Increases are normally announced in April but there is no obligation on the Secretary of State to change the limit (see Chapter 26 for commentary on the Government's proposals for removal of this cap on compensation).

Statutory Maximum may be exceeded where there has been a failure to comply with an order to reinstate or re-engage

10–03 Section 124(4) ERA provides a basis for the statutory maximum to be exceeded in limited circumstances. Where an order for either form of re-employment has been made, but the complainant is not re-instated or re-engaged in accordance with the order, the complainant is entitled to the basic award and the compensatory award. He is also entitled to an additional award (s.117(3)(a) ERA) unless the tribunal is satisfied that it was not practicable to comply with the order (s.117(3)(b) and (4) ERA). (Note also the limited circumstances in which a special award is made instead of an additional award (see para. 8–49)).

10–04 If, in such circumstances, the tribunal concludes that an additional award is payable then the limit on the compensatory award may be exceeded in order to ensure that the complainant receives as much from the compensatory and additional awards as he would have got had he been reinstated or re-engaged in respect of compensation for the period between dismissal and re-employment (under s.114(2)(a) ERA in respect of reinstatement or s.115(2)(d) ERA in respect of re-engagement).

This provision has been considered by the EAT in the case of *Selfridges Ltd v. Malik* [1997] I.R.L.R. 577. In that case the tribunal ordered reinstatement and calculated the amount he should receive to compensate him for loss suffered between dismissal and reinstatement as £25,042.89. The Company failed to reinstate Mr Malik and so the tribunal had to determine what compensation was due. Being satisfied that it was practicable to comply with the order for reinstatement the tribunal awarded an additional award of £5,460.

10–05 The EAT, applying s.124(4) held that the compensatory award should be £19,582.89 so that this plus the additional award totalled the amount he would have received in respect of the period between dismissal and reinstatement had he indeed been reinstated, *i.e.* £25,042.89. This interpretation can effectively mean that there is no penalty for failing to re-instate where a large loss has built up since dismissal. Why bother, a respondent might ask, to reinstate if the maximum you will have to pay out for failing to reinstate equals the amount you have been, in any event, ordered to pay to compensate for loss since the dismissal?

Statutory Maximum applies after deducting any *ex gratia* payment made by the employer

10–06 It is very important to understand that in cases where the employer has made some sort of payment to the complainant on termination of employment this sum is deductible from the total loss before the statutory maximum is applied (s.124(5) ERA). For example, the complainant has received a £5,000 *ex gratia* payment on termination of employment but his total assessed loss (including future loss) is £20,000. The £5,000 *ex gratia* payment is deducted from the total loss of £20,000 leaving a sum of £15,000. This sum is then subject to the statutory maximum (currently £12,000). The net effect of this is that the employer receives no benefit for having made the *ex gratia* payment (see *McCarthy v. British Insulated Callenders Cables plc* [1985] I.R.L.R. 94 EAT). Note that a similar principle applies where the tribunal reduces the compensatory award for any reason. The reduction is applied first then the statutory maximum.

No Cap on Maximum Weekly Pay

10–07 Unlike the basic award, the compensatory award is not subject to any limitation on the amount of lost weekly pay and other benefits which can be awarded to the complainant (subject, of course, to the overall statutory maximum). So someone with a remuneration package worth £2,000 per week net who is unfairly dismissed and out of work for four weeks is entitled to £8,000 (plus any further sums for expenses incurred in finding work, loss of statutory rights, future loss, etc.).

Net Pay and Net Value of Other Benefits

10–08 The award is intended to compensate for actual loss suffered. The calculation of loss is therefore based on net "take home" pay and the net value of all other benefits lost (see *British Transport Commission v. Gourley* [1955] 3 All E.R. 796 and commentary at para. 11–02).

No Award for Injured Feelings—Just Financial Loss

10–09 The compensatory award is intended to compensate for financial loss suffered. "The object is to compensate, and compensate fully, but not to award a bonus" Sir John Donaldson, *Norton Tool Co. Ltd v. Tewson* [1973] 1 All E.R., [1972] I.R.L.R. 86 NIRC.

No punishment of the employer is involved and the former employee does not receive extra compensation because of especially blameworthy conduct by the employer. Sir John Donaldson considered this point in the *Norton Tool* case in relation to the discretionary element in the statutory formulae for assessing the compensatory award. "The discretionary element is introduced by the words 'having regard to the loss'. This does not mean that the tribunal can have regard to other matters but rather that the award of the compensation is not precisely and arithmetically related to the proved loss" Sir John Donaldson, *Norton Tool Co. Ltd v. Tewson.*

Manner of Dismissal

10–10 The manner of dismissal may, however, be relevant in assessing the likely extent of total loss if it was such that it has damaged the complainant's reputation or health, making it more difficult to get other work. "We need only consider whether the manner and circumstances of dismissal could give rise to any risk of financial loss at a later stage by, for example, making him less acceptable to potential employers or exceptionally liable to selection for dismissal" (Lord Donaldson, *Norton Tool Co. Ltd v. Tewson*). Clear evidence will need to be produced to show this.

In *Lifeguard Assurance Ltd, v. Zadrozny* [1977] I.R.L.R. 56, the EAT said the tribunal was wrong to have operated "in a general, benevolent manner according to their conception of what they think would be fair in the circumstances" (Phillips J.). Any loss awarded must have been "consequent upon the dismissal".

Supplementary Award

The Employment Rights (Dispute Resolution) Act 1998 (s.13) introduced a new s.127A to the ERA, the aim of which is to encourage employers to offer dismissed employees the right to use an internal appeals procedure and also to encourage employees to pursue such an appeal. If the employee fails to appeal, having been offered the chance, then compensation can be reduced by up to two weeks' pay (see para. 11–01 for commentary). If, however, the employer provides a procedure for appealing against dismissal but prevents the dismissed employee from using it then the tribunal shall make a supplementary award of up to two weeks' pay (provided, of course, that the tribunal finds the dismissal unfair). In deciding how much the supplementary award should be, the tribunal must "have regard to all the circumstances of the case, including the chances that an appeal ... would have been successful" (s.127A(3)). There is no cap on the calculation of a week's pay as there is in calculating the basic award. However, the week's pay is assessed at the same "calculation date" as with the basic award (see para. 9–09) (see Chapter 24 for commentary on "week's pay").

Trade Union Cases

Note that where the unfair dismissal claim is based on trade union grounds the award of compensation (both basic and compensatory awards and any special award) may be ordered to be paid in whole or in part by a trade union or other third party after they have been joined as a party to the proceedings (s.160 TULR(C)A). This may happen if either the complainant or the employer claims that the employer was induced to dismiss the complainant by pressure from a trade union or other person. The pressure envisaged is the calling, organising, procuring or financing of a strike or other industrial action, or by threatening to do any of these things. The pressure must have been exercised because the complainant was not a member of any trade union or of a particular trade union or of one of a number of particular trade unions. Either the complainant or the employer can request the tribunal to direct that the trade union or other person be joined as a party.

General Approach of Tribunal in Determining Loss

10–11 Compensation must not be dispensed "arbitrarily" (Sir John Donaldson, *Norton Tool Co. Ltd v. Tewson*) but it has a discretionary element and "is not to be assessed by adopting the approach of a conscientious and skilled cost accountant or actuary ... That discretion must be exercised judicially and on the basis of principle ... The common law rules and authorities on wrongful dismissal are irrelevant." The measure of damages is to be based on the wording of the statute.

Heads of Loss

10–12 The compensatory award can be broken down into four heads of loss and it would be sensible when drafting the schedule of loss to use these widely accepted categories. Sir John Donaldson in the *Norton Tool* case said that tribunals should break down the compensatory award into separate heads of loss so that the parties can see how compensation has been calculated. The heads of loss are as follows:

1. Immediate loss of earnings and other benefits up to the date of the remedy hearing

2. Future loss of earnings and other benefits

3. Expenses incurred as a result of the dismissal (for example in seeking to mitigate loss)

4. Loss of pension rights

10–13 At paras 3–10 to 3–47 we considered the various benefits and pay which can be taken into account and at paras 3–52 to 3–60 guidance is given on expenses recoverable. The tribunal itself has a duty to investigate each head of loss but it is the responsibility of the aggrieved person, once the categories have been investigated, to prove the loss (see *Tidman v. Aveling Marshall Ltd* [1977] I.R.L.R. 218).

Loss of Statutory Rights

10–14 Note that the tribunal will normally award a standard sum (currently approximately £200) to compensate the complainant for the loss of statutory rights enjoyed in employment. The most significant of such rights is, of course, the right not to be unfairly dismissed. In *Muffett Ltd v. Head* [1986] I.R.L.R. 488, the EAT overturned the tribunal's decision to award £20 in respect of his loss. At that time, the EAT considered that £100 was the appropriate sum (this after consultation with the President of the EAT). The sum should be increased over the years to take account of inflation.

Loss must be attributable to action taken by the employer

10–15 The statutory formula for determining the compensatory award states that for loss to be recoverable it must be "attributable to action taken by the employer" s.123(1) ERA. In the case of *Simrad Ltd v. Scott* [1977] I.R.L.R. 147, Ms Scott had been employed by the respondent company as an electronic technician. Following her dismissal (which was adjudged to be unfair) she failed to find other similar work but managed to get a lower paid job with no career prospects. After some time she took the decision to retrain as a nurse. She left the lower paid job and started a three-year course. The tribunal awarded compensation including a sum for future loss of fifteen months based on the difference between the net pay she earned when working for the respondent company and the grant she received whilst on her course.

10–16 The EAT overturned this decision on the basis that loss which resulted from her decision to retrain as a nurse was too remote "both in time and content, to be directly linked to the dismissal" (Lord Johnston). The EAT said that the assessment of the compensatory award under what is now s.123(1) ERA was a three-stage process as follows:

1. A factual quantification of losses claimed.

2. Determining the extent to which "any or all of those losses are attributable to the dismissal or action taken by the employer".

3. Applying the "just and equitable" test in s.123(1) ERA the tribunal should look at the conclusions they have drawn from the first two questions and determine whether, in all the circumstances, it remains reasonable to make the award.

The question of whether the complainant had mitigated his loss is considered at this third stage (for commentary on mitigation see Chapter 19).

10–17 Lord Johnston said that the tribunal had failed to direct themselves to the second stage of the process "but had merely looked at the question of the career change in the context of a reasonable decision by the employee or not, as the case may be". The second stage of determining whether loss is attributable to the dismissal involves asking whether there is a "direct and natural link between the losses claimed and the conduct of the employer in dismissing". It is not enough to simply conclude that, but for the dismissal, the loss would not have arisen. "If that is the only connection, the loss is too remote."

10–18 Lord Johnston made it clear that the EAT did not find it easy "to determine whether or not ... [Ms Scott's] decision to embark upon a nursing career is sufficiently directly linked to the original dismissal to meet the test of attribution". The EAT took into account the intervening period of employment at a lower rate of pay and concluded "with some hesitation" that the loss which followed her decision to train as a nurse was too remote. "It was her decision, no doubt reasonable in the context of the position in which she found herself but not one which, in our opinion, can be properly attributable to the conduct of the employers within the meaning of [s.123(1) ERA] as we have defined it" (see paras 10–60 to 10–63 and 19–53 to 19–56 for further commentary on the effect of a dismissed employee going on a training course). This decision leaves open the possibility that a dismissed employee's decision to retrain may, in the particular circumstances, be attributable to the dismissal and that loss can therefore continue to be recoverable.

10–19 In another case later in the same year, *(1) Strathclyde Buses Ltd v. Leonard & ors (2) Ellum & ors v. Strathclyde Buses Ltd* (1997) EAT (507 & 515/97) and IDS Brief 600, November 1997, the EAT again had to consider whether a loss claimed was attributable to action taken by the employer. The employees had shares in the company which had to be sold back to the company when they were dismissed. Some time after their dismissal the company was sold. The purchasing company paid a much higher price for the shares than the dismissed employees had received. The tribunal awarded compensation for the loss of the enhanced value of the shares. The EAT, however, said that the shares increased in value as a direct result of the action of the purchasing company. The takeover could not have been foreseen at the time of the dismissals.

There was, therefore, no direct and natural link between the loss of the enhanced value of the shares and the action of the employer in dismissing the employees—the loss was not attributable to the action of the employer and was not recoverable.

WHAT PERIOD OF LOSS CAN BE RECOVERED?

10–20 In this section, we consider how long a period of loss may be awarded by the tribunal. This may be made up partly of immediate loss—loss between the date of dismissal and the date of the remedy hearing—and future loss. The only real difference between these two heads of loss is that, inevitably, future loss is speculative whereas loss which has already occurred can be assessed with much greater precision. Assessing past loss is a fact finding exercise (subject to an assessment of whether the complainant has mitigated his loss).

Loss has to be proved. "It is for the aggrieved person to prove the loss", (Kilner Brown J. in *R.W. Tidman v. Aveling Marshall Ltd* [1977] I.R.L.R. 218 EAT). The need to satisfy the tribunal that the complainant has made efforts to mitigate her loss may have a crucial bearing on the period of loss awarded (see Chapter 19). Proving loss is of course particularly problematic in the case of future loss.

Period of future loss

10–21 In *Adda International Ltd v. Curcio* [1976] I.R.L.R. 425 a familiar problem arose. The parties had focused on liability "and not with what the appropriate amount of compensation" should be. The EAT made clear in (*obiter*) comments that there must be some evidence of future loss and the scale of future loss to enable the tribunal to make any award under this head. The tribunal must have something to bite on, and if the complainant produces nothing for it to bite on he will have only himself to thank if he gets no compensation for loss of future earnings.

But it is also clear that there is no artificial limit on the period of future loss. It will depend on the evidence. In *Scottish & Newcastle Breweries v. Halliday* [1986] I.R.L.R. 291 EAT, Sir Ralph Kilner Brown said: "This exercise involves both a look backwards to see what has happened and a look forward in order to make a reasonable estimate as to what is likely to happen in the future. In order to keep the amount of compensation within bounds, it has been the practice for many years to express the forward period in terms of months. This is often six months but with mass unemployment it is now frequently extended to twelve months or even more."

10–22 In *Morganite Electrical Carbon Ltd v. Donne* [1987] I.R.L.R. 363, an argument that the tariff for periods of loss should be 6–12 months was rejected. "Having regard to the terms of the statute ... we can see no justification for saying that there is any specific limit or that practice has decreed that there should be some limit." Subject to the statutory maximum "the range must be determined by the evidence in any particular case". In that case, 52 weeks of future loss (on top of 30 weeks up to the date of assessment) was not excessive. They took into account the "employment situation in the country generally" and in that area in particular (South Wales) and also the complainant's medical history—which would make getting another job more difficult.

10–23 It is fair to say that tribunals tend to award more limited periods of future loss—perhaps in the range of three to nine months—but, as stated, it must depend on the evidence. The lesson to learn from this guidance is that if there is a case for claiming a long period of future loss, it should be included in the schedule of loss but evidence must be given to support it.

Delayed Hearing on Compensation

10–24   Sometimes, for unavoidable reasons, the hearing to consider compensation may be delayed long after the dismissal and possibly long after the finding of unfair dismissal. It is often the case that the tribunal will not consider remedies immediately after determining liability. The hearing may be adjourned to allow the parties to try to negotiate a settlement which subsequently proves unattainable. There may be an appeal against liability or a successful appeal by the applicant against a finding that the dismissal was fair. Also, the delay may be a result of the case-load at the Regional Tribunal hearing the case. Whatever the reason, the result may be that, by the time the tribunal does get to consider compensation, the complainant may have been out of work for a long period of time.

10–25   In *Gilham & others v. Kent County Council* [1986] I.R.L.R. 56, the compensation hearing took place two years and nine months after the dismissals. The EAT rejected the decision of the tribunal that loss should be limited to one year because the complainants would have been dismissed then anyway. This flew in the face of the evidence. Loss could, subject to satisfying the rules on mitigation, extend up to the compensation hearing.

Examples: Period of loss

Local Job Market

10–26   *Welburn v. Luxihomes Ltd COIT 3088/232* The local job market was highly seasonal being a resort town. The tribunal decided to award 45 weeks' loss up to the start of the next holiday season.

Nature of Dismissal/No Reference

10–27   The circumstances of the dismissal may make it particularly difficult to find other work. An unjustified dismissal for gross misconduct with no reference could make someone unemployable for a considerable length of time. Evidence of repeated failures to get jobs applied for would be helpful.

Gerbaldi v. Jones t/a Milton Business Products COIT 3132/243 where a failure to give a reference made it more difficult to get other work resulting in an award of 52 weeks' future loss.

Access to Employment Opportunities

10–28   A woman who lived in a rural area and had no car had difficulty getting other work. This could be taken into account in determining the period of future loss (*Haslam v. Manchetts Cleaning Supplies Ltd* COIT 3130/19).

Issues Personal to the Applicant

10–29   For an Afro-Caribbean with no qualifications and poor communication skills the tribunal accepted it would be very difficult to get other work. These factors could be taken into account in determining the period of loss (see *Malcolm v. Balmstore Ltd t/a Thompson's Bakery* COIT 3169/50).

Discrimination in the Labour Market

10–30 This raises the issue as to whether tribunals can recognise the reality that ethnic minorities may find it more difficult to find alternative employment because of discrimination in recruitment. Equally, a woman with a small child or who is pregnant may have additional problems in finding new work. Clear evidence of a potential employer discriminating against someone in refusing to give her a job on grounds of race, sex or disability could clearly "break the chain of causation" and provide a fresh basis of claim.

However, if such evidence does not exist a tribunal may reasonably reach the view that a particular complainant may, for such reasons, find it harder to get other work and therefore award a longer period of future loss. (See *Bennett v. Tippins* EAT 361/89 where it was accepted that a pregnant woman is likely to find it difficult to find new employment. In *MOD v. Hunt & Others* [1996] I.R.L.R. 139 it was accepted that a woman with a baby or young child and who has responsibility for child care is likely to have the same problem. See paras 19–12 to 19–13 for further commentary).

Age

10–31 Age is clearly a factor affecting the chances of getting new work. The older the applicant, and the closer they are to retirement age, the harder it is likely to be to find new work. This will, therefore, lengthen the period of future loss which the tribunal may be willing to award.

In *Isle of Wight Tourist Board v. Coombes* [1976] I.R.L.R. 413, Mrs Coombes recovered two years' loss up to what would have been her retirement date because the tribunal accepted she was unlikely to get another job. The tribunal also accepted that, had she not been dismissed, she would have stayed until her retirement date. The EAT accepted the fact that the tribunal could take into account the fact that with someone approaching retirement age "the significance of the [sixtieth] birthday becomes rather greater in the equation" with the imminence of "cheap bus fares, pensions and so on" tending to encourage the employee to stay on until then, perhaps, despite temptations to leave sooner.

10–32 In *Penprase v. Mander Bros. Ltd* [1973] I.R.L.R. 167 the tribunal awarded compensation for three-and-a-half years up to the date when he would have retired had he not been dismissed. The tribunal took into account the fact that he had been unable to obtain any further employment "and we think it unlikely that he will do so before the age of 65".

However, in circumstances where there is evidence that age is not an impediment to getting new work the tribunal may award only a short period of loss. In *Machan v. New Longmoor Club* COIT 1921/31, a 53-year-old cleaner was dismissed. Evidence suggested that the average age of cleaners was over 50 and that there was, generally, a rapid turnover of staff. The tribunal decided that the complainant should be able to get work almost immediately and awarded no future loss.

Compensation may be awarded for a period beyond retirement age

10–33 In *Barrel Plating and Phosphating Co. Ltd v. Danks* [1976] I.R.L.R. 262 the tribunal found that Mrs Danks would have stayed in her job six months beyond her normal retirement age had she not been dismissed. The EAT confirmed that if, on the facts, employment would have continued, but for the dismissal, beyond the normal retirement age then compensation can be awarded for that period (despite the fact that someone dismissed after they have reached normal retirement age has no claim).

Health

10–34 Ill health can be a double edged sword for the complainant seeking compensation for loss following dismissal. Ill health could result in the tribunal reaching the conclusion that there may, in due course, have been a fair basis for dismissing the complainant and thereby limit loss to the period up to the point when he might have been fairly dismissed (see paras 11–25 to 11–27). It should, of course, be borne in mind that someone suffering ill health may have a disability under the terms of the Disability Discrimination Act 1995 and that, accordingly, they may have more protection against dismissal. However, each case has to be considered on its merits.

10–35 On the other hand, ill health caused by the dismissal may lead to a lengthy period of loss if it prevents the complainant from getting another job.

In *Devine v. Designer Flowers Wholesale Florist Sundries Ltd* [1993] I.R.L.R. 577, Mrs Devine "suffered anxiety and reactive depression" and the tribunal found that this was as a result of her dismissal. The EAT made clear that the personal circumstances of the employee "including the effect of the dismissal on her health" should be taken into account in ascertaining the appropriate amount of compensation. The complainant may not necessarily be awarded compensation for the whole period of any such incapacity. That depends on how far it is attributable to action (*i.e.* dismissal) taken by the employer. There may be evidence that the unfitness "might have manifested itself in any event". The tribunal must arrive at a sum which is just and equitable. The medical condition may also disqualify the complainant from certain sorts of work, for example managerial, but not other less stressful and perhaps less well-paid work. This must be considered by the tribunal in assessing whether the complainant may be able to partially mitigate his loss in such a way (see Chapter 19 for discussion on mitigation).

Pre-existing medical condition at date of dismissal

10–36 In the case of *Fougere v. Phoenix Motor Co.* [1976] I.C.R. 495, the complainant had pre-existing medical problems at the date of dismissal. Mr Fougere was 58 years old and suffering from a hernia and bronchitis. His ill health prevented him from getting other work for a long time. The EAT said that for loss to be recoverable it must have been sustained in consequence of the dismissal (see s.123(1)—attributable to action taken by the employer). Clearly, in the EAT's view, the loss resulted from his dismissal. However, they noted that ill health might have subsequently enabled the employer to dismiss him fairly.

Note also that ill health following dismissal may reduce the amount recoverable. If the employee had not been dismissed and had been off work on sickness absence then, depending on sick pay rules in that employment, he might have received less pay during those periods of absence. For example, he may only have been entitled to Statutory Sick Pay. If, because of such absences, his total pay over a period would have been reduced had he not been dismissed, his total loss for that period following dismissal will be less (see *Curtis v. James Paterson (Darlington) Ltd* [1973] I.C.R. 496 NIRC, [1974] I.R.L.R. 88).

The Effect of a New Job on the Calculation of Loss

10–37 There are a number of different scenarios relating to the potential impact on compensation of the complainant getting a new job.

Special Rules for Notice Period

Complainant has been unfairly dismissed without receiving notice or pay in lieu of notice

10–38 The complainant can claim net pay for the notice period without having to set off any earnings received from other employment.

In *Norton Tool Co. Ltd v. Tewson* [1973] 1 All E.R. 183, [1972] I.R.L.R. 86, Mr Tewson was sacked unfairly with no notice or pay in lieu. He was entitled to six weeks notice. After four weeks he got another job at slightly higher pay. He was entitled to be compensated for net wages for the full six weeks notice. It was "good industrial practice" to give notice or a payment in lieu and had he been paid his "six weeks wages in lieu, the employee would not have had to make any repayment if he had obtained further work within the notice period" (Sir John Donaldson).

10–39 This general rule might not apply in a limited number of cases if the notice period is very long and the complainant is likely to be able to find new work during that period. This point was made by Gibson L.J. in *Babcock FATA Ltd v. Addison* [1987] I.R.L.R. 173 CA. The argument seems to be that where there is a very long notice period, good industrial practice would not necessarily require a payment in lieu equivalent to the wages for the full period of notice. A smaller sum may be justified on the basis of an expectation that the dismissed employee will be able to mitigate his loss by getting new work during the notice period. This begs the question in any particular case as to what sum the tribunal considers should be paid by the employer in accordance with good industrial practice.

10–40 In *Babcock*, Gibson L.J. gave an example of a situation where an employee is entitled to six months' notice but the employer hands over only two months' pay in lieu of notice. That might not offend good industrial practice if the employee is likely to get another job quickly. If this was found to be so, any wages earned by the dismissed employee during the first two months would not have to be offset against compensation in lieu of notice but wages earned beyond that period might legitimately be offset against further compensation.

Another situation where an exception to the general rule in *Norton* would apply is where there is an early termination of a fixed term contract with a substantial unexpired period. In *Isleworth Studios Ltd v. Rickard* [1988] I.C.R. 482, Mr Rickard was dismissed with 29 weeks left to run on his one-year fixed term contract. The day after his dismissal he started trading in his own business. During the next 29 weeks he earned £10,000 more than he would have earned had he not been dismissed. He suffered no loss. The EAT ruled that he was entitled to no compensation. It cannot have been intended that section 123 ERA (as it is now) could allow the payment of compensation where no loss had been sustained and where substantial profit has been made.

10–41 There appears to be no sound argument in principle that the general rule set out in *Norton Tool Co. Ltd v. Tewson* should be limited to the statutory notice period in circumstances where there is a longer contractual notice. Subject to the exceptional circumstances described in *Babcock*, it would seem that wages from a new job do not generally have to be set off against entitlement to compensation for the contractual notice period. For example, someone employed for just over two years may have a contractual notice entitlement of four weeks. Good industrial practice could well require the employer to pay the full four weeks' wages in lieu of notice and if he does not do so the complainant should, under the *Norton* principle, be entitled to compensation for the full period of notice without having to offset any wages earned from a new employer during that four-week period. The statutory minimum notice of two weeks for someone of two years' standing appears to be irrelevant to the application of the principle in *Norton* to these facts.

Applicant has been unfairly dismissed without notice but with pay in lieu of notice

10–42   Credit must be given to the employer for sums paid in lieu of notice. The complainant cannot be compensated again for the period of notice. This was confirmed by the Court of Appeal in *Babcock FATA Ltd v. Addison* [1987] I.R.L.R. 173 CA. If, having received a payment in lieu of notice, the complainant then secures another job during that period, he does not have to give credit for these new earnings (during the notice period) in the calculation of loss (Gibson L.J. *Babcock FATA v. Addison*). "Whether the wages in lieu of notice are paid or not, the employee need not give credit for sums earned in new employment during that period."

10–43   In the exceptional circumstances of a long notice period where a partial payment in lieu of notice is given and where the tribunal accepts that this was reasonable in accordance with good industrial practice, it seems that only new wages earned during the part of the notice period covered by the partial payment in lieu would not have to be offset (see earlier commentary on *Babcock* at paras 10–39 to 10–40).

New Job outside the notice period

10–44   Subject to these special rules relating to the notice period, a number of further situations need to be considered. The effect of a new job on assessment of compensation has been the subject of contradictory decisions in the past. A particular problem arises when, at some stage prior to the remedy hearing, the complainant gets new employment at a higher rate of pay than he had before he was dismissed. Do those higher wages have to be set against the lost earnings or does the calculation of loss stop at the point he gets the new job?

A recent EAT decision sought to remove some of the uncertainty in this area. In *Whelan and another t/a Cheers Off Licence v. Richardson* [1998] I.R.L.R. 114, Mrs Richardson was unfairly dismissed from her job as a shop assistant on August 4, 1995. She had earned £72 per week. She was then unemployed for two weeks before getting other shop work earning £51.60 a week. This job lasted for eighteen weeks. On December 27 she got a permanent job earning an average of £95.82 per week. She still had this job at the date of the remedy hearing in November 1996.

10–45   The tribunal considered whether to calculate loss of earnings up to December 27, 1995, when she got higher paid "permanent" work, or up to the date of the remedy hearing with credit being given for all earnings between dismissal and the hearing.

Using the first approach the loss of earnings totalled £511.20. Adopting the second approach the earnings since December 27 more than cancelled out the loss up to that date. The tribunal opted to calculate loss up to December 27, 1995. The EAT upheld the tribunal's approach. In doing so Clarke J. assessed the conflicting case law and then gave guidance to tribunals on various scenarios.

10–46   The cases considered by Clark J. in *Whelan and Another v. Richardson* were as follows:

Ging v. Ellward (Lancs) Ltd [1978] 13 I.T.R. 265 EAT
Mr Ging was unfairly dismissed on January 23, 1976. In September 1976 Mr Ging got a job on an oil rig. Four weeks later it was destroyed by a storm and he lost his job.

By then he had earned £1,200 net. He got another job in November 1976 which he still had by the time of the remedy hearing in July 1977.

The tribunal looked at loss up to the date Mr Ging got "permanent" work in November 1976. The earnings on the rig extinguished his loss suffered prior to September 1976.

On appeal, Arnold J. ruled that the tribunal had got it wrong. Compensation should be assessed up to the date of the remedy hearing. He said there was no distinction between the effect of temporary and permanent employment for the purpose of assessing compensation. The effect of this analysis was that the earnings up to the remedy hearing outweighed the loss suffered as a result of dismissal. Mr Ging received no compensation.

Courtaulds Northern Spinning Ltd v. Moosa [1984] I.R.L.R. 43

10-47   Mr Moosa was unfairly dismissed on June 8, 1979. On October 1, 1979 he got alternative work but was eventually made redundant on March 21, 1981. He was then out of work for a long time. The remedy hearing took place on January 14, 1983. He was still unemployed. In this case, loss would have been much greater if it had been calculated for the full period up to the remedy hearing (following the *Ging* approach). The tribunal followed this approach and also awarded a further twenty-six weeks' future loss of wages. The EAT overturned the tribunal's decision. Reference was made to the approach taken in wrongful dismissal cases (this is now dealt with in McGregor on Damages, 16th Edition, 1977). "Loss is treated as at an end when the employee secures alternative permanent employment at the same or greater wage than he earned with the defendant prior to dismissal" (Clark J. in *Whelan*). The EAT therefore said that loss should be calculated to October 1, 1979 when he got permanent employment.

Lytlarch Ltd v. Reid [1991] 1 C.R. 216 EAT

10-48   This was a Scottish EAT decision which followed *Moosa*, calculating loss up to the date Mr Reid got "permanent" new employment and not up to the date of hearing.

Fentiman v. Fluid Engineering Products Ltd [1991] I.R.L.R. 150 EAT

The EAT in this case again followed the *Moosa* approach. Compensation was calculated up to the date Mr Fentiman got a much better paid job, rather than up to the date of hearing. The difference was that Mr Fentiman got the statutory maximum which was then £8,925. Had the *Ging* approach been used, loss up to the date of hearing (taking into account his new higher earnings) came to £2,373.

After reviewing these decisions, Clark J. in *Whelan* made the observation that a dismissed employee "should not be discouraged from doing [temporary work] because he appreciates that at the end of that temporary employment he will have no continuing claim against his former employer".

10-49   He then made a series of propositions aimed at giving guidance but stressing that he did not seek to fetter the exercise of discretion by the tribunal on the facts of a particular case. First he said that assessment of loss is to be judged on the basis of facts as they appear at the date of the remedy hearing (assessment date). Then he set out various scenarios:

Complainant unemployed up to assessment date

10-50   Subject to recoupment and the duty to mitigate, complainant will recover full net loss. There may also be future loss.

Complainant gets lower paid work prior to assessment date

10–51   The complainant will be compensated for full net loss up to the date he gets the new job and for partial loss (difference between earnings in old and new jobs) up to the assessment date (although Clark J. did not say so, the complainant may also recover future loss).

Complainant gets temporary work prior to the assessment date

10–52   If the complainant gets a job for a "limited duration" he can claim for loss following the end of that job up to the assessment date (and again for any future loss). Earnings in the temporary job are set against the full loss from dismissal up to the assessment date or up to when he gets permanent work. Although Clark J. does not say so, the reasoning dictates that loss would only then stop if the permanent job was at the same or better money than the job from which he had been dismissed.

Complainant gets a "permanent" job paying the same or more than pre-dismissal earnings

10–53   If the complainant gets a permanent job on the same or better earnings, "loss attributable to the action taken by the respondent employer ceases" and cannot be revived if he loses that job, whatever the circumstances. The increased earnings are not set against loss previously suffered so as to reduce the loss.

By adopting this approach, Clark J. was rejecting the EAT's analysis in *Ging v. Ellward (Lancs) Ltd* [1978] 13 I.T.R. 265 and following *Courtaulds Northern Spinning Ltd v. Moosa* [1984] I.R.L.R. 63 together with the general approach taken in wrongful dismissal cases. Note, however, the more recent Court of Appeal decision in *Dench v. Flynn & Partners (a firm)* CA 9.6.98e IDS Brief 621 September 1998 considered at paragraph 10–56.

Can further loss ever be recovered following termination of a permanent job?

10–54   One scenario which Clark J.'s guidelines are not clear on is where, just as in *Ging*, the complainant gets a job which appears to be permanent but, in fact, ends relatively soon after it has started, and in circumstances where no fault can be attached to the complainant.

What is a permanent job? This issue, according to Clark J., "will be a question of fact for the ... tribunal". Brown-Wilkinson J. in *Moosa* took the view that the short duration of the job Mr Ging obtained on the oil rig was such that one could not describe it as permanent.

10–55   This suggests that in determining whether a job is temporary or permanent the tribunal can look not only at what the expectation was at the start of the job but how long it actually lasted. If the period in the new job lasts for any length of time it is unlikely that the tribunal would regard loss which results from the subsequent termination of that employment as being attributable to the action of the original employer. In *Courtaulds Northern Spinning Ltd v. Moosa* [1984] I.R.L.R. 443 Mr Moosa was employed by Fashion Flow for nearly eighteen months following his dismissal from Courtaulds. His dismissal on grounds of redundancy from his new employment was "attributable to action taken by Fashion Flow and not at Courtaulds" (Browne-Wilkinson J).

10–56   In *Mabey Plant Hire Co Ltd v. Richens* (1992) EAT February 4, IDS 468 May 1992, the unfairly dismissed employee found new work from which he was subsequently dismissed for failing to comply with company regulations. The EAT criticised the tribunal for reducing the complainant's compensation by 50 per cent for the period following the dismissal from the new job. Such dismissal either meant that there should be no further compensation because subsequent loss was not attributable to the dismissal by the original employer, or that the dismissal was not enough to interrupt the respondent's liability for loss for the whole period up to the date of assessment of loss. There could not be a compromise between the two positions. That issue was remitted to the tribunal.

In the recent case of *Dench v. Flynn & Partners (a firm)* CA 9.6.98 and IDS Brief 621, September 1998 the Court of Appeal has reinforced the fact that the normal rule in Whelan (that loss ceases when the complainant obtains alternative employment at the same or better pay) is not cast in stone. To always cut off loss in this way may result in compensation being awarded which is not just and equitable in accordance with the statutory basis for calculating the compensatory award set out in s.123(1) ERA. If subsequent and apparently permanent loss flowing from the original dismissal. In this case a solicitor was given three months notice in June 1995. In October 1995, she accepted a new post in a small husband and wife partnership. She had real misgivings having been warned of the potential problems working for sole practitioners. The job did not work out and she left on 31st December, 1995. The tribunal had held that Ms Dench was not entitled to compensation beyond October 1995. The Court of Appeal remitted the case to the tribunal so that they could determine the total loss suffered by Ms Dench taking into account the earnings she received between October and December and any other subsequent earnings from part time work.

In summary, the guidance given by Clark J in *Whelan* (see paras 10–49 to 10–53) is generally sound but with the important proviso that the overriding principle is that compensation must be that which is just and equitable (s.123(1) ERA) and that therefore in some cases an apparently permanent job on the same or better pay will not necessarily stop the period of loss if the complainant loses that job through no fault of their own.

Dismissal From New Job—Continuing Loss

10–57 Note that if the complainant secures a new job on lower pay but is subsequently dismissed in circumstances where the tribunal considers that loss resulting from that dismissal cannot be attributed to the respondent, the complainant can claim the continuing loss that he would have suffered in any event had he not been dismissed from his new job—*i.e.* the difference between his pay with the respondent and pay in the new job.

Part-time Work

10–58 Any earnings from part-time work carried out by the complainant following an unfair dismissal should, of course, be set-off against total loss in the normal way (see *Justfern Ltd v. D'Ingerthorpe and others* [1994] I.R.L.R. 164).

Resignation from new job

10–59 There may be circumstances in which the complainant takes on new work but soon recognises that the work is unsuitable for one reason or another. This may not necessarily break the chain of causation. He may have taken the job specifically to reduce his losses and if it turns out to be unsuitable work he should not be penalised for making proper efforts to mitigate his loss. It may reasonably be said that the losses which follow such a decision could be attributable to the actions of the respondent employer and, further, such a decision may be reasonable in the overall context of the duty to mitigate (see paras 19–49 to 19–50 for further commentary and case law on mitigation).

Retraining / College Courses

10–60   Difficult issues of both remoteness and of the duty to mitigate loss arise in circumstances where the dismissed employee decides to enrol on a course to retrain or to gain further education. Can the complainant in the circumstances recover compensation for loss suffered following such a decision? In *Simrad Ltd v. Scot* [1977] I.R.L.R. 147 (discussed in more detail at para. XX) the EAT decided that Ms Scott's decision to retrain as a nurse was not sufficiently directly linked to the original dismissal to meet the test of attribution. Further losses were not attributable to the dismissal but to her decision to retrain. It may, however, be the case that a decision to retrain is directly linked to the dismissal. For example, the complainant may conclude that he cannot get other similar work and that he has to retrain to get back into employment. It will then be a question of the tribunal deciding whether the steps taken were reasonable in order to mitigate his loss.

10–61   In addressing these questions, it is necessary to analyse the complainant's motivation for the particular course of action he pursues. If the complainant independently decides that having been dismissed he will take the opportunity to do something different, this is likely to "break the chain of causation". Further losses which result from the decision to retrain are too remote to be recovered from the respondent. It may be a perfectly reasonable decision for the complainant to make but losses following from that decision are not attributable to action taken by the respondent.

10–62   If the motivation for retraining is, on the other hand, directly aimed at limiting loss by seeking to become more employable then further loss should not be too remote and it then becomes a question of whether the steps actually taken by the complainant were reasonable in order to mitigate loss. These issues have arisen in a number of cases considered by the EAT.

In *Holroyd v. Gravure Cylinders Ltd* [1984] I.R.L.R. 259, Mr Holroyd took up a 12 month postgraduate course some time after his constructive dismissal. The EAT considered that by doing this he had taken himself out of the labour market. "Any suggestion of future loss at the termination of his university course is so remote as to be incapable in our view of calculation" (Lord McDonald).

In *Justfern Ltd v. D'Ingerthorpe* [1994] I.R.L.R. 164 the complainant, following his constructive dismissal, took a course, qualifying for an educational grant of £4000 to finance it. The EAT considered that this was a proper step to take in seeking to mitigate his loss. Taking up the course did not break the chain of causation. Further, the educational grant was sufficiently remote that it would not in all the circumstances be just and equitable to deduct that sum from the compensatory award.

10–63   In reality, the longer the course, the more likely it is that this will be seen as an independent decision by the complainant which breaks the chain of causation. If the course is short and is directly related to a proposed course of action aimed at mitigating loss, the chain of causation should not be broken. Further losses should be recoverable provided the complainant acts reasonably.

In *Glen Henderson Ltd v. Nisbet* EAT 34/90 the EAT accepted that the complainant should be compensated for the period of five weeks when she was on a business enterprise course with the aim of becoming self-employed. She was also awarded a further year's loss because of low self employed earnings.

Self Employment Following Dismissal

10–64 Just as with earnings from employment subsequent to an unfair dismissal, earnings from self employment have to be set against loss. If the complainant chooses to set up a business rather than look for new employment the question of whether this is reasonable in order to properly mitigate loss well may arise (see paras 19–51 to 19–52 for further commentary on mitigation of loss).

In *Glen Henderson v. Nisbet EAT 34/90* the EAT upheld a decision to award loss for a period of a year from when the complainant set up in business on the basis of low self employed earnings.

10–65 In *Oliver v. Panayi t/a Criss Hair Dressers* COIT 834/132, the complainant set up her own business. She was awarded one year's loss of earnings on the basis that it would take a year to build up her earnings to the level she earned whilst in employment.

In *Gardiner-Hill v. Roland Berger Technics Ltd* [1982] I.R.L.R. 498, Mr Gardiner-Hill set up his own business following his dismissal. The EAT was satisfied that it was reasonable for him to seek to establish himself in an alternative business. There had been no failure to mitigate. He was 55 years old and for sixteen years had been sole managing director of a specialist business. It was "prudent of him to seek to exploit his own expertise by conducting his own business" (Brown-Wilkinson J.).

Higher Self-employed Earnings

10–66 If self employed earnings are higher than previous earnings in employment at the date of the tribunal hearing fixed to consider compensation, the tribunal should follow the same principles as those relating to earnings from employment (see paras 10–44 to 10–56).

Costs of Setting Up Business

10–67 Provided the tribunal is satisfied that the decision to set up in business is reasonable in terms of the duty to mitigate loss, then costs incurred in setting up the business may be recoverable.

In *Sparkes v. E.T. Barwick Mills Ltd* COIT 6111/68, Mr Sparkes set up in business as a commission agent. He was awarded two years' interest on capital which he borrowed to establish the business. He was also compensated for the down-payment on a car which he required for the business (having presumably had a company car).

CHAPTER 11

Unfair Dismissal: The Tribunal's Powers to Reduce or Limit the Compensatory Award

11–01 At paras 10–20 to 10–66 we considered guidance on the period of loss which the tribunal may award by virtue of the compensatory award. Now we look at the ways in which the tribunal may reduce the loss which is awarded to the complainant. The tribunal has the power to reduce or limit the compensatory award for a number of different reasons. They are all as follows:

1. Just and equitable to limit the award (s.123(1) ERA);

2. Contributory fault by the employee (s.123(6) ERA);

3. Loss not attributable to the employer (remoteness) (s.123(1) ERA) (see paras 10–15 to 10–19);

4. Failure by the complainant to mitigate his loss (s.123(4) ERA) (see Chapter 19);

5. Failure to make use of an internal appeal procedure where written notice of procedure has been given at or soon after the date of dismissal. Compensation shall be reduced by "such amount (if any) as the tribunal considers just and equitable". The reduction must not exceed the amount of two weeks' pay. In determining the amount of the reduction the tribunal must have regard to all the circumstances of the case, including the chances that an appeal would have been successful. The week's pay is not capped. The calculation date is the same as with the basic award (see para. 9–09). (s.13 Employment Rights (Dispute Resolution Act 1998 (inserting a new s.127A ERA)) This provision is in force from January 1, 1999.

   Note also that if an employer fails to allow a dismissed employee the chance to use an appeal procedure provided by him, then the award of compensation "shall include a supplementary award of such an amount (if any) as the tribunal considers just and equitable". The same considerations apply when determining the size of the supplementary award as when deciding how much to reduce the compensatory award where an employee has failed to pursue an appeal. The maximum supplementary award is two weeks' pay but the week's pay is not capped (see also para. 10–10).

In this section we focus on 1 and 2 above.

Reductions/limitations and the Statutory Maximum

11–02 It is important to note that the tribunal's task is to determine whether there should be any reduction or limit to the total loss before subsequently applying the statutory maximum (currently £12,000). For example, an unfairly dismissed employee suffers a total loss of £30,000. The tribunal decides that he contributed to his dismissal and accordingly applies a 50 per cent reduction to reflect this. The total loss will be reduced to £15,000. The tribunal then applies the statutory maximum and the complainant is awarded £12,000.

Order of Reduction/Set off

It is also important to consider what sums are to be set off against the loss suffered and the vexed question of the order in which the tribunal shall apply reductions where such a sum is set off against loss (full commentary on this issue is in Chapter 15).

JUST AND EQUITABLE REDUCTIONS

11–03 As we have seen, s.123(1) ERA provides that the compensatory award shall be an amount that the tribunal considers just and equitable in all the circumstances having regard to the loss sustained by the complainant. This gives the tribunal the discretion to limit or reduce the award. Such a broad discretion is not available when determining the basic award (see paras 9–23 to 9–25). There are two broad categories of cases where tribunals effectively reduce the compensatory award on this basis.

1. *Procedural failures*
    Where there has been some procedural failure by the employer and the tribunal concludes that had a fair procedure been followed there might have been a fair dismissal.

2. *Misconduct discovered following dismissal*
    The employer satisfies the tribunal that the employee was guilty of misconduct which, although it might have been discovered after the dismissal, could have justified dismissal.

Justice and Equity: Procedural Failures

11–04 The basic principle is that if the tribunal decides that a flawed procedure renders a dismissal unfair, it is just and equitable then to consider, in determining the level of compensation, whether, had a fair procedure been used, it would have made any difference.

Prior to the House of Lords decision in *Polkey v. A.E. Dayton Services Ltd* [1987] I.R.L.R. 503, tribunals used a "no difference rule". Under this rule, if the employer could show, on a balance of probabilities, that a fair procedure would have made no difference to the decision to dismiss, then the dismissal, despite procedural irregularities, was likely to have been fair. This, thought the House of Lords in *Polkey*, misapplied the test of fairness in what is now s.98(4) ERA 96. This provides that the determination of whether a dismissal for a potentially fair reason is fair or unfair depends on whether in the circumstances "the employer has acted reasonably or unreasonably".

11–05 Culpability is determined on the basis of what the employer did, not what he might have done. So, post *Polkey*, procedural irregularities are likely to render a dismissal unfair. Now, the extent to which a fair procedure might have affected the outcome is relevant in determining the level of compensation applying the "just and equitable" test in s.123(1) ERA.

"Utterly Useless" or "Futile" Exceptions

11–06 In very limited, extreme circumstances procedural failures may still be disregarded by the tribunal. Lord Mackay of Clashfern in *Polkey* said that "if the employer could reasonably have concluded in the light of the circumstances known to him at the time of the dismissal that consultation or warning would be utterly useless [Lord Bridge in the same case used the word 'futile'] he might well act reasonably even if he did not observe the provisions of the Code". In these limited circumstances a dismissal could still be fair despite procedural failures. This, however, is very much the exception rather than the rule.

The Percentage Chance Approach

11–07 The *Polkey* approach provides for flexibility in determining the level of compensatory award. Applying the general principle of "justice and equity" the tribunal can determine the likelihood that the dismissal would have occurred in any event (had a fair procedure been used) and, accordingly, apply a percentage reduction to the total loss resulting from the dismissal. Lord Bridge in *Polkey* approved this approach enunciated by Browne-Wilkinson J. in *Sillifant v. Powell Duffryn Timber Ltd* [1983] I.R.L.R. 91. "There is no need for an 'all or nothing' decision. If the tribunal thinks there is a doubt whether or not the employee would have been dismissed, this element can be reflected by reducing the normal amount of compensation by a percentage representing the chance that the employee would still have lost his employment."

> *Example:* Redundancy Dismissal.
> An employee has been made redundant without warning or consultation. The tribunal finds that the dismissal is unfair. If the tribunal concludes that had the employee been consulted there was a 50/50 chance that he would still have been dismissed then the loss is reduced by 50 per cent.

Percentage Reduction—Can it be up to 100 per cent?

11–08 The extent of the percentage reduction is a matter for the tribunal's discretion applying the test of what is just and equitable. In appropriate circumstances, the tribunal may conclude that it would not be just and equitable to make any compensatory award. In *Polkey*, Lord Bridge said: "If it is held that taking the appropriate steps which the employer failed to take before dismissing the employee would not have affected the outcome, this will often lead to the result that the employee, though unfairly dismissed, will recover no compensation." Two cases in the redundancy context provide examples of this.

11–09 In *Jackson v. Greenock Morton Football and Athletic Club Ltd* EAT 395/84 the assistant manager was dismissed. Unfair, said the tribunal because he had not been given the chance to consider alternative employment. The tribunal, however, awarded nil compensation because they concluded on the facts that Mr Jackson would have turned down the alternative post had he been offered it. The EAT upheld this decision.

In *Hunter Timber Group Ltd t/a Hunter Timber Hardwood v. Newcombe* EAT 294/92, Mr Newcombe was selected for redundancy having achieved a very low score in the company's redundancy assessment procedure. Because there had been no individual consultation the tribunal found that he had been unfairly dismissed. His compensatory award was reduced by 50 per cent because they concluded that had he been consulted it was likely he would still have been made redundant. The EAT held that the very low score achieved by Mr Newcombe applying an assessment procedure which was fair and objective indicated that consultation would have made no difference. Accordingly the compensatory award should have been reduced by 100 per cent.

The Tribunal's Duty

11–10 Where procedural failures have led to a finding of unfair dismissal the tribunal must conduct its own investigation and reach its own conclusion to determine whether the result would have been the same had a fair procedure been used. The tribunal should assess what, if any, percentage chance there was of the dismissal occurring even with a fair procedure, and then, if appropriate, reduce compensation accordingly. A failure to go through this process is likely to make the tribunal's decision flawed and therefore appealable (see *Fisher v. California Cake & Cookie Ltd* [1997] I.R.L.R. 212.

In *Hepworth Refractories Ltd v. Lingard* EAT 555/90, the EAT said that in redundancy cases the tribunal must consider whether it would be just and equitable to award full compensation where there had been no consultation. Not to do so would be wrong in law.

11–11 Note that the burden of proving that the employee would still have been dismissed had a fair procedure been followed falls on the employer. In *Britool Ltd v. Roberts and others* [1993] I.R.L.R. 481, the EAT described the steps as follows:

> First the employee must show what loss he has suffered due to the dismissal. Then the evidential burden shifts to the employer to show that the dismissal could, or would be likely to, have occurred in any event. All the employee has to do is put forward an arguable case that but for the lack of consultation or warning he would have kept his job. The employer should adduce evidence at the tribunal to demonstrate that a fair procedure would equally have led to the employee's dismissal. If this issue has not been dealt with at the stage of the tribunal considering liability or if there has been no finding on the issue then the employer should call such evidence at the remedy hearing.

In this case the employer had not adduced evidence to show that a fair procedure would have led to the employee's dismissal and so no *Polkey* deduction was made.

11–12 There may not be the same duty on the tribunal, on its own motion, to consider and evaluate the possibility of a reduction in the compensatory award where the unfair dismissal results from the employer positively taking some step which he ought not to have done (rather than simply failing to carry out a procedural requirement such as consulting with the employee). In *Boulton & Paul Ltd v. Arnold* [1994] I.R.L.R. 532 EAT, the employer had taken into account, in selecting Mrs Arnold for redundancy, genuine sickness absences which their agreed procedure did not permit. In such circumstances it is up to the employer to produce positive evidence that a fair application of the criteria would have led to the same result. Without such evidence the tribunal was right not to reduce the compensatory award.

Compensation for the period of consultation

11–13 Where an employee has been made redundant without consultation, the tribunal may conclude that, although this makes the dismissal unfair, they are satisfied that dismissal would have occurred following a proper consultation process. In such circumstances the tribunal might properly award compensation only for the period during which consultation should have taken place. Commonly this is assessed as a period of four weeks.

In *Mining Supplies (Longwall) Ltd v. Baker* [1988] I.R.L.R. 417, the tribunal found that the employee would still have been dismissed even if there had been individual consultation, but that the lack of consultation made the dismissal unfair. The EAT took the view that in such circumstances the *Polkey* decision did not require them to award nil compensation. The EAT decided that consultation would have taken two weeks and awarded compensation on that basis.

Loss for consultation period followed by percentage reduction in future loss

11–14   Equally, the tribunal can award compensation for the period during which consultation should have taken place and thereafter award further loss subject to a percentage reduction if they conclude that there was a chance that the employee could have been fairly dismissed at that point.

Example:
The employee is dismissed without consultation. His net weekly earnings are £100 and he is unemployed for six months before getting another job on the same wage. The tribunal decides that he was unfairly dismissed and that proper consultation would have taken four weeks. They also decide that there was a 25 per cent chance that, after consultation, he could have been fairly dismissed on grounds of redundancy.

His compensatory award for lost earnings will be calculated as follows:

	£	£
4 weeks at £100 per week (for consultation period)		400
22 weeks at £100 per week further period of loss	2,200	
Reduce by 25% to reflect chance that he could have been fairly dismissed	550	1,650
Total		£2,050

11–15   This approach was followed in the case of *Walker & ors v. (1) Dysch Rosen Shoes Ltd (2) Secretary of State for Employment* EAT 341 & 342/90. The EAT held that there should be full compensation for the period during which consultation should have taken place. To assess compensation beyond this point the tribunal had to assess the likelihood of dismissal occurring even if proper consultation had taken place and, accordingly, apply a percentage reduction to further loss.

In what circumstances will the tribunal apply the percentage chance approach where there are procedural or other errors by the employer?

11–16   There has been some uncertainty as to whether a distinction can be drawn between errors of procedure and errors of substance. In *Steel Stockholders (Birmingham) Ltd v. Kirkwood* [1993] I.R.L.R. 515, the EAT drew this distinction stating that if the error by the employer was one of substance rather than being merely procedural there should be no percentage reduction in the compensatory award.

This approach was criticised by Gibson, L.J. in the Court of Appeal case of *O'Dea v. ISC Chemicals Ltd (t/a Rhone -Poulenc Chemicals)* [1995] I.R.L.R. 599: "I do not regard it as helpful to characterise the defect as procedural or substantive." In that case, Mr O'Dea was made redundant when the packaging department where he worked was closed down. He had been a senior shop steward and had spent 50 per cent of his time on union activities. He applied for five vacant posts within the company but was turned down for all of them. The tribunal found that, although he had been told he would have to give up his union activities in any new post, the employers had not made that clear to those interviewing him. On this basis the tribunal found he had been unfairly dismissed. However compensation was reduced, using the percentage chance approach, on the basis that even if the procedural defect had not occurred, he only stood a good chance of obtaining one of the five vacancies for which he had applied. The Court of Appeal upheld the 80 per cent reduction in compensation.

11–17 There must be some doubt as to the logic of this percentage reduction. If he stood a good chance of obtaining just one of the jobs he applied for it surely makes no difference that he, in fact, applied for four others where he had no chance. A reduction in the compensatory award of 80 per cent appears to be incompatible with a finding that, but for the defect on the employer's part, he stood a good chance of getting one of the jobs he applied for. The percentage reduction should be based on an assessment of the chance of getting any alternative job, not on the basis of finding that he had a good chance in one in five of the jobs he applied for. If there was, say, an 80 per cent chance of him getting one of these five jobs, but for the failure by the employer to properly inform those interviewing him of the full facts, then presumably compensation should only be reduced by 20 per cent.

11–18 It is clear, therefore, that the tribunal can consider errors by the employer in such matters as the criteria for selection, the pool of employees from which to select, and the extent to which the employer examined the possibilities of alternative employment in determining whether there should be a percentage reduction to the compensatory award based on "justice and equity".

For example, X is made redundant. He was one of two people doing the same job. No proper selection criteria was used. If the tribunal concludes that *had* a fair basis for selection been used there was a 50 per cent chance that X would still have been made redundant, he would receive 50 per cent of his loss as the compensatory award (however, note *Chloride Ltd v. (1) Cain (2) Hewitt* EAT 564/94 at para. 11–19).

The question of whether to limit compensation in this way is a matter for the discretion for the tribunal. The more the defect goes to the root of the dismissal the less likely it is that the tribunal will decide that it is just and equitable to reduce the award. In other words, if the failure by the employer is so serious that it makes it impossible for the tribunal to conclude that a proper procedure may have led to the same result then no reduction should be made.

11–19 An example of this limitation to the application of a *Polkey* principle was the case of *Chloride Ltd v. (1) Cain (2) Hewitt* EAT 564/94. There had been no consultation, no objective criteria for selection and no exploration of alternative employment. The EAT decided that the tribunal was right to conclude that as unfair criteria had been used to select the employees for redundancy it was not right on the basis of justice and equity to reduce the compensatory award. Also, the case of *Eclipse Blinds Ltd v. Bill* EAT 818/92 EAT is a reminder that all the circumstances need to be taken into account, not just one particular isolated factor such as consultation.

Percentage Chance and Alternative Employment

11–20   It is often the case that a complainant will argue that he should have been offered some alternative post which was available at the time of a redundancy dismissal even though it was on a lower salary. If the tribunal concludes that the dismissal was unfair, they then consider whether the employee should have been offered such alternative work. They might conclude that had the employer acted fairly he should have offered the post to the redundant employee, in which case the loss suffered will be the wages he would have earned in that alternative employment. Again, the tribunal should use the percentage chance approach in determining the likelihood of the employee being offered and accepting the alternative post. If the tribunal decides that there was, for example, a 75 per cent chance that he would have been chosen for that alternative post then the compensation would be based on 75 per cent of the wages in that alternative post.

> *Example*
> X is dismissed for redundancy. The dismissal is unfair because he should have been considered for alternative employment. He earned £400 net per week.
>
> A job was available within the Company at the date of dismissal at £300 net per week. There are four applicants for the job. The tribunal concludes that X would have had a 25 per cent chance of being appointed. His compensation is calculated by multiplying £300 by 25 per cent = £75.00 per week.

11–21   The question of how tribunals should deal with the possibility of alternative employment and the application of the percentage chance approach in such circumstances has been considered by the EAT.

In *Red Bank Manufacturing Co. Ltd. v. Meadows* [1992] I.R.L.R. 209 the EAT said that in circumstances where the employer had failed follow a fair procedure in a redundancy situation the tribunal should ask a two stage question when calculating compensation.

"If a proper procedure had been followed, and if consultation had taken place, would it have resulted in an offer of employment?". If it might have done then the tribunal has to ask what that employment would have been and what wage would have been paid in respect of it. The tribunal should then consider making a percentage reduction in the award "to reflect the chances that the outcome might have been the same even if consultation had taken place". (Tucker J.)

Procedural failures in misconduct and capability dismissals

11–22   As will be clear from the discussion above, the percentage chance approach, applying the just and equitable requirement, is most commonly seen in redundancy dismissals where there has been some failure of procedure by the employer. The principle can, however, equally apply to other sorts of dismissal.

Misconduct Dismissals

11–23   In *Fisher v. California Cake and Cookie Ltd* [1997] I.R.L.R. 212, Mr Fisher was dismissed because of suspected theft of money from his employer. Statements made by other employees in the course of the employer's investigation were not disclosed to him and he was not made aware of the detailed contents. Because of this the tribunal held that he had been unfairly dismissed but then concluded on the evidence that disclosure of the statements would have made no difference to the outcome. Accordingly, on the basis of justice and equity they awarded no compensation. The EAT agreed, and again confirmed that where evidence at least supports a view that dismissal would have occurred in any event, the tribunal should assess as a matter of probability in percentage terms the chance that dismissal would actually have occurred had a fair procedure been followed. The EAT also reiterated the point that in considering the hypothetical question as to whether a fair procedure would have made any difference, the tribunal must conduct its own investigation and reach its own conclusion (see also paras 11–10 to 11–12).

11–24   In *Cormack v. Saltire Vehicles Ltd* EAT 209/90 the EAT upheld a tribunal's decision to award no compensation to Mr Cormack. He was employed as a mechanic. He failed to carry out an MOT test adequately and another vehicle was left in a dangerous condition. He was denied his contractual right to an appeal against dismissal, but the EAT was satisfied that an appeal would have made no difference. In such circumstances it would not be just and equitable to make a compensatory award.

Just as with redundancy dismissals, there may be a percentage reduction of less than 100 per cent to reflect the possibility that a fair procedure would have made a difference. In *Church of Scotland Board of Social Responsibility v. Forsyth* EAT 699/87, Mr Forsyth was dismissed for disobedience. The disciplinary procedure was flawed as he had no representation and was not given certain information. The EAT held that the tribunal should have considered the chances of Mr Forsyth being dismissed even if a fair procedure had been used. His compensatory award was reduced by 35 per cent to reflect this chance and by a further 15 per cent because of contributory fault (see also paras 11–38 to 11–87 for commentary on reductions for contributory fault).

Ill-Health Dismissals

11–25   In order to fairly dismiss an employee on grounds of ill health it is generally necessary to fully investigate the medical facts, warn the employee of the probability of dismissal and consult the employee, particularly with regard to the implications of a medical report. Further, the possibilities of alternative employment should also be considered. A failure to follow any of these procedural requirements is likely to result in a finding of unfair dismissal but, again, the tribunal, in applying the test in s.123(1) ERA requiring the compensatory award to be just and equitable, may consider whether, had proper procedural steps been taken, the result would have been just the same.

In *Slaughter v. C.Brewer & Sons* [1990] I.C.R. 730 Wood J said, "A dismissal may be unfair on procedural grounds yet it may be quite apparent from the medical evidence that an applicant was, at the date of dismissal, quite incapable of carrying out her or his function." This can lead to a reduction under s.123(1) ERA to reflect the chance that had a fair procedure been followed the dismissal might still have occurred.

Compensation for period it would have taken to obtain medical report

11–26   Wood J. in *Slaughter* (see above) gave another example of where there has been insufficient medical evidence and therefore unfairness "but the subsequent investigation would have shown that the dismissal was inevitable. In such a case a possible view might be that such an investigation would have taken some days or weeks and that compensation should cover that period."

In *Rao v. Civil Aviation Authority* [1994] I.R.L.R. 240, Mr Rao, an air traffic controller, was dismissed from his job for poor attendance. He pursued an internal appeal at which the managing director agreed to postpone a decision pending receipt of a medical report. The managing director then discovered that Mr Rao had issued tribunal proceedings and immediately dismissed the appeal. The Court of Appeal upheld the approach taken by the tribunal in concluding that, but for the unfair dismissal because of the flawed procedure, Mr Rao would have been employed up until receipt of the medical report and in assessing his chances of remaining in employment beyond that date applying an 80 per cent reduction to his continuing loss. (Note that in this case there was also a reduction for contributory fault (see para. 11–37).

Alternative Employment

11–27   If a tribunal decides that an employee unfairly dismissed for ill health could have been offered alternative employment then they can award compensation based on the earnings the employee would have received in that alternative post. If the chances of alternative employment are not certain then the tribunal can use the percentage chance approach to assess the likelihood of the employee being able or willing to do that alternative job.

> *Example:*
> X is dismissed on grounds of ill health. The dismissal is unfair because no consideration was given to the possibility of alternative employment which might be less onerous and X could have done given his medical condition. They also decide that there was a 50 per cent chance that, had a fair procedure been used, X would have been offered and accepted such alternative employment.

The compensatory award would be calculated on the basis of 50 per cent of the earnings X would have received in that other job.

Capability: Poor performance dismissals

11–28   Lack of capability on the basis of poor performance is a potentially fair reason to terminate employment. But it will generally be unfair under s.98(4) ERA if the employer has not consulted with the employee and given him or her a chance to improve. If the dismissal is unfair on this basis, the tribunal may be entitled to limit the compensatory award on the basis of justice and equity if they conclude that a fair procedure may not have made any difference.

In *Winterhalter Gastonom Ltd v. Webb* [1973] I.R.L.R. 120, Mr Webb, a director, was dismissed following disappointing sales resulting in the company making a loss. Because he had received no warning, his dismissal was unfair. The EAT said that the correct approach in such circumstances was for the tribunal to decide what would have been a fair period for the employee to improve his performance following a warning and then evaluate the chance that he would have been able to improve his sales performance to a satisfactory level within that period and so retain his position as sales director. The EAT took the view that three months would be a fair period in which to improve. He should have been awarded compensation for that period. Then the tribunal should have assessed the chance that he would have been able to continue in his employment following the warning period. The EAT, in this pre-*Polkey* case, awarded some £418 for the lost chance of continued employment, judging that the chances of him improving sufficiently to keep his job were low. Post-*Polkey*, the proper approach would be to determine the percentage chance of continued employment and reduce future loss accordingly.

11–29   In *Mansfield Hosiery Mills Ltd v. Bromley* [1977] I.R.L.R. 301, Mr Bromley, a boiler service fitter, was dismissed following a number of complaints about poor work performance. The dismissal was unfair because he had not been warned about his shortcomings or been given the opportunity to improve. They also found, however, that it was unlikely that Mr Bromley would have been able to make any improvement in his performance and that if his employment had been reviewed two months later he would then have been dismissed fairly. Accordingly he was awarded two months loss of earnings. The EAT upheld this approach.

Justice and Equity: Misconduct discovered following dismissal

11–30   The other situation in which a tribunal can limit or "cancel out" the compensatory award on the basis of justice and equity under s.123(1) ERA is where misconduct, which is only discovered after dismissal, would, if it had been known about at the date of the dismissal, have justified a fair termination of employment.

The case of *W. Devis & Sons Ltd v. Atkins* [1977] I.R.L.R. 314 HL is an example of this. Mr Atkins had been manager of an abattoir. He was dismissed due to dissatisfaction with his method of making purchases. Following the dismissal, information came to light that he had been dishonestly dealing in live animals. Although he was found to have been unfairly dismissed, the House of Lords upheld the tribunal's decision to make a nil compensation award. The evidence indicated that had the employer known about the dishonest conduct they could have fairly dismissed him. It was not just and equitable for him to receive a compensatory award.

Where the tribunal concludes that a fair dismissal might have resulted had misconduct been discovered earlier, then they should assess the percentage chance of that occurring and reduce compensation accordingly.

Conduct following dismissal

11–31   Culpable conduct following dismissal will not, however, provide a basis for reducing the compensatory award.

In *Saros & anor v. Davison & anor* [1994] I.R.L.R. 264, Mr and Mrs Davison were dismissed from their employment as domestic servants. They then sold information about their employment to the Sun newspaper. The EAT held that their conduct following dismissal (which the tribunal had found amounted to a breach of the implied term of confidentiality) was not relevant to the assessment of compensation under what is now s.123(1) ERA. The assessment of what sum would be just and equitable to award the complainant can take into account conduct during employment, but not after.

In *Abbey Motors (Hemel Hempstead) Ltd v. Carta* EAT 403/95, the complainant misled the tribunal as to the extent of loss he had suffered. The EAT upheld the tribunal's decision that they could not reduce the compensatory award simply because of such conduct, although they could properly decide what loss had been suffered.

Reneging on an agreement to settle claims

11–32   Section 203 ERA makes void any agreement which precludes a person from bringing proceedings under the Act to a tribunal. The exceptions are where the employer and employee enter a compromise agreement or concludes an agreement through ACAS (see para. 6–16). So any other agreement between employer and employee, even if stated to be in full and final settlement of all claims, cannot stop an employee issuing or continuing proceedings. But it may have an effect on the employee's entitlement to compensation if the tribunal concludes that it would not be just and equitable (under s.123(1) ERA) to award further compensation.

11–33 In *Courage Take Home Trade Ltd v. Keys* [1986] I.C.R. 874, the tribunal found that Mr Keys' dismissal was unfair. The question of remedy was adjourned. Prior to the adjourned hearing the employee accepted £9,500 as a full and final settlement of his claim. But he then pressed on to the remedy hearing. Although the agreement was subsequently found by the tribunal to be void, they decided that it would not be just and equitable to award any compensation even though Mr Keys' loss exceeded the sum already paid. The EAT agreed. Popplewell J. said: "it would be unjust and inequitable in all the circumstances if this employee were allowed to take advantage of the employers." Popplewell J. made clear that if an employer had "unduly persuaded an employee to accept a settlement, or brought pressure on him" the tribunal may conclude that "the employer could scarcely be heard to say that it was unjust or inequitable if he were called on to pay a further sum".

Other potentially fair reasons to dismiss

11–34 We have seen that misconduct discovered after dismissal which could have justified a fair dismissal may be taken into account on a just and equitable basis to limit or extinguish the compensatory award. What about the situation where the employer knew of another potentially fair reason to dismiss at the time of actual dismissal but chose not to proceed on that basis?

For example, X is dismissed on grounds of ill health but without proper investigation of the medical facts. At the time of dismissal there was ample evidence to dismiss simply because of his attendance record, which was so bad that the employer could not be expected to tolerate it. The dismissal is held to be unfair because, relying on incapability, the employer had not actually investigated the medical facts or consulted the employee to establish whether such a basis was justified.

11–35 In *Trico-Folberth Ltd v. Devonshire* [1989] I.R.L.R. 396, which involved similar facts to those in the above example, the Court of Appeal said that the fact that there was a potentially fair basis for dismissal known to the employer at the time of the dismissal will not be taken into account as a basis for reducing the compensatory award on just and equitable grounds if, in fact, they decided not to dismiss on that basis (believing wrongly at that time that it would not be a fair basis to dismiss). "It cannot be just and equitable for an employee to be deprived of the compensation to which she would otherwise be entitled if the employer himself would not have relied on that other ground." (Nourse L.J.).

Now consider another example. At the time of dismissal the employer believes that there are alternative reasons to dismiss the employee and makes clear that he could dismiss on either ground. He chooses one of these grounds to justify dismissal. If the tribunal subsequently finds that the dismissal was unfair, it seems, on the basis of the reasoning in *Trico Folberth*, that the employer could seek to argue that the alternative basis for dismissal would have been a fair basis and that, accordingly, compensation should be reduced or extinguished on "just and equitable" grounds.

Relationship between "just and equitable" reductions and reductions for contributory fault

11–36 The compensatory award can then be reduced both on the basis that it would be just and equitable to do so (under s.123(1) ERA, (see paras 11–03 to 11–35) and also on the basis that the employee has contributed to his dismissal (contributory fault under s.123(6) ERA, (see 11–38 to 11–87). If there is a basis for reducing the compensatory award on both these grounds then the tribunal can make two reductions.

Example
An employee is dismissed for misconduct. The employer fails to follow a fair procedure by not giving the employee the right to an appeal against dismissal. The tribunal may conclude that had an appeal been provided there was a 50 per cent chance that he would still have been dismissed. The tribunal also concludes that it would be just and equitable to reduce the compensatory award by 30 per cent because the employee contributed to his dismissal by his conduct. This would mean a total reduction of 80 per cent in the compensatory award.

11–37 The case of *Rao v. Civil Aviation Authority* [1994] I.R.L.R. 240 provides guidance on the relationship between these two types of reductions and how the tribunal should go about its task of calculating the compensatory award in such circumstances.
The following points emerge:

1. The tribunal can properly apply both reductions;

2. The tribunal should first decide what, if any, reduction to make on the "just and equitable" basis (s.123(1) ERA), for example because there has been a failure of procedure and the tribunal concludes that, had a proper procedure been used, the result might have been the same (see paras 11–03 to 11–35);

3. The tribunal should then decide whether to make a further reduction on the basis of contributory fault (s.123(6) ERA), but at this stage the tribunal should take into account the fact that a reduction has already been made. s.123(6) ERA requires the tribunal to reduce the compensatory award where there is contributory fault "by such proportion as it considers just and equitable having regard to that finding". In making this judgement of what further "just and equitable" reduction should be made for contributory fault the tribunal might conclude that the fact that there has already been a reduction may "have a very significant bearing on what further reduction may fall to be made", (Sir Thomas Bingham in *Rao v. Civil Aviation Authority*). This is one reason why a reduction to the compensatory award for contributory fault may be different from the reduction to the basic award because of fault on the part of the employee (see paras 9–27 to 9–31).

CONTRIBUTORY FAULT BY THE EMPLOYEE

Statutory Provision

11–38 Section 123(6) ERA provides as follows "Where the tribunal finds that the dismissal was to any extent caused or contributed to by any action of the complainant, it shall reduce the amount of the compensatory award by such proportion as it considers just and equitable having regard to that finding."
Note that the basic award and the special award can also be reduced because of contributory fault by virtue of s.122(2) ERA and s.125(4) respectively (see 8–56 to 8–59 and 9–23 to 9–35). However, those provisions are wider than s.123(6) because under them the tribunal can take into account any conduct of the complainant before

the dismissal (or, if on notice, before notice of dismissal was given), not just conduct which caused or contributed to the dismissal. Nonetheless, given that s.122(2) and s.125(4) clearly cover, within their scope, circumstances where the employee has caused or contributed to his dismissal, the commentary in this section on contributory fault is also relevant to the basic award and special award.

How Will the Tribunal Consider Contributory Fault?

11–39   Two approaches are possible. The tribunal may hear evidence and allow argument on the issue of contributory fault during the main hearing on liability. Alternatively, it may have a split hearing whereby all evidence and argument on contributory fault is heard only if there is a finding of unfair dismissal, in which case it would be considered at the same time as all other compensation issues at the remedy stage. The tribunal must state clearly which approach it intends to take.

The tribunal should only make a reduction if there is sufficient evidence of fault on the part of the employee which caused or contributed to the dismissal. In *Tele-Trading Ltd v. Jenkins* [1990] I.R.L.R. 430, the Court of Appeal held that the tribunal was right not to reduce the compensatory award because at the time of dismissal the employer did not have reasonable grounds for their belief in the employee's guilt (see also para. 11–30 for commentary on the power to reduce compensation on "just and equitable" grounds where misconduct is only discovered after the dismissal).

Broad Common Sense View

11–40   The case of *Morrison v. Amalgamated Transport & General Workers Union* [1989] I.R.L.R. 361 confirmed the following principles:

1.   The tribunal should adopt a broad, common-sense view of the situation;

2.   That broad approach should not necessarily be confined to a particular moment, even the terminal moment of employment (Note that in *Dundon v. GPT Ltd* [1995] I.R.L.R. 403 conduct over a long period of time had contributed to Dundon's selection for redundancy. This conduct led to a reduction in compensation).

For the avoidance of doubt, if a tribunal finds that the employee was, for example, 50 per cent to blame, then compensation is reduced by 50 per cent.

THE PRINCIPLES

11–41   The Court of Appeal in *Nelson v. BBC (No.2)* [1979] I.R.L.R. 346 gave guidance on the findings a tribunal must make for there to be a reduction for contributory fault.

1.   Culpable or blameworthy conduct by the employee.

2.   That conduct must have caused or contributed to the dismissal.

3.   It is just and equitable to reduce the assessment of loss to a specified extent.

Culpable or blameworthy conduct

11–42 The conduct must be culpable or blameworthy to some extent. "If a man is blameless it can be neither just nor equitable to reduce his award for an unfair dismissal" Sir Hugh Griffiths in *Morrish v. Henlys (Folkestone) Ltd* [1973] I.R.L.R. 61 NIRC.

In *Nelson v. BBC (No.2)* [1979] I.R.L.R. 346, Brandon LJ considered the scope of culpability or blameworthiness. The following points emerge:

1. The conduct need not amount to a breach of contract or a tort but it includes such conduct;

2. It includes conduct which is "perverse or foolish";

3. It may simply be unreasonable conduct in all the circumstances, (but not all unreasonable conduct is culpable or blameworthy—it depends on the degree of unreasonableness).

11–43 Misconduct in its various guises will generally be blameworthy to some extent. The following are some specific examples of blameworthy conduct:

1. Returning to work drunk after Christmas lunch. Subsequent dismissal was procedurally unfair but employee contributed to his dismissal.

   Reduction: 75 per cent. *Ardyne Scaffolding Ltd v. Rennie* EAT 688/93.

2. HGV driver dismissed for capability. He failed driving assessment and refused offer of another independent assessment. Although unfair dismissal, compensation reduced by 100 per cent primarily because of refusal of independent assessment. Overturned on appeal: EAT held that tribunal had not given detailed findings of why such a large reduction was justified. It would be only in extremely rare cases that a 100 per cent contribution would be found. *White v. Summerfield (Contract Hire) Ltd* EAT 494/93, IDS Brief 521, July 1994.

3. Salmon, a union representative, was dismissed for organising a meeting in work time which caused substantial disruption. Dismissal was unfair because of insufficient investigation and no reasonable grounds for concluding that he was the main instigator of the meeting at that time. Tribunal decided he was responsible along with two other officials. Held that he had contributed to his dismissal and reduced compensation by 60 per cent. Upheld by the EAT. Irrelevant that two other union representatives had been treated differently. *Salmon v. Ribble Motor Services Ltd* EAT 23.11.92 (51/91), IDS Brief 496, July 1993.

11–44

4. Slack was dismissed after a fight at work with another employee. Although unfair dismissal, each employee was 50 per cent to blame and therefore Slack's compensation reduced by 50 per cent. Irrelevant what happened to other employee in determining reduction for contributory fault. *Parker Foundry Ltd v. Slack* [1992] I.R.L.R. 11.

5. White and another employee dismissed after being filmed taking sweets from stockroom. Unfair dismissal finding because of procedural failures by employers. EAT upheld tribunal's decision to reduce basic award by 50 per

cent because of culpable, blameworthy conduct and compensatory award by 100 per cent because of contributory fault (under what is now s.123(6) ERA). The basic and compensatory awards could be reduced by different amounts (see also para. 9–28). It was reasonable for the tribunal only to reduce the basic award by 50 per cent because the employees had been denied the important right to a fair procedure. *Charles Robertson (Developments) Ltd. v. White & anor* [1995] I.C.R. 349 EAT.

6.   Ms Morrison resigned from her employment with a union and claimed constructive dismissal because she had been suspended without pay for five weeks in breach of contract. Held: Unfair dismissal but compensation reduced by 40 per cent because of contributory conduct in that she had provoked and precipitated the unlawful reaction by her employer (she had acted in disregard of instructions and flouted the authority of the finance director). Upheld by EAT. *Morrison v. Amalgamated Transport and General Workers Union* [1989] I.R.L.R. 361.

11–45

7.   Goods were stolen by a van driver. Mr Warrilow, a fork lift truck driver, was dismissed after it was alleged he was involved. The dismissal was unfair but the tribunal found that he had not been alert or taken steps to safeguard the goods. He was, therefore, blameworthy and had his compensation reduced by 80 per cent. Upheld by EAT. *Warrilow v. Robert Walker Ltd* [1984] I.R.L.R. 304.

8.   Barnes was dismissed from a casino after being charged with growing and possessing cannabis. At the tribunal hearing prior to the hearing in the Crown Court, found unfairly dismissed because of no proper investigation. Awarded full compensation. Subsequently convicted in Crown Court. EAT held that tribunal should have allowed a review. 100 per cent contribution to dismissal by Barnes, *Ladup Ltd v. Barnes* [1982] I.R.L.R. 7.

9.   Smith dismissed for absence from work and failing to tell employer about the absence or reasons for it. Unfair dismissal for procedural failure but Smith had caused his dismissal. 100 per cent reduction upheld by EAT. *Smith v. Lodge Bros. (Funerals) Ltd* EAT IDS 411, 19.10.89.

11–46

10.   Nairne was employed by the Highlands and Islands Fire Brigade for 22 years. It was necessary that he could drive. He was convicted of drink driving and disqualified for 12 months. He kept his job but, after regaining his licence, he was banned again for three years. His subsequent dismissal was held to be unfair because of procedural failures by the employer. The EAT increased the contributory fault reduction from 25 per cent to 75 per cent. Only the procedural flaws made it an unfair dismissal. The fact that he might have been able to persuade his employer to keep him on justified reduction being 75 per cent rather than 100 per cent (which might otherwise have been justified). *Nairne v. Highlands & Islands Fire Brigade* [1989] I.R.L.R. 366.

11.   Coalter was a receptionist at a funeral directors. Two bodies got mixed up and placed in the wrong coffins. It was her job to check. She did not and was dismissed. Although unfairly dismissed, her negligence resulted in a reduction for contributory fault. The EAT changed the reduction from 50

per cent to 25 per cent because it was her first offence and it was unintentional. She had had no detailed written instructions as to what she had to do and the nametags had been written in long hand and looked similar. *Coalter v. Walter Craven Ltd* [1980] I.R.L.R. 262 EAT.

11–47

12. A failure to explain or justify behaviour at a disciplinary meeting could justify a reduction. In *Kwik Save Stores Ltd v. Clerkin* EAT 295/96 the tribunal accepted Clerkin's version of events but he had not provided this explanation at the disciplinary meeting. He contributed to his dismissal and had his compensation reduced by 40 per cent. Similarly, a failure to attend a disciplinary meeting was held to be blameworthy conduct in *London Dungeon Ltd v. Belacel & anor* EAT 52/89.

13. An employee may be guilty of blameworthy conduct on the basis of the acts of his agent or representative. In *Allen v. Hammett*, EAT 245/81, Mr Allen should have returned money to an insurance company paid in respect of sick leave because he had already received sick pay from his employer. On the advice of a solicitor he refused to repay the money. Ultimately, he was dismissed. The tribunal held that his failure to repay the money was a factor contributing to his dismissal and reduced compensation by 60 per cent. The tribunal should adopt "a broad common sense view" in assessing whether there was blameworthy conduct. Just as in other contexts, a man should be "held responsible for the acts of his agents." Mr Allen's remedy, if any, was to seek compensation from his solicitor.

11–48

14. A refusal by an employee to provide names of employees who he knew to be guilty of misconduct was found to be blameworthy conduct in *Simpson v. British Steel Corporation*, EAT 594/83.

15. Daykin was guilty of an aggressive response to final warning given by employer. This was blameworthy conduct. *Daykin v. IHW Engineering Ltd* COIT 1440/117.

16. Mr Wall walked out of a meeting arranged to discuss his terms and conditions of employment. Blameworthy conduct said the EAT. *Wall v. Brookside Metal Co. Ltd* EAT 579/89.

Blameworthy Conduct: Ill Health Dismissals

11–49 It will be rare that a tribunal will find that there has been contributory fault where the dismissal is because of ill health. However, if an employee has blatantly and persistently refused to obtain appropriate medical reports or attend for medical examination a reduction could be justified (see *Slaughter v. C Brewer & Sons Ltd* [1990] I.R.L.R. 426, see also paras 11–25 to 11–26 for commentary on just and equitable reductions under s.123(1) ERA in ill health cases).

Blameworthy Conduct: Contributory Fault and Redundancy Dismissals

11–50 Just as with ill health dismissals, reductions for contributory fault where the dismissal is on grounds of redundancy will be rare, but there are circumstances where such a reduction might be just and equitable. Take, for example, a redundancy situation in which the employer used objective criteria for selection, including disciplinary records. If someone is, accordingly, selected for redundancy because, or partly because of, an appalling disciplinary record (for example persistent unjustified absences from work which might in itself be part of a fair basis for selection) then it could be said that he has contributed to his dismissal. If the dismissal is unfair because, for example, the employer fails to consult, then the employee could face a reduction for contributory fault.

11–51   In *Dundon v. GPT Ltd* [1995] I.R.L.R. 403, Mr Dundon, a union representative, was selected for redundancy on grounds of union activities. However, the EAT was satisfied that his conduct was blameworthy. He had often been late for work. He had failed to honour his side of agreements with regard to the split between union activities and working time. He had not even tried to comply with his employer's wishes. All these maters were "causative of his dismissal" (Smith J.).

Another possible situation where a reduction for contributory fault might apply in a redundancy situation is where the employee has refused to attend meetings arranged for the purposes of consultation about the redundancy. According to the guidance in *Nelson v. BBC (No.2)* [1979] I.R.L.R. 346 CA, (see para. 11–42) this behaviour may be regarded as "perverse or foolish" or "bloody-minded".

Blameworthy Conduct: Capability Dismissals

11–52   Where an employee is dismissed for failing to measure up to the requirements of the job despite his best efforts, there should be no reduction for contributory fault. There is no "blameworthy" conduct in the sense that the employee's inadequate performance is beyond his control. He is doing his best.

Kilner Brown J. in the case of *Kraft Foods Ltd v. Fox* [1977] I.R.L.R. 431 drew a distinction between such circumstances and those where the employee has some control over events. "In the case of a man who falls short, he may not try. He may not be doing his best. That is something over which he has control" and could lead to a reduction for contributory fault.

11–53   This distinction was somewhat blurred in the case of *Moncur v. International Paint Co. Ltd* [1978] I.R.L.R. 223, in which Phillips J. said that "in practice it is extremely difficult to divide acts, or failures to act, into those which are the result of a failure within the power of the applicant to control and those which are not." Mr Moncur was a manager. He was not always successful, or tactful, in getting on with his superiors. He was also judged to be deficient in powers of day-to-day management and administrative control. Phillips J. made the point that some of these complaints might not have been outside Mr Moncur's power to control.

11–54   This case makes the reasonable point that the distinction between acts within the control of an employee and those outside is often difficult to discern. In the grey area between poor performance and misconduct there are plenty of situations where an employee's failings in his job could, for example, be due to laziness or carelessness or, alternatively, entirely beyond his control. Nonetheless, the Court of Appeal case of *Nelson v. BBC (No.2)* [1979] I.R.L.R. 346 requires blameworthy conduct and so it must be for the tribunal to make a finding of fact, on the evidence available, as to whether the employee was in any way to blame.

This judgment had to be made in the case of *Sutton & Gates (Luton) Ltd v. Boxall* [1978] I.R.L.R. 486: "Where the incapability so-called was due to the person's own fault, in the sense that he was lazy, negligent or idle or did not try to improve, the degree of contribution may well be very high indeed" (Kilner Brown J.).

Blameworthy Conduct: Industrial pressure from other employees to dismiss

11–55 If the employee is culpable or blameworthy to some extent in causing pressure from other employees to dismiss him then this can properly be taken into account.

In *Colwyn Borough Council v. Dutton* [1980] I.R.L.R. 420, Mr Dutton was convicted of careless driving. Other employees subsequently refused to go out with him. He was offered, but refused, other work and was dismissed. The EAT held that his dangerous driving contributed to or caused the threat from employees, which in turn led to the dismissal. This could justify a reduction in compensation for contributory fault.

Blameworthy Conduct: Industrial Action

11–56 If an employee is dismissed for participating in industrial action he cannot bring a claim for unfair dismissal unless another employee has not been dismissed or was re-engaged within three months (s.238 TULR(C)A). If an employee has, however, been selectively dismissed or refused re-engagement then he can pursue a claim. In such circumstances, it is clearly established that compensation cannot be reduced for contributory fault merely for taking part in that action. "It has always been accepted that the general intention of Parliament ... is to prevent ... tribunals from going into the merits or demerits of collective action" Browne-Wilkinson J. in *Courtaulds Northern Spinning Ltd. v. Moosa* [1984] I.R.L.R. 43 EAT).

11–57 However, it now appears as if a distinction can be drawn where there is some conduct on the part of the employee above and beyond merely taking part in the action. This is as a result of the House of Lords decision in *Crosville Wales Ltd v. Tracey & others (No. 2)* [1997]I.R.L.R. 691. Browne-Wilkinson J. in the *Courtaulds* case had already pointed to a possible scenario where an employee dismissed whilst on strike might have his compensation reduced for contributory fault. If whilst on strike an employee was, in fact, dismissed for other reasons then the conduct which caused the dismissal may merit a reduction for contributory fault.

11–58 In *Crosville Wales Ltd. v. Tracey and Others* the House of Lords (following the decision of the Court of Appeal) goes further. There can be a reduction for contributory fault where the dismissal was for the taking part in the industrial action where there has also been "individual blameworthy conduct additional to or separate from the mere act of participation in industrial action".

In the Court of Appeal hearing of the *Crosville* case [1996] I.R.L.R. 91, Waite L.J. highlighted the possibility of the spotlight falling particularly on the leaders of a strike or other industrial action. "Their particular activities as leaders would represent conduct which could properly be made the subject of separate investigation by the tribunal, independently of any general action which it had inspired ... If they were judged to have been over hasty and inflammatory, there would seem to be no logical reason why the tribunal should not be free to say what contribution they are to be found to have made to their own dismissal and what abatement in their compensation is called for in justice and equity."

11–59 One problem with this analysis is that, in practice, if the employer has dismissed all employees on strike then it is likely that the cause of the dismissals is the strike—not the "additional" behaviour of certain individuals. Is it likely that certain "additional" behaviour by a number of individuals caused or contributed to their dismissals, when other employees, also dismissed, were not involved? The key point which has to be remembered is that there must be some causal link between the conduct and the dismissal in order for there to be a reduction for contributory fault.

11–60 Another problem is the practical difficulty of separating off additional blameworthy conduct from the conduct of the dispute itself. Note that the individual blameworthy conduct must predate the dismissal—must have caused or contributed to the dismissal. Any conduct on the part of the employee which resulted in him not being re-engaged cannot be taken into account so as to reduce compensation—it did not cause or contribute to the original dismissal.

Blameworthy Conduct: Trade Union Dismissals

11–61   When the tribunal is deciding compensation in respect of a dismissal which is automatically unfair by virtue of s.152 or s.153 TULR(C)A (trade union dismissals), they must disregard the immediate circumstances giving rise to the finding of unfair dismissal in deciding whether the compensatory award should be reduced because of the conduct of the complainant (s.155 TULR(C)A). So, for example, if the complainant has been dismissed for joining a union, the conduct itself in joining the union cannot be taken into account in deciding whether to reduce compensation. However, if the complainant acted in a way which was deliberately confrontational and unreasonable this may be taken into account.

11–62   The tribunal can distinguish between that which is done by the complainant (joining the union, for which no reduction can be made) and the way in which it is done (which can be taken into account in considering a reduction for contributory fault) (see *TGWU v. Howard* [1992] I.R.L.R. 170).

Findings of No Blameworthy Conduct

11–63   Not every breach of contract by an employee will amount to "blameworthy conduct" resulting in a reduction for contributory fault. In *Glenrose (Fish Merchants) Ltd v. Chapman & Others* EAT 467/91, employees refused to do overtime because of what they considered to be a unilateral variation to their contracts of employment. Although the overtime refusal was a breach of contract, the EAT agreed with the tribunal that in these particular circumstances it would not be just and equitable to reduce compensation because of contributory fault.

11–64   A refusal to comply with an unreasonable order where there is no fault on the part of the employee will not justify a reduction in compensation. In *L G Morrish v. Henlys (Folkestone) Ltd* [1973] I.R.L.R. 61, Mr Morrish refused to go along with an alteration to the records of the amount of diesel he had used. His manager had increased the amount shown on the records to cover for a discrepancy on the forecourt. Mr Morrish objected and was dismissed. "If a man is blameless it can be neither just nor equitable to reduce his award for unfair dismissal." (Sir Hugh Griffiths).

A refusal to disclose spent convictions was held not to justify a reduction for contributory fault in *Property Guards Ltd v. Taylor & Kershaw* [1982] I.R.L.R. 175, "No question of contribution can arise because there is no obligation to disclose and there is no question of any fault by the applicants" (Neill J.).

A failure to call a particular witness to a disciplinary hearing did not justify a reduction for contributory fault in *British Steel Corporation v. Williams* 776/82.

Conduct of Other Employees and Employer Irrelevant

11–65   The behaviour of the employer and whether he has acted consistently as between employees may be of central importance in determining whether there has been a fair dismissal (applying the test in s.98(4) ERA). Such matters are not relevant, however, when considering the issue of contributory fault such as to justify reducing the compensatory award. As a basic rule one looks simply at the conduct of the dismissed employee.

In the case of *Parker Foundry Ltd v. Slack* [1992] I.R.L.R. 11, the fact that the employer had not dismissed the other employee involved in a fight had no bearing on whether Mr Slack had contributed to his dismissal. However, the other employee's conduct was in one sense relevant in that the tribunal found each employee 50 per cent to blame and accordingly reduced Mr Slack's compensation by that amount. Had the other employee been more than 50 per cent to blame, presumably the reduction in Mr Slack's compensation would have been less.

Objective Test of Blameworthy Conduct

11–66 In deciding whether there has been contributory fault the tribunal should consider the employee's conduct rather than their state of mind. In the case of *Ladbroke Racing v. Mason* [1978] I.C.R. 49, two employees planned to buy two of their employer's shops and operate them whilst still working for the respondent company. Whilst there was some evidence that they did not consider they were doing anything wrong, the fact was that their action amounted to a "grave breach of trust". "What they may have believed is almost, if not entirely, irrelevant" Kilner Brown J. The EAT accordingly reduced compensation by 50 per cent.

11–67 However, it is for the tribunal to determine in any particular case, on the facts, the degree of blameworthiness and there may be cases where the "belief of a man that he is not misbehaving is to be taken into consideration" (Kilner Brown J. in *Ladbroke Racing*).

Conduct Caused Or Contributed To The Dismissal

11–68 The second limb of the analysis in *Nelson v. BBC No.2* [1979] I.R.L.R. 346 (see para. 11–41) of whether there has been contributory fault such as to justify a reduction in compensation is to establish a causal link between the conduct and the dismissal. Note that the conduct can either cause or contribute to the dismissal. The conduct does not have to have been the prime reason for dismissal but it must have been a contributory factor.

11–69 In *Robert Whiting Designs Ltd v. Lamb* [1978] I.C.R. 89, Mr Lamb was dismissed after he admitted he had improperly arranged for bonus payments to be made to him. The tribunal found that the real reason for his dismissal was poor performance rather than dishonesty. He was found to have been unfairly dismissed because of a flawed procedure but a 10 per cent reduction was made because of his own conduct. The EAT increased the reduction to 20 per cent. The tribunal could properly take into account the employee's conduct if it "played any part at all in the history of events leading to dismissal". It clearly had in this case. His conduct was "a factor in the minds of the employers" when they decided to dismiss (Kilner Brown J.). There must, therefore, be a careful analysis of whether conduct complained of actually contributed to the dismissal.

11–70 In *Smith & Smith v. McPhee and Stewart* EAT 338/339/89, Mrs McPhee, who was a hotel barmaid, was given permission to take home some caustic soda. Another employee decanted some into a lemonade bottle. Unfortunately, Mrs McPhee forgot to take it home, leaving it in reception. The next day the employer used the caustic soda to clean a sink and then left it in the lounge bar. Later an unsuspecting customer was served up a whisky and caustic soda severely burning his mouth! Mrs McPhee was dismissed. The tribunal decided that the real reason for the dismissal was to divert attention from the actions of the employer and to preserve the hotel's reputation. Although her actions in leaving the bottle at the hotel overnight were reprehensible, they did not actually contribute to the real reason for dismissal.

11-71 The tribunal cannot simply identify misconduct by the employee as a justification for reducing compensation for contributory fault. In *Hutchinson v. Enfield Rolling Mills Ltd* [1981] I.R.L.R. 318, Mr Hutchinson was dismissed for attending a union demonstration in Brighton whilst on sick leave. The tribunal reduced compensation by 100 per cent on the basis that Mr Hutchinson had been a trouble-maker throughout his employment, that his attitude during the tribunal hearing was symptomatic of the same trouble-making attitude, that his political views affected his attitude to work and that he had nothing but contempt for his employers. However, the EAT said that the tribunal had got it wrong. There had to be a causal link between the blameworthy action of the employee and the dismissal. The factors leading the tribunal to reduce the award had not been alleged by the employer and were not generally supported by the evidence. They reflected "little more than an extremely adverse view taken by the tribunal personally of Mr Hutchinson" (Brown Wilkinson J.).

Constructive dismissal and the causal link

11-72 In constructive dismissal cases there may have been a chain of events which starts with some culpable conduct by the employee and ends with a breach of contract by the employer entitling the employee to resign. Provided there is such a chain of events, the original culpable conduct by the employee may justify a reduction for contributory fault.

In *Polentarutti v. Autokraft Ltd* [1991] I.R.L.R. 457, Mr Polentarutti's work involved machining parts for sports cars. Twenty-three out of a batch of 24 rear hubs he machined were defective. The company had to bring in a sub-contractor to make good the damage. By way of recovering the extra cost they decided not to pay overtime due to Mr Polentarutti. He resigned and claimed constructive dismissal. Finding the dismissal unfair, the tribunal made a reduction of 66.6 per cent on the basis that he had contributed to his dismissal. Despite his conduct not being the direct or sole cause of dismissal, there was a causal link and this was enough.

11-73 However, when the causal link is missing between the culpable conduct and the constructive dismissal there can be no reduction for contributory fault. In British Rail Staff Association (Newcastle Central Branch) v. Robson EAT 10.7.90 and IDS Brief 431 October 1990, Mrs Robson worked as a steward at the Staff Association Club. She eavesdropped a meeting of the committee during which she felt there were veiled criticisms of her. She tried to get the committee to resolve what she felt was the root of the problem, a bad working relationship with the Treasurer. Nothing happened. She resigned and successfully claimed unfair dismissal. The tribunal reduced her compensation because of contributory fault (eavesdropping the meeting). However, the EAT overturned this finding because there was no causal link between her conduct and the dismissal.

11-74 There had been judicial support for the view that contributory fault would only be found in exceptional cases where there was a constructive dismissal. However the Northern Ireland Court of Appeal in *Morrison v. Amalgamated Transport and General Workers Union* [1989] I.R.L.R. 361 made clear that an unfairly constructively dismissed employee may be held to have contributed to that dismissal. For a summary of the facts of this case see para. 11-44. The employee's culpable bad conduct had led to a suspension without pay. This was a breach of contract by the employer entitling her to resign and claim constructive dismissal. It was an unrealistic refinement to argue that the culpable conduct only related to her suspension and not to her ultimate constructive dismissal. The culpability or unreasonable conduct contributed to or played a part in her dismissal. The EAT held that the tribunal had not erred in assessing her contribution at 40 per cent.

Causal Link: Conduct must be prior to the decision to dismiss

11–75 Only conduct by the employee prior to dismissal self-evidently can have caused or contributed to it. Therefore a decision by an employee not to appeal to the employer against dismissal will not lead to a reduction for contributory fault.

If, however, an employer's procedures provide that the dismissal will not take effect until after an opportunity for appeal has been given, a failure to pursue an appeal could potentially lead to a reduction for contributory fault. "In such cases no doubt it would be right for the appeal procedures and all circumstances concerned with it to be taken into account by the tribunal" (Talbot J. in *Hoover Ltd v. Forde* [1980] I.C.R. 239).

11–76 For the same reason, if misconduct occurs during the notice period, this cannot have caused or contributed to the dismissal and the tribunal is not entitled to reduce compensation for contributory fault. In *Bell v. Service Engines (Newcastle) Ltd* COIT 1660/185 and IDS Brief 309, Bell committed various acts of theft during the notice period which led to a conviction and a fine. But the employer had already served notice terminating his employment when the thefts occurred and so they could not have caused or contributed to the decision to dismiss. However, the tribunal nonetheless decided that it would not be just and equitable (under what is now s.123(1) ERA) to make any compensatory award (see paras 11–03 to 11–37).

Just And Equitable Reduction

11–77 If the tribunal decides that there has been blameworthy conduct on the part of the dismissed employee and that that conduct caused or contributed to the dismissal, s.123(6) ERA provides that the tribunal shall reduce the compensatory award by such proportion as it considers just and equitable. Likewise, the similar but wider provisions relating to the basic award (s.122(2) ERA) and the special award (s.125(4)) impose a duty on the tribunal to reduce the award. The wording is, though, subtly different. Those provisions refer to conduct which would make it just and equitable to reduce the award. If there is such conduct then the tribunal shall reduce the award "accordingly" (see also paras 8–56 to 8–59 (special award) and 9–23 to 9–35 (basic award)).

How much should the reduction be?

11–78 Note that there are circumstances in which the basic award may be reduced by a different amount to the Compensatory Award (see paras 9–27 to 9–31). However, the case law referred to in this section is relevant to both basic and compensatory awards.

Amount of reduction is within tribunal's discretion

11–79 The proportion by which compensation is reduced because of contributory fault is a matter for the tribunal and is only appealable if the tribunal has failed to appreciate some material aspect of fact or if an improper emphasis has been laid on particular facts (see *Warrilow v. Robert Walker Ltd* [1984] I.R.L.R. 304 EAT). This is the same approach as that under the Law Reform (Contributory Negligence) Act 1945.

In *Hollier v. Plysu Ltd* [1983] I.R.L.R. 260, the Court of Appeal (Stephenson L.J.) said that the apportionment of responsibility was "so obviously a matter of impression, opinion and discretion." There must be either a plain error of law, or something like perversity, to entitle an appellate tribunal to interfere with the decision of the tribunal.

Examples of where percentage reduction has been changed on appeal:

11–80

1. Funeral directors' receptionist failed to check bodies which had been put in wrong coffins (see para. 11–46 for facts of case). Reduction for contributory fault reduced from 50 per cent to 25 per cent. First offence, unintentional mistake and had received no detailed written instructions. Nametags had been written in longhand and looked similar. *Coalter v. Walter Craven Ltd* [1980] I.R.L.R. 262 EAT.

2. An HGV driver dismissed for capability (failing a driving assessment and then refusing to have an independent assessment). 100 per cent reduction overturned on appeal because the tribunal had not given detailed findings on why such a large reduction was justified. *White v. Summerfields (Contract Hire) Ltd* EAT 494/93 and IDS Brief 521 (see also para. 11–43).

3. Nairne was convicted of drink driving for a second time and banned for three years. He was dismissed from his job with the Highlands and Islands Fire Brigade. EAT increased the reduction for contributory fault from 25 per cent to 75 per cent ⁢Nairne v. Highlands and Islands Fire Brigade [1989] I.R.L.R. 366 (see also para. 11–46).

Guidance on extent of reduction:

11–81 The EAT in *Hollier v. Plysu Ltd* EAT 431/86 provided some general guidelines to assist tribunals in determining the extent of the reduction for contributory fault. The guidelines are also set out in the Court of Appeal judgment in the same case ([1983] I.R.L.R. 260).

The EAT identified four broad categories of cases:

1. The employee was wholly to blame; reduction could be 100 per cent.

2. The employee was largely responsible; "nobody would quarrel with the figure of 75 per cent".

3. Both parties equally to blame; reduction 50 per cent.

4. Employee to a much lesser degree to blame; reduction 25 per cent.

The examples of cases where there has been blameworthy conduct set out at paragraphs 11–42 to 11–48 demonstrate that these are only broad guidances and that the tribunal can properly determine a different reduction.

Examples of the range of reduction

11–82   100 per cent Reduction—Employee Wholly to Blame   A major procedural defect by the employer resulting in a finding of unfair dismissal will not necessarily prevent the tribunal reducing compensation by 100 per cent if they have also concluded that the employee caused the dismissal by his conduct and that he was wholly to blame. This was the case in *Smith v. Lodge Bros. (Funerals) Ltd* EAT 92/88 and IDS Brief 411. Smith was dismissed by letter without having any opportunity to state his case. His dismissal was for absences from work and for failing to inform the company about his absence or the reasons for it. The tribunal decided on the facts that it would be just and equitable to reduce his compensation by 100 per cent.

In *Chaplin v. Rawlinson Ltd* [1991] I.C.R. 553, Mr Chaplin was unfairly dismissed because of procedural failings by the employer. However, Mr Chaplin's misconduct which led to his dismissal was that he had urinated on wheat he was delivering to Buxted Chicken. At the time there was great concern about salmonella affecting chickens. The tribunal awarded nil compensation. The EAT dismissed Mr Chaplin's appeal stating that the tribunal was "perfectly entitled to reach the conclusion that it did and that no injustice was suffered at all". See also *Charles Robertson (Development) Ltd v. White and anor* EAT [1995] I.C.R. 349 (see para. 11–44).

11–83   90 per cent Reduction: It is clear that a 100 per cent reduction may be appropriate in cases where the tribunal reaches the conclusion that the employee was wholly to blame for his dismissal, despite the employer being guilty of procedural errors. There may also be circumstances in which the procedural errors are such that something less than a 100 per cent reduction should be applied.

In *Gibson v. British Transport Docks Board* [1982] I.R.L.R. 228, a serious procedural error caused or contributed to the dismissals despite the employees being over-whelmingly to blame. The employers had failed to consider the individual involvement of 10 employees following a fracas which took place on a picket line. All were dismissed. Had the tribunal examined each individual's involvement the results could have been different. The EAT assessed the employees contribution to their own dismissal at 90 per cent and accordingly decided that compensation should be reduced by that amount.

11–84   75 per cent Reduction: In *Nairne v. Highlands and Islands Fire Brigade* [1989] I.R.L.R. 366, the EAT decided that Mr Nairn's compensation should be reduced by 75 per cent because of contributory fault (see para. 11–46 for summary of facts). Procedural flaws rendered the dismissal unfair. Had a fair procedure been followed there was a chance he could have persuaded his employer to keep him on and, therefore, a 75 per cent reduction was justified rather than 100 per cent.

11–85   50 per cent Reduction: In *Parker Foundry Ltd v. Slack* [1992] I.R.L.R. 11 (see also para. 11–44), two employees were equally to blame for a fight. One was dismissed. As he was 50 per cent to blame his compensation for unfair dismissal was reduced by 50 per cent.

11–86   25 per cent Reduction: In *Coalter v. Walter Craven Ltd* [1980] I.R.L.R. 262, the EAT decided that Ms. Coalter's compensation should be reduced by 25 per cent (see also para. 11–46). She was dismissed from her job as receptionist at a funeral directors for failing to check that two bodies had been placed in the right coffins. Although the negligence was serious, it was her first offence and the employers had been at fault in failing to give clear instructions. Also, the name tags had been written in longhand and were unclear.

11–87   Minor Fault: Where the fault on the part of the employee is minor or insignificant then the tribunal can reach the view that it would not be just and equitable to reduce the award at all. So in *York v. Brown* EAT 262/84 IDS Brief 309, the EAT decided that a contribution to dismissal of only 10 per cent could be *de minimus* and therefore not worth effecting a reduction.

But a reduction as low as 10 per cent can be made by the tribunal acting properly within its discretion. In *McNicholas v. AR Engineering* COIT 1672/67, Mr McNicholas was dismissed following verbal abuse of his foreman. This was a minor breach of company rules, and although it could be said that he had contributed to his dismissal, the contribution was modest. A 10 per cent reduction was appropriate.

CHAPTER 12

Interim Relief

Re-employment or continuation of contract

12–01   A powerful, but rarely used, additional remedy is available in respect of a limited category of automatic unfair dismissal cases. If an employee considers that he has been dismissed for a reason which falls within one of these categories he can apply to the tribunal for interim re-employment. If the application is successful but the employer refuses to reinstate or re-engage pending the full hearing of the unfair dismissal claim then the tribunal will order what, in effect, amounts to suspension on full pay. Strict rules apply to such applications. These will be explained in this section. However, in appropriate cases, interim relief of this sort is a valuable remedy which should be considered immediately the dismissal takes effect. Timing, as we shall see, is critical.

When is interim relief available?

12–02   The categories of cases where interim relief is available is the same as for the special award (see paras 8–47 to 8–48 for a fuller description of such categories of case). There is, however, one major exception. Interim relief is not available where an employee has been selected for redundancy for one of these inadmissible reasons. The category of cases where interim relief is available is as follows:

Reason for dismissal	**Statutory provision**
1. Carrying out (or proposing to carry out) designated health and safety activities.	s.100(1)(a) ERA
2. Performing (or proposing to perform) functions as a health and safety representative or member of a safety committee.	s.100(1)(b) ERA
3. Performing (or proposing to perform) functions as a trustee of an occupational pension scheme.	s.102(1) ERA
4. Performing (or proposing to perform) functions/ activities as a candidate or elected representative in respect of collective redundancy consultation or transfer of undertakings consultation.	s.103 ERA
5. Refusing (or proposing to refuse) to comply with a requirement imposed by the employer in contravention of the Working Time Regulations 1998 or refusing (or proposing to refuse) to	s.101A ERA

forego a right conferred by those regulations or failing to sign a workforce agreement or to enter into, or agree to vary or extend any other agreement with his employer provided for by those regulations or performing (or proposing to perform) functions/activities as a candidate or as an elected representative for the purposes of those regulations.

6. Being (or proposing to become) a trade union member, taking part (or proposing to take part) in trade union activities, not being a member of a trade union or refusing (or proposing to refuse) to become or remain a member.   s.152 TULR(C)A

7. Worker making a protected disclosure (New protection provided by Public Interest Disclosure Act 1998, effective from 1st January 1999).   s.103A ERA

Statutory provisions governing interim relief

12–03   The provisions governing the right to apply for interim relief in respect of those categories of cases listed above in the ERA are ss.128–132 ERA. With regard to the TULR(C)A category, the provisions on interim relief are ss.161–167 TULR(C)A.

Procedure

12–04   The application for interim relief must be presented to the tribunal "before the end of the period of seven days immediately following the effective date of termination (whether before, on or after that date)" (s.128(2) ERA and s.161(2) TULR(C)A). Note that this wording allows the application to be made before the effective date of termination. So far as the deadline is concerned, if, for example, the date of termination was a Wednesday, the application must be with the tribunal by the end of the following Wednesday. There is no discretion to extend the time limit in any circumstances.

12–05   The application on the ITI should claim that the dismissal was unfair and clearly identify a reason falling within one of the categories set out at para. 12–02. It should also specify clearly that the complainant seeks interim relief. Note that it may be possible to amend an application after the expiry of the seven-day period so as to add further detail. In *Barley & ors v. Amey Roadstone Corporation Ltd* [1977] I.C.R. 546 EAT, the complainant had referred to unfair dismissal and had requested interim relief but had not set out details of the alleged trade union reasons. The EAT allowed amendment to the application following the seven-day period.

Special additional requirement: trade union cases

12–06   If the complainant alleges that the reason for the dismissal fell within s.152(1)(a) or (b) TULR(C)A, (being or proposing to become a trade union member or taking part/proposing to take part in trade union activities) then he must also present to the tribunal within the same seven day period a written certificate signed by an authorised trade union official. The certificate must state:

1. that on the date of dismissal the complainant was, or proposed to become, a member of that union;

2. that there appear to be reasonable grounds for supposing that the reason for his dismissal (or, if more than one, the principal reason) was one alleged in the complaint (s.161(3) TULR(C)A).

Authorisation

12–07 S.161(4) TULR(C)A states that the trade union official who signs the certificate must be authorised by the union specifically to act for this purpose.

In *Farmeary v. Veterinary Drug Co. Ltd* [1976] I.R.L.R. 322 the tribunal made the point that it was not enough just to be an official of the union validly appointed to his office. The union executive should decide who has authority to sign for the union. The tribunal also advised that officers should be appointed before "any trouble arises" in view of the seven day time limit for submitting the certificate to the tribunal (see para. 12–04).

12–08 Note that s.161(5) TULR(C)A provides that a document purporting to be an authorisation for a trade union official to sign a certificate on behalf of the union shall be accepted as such unless the contrary is proved. Further, a document purporting to be a certificate signed by an official shall be taken to be signed by him unless the contrary is proved. It appears as if the certificate does not actually have to state that the signatory is authorised by the union (see *Sulemany v. Habib Bank Ltd* [1983] I.C.R. 60).

If the employer challenges the authorisation then it is up to the official to prove that he has the authority of the union. It seems that authority may be implied. An official who is authorised by the union to conduct tribunal cases may have such implied authority (see *Hird v. ITS Rubber Ltd* COIT 1873/246).

Reasonable grounds

12–09 Note that s.161(3)(b) TULR(C)A provides that the certificate must state that the union official believes that there appear to be reasonable grounds for supposing that the reason for dismissal was trade union membership or activities. However, it seems that the application will not fail because of minor irregularities. In *Bradley v. Edward Ryde & Sons* [1979] I.C.R. 488, the official left out the word "reasonable". This did not invalidate the certificate.

It may also be possible to read the certificate together with the unfair dismissal/interim relief complaint (see *Sulemany v. Habib Bank Ltd*). Note that the Act clearly requires the official to carry out some investigation into the claim rather than simply "rubber-stamping" the complainant's application. The official has to believe that there are "reasonable grounds".

Determination of application as soon as practicable

12–10 There is a duty imposed on the tribunal to determine the application "as soon as practicable" after receiving it (and the certificate where appropriate) (s.128(3) ERA and s.162(1) TULR(C)A).

The employer must have at least seven days' notice of the hearing and must receive a copy of the application (and certificate if appropriate) with this much notice (s.128(4)

ERA and s.162(2) TULR(C)A. Note that in trade union cases, a request may be made by the employer or the complainant to joint a third party to the proceedings because they are alleged to have induced the employer to dismiss by, for example, calling a strike. If such a request is made at least three days before the hearing the tribunal must give to the third party, as soon as reasonably practicable, a copy of the application and certificate and notice of the date of the hearing (s.162(3) TULR(C)A).

Postponement

12–11   Postponement of the hearing will only be permitted if special circumstances exist to justify it (s.128(5) ERA and s.162(4) TULR(C)A.

Tribunal hearing

12–12   The tribunal has to decide whether it is "likely" that the complainant will win his unfair dismissal complaint on the basis of one of the reasons set out at para. 12–02 (s.129(1) ERA and s.163(1) TULR(C)A. This test was considered by the EAT in the case of *Taplin v. C. Shippam Ltd* [1978] I.R.L.R. 450. At this interim stage the test is much tougher than when it comes to actually determining the unfair dismissal claim. "We do not think that Parliament intended that an employee should be able to obtain an order under this section unless he achieved a higher degree of certainty in the mind of the tribunal than that of showing that he just had 'reasonable' prospects of success." (Slynn J.)

12–13   The EAT also rejected the suggestions that "likely" meant "on a balance of probabilities" or "a real possibility of success". The right approach was for the tribunal to "ask itself whether the applicant has established that he has a 'pretty good' chance of succeeding in the final application to the tribunal". Evidence of hostility to trade unions may be taken into account in appropriate cases in considering the prospects of success.

Possible orders

12–14   If it appears to the tribunal that ultimate success in the unfair dismissal claim is likely then the following steps must be followed (s.129(2) ERA and s.163(2) TULR(C)A.

1.   The tribunal announces its findings and explains to the parties what powers it may exercise.

2.   The tribunal asks the employer whether he is willing to reinstate the employee pending the full hearing.

3.   If the employer is willing to reinstate, the tribunal makes an order to that effect (s.129(5) ERA and s.163(4) TULR(C)A).

4.   If the employer is not prepared to reinstate, the tribunal goes on to ask if he is willing to re-engage the employee in another job on terms and conditions not less favourable than the employee enjoyed before dismissal.

5.   If the employer is willing to re-engage on specified terms and conditions, the tribunal must ask the employee if he is willing to accept (s.129(6) ERA and s.163(5) TULR(C)A).

6.   If the employee is so willing, the tribunal makes an order to that effect (s.129(7) ERA and s.163(5)(a) TULR(C)A).

7. If the employee refuses, the tribunal has to decide whether the refusal is reasonable. If it reaches the view that it was reasonable to refuse then the tribunal makes an order for the continuation of the contract of employment (s.129(8) ERA and s.163(5)(b) TULR(C)A).

8. If the tribunal considers the refusal to be unreasonable it makes no order (s.129(8)(b) ERA and s.163(5)(b) TULR(C)A).

9. If the employer fails to attend the hearing or if he refuses to reinstate or re-engage then, again, the tribunal will make an order for the continuation of the contract of employment (s.129(9) ERA and s.163(6) TULR(C)A).

Order for continuation of contract of employment

12–15 This amounts to suspension on full pay. Continuity of employment is maintained (s.130(1)(b) ERA and s.164(1)(b) TULR(C)A). Pay, pension rights, seniority and any other benefits are also maintained (s.130(1)(a) ERA and s.164(1)(a) TULR(C)A. Arrears back to the date of dismissal are covered (s.130(1) ERA and s.164(1) TULR(C)A).

The order must specify the amount which is to be paid by the employer for each pay period from dismissal to determination of the complaint (s.130(2) ERA and s.164(2) TULR(C)A).

12–16 The amount specified as payable shall be what the employee could reasonably have expected to earn. This, therefore, would include anticipated overtime, bonuses, etc., (s.130(3) ERA and s.164(6) TULR(C)A). Sums paid in lieu of notice or by way of damages for breach of contract are set off against the amount otherwise due (s.130(6) ERA and s.164(6) TULR(C)A). Also set off are sums received from another employer during the period since dismissal (s.130(5) ERA and s.164(5) TULR(C)A).

Application for variation or revocation

12–17 If there is a change in circumstances since the order was made then either the employee or the employer can apply for the order to be revoked or varied (s.131 ERA and s.165 TULR(C)A). Such an application is most likely to be made by the employer on the basis that the employee has got a new job. An application to vary or revoke can be made at any time right up to determination of the complaint. This might include the period during which the unfair dismissal claim is being heard.

12–18 The application can be considered by another tribunal. It does not have to be the same panel as that which considered the original interim relief application (see *British Coal Corporation v. McGinty* [1988] I.R.L.R. 7 EAT). The EAT in that case also made the *obiter* observation that a differently constituted tribunal should hear the main application for unfair dismissal to the tribunal which considered the interim relief application.

Failure to comply

12–19 If the employer fails to comply with an interim order for reinstatement or re-engagement then the employee can apply again to the tribunal (s.132 ERA and s.166 TULR(C)A). If the tribunal is satisfied that the employer has not complied then it shall make an order for continuation of the contract of employment. In addition, the tribunal shall order the employer to pay compensation to the employee of such amount as the tribunal considers just and equitable in all the circumstances, having regard to:

(a)   the infringement of the employee's right to be reinstated or re-engaged, and

(b)   any loss suffered by the employee in consequence of non compliance.

(s.132(2) ERA and s.166(1)(b) TULR(C)A)

(See para. XX for commentary on similar provisions for awards of compensation in respect of action short of dismissal.)

12–20   If the tribunal is satisfied (following an application by the employee) that the employer has failed to comply with an order for continuation of the contract of employment, it shall determine the amount owed by the employer. If this determination is made on the same date as the tribunal determines the employee's complaint that he has been unfairly dismissed, the tribunal must separately specify the sum due as a result of non-compliance. In any other case, the tribunal shall order that the employer pays compensation of an amount the tribunal considers "just and equitable in all the circumstances having regard to any loss suffered by the employee in consequence of the non-compliance" (s.132(5) and (6) ERA and s.166(4) and (5) TULR(C)A).

CHAPTER 13
Remedies in Discrimination Cases

13–01 Essentially the same rules with regard to remedies apply to race, sex and disability discrimination cases. The three relevant Acts are the Sex Discrimination Act, 1975 (SDA), the Race Relations Act, 1976 (RRA) and the Disability Discrimination Act, 1995 (DDA). In each case, if the tribunal finds that the complaint of discrimination is well-founded it must take such of the following steps as it considers *just and equitable.*

1. Make a declaration of the rights of the complainant and respondent.

2. Order the respondent to pay compensation to the complainant.

3. Recommend that the respondent takes some action with the purpose of obviating or reducing the adverse effects on the complainant of any matter to which the complaint relates. The tribunal will specify a time period, within which such action should be taken.

See s.65(1) SDA, s.56(1) RRA and s.8(2) DDA.

ORDERS IN RESPECT OF NAMED INDIVIDUAL RESPONDENTS

13–02 Note that the three steps that the tribunal can take under the discrimination Acts—the declaration, the order for compensation and the recommendation—are in respect of the respondent. The respondent may be a named individual and/or the employer.

Particularly in cases of harassment, proceedings are often brought against both the alleged harasser and against the employer, who may also be liable as a result of vicarious liability (s.41(1) SDA, s.32(1) RRA and s.58(1) DDA). In such circumstances, compensation can be awarded against both the employer and the named individual, although the complainant cannot recover double compensation for financial loss. Awards for injury to feelings can be made against both respondents. Whether compensation for injury to the feelings is awarded against named individual respondents as well as against the employer is a matter for the tribunal's discretion.

13–03 In *Deane v. London Borough of Ealing* [1993] I.R.L.R. 209 EAT, no award was made against a Mr Crofton who was director of housing at Ealing and a named respondent. Mr Deane was found to have suffered race discrimination in not being promoted to a more senior position in the housing department. Mr Deane was white and Mr Crofton wanted an Asian or black employee in this particular post which was based in an area with a substantial Asian population. The EAT agreed with the tribunal that as Mr Crofton was acting in the course of his employment, any award of damages should be made against the Borough.

This decision was considered in the later EAT case of *Armitage, Marsden and HM Prison Service v. Johnson* [1997] I.R.L.R. 162. Mr Johnson, a black auxiliary prison officer suffered from a "campaign of appalling treatment" and was awarded £20,000 compensation for injury to feelings against the Prison Service together with a further £7,500 aggravated damages and £500 against each of the named prison officers.

13–04   The EAT upheld this award and rejected an argument, based on the *Deane* decision, that no award should be made against the two prison officers. "We do not think that *Deane* is authority for the general proposition that wherever it is possible to order the employer to pay by finding him vicariously liable for his employee's act, it will necessarily follow that that should be done. In our view, it is a question for the discretion of the tribunal. The exercise of the tribunal's discretion was perfectly proper in *Deane's* case where Mr Crofton was acting bona fide in the best interest of his employer. He did not intend to discriminate on racial grounds. He was doing his best but was in this respect misguided. In the present case, the facts are very different. The second appellant acted out of sheer malice and the first appellant victimised [Mr Johnson]. In our view the tribunal were quite entitled to make separate awards" (Smith J.).

In summary, therefore, in cases of harassment, and also possibly victimisation, where a named individual respondent is personally culpable, it is likely that the tribunal will exercise its discretion and make separate awards for injury to feelings against those named respondents. At the other end of the scale, in a case where the individual respondent was simply carrying out the policy of his employer and personally intends no discrimination, then the tribunal's discretion may well be exercised against making any award in respect of the individual respondent. Just as with awards of compensation, declarations and recommendations can also potentially be made against named respondents as well as against a respondent employer.

DECLARATION OF RIGHTS

13–05   (See s.65(1)(a) SDA, s.56(1)(a) RRA, s.8(2)(a) DDA). In most cases the main objective of the complainant is to recover compensation for a wrong allegedly committed. However, in cases where a policy or practice of the employer is being challenged as having indirect discriminatory effect, a declaration that the policy/practice is unlawful may be very important. First, it may be sufficient to ensure that the discrimination comes to an end (note also the power to make a recommendation— see para. 13–07). Secondly, it may have an important bearing on subsequent entitlement to compensation. This is for the following reason.

No compensation can be awarded for indirect race discrimination unless the respondent intended treating the complainant less favourably on racial grounds. Note that in cases of indirect sex discrimination compensation can now be awarded without having to prove intention.

13–06   However, if a declaration has been made that a particular "requirement or condition" is indirectly discriminatory, but the employer continues to apply it, it will be hard to argue in any subsequent claim that it was unintentional (see also paras 13–34 to 13–36).

RECOMMENDATION

13–07   (See s.65(1)(c) SDA, s.56(1)(c) RRA, s.8(2)(c) DDA).

The power in the DDA is to recommend that the respondent takes action appearing to the tribunal to be reasonable in all the circumstances of the case with the purpose of obviating or reducing the adverse effect on the complainant of any matter to which the complaint relates. In the case of the SDA and RRA, the power is to recommend action appearing to the tribunal to be *practicable* for the same purpose.

13–08 It is not clear whether this distinction has much practical effect. The reference in the DDA to action which is "reasonable" is consistent with the obligation in the Act to make "reasonable adjustments" where arrangements or physical features of the premises place a disabled person at a "substantial disadvantage" (see s.6 DDA). The sort of action which a tribunal might recommend to the employer where there is a finding of disability discrimination is likely to equate to the range of reasonable adjustments envisaged by s.6 DDA and by the Code of Practice which has been issued by the Secretary of State under s.53 DDA.

Purpose of recommendation

13–09 The recommendation can only be for the purpose of obviating or reducing the adverse effect on the complainant of the discrimination.

Examples of recommendations

13–10 The following are examples of recommendations which have been made by tribunals.

1. Training/career development for the complainant.

2. That a note be placed on file so as to ensure that if a reference is requested for a dismissed employee who suffered discrimination, the prospective employer is informed that no fault attaches to the former employee and that the employer was found to have discriminated against him (*Bayoomi v. British Railways Board* [1981] I.R.L.R. 431).

3. That the employer offers an apology to the complainant (see *Clayton-Naute v. The Governors of Catherine Infant School* COIT 3270/139).

4. That a supervisor who sexually harassed the complainant be transferred to another job and until the transfer was effected that he be suspended on full pay (*Whittington v. P. Morris and Greenwich Health Authority*—COIT 17846/89).

13–11 In the case of *Hyatt v. IMI Refiners Ltd* Case No. 1301315/96, 4.6.97 (Discrimination Law Association Briefing No.45, October 1997) the tribunal made a recommendation that the complainant be re-engaged on the following terms,

> He should be treated as if his employment had not been terminated as to his rate of pay, employer's contributions to his company pension scheme, access to any share option scheme and in continuity of employment.

The tribunal had found that there was a vacancy. The respondent's organisation was large, there was a flexible workforce and the complainant's record was exemplary. They decided, therefore, that it was practicable to recommend re-engagement. The tribunal warned the respondent company that if they failed to comply with the recommendation the tribunal could increase compensation and that the total compensation was likely to exceed £40,000. Note that, unlike unfair dismissal, there is no specific remedy of reinstatement or re-engagement in any of the discrimination Acts. Whether the tribunal had the power to make this recommendation must be open to doubt (see para. 13–17 where there is commentary on the Court of Appeal case of *Irvine v. Prescott Ltd* [1981] I.R.L.R. 28 CA. The Court of Appeal rejected a recommendation for the complainant to be paid the difference between her salary and what she would have received had she been promoted.

13–12   The tribunal also recommended "as strongly as we can" that Equal Opportunities training be given to managers and supervisors concerned with the complainant. This was on the basis that it would "obviate the effects of discrimination on this complainant" (once he was working for the company again). Note, however, that a tribunal should not recommend a course of action which might amount to a breach of the contract of employment. A transfer to another job may not be permitted by the contract and, unless it could be done with the consent of the employee concerned, would amount to a breach of contract. Such a recommended course of action would not be "practicable" in accordance with the statutory test (or "reasonable" in the case of the DDA) (see paras 13–07 to 13–08).

Limits to the power to make recommendations

Recommendation must not be general

13–13   Because the recommendation must be to take action to obviate or reduce the adverse effect of the discrimination on the complainant, general recommendations which do not achieve this objective are not permitted.

In *Ministry of Defence v. Jeremiah* [1978] I.R.L.R. 402 EAT, the tribunal had made a general recommendation relating to facilities for "women in like employment with the applicant". This was overturned by the EAT. It was neither "necessary [nor] desirable" to make such a recommendation. In fact, the EAT should probably have gone further than this and found that such a recommendation was not permitted (given that the recommendation must be directed at obviating or reducing the adverse effect *on the complainant* of the discrimination and not simply to improve practices generally).

In *Record Production Chapel & Others v. Turnbull & anor* EAT 955/83, the EAT overturned a general recommendation that a trade union overhaul its selection procedures.

13–14   In *Bayoomi v. British Railways Board* [1981] I.R.L.R. 431, Mr Bayoomi suffered race discrimination when he was dismissed by the Board. The tribunal recommended that an entry be made on its files so as to ensure that if the Board was asked for a reference for Mr Bayoomi, any potential employer was informed that he left in circumstances which reflected no discredit on him and that a tribunal had found that he had suffered race discrimination. The tribunal rejected a proposal to make "sweeping and general" recommendations about the Board's employment practices so far as they affect people of minority racial groups. They had no power to do this.

What the tribunal may, in practice, do is to give informal guidance about practices or procedures. They may, for example, suggest that an equal opportunities policy should be introduced. Such advice has no force of law but may, nonetheless, be helpful.

Recommendation cannot have the effect of positive discrimination

13–15   In *British Gas plc v. Sharma* [1991] I.R.L.R. 101, Mrs Sharma suffered race discrimination in respect of a failed promotion application. As well as awarding compensation, a recommendation was made that British Gas should promote Mrs Sharma to the next suitable vacancy at a particular grade. The EAT overturned this recommendation on the basis that the RRA does not permit positive discrimination and to promote Mrs Sharma without considering other applicants who may have superior qualifications could in itself amount to direct discrimination. The EAT also made the point that the power to make a recommendation envisages a time limit for the action to be taken. A vacancy could occur at any time and so a time limit would be impossible to impose. Note that this prohibition does not necessarily apply to cases under the DDA where there is no bar on positive discrimination, although, of course, the recommendations must be "reasonable" (s.8(2)(c) DDA).

Recommendation to appoint to future vacancy

13–16 In *Noone v. North West Thames Regional Health Authority (No.2)* [1988] I.R.L.R. 530, the Court of Appeal rejected a recommendation that the Health Authority should seek the Secretary of State's authorisation to dispense with its statutory obligations to advertise its next vacancy for a consultant post. Dr Noone had suffered race discrimination in respect of a previous vacancy. Lord Justice May said that "any such recommendation would set at nought the statutory procedure set out for the benefit of the NHS, the various professions concerned in that service, the public and others qualified for the vacant post". No doubt, just as in the *Sharma* case, it could also have led to direct discrimination in respect of other excluded potential applicants.

Recommendations to increase pay or benefits

13–17 In *Irvine v. Prestcold Ltd* I.R.L.R. [1981] 281 CA, the Court of Appeal made clear that monetary compensation is fully provided for in s.65(1)(b) SDA—the general power to award compensation for sex discrimination. The power to make a recommendation does not extend to the remuneration to be paid to an employee. Therefore a recommendation by the tribunal which, amongst other things, provided for the employee to receive the difference in salary between her job and one to which she should have been promoted, was overruled.

Further compensation: Failure to comply with recommendations

13–18 If the respondent fails, without reasonable justification, to comply with a recommendation made by the tribunal, the tribunal can, if it considers it just and equitable to do so, increase the award of compensation or make an award of compensation, if no such order was originally made (see s.8(5) DDA, s.65(3) SDA, s.56(4) RRA, see also commentary on failure to comply with recommendations in case of indirect race discrimination at paras 13–39 to 13–40).

Steps to Take

13–19 In circumstances where a respondent has failed to comply with a recommendation, the complainant should write to the tribunal setting out the circumstances and details of the alleged failure. The tribunal chairman may ask the respondent to respond to the complaint, but will then fix a further hearing date when the parties can give evidence and make submissions. Note that the respondent has a potential defence to an award of further compensation if he can show that he has "reasonable justification" for non compliance (see *Nelson v. Tyne and Wear Passenger Transport Executive* [1978] I.C.R. 1183 EAT).

COMPENSATION

13–20   The general principles relating to the power of the tribunal to award compensation are the same for sex, race and disability discrimination. In cases of indirect discrimination, however, the rules on compensation are different for sex and race cases (see paras 13–32 to 13–41). There is no concept of indirect discrimination in the Disability Discrimination Act.

Statutory Provisions

13–21   Section 65(1) of the SDA provides that where a tribunal finds that a complaint is well founded the tribunal *shall* make such of the following as it considers just and equitable:

> (b)   an order requiring the respondent to pay to the complainant compensation of an amount corresponding to any damages he could have been ordered by a County Court or by a Sheriff Court to pay to the complainant if the complaint had fallen to be dealt with under s.66

s.65(1) (a) and (c) provide for the power to declare the rights of the parties and the power to make a recommendation—see paras 13–05 to 13–19). (Section 56(1)(b) RRA and s.8(2)(b) DDA give the same power to the tribunal to award compensation for race and disability discrimination).

13–22   Section 66(1) SDA and the corresponding provision in the RRA (s.57(1)) provides that claims of discrimination "may be made the subject of civil proceedings in like manner as any other claim in tort or (in Scotland) in reparation for breach of statutory tort." Both these Acts, therefore, treat unlawful acts of discrimination as statutory torts and compensation must be calculated in the same way as damages in tort.

The language of the DDA is simpler. Section 8(3) states that "the amount of compensation shall be calculated by applying the principles applicable to the calculation of damages in claims in tort or (in Scotland) in reparation for breach of statutory duty".

In each of the three discrimination Acts it is made clear that compensation may include compensation for injury to feelings "whether or not it includes compensation under any other head". (s.66(4) SDA, s.57(4) RRA, s.8(4) DDA, see paras 13–96 to 13–183). Note also the power to award interest (see paras 13–42 to 13–54).

"Just and Equitable" Test

13–23   It is important to note a crucial distinction between the relevance of the words "just and equitable" in the award of compensation under the three discrimination Acts on the one hand and the calculation of the "compensatory award" in an unfair dismissal claim on the other hand.

In the discrimination Acts, if the tribunal decides that a claim is well-founded it shall award compensation if it considers it just and equitable to do so (s.65(1)(b) SDA, s.56(1)(b) RRA, s.8(2)(b) DDA). Once the tribunal decides it is just and equitable to award compensation, the award itself is not to be limited by any statutory concept of justice and equity. The tribunal simply follows the principles for determining damages in tort (see *Hurley v. Mustoe (No.2)* [1983] I.C.R. 422 EAT). Contrast this with the assessment of the compensatory award in an unfair dismissal claim where the award itself "shall be such amount as the tribunal considers just and equitable"—s.123(1) ERA 96, see paragraphs 10–01 and 11–03 to 11–37.

Tortious Measure of Damages

13–24 "The correct measure of damages is based on the principle that, as best as money can do it, the applicant must be put in the same position she would have been in but for the unlawful conduct" of the respondent (Mr Justice Morison in *MOD v. Cannock and Others* [1994] I.R.L.R. 509 EAT).

Foreseeable Loss

13–25 As with the assessment of damages in other torts, the test of foreseeability applies to compensation for discrimination. The test is whether "judged by the standard of the reasonable man ... he ought to have foreseen" the "natural or necessary or probable consequences of his act" *The Wagon Mound* [1961] 1 All E.R. 404 PC at 423.

The respondent is responsible for any type of damage which ought to have been foreseen by the reasonable man (see *The Wagon Mound (No.2)* [1966] 2 All E.R. 709 at 714) and if a particular type of injury was foreseeable then the respondent is responsible for an unforeseeable form of that injury. In the discrimination context, this means that if injury to feelings was a foreseeable consequence of an act of discrimination, then it does not matter that a particularly extreme reaction (for example the complainant suffering severe depression as a result of harassment) was, in itself, unforeseeable. The respondent would be liable for compensation based on the degree of suffering actually experienced by the complainant (see *Hughes v. Lord Advocate* [1963] 1 All E.R. 705 HL).

The complainant should also recover compensation for the unforeseeable consequences of a foreseeable type of injury (see *Smith v. Leech Brain & Co. Ltd* [1961] 3 All E.R. 1159, a personal injuries case, where the plaintiff suffered a burn on his lip which resulted in him getting cancer, see also paras 13–96 to 13–183 on Injury to Feelings).

No limit on compensation

13–26 The decision in *Marshall v. Southampton and South-West Hampshire Area Health Authority (No.2)* [1993] I.R.L.R. 445 ECJ, was that the statutory cap on compensation for sex discrimination was contrary to the Equal Treatment Directive. Interpreting Article 6 of the Directive, the European Court said that the objective "is to arrive at real equality of opportunity and cannot therefore be attained in the absence of measures to restore such equality when it has not been observed". Where "financial compensation is the measure adopted in order to achieve the objective ... it must be adequate in that it must enable the loss and damage actually sustained as a result of the discriminatory dismissal to be made good in full." This decision forced the Government to remove the cap on compensation (see Sex Discrimination and Equal Pay (Remedies) Regulations 1993 (S.I. 1993 No.2798) Reg 2).

13–27 This, however, left a glaring disparity between sex and race cases (where the cap remained because the Equal Treatment Directive does not address race discrimination). The cap was, however, subsequently removed in race cases as a result of the Race Relations (Remedies) Act 1994 with effect from July 3, 1994. The DDA mirrors the position with race and sex, having no upper limit on compensation. The lifting of the lid on compensation led very quickly to some very substantial awards, particularly in the MOD pregnancy dismissal cases. Tribunals had to grapple for the first time with claims for compensation for loss suffered over many years.

13–28   Mrs Cannock, for example, was awarded £172,939 and Mrs Hadley £174,430. Both these women had been officers in the armed forces who were discharged unlawfully when they became pregnant. When the EAT considered these and other cases (*MOD v. Cannock and others* [1994] I.R.L.R. 509 EAT), Morison J. laid down some general guidance "to assist [tribunals] in assessing compensation in other sex discrimination cases in the future." With regard to the overall size of awards, he sought to distinguish the case of a woman discharged as a result of pregnancy who would have been "ready, willing and able to resume her ... duties ... six months after the child was born" from the circumstances where a person has some kind of long term disability.

13–29   He went on to suggest "that tribunals do not simply make calculations under various different heads, and then add them up and award the total sum. A sense of due proportion involves looking at the individual components of any award and then looking at the total to make sure that the total award seems a sensible and just reflection of the chances which have been assessed." He also encouraged a comparison with the assessment of loss in general unfair dismissal cases stating that in discrimination cases "their compensation for loss of earnings is not likely to be different from the thousands of cases of unfair dismissal with which the [tribunals] are having to deal with each year, albeit that there is no cap on the award."

13–30   This approach does not, however, seem to accord either with the principles of damages assessment in tort or with the requirements of European law in the light of *Marshall (No.2)*. In a subsequent pregnancy dismissal case *MOD v. Hunt and others* [1996] I.R.L.R. 139, Kay J. made clear that the obiter guidelines in *Cannock* "are not tramlines and individual cases must be decided upon the evidence and factual findings in them".

With regard to the particular passage suggesting that tribunals "do not simply make calculations under various different heads and then add them up and award the total sum", this caused Kay J. concern. If the tribunal properly determines that a complainant is "entitled to £X in respect of injury to feelings, £Y in respect of loss of earnings and £Z in respect of loss of pension entitlement, she is prima facie entitled to an award of not less than £X + Y + Z and appropriate interest."

13–31   Referring to *Marshall (No.2)* he concluded: "It seems to us that a general approach which required reconsideration of the figure produced by aggregating the constituent heads of damage would be to introduce a judicial cap in an area where there is no statutory cap and would be contrary to *Marshall (No.2)*".

In summary, whilst it is clear that in the majority of cases awards of compensation are going to be more modest than in personal injury cases involving permanent incapacity, each case has to be judged on its own facts. If, for example, a woman suffers serious harassment which results in post traumatic stress disorder or a nervous breakdown, the scale of her losses could be very substantial, particularly if she has lost a well paid job with pension rights and had had good career prospects.

INDIRECT DISCRIMINATION

13–32   It is important to note the special rules applying to compensation for indirect race and sex discrimination. There is no equivalent concept of indirect discrimination in the DDA.

What is indirect discrimination?

13–33   Section 1(1)(b) SDA provides that where an employer

(a)   applies a requirement or condition to a person which applies equally to men and women,

(b)   but the proportion of women who can comply with it is considerably smaller than the proportion of men, and

(c)   he cannot show that the requirement or condition is justifiable, irrespective of the sex of the person to whom it is applied, and

(d)   the requirement or condition is to her detriment because she cannot comply with it,

he unlawfully indirectly discriminates against her. This rule applies equally to men as it does to women.

Section 1(1)(b) RRA similarly provides for indirect race discrimination where one racial group is disproportionately affected by a requirement or condition. Otherwise, the framework of the equivalent provision is the same.

Unintentional Indirect Race Discrimination

13–34   Under the RRA, if the respondent can prove that the requirement or condition was not applied with the intention of treating the complainant unfavourably on racial grounds then there can be no award of damages (s.57(3) RRA).

However, knowledge of the discriminatory effect is enough to amount to an "intention". In *J. H. Walker Ltd v. Hussain & ors* [1996] I.R.L.R. 11 EAT, the company imposed a new rule that non-statutory holidays could not be taken during their busiest period—May, June and July. Seventeen Muslim production workers, including Mr Hussain, were found to have suffered indirect race discrimination when they were disciplined for taking a day off work to celebrate Eid, one of the most important religious days in the Muslim calendar, which in that year fell on June 11. They had always previously been permitted to take a day's holiday for this purpose.

13–35   The EAT upheld the tribunal's decision that the complainants were entitled to compensation. The respondent "intends to treat the complainant unfavourably on racial grounds if he:

(a)   wants to bring about the state of affairs which constitutes the prohibited result of unfavourable treatment on racial grounds, and

(b)   knows that that prohibited result will follow from his actions.

"The fact that the company's reason or motive in adopting and applying the holiday policy was to promote its business efficiency does not, in our view, either displace the company's knowledge of the consequences which follow from applying that condition or requirement, or prevent the tribunal from inferring that the company wanted to produce a state of affairs in which the applicants were in fact treated unfavourably on racial grounds" (Mummery J.).

The complainants had suffered no financial loss but were awarded £1000 each for injury to feelings.

13–36   Also in *London Underground Ltd v. Edwards* [1995] EAT 355, a single parent suffered indirect sex discrimination when a new rostering arrangement was introduced which she could not comply with. The EAT upheld the tribunal's conclusion that the company had failed to prove that there was no intention of treating Mrs Edwards unfavourably on grounds of her sex. "It was open to the tribunal to infer that the requirement or condition was applied with knowledge of its unfavourable consequences for her as a single or lone parent. An intention to produce those consequences could be inferred" (Mummery J.). Note that compensation can now be awarded in any event for unintentional sex discrimination (see para. 13–41) but the *Edwards* case is still relevant by analogy to race cases.

Burden of Proof in showing no intention

13–37   Note that it is the respondent who has to prove that he did not apply the requirement or condition with the intention of treating the complainant unfairly on racial grounds.

Failure to remedy indirect race discrimination following declaration by the tribunal

13–38   Section 56(1)(a) RRA provides that where the tribunal finds that there has been unlawful race discrimination, it may make an order declaring the rights of the parties in relation to the act complained of. So, in a case of unintentional indirect race discrimination the tribunal may make a declaration to that effect but it may not, as we have seen, award compensation. However, if the respondent then continued to apply the unlawful requirement or condition, a tribunal faced with a subsequent complaint would be likely to infer that the respondent "intended to treat [the] employee unfavourably on racial grounds, even through his reason or motive for persisting in the action was one of business efficiency" (Mummery J. in *J.H. Walker Ltd v. Hussain and Others* [1996] I.R.L.R. 11 EAT). See also paras 13–05 to 13–06 for commentary on the power to make a declaration.

Failure to comply with a recommendation

13–39   Section 56(1)(c) RRA provides that where the tribunal finds that there has been unlawful race discrimination it may make a recommendation that the respondent take specified action to obviate or reduce the adverse effect on the complainant of the discrimination. A recommendation can be made in a case involving indirect race discrimination (see also paras 13–07 to 13–19 for commentary on the power to make a recommendation). If the respondent then fails to comply with such a recommendation, the tribunal can, if it thinks it just and equitable to do so, either increase compensation or, if an award of compensation "could have been made but was not" the tribunal may make such an award, s.56(4)(a) and (b).

13–40   The problem is that if the discrimination was unintentional and indirect, the tribunal had no power to award compensation in the first place and so it is not a case where an award of compensation "could have been made but was not". So if a recommendation is made in a case of unintentional indirect race discrimination the tribunal does not appear to have the power to subsequently award compensation if the recommendation has been ignored.

It seems, then, that we have a somewhat perverse situation. If the tribunal simply makes a declaration that a particular requirement or condition gives rise to unintentional indirect race discrimination and the respondent subsequently does nothing to remove that requirement or condition, a further complaint to the tribunal could lead to an inference being drawn that the discrimination was now intentional (see para. 13–38) and so compensation can be awarded. If, however, the tribunal had made a recommendation which is not complied with, it appears as if the tribunal has no power to then award compensation because under s.56(4)(b) it can only do so if, on the original complaint, compensation could have been awarded but was not.

Indirect Sex Discrimination

13–41 Although the rules used to be the same for unintentional indirect sex and race discrimination—no power to award compensation—the position has now changed in cases involving indirect sex discrimination. The change was introduced by means of the Sex Discrimination and Equal Pay (Miscellaneous Amendments) Regulations 1996 (S.I. 1996 No.438) which inserted sub-sections 1A and 1B into s.65 SDA. These amendments introduced a power to award compensation for unintentional indirect sex discrimination if the tribunal considers it just and equitable to do so, as well as making a declaration and/or a recommendation. The change was introduced to ensure compliance with the Equal Treatment Directive.

ENTITLEMENT TO INTEREST

13–42 The case of *Marshall v. Southampton and South West Hampshire Area Health Authority (No.2)* [1993] I.R.L.R. 445 concluded that in order to comply with the Equal Treatment Directive "the award of interest ... must therefore be regarded as an essential component of compensation for the purposes of restoring real equality of treatment." Whilst this only applied to sex discrimination cases, the Government acted to provide for the same entitlement to interest in race and disability cases. The rules on entitlement to interest are now set out in the Industrial Tribunal (Interest on Awards in Discrimination Cases) Regulations, 1996 (S.I. 1996 No.2803). The regulations also apply to equal pay claims under the Equal Pay Act, 1970.

Contrast with entitlement to interest in unfair dismissal cases

13–43 A successful complainant in an unfair dismissal case can only claim interest on compensation if it remains unpaid for 42 days after promulgation of the award. However, under the 1996 discrimination regulations interest runs from the date of the discriminatory act.

No requirement to apply for interest

13–44 Whilst it is advisable to include in the application to the tribunal (the ITI) a claim for interest in accordance with the 1996 regulations the tribunal is under a duty to consider awarding interest whether or not an application for interest has been made (Regulation 2(1)(b)). Regulation 2(1)(a) provides that the tribunal "*may* ... include interest on the sums awarded".

Note, however, that in the case of sex discrimination, a failure to award interest would probably fall foul of the principle in *Marshall (No.2)* that "interest is an essential component of compensation" under the Equal Treatment Directive. Tribunals should therefore exercise their discretion in a way which is consistent with the ETD. If the parties agree the amount of interest, the tribunal may make an award in that sum (Regulation 2(2)).

Simple Interest

13–45   Interest is calculated as simple interest which accrues from day to day. (See Regulation 3(1)). Since June 1987, daily interest has been calculated on the basis of 1/365 irrespective of whether or not the relevant year is a leap year.

Rate of Interest

13–46   The rate (in England and Wales) is the rate prescribed for the Special Investment Account (See Rule 27(1) Court Fund Rules, 1987). In Scotland the rate is that fixed by the Act of Sederunt (Interest in Sheriff Court Decrees or Extracts) 1975. See Regulation 3(2)).

The rate is currently eight per cent. This has not changed since February 1, 1993. Where, over the relevant period, the rate has varied, the tribunal may, to keep things simple, apply a median or average of those rates as seems appropriate.

13–47   A table representing the total rates from January 1980 is published annually in the Law Society Gazette (see Appendix M). The table records the month from which interest is assumed to run, together with the percentage interest rate accumulated from the first day of each month up to October 1, 1998. For calculation dates after October 1, 1998 the percentages quoted are simply increased by adding 1/365 of the special account rate from October 1, 1998 for each day up to the appropriate calculation date.

Calculation of Interest

13–48   The calculation of interest is different for financial loss and compensation for injury to feelings. In the case of injury to feelings compensation, interest is calculated on the full period from the date of the discriminatory act to the date when the calculation is made by the tribunal (Regulation 6(1)(a)).

Interest on compensation for financial loss is calculated for half this period starting on the "mid-point date" and ending on the date of calculation (Regulation 6(1)(b)). The mid-point date is the day which falls half way through the period starting with the discriminatory act and ending on the date of calculation (Regulation 4(2)). The reason for this is that financial loss does not all occur at the date of the discriminatory act (for example, a dismissal) but accrues over a period of time, and is often still accruing at the date of the tribunal hearing. To achieve a "rough and ready" fairness, the regulations provide for interest over half this period. This follows the approach taken in personal injuries cases (see *Dexter v. Courtaulds Ltd* [1984] 1 W.L.R. 372).

13–49   If the respondent has paid all or part of the compensation prior to the date when the tribunal assesses interest then the mid point would be the date half way between the date of the discriminatory act and the date of payment (The normal mid point would still apply in respect of any part of the compensation not yet paid by the respondent, Regulation 6(2)).

The regulations do give the tribunal a discretion to award interest for a different period if a "serious injustice" would be caused using the standard method of calculation (Regulation 6(3)). This may be the case where loss has accrued over a period which ended many years prior to the tribunal hearing. This was sometimes the case with the MOD pregnancy dismissal claims where women had been discharged up to 16 years prior to the claims being heard by the tribunal.

13–50   In *MOD v. Cannock and others* I.R.L.R. [1994] 509 EAT, one of the "others" was Ms Skellon. Her losses accrued between August 1, 1980 and April 15, 1983. The tribunal exercised its discretion to award interest for the period starting half way through the period of loss and ending with the date of calculation in 1993. The EAT upheld the tribunal's exercise of its discretion. Note that at the time when the EAT considered this matter the interest regulations then in force were the Sex Discrimination and Equal Pay (Remedies) Regulations 1993. They provided that the tribunal could exercise its discretion to change the period over which interest is calculated in "exceptional" cases. The 1996 regulations do not make such a reference, referring instead to cases where there would be "serious injustice" if the standard method of calculation of interest was used.

13–51   Morison J. in Mrs Skellon's case noted that, had the period between the end of the loss and the date of hearing been shorter, or if there had been a delay which was the complainant's fault, then the tribunal might well have decided to apply the standard method of calculation.

The tribunal has the discretion under Regulation 6(3) to award interest for a different period from the standard basis in respect of either all or part of the award as it considers appropriate.

13–52   Set out below is an example of an interest calculation using the table set out in Appendix M.

Example
Financial loss: £10,000
Injury to feelings: £5,000

Date of discrimination: January 1, 1998
Date of hearing/calculation: December 10, 1998
Mid point date between discrimination/hearing: June 21, 1998
Using Nelson Jones Table at Appendix M published 23.9.98:

Financial loss
Total interest from mid point to end of September 1998 = 2.67%

The rate has remained at 8% per annum. So, the additional interest for the period from the end of September 1998 (which is the date up to which the Nelson Jones Tables applies) to December 10, 1999 must be added. This equates to an additional 71 days. (The table of accumulated days October 1998–March 1999 at Appendix M can be used to assist in this calculation).

The appropriate addition is therefore:
   $8\% \times 71 \div 365 = 1.56\%$

Total interest on £10,000 from 21.6.98 will be:
   $2.67\% \times 1.56\% = 423\%$
   $£10,000 \times 4.23\% = £423$

The same calculation is used for injury to feelings but from the date of discrimination on January 1, 1998 as follows:
   $5.89\% + 1.56\% = 7.54\%$
   $£5,000 \times 7.54\% = £377$

Interest on Future Loss

13–53 No interest can be awarded in respect of any future losses which may occur after the date of calculation (Regulation 5). The EAT in *MOD v. Cannock and others* confirms that this means that no award of interest can be made in respect of compensation for pension loss.

Written Reasons

13–54 The tribunal's written statement of reasons must set out the total amount of interest and a table showing how it has been calculated or a description of the method of calculation. Only the total need be stated if the parties have agreed the amount of interest (Regulation 7(1)). If no interest is awarded, reasons must be given by the tribunal (Regulation 7(2)).

HEADS OF LOSS

13–55 There are essentially two heads of loss in discrimination cases: financial loss and non-financial compensation, akin to general damages. Each of these are considered below. In this section we will consider compensation for both financial loss and non-financial loss—primarily compensation for injury to feelings.

Financial Loss

13–56 The tribunal's task is two-fold. First, it will have to decide what losses the complainant has suffered since the discriminatory act (whether it is a failure to recruit, a failure to promote, a dismissal or a resignation following on from discrimination such as harassment). Just as with an unfair dismissal claim, the complainant should provide a schedule of loss setting out all the elements of loss—lost earnings, fringe benefits, pension, expenses incurred (see paras 3–14 to 3–60 for commentary on last pay and benefits, etc., and expenses incurred which can be recovered. See also Chapter 5 for preparation of schedule of loss and Chapter 4 for gathering evidence). Unlike the compensatory award there is no award for loss of statutory rights. Great care should be taken to ensure that all available evidence is presented to the tribunal to prove all elements of loss.

13–57 Secondly, once the tribunal is satisfied as to the elements making up the loss suffered by the complainant, the tribunal then has to consider, applying the principles relating to damages for tort, how much compensation for both past and future loss should be awarded.

The Percentage Chance Approach

13–58 In many cases of unlawful discrimination the loss suffered by the complainant is the loss of a chance : the loss of a chance to be recruited to a post, the loss of a chance of promotion, the loss of a chance to return after maternity leave if dismissed on pregnancy. Even where there has been a clear discriminatory dismissal not involving any lost chance, the tribunal still has to look at what would have happened had the dismissal not occurred. Was there a chance, for example, that at some future date the complainant would have been made redundant fairly? This chance needs to be assessed and reflected in the award of compensation. (Note that in unfair dismissal cases the tribunal often has to assess chances in a similar way. With unfair dismissal, however, the tribunal has to apply the statutory rules set out in s.123 ERA. See paras 11–03 to 11–37 for commentary on percentage reductions on "just and equitable" grounds).

13–59 The tribunal's task then, in assessing compensation for financial loss, over a period of time, which results from discrimination is not to ask what did happen in the past. "In assessing damages which depend upon its view as to what will happen in the future or would have happened in the future if something had not happened in the past [*i.e.* in this context, the act of discrimination], then the court must make an estimate as to what are the chances that a particular thing will or would have happened and reflect those chances, whether they are more or less even, in the amount of damages which it awards" (Lord Diplock in *Mallett v. McMonagle* [1970] A.C. 166, referred to by Morison J. in *MOD v. Cannock and others* [1994] I.R.L.R. 509). The case in fact was a claim by a widow of a victim killed in an accident. The court had to ask what would have happened but for the death of the deceased: "All the chances and the changes of the future must be assessed" (Lord Morris).

13–60 Once the chance of a particular course of events has been assessed this then has to be reflected in the compensation awarded. So, for example, in the case of a woman dismissed because she is pregnant the tribunal might assess the chance that she would have returned following a period of maternity leave as 80 per cent likely. To reflect this chance in the award of compensation the tribunal will award 80 per cent of her post-dismissal losses. It should be noted that in the same case other chances may need to be assessed which could also affect the compensation awarded (see paras 13–62 to 13–70). The application of the percentage chance approach to different types of claim is considered below.

Pregnancy Dismissals

13–61 The general guidance given by Morison J. in *MOD v. Cannock and others* [1994] I.R.L.R. 509 EAT has wider application although the length of the period of loss in the MOD cases is unusual (probably because it was easier for tribunals to look back and analyse what had actually happened following discharges many years ago, and partly also because they had often lost the benefit of fixed period engagements with good pay and excellent pension benefits and so the chances of continuing losses, even for those women who secured good alternative employment, were high).

13–62 Morison, J. said that the tribunal had to consider a series of hypothetical questions.

1. What are the chances that had the woman been given maternity leave, and an opportunity to return to work, she would have returned?

The question has to be answered on the basis "of the best assessment that a [tribunal] can make having regard to all the available material" Morison J. suggested that the statistics of the number of women actually returning to a particular sort of work were important in making this assessment. Whilst the tribunal may be right to consider such evidence the essential question is what the particular complainant would have done. In assessing this, general statistics are likely to be of strictly limited value. In *Greaves v. MOD* COIT (Case No. 7423/92), the tribunal considered statistics of women opting for maternity leave in the armed forces once the right to take it was introduced. Their conclusion was: "They are not helpful. In so far as they show that 49 per cent of qualifying pregnancies opted for maternity leave we take note. However, we are urged to use them as a starting point, a 'signpost'. We do not follow that advice. Like the figure of 90 per cent of ex-service personnel finding employment, such generalisations are statistically irrelevant."

13–63 Morison J. also made the point that "many women ... do not take up the right to return to work because as things turn out ... they choose to spend time with the child during the tender years". However, care should again be taken not to make assumptions which are in themselves gender based.

Another factor which is becoming increasingly relevant is that many women, who may in the past have not returned to a full time job, may now seek to return part time. (Note that a refusal by an employer to agree to a woman's request to return part time may be indirect sex discrimination). If a tribunal concludes, based on the evidence available, that there was, for example, an 80 per cent chance that she would have returned part time, then the compensation would be 80 per cent of what the part time earnings would have been.

13–64 The tribunal will also look at what the woman has in fact done since the birth of her child, because this may "shed some light on what the applicant might have done had she had the opportunity to return to work".

A woman who has made clear efforts to mitigate her loss by trying to find other work will also have a strong case for arguing that this demonstrates that there was a high percentage chance—or even a near certainty—that she would have returned to work had she been able to take maternity leave.

13–65 Note that in both *MOD v. Hunt* [1996] I.R.L.R. 139 EAT and *MOD v. Mutton* [1996] I.C.R. 590, Kay J. accepted that it was possible that the chance that a woman would have taken maternity leave and returned to work can, if there is evidence to support it, be assessed at 100 per cent. There may even be "exceptional and unusual" cases where the tribunal properly concludes that there was a 100 per cent chance that the woman in question would have gone on to complete many further years of service (*Hunt*).

> "When considering whether the woman in question would have availed herself of maternity leave had it been provided and would then have returned to service, an assessment of the chance at 100%, based on an assessment of all the evidence, would not strike us as exceptional or even unusual. At the other end of the scale, however, the assessment of the chance that she would have then proceeded to complete 10 or 22 years further service as 100% would strike us as exceptional and unusual. But that does not necessarily mean that such an assessment must be perverse." (Kay J.)

13–66 Note, however, that a differently constituted EAT in *MOD v. Nathan, The Times*, February 13, 1996 concluded that it had been "irrational" for the tribunal to find that a woman discharged on grounds of pregnancy would have continued in the armed forces from 1995 to 2004. The further into the future one looks the more uncertain it is as to what would have happened but for the discriminatory act.

13–67   2.   The second hypothetical question which Morison J. said the tribunal should ask is: What are the chances that the woman would have been in a position to return to work, had she been given the opportunity? This question is clearly linked to the first and is rarely likely to add very much by being considered separately.

      Note, also, that since the decision of the Court of Appeal in *Kwik Save*

Stores Ltd v. Greaves, and *Crees v. Royal London Mutual Insurance Society Ltd(2)* [1998] I.R.L.R. 245 CA, a woman can exercise her right to return to work following maternity leave by giving the required notice, even though she is physically unfit to return at the end of the maternity leave period. In such circumstances she could claim Statutory Sick Pay together with any Contractual Sick Pay to which she may be entitled.

As a result of this development, an argument by a respondent employer that the woman was not in a position to return to work because of ill health would be unlikely to succeed, provided the tribunal is satisfied on the evidence that she would have exercised her right to return by serving the statutory notice.

13–68   3.   The third question relates to the length of service which the woman has hypothetically lost.

This question was particularly relevant in the armed forces pregnancy dismissal cases because of the long fixed term engagements which women lost by being discharged. It may, however, also be relevant in some civilian cases where, for example, a woman has suffered a nervous breakdown as a result of harassment and is likely to be unable to work for a considerable period of time. In such circumstances the tribunal will again have to consider the hypothetical situation of what would have happened over that period had she not suffered harassment. There may be evidence of redundancies having occurred since she left her job or there may be some other evidence that at some stage she may have left that job in any event. The chances of this happening would be assessed by the tribunal as a percentage (see para. 13–71 for commentary on cumulative percentage chances).

13–69   4.   The next hypothetical question relates to the issue of promotion. What was the chance that the woman would have been promoted to a higher paid job had she not been discharged?

This may be a relevant question in the civilian context, particularly in organisations with fairly rigid career structures where employees are regularly assessed for promotion potential. Documentary evidence may be available from the personnel file, as was the case in the MOD pregnancy dismissal cases, which might shed light on the promotion prospects of the woman had she not been dismissed.

If, for example, the tribunal assesses the chance of promotion at a particular point in time as 50 per cent then she would be entitled to be compensated for 50 per cent of the additional pay she would have received from that point onwards.

Other Contingencies: Birth of a Second Child

13–70   Morison J. in *MOD v. Cannock and Others* also referred to the other contingency of the birth of a second child. In the MOD pregnancy dismissal cases, tribunals frequently decided, on the evidence available, that the chance of the woman remaining in her job, had she not been discharged, after the birth of a second child were lower. There may, however, also be evidence put forward by the woman that, had she not been discharged/dismissed from her chosen career, she would not have had another child. Again the chance of this would have to be assessed by the tribunal.

Cumulative Percentage Chance

13–71   In circumstances where the tribunal has decided that there was a particular percentage chance of the woman taking maternity leave and returning to work but has also found that at a particular point thereafter there was a reduced percentage chance that the woman would have continued in her original employment, then the tribunal has to make a "cumulative calculation on the basis of a percentage of a percentage" (Kay J. in *MOD v. Hunt* and others [1996] I.R.L.R. 139 in relation to another complainant, Mrs Donald). "The proper approach is for the tribunal first to quantify the percentage chance or chances. They should do that before considering the consequential arithmetic. Having arrived at differential percentage chances, it is then incumbent upon the tribunal to make a cumulative calculation." So if the chance that the woman would have returned following maternity leave is assessed at 80 per cent and then if the chance that she would have then returned to work following the birth of a second child is assessed at 50 per cent, compensation for the period following the birth of the second child is subject to a percentage chance of 50 per cent of 80 per cent = 40 per cent.

The Court of Appeal later considered the same issue and agreed with the EAT that the cumulative percentage chance approach should be adopted (*MOD v. Wheeler and others* I.R.L.R. [1998] 22 CA).

Recruitment

13–72   The percentage chance approach is also used in circumstances where an employer has discriminated against someone in the recruitment process. If the tribunal concludes that, but for the discrimination, the complainant would have been offered the job, then full compensation for financial loss can be awarded (a 100 per cent chance). However, the tribunal might instead conclude that the discrimination in the recruitment process has led to the applicant losing the chance of being offered the job and that the "chance" is rated at less than 100 per cent.

If, for example, there were two good applicants for a job, the tribunal might conclude that, but for the discriminatory exclusion of one female applicant, there was a 50 per cent chance that she would have been recruited. Compensation would then be based on 50 per cent of the financial loss suffered.

13–73   In the unusual circumstances that the man or woman suffers financial loss over a number of years as a result of such a discriminatory refusal to offer the post, then similar hypothetical questions may have to be asked as outlined by Morison J. in *Cannock* (See paras 13–62 to 13–69). For example, what was the chance of her remaining in the post beyond the end of the probationary period, or for any particular further period of loss claimed?

In cases of disability discrimination involving recruitment, the disadvantages that some disabled people may suffer in the job market may mean that a substantial period of loss might result from a discriminatory failure to recruit. The following example demonstrates how the percentage chance approach might be applied in a disability discrimination case involving recruitment.

13–74   "A" is not recruited to a post because he is partially sighted. The company fails to consider making "reasonable adjustments" to the job which might have removed the "substantial disadvantage" suffered by "A" as a result of his disability (see s.6(1) DDA: duty to make reasonable adjustments). The tribunal might conclude that had the company made reasonable adjustments to the nature of the job, there was a 50 per cent chance that "A" would have been recruited. Thus his compensation would be reduced by 50 per cent. The tribunal might also decide that there was a 50 per cent chance that "A" would have been employed for, say, two years had he been recruited. Using the cumulative percentage chance approach he would be awarded 50 per cent of 50 per cent = 25 per cent × his financial loss for two years less any earnings or benefits actually received by way of mitigation.

In the case of some disabilities the tribunal might, on the evidence available, decide that there was a chance that he would have been recruited but for the discrimination, but that the nature of the disability is such that there was a chance that the employer might have to subsequently terminate his employment because he becomes unfit to work. The tribunal can assess the percentage chance of this happening and reduce compensation accordingly.

Lost Chance of Promotion

13–75   Where the complainant has lost the chance of promotion as a result of unlawful discrimination, the tribunal will assess that chance on a percentage basis. The tribunal might conclude that there was a 100 per cent chance that the complainant would have been promoted but for the discrimination and accordingly award the full difference in salary between the two jobs. Alternatively, the tribunal might find, on the evidence, that there was a percentage chance of less than 100 per cent.

In *Atkinson and Tomlinson v. East Birmingham Health Authority* Case No 9474–5/89 the applicants were senior female radiographers. They applied for promotion to a senior 1 post. The job went to a male colleague on a lower grade. The tribunal found that they had both suffered sex discrimination. Assessing the chance that each of them would have been appointed had an objective approach been taken the tribunal found that there was a 90 per cent chance that Ms Tomlinson would have been promoted.

13–76   Assessing Ms Atkinson's chances separately the tribunal found that there was a 20 per cent chance that she would have been promoted. (This particular conclusion must be open to some doubt). In each case the tribunal found that suitable promotion posts occurred, on average, every seven years and accordingly the loss was assessed over a seven-year period and then reduced by the appropriate percentage (10 per cent reduction in the case of Ms Tomlinson and 80 per cent in the case of Ms Atkinson).

In *Williams v. Newport Borough Council* COIT 1908/128, Mrs Williams suffered sex discrimination in not being considered for promotion. The tribunal then concluded that there was only a 25 per cent chance of promotion. She was likely to be promoted in two years' time and so she was awarded 25 per cent of the difference in net salary for two years.

Child Care Costs

13–77   In cases involving pregnancy dismissals, when the tribunal assesses the loss suffered, they will take into account the question of whether, had the woman been able to take maternity leave and return to work, she would have incurred child care costs. If such costs would have been incurred then the lost wages suffered will be reduced by the full amount of the child care costs. The tribunal should not take into account the possibility that a husband or partner might have met half the cost. "It seems to us obvious that if only half the notional costs are allowed for, there will be over-compensation" Morison J. in *MOD v. Cannock and others* [1994] I.R.L.R. 509 EAT.

Mitigation

13–78 The common law rules on mitigation apply in exactly the same way in discrimination cases as in unfair dismissal cases. Commentary on mitigation is set out in Chapter 19.

Remoteness

13–79 Issues relating to remoteness of loss are considered at paragraphs 10–15 to 10–19 in the context of unfair dismissal cases. Similar principles apply. If some event occurs following the act of discrimination which breaks the "chain of causation" then further losses will not be the responsibility of the respondent.

Order of Deductions/Reductions

13–80 In both discrimination and unfair dismissal cases, if the tribunal concludes that there should be some percentage reduction in compensation (see Chapter 11 re. unfair dismissal and paras 13–58 to 13–76 re. discrimination) then issues may arise as to whether that reduction should be applied before or after deducting payments from the employer or payments received from other sources by way of mitigation of loss. The method used can have a significant bearing on the ultimate level of compensation. These issues are considered in Chapter 15.

Future Loss

13–81 If, at the date of the tribunal hearing, the complainant has managed to secure fresh employment with a remuneration package at least as good as in the job which he lost as a result of the discrimination, then the tribunal will only need to consider past-loss. (An exception to this may be where the new job is temporary and evidence is produced to the tribunal that it is likely to come to an end soon. For example, the complainant may produce a letter or affidavit from the new employer which confirms that the new post will come to an end shortly. In such circumstances the tribunal would need to consider the possibility of future losses.) If, however, the loss is still continuing because the complainant has failed to find work or because she is earning less than in her previous employment, the question of assessment of future losses arises. Just as with unfair dismissal, the task facing the tribunal is inevitably speculative. It cannot be an exact science.

13–82 If the anticipated period of future loss is limited—perhaps a period of a few months up to say two years—the approach taken can be straightforward. The tribunal would first assess the total net loss which is likely to be suffered over the relevant period, deducting any earnings which the complainant is likely to receive, or if the tribunal believes there has been a failure to mitigate, (see Chapter 19) deducting earnings which he would have received had he properly mitigated his loss.

13–83 Then the tribunal applies any percentage reductions in accordance with the principles of assessing the chances of what would have happened had there been no discrimination (see paras 13–58 to 13–76). There may also be an additional element of loss if the tribunal has assessed the percentage chance that the complainant would have secured promotion had he not suffered discrimination. The tribunal may then make some reduction in the resultant total loss to take account of early payment.

> *Example: Pregnancy Dismissal*
>
> | | | |
> |---|---|---:|
> | Total lost net wages from previous employment over 2 years | | 20,000 |
> | *Less*: Net earnings from new employment | | 10,000 |
> | | | 10,000 |
> | Percentage chance that woman would have returned to work after maternity leave | | 80% |
> | | Total | 8,000 |
> | *Less*: £1,000 for early payment | | 1,000 |
> | **Award for financial loss** | | **£7,000** |

Long Periods of Future Loss

13–84   The position is more complicated if the tribunal has found that there is likely to be a long period of future loss. Given that the basis for assessing compensation in discrimination cases is the measure of damages in tort, some guidance can be gained from personal injuries cases. It is, of course, always important to ensure that, in translating the principles used in personal injuries cases to the discrimination field, one makes relevant comparisons. Morison J. in *MOD v. Cannock and others* [1994] I.R.L.R. 509 EAT said in relation to assessment of compensation in a pregnancy dismissal case "... a Tribunal should not make an award of a size which is more appropriate to compensate a person who has some kind of long-term disability".

13–85   This, of course, does not address the fact that, in some discrimination cases, the complainant may have suffered a long-term disability as a result of the discriminatory act—for example a nervous breakdown following serious harassment. In disability cases, despite the increased protection afforded by the DDA, the complainant may well have a serious disadvantage in the labour market making it more difficult to mitigate loss and making a long period of future loss more likely (see 19–10 to 19–13 for commentary on how tribunals recognise that personal characteristics and discrimination in the labour market might affect the chances of getting other work following dismissal).

Another example of a situation in which a long period of future loss might occur is where the complainant has lost a career with high earnings and good promotion prospects. This was the case with several of the MOD pregnancy dismissal claims (where the complainant had also lost the benefit of a fixed period engagement or commission). The complainant may well be expected to secure new employment but if the earnings are lower and if this is likely to continue then a substantial period of future loss may have to be assessed.

The Multiplier/Multiplicand

13–86   If the tribunal finds that there is likely to be a long period of future loss stretching over a number of years it is no good simply multiplying the annual loss by the total number of years of anticipated future loss. This would over-compensate the complainant because he will be able to invest the lump sum received and will receive interest on that investment. The assumption is that, in order to compensate the complainant for the full period of loss, the complainant would draw the interest from the invested lump sum plus an element of the capital. As each year goes by, the interest element reduces (as the lump sum gets smaller), and so more capital has to be taken until at the end of the period of loss the lump sum is exhausted. The challenge for the tribunal is to try to determine the lump sum necessary to compensate for the loss on the basis of the complainant acting in the way described above.

13–87 The approach used in personal injuries cases is to ascertain the annual loss as at the date of the assessment of compensation. This is called the multiplicand. A multiplier is then applied to the multiplicand to determine the total sum. The crucial question is how to determine the size of the multiplier. In personal injuries cases where the court may have to ascertain loss for the remainder of a person's normal working life, a multiplier of 14 or 15 is often used for a plaintiff in their mid-thirties. In personal injury cases, the court's approach is first to determine the appropriate rate of interest which the plaintiff will obtain on investing the lump sum. It seems that 4.5 per cent is generally regarded as an appropriate rate to use (see the *Wells v. Wells* [1997] P.I.Q.R. QI CA, although leave has been given to appeal to the House of Lords).

13–88 In the discrimination context, Morison J. in *MOD v. Cannock and others* [1994] I.R.L.R. 509 EAT said "The multiplier will reflect the court's practice of using an assumed real rate of return of between 4 per cent and 5 per cent, normally 4.5 per cent". If the court is assessing loss up to retirement age, the court is likely to use tables produced by a working party chaired by Sir Michael Ogden to determine the appropriate multiplier on the basis of the rate of interest of say 4.5 per cent (see Appendix N for Ogden tables). Using these tables one can ascertain the appropriate multiplier by reference to the plaintiff's age and the selected rate of interest.

The approach of using a multiplicand/multiplier in discrimination cases was, as we have seen, endorsed by Morison J. in *MOD v. Cannock and others* [1994] I.R.L.R. 509 EAT. The tribunal should normally calculate damages for future loss of earnings "having regard to the matters we have referred to [in other words the hypothetical questions of what would have happened had the discrimination not occurred (see paras 13–62 to 13–69)] by using the usual multiplicand and multiplier method adopted by the courts."

13–89 So, for example, if the tribunal in a pregnancy dismissal case decides that there is a 50 per cent chance that the woman would have returned after maternity leave, then the annual net loss is reduced by 50 per cent to determine the multiplicand. This is then multiplied by the appropriate multiplier. Deciding what the multiplier should be may be a difficult task.

In many of the MOD pregnancy dismissal cases tribunals adopted a rough and ready approach of dividing the number of years of future loss by two and adding one to determine the multiplier. For example, if the tribunal decided that the complainant should be compensated for future loss for a period of five years, the calculation would be as follows:

Future Loss 5 years
Divide by 2 $2\frac{1}{2}$
Add 1 $3\frac{1}{2}$
Multiplier = $3\frac{1}{2}$

13–90 Morison J. in *Cannock* said that such an approach was "not sufficiently accurate to be reliable in every case". This suggests that it may be an approach which is acceptable in some cases. The following factors may be taken into account by the tribunal in determining whether there should be a discount or an enhancement applied to the multiplier in any particular case—the job prospects taking into account the type of work of the complainant, levels of unemployment, the complainant's state of health, and promotion prospects.

The extent of guidance on the use of the multiplicand/multiplier approach in discrimination cases is unfortunately still very limited. Set out below is an example of the calculation of future loss in a pregnancy dismissal case where compensation was settled:

Annual Loss	£19,622.40
Less 25 per cent for tax and NI (agreed basis between parties)	−£4,716.80
	£14,716.80
Less current net earnings	−£3,750.00
	£10,996.80
Apply percentage chance 80 per cent	8,773.44
Multiplier Based on $7\frac{1}{2}$ years future service 4.35 =	£38,164.46

13–91 In *Thompson v. MOD* COIT 51863/93 the tribunal considered future loss of seven and a half years. They also decided that there was a 65 per cent chance that the complainant would have stayed in the army throughout that period which would have taken her up to the end of her engagement. The tribunal therefore calculated her current annual loss before applying the 65 per cent chance and using a multiplier of 4.5. The calculation for future loss was as follows:

	£	£
Gross annual earnings if in Army		21,177.30
Less 1) Tax and NI	5,294.33	
2) Average net earnings	7,286.64	
		12,580.97
Multiplicand		8596.30
Using Multiplier of 4.5 =		38,683.49
65% chance		£25,144.28

13–92 In the case of *D'Souza v. London Borough of Lambeth* [1997] I.R.L.R. 677, the question of the appropriate multiplier was considered by the EAT. Mr D'Souza had suffered racial discrimination. His compensation included future loss for the rest of his working life, which was four years and ten months. The tribunal had used a multiplier of 4.5 in order to determine compensation for this future loss. The EAT said that this multiplier could not be justified. "Applying the Ogden tables, it seems to us that a fair multiplier would be in the order of 4.16 which would produce a total figure (in round terms) of £150,000" (Morison J.).

Compensation for net loss

13–93   Compensation for financial loss is based on net loss suffered by the complainant. If the total loss exceeds £30,000 then account must be taken of the fact that compensation above this figure will be subject to tax even though it is based on net loss. To avoid what would effectively be double taxation, a grossing up exercise must be carried out on compensation above £30,000. This is considered at paras 6–67 to 6–72.

Pension Loss

13–94   If the complainant has lost the benefits of a pension scheme as a result, for example, of a discriminatory dismissal then she should be compensated for that loss (see Chapter 20 for commentary on assessment of compensation for pension loss).

Level of Discrimination Awards

13–95   Median or average levels of award may be of general interest, but they are of no real assistance in determining compensation in any particular case. Kay J. in *MOD v. Hunt and others* [1996] I.C.R. 554 said that "an average figure tends to conceal as much as it discloses when put forward simply as a raw average". For what it is worth, the latest annual survey carried out by Equal Opportunities Review (reported in Issue 8, number 81, September/October, 1998) found that average compensation awards were £4,556 (sex discrimination), £8,220 (race discrimination) and £3,743 (disability discrimination).

What these figures do not show is what happened in all those cases which were settled. ACAS statistics show that of 5,245 sex discrimination cases in 1996 39 per cent resulted in settlement. Of 2,711 race discrimination cases in the same year 29 per cent settled. The latest Annual Reports of the Equal Opportunities Commission and the Commission for Racial Equality show that in cases which they assisted the average awards were £17,142 and £7,933, respectively.

GENERAL DAMAGES—NON FINANCIAL LOSS

Injury to Feelings

Statutory Provisions

13–96   The basis for the assessment of compensation under all three discrimination Acts (the SDA, RRA and DDA) is the measure of damages in tort (see para. 13–24). There is, therefore, an entitlement to general damages for non-pecuniary loss as well as compensation for financial loss. In personal injuries cases compensation can be awarded for pain and suffering, and loss of amenity and enjoyment of life, and loss of congenial employment. The three discrimination Acts specifically provide for compensation for injury to feelings (s.66(4) SDA, s.57 (4) RRA and s.8(4) DDA).

Sections 66(4) SDA and 57(4) RRA both state:

> "For the avoidance of doubt it is hereby declared that damages in respect of an unlawful act of discrimination may include compensation for injury to feelings whether or not they include compensation under any other head".

The wording only is insignificantly different in s.8(4) DDA.

Action Short of Dismissal

13–97　It is now established that an employee who has suffered action short of dismissal as a result of trade union activities (s.146(1) TULR(C)A1992) is entitled to recover compensation for injury to feelings as well as for financial loss. Note that there are a number of provisions Part V of the ERA which give rise to a claim for compensation as a result of suffering a detriment during employment. They are as follows:

Section 44　Health and Safety cases

Section 45　Sunday working for shop and betting workers

Section 45A　Working Time Regulation cases

Section 46　Trustees of occupational pension schemes

Section 47　Employee Representatives

In all these cases therefore it seems as if the complainant can claim compensation for injury to feelings (see also paras 22–02 to 22–15). The guidance in this section is relevant to awards for injury to feelings in cases of action short of dismissal/detriment during employment.

Preparing evidence in support of a claim for compensation for injury to feelings

13–98　At paras 3–26 to 3–31, guidance is given on the task of compiling evidence to support a claim for injury to feelings. Evidence to support the claim is very important because it is for the complainant to demonstrate to the tribunal the nature and extent of the injury to feelings.

Onus on complainant to establish claim

13–99　It is for the complainant to establish the heads of claim including injury to feelings. However, in *Murray v. Powertech (Scotland) Ltd* [1992] I.R.L.R. 257, Lord Mayfield said that all that is required of a complainant is to state the claim for injury to feelings: "In our view it is almost inevitable in sex discrimination cases that a claim for hurt feelings be made". The tribunal had found that Ms Murray had been "shocked" by her dismissal when she was pregnant. That was probably a "sufficient indication ... that the matter of hurt feelings had been raised". The "head of claim for hurt feelings is so fundamental to a sex discrimination claim that it is quite often the only head of claim". The same reasoning applies to race and disability cases. However, in order to be adequately compensated for hurt suffered, it is incumbent upon the complainant to do more than simply raise the issue. As we have seen in paras 3–26 to 3–31 evidence should be carefully considered so as to ensure that the tribunal gets the full picture.

Award for injury to feelings not automatic

13–100　Despite the strong prospect of some award for injury to feelings if the complainant has raised the issue, an award does not automatically follow a finding of unlawful discrimination.

In *Alexander v. Home Office* [1988] I.R.L.R. 190, May L.J. said "Whilst I agree that in the substantial majority of discrimination cases the unlawful conduct will cause personal hurt, in the sense of injury to feelings, ... I do not think that this must 'inevitably' follow". The court or tribunal may draw an inference that the discrimination will cause "hurt" but simply proving race discrimination "is not in itself a factor affecting damages".

In *MOD v. Cannock and others* [1994] I.R.L.R. 509 EAT, Morison J. supported this analysis confirming that "injury must be proved". He also observed that it "will often be easy to prove, in the sense that no tribunal will take much persuasion that the anger, distress and affront caused by the act of discrimination has injured the applicant's feelings".

Award must compensate but not have a deterrent element

13–101 Awards for injury to feeling should not include an element specifically designed to act as a deterrent to the employer. The award should simply be to compensate the complainant for the injury to her feelings. Morison J. in *MOD v. Cannock* referred to the importance of compensation being full, and not subject to a cap (*Marshall (No.2)*). This applies equally to injury to feelings as it does to compensation for financial loss. However, the EAT rejected the suggestion that this meant the award could include a factor in respect of deterrence.

Knowledge of discrimination

13–102 It seems clear that to recover compensation for injury to feelings the complainant does not have to demonstrate that at the time of the discriminatory act she knew that it was unlawful. The suggestion that such knowledge was necessary was made obiter by Lawton L.J. in *Skyrail Oceanic Ltd v. Coleman* CA [1981] I.C.R. 864. However, in all the MOD pregnancy dismissal cases, women were discharged long before it was established that the practice of dismissing women when they got pregnant was unlawful. This was no impediment to the recovery of compensation for injured feelings. If distress, hurt or suffering is experienced as a result of something the employer does it does not matter that she only subsequently discovers that the employer's behaviour was unlawful. She has suffered hurt feelings as a result of action taken by the employer which is unlawful. It is, of course, possible that knowledge that particular behaviour was unlawful may cause added distress and therefore a higher award of compensation. That, of course, is a question of fact for the tribunal to consider.

Loss of Congenial Employment

13–103 In personal injury cases, "loss of congenial employment" is a recognised head of damage (see *Hale v. London Underground* [1993] P.I.Q.R. Q30—fireman's loss of job and *Morris v. Johnson Matthey* [1968] 112 S.J. 32 which related to the loss of a satisfying, skilled job).

What is loss of congenial employment?

13–104 Morison J. in *MOD v. Cannock and others* [1994] I.R.L.R. 509 EAT described "loss of congenial employment" as "loss of job satisfaction". He also quoted Lord Williams QC in *Saunders v. London Fire and Civil Defence Authority* (unreported) "He enjoyed his work not only because it provided him with employment and a wage but because he had a pride in it, he did it well, he liked the companionship of his fellows and, indeed, took a prominent part in the social life of the fire station. It is not to be overlooked this item, the value of amenity in chosen work at which he excels".

In the discrimination context, Morison J. considered that there is "sufficient overlap" between loss of congenial employment and injury to feelings for it to be appropriate to make one award which can include an element for "loss of a chosen career which gave job satisfaction".

Note, therefore, the importance of giving evidence in support of an assertion that a discriminatory act has led to the loss of employment which the complainant found to be congenial, which he took pride in, etc. (see para. 3–28 for guidance on evidence).

Loss of Career Prospects

13–105   There is, however, no head of damages to compensate a complainant for loss of career prospects and the award for injury to feelings should not include any element to reflect such loss. This is to be dealt with as financial loss applying the principles set out in paragraphs 13–56 to 13–95 (Morison J. in *Cannock*).

Separate Awards Against Individual Respondents

13–106   The tribunal may make awards in respect of injury to feelings against not only the respondent employer (or former employer) but also against other named respondents who may, for example, have been the perpetrators of serious harassment. In *Armitage, Marsden and HM Prison Service v. Johnson* [1997] I.R.L.R. 162 EAT, a case involving racial harassment of a prison officer, awards of £500 for injury to feelings were made against two officers. The tribunal considered that they should be "personally responsible for their unlawful acts of discrimination". One had acted out of "sheer malice", the other had "victimised" Mr Johnson. The Prison Service was ordered to pay £20,000 for injury to feelings and a further £7,500 for aggravated damages.

This case follows the usual pattern where individual respondents have relatively modest awards made against them. However, this does not have to be the case. If the tribunal concludes, on the basis of applying the principles set out in this section, that the injury to feelings is substantial and a particular individual respondent is primarily responsible, then it can exercise its discretion to make a larger award against that person.

Foreseeability

13–107   As stated at para. 13–25, the test of whether damages are recoverable in tort is foreseeability. This applies equally to the question of compensation for injury to feelings as it does to compensation for financial loss. The injured feelings must relate directly to the discriminatory act (*Coleman v. Skyrail Oceanic Ltd* [1981] I.R.L.R. 398 CA).

In the context of "injury to feelings", the complainant can recover compensation in respect of an unforeseeable form of a foreseeable type of injury and for unforeseeable consequences of a foreseeable type of injury (see, in respect of personal injury cases, *Hughes v. Lord Advocate* [1963] A.C. 837, *Bradford v. Robinson Rentals Ltd* [1967] 1 All E.R. 267 and *Smith v. Leech Brown & Co Ltd* [1962] 2 Q.B. 405).

If, therefore, it is foreseeable that an employee will suffer some sort of nervous distress or disorder as a result of discriminatory behaviour, but she actually suffers a nervous breakdown which might not itself have been foreseeable, the respondent is likely to be liable to pay compensation in respect of that breakdown.

Take the victim as you find them: subjective test

13–108   Linked to the above is the fact that the respondent must take the victim as he finds him or her. One employee may suffer distress as a result of behaviour which would have little or no effect on someone else. Compensation must relate to the detriment actually suffered by the complainant.

The test, then, appears to be largely subjective but in *Snowball v. Gardner Merchant Ltd* [1987] I.R.L.R. 397, Sir Ralph Kilner-Brown indicated that the test has both a subjective and an objective element. "There has to be an assessment of injury to the woman's feelings, which must be looked at not only subjectively with reference to her as an individual but objectively with reference to what any ordinary reasonable female employee would feel."

Evidence of Woman's Character in Sexual Harassment Cases

13–109   The tribunal has to assess the extent to which the complainant has actually suffered a detriment in determining compensation for injury to feelings. In sexual harassment cases, the respondent may seek to argue that evidence of a woman's attitude to sexual matters demonstrates that she might not have found particular behaviour very upsetting and therefore might not have suffered much of a detriment. The issue may be relevant to both liability and to the level of compensation.

In *Snowball v. Gardner Merchant Ltd* [1987] I.R.L.R. 397, the EAT held that such evidence might be relevant and that a tribunal was entitled to decide to hear it. At the tribunal, Ms Snowball had been cross-examined about her sexual attitudes. She had, it was alleged, talked to other employees about her bed as a "play-pen" and about her black satin sheets. The employer wanted to call evidence to establish the truth of the allegations. The appeal to the EAT was against the Chairman's ruling that such evidence was admissible.

13–110   In the case of *Wileman v. Minilec Engineering Ltd* [1988] I.R.L.R. 144 EAT, the tribunal took into account evidence that Miss Wileman on occasion wore clothes which were "scanty and provocative". She had also put up with sexual harassment by a director for over four years and had found it only an irritation but was not upset by it, decided the tribunal.

The EAT accepted that, in other cases, the remarks made by the director may constitute "very great discrimination and cause very great detriment". However, that is for the tribunal to decide having seen and heard the witnesses. The EAT said that the tribunal was entitled to take into account evidence of how Miss Wileman dressed, "as an element in deciding whether the harassment to which she was subjected really did constitute a detriment", Popplewell J.

Needless to say, such evidence needs to be treated with great caution and tribunals will be wary of making assumptions about how a woman copes with sexual harassment on the basis of what she chooses to wear.

Compensation for Personal Injury

13–111   If the complainant suffers a physical or mental injury as a result of a discriminatory act such as harassment, then the tribunal may, it seems, award compensation specifically under the head of loss for personal injury. This is in accordance with the assessment of damages in tort.

In the case of *Thomas v. London Borough of Hackney* Case No. 49261/93, EOR 34, a London North Industrial Tribunal awarded £7,000 for injury to feelings and a further sum of £10,000 for personal injury. The case involved a dispute over the completion of an expenses claim. Mr Thomas, a Jamaican of Indian descent, was employed as a social worker by the council. His manager, Mr O'Deane, a West Indian of African descent, refused to authorise the claim because it had not been completed correctly. This lead to tension between the two men. Mr Thomas felt humiliated. He swore at Mr O'Deane which led to Mr O'Deane pursuing a grievance claim. A more senior manager arranged a meeting to try to resolve the problem. During the meeting, Mr O'Deane lost his temper. He racially abused and physically attacked Mr Thomas. Mr Thomas was physically injured and traumatised. Three months later he left his job and had not worked again by the date of the tribunal hearing.

13–112 The tribunal considered an expert psychological report which stated that Mr Thomas was still suffering severe depression and moderate levels of anxiety. He also had suicidal thoughts caused, in part, by the physical trauma of the assault, the racial insults and the failure by the council to respond adequately. The recommended treatment was that Mr Thomas should be given therapy and that he take anti-depressants. The tribunal found that Mr Thomas was suffering "moderately severe psychiatric damage which appears to have had a lasting effect". In assessing the appropriate level of compensation the tribunal took account of the Judicial Studies Board guidelines for assessment of general damages. (These guidelines are published annually to assist judges and practitioners in the assessment of general damages for the range of injuries which might be sustained.)

Behaviour of the Respondent in the Course of the Litigation

13–113 The impact of a discriminatory act, (particularly in certain serious cases of harassment), may continue for a considerable period of time. It may also be made worse by the way in which the respondent behaves in the course of tribunal proceedings brought by the complainant in order to obtain some remedy. On the other hand, if a respondent employer readily accepts that discrimination has been suffered and offers an apology this is likely to limit the extent of the distress and, accordingly, limit the scale of compensation for injured feelings.

In *Orlando v. Didcot Power Station Sports and Social Club* [1996] I.R.L.R. 262 EAT, Morison J. said "the willingness of the respondent to admit that he has acted in breach of the discrimination legislation may well help to reduce the hurt which is felt. Here the employers made such an admission almost immediately after the allegation had been made against them for the first time. Mrs Orlando was therefore spared the indignity and further hurt of having to rehearse the nature of her treatment." Note also that in *Armitage, Marsden and HM Prison Service v. Johnson* [1997] I.R.L.R. 162 EAT, Smith J. accepted that the respondent could take steps which could mitigate the award of compensation. "However we would think that the greatest mitigation would have been an apology which we are told has never been offered."

13–114 However, in *McConnell v. Police Authority for Northern Ireland* [1997] I.R.L.R. 625, the Northern Ireland Court of Appeal cautioned against increasing compensation simply because an employer defends a claim in the tribunal. Where a defence is "honestly put forward and the complainant is treated with propriety in the proceedings, the fact that his case or his recollection may be challenged is an insufficient reason without more to regard the employer's conduct as aggravating the damages". In this case, the Northern Ireland Court of Appeal ruled that there should be a single award which may "include any features which may have had the effect of aggravating the sense of injury felt by the complainant. The final result of this assessment will be a single figure reflecting the total injury to his feelings which may in appropriate cases include an element of aggravation" (Lord Chief Justice Carswell) (see also paras 13–126 to 13–134 on Aggravated Damages).

Summarising the guidance from these cases, the important issue is the assessment of the extent of the complainant's injured feelings. A speedy recognition of wrongdoing, together with an apology, self evidently is likely to limit the complainant's hurt feelings. If the litigation has been honestly conducted, and the complainant treated properly, then it may be unlikely that the injury is aggravated, although the Court of Appeal in *McConnell* left open the possibility that there may be some cases in which it could.

13–115   However, where the respondent's behaviour in the litigation and in the tribunal hearing itself falls below acceptable standards then this is likely to aggravate the injury suffered by the complainant and thereby increase the award of compensation. This is generally characterised as aggravated damages which is considered further at paras 13–126 to 13–134.

An example of the respondent's conduct of litigation increasing the award of compensation is the case of *Elmi v. Harrods* 13 November 1997 Case no. 23329/93 and EOR 35. Mrs Elmi applied for a post with a company which had a florist concession at Harrods. She could not take up the job because Harrods refused store approval. The case went to the Court of Appeal where it was established that Mrs Elmi and other staff employed by concessionaires at Harrods were protected against discrimination on the part of Harrods. The original tribunal had decided that the refusal to give store clearance was on racial grounds. When it went back to the tribunal to consider the issue of compensation, £15,000 was awarded for injury to feelings and aggravated damages.

13–116   The aggravated damages element of £7,500, reflected the tribunal's view of the way in which Harrods had conducted itself in the litigation. "There was lying and deceit on the part of Harrods personnel to conceal that act of discrimination. Even the documentary evidence was manipulated. At the hearing of the case, there was dishonest testimony and a humiliating counter-attack against the applicant. She was wrongly described as unclean, unkempt and having untamed hair and unpolished speech and that was a very injurious attack to make upon her in public. It was all part of the malicious way in which Harrods personnel decided to contest the complaint. Finally ... there has been no apology. We could understand the absence of an apology while the issue of liability was pending. Once the Court of Appeal had given its decision, it was open to Harrods to accept that there had been discrimination both on the facts and in law and to give an apology to Mrs Elmi to mitigate the damage to her."

Such damages in respect of the respondent's conduct of the litigation must, as already stated, be assessed on the basis of compensating the complainant and not punishing the defendant (see para. 13–131 on aggravated damages).

Size of Awards for Injury to Feelings

13–117   Prior to the statutory cap on compensation for sex and race discrimination being lifted (see paras 13–26 to 13–31) it appeared as if the cap had the effect of putting an artificial limit on compensation for injury to feelings. In *Noone v. North West Thames Regional Health Authority* [1988] I.R.L.R. 195, the Court of Appeal specifically made reference to the statutory limit (which was then £7,500) when assessing the appropriate level of compensation for injury to feelings—set at £3,000 in that case which concerned the failure to appoint Dr Noone to a post. This amounted to race discrimination.

Now the cap has gone and although, initially, cases which preceded the lifting of the cap were still used as guidance (see *Orlando v. Didcot Power Station Sports and*

Social Club [1996] I.R.L.R. 262, in which the EAT followed the guidance of the Court of Appeal in *Noone*) there has recently been an upward trend in the amount that tribunals will award particularly for serious harassment. It is also clear that tribunals no longer feel themselves constrained in the way they may have done prior to the lifting of the cap. Smith J. in *Armitage, Marsden and HM Prison Service v. Johnson* [1997] I.R.L.R. 162, specifically said "We think the award in Noone might well have been higher had there been no statutory limit."

Guidance

13–118   The EAT in *Armitage* summarised the principles for assessing the level of compensation for injury to feelings. The principles were drawn from two particular authorities: *John v. MGN* [1996] 3 W.L.R. 593, a libel case involving Elton John in which the Court of Appeal reduced compensatory damages from £75,000 to £25,000 stating that libel juries should have some regard to the level of awards in personal injury cases; and *Alexander v. Home Office* [1988] I.R.L.R. 190, a case of racial discrimination by prison officers against a prisoner. The principles should apply equally to sex, race and disability cases. The principles were set out as follows:

1.   Awards for injury to feelings are compensatory and should be just to both parties. They should compensate fully without punishing the tortfeasor. Feelings of indignation at the tortfeasor's conduct should not be allowed to inflate the award.

2.   Awards should not be too low. That would diminish respect for the policy of anti-discrimination legislation. Society has condemned discrimination and awards must ensure that it is seen to be wrong. On the other hand, awards should be restrained as excessive awards could be seen as the way to untaxed riches.

3.   Awards should bear some broad general similarity to the range of awards in personal injury cases, not by reference to any particular type of injury award but to the whole range of such awards.

4.   In exercising their discretion in assessing the sum, tribunals should remind themselves of the value in everyday life of the sum they have in mind, either by reference to purchasing power or by reference to earnings.

5.   Tribunals should bear in mind the need for public respect for the level of awards made.

Minimum Awards

13–119   Whilst each case is to be judged on its own merits, a general rule of thumb is that £500 is regarded as a minimum level of compensation if some injury to feelings has been suffered. This was the view of the EAT in *Sharifi v. Strathclyde Regional Council* [1992] I.R.L.R. 259 EAT.

Also in *MOD v. Hunt and others* [1996] I.R.L.R. 139, Kay J. said (in relation to one of the other women, Mrs Anderson, whose case was also subject to appeal) "A perusal of recent authorities ... in cases of race discrimination (*Sharifi, Deane v. London Borough of Ealing and another* [1993] I.R.L.R. 209 and *Alexander v. Home Office* [1988] I.R.L.R. 190) establishes that there is an emerging picture of £500 being at or near the minimum".

13–120   Given that in *Armitage* the EAT said that tribunals should remind themselves of the value in everyday life of the sum they have in mind, it may be that tribunals will progressively uplift this "minimum" figure somewhat to take account of the increase in the cost of living and in wages. It will be noted, however, from the Case Digest at paras 13–137 to 13–183 that tribunals do sometimes exercise their discretion to award lower sums than £500.

Tribunal's discretion

13–121   The tribunal has to exercise its discretion in assessing the level of compensation for injury to feelings, applying the principles set out above. The exercise of that discretion will not be interfered with on appeal unless the tribunal has "acted on a wrong principle of law or have misapprehended the facts or . . . have made a wholly erroneous estimate of the damage suffered" (Lord Justice Lawton in *Coleman v. Skyrail Oceanic Ltd* [1981] I.R.L.R. 398).

See also *Suraju Deen Tiyamiyu v. London Borough of Hackney and others* (1998) (LTL 20/2/98) in which the Court of Appeal reinstated the tribunal's original award for injury to feelings of £13,500 after the EAT had reduced it to £7,500. The tribunal's award had not been perverse (see also case digest at para. 13–178).

Guidance on injury to feelings awards: termination of pregnancy cases

13–122   Up until 1991, women in the armed forces who became pregnant were discharged by the Ministry of Defence. This policy was subsequently accepted as unlawful, being contrary to the Equal Treatment Directive. Most of the subsequent litigation involved women who were discharged in accordance with this unlawful policy. Many other women chose to have their pregnancies terminated and some of them pursued claims asserting that they, too, had been discriminated against as a result of the unlawful policy and that they had suffered a detriment—the loss of their unborn child. Those women had not suffered financial loss because they had kept their employment but they claimed compensation for injury to feelings.

The cases of *MOD v. O'Hare* and *MOD v. Lowe* were considered by the EAT ([1997] I.C.R. 306) following appeals by the MOD against quantum. The EAT upheld awards of compensation for injury to feelings of £10,000 and £500 respectively and gave guidance on how tribunals should go about the task of assessing compensation.

13–123   Pugsley J. made it clear that the EAT did not seek to impose a mandatory requirement that tribunals should pursue a particular approach. The tribunal's discretion should not be fettered when dealing with a wide range of factual circumstances. Subject to this constraining note, Pugsley J. suggested that there were two elements to the loss suffered (following the approach taken by the Exeter tribunal in another case, *MOD v. Pope* [1997] I.C.R. 296):

1.   the dilemma of having to make the decision on whether to terminate the pregnancy;

2.   the consequences of making that decision.

13–124   The EAT's guidance in respect of the dilemma of having to make the decision in the context of losing one's job was that compensation for injury to feelings should be in the order of £2,000. The particular facts of the case could increase or reduce this sum. There may have been other factors apart from the loss of employment which influenced the woman's decision. This could result in a reduction in the award. If the threat of loss of employment was the sole cause of the decision to terminate the pregnancy then it would be appropriate to increase the compensation.

With regard to compensation for injury to feelings consequent upon having an abortion, Pugsley J. suggested that where the "injury" is "relatively transient" compensation in the order of £1,500 to £3,000 would be appropriate. Where the impact on the woman is "more durable", £3,000 to £7,500 would be the normal range. These two elements should then be added together.

13–125 The EAT took the view therefore that compensation of £10,000 for Mrs O'Hare was at "the upper end" of the scale but should not be overturned. The tribunal had found that "to have the pregnancy terminated involved an agonising personal decision, further affected by her endeavouring to have regard for the point of view of her [Roman Catholic] husband". The termination itself was "deeply distressing". "The further consequences were even more serious. Her husband realised that he had made a grave error of judgement. The applicant's distress continued. The personal and physical relationship was seriously impaired. For a time they separated." The tribunal also found that the "long term effects have sadly continued".

With regard to Mrs Lowe there were other factors, which had nothing to do with the Ministry's unlawful policy, which had "weighed heavily with Mrs Lowe in deciding to terminate the pregnancy". However, the unlawful policy was a factor in her decision and the tribunal was "entitled to award her some figure for her injury to her feelings in that this was an added dimension to the dilemma in which she was placed" (Pugsley J.). £500 was an appropriate figure.

These guidelines are potentially of relevance to any case where a woman is forced to terminate her pregnancy in order to keep her job.

Aggravated Damages

13–126 The Law Commission, in its Consultation Paper No. 132, "Aggravated, Exemplary and Restitutionary Damages" summarised the basis on which aggravated damages may be granted (para. 3.3).

> In *Rookes v. Barnard* [1964] A.C. 1129 HL, Lord Devlin said that aggravated damages were appropriate where the manner in which the wrong was committed was such as to injure the plaintiff's proper feelings of pride and dignity, or give rise to humiliation, distress, insult or pain. Examples of the sort of conduct which would lead to these forms of intangible loss were conduct which was offensive, or which was accompanied by malevolence, spite, malice, insolence or arrogance ... It would therefore seem that there are two elements relevant to the availability of an aggravated award: first exceptional or contumelious conduct or motive on the part of the defendant in committing the wrong; and secondly intangible loss suffered as a result by the plaintiff, that is injury to personality.

Causal Link

13–127 In analysing this summary, the EAT in *MOD v. Meredith* [1995] I.R.L.R. 539, stressed the importance of establishing a causal connection between the exceptional or contumelious conduct or motive in committing the wrong and the intangible loss (the injury to feelings) suffered by the plaintiff.

"We consider that for the plaintiff's feelings to have suffered an increased or aggravated hurt, he or she must have had some knowledge of the conduct or motive which caused that increase. It may not be necessary for him to know all the details of that conduct or motive but there must be either knowledge or suspicion of it for the causal link to exist" (Smith J.). This must be right because if the complainant was entirely unaware, for example, of a particular malice which led an employer to commit an act of discrimination, his injured feelings cannot have been aggravated by that malice.

13–128   More controversial is the question of whether the complainant must actually know that the act complained of was unlawful. The Court of Appeal in *Alexander v. Home Office* [1988] I.R.L.R. 190 suggested that this was necessary and referred to the Court of Appeal decision in *Coleman v. Skyrail Oceanic Ltd* I.R.L.R. [1981] 398, in support (in relation to sex discrimination).

However, in *MOD v. Meredith* [1995] I.R.L.R. 539 EAT, after reviewing these authorities, Smith J. said that the extent of knowledge required is unclear. "Whether it is sufficient that the employee knows that he has been dismissed or whether he must also know that the dismissal was unlawfully discriminatory is not clear."

To require actual knowledge that the act complained of is unlawful seems to go too far. It is not suggested as an essential element for the award of aggravated damages by the Law Commission (see para. 13–126, see also para. 13–102 in respect of "knowledge" and injury to feelings generally).

13–129   Indeed, there will be numerous cases in which an employee feels that he has been outrageously treated but does not know at the time whether the treatment was actually unlawful. To exclude such a person from entitlement to compensation for injury to feelings or aggravated damages would not, it is submitted, be following the normal principles for the award of damages in tort or the principle of full compensation in *Marshall v. Southampton and South-West Hampshire Area Health Authority (No.2)* [1993] I.R.L.R. 445 (see also paras 13–26 to 13–31).

Application of principles in discrimination cases

13–130   The Court of Appeal in *Alexander v. The Home Office* [1988] I.R.L.R. 190, made clear that aggravated damages were available in discrimination cases. (This case involved a black prisoner who was refused a job in the kitchen, such refusal amounting to race discrimination.) May L.J. said that "compensatory damages may and in some instances should include an element of aggravated damages where, for example, the defendant may have behaved in a high-handed, malicious, insulting or oppressive manner in committing the act of discrimination".

In *MOD v. Meredith* [1995] I.R.L.R. 539, the EAT commented that it was "common ground" that in discrimination cases (both sex and race—and, by analogy, disability, although the DDA was not yet in force at that time) "an award for injury to feelings may include an element of aggravated damages".

Compensatory damages not punitive

13–131   Note that an award for aggravated damages is not intended to punish the respondent. In *Rookes v. Bernard* [1964] A.C. 1129 HL Lord Devlin drew a distinction between exemplary damages the object of which is to punish and deter (see paras 13–135 to 13–136) and aggravated damages, "which are compensatory in nature".

This was confirmed in the discrimination context in *Alexander v. Home Office* (see para. 13–130) and in *McConnell v. Police Authority for Northern Ireland* [1997] I.R.L.R. 625 EAT. In that case Lord Chief Justice Carswell quoted from *Winfield and Jolowicz on Tort* (14th ed., p. 637): "aggravated damages may be regarded as truly compensatory, despite the difficulty in quantifying that for which they are awarded . . . it is now clear that, except in rare cases where exemplary damages are still allowed, any award must be strictly justifiable as compensation for the injury sustained."

It follows that any feelings of revulsion, on the part of the tribunal, at the behaviour of the respondent, should be put to one side. The only relevant issue is the extent to which that behaviour has aggravated the "injury" suffered by the complainant.

Part of the award for injury to feelings or separate?

13–132   It will be noted from the case digest on "injury to feelings" and "aggravated damages" at paragraphs 13–137 to 13–183 that in most of those cases where the tribunal has found that the respondent's behaviour has aggravated the complainant's injury to feelings, they have gone on to make a separate award for aggravated damages.

However, the recent case of *McConnell v. Police Authority for Northern Ireland* [1997] I.R.L.R. 625 CA, states that tribunals should make one award for "injury to feelings" which may, where appropriate, include an element to reflect the extent to which the respondent's behaviour has aggravated the "injury". There should not be a separate award. This is, of course, a Northern Ireland Court of Appeal case and, therefore, is not binding on tribunals in Great Britain. Nonetheless, it may be followed. The principle emerging from this decision is the importance of avoiding "duplication in the assessment of compensation".

13–133   Lord Chief Justice Carswell put it as follows: "aggravated damages should not be an extra sum over and above the sum which the tribunal of fact considers appropriate compensation for the injury to the claimant's feelings. Any element of aggravation ought to be taken into account in reckoning the extent of the injury to his feelings, for it is part of the cause of that injury. It should certainly not be treated as an extra award which reflects a degree of punishment of the respondent for his behaviour. If Smith J. intended to express approval of any different approach in *Armitage, Marsden and HM Prison Service v. Johnson* [1997] I.R.L.R. 162 EAT where separate awards were made for injury to feelings and for aggravated damages, I should not find it possible to agree."

The tribunal's task, according to Lord Chief Justice Carswell was to "weigh the evidence and form a view as to the level of distress and humiliation caused by the act or acts of discrimination, having regard to all the circumstances." That may include features which have the effect of aggravating the sense of injury. "The final result of this assessment will be a single figure reflecting the total injury to his feelings which may in appropriate cases include an element of aggravation." This analysis has the merit of logic and helps to avoid the risk of tribunals either duplicating compensation or punishing the respondent, by making a separate award for aggravated damages.

How much should compensation be increased if aggravating factors are found?

13–134   Whether the tribunal makes a separate award or enhances the award for injury to feelings it is still necessary to consider the extent to which aggravating factors should add to the compensation awarded. The decided cases demonstrates a wide range of awards for aggravated damages. For examples of awards of aggravated damages see the case digest at paragraphs 13–137 to 13–183.

Exemplary Damages

13–135   Exemplary damages, which are punitive in nature, rather than compensatory, are not available in discrimination cases. Such damages are only available in respect of torts in existence prior to 1964 and for which exemplary damages had been awarded prior to that date. This is the effect of *Rookes v. Barnard* [1964] A.C. 1129 and *Broome v. Cassel & Co. Ltd* [1972] A.C. 1027.

This analysis was confirmed in the race discrimination case of *Deane v. London Borough of Ealing and another* [1993] I.R.L.R. 209.

13–136 Further, the EAT in *MOD v. Meredith* [1995] I.R.L.R. 539 ruled that exemplary damages were not available for breach of the Equal Treatment Directive, 1976 (76/207). The tort of breach of the 1976 Directive has self-evidently come into existence since 1964. Smith J. also made the point that "as exemplary damages are not available as compensation for [the tort of discrimination under the SDA] they cannot be available for breach of the Directive under the criterion of comparability".

The Law Commission has recently recommended that exemplary or punitive damages, as the Commission describes them, should be available in discrimination cases where the respondent's conduct "showed a deliberate and outrageous disregard" of the complainant's rights. Such damages should be limited to cases where "other remedies awarded would be inadequate to punish" the respondent for their conduct (see "Aggravated, exemplary and restitutionary damages" Law Commission No. 247).

CASE DIGEST: INJURY TO FEELINGS/AGGRAVATED DAMAGES

13–137 Set out below are details of recent cases categorised by the type of discrimination involved. These cases should give some guidance on the way in which tribunals are currently exercising their discretion and, in some cases, how appeal courts have interpreted the principles. Details are not given of awards for financial loss.

Harassment: Race Discrimination
Armitage, Marsden and H.M. Prison Service v. Johnson [1997] I.R.L.R. 162 EAT

13–138 Facts The respondent was a black auxiliary prison officer at Brixton Prison. The tribunal found he had been subjected to a campaign of racial harassment and discrimination from mid 1991. It was still continuing at the time he presented his application to the tribunal in March 1993. The campaign of harassment involved the following:

In mid 1991, Mr Johnson saw a black prisoner manhandled by prison officers. He mentioned it to a colleague because he thought it was wrong. He was advised not to get involved. This led to the other officers not speaking to him and turning away. After a while he informed his supervisor of this and he was transferred to another wing. The ostracism continued. Various further incidents occurred which Mr Johnson believed amounted to racial harassment. He suffered false accusations, he was sent on "wild-goose chases" by more senior officers; he was unfairly deprived of overtime; on occasions he arrived for overtime to be told he was not wanted. He sought the help of Brixton Advice Centre which merely antagonised the senior officers and increased the hostility to him. He suffered racial remarks. He was told "to sing because all you guys can sing" and to run because "all you guys are athletes". He was reprimanded for not producing a medical certificate on the eighth day of absence—only a day after the self certification expired. The reprimand was officious and humiliating. He was warned for sickness absence when a white officer who had far worse absences was not called to account.

13–139 Eventually, in November 1992, he made a formal complaint to the governor. However, the officer given the task of investigating the complaint quickly reached the assumption that Mr Johnson was obsessed with his colour and that all the troubles were in his own mind. The tribunal concluded that the investigation was a travesty of what it should have been. When the result of the investigation was communicated to Mr Johnson the problems were put down to a clash of personalities and not racial discrimination. Mr Johnson's tribunal application was triggered by a further incident when he was reported for leaving his shift early because those on the next shift had already arrived. This was a common practice amongst officers. He received what amounted to a written reprimand and warning of future formal disciplinary action. No action was taken with regard to his complaint about other officers. He made a formal complaint of discrimination to the governor. The tribunal concluded that one officer had acted out of "sheer malice" with the intention of causing trouble for Mr Johnson and that the warning which followed the complaint about leaving his shift early amounted to victimisation.

13–140   The tribunal recognised the amount of stress caused by working in such an environment. The treatment Mr Johnson received had affected him and his home life. They accepted that he had been placed in fear—a fear of being alone because he might not get support from colleagues if attacked. One of the main factors taken into account by the tribunal in the award of aggravated damages had been the way his complaints had been dismissed and put down to defects in his personality. There had never been any apology.

> "This was a campaign of discrimination over a period in excess of 18 months involving exposure to humiliation, ostracism, ridicule and contempt at [Mr Johnson's] place of work ... It is certainly a very serious [case]."

Award

	20,000	Injury to feelings against Prison Service
	2 × 500	Injury to feelings against each of named officers
	7,500	Aggravated damages against Prison Service
Total	£28,500	

Harassment: Race discrimination

Bhalla v. M. Firkin Ltd October 7, 1997. Case No. 1301024/96 EOR (DCLD) 34

13–141   Facts   Mr Bhalla suffered racial harassment. In investigating his complaints the company had "failed totally to take [his] complaints seriously so that the injury that was caused initially by the name-calling and insulting remarks, instead of being remedied by management, was made worse by their failure to take these complaints seriously". Mr Bhalla had been "cross-examined on the basis that he was making-up the history of complaints of which he told us, but we have heard almost no evidence from those who could have said that it was not true ... We think that too was an aggravating feature."

Award

£10,000   Injury to feelings
£ 2,500   Aggravated damages

Harassment: Race discrimination, forced medical retirement
Chan v. London Borough of Hackney [1997] I.C.R. 1014

13–142 Facts From 1981 to 1991 Mr Chan had been promoted twice in the valuer's department. He became team leader and had also been temporarily promoted to group valuer. He received praise for his work. Then Mrs Collins was appointed Borough Valuer. She soon decided that he was "lazy, incompetent and a liar". She gave him a heavy work load and was unsympathetic to his concerns. When Mr Chan tried to arrange a meeting with his line manager to discuss the treatment he was receiving from Mrs Collins it ended up with him being given notice of a disciplinary meeting for him to attend. It was alleged that he was guilty of inadequate and negligent work and also of refusing to obey instructions. Mr Chan went off on sick leave and lodged a formal race grievance with Mrs Collins' manager. The complaint was not dealt with and Mr Chan's letter was not acknowledged. Instead, a proposal was communicated to Mr Chan that if he dropped his grievance the Council would not proceed with the disciplinary matter and he would seek medical retirement. He was given the impression that the disciplinary process could lead to dismissal. Reluctantly he accepted the offer. The tribunal took the view that the award in respect of injury to feelings should be very much at the top end of the awards and that an element in respect of aggravated damages would be appropriate. Mr Chan had been "subjected to humiliating treatment by Mrs Collins on a daily basis from the moment of her arrival in March 1991 to the date of the termination of his employment (July 31, 1992). This was in stark contrast to the way she had treated Mr John Edmonds, his white comparator. She had undermined the applicant's authority … [and he was] put under extreme pressure. The applicant's grievance was not dealt with by [Mrs Collins' line manager] who ignored it … He was treated … in a high-handed, insulting and aggressive manner."

Award

£25,000   Injury to feelings (including £5,000 for aggravated damages)

Harassment: Sex/Race discrimination
Reid v. Swinton Group Ltd July 16, 1997. Case No. 46558/93 EOR (DCLD) 31

13–143 Facts Ms Reid suffered racial and sexual harassment over a period of at least 16 months.

Award

£10,000   Injury to feelings

Harassment: Race/Sex discrimination
Hutchinson v. Edward Lloyd t/a Marriotts Case No. 3247/110

13–144 Facts Ms Hutchinson suffered both sex and race discrimination. She was humiliated by treatment in front of other employees and customers such as being told she was "typically Polish" and a "stupid woman". She was told she could not use her first name "Bogna" because it "sounded like a second-rate English seaside town". She had to go to hospital after her employer deliberately stood on her foot. She had keys and a book thrown at her which cut her cheek leaving a small scar. This all led to her becoming depressed and unsure of herself. Her loss of confidence made her afraid to go out and meet people. The "blatant" and "malicious" nature of her employer's conduct aggravated her injury.

Award

£15,000   Injury to feelings
£ 2,500   Aggravated damages

Harassment: Race discrimination

Otu v. United Artists Communications June 25, 1996. COIT 3270/183 IDS Brief 598

13–145   Facts   Disciplinary proceedings were pursued against Mr Otu. In a break during one disciplinary meeting his manager said to him "you are a loud-mouth fucking nigger and I am going to kick your fucking head in very soon you fucking black cunt". This was, found the tribunal, a one-off incident, with no evidence of a substantial campaign against Mr Otu.

Award

£1,000   Injury to feelings

Harassment: Race discrimination

Quaid v. L. Williamson (Shetland) Ltd t/a Sheltie March 13, 1996. COIT 3208/16 IDS Brief 598

13–146   Facts   For six years of employment Mr Quaid suffered racist comments such as "black bastard" and "nigger". The Managing Director had once pointed to a screened-off area and commented: "That's where we put fucking niggers who tell tales". This racist abuse was of a very serious nature and caused great offence to Mr Quaid, found the tribunal. The company employed 70–90 people but had no equal opportunities policy and denied knowledge of race relations legislation.

Award

£7,500   Injury to feelings

Harassment: Sex discrimination

M v. The Ministry of Defence March 19, 1997. Case No. 555 42/95 EOR (DCLD) 33

13–147   Facts   A wren suffered four years of sexual harassment leading to her developing a depressive illness which in turn led to her discharge from the Navy. She joined the Navy at the age of 17. During the next four years she had had to endure constant sexual harassment including being sexually assaulted, forced to simulate oral sex, required to jump into water making her clothes translucent, and having her breasts squeezed in public. She suffered deteriorating health as a result of this bullying and harassment. Her male colleagues then started to call her a "sick bay ranger". In July 1994, she was diagnosed as suffering clinical depression which then intensified. She had severe headaches, sleeping problems and a lack of energy and enthusiasm. She regularly cried. Eventually, she took an overdose of paracetamol. She was then discharged because of being temperamentally unsuitable for service in the Navy. Her complaint to the tribunal was contested but during the course of the hearing the Navy accepted unlawful sex discrimination and that the harassment had led to her discharge.

The tribunal took into account in assessing the award for injury to feelings "the humiliation and stress suffered, an element relating to the personal injury arising directly from the harassment in the form of depression and an element for the loss of congenial employment". There was no award for aggravated damages. The tribunal found that the Navy had not acted high-handedly nor arrogantly. "There was no evidence ... that the [Navy] had aggravated the situation by its behaviour."

Award

£25,000   Injury to feelings (including element relating to personal injury suffered)

Harassment: Sex discrimination
Jones & Childs v. Seasons Holidays plc COIT 16002/12/98 and 1600213/98
Employment Lawyer Issue 2, June 1998

13–148   Facts   Ms Jones and Ms Childs were sales executives. They suffered a number of incidents of sexual harassment from senior managers and other sales executives during October and November, 1997. There were gestures made and invitations to conduct sexual acts. Comments were made about their clothes and their bodies. The tribunal held that Ms Jones suffered significant injury to her feelings. Ms Childs' injury to feelings and suffering was particularly serious and included severe emotional trauma and anxiety.

Award

Ms Jones: £750   Injury to feelings
Ms Childs: £1,500   Injury to feelings

Harassment: Sex discrimination
Smith v. Trafalgar Communications Ltd 2802/109/97 Employment Lawyer
Issue 1; May, 1998

13–149   Facts   From July 1977, Ms Smith did administrative work and then was transferred to telesales. Her line manager pursued a campaign of harassment which the tribunal decided was based on gender. She suffered unpleasant comments of a sexual nature, a series of assaults, and being hit by "blue tack" pellets fired out of a blowpipe. She was then taken into an empty office. When she tried to go, the line manager slapped her leg. The tribunal held that this was far from trivial. It was unpleasant, and occasionally frightening, but was not one of the most serious examples of harassment. It did not go on for too long because she got alternative employment.

Award

£2,500   Injury to feelings

Harassment: Sex discrimination
Evans v. Stobbart COIT 18351/96 Employment Lawyer Issue 1, May 1988

13–150   Facts   On the first day of her job Miss Evans arrived with her mother. Whilst her mother was nearby, Mr Stobbart grabbed her and asked her to kiss him. She told him to "get off". She did not complain to her mother at the time and mentioned it for the first time when she was dismissed five weeks later. She claimed that Mr Stobbart's behaviour on her first day was the reason for her dismissal. The tribunal took the view that had she not been dismissed no mention would have been made of the allegations. She was planning to leave in any event in two weeks to go to college. Taking all these facts into account the tribunal decided that this was not a very serious matter.

Award

£100   Injury to feelings

Harassment: Sex discrimination
McDonald v. Seldon March 23, 1994. COIT 12355/93 IDS Brief 598

13–151   Facts Ms McDdonald worked for eight days for Seldon as a kitchen assistant. Her employer, Mr Seldon, an experienced businessman made sexual comments to her and grabbed her from behind. The tribunal considered this to be a particularly bad case of harassment of a young woman.

Award

£3,000   Injury to feelings

Harassment: Sex discrimination
Young v. (1) McLeod (2) John McLeod & Co. June 20, 1995. COIT 3091/80

13–152   Facts Mrs Young went to work for a firm of solicitors on a temporary basis. On her first day the Agency confirmed with the firm that it would be acceptable for her to deal with some urgent personal matters. After making a telephone call, one of the partners pushed her against a wall, calling her a "slag" and a "scrubber".

Medical evidence was given at the tribunal indicating lasting psychological effects. The tribunal considered the partner's behaviour to be very serious.

Award

£8,000   Injury to feelings

Recruitment: Race discrimination
Hussain v. (1) Harrison and (2) Bramall (Bradford) Ltd June 20 and November 25, 1997. Case No. 1800 810/97 EOR (DCLD) 35

13–153   Facts Mr Hussain applied for a position as a fleet sales administrator with a Ford dealership. He received a rejection letter from Mr Harrison, the General Manager. He then submitted a further application using a fictitious name purporting to be a white female with similar qualifications. This time an interview was offered. The tribunal found that there had been race and sex discrimination. The General Manager's explanation was inconsistent. The respondents had "cobbled together an explanation to excuse the way in which they had dealt with the applicant."

Award

£1,250   Injury to feelings
£2,500   Aggravated damages

Recruitment: Race discrimination

Hussain v. (1) JCT 600 Ltd and (2) Oram November 12, 1997. Case No. 1801
653/97 EOR (DCLD) 35

13–154 Facts The same applicant as in the previous claim. He also applied for a
post with the first respondent company. He seeks to expose race discrimination by
making applications to companies and examining how they are treated. The tribunal
said that having been "discriminated against before and having been to a tribunal
successfully before does not diminish the distress caused by further discrimination".
Aggravated damages were awarded because of additional distress caused when the
respondents mentioned at the end of the first day at the tribunal that there was a
rumour that the police were investigating his involvement in repeated tribunal
applications. The rumour was not true. There were no such investigations but because
the press were present at the tribunal it had been widely reported.

Award

£3,000	Injury to feelings
£1,000	Aggravated damages

Recruitment: Race discrimination

Widlinski v. Racial Equality Council of Cleveland and others December 10,
1996. Case No. 38275/96 EOR (DCLD) 33

13–155 Facts Mr Widlinski worked for Cleveland REC, first of all as a part time
volunteer and then as a full time volunteer. He then became a race equality officer
and was employed on a fixed term contract. Subsequently, he was interviewed for a
new post. Having been given an unconditional offer he was then informed by the
chair of the interviewing panel, Mr Husaini, that he was in fact the second choice.
He was instead offered an extension to his fixed term contract. About three months
later the REC repeated the selection process. This time Mr Husaini's wife chaired the
panel. A different format was followed for the interview. The result was that an Asian
female was chosen instead of Mr Widlinski. The tribunal found that the failure to
appoint him was race discrimination. The tribunal awarded aggravated damages
because of the respondent's "insulting behaviour".

Award

£10,000	Injury to feelings
£ 5,000	Aggravated damages

Recruitment: Race discrimination

Stuart v. Excellence Enterprises Ltd t/a Vaticano Restaurant April 3, 1996.
COIT 3231/10 IDS Brief 598

13–156 Facts Ms Stuart worked as a full time waitress but she wanted evening
work as well. She saw a job advertised at a restaurant and went in to enquire about
it. She was told that the vacancy had been filled. She was black. The following day a
white waitress she worked with enquired about the job and was handed an application
form. The tribunal concluded that Ms Stuart had been upset by the discrimination
but was a particularly resilient type of person.

Award

£500   Injury to feelings

Recruitment: Race discrimination
Silvera v. The Dominion Hotel October 14, 1996. COIT 3272 197 IDS Brief 598

13–157   Facts   Ms Silvera, a black student, applied for part time waitress work and was offered the job. This offer was then withdrawn. Two white waitresses were offered work. One of them had been interviewed after Ms Silvera. Ms Silvera had been badly let down and was justifiably angry.

Award

£3,000   Injury to feelings

Recruitment: Sex discrimination
Fitzgerald v. (1) Staffordshire County Council and (2) Board of Governors, Knutton Infants School October 2, 1996. Case No. 15152/96 EOR (DCLD) 33

13–158   Facts   Ms Fitzgerald was appointed to a temporary teaching position for two terms. Prior to starting she informed the headmistress that she had discovered she was pregnant and was due to give birth about one and a half months before the end of the contract. She was not taken on.

Award

£1,000   Injury to feelings

Recruitment: Sex discrimination
Ul-Haque v. Fancy & another t/a Food Fax August 16, 1996. COIT 3304/131 IDS Brief 598

13–159   Facts   Mr Ul-Haque was not interviewed for a job as a catering assistant. The tribunal held that this was on grounds of his sex. However, he suffered minimal injury to feelings and only pursued a claim because the job centre referred him to the CAB.

Award

£100   Injury to feelings

Recruitment: Sex discrimination
Ryan v. (1) Wickes (2) T Parker & Sons (Turf Management) Ltd June 3, 1996. COIT 3137/82 IDS Brief 598

13–160   Facts   Mr Ryan was not interviewed for a job as an office assistant. The employer wanted a "young lady". He was 33 years old and the tribunal found that he "did not have the resilience of a younger person to help him in overcoming such an incident". He had spent 12 months gaining the qualifications and experience for such work. The company's treatment of him seriously undermined his confidence.

Award

£2,000   Injury to feelings

Recruitment: Sex/Race discrimination
Nwoke v. (1) Government Legal Service (2) Civil Service Commissioners
December 2, 1996. COIT 4302/94 IDS Brief 598

13–161 Facts Ms Nwoke, a solicitor, failed to get a post with the government's legal services. The low mark she received after interview had the effect of barring her from getting any similar post in the future. She suffered professional humiliation for the race and sex discrimination suffered.

Award

£2,000   Injury to feelings

Dismissal/Redundancy: Race discrimination
Onwuagbusi v. Sunlight Textile Services Ltd October 17, 1996. Case No. 12636/93 EOR (DCLD) 33

13–162 Facts Aggravated damages were awarded after the tribunal heard evidence from management which included a derogatory account of the complainant which was "blatantly not genuine". They showed no contrition and hence aggravated the wrong done to the complainant. "It is our view that their continued arrogance and insistence on the opinion which we have found to be discriminatory must substantially increase and aggravate the insult and injury to the applicant."

Award

£2,000   Aggravated damages

Dismissal/Redundancy: Race discrimination
Campbell v. Ecclestone and Others February 14, 1996. COIT 3186/126 IDS Brief 598

13–163 Facts Ms Campbell worked for the respondent for six months. She was called a "coon" behind her back and was then dismissed without the proper procedures being used. When senior management discovered what had happened she was reinstated. For months she felt badly about what had happened and about her treatment. She subsequently suffered from a serious illness. The tribunal could not establish whether the distress and anxiety she suffered was caused by the unlawful treatment or by her illness. However, they found that she was incensed by her treatment. The description "coon" was disparaging and demeaning and would have caused feelings of a lack of self-worth. She did not, however, suffer discrimination on a day to day basis.

Award

£2,000   Injury to feelings

Pregnancy Dismissal: Sex discrimination
Coe v. Tee Gee Snacks Ltd COIT 3198/46

13–164   Facts   Ms Coe worked as a management accountant at the company's Leeds administration centre. She informed her employer that she was pregnant but soon after found she had cancer. Her baby was born prematurely. She was also having treatment for potentially terminal cancer. During her maternity leave her employer wrote to her to inform her that the Leeds centre was closing due to a restructuring and that accordingly her employment was terminated. The tribunal described this as an "appalling" case. The employer's callous way of dismissing her without any discussion had aggravated her injury.

Award

£11,000	Injury to feelings
£ 4,000	Aggravated damages

Pregnancy Dismissal: Sex discrimination
Davison v. Pilling t/a Poshwash COIT 2405076/97 Employment Lawyer Issue 1, May 1998

13–165   Facts   Ms Davison became pregnant and informed her employer. She attended ante-natal appointments but was not initially paid for the time she had off. She went off on maternity leave but did not receive SMP. When she telephoned to enquire about payment she was first told there was no money to pay staff wages. She was then offered a cheque. She said she wanted cash. She asked to see Mr Pilling and at the meeting which was arranged she took a letter outlining the employer's duties. The manager "went mad". She was told to "go off and have her fucking baby". She was dismissed and told that she was not "going to get any more money out of him". The tribunal found that she was hurt and upset by her dismissal and non-payment of SMP would put financial strain on the family and affected her relationship with her husband. It had spoilt her excitement of giving birth to her first child. She was signed off work for a month.

Award

£2,500	Injury to feelings

Pregnancy Dismissal: Sex discrimination
Jones v. Goldcrest Aviation Ltd September 18, 1995. COIT 3126/211 IDS Brief 598

13–166   Facts   Ms Jones who worked as a sales executive was made redundant. She was selected because she was pregnant. She was upset and distressed and suffered feelings of uncertainty and insecurity.

Award

£2,250	Injury to feelings

Dismissal/Redundancy: Disability discrimination
Kirker v. British Sugar plc December 5, 1997 & January 9, 1998. Case No. 2601 249/97 IDS Brief 609

13–167   Facts   Mr Kirker was selected for redundancy. The tribunal held that his selection amounted to unlawful disability discrimination. He was awarded substantial compensation for financial loss (total award £103,146.49). The award included compensation for injury to feelings. The dismissal substantially undermined his confidence. He had also lost congenial work which it would be very hard to replace. Decision now upheld on appeal by EAT.

Award

£3,500   Injury to feelings

Dismissal: Disability discrimination
Mansfield v. Saunders November 19, 1997. Case No. 1401315/97 IDS Brief 609

13–168   Facts   This case concerned the dismissal of Ms Mansfield in circumstances which amounted to disability discrimination. The award for injury to feelings reflected the fact that she was upset at losing her job. The tribunal considered that it was not one of the most serious cases of discrimination, stating that injury to feelings awards were much higher where the discrimination was, for example, coupled with humiliation. Awards for injury to feelings in disability cases should be comparable with those made in race and sex cases.

Award

£1,000   Injury to feelings

Dismissal: Disability discrimination
Holmes v. Whittingham and Porter Ltd October 8, 1997. Case No. 1802799/97 IDS Brief 609

13–169   Facts   Mr Holmes had been an epileptic throughout his 31 years' employment with the company. In March 1997, he collapsed for the first time in his office. The company got a medical report which gave advice about certain types of work he should not do. Subsequent dismissal amounted to disability discrimination. The tribunal's award for injury to feelings reflected his length of service and dismissal at the age of 59, and the fact that he was admitted to hospital because of his distressed mental state which was caused by his dismissal.

Award

£4,250   Injury to feelings

Dismissal: Disability discrimination
Lang v. Redland Roofing Systems Ltd October 31, 1997. Case No. S/400788/97 IDS Brief 611

13–170   Facts   Ms Lang suffered bi-polar affective disorder—a clinically recognised mental disorder. The tribunal held that she was unlawfully dismissed on account of disability discrimination. The award for injury to feelings was, according to the tribunal, at "the lower end of the scale". The tribunal took into account Ms Lang's evidence that she was happier in her new job and that there was no evidence of substantial injury to feelings.

Award

£1,000   Injury to feelings

Dismissal: Disability discrimination
Coleman v. Seceurop (UK) Ltd March 2, 1998. Case No. 2502841/97 IDS Brief 611

13–171   Facts   Mr Coleman was recruited after informing his employers that he had a disability which caused problems with writing. On his first day in the job the company discovered his handwriting was completely illegible. He was dismissed the following day. The company admitted disability discrimination. The award for injury to feelings took into account the fact that Mr Coleman did not appear distressed, nor did he raise any grievance before instituting tribunal proceedings.

Award

£750   Injury to feelings

Dismissal: Disability discrimination
Calvert v. Jewelglen Ltd October 21 & 31, 1997. Case No. 2403989/97 EOR (DCLD) 34

13–172   Facts   Mr Calvert is epileptic but, with medication, had been free of attack or fit for 18 years. Having been recruited as a care assistant, with the matron of the nursing home fully aware of his medical condition, he suffered a dizzy spell and was sent home. The part-owner of the company then dismissed him. The tribunal found he had suffered disability discrimination. "The decision to dismiss him was taken because of the concerns of one woman, whose concerns were not properly investigated through the appropriate managerial channels, and by the proprietor, in effect, of the business who failed to make any proper enquiry of appropriate independent sources in order to satisfy himself as to the real facts". The tribunal found that Mr Calvert "was extremely hurt" by the "demeaning and degrading" treatment he received and that his injured feelings were aggravated "by reason of the manner in which it was handled and the way in which the dismissal was carried out."

Award

£2,500   Injury to feelings
£1,000   Aggravated damages

Dismissal: Disability discrimination
Howden v. Capital Copiers (Edinburgh) Ltd July 30, 1997. Case No. S/400005/97 EOR (DCLD)33

13–173   Facts   Mr Howden had frequent sickness absence due to abdominal pains. He was employed for just over two years. His disability caused him a severe gripping pain; he was unable to walk, and lost the use of his hands. He was dismissed without warning.

Award

£1,000   Injury to feelings

Dismissal: Disability discrimination
O'Connor v. Spankers Ltd December 5, 1997. Case No. 1804372/97
Discrimination Law Association Briefing 70, March 1998

13–174   **Facts**   Ms O'Connor was disabled from birth with curvature of the spine. She got work with Spankers Ltd as a machinist on an hourly rate. Other workers were paid by piece rate. After a few months the company complained about her output. She was transferred to piece rate on a trial basis. She tried to increase her speed but as a result became ill. She was dismissed. The tribunal found that she had suffered disability discrimination. Her dismissal, which was clearly on the basis of her disability, "must have caused considerable injury to her feelings".

Award

£2,500   Injury to feelings

Dismissal: Disability discrimination
Tarling v. Wisdom Toothbrushes Ltd June 24, 1997. Case No. 1500148/97
EOR (DCLD) 33

13–175   **Facts**   Mrs Tarling suffered from club foot. She had worked for the company for 18 years. The condition got worse, causing her pain and discomfort. The company got expert advice proposing the use of a special chair which would have cost £1,000. Instead of buying the chair, they dismissed her for not achieving production targets. This, the tribunal held, amounted to disability discrimination. She also succeeded in an additional claim of unfair dismissal for which the tribunal ordered re-instatement.

Award

£1,200   Injury to feelings

Dismissal/Redundancy: Race discrimination
Nazir v. Sampson Foods Ltd March 14, 1996. COIT 3208/62 IDS Brief 598

13–176   **Facts**   Mr Nazir was selected for redundancy. Another employee who was white had less service. The tribunal's inference was that the selection was based on race. However, although they found that he was "bitter" at the way he had been treated, he was not greatly hurt.

Award

£500   Injury to feelings.

Victimisation: Race discrimination
Mensah v. (1) Bell (2) Sheard May 10, 1996. COIT 3231/134 IDS Brief 598

13–177   **Facts**   Ms Mensah was a midwife. She made several applications to go onto the "bank" of midwives but got nowhere. She then wrote asking for the shortlisting criteria and for information about ethnic minority employees. She stated that she believed she was suffering race discrimination. The reply stated that the hospital could not be forced to employ her and that she should stop applying for work. The tribunal found the reply to be offensive and abrupt and that Ms Mensah was hurt and distressed by the letter and that she was "in despair".

Award

£1,750   Injury to feelings

Victimisation: Race discrimination/dismissal
Suraju Deen Tiyaniyu v. London Borough of Hackney and others (1998) LTL February 20, 1998 (LAWTEL report)

13–178   Facts   Mr Suraju was the council's principal finance officer in the support services section of the Leisure Department. In 1993 there was a reorganisation in which Mr Suraju was dismissed. He refused an offer of re-engagement. The tribunal concluded that he had suffered race discrimination and victimisation. The EAT reduced Mr Suraju's compensation for injury to feelings from £13,500 to £7,500 but the Court of Appeal restored the tribunal's award. Although the tribunal's award was high it had not been perverse. It was at the top end of the scale for race cases.

Award

£13,500   Injury to feelings

MISCELLANEOUS

Refusal of Promotion, Study Leave and Related Matters: Race Discrimination

Qureshi v. Victoria University of Manchester and Brazier November 21, 1997. Case No. 01 359/93 EOR (DCLD) 35

13–179   Facts   Dr Qureshi was a lecturer in the Faculty of Law. Between 1992 and 1994 he complained that he had been refused consideration for promotion in annual promotion exercises, and refused study leave. He also complained about the conduct of an examination scrutiny meeting. He had earlier raised equal opportunities issues with senior faculty members which had not been taken seriously. He found hostility and apathy to his concerns. He suffered personal isolation within the faculty and a lack of support from both the faculty itself and colleagues.

In determining the compensation for injury to feelings the tribunal found that the background of earlier events were highly relevant. "It demonstrated the university's approach to equal opportunities issues raised by the applicant, and as a result heightened the applicant's subsequent sense of injustice and frustration which became cumulative at every setback he received." The tribunal made a single award in respect of all acts complained of (he had made eight complaints of race discrimination and victimisation in two separate applications). The award was to reflect "the extremely long period of stress, frustration and sense of injustice which mounted and accumulated over a period of many years, starting in 1989 and continuing through to the decision of the tribunal". With regard to aggravated damages, the tribunal found that the manner of committing the wrong led to further injury to the applicant's feelings of dignity and pride. The award was based on the university's "lack of perception or apparent interest in equal opportunities issues and the responses of the faculty to the raising of such issues was negative, inadequate, hostile and showed a lofty disregard." Also, "double standards were applied and emphases were changed according to needs.

When the applicant objected, nothing was done to answer his objections or assuage his feelings. Correspondence addressed to the applicant was often brusque, dismissive and critical". No apology had been forthcoming.

Award

£25,000	Injury to feelings against the University
£ 1,000	Injury to feelings against Professor Brazier
£ 8,000	Aggravated damages against the University

Access to Benefits: Race discrimination
Ahmed v. Derby Pride Ltd November 26, 1996. COIT 3231/147 IDS Brief 598

13–180   Facts   Ms Ahmed worked as a junior manager. She complained that she had been excluded from interviews to recruit someone for her team. She also complained about the way disciplinary proceedings had been pursued against her. She said that employees in her department described her as a "token black person". Following the disciplinary proceedings she suffered from stress. She noticed her hair was falling out and she had to take sick leave and receive medical treatment. The tribunal said that the effect of the discrimination on her was "at a high level".

Award

£5,000	Injury to feelings

Promotion: Sex discrimination
Bamber v. Fuju International Finance plc April 26, 1996. COIT 3258/168 IDS Brief 598

13–181   Facts   Over a number of years Ms Bamber had not been promoted because of her sex. Depression increased and she felt downtrodden, angry, hurt and humiliated. The tribunal found that she had suffered real distress. At an interview with a manager she had become tearful.

Award

£ 5,000	Injury to feelings
£20,000	Aggravated damages

Refusal of Job Share: Sex discrimination
Given v. Scottish Power plc January 20, 1995. COIT S/3172/94 IDS Brief 598

13–182   Facts   Ms Given was refused the chance to work on a job share basis after returning from maternity leave. She had worked for the company from 1979 to 1994. She resigned. This indirect discrimination was exacerbated by the way she was treated. Her career was brought to an end.

Award

£5,000	Injury to feelings

Disciplinary Action: Sex discrimination

White v. Commissioner of Police for the Metropolis February 19, 1996. COIT 3059/89 IDS Brief 598

13–183   Facts   Mr White, a police sergeant, was compulsorily transferred following a grievance lodged against him by a WPC. The tribunal found this amounted to sex discrimination. He had suffered considerable stress and trauma; he had lost confidence in dealing with women police officers and he had also lost confidence in senior police officers. His relationship with his partner broke down (the tribunal reached no conclusion as to whether the discrimination had caused this).

Award

£15,000   Injury to feelings

EQUAL PAY

13–184   This section considers the remedies available under the Equal Pay Act 1970. The law on equal pay generally is beyond the scope of this book.

Complaints to the tribunal

An employee may present a complaint to the tribunal alleging contravention of a term modified or included by virtue of an equality clause, including a claim for arrears of remuneration or damages which results from the contravention (s.2(1) EPA). Note that s.1 EPA implies into every contract an equality clause so that if a woman can show that she is employed on like work or on work which is rated as equivalent or on work of equal value to a man who is in the same employment then her contract is changed so that none of the terms and conditions of employment are less favourable than equivalent terms and conditions in the man's contract of employment.

The complainant to the tribunal can achieve two objectives:

1. A declaration can be made modifying less favourable terms or introducing into her contract any term of the man's contract which is more favourable to him.

    The tribunal does not look at the entirety of the contract. It looks at each individual term to ask whether it is less favourable. Any less favourable term is modified by the equality clause whether or not the woman has claimed this. The contract is not modified, however, to introduce a right to any element of the man's pay which relates to some feature of his employment which affects him but not her. For example, if the man is working on a night shift and the woman on days then she is not entitled to receive any night shift bonus paid to him (see *Dugdale & others v. Kraft Foods Ltd* [1976] I.R.L.R. 368.

    13–185   The case of *Enderby v. Frenchay Health Authority and Secretary of State for Health* [1993] I.R.L.R. 591, is authority for the principle that a woman may succeed in achieving entitlement to pay which is "proportionate" to her male comparator if the employer succeeds to some extent in objectively justifying the difference in pay. Once the contract has been modified it remains modified until it is later varied, for example, by an agreement between employer and employee.

If the complaint relates to access to an occupational pension scheme the tribunal may declare that the person has a right to be admitted to the scheme with effect from a date no earlier than two years before the institution of proceedings (s.2(6D) EPA). If the complaint relates to the terms on which members of the scheme are treated, the tribunal may declare that a member has a right to equal treatment in respect of such a period as it may specify provided that the period does not begin before May 17, 1990 (s.2(6E) EPA). If the woman is able to retrospectively join a pension scheme she cannot avoid having to pay employee contributions for the relevant period (see *Fisscher v. Voorhuis Hengelo BV and Stichting Bedrijfspensioenfonds voor de Detailhandel* [1994] I.R.L.R. 662.

2. *Damages/Award of back pay*

13–186   The tribunal will make an award for arrears of remuneration to be paid to the woman where she is being paid less than her male comparator. If she is being treated less favourably by receiving inferior benefits in kind (for example, not having a company car) then the tribunal awards damages for breach of contract. Note that s.2(5) EPA limits an award of damages or arrears of remuneration to a period of two years prior to the date that proceedings were instituted. Also, Regulation 9 of the Occupational Pension Schemes (Equal Treatment) Regulations 1995 (S.I. 1995 No 3183) amends the Equal Pay Act by introducing the following: "A woman shall not be entitled ... to be awarded any payment by way of arrears of benefits or damages" where the claim is made in respect of a breach of an equality clause relating to membership of or rights under a pension scheme. The tribunal can, however, award payment of arrears or damages in breach of contract in respect of "pensioner members" (See s.124(1) Pension Act 1995). Regulation 1 of the Occupational Pension Schemes (Equal Treatment) Regulations 1995 states that a "pensioner member" includes a person who is entitled to the present payment of pension or other benefits derived through a member.

Challenge to the two year limit (s.2(5) EPA)

13–187   Note that the EAT has asked the ECJ to rule on whether the two year rule conflicts with Article 119 of the EEC Treaty and Equal Pay Directive 75/117. In the case of *Levez v. T.H. Jennings (Harlow Pools) Ltd* [1996] I.R.L.R. 499, the majority of the EAT took the view, in making the referral, that the appropriate comparisons with limitations applicable under national law for other similar claims were in the field of employment law such as the limitation periods for race and sex discrimination and for breach of contract. Note that breach of contract claims can be brought within six years of the date of the breach. The majority of the EAT also referred to the decision in *Marshall v. Southampton & South-West Hampshire Area Health Authority (No. 2)* [1993] I.R.L.R. 445 ECJ which ruled that the limit on damages for sex discrimination in claims under the Sex Discrimination Act were contrary to Article 6 of the Equal Treatment Directive. Article 2 of the Equal Pay Directive is in terms effectively equivalent to Article 6 of the Equal Treatment Directive. A decision is awaited.

Time limit for complaints

A complaint must be made no later than six months following the termination of employment to which the complaint relates. A complaint can, of course, be made during that employment (s.2(4) EPA).

CHAPTER 14
Trade Union Discrimination

14–01 It is unlawful to refuse employment to someone on various trade union grounds. The rules are contained in Part III of TULR(C)A. It is also unlawful for an employment agency to refuse someone any of its services on trade union grounds. Section 137 TULR(C)A deals with refusal of employment. Section 138 TULR(C)A concerns refusal of the service of an employment agency. Section 137(1) TULR(C)A sets out the grounds upon which it is unlawful to refuse employment:

(a) because he is, or is not a member of a trade union, or

(b) because he is unwilling to accept a requirement

    (i) to take steps to become or cease to be, or to remain or not to become, a member of a trade union, or

    (ii) to make payments or suffer deductions in the event of him not being a member of a trade union.

The same grounds apply (with the exception of (b)(ii)) to cases involving the refusal of services of an employment agency.

Remedies

14–02 s.140 TULR(C)A sets out the remedies available where a tribunal finds a complaint under s.137 or s.138 well-founded. The remedies are as follows:

Declaration

14–03 The tribunal shall make a declaration to the effect that the complaint is well-founded (s.140(1) TULR(C)A).

Further Orders

14–04 The tribunal shall then make such of the following as it considers just and equitable:

1 Compensation

An order requiring the respondent to pay compensation to the complainant of such amount as the tribunal may determine (s.140(1)(a) TULR(C)A). Compensation is to be assessed on the same basis as damages for breach of statutory duty and may include compensation for injury to feelings (s.140(2) TULR(C)A).

The effect of this provision is that compensation is to be assessed in the same way as compensation for race, sex or disability discrimination (see Chapter 13 for commentary on compensation in discrimination cases. Note, however, that in these cases of trade union discrimination there is a statutory cap which is the same as that applying to the compensation award for unfair dismissal (s.140(4) TULR(C)A, see paras 10–02 to 10–06).

Note also, however, that just as with other forms of discrimination the test of justice and equity does not apply to the size of the compensation awarded. The tribunal shall order compensation if it considers it just and equitable to do so (s.140(1) TULR(C)A. Once the tribunal decides, on this test, to award compensation it cannot limit compensation because it considers it just and equitable so to do (see, by way of contrast, s.123(1) ERA in relation to the compensatory award for unfair dismissal considered at paras 11–03 to 11–37).

2 Recommendation

14–05 Just as with other forms of discrimination the tribunal can also make a recommendation if it considers it just and equitable so to do (s.140(1)(b) TULR(C)A.

The recommendation is that the respondent "take within a specified period action appearing to the tribunal to be practicable for the purpose of obviating or reducing the adverse effects on the complainant of any conduct to which the complaint relates". (See paras 13–07 to 13–19 for commentary on the application of the power to make a recommendation in relation to other forms of discrimination.)

Failure to comply with a recommendation

14–06 Just as with other forms of discrimination, s.140(3) TULR(C)A provides that where a respondent fails, without reasonable justification, to comply with a recommendation to take action, the tribunal may increase its award of compensation or, if it has not made such an award, make one (see also paras 13–18 to 13–19 in respect of this power with regard to other forms of discrimination).

Action against both prospective employer and employment agency

14–07 A complaint to a tribunal can be brought against both a prospective employer and an employment agency where the complaint arises out of the same facts (s.141(1) TULR(C)A). Equally, either an employment agency or a prospective employer can be joined in proceedings brought against the other (s.141(2)). The tribunal then has power to award compensation against either or both as the tribunal considers just and equitable in the circumstances (s.141(3) TULR(C)A). Compensation for financial loss cannot, however, be ordered twice over. It may be "shared" between the two respondents.

Awards against third parties

14–08 If either the complainant or the respondent claims that a third party, such as a trade union, induced the respondent to act in the way complained of by pressure by calling, organising, procuring or financing a strike or other industrial action, or by threatening to do so, then they can apply to have the third party joined as a party to the proceedings (s142(1) TULR(C)A). Again, the tribunal has power to award all or part of the compensation (as it considers just and equitable) to be paid by the third party.

CHAPTER 15

Payments Received from Employer or by Way of Mitigation

ORDER OF REDUCTIONS: UNFAIR DISMISSAL AND DISCRIMINATION

15–01 Where a payment has been made by the employer to the employee on termination of employment that payment must be taken into account in determining the award to be made to the employee. In determining the compensatory award in an unfair dismissal claim the employee is compensated for loss suffered as a result of dismissal. Likewise, an award of compensation for race, sex or disability discrimination compensates the employee for loss suffered as a result of the discriminatory dismissal. In either case if the employer has made an *ex gratia* payment on termination of employment that payment must be set off against the loss to determine the net loss suffered (see para. 10–06) for the impact of the statutory maximum compensatory award for unfair dismissal where such a sum has to be set off.)

15–02 Problems arise in cases where the tribunal has also made a percentage reduction to the award of compensation, for example, on the basis that it would be just and equitable to reduce the compensatory award (s.123(1) ERA, see XX) or because of contributory fault (s.123(6) ERA). In discrimination cases the tribunal also has power to make a percentage reduction to compensation for loss in certain circumstances (see paras 13–58 to 13–76). For example, a percentage chance can be applied to take account of the possibility that had no discrimination occurred the employee would not have continued in employment in any event. The order in which the payment by the employer and the percentage reduction is applied to the figure for total loss can have a significant impact on the amount of compensation awarded to the employee. For example, X is dismissed for incompetence. He receives an *ex gratia* payment of £5,000 on termination of employment. The tribunal finds that the dismissal was procedurally unfair but that there was a 50 per cent chance that, had a fair procedure been followed, he would have been dismissed anyway. His total loss of earnings and other benefits is assessed at £15,000.

15–03 If the *ex gratia* payment of £5,000 is deducted from the total loss of £15,000 before the 50 per cent reduction is applied the result is as follows:

$$
\begin{array}{rr}
 & £15,000 \\
\text{less} & \underline{5,000} \\
 & £10,000
\end{array}
$$

$$£10,000 \times 50\% \quad = \quad \textbf{Award: £5,000}$$

If, on the other hand, the percentage reduction is applied to the total loss before the *ex gratia* payment is deducted the result is different:

$$
\begin{array}{lr}
£15,000 \times 50\% \quad = & £7,500 \\
\text{Less } \textit{ex gratia} \text{ payment} & \underline{£5,000} \\
\textbf{Award:} & \textbf{£2,500}
\end{array}
$$

These competing methods have been the subject of much dispute over recent years and guidance from case law has been contradictory. Unfortunately, the position is still not settled.

Unfair Dismissal

Enhanced Redundancy Payment

15–04 A recent Court of Appeal decision has confirmed that in calculating the compensatory award for unfair dismissal the treatment of enhanced redundancy payments depends on the specific wording of s.123(7) ERA (*Digital Equipment Co. Ltd v. Clements (No.2)* [1998] I.R.L.R. 134). If an employee is unfairly dismissed on grounds of redundancy, but received the statutory redundancy payment, that payment is set off against his entitlement to the basic award. However, if the employee receives an enhanced redundancy payment (whether by virtue of a contractual entitlement to an enhanced payment or as an *ex gratia* payment) that excess amount over and above the amount of basic award "goes to reduce the amount of the compensatory award" (s.123(7) ERA).

15–05 Note that s.123(7) ERA requires that the enhanced redundancy payment is set off against "the compensatory award" and is not simply to be taken into account in assessing loss. The Court of Appeal in *Digital Equipment Co. Ltd v. Clements (No.2)* [1998] I.R.L.R. 134 said that this was an important distinction. In that case, Mr Clements had been unfairly made redundant. Had a fair procedure been followed there was a 50 per cent chance that he would have been retained. He received a contractual redundancy payment which exceeded his statutory entitlement by £20,685. Mr Clement's loss was assessed at £43,136.

15–06 If the enhanced redundancy payment was deducted from the total loss this would leave £22,451 to which the 50 per cent reduction would then be applied. This would have left Mr Clements being awarded what was then the statutory maximum of £11,000. However, the Court of Appeal found that the language used by Parliament in s.123(7) was clear. The enhanced redundancy payment is applied to the compensatory award, not to the total loss as in the method set out above. The result of this is that the percentage reduction should first be applied to the figure for total loss of £43,136 leaving £21,568. This is what would have been the compensatory award had there been no enhanced redundancy payment (and subject, of course, to the statutory maximum). Then the enhanced payment (in this case £20,685) "goes to reduce the amount of the compensatory award".

Loss	£43,136
Reduce by 50%	£21,568
Less enhanced redundancy payment	£20,685
Award =	**£883.00**

The difference is dramatic. Instead of the employee receiving the statutory maximum, he receives just £883.00. The employer gains the full benefit of the enhanced redundancy payment.

15–07 There may be one exception to this principle. By way of example, an employee has been dismissed ostensibly for redundancy and receives an enhanced "redundancy" payment. The tribunal subsequently decides that the dismissal was not on grounds of redundancy but was for some other reason. The employee should be able to argue that the enhanced payment was not in reality a redundancy payment and therefore the special rules applying to redundancy payments in s.123 (7) should not apply. In *Boorman v. Allmakes Ltd* [1995] I.R.L.R. 553, Mr Boorman was dismissed and received a "redundancy" payment. The tribunal held that Mr Boorman was not redundant and that he had been unfairly dismissed. The Court of Appeal held that the normal rule (in what is now s.122(4) ERA) that the redundancy payment is set off against the basic award only applies where the dismissal was, in fact, by reason of redundancy. Applying this reasoning it is arguable that if the dismissal is held not to be on grounds of redundancy, an enhanced payment should not be set off against the compensatory award under s.123(7) but should be treated like any other payment by the employer (see paras 15–08 to 15–10. Unfortunately, as we shall see the position with regard to other payments is still not clear).

Unfair Dismissal

Other Payments Made by the Employer

15–08   Until the recent case of *Heggie v. Uniroyal Engelbert Tyres Ltd* EAT [1998] I.R.L.R. 425 (see para. 15–10) it seemed as if we might have reached a settled position that other payments made by the employer are to be treated differently from enhanced redundancy payments—to the advantage of the employee. The Court of Appeal in the *Digital* case (see paras 15–04 to 15–06) based its decision in relation to enhanced redundancy payments specifically on the working of s.123(7) which provides that the excess of a redundancy payment "shall go to reduce the amount of the compensatory award".

> "I think that Parliament has drawn a clear distinction in the treatment of the excess of redundancy payments which have actually been made by the employer and the other elements which go to make up the loss". (Beldam L.J.)

15–09   However, no such special provision applies to any other payment made by the employer such as pay in lieu of notice or an *ex gratia* payment unrelated to redundancy. It seems, therefore, that in the case of such payments the correct approach is to set them off against the total loss suffered before applying any percentage reduction determined by the tribunal. This was the clear view of the EAT in *Digital Equipment Co Ltd v. Clements (No.2)* [1997]I.C.R. 237. The Court of Appeal, in distinguishing the treatment of redundancy payments, appears to support the EAT's view with regard to other non-redundancy payments. The effect of this is somewhat strange. The employer will get the full benefit of enhanced redundancy payments— (because the total enhanced payment is deducted after any percentage reduction has been applied) whereas the employer does not in this sense get the full benefit of any other payment made by him because, in effect, it is reduced by the same percentage as the loss suffered by the employee.

Example:
   15–10   Two employees are unfairly dismissed. Both suffering the same loss (£10,000). One has been dismissed for redundancy and receives a £5,000 enhanced redundancy payment (over and above the statutory redundancy payment). The other has been dismissed for lack of capability but receives an *ex gratia* sum of £5,000. In each case the tribunal decides that there should be a 50 per cent reduction under s.123(1) on the basis that had a fair procedure been used there was a 50 per cent chance that they would have been dismissed anyway.

Redundancy Case		Capability Case	
Loss	£10,000	Loss	£10,000
Apply percentage reduction	50%	Deduct *ex gratia* payment	£ 5,000
	£ 5,000		£ 5,000
Deduct enhanced redundancy payment	−£ 5,000	Apply percentage reduction	50%
	Nil		£ 2,500
The employee receives NIL compensatory award		The employee receives £2,500 compensatory award	

The position has, however, been thrown into doubt again by the EAT in the case of *Heggie v. Uniroyal Engelbert Tyres Ltd* [1998] I.R.L.R. 134. This case involved a finding that Mr Heggie had contributed to his dismissal and that accordingly there should be a reduction for contributory fault. The EAT upheld the tribunal's decision to apply this percentage reduction to the loss suffered by Mr Heggie before deducting the sum paid by his employers in lieu of notice. The EAT took the same approach as the Court of Appeal had done in *Digital Equipment Co Ltd v. Clements (No 2)* [1998] I.R.L.R. 134 when considering an enhanced redundancy payment. However, as we have seen, there is a special position dealing with enhanced redundancy payments (s.123(7) ERA—see paras 15–04 to 15–06) which does not apply to any other sort of payment made by the employer. In the Heggie case, Lord Johnston stated: "Justice between the parties, in our view, dictates that the relevant sum should be applied to whatever potential award calculation has been made after the percentage (whatever it may be) deduction has been, made to reflect contributory fault. This approach reflects what we consider to be a distinction, even if the result is the same, between the test to be applied with regard to excess redundancy payments which is laid down in subsection (7), and plainly, in our view, requires the employer to get the full benefit of any excess payment he has made, and the approach to be adopted in cases of contributory conduct, where resort finally has to be had to the overriding considerations of justice and equity, to be found in subsection (1)". The decision has been subject to criticism (see I.R.L.R. Volume 27, Number 8, August 1998 "Highlights" and IDS Brief 619, August 1998). It is unlikely to be the end of the matter.

Payments by the Employer in Discrimination Cases

15–11 In discrimination legislation there is no special provision relating to redundancy cases. Although the issue has not been tested in appeal cases it would seem that in the absence of any special provision such as s.123(7) (see paras 15–04 to 15–06) any payment by the employer—including an enhanced redundancy payment would be set-off against loss suffered by the employee as a result of unlawful sex, race or disability discrimination before any percentage reduction was applied (see paras 13–58 to 13–76 for application of the percentage chance approach in discrimination cases). For example, a woman is unlawfully discriminated against by being selected for redundancy because she is pregnant. The employer makes an *ex gratia* enhanced payment of £1,000 to the employee on termination of employment. The tribunal decides that had she not been dismissed there was a 50 per cent chance that she would have taken maternity leave and returned to work. Her total loss is £10,000. Compensation would, it seems, be calculated as follows:

Loss	£10,000
Deduct *ex gratia* redundancy payment	£ 1,000
	£ 9,000
Apply 50% reduction	£ 4,500
Compensation	**£ 4,500**

Payments Received by way of Mitigation of Loss

15–12   If, following dismissal, the employee gains new employment, those earnings also have to be taken into account in determining the level of compensatory award in an unfair dismissal case or the level of compensation in a discrimination case. The calculation of compensation where the employee has new earnings but where the tribunal also decides that there should be some percentage reduction was considered in *Ministry of Defence v. Wheeler and others* [1998] I.R.L.R. 23. Servicewomen had been unlawfully discharged from the armed forces because of pregnancy. All the women in this appeal had managed to get new employment. The tribunals in each case had had to decide the percentage chance of the women remaining in the armed forces following a period of maternity leave had they not been unlawfully discharged (see paras 13–16 to 13–76 for further commentary on percentage chance approach). The MOD had argued that any percentage reduction should be applied to the total earnings the women would have received had they remained in the armed forces and that any new earnings should then be deducted from this reduced figure.

15–13   The Court of Appeal rejected this approach. First you should calculate total loss by deducing any new earnings from the loss suffered as a result of the unlawful discharge. Then you apply any percentage reduction.

Example

Woman unlawfully dismissed when pregnant	
Total lost wages and other benefits	£10,000
Earnings from new job	£ 5,000
	£ 5,000
Percentage reduction of 50 per cent on basis that the tribunal	50%
decides that had she not been dismissed there was a 50 per cent chance that she would have returned to her job after maternity leave	

Award: £2,500

This is the approach used in personal injury litigation and other litigation where courts have to grapple with the effects of a lost chance (see *Hartle v. Laceys (a firm)* unreported transcript February 28, 1997—referred to by Swinton Thomas LJ in *MOD v. Wheeler* which concerned the lost chance of the sale of a property).

15–14   An example given by Swinton Thomas LJ of the calculation of compensation in a personal injuries case was as follows:

A man earning £10,000 per year is injured in an industrial accident. He can no longer do this work but gets alternative employment at £5,000 per year. The court decides that employer and employee were each 50 per cent to blame for the accident.

If the 50 per cent reduction for contributory fault is applied first to the loss of earnings of £10,000 this gives £5,000. Deduction from this of his earnings of £5,000 would result in nil compensation. This is clearly wrong because "quite plainly the employee has suffered a continuing loss for which he should be compensated".

This analysis is relevant to both the calculation of loss in a discrimination claim and the calculation of the compensatory award for unfair dismissal.

Summary

15–15 Whilst it is always possible that further appeal decisions will revisit these issues the current approach can be summarised as follows:

1. Calculate total loss of earnings and other benefits from previous employment and expenses incurred.

2. Set off against this any earnings/benefits from new employment.

3. Also set off against this any "non redundancy" *ex gratia* payments and any pay in lieu of notice received from former employer. (It is arguable that in a discrimination claim an enhanced redundancy payment should also be set off at this stage.) (Note Heggie v. Uniroyal Englebert Tyres Ltd [1998] I.R.L.R. 425 found that in an unfair dismissal case involving a reduction for contributory fault, that reduction should be made before this stage (see commentary at paras 15–08 to 15–10)).

4. Apply any percentage reduction—for example in a discrimination case, the lost chance of continued employment had the discrimination not occurred, or in an unfair dismissal case, a *Polkey* reduction (see under s.123(1) ERA).

5. Apply any further reduction (unfair dismissal cases) for contributory fault (s.123(6) ERA).

6. Deduct any enhanced redundancy payment (s.123(7) ERA (unfair dismissal cases)).

7. Apply the statutory maximum (currently £12,000) in unfair dismissal cases.

CHAPTER 16

Impact of State and Other Benefits Received in Assessment of Compensation

16–01   In the period following either an unfair dismissal or a dismissal or resignation in circumstances where the employee has suffered unlawful discrimination, he may have been in receipt of one or more of a range of state benefits such as:

1. Jobseekers Allowance

2. Income Support

3. Invalidity Benefit

4. Housing Benefit

The total sum received in the period up to the point at which the tribunal decides compensation may be substantial. It is, therefore, important to understand how such benefits are treated in the assessment of compensation. The rules are different for unfair dismissal and discrimination cases and are therefore considered separately below.

UNFAIR DISMISSAL: WHICH BENEFITS ARE DEDUCTED FROM LOSS?

Income support and Jobseekers Allowance: The Recoupment Regulations

16–02   Special rules apply in the case of income support and the jobseekers allowance. Regulation 4(1) of the Employment Protection (Recoupment of Jobseekers Allowance and Income Support) Regulations 1996 (S.I. 1996 No.2349) states:

"Where these Regulations apply, no regard shall be had, in assessing the amount of a monetary award, to the amount of any Jobseekers Allowance or any income support which may have been paid to or claimed by the employee for a period which coincides with any part of a period to which the prescribed element is attributable".

The Schedule to the Regulations confirms that they apply to the compensatory award for unfair dismissal. (See para. 16–30 for full list of awards that the Regulations apply to and para. 16–20 for commentary on the "prescribed element".)

16–03   The effect of Regulation 4(1) is that, in calculating loss from the date of dismissal to the date of the tribunal remedy hearing, income support or Jobseekers Allowance received during that period is not deducted from loss suffered. The reason for this is that the employer is under a duty to retain a sufficient sum, out of the compensation awarded, to repay benefits received by the complainant to the Secretary of State (see para. 16–24). Note, however, that there is no duty to repay benefits received where an unfair dismissal claim is settled. This is the case even if the settlement is achieved after a finding of unfair dismissal. The rules on recoupment of benefit only apply to awards of the tribunal (see paras 16–18 to 16–30 for further commentary on recoupment).

16–04   The schedule to the regulations states that the period of loss to which recoupment of benefits applies is the period up to the conclusion of tribunal proceedings.

If the tribunal makes an award for future loss the complainant will lose entitlement to benefits for this period (see Regulation 7(1)(k)(iv) Social Security (Unemployment, Sickness and Invalidity Benefit) Regulations 1983 (S.I. 1983 No.1598)). (Jobseekers Act, 1995) By virtue of this provision, days for which compensation is awarded cannot count as days of unemployment. The period of disallowance to benefit is limited to one year from the date of termination of employment. If the compensation is not paid by the respondent, or the respondent becomes insolvent, the complainant will not lose entitlement to benefits.

Housing Benefit

16–05   It is possible that, as a result of the loss of income following dismissal, the dismissed employee will be able to recover all or part of his (and his family's) housing costs by way of a claim for housing benefit. The question of whether housing benefit received following dismissal should be taken into account in the assessment of compensation was considered in the recent case of *Savage v. Saxena* [1998] I.R.L.R. 182 EAT. The majority of the EAT (including Hargrove J.) held that housing benefit should not be taken into account. This should not result in a double benefit for the complainant because the Housing Benefit (General) Regulations 1987 provide for repayment of benefits received in circumstances where the claimant's financial situation changes (such as where compensation for financial loss is received). The duty is on the claimant of housing benefit to notify the housing benefit office of his changed circumstances.

16–06   Hargrove J. pointed out that if housing benefit was deducted by a tribunal in assessing financial loss, this would not stop the authority responsible for reassessing housing benefit from recovering sums apparently overpaid on the basis of the compensation recovered. In this way the complainant could lose out twice—by having housing benefit deducted from financial loss suffered in the assessment of compensation and by having to repay housing benefit received if the compensation he does get disentitles him to benefit for the period concerned.

The EAT also held that "housing benefit ... is not sufficiently proximate to the loss sustained in consequence of the dismissal in so far as that loss is attributable to the action taken by the employer. Housing benefit results from the inability of an applicant to meet reasonable housing needs from his resources. Furthermore, it is paid not in respect of the individual but in respect of the needs of the household. In this way it differs markedly from invalidity benefit" (Hargrove J.).

Hargrove, J. also made the point that, if housing benefit were to be deducted from financial loss suffered, the respondent would "derive a profit in that the sum that has been utilised, housing benefit, will be credited to him". That could not be right.

Future Loss

16–07   So far as future loss is concerned, the position is that compensation received by the complainant will be taken into account in determining future entitlement to housing benefit.

Invalidity Benefit

16–08   The treatment of invalidity benefit in the assessment of compensation for unfair dismissal has been the subject of conflicting decisions of the EAT. In fact, three divisions of the EAT have managed to come up with different solutions.

In the case of *Hilton International Hotels (UK) Ltd v. Faraji* [1994] I.C.R. 259, the EAT took the view that invalidity benefit should be included within the category of insurance benefits which should not be taken into account in the assessment of loss. Invalidity benefit arises as a result of the national insurance scheme. Payments made by employees in respect of national insurance can be classified as insurance premiums. Invalidity benefit depends to some extent on the amount of payments made.

16–09   Insurance benefits of this sort were an exception to the general principle that an award should put the injured party in the same position as he would have been if he had not sustained the injury. Accordingly, invalidity benefit received should not be deducted from financial loss suffered in determining the compensatory award.

However, then came the case of *Puglia v. C. James & Sons* [1996] I.R.L.R. 70 EAT. In this case, the EAT held that the full amount of invalidity benefit should be deducted. Mummery J. took the view that the *Hilton* case should not be followed. Their attention had not been drawn to all the relevant authorities. In particular, in the case of *Palfrey v. Greater London Council* [1985] I.C.R. 437 (a personal injuries case), the judge, Mr Piers Ashworth QC, said "It seems to me ... that the common law position is that benefits received from the state must be taken into account in the assessment of damages ... I do not think that any valid distinction can be drawn between unemployment benefit, supplementary benefit, sickness benefit, industrial injury benefit and so on." It is only the recoupment regulations in the employment law context which require Jobseekers Allowance (which replaces unemployment benefit) and income support (which replaces supplementary benefit) to be treated differently (see paras 16–02 to 16–03).

16–10   The third of the recent EAT cases considering this issue is *Rubenstein & another (t/a McGuffies Dispensing Chemists) v. McGlaughlin* [1996] I.R.L.R. 557 EAT. The EAT in this case decided that one-half of the invalidity benefit received should be deducted from financial loss suffered in order to determine the compensatory award. Hicks J. reached this conclusion for the following reasons.

What is now s.123(1) ERA requires tribunals to award what is "just and equitable". That "releases it from the straight-jacket of the 'all or nothing' approach of common law."

Secondly, Hicks J. pointed to the situation in which Parliament had mitigated the "extremity of the common law" by adopting "solutions which involved treating employer and employee equally, either by dividing the value of the benefits between them by the device of half deduction or by removing from both by requiring recoupment". This provided strong support for adopting an intermediate course.

16–11   Thirdly, they took the view that while invalidity benefit was not in the category of pure insurance moneys, the employee had contributed to it by making National Insurance payments. The just and equitable solution was to deduct half.

This last case is the most recently argued and the EAT carried out a comprehensive review of the authorities. To that extent, it is likely to be followed by tribunals until the issue is determined by the Court of Appeal.

DISCRIMINATION CASES

16–12 The Recoupment Regulations do not apply to discrimination cases. Compensation is calculated in accordance with common law principles in cases of tort.

In the personal injuries case of *Palfrey v. Greater London* Council [1985] I.C.R. 437 (see also para. 16–09) it was confirmed that the normal common law rule is that any benefits recovered from the state must be taken into account in the assessment of damages. It would seem that an exception to that principle should be housing benefit, on the basis that it is not sufficiently proximate to the loss sustained as a result, for example, of a discriminatory dismissal and because the local authority is obliged to recover housing benefit paid if the claimant's circumstances change (see paras 16–05 to 16–07 in respect of *Savage v. Saxena* [1998] I.R.L.R. 182 EAT—an unfair dismissal case).

EARLY RETIREMENT PENSIONS, AND OTHER INSURANCE PAYMENTS: UNFAIR DISMISSAL AND DISCRIMINATION CLAIMS

16–13 If the dismissed employee qualifies for an early retirement pension or an ill-health pension by virtue of having been a member of a pension scheme, payments of such a pension should not, it seems, be deducted from financial loss suffered as a result of the dismissal. This rule appears to apply to both unfair dismissal and to discrimination cases. Similarly, if the dismissed employee has chosen to obtain insurance to cover payments under a mortgage or the repayments of any other loan in the event of certain kinds of dismissal, such as redundancy, then the payments recovered by the employee from such an insurance policy should not be taken into account in the assessment of compensation.

16–14 The case law all relates to common law claims which, of course, is the basis of assessment of compensation for discrimination. It is logical to apply the same approach to unfair dismissal cases subject to the important proviso that the tribunal has the discretion to determine what is "just and equitable" in assessing the compensatory award (s.123(1) ERA).

In the case of *British Transport Commission v. Gourley* [1956] A.C. 185 the following statement was made:

> "The broad general principle which should govern the assessment of damages in cases such as this is that the tribunal should award the injured party such sum of money as will put him in the same position as he would have been in if he had not sustained the injuries ... There are, no doubt, instances to be found in the books of exceptional cases as ... for instance, in cases of insurance."

The principle that where a plaintiff recovers under an insurance policy, for which he has paid the premiums, any insurance moneys received are not deductible from damages was established in the case of *Bradburn v. Great Western Railway Co.* [1864] L.R. 10.

16–15 The principle that where a plaintiff receives money from the benevolence of third parties out of sympathy for his misfortune, such sums are not deductible was established in *Redpath v. Belfast and County Down Railway* [1947] N.I. 147.

In *Parry v. Cleaver* [1970] A.C. 1, Lord Reid considered further the exceptions to the general principle explained in *Gourley*. The plaintiff, in this case, had received a pension as a result of the accident (which was the basis of the personal injuries claim). He stated:

> "In two large classes of case such sums were disregarded—the proceeds of insurance and sums coming to him by reason of benevolence. If *Gourley's* case had any bearing on this matter it must have impinged on these classes. But no one suggests that it had any effect as regards sums coming to the plaintiff by reason of benevolence, and I see no reason why it should have made any difference as regards insurance."

Mr Parry had to make contributions to the pension scheme as a condition of his contract of employment.

16–16 In *Smoker v. London Fire and Civil Defence Authority* [1991] I.C.R. 449 (HL), it was held that, even in circumstances where the defendant in the claim and the insurers were identical, the same rule applied: payments received as a result of insurance should not be deducted from lost earnings in the assessment of damages. In this case, Lord Templeman said that "*Parry v. Cleaver* established clearly that pension benefits are not deductible". A distinction does, however, appear to be drawn in the case of permanent health insurance provided by the employer. Payments received under such a scheme should, it seems, be deducted in the assessment of compensation.

16–17 This was the decision of the House of Lords in *Hussain v. New Taplow Paper Mills Ltd* [1988] I.C.R. 259. Lord Bridge of Harwich said that "it has always been assumed as axiomatic that an employee who receives under the terms of his contract of employment either the whole or part of his salary or wage during a period when he is incapacitated for work cannot claim damages for a loss which he has not sustained."

The distinction, if there is one, appears to be based on the nature of the payments. The payments under the permanent health insurance policy in *Hussain* could be equated to wages. In *Smoker v. London Fire Authority*, Lord Templeman took this view: "The cases on which the defendants rely are mainly those in which the courts have decided that payments which correspond to wages must be taken into account when assessing loss of wages".

THE RECOUPMENT REGULATIONS

16–18 We have already considered the rule that payments of income support (IS) and Jobseekers Allowance (JSA) are not to be taken into account in the assessment of compensation for unfair dismissal (see paras 16–02 to 16–04 and Regulation 4(1) Employment Protection (Recoupment of Jobseeker's Allowance and Income Support) Regulations, 1996 (1996 Regulations)). The 1996 Regulations then set out the rules which require the payments of IS and JSA to be repaid, out of compensation awarded, to the Secretary of State.

The Recoupment Process

16–19 The tribunal is required to assess the monetary award without deduction of JSA or IS. The tribunal is then under a duty (Reg 4(3) 1996 Regulations) to set out in any decision which includes a monetary award the following particulars:

    (a)   the monetary award

(b) the amount of the prescribed element, if any

(c) The dates of the period to which the prescribed element is attributable

(d) The amount, if any, by which the monetary award exceeds the prescribed element.

What is "the prescribed element"?

16–20 The prescribed element in unfair dismissal cases is the amount of compensation for lost wages up to the conclusion of the tribunal proceedings (see Reg 3(1)(a) and schedule to the regs). If the period of lost wages for which the complainant is to be compensated is shorter than the full period up to the conclusion of the tribunal proceedings then just that shorter period applies. If, therefore, the tribunal awards compensation for six weeks' lost wages but the complainant continues, after that, to receive benefit up to the date of the hearing, only the benefit paid during the period of six weeks' loss awarded can be recouped. Note that pension contributions are not taken into account in calculating lost wages.

Percentage Reduction

16–21 It is important to note the provision of regulation 4(2) of the 1996 Regulations:

"Where the ... tribunal in arriving at a monetary award makes a reduction on account of the employee's contributory fault or on account of any limit imposed by or under the 1992 Act or 1996 Act a proportionate reduction shall be made in arriving at the amount of the prescribed element."

Note that no reference is made to percentage reductions on the basis of what is "just and equitable" by virtue of s.123(1) ERA (see paras 11–03 to 11–37).

In *Mason v. (1) Wimpey Waste Management Ltd (2) Secretary of State for Employment* [1982] I.R.L.R. 454 EAT, compensation was assessed in the sum of £7,712. Of this, the compensation for loss suffered up to the hearing was £5,918. The statutory maximum at that time was £5,200. The total compensatory award, of course, therefore, had to be reduced to £5,200, to the statutory maximum.

16–22 The EAT confirmed that the prescribed element had to be reduced to a similar extent as the total compensatory award had been reduced to bring it down to the statutory maximum. Therefore, loss up to the date of the final tribunal hearing, £5,918, was reduced to £3,991 to determine the prescribed element out of which benefits would be recouped. It may, of course, be the case that the prescribed element is reduced to a lower figure than the total sum of benefits received. If this is the case then not all the benefits are recouped.

Date of tribunal hearing to determine prescribed element

16–23 The case of *Mason v. (1) Wimpey Waste Management Ltd (2) Secretary of State for Employment* (see paras 16–21 to 16–22) also confirms that the prescribed element applies to compensation for loss of wages for a period up to the final compensation hearing (even if there has been an appeal in the meantime). The schedule to the regulations states that the prescribed element covers lost wages up to the "conclusion of the tribunal proceedings". Regulation 2(3) states that the conclusion of the proceedings is taken to occur:

(a)   where the tribunal at the hearing announces the effect of its decision to the parties, on the date on which that announcement is made;

(b)   in any other case, on the date on which the decision of the tribunal is sent to the parties.

Regulation 2(5) makes specific reference to further hearings following an appeal. This, said the EAT, meant that the relevant period for the determination of the prescribed element ended with the conclusion of the final hearing which in the *Mason* case followed a successful appeal against the first hearing.

Informing the Secretary of State

16–24   Once the tribunal has announced the details set out at para. 16–19, the Secretary of the tribunal notifies the Secretary of State of the monetary award including a prescribed element and of the other details set out at para. 16–19. The Secretary also sends the Secretary of State the written decision (Reg 4(5) and (6)). (These steps are only required if the complainant has received JSA or IS—Reg 4(8)). The employer must not send the complainant the prescribed element until he receives a recoupment notice from the DSS or, alternatively, a written notice confirming that the DSS does not intend to serve a notice (Reg 7).

16–25   The Recoupment Notice must be served on the employer (or the notification confirming that the Secretary of State does not intend service a Notice) within 21 days of the tribunal's announcement of the decision at the hearing or within nine days of the decision being sent to the parties, whichever is later (Reg 8(6)(a)). If it is a reserved decision the Notice must be sent to the employer within 21 days of the written decision being sent to the parties (Reg 8(6)(b)). The complainant also receives a copy of the Recoupment Notice (Reg 8(4)).

In response to the Recoupment Notice, the employer must pay to the Secretary of State the "recoupable amount" (Reg 8(8)). This is the total sum of JSA or IS paid to the complainant during the period to which the prescribed element relates, but subject to the maximum of the prescribed element (Reg 8(2)(a)) (whichever is the lesser of either the amount of the prescribed element less tax and National Insurance; or (b) the actual amount of JSA or IS paid during the period).

Employee's right to challenge Recoupment Notice

16–26   If the employee does not accept the amount set out in the recoupment notice to be recouped, he can, within 21 days of receiving a copy of the recoupment notice, serve notice on the Secretary of State (Reg 10(1)). The Secretary of State can accept a late notice if there are "special reasons" (Reg 10(1)). If such a notice is served, an Adjudication Officer is asked to review the amount fixed for recoupment.

There is then a right of appeal to the Social Security Appeal Tribunal against the Adjudication Officer's decision and, where appropriate, to the Social Security Commissioner (Reg 10(2)). If the employee succeeds in his challenge he recovers any excess amount recouped (Reg 10(3)). Also, if the decision of the tribunal is successfully appealed, resulting in a reduction in the amount which should have been recouped, then the Secretary of State must repay either the employer or the employee as required (Reg 10(4)).

Special procedural rules for protective awards

16–27 Regulation 5 sets out special procedural requirements in respect of protective awards. Where a tribunal at the hearing announces the effect of a decision to make a protective award, or if no announcement has been made and the tribunal sends a decision to make such an award to the parties, the Secretary of the tribunals must straight away send the following particulars to the Secretary of State:

1. The date of the announcement or the date the decision was sent to the parties;

2. The location of the tribunal;

3. The name and address of the employer;

4. The description of employers to whom the award relates;

5. The dates of the protected period.

(Regulation 5(1)).

16–28 If the tribunal announces the award, they must also explain to the employer the steps he must take. In any event, those steps must be set out in the decision sent to the parties (Reg 5(2)(a) and (b)). The employer must give the Secretary of State the following written information:

1. name, address and NI number of every employee to whom the award relates;

2. the date of termination (or proposed termination) of employment of each such employee (Reg 6(1)).

This information must be given within 10 days of the oral announcement of the effect of the decision or (if no announcement was made) of the date the decision was sent to the parties (Reg 6(2)). If it was not reasonably practicable for the employer to provide the information within this time scale, he must supply it as soon as reasonably practicable (Reg 6(3)).

16–29 Regulation 7(2) requires the employer not to make any payments to the employees entitled to the protective award until the Recoupment Notice is served instructing the employer how much recoupment is required in respect of each employee. The Recoupment Notice must be served by the Secretary of State within 21 days of having received the information required under Regulation 6(1) from the employer. (Reg 8(7)). Regulation 7(3) provides that the obligation on the employer not to pay the protective award until he has received the recoupment notice does not stop the employee from presenting a complaint to a tribunal in respect of the employer's failure to pay the award. This right to complain is provided for by s.192 TULR(C)A.

Tribunal Awards subject to recoupment

16–30 The Schedule to the Recoupment Regulations sets out all of the awards to which the rules on recoupment apply. They are as follows:

1. guarantee payments (s.28 ERA);

2. payments under a collective agreement providing for guaranteed pay where

an exemption order has been made under s.35 ERA excluding statutory guarantee payments;

3. payments of remuneration for a period of suspension on medical grounds (s.64 ERA and s.108(2) ERA, see paras 22–42 to 22–45);

4. payments of remuneration for a period of suspension on maternity grounds (s.68 ERA, see paras 22–42 to 22–45);

5. payments under reinstatement or re-engagement order in respect of unfair dismissal (s.114(1) and s.117(8), see paras 8–17 to 8–38);

6. compensatory awards for unfair dismissal (see Chapter 10);

7. additional awards where reinstatement or re-engagement order not complied with (see paras 8–39 to 8–46);

8. payment under interim order for reinstatement or re-engagement (s.163(4) and s.163(5)(a) TULR(C)) (see Chapter 12);

9. payment under order for continuation of employment (s.163(5), s.163(6), s.166(1) and (2) TULR(C)A, (see Chapter 12);

10. payments of compensation where order for continuation of contract of employment not complied with (s.166(3)–(5) TULR(C)A, see Chapter 12);

11. payments due under protective award or where employer fails to pay protective award (s.192 TULR(C)A).

CHAPTER 17

Recovery of Costs

17–01 An award of costs in tribunal proceedings is the exception rather than the rule. There is no general power to award costs. Such an award will only be made in strictly defined circumstances. Nonetheless, it is important for litigants and their advisers to be fully conversant with the rules relating to costs and for the issue to be properly considered throughout the course of any litigation. Whilst recognising the limited circumstances in which an award of costs will be made, it is clear that such an award can be a valuable remedy. As has been noted at para. 6–05, it may be appropriate for the complainant, during the preparation stage, to warn the other party that you consider that their conduct of the proceedings will provide a basis for claiming costs and to put them on notice that you will make such an application.

PRELIMINARY CONSIDERATIONS: TIMING OF APPLICATION

17–02 An application for costs should be made within a reasonable time (see *Colin Johnson t/a Richard Andrew Ladies Hairstylists v. Baxter* [1985] I.R.L.R. 96). It should preferably be made at the tribunal hearing, unless the tribunal reserves its decision. Even then it may be appropriate to make the application so that the tribunal can consider the issue and include its decision on costs along with their findings on liability. This *obiter* guidance was given by the EAT in *Colin Johnson t/a Richard Andrew Ladies Hairstylists v. Baxter* [1985] I.R.L.R. 96. Bearing in mind that cases frequently settle at the tribunal, sometimes following a finding of liability, it may be wise to take to the tribunal a clear breakdown of costs incurred either to present to the tribunal or for use in negotiations to settle the claim. There is no reason for not raising a claim for costs in such negotiations. If there is a basis for an award of costs then the issue should be taken into account in deciding whether a settlement offer is acceptable (see para. 17–18 for the costs orders which can be made).

STATUTORY PROVISIONS

17–03 The provisions dealing with costs are set out in Rule 12 of Schedule 1 to the Industrial Tribunals (Constitution and Rules of Procedure) Regulations 1993 (S.I. 1993 No.2687). Subject to a special provision relating to equal pay claims (see para. 17–23) the rules apply generally to all proceedings in the tribunal considered in this book. The key provision is set out in Rule 12(1):

> "Where, in the opinion of the tribunal, a party has in bringing or conducting the proceedings acted frivolously, vexatiously, abusively, disruptively or otherwise unreasonably, the tribunal may make—
>
> (a)   an order containing an award against that party in respect of the costs incurred by another party;

(b) an order that that party shall pay to the Secretary of State the whole, or
    any part, of any allowances (other than allowances paid to members of
    tribunals) paid by the Secretary of State … to any person for the purposes
    of, or in connection with, his attendance at the tribunal."

It is worth noting that prior to the introduction of the current rules, specific reference
was made to the fact that an award of costs was not normally to be made. Now no
such presumption is stated. Nonetheless, the strict criteria set out in Rule 12(1) still
have to be met. Note also that the tribunal has a discretion to award costs in the
circumstances set out in Rule 12(1). It may make such an order.

Awards against either party

17–04   Rule 12(1) applies equally to the conduct of the complainant and the
respondent in tribunal proceedings, although the reference to bringing proceedings
self-evidently refers to the complainant.

Frivolous or vexatious conduct

17–05   Originally the rule only referred to frivolous or vexatious conduct and did
not include any reference to acting unreasonably. This addition has extended the scope
of the rule considerably and is considered at paras 17–08 to 17–11. Conduct which is
frivolous or vexatious is hard to establish. With regard to the complainant, Sir Hugh
Griffiths in *E.T. Marler Ltd v. Robertson* [1974] I.C.R. 72, NIRC described the sort of
conduct covered:

Frivolous conduct

17–06   If the complainant "knows that there is no substance to his claim and that
it is bound to fail, or if the claim is on the face of it so manifestly misconceived that
it can have no prospect of success, it may be deemed frivolous and an abuse of the
procedure of the tribunal to pursue it". (See also Carr v. Allen-Bradley Electronics Ltd
[1980] I.R.L.R. 263 EAT at para. 17–07).

Vexatious conduct

17–07   If the claim is "hopeless", brought with no expectation of recovering
compensation but "out of spite to harass his employers or for some other improper
motive, he acts vexatiously". Such findings by the tribunal will "generally involve bad
faith" on the part of the complainant. One would expect the tribunal's discretion "to
be sparingly exercised".

These interpretations of the law have been accepted in subsequent cases. In *Cartiers
Superfoods Ltd v. Laws* [1978] I.R.L.R. 315 EAT, Phillips J. made the point that it
was not desirable to multiply authority. He was content to accept as a general
statement of the law what was said by Sir Hugh Griffiths in *Marler Ltd v. Robertson*.

It was also accepted in *Carr v. Allen-Bradley Electronics Ltd* [1980] I.R.L.R. 263
EAT. In that case there had been no vexatious behaviour by the complainant. However,
the tribunal had found that this was "a meritless claim which should never had been
brought in view of the applicant's deplorable attendance record" and the respondent's
"admirable personnel procedures" and consultations with the union. The claim "did
not leave the starting post". The EAT upheld the tribunal's decision. The claim could
be characterised as frivolous.

Unreasonable conduct

17–08 The introduction into the statutory criteria for awarding costs of the concept of unreasonable conduct has substantially widened the scope of the rules.

Unreasonable conduct of the complainant

17–09 Note that the conduct of the complainant which can be considered in this context includes both the bringing and the conducting of proceedings.

In *Stein v. Associated Dairies Ltd* [1982] I.R.L.R. 447 EAT, the complainant's representatives had been warned by the respondent's solicitor before the hearing that another employee who had been dismissed on the same day for the same offence had lost his claim for unfair dismissal and had had costs awarded against him. The solicitor had put them on notice that in the event of success he reserved the right to claim costs. The EAT upheld the tribunal's decision to award costs against the complainant on the grounds that he had acted unreasonably.

Conduct of the respondent

17–10 The respondent might act unreasonably (or frivolously or vexatiously) in defending the claim, in his conduct thereafter in continuing his defence and in his conduct at the hearing. Note, first of all, that costs should not be awarded as a punishment of the respondent. The purpose of an award of costs is to compensate the complainant in the limited set of circumstances where costs can be awarded. (See *Davidson v. John Calder (Publishers) Ltd and Calder Educational Trust Ltd* [1985] I.R.L.R. 97 "In our judgment it is contrary to the whole basis on which costs are awarded to think of the problem in terms of punishment of the loser, not compensation to the winner for what it has cost him to get justice").

Conduct in relation to the dismissal

17–11 In the unfair dismissal context, the conduct of the respondent in dismissing the complainant or in terms of the nature of the dismissal is not a basis for awarding costs against the respondent (*Davidson v. Calder*). Clearly, however, these issues obviously have a bearing on whether it is reasonable for the respondent to defend the claim and so, to this extent, they are relevant. For example, an employer who dismisses an employee for a minor act of misconduct without conducting a disciplinary hearing may well act unreasonably in defending the claim and continuing to defend it all the way to a tribunal hearing. If the complainant, or his representative, considers that there is no proper basis for the respondent to defend the claim then he should put the respondent on notice that in the event of the claim succeeding, an application will be made for costs (see also para. 6–05).

Postponement or adjournment of hearing

17–12 Special provision is made for an award of costs where a hearing is postponed or adjourned. Rule 12(4) provides:

> "Where the tribunal has on the application of a party postponed the day or time fixed for or adjourned the hearing, the tribunal may make [an order for costs or for repayment of allowances] against or, as the case may require, in favour of that party as respects any costs incurred or any allowances paid as a result of the postponement or adjournment."

Note then, that an award of costs in such circumstances is at the discretion of the tribunal. Note also that costs can be awarded either against or in favour of the party making the application for postponement or adjournment. This will, of course, depend on the circumstances of the particular case. For example, a party might apply for an adjournment either in circumstances where he is at fault, perhaps in not being ready to proceed, or, alternatively, in circumstances where he alleges that the other party is at fault, for example by revealing documents late in the day or responding late to an order for further and better particulars (see also Chapter 4 for commentary on the tribunal's powers to obtain information and documents from the other side).

17–13   For example, in *Ladbroke Racing Ltd v. Hickey* [1979] I.R.L.R. 273 EAT, the respondent delivered a large bundle of documents to the employee's representative 45 minutes before the hearing. This led to an application for an adjournment by Mr Hickey's representative so as to give time to consider these documents. The EAT upheld the tribunal's decision to award costs against the respondent. It was his conduct which had led to the need for an adjournment. Bristow J. in *Ladbroke Racing Ltd v. Hickey* also drew attention to the fact that the specific power to award costs in the case of adjournments and postponements is not restricted to cases of conduct which is frivolous, vexatious or unreasonable. In this context "the tribunal is vested with the ordinary power of the court to award costs ... against a party which it considers to have been responsible for the necessity for the adjournment".

Finally, note that the power to award costs is in respect of costs "incurred or any allowances paid *as a result* of the postponement or adjournment". Costs of actually preparing the claim have nothing to do with an adjournment and should not be awarded. They would be incurred in any event and not as a result of the adjournment.

Special rules where there is an application for reinstatement or re-engagement / Return to work after maternity leave (unfair dismissal claims)

17–14   If the complainant has applied for reinstatement or re-engagement and the respondent has been notified of such application at least seven days before the hearing or where the respondent has failed to allow the complainant to return to work after maternity leave and a postponement or adjournment is necessary because the respondent has failed, without special reason, to adduce reasonable evidence as to the availability of the job from which the complainant was dismissed (or which the woman had before maternity leave) or of comparable or suitable employment, then costs shall be awarded against the respondent (Rule 12(5)). Note that in this case the tribunal does not have a discretion. It shall make an award of costs if the circumstances set out in Rule 12(5) apply (see Chapter 8 for commentary on reinstatement and re-engagement).

Deposit paid by complainant

17–15   Power exists by virtue of Rule 7 of Schedule 1 to the 1993 Procedure Regulations to order the complainant or respondent to pay a deposit of up to £150 as a condition of being permitted to take part in the proceedings. This occurs following a pre-hearing review if the tribunal is of the view that that party "has no reasonable prospect of success" (Rule 7(4)). If that party proceeds, having paid the deposit, and subsequently loses and if there has been no other award of costs made against that party, the tribunal is obliged to consider whether to award costs on the basis that he "conducted the proceedings ... unreasonably in persisting in having the matter determined by a tribunal" (Rule 12(7)).

17–16   Note, however, that before making such an award the tribunal must consider the written decision relating to the deposit. An award should then only be made if the tribunal is of the opinion that the reasons that led to the tribunal finding against the party were "substantially the same" as the reasons recorded when the decision was made in respect of the deposit (Rule 12(7)). Rule 12(8) provides that the deposit monies can be used to pay an award of costs made against the party who has paid the deposit. The award of costs may be in respect of other proceedings considered at the same time (for example, discrimination and unfair dismissal claims considered together). An apportionment is made as the tribunal considers fit where an award of costs is made in favour of more than one party (Rule 12(8)(b)). Any balance is refunded to the party paying the deposit (Rule 12(8)(b)).

Extension of time for presenting Notice of Appearance

17–17   As a result of an amendment in 1996 to the Procedure Rules, the respondent now has twenty one days to present the notice of appearance (Rule 3). As well as potentially losing the right to take part in the proceedings by failing to meet this deadline there may also be a financial penalty to pay in the form of an order for costs if an application for an extension of time is successful (Rule 3(4)). If the tribunal chairman who grants such an application for an extension of time determines that it would have been "reasonably practicable" for the respondent to present his notice of appearance within the twenty one days permitted, the respondent "shall be treated as having acted unreasonably" for the purposes of Rule 12(1). The chairman then shall make an order for costs under Rule 12(1) if he considers it appropriate (see paras 17–03 to 17–10). Note, however, that the order under Rule 12(1) is in respect of costs incurred by the other party. The complainant would therefore have to show costs which had been incurred as a result of the respondent's unreasonable conduct in failing to present his notice of appearance in time in order to get an award of costs.

THE AWARD OF COSTS

17–18   The powers of the tribunal in respect of the award of costs which it can make are set out in Rule 12(3). The award against a party shall be:

(a)   where the tribunal thinks fit, an order that the party pay a specified sum not exceeding £500;

(b)   where the parties agree on a sum, the tribunal shall order that sum to be paid; or

(c)   in any other case, an order that the party pay the whole or a specified part of costs incurred as taxed (if not otherwise agreed).

If an order is made for costs to be taxed they may be taxed in the County Court using County Court scales as directed by the tribunal order (Rule 12(6)). The effect of these rules is that if the party who would receive the award of costs wants to pursue a sum in excess of £500 then he either has to agree it with the party against whom the order is to be made or wait for his costs to be taxed.

The tribunal's discretion in the award of costs

Means of the party

17–19   The tribunal can take into account the means of the party against whom the order for costs is to be made. In the case of *Wiggins Alloys Ltd v. Jenkins* [1981] I.R.L.R. 275, the complainant was imprisoned for six years as a result of theft from his employer. His unfair dismissal claim, not surprisingly, failed, but the tribunal made no award of costs because he was not in a position to pay any costs. The EAT upheld this decision but noted that each case depended on its own circumstances. The "mere fact that for the time being an applicant is penniless" does not lead inevitably to the decision not to award costs. The issue is within the discretion of the tribunal. Frequently a respondent will decide that it is not worth pursuing an order for costs against an unemployed complainant with no obvious assets. Where, however, the award of costs is to be made against the respondent, ability to pay is unlikely to be an issue.

In Omar v. Worldwide News Inc [1998] I.R.L.R. Smith J said that "tribunals *must* look at an applicant's personal means to pay before making an order for costs against him as a party".

Disregard the means of a union supporting the complainant

17–20   In the case of *Carr v. Allen-Bradley Electronics Ltd* [1980] I.R.L.R. 263, the EAT overturned an order for costs to be taxed on Scale 4 by the County Court. This decision had been reached taking into account the means of the union which had supported the complainant. Although the tribunal had been right to order costs against her as a result of her conduct, the order should only take into account her means and not those of the union (the EAT left open the possibility of taking into account the means of the union in some circumstances where the union appears culpable).

In the Omar case (see para. 17–19) Smith J said that it is only in "exceptional cases" that the tribunal can take into account the means of the trade union. He then defined two categories of such cases

1.   "where the union ... has brought or conducted a claim before [a tribunal] on behalf of its member which to the union's knowledge or means of knowledge is without any merit"

2.   "where the union has pursued a particular case as a 'lead' or 'test' case, involving an important point of principle for its membership and where unusually it has offered an indemnity as to costs to the applicants concerned in such case"

In support of this exception Smith J referred to the case of *Dorney and others v. Chippenham College* EAT 10/97.

In-house lawyers

17–21   The EAT in the case of *Wiggin Alloys Ltd v. Jenkins* [1981] I.R.L.R. 275 held that "legal costs incurred in litigation by the use of in-house lawyers are as much recoverable as are the costs incurred by employing independent solicitors".

Repayment of Allowances

17–22   Note that Rule 12(1) provides for the repayment of allowances as well as the making of an award of costs where the criteria under that rule are met. The allowances referred to are those paid to parties or witnesses attending the hearing (claim forms are available from the tribunal). So the party against whom an order is made under Rule 12(1) may have to repay to the Secretary of State allowances paid to witnesses on both sides and those paid to both parties.

Equal Pay Cases

17–23   Rules on costs in equal pay cases are set out in Rule 12 of Schedule 2 to the 1993 Regulations. The rules are essentially the same but it should be noted that costs can include the expenses of instructing an expert to investigate and prepare a report (Rule 12 (2A)).

CHAPTER 18

Interest on Late Payment of Awards

18–01 The rules relating to the right to interest from the date of an act of discrimination are dealt with at paras 13–42 to 13–54. There is no equivalent right to interest in respect of awards for unfair dismissal, or other claims such as unlawful deduction from wages or in breach of contract claims. This section considers the right to claim interest where there has been a late payment of an award. This applies to discrimination awards as well as to other monetary awards including unfair dismissal. Note, however, that the rules on calculation of this interest are different in discrimination cases (see para. 18–07).

Statutory Provision

18–02 The current rules are contained in the Industrial Tribunal (Interest) Order 1990 (S.I. 1990 No.479). The right applies to "any award or other determination of the tribunal" where one party is required to pay a sum of money to another party. Excluded from this are sums in respect of costs or expenses (Article 2(1)). One also disregards any part of an award which is subject to recoupment and any sum which the respondent has to deduct and pay to the Revenue (or National Insurance). The sum of money has to be specified "in an award or other determination of the tribunal" or "in an order or decision of an appellate court". Alternatively, it must be "otherwise ascertainable, solely by reference to the terms of an award or determination or to terms of an order or decision of an appellate court". (Article 2(2). In other words, if the tribunal finds in favour of the complainant but leaves open the question of compensation to be determined either by agreement between the parties or by the tribunal at a later hearing, interest will not run unless and until the tribunal subsequently determines a figure for compensation and states it in an award.

The Right to Interest

18–03 Article 3 provides that if all or part of a sum of money awarded by the tribunal remains unpaid for 42 days after promulgation of the award then interest starts to accrue on the amount unpaid. Note that it only starts to accrue from the 42nd day after promulgation. Promulgation is when the written decision confirming the monetary award is sent to the parties (note, however, that different rules apply in discrimination cases—see para. 18–07).

Rate of Interest

18–04 The rate of interest is as specified in the Judgements Act 1838. The current rate is eight per cent. Interest is simple interest accruing from day to day (Article 4).

Reviews and Appeals

18–05 If the decision of the tribunal is reviewed or appealed then the following rules apply:

1. If there is an application for review of the original decision which contains a promulgated award, interest runs from 42 days after promulgation of the original award. If the review, or a re-hearing following a review, results in the sum awarded being varied then interest is calculated on that varied sum (arts. 5 and 11)

2. If the decision is appealed, and if that original decision contained a promulgated award, interest will accrue from 42 days after that original decision is promulgated (arts. 6 and 7)

3. If in that situation the sum awarded is varied then the interest will be calculated on that varied sum but still for the period starting from 42 days after the original decision was promulgated (arts. 6, 7, 11)

4. If there are further appeals the same principle applies (art. 7).

5. If, following appeal, the case is remitted to a fresh tribunal hearing to re-assess the sum payable and the tribunal varies the amount of compensation, interest is calculated on the varied sum but still from 42 days after the original award was promulgated (art. 6).

6. If a tribunal decision is appealed but no award has been promulgated by the tribunal (for example the tribunal's decision only deals with liability) then interest will only accrue 42 days after either the appellate court has promulgated an award of compensation or, if the appeal court remits the case to the tribunal, 42 days after the tribunal which considers the case further, promulgates an award (art. 8).

Part Payment of sum awarded

18–06 If, following the period of 42 days after promulgation of the decision, part of the sum due is paid then, from that date on, interest continues to accrue on the part of the award which remains unpaid (art. 3(2)).

Discrimination Cases

18–07 An important variation to the above rules applies in discrimination cases by virtue of the Industrial Tribunal (Interest on Awards in Discrimination Cases) Regulations 1996 (S.I. 1996 No.2803) (the 1996 Regulations). First, where an award in a discrimination case remains unpaid for 14 days following promulgation of the decision, interest becomes payable on that award (art. 8(2), 1996 Regs). Further, interest runs from the day following promulgation of the decision rather than from 42 days after that date as in other claims (see para. 18–03) (article 8(1) 1996 Regs). The same rate of interest applies. Finally, interest on late payment in discrimination cases is calculated on the full award unpaid including on any interest awarded as part of the compensation (art. 8(2), 1996 Regs) (see paras 13–42 to 13–54).

CHAPTER 19
Mitigation of Loss

19–01 The principle of the duty to mitigate loss has assumed greater importance in the tribunal with the lifting of the lid on compensation in discrimination cases. With potentially large awards of compensation now possible the tribunal frequently has to consider periods of loss stretching over a number of years. In the litigation involving women unlawfully discharged from the armed forces as a result of pregnancy, tribunals often had to consider cases where the woman had left the forces several years previously. Identifying the steps which the woman had taken, following discharge, to mitigate her loss was crucial to the proper assessment of compensation. If the cap on compensation for unfair dismissal is raised substantially or lifted altogether (see Chapter 26) then the principles of mitigation will assume greater significance for unfair dismissal compensation as well.

Statutory Provisions

19–02 In assessing the compensatory award for unfair dismissal and compensation for unlawful sex, race or disability discrimination the tribunal applies the same rule with regard to mitigation. In all such cases the complainant has a duty to mitigate his loss and the normal common law principles apply. With regard to unfair dismissal, s.123(4) ERA specifically provides that the tribunal must apply the common law principle that a person has a duty to mitigate his loss. Sex, race and disability discrimination are all statutory torts and the same common law duty to mitigate applies.

WHAT IS THE DUTY TO MITIGATE?

19–03 The duty to mitigate is based on the principle that a plaintiff should only be compensated for unavoidable loss. If the loss could reasonably have been avoided by the plaintiff taking certain steps then he should not be able to recover compensation from the defendant. Halsbury's Laws (Fourth Edition) Volume 12 paragraph 1193 states:

> "The plaintiff must take all reasonable steps to mitigate the loss which he has sustained consequent upon the defendant's wrong, and, if he fails to do so, he cannot claim damages for any loss which he ought reasonably to have avoided."

The law on mitigation was considered by the EAT in the MOD pregnancy dismissal appeal: *MOD v. Hunt, Wheeler, George, Donald and Anderson* [1996] IRLR 139.

19–04 Kay J. said "The legal framework in this area is clear. A person who seeks compensation is under a duty to mitigate his loss. Mitigation is essentially a question of fact. The burden of proving a failure to mitigate is upon the person who asserts it, in this case the Ministry of Defence. However, those charged with the duty of finding the facts must not be too stringent in their expectations of an injured party."

The following principles emerge:

(i) *Finding of Fact* It is for the tribunal to decide as a question of fact whether the complainant has mitigated his loss. This means that the finding that the tribunal makes will only be overturned on appeal if it is perverse. A failure to consider the issue of mitigation or applying the principle incorrectly could also, of course, be challenged on appeal as a misdirection in law.

(ii) *Burden of Proof* The burden of proving that the complainant has failed to mitigate his loss rests with the respondent.

19–05 In the *MOD v. Hunt and others* case, the EAT pointed out that in some of the pregnancy dismissal cases they had considered a recurrent theme had been "an absence of evidence from the Ministry of Defence coupled with little or no cross-examination of the applicant herself on this issue ... In our judgement and as a matter of general observation it lies uneasily in the mouth of the MOD to criticise an Industrial Tribunal in a case where it has taken few if any steps in the presentation of its case to fill an evidential vacuum in respect of which it bears the burden of proof." (Kay J.). The tribunal must be provided with evidence with which to consider the question of a possible failure to mitigate, either by way of evidence called by the respondent or arising from cross-examination: "A vague submission of failure to mitigate unsupported by any evidence is unlikely to succeed."

19–06 In *MOD v. Mutton* [1996] I.C.R. 590, Mrs Mutton decided to undertake retraining as a teacher some years after her unlawful discharge from the army. The retraining would have taken about four years. She was only part way through when the tribunal considered her compensation. The EAT was satisfied that the MOD had failed to prove that this amounted to a failure to mitigate her loss. Further, in assessing compensation the tribunal took no account of her likely future earnings as a teacher. Mrs Mutton had not been cross-examined on the issue. The EAT rejected the proposition from the MOD that in the absence of evidence the tribunal should have filled the evidential vacuum (see also *Kumchyk v. Derby City Council* [1978] I.C.R. 1116, where the EAT said that the duty was on the parties to ensure that all relevant evidence was put before the tribunal).

19–07 However, whilst the burden of proof might be on the respondent, the complainant clearly needs to be in a position to demonstrate in response to a challenge by the respondent that he has mitigated his loss (see paras 3–49 to 3–51 for guidance on preparation of evidence prior to the hearing). The complainant must be able to give evidence verbally and produce, if possible, documentary evidence to support the contention that he has mitigated his loss.

In the case of *Fyfe v. Scientific Furnishings Ltd* [1989] I.R.L.R. 331, the EAT made it clear that in unfair dismissal proceedings the tribunal may raise the issue of mitigation itself. Once raised, the common law principles clearly apply.

Extent of the duty to mitigate

19–08 Not too high a burden must be placed on the complainant to demonstrate that he has mitigated his loss. *McGregor on Damages* (15th ed., para. 311) states "Although the plaintiff must act with the defendant's as well as with his own interests in mind, he is only required to act reasonably, and the standard of reasonableness is not high in view of the fact that the defendant is an admitted wrongdoer".

In the discrimination field, the same principle applies: "Those charged with the duty of finding the facts must not be too stringent in their expectations of an injured party"

(Kay J. in *MOD v. Hunt and others*; see para. 19–04). In this case, Kay J. also quoted Lord Macmillan in *Banco de Portugal v. Waterlow and Sons Limited* [1932] A.C. 452.

> "Where the sufferer from a breach of contract finds himself in consequence of that breach placed in a position of embarrassment the measures which he may be drawn to adopt in order to extricate himself ought not be weighed in nice scales at the instance of the party whose breach of contract has occasioned the difficulty. It is often easy after an emergency has passed to criticise the steps which have been taken to meet it, but such criticism does not come well for those who have themselves created the emergency. The law is satisfied if the party placed in a difficult situation by reason of a breach of a duty owed to him has acted reasonably in the adoption of the remedial measures and he will not be held disentitled to recover the costs of such measures merely because the party in breach can suggest that other measures less burdensome to him might have been taken."

So the complainant must, then, take reasonable steps to mitigate his loss and the mere fact that he could, with the benefit of hindsight, have taken some other step which might have more successfully reduced his loss will not lead to a finding that he has failed to mitigate if he can show that he has acted reasonably in the steps he has actually taken.

Personal Characteristics: Subjective or Objective Test

19–10   In *Archbold Freightage Ltd v. Wilson* [1974] I.R.L.R. 10 NIRC, Sir John Donaldson described the extent of the duty as follows: It is "to act reasonably and to act as a reasonable man would do if he had no hope of seeking compensation from his previous employer. It follows from that that he should accept alternative employment if, taking account of the pay and other conditions of that employment, it is reasonable so to do."

That suggests an objective test: the test of what a reasonable man would have done. However, it is clear that the question of whether a particular complainant has acted reasonably must be judged subjectively. Has that particular person taken reasonable steps to mitigate his losses?

19–11   In *Fougere v. Phoenix Motor Co. Ltd* [1976] I.R.L.R. 259 EAT, Phillips J. said that "when looking to see what loss has been sustained in consequence of the dismissal, one does not ... ignore ... the personal characteristics of the dismissed employee." In this case, the complainant was 58 years of age and in poor health. If personal circumstances put the complainant at a disadvantage in the labour market this must be taken into account in determining whether that person has acted reasonably in seeking to mitigate their loss. As in the case of Fougere, someone nearing retirement age is likely to find it much more difficult to get other work or to get work at a comparable salary.

19–12   A pregnant woman is also likely to find it difficult to find new employment. This was accepted in the case of *Bennett v. Tippins* EAT 361/89. Similarly, a woman with a baby or young child and with responsibility for child care is likely to have the same problem. This was considered by the EAT in *MOD v. Hunt and others* (see paras 19–03 to 19–05). The tribunal had acknowledged the difficulties of getting work when the person is in some way "disadvantaged in the eyes of [the labour] market" (whether by reason of having a baby to care for or because of age or for some other problem). The EAT agreed. The tribunal was not making a gender based assumption that it was for the woman to stay at home. The tribunal was simply acknowledging at the time in question, and notwithstanding the legislation, that there was a disadvantage in the labour market in being a woman with a young child or children. "This seems to us to be no more and no less than the tribunal acting as 'industrial jury' and applying collective common sense to historical circumstance" (Kay J.).

19–13 The same logic could be applied in the case of race discrimination. If it is an objective fact that a particular ethnic minority is at a disadvantage in the labour market and a particular individual has suffered from that, it is reasonable to take this into account in determining whether he has taken reasonable steps to mitigate his loss and, given such reasonable steps, how long it will take to find other work. In the case of disability discrimination, it is again reasonable to take into account the particular difficulties faced by a disabled person in securing alternative employment (see also commentary in relation to unfair dismissal at paras 10–26 to 10–36).

Steps the Tribunal takes in deciding whether there has been a failure to mitigate

19–14 After hearing evidence and cross-examination on the issue of mitigation the tribunal has to decide whether there has been a failure to mitigate. If the tribunal does decide that the complainant has failed to mitigate his loss it is not appropriate for the tribunal to make a percentage reduction to compensation. The correct approach was summarised by the EAT in *Gardiner-Hill v. Roland Berger Technics Ltd* [1982] I.R.L.R. 498. Browne-Wilkinson J. said that to show a failure to mitigate,

> "it has to be shown that if a particular step had been taken, Mr Gardiner-Hill would, after a particular time, on a balance of probabilities, have gained employment; from then onwards the loss flowing from the unfair dismissal would have been extinguished or reduced by his income from that other source. In fixing the amount to be deducted for failure to mitigate, it is necessary for the tribunal to identify what steps should have been taken; the date on which that step would have produced an alternative income and, thereafter, to reduce the amount of compensation by the amount of the alternative income which would have been earned."

Note that a finding of a failure to mitigate at any particular point in time does not necessarily extinguish further compensation. As the explanation of the principle by Browne-Wilkinson J. demonstrates, if the alternative income which the complainant would have received had he reasonably mitigated his loss is lower than the income he received prior to dismissal, there is a continuing loss which should be compensated.

Failure to Mitigate can only lead to reduction in Compensatory Award in Unfair Dismissal Claims

19–16 In the case of *Lock v. Connell Estate Agents* [1994] I.R.L.R. 444 EAT, the tribunal had reduced both the compensatory award and the basic award because they had concluded that the complainant had failed to mitigate his loss. The EAT, however, made it clear that the duty to mitigate provided for, in what is now s.123(4) ERA, relates only to the compensatory award and not the basic award.

APPLICATION OF THE PRINCIPLE OF THE DUTY TO MITIGATE

19–17   In this section, a number of factual situations are considered in the context of the duty to mitigate. Unless otherwise stated, the law described here may be of relevance to both unfair dismissal and discrimination claims.

Failure to Appeal against Dismissal

19–18   The most recent EAT decision on the issue makes clear that a failure to appeal to the employer against dismissal will not give rise to a finding that the complainant has failed to mitigate his loss.

In *Lock v. Connell Estate Agents* [1994] I.R.L.R. 444, Hull J, QC considered that a failure to follow an internal appeals procedure cannot, as a matter of law, amount to a failure to mitigate. He pointed out that if the decision to dismiss had been "a careful and responsible one, then the prospects of it being reversed on appeal must be remote." But the prospects would be "even more remote" if the decision to dismiss was an irresponsible and hasty one. What confidence could the employee then have in the integrity of the employer? A plaintiff is "not generally required to engage in hazardous litigation". You cannot expect the employee to appeal to the appropriate party himself. In discrimination cases, the same principle probably applies.

Employee Rights (Dispute Resolution) Act 1998

19–19   Instead of the complainant being under a duty to pursue an internal appeal in order to mitigate his loss, the Employment Rights (Dispute Resolution) Act 1998 provides a new and different incentive for employees to pursue an internal appeal. Section 13, which inserts a new s.127A into the ERA, provides that in an unfair dismissal claim the tribunal must reduce the compensatory award if the employee has failed to pursue an internal appeal (provided the employer has properly notified him in writing of this right). The award can be reduced in such circumstances by up to a sum equivalent to two weeks' pay. Equally, if the employer has prevented an employee from using an appeal procedure provided by him then the award can be enhanced by up to the same amount (see paras 10–10 and 11–01 for further commentary). These provisions come into force on January 1, 1999.

Offer of re-employment or alternative employment prior to termination of employment

19–20   The duty to mitigate loss only applies following termination of employment. Therefore a refusal to consider an offer of re-employment or of alternative employment prior to the dismissal actually taking effect cannot amount to a failure to mitigate. Note, however, that in unfair dismissal claims it could result in a reduction in compensation on the basis that it would be just and equitable to reduce it under s.123(1) ERA (see paras 11–03 to 11–37).

19–21   In *Savoia v. Chiltern Herb Farms Ltd* [1981] I.R.L.R. 65 EAT, the company had wanted to reorganise. Mr Savoia was offered an alternative job at a higher salary. He refused but was not permitted to continue with his old job. He resigned and claimed constructive dismissal. The EAT found that the refusal to accept the offer of an alternative job prior to the termination of his employment could not amount to a failure to mitigate. However, in the case of *Plewinski v. McDermott Engineering* EAT 6.12.88 (465/88) IDS Brief 392 (1989), the EAT accepted that Mr Plewinski had failed to mitigate his loss by resigning in response to a substantial cut in the overtime rate.

The EAT stated that his loss was due to his own ill-judged action in giving up a good job as a long-serving employee to become self-employed with poor prospects. This decision seems hard to reconcile with the principle that the duty to mitigate only arises following dismissal.

Offer of reinstatement or re-engagement following termination of employment

19–22 A refusal of an offer by the employer either to reinstate the employee or to re-engage him in some other job can amount to a failure to mitigate (see also paras 9–21 to 9–22 for powers to reduce the basic award where there is an unreasonable refusal of offer of reinstatement). Whether such a refusal does amount to a failure to mitigate turns on the question of reasonableness. This will depend on:

(1)   the circumstances in which the offer was made,

(2)   the attitude of the employers and the way the complainant had been treated, and

(3)   other surrounding circumstances.

See *Fyfe v. Scientific Furnishings Ltd* [1989] I.R.L.R. 331:

> "It is trite law that in the sphere of contracts which involve personal relationships, not every refusal of an offer which would have the result of mitigating damage is unreasonable. It is important to examine the surrounding circumstances" (Wood J.).

19–23 The test of reasonableness in refusing an offer of re-employment is subjective (see *Johnson v. Hobart Manufacturing Co. Ltd* EAT 20.7.90 (210/89) and IDS Brief 433, Nov 1990). This does not give the complainant the right to turn down an offer because of "any whim or fancy". However, the suitability of the job must be looked at in relation to the complainant's particular circumstances. "It is no good saying objectively that a particular job is perfectly satisfactory for nine men out of ten if the job is manifestly unsuitable for the man in question."

Application of Reasonableness Test

19–24 The following section gives guidance on determining whether a complainant has acted reasonably in refusing an offer of re-employment.

Re-instatement or Re-engagement

19–25 The nature of the employer's offer is clearly relevant. If the complainant is being offered his old job back with continuity of service (in other words, full re-instatement) then, depending on other factors considered below, it is more likely to be unreasonable to turn down such an offer than an offer of re-engagement to another job. However, because one looks at all the circumstances, this will not always be the case. Where a particular working relationship has broken down, perhaps with a line manager, then an offer of alternative employment elsewhere in the organisation may be an attractive offer which it would be unreasonable to turn down.

Terms of offer of re-engagement/alternative employment

19–26 The terms of the offer of re-engagement or alternative employment are certainly relevant considerations. The tribunal will compare the terms of the offer with the job from which the employee was dismissed. They may take into account salary, status, hours, job location and benefits.

In *Ballie Brothers v. Pritchard* EAT 59/89, the alternative job offer was at a lower rate of pay and there would no longer be a van available to travel to and from work. Further, Mr Pritchard would have lost continuity of employment (the offer had been made months after the dismissal). The EAT held there was no failure to mitigate by refusing the offer.

19–27 In *Johnson v. Hobart Manufacturing Co. Ltd* EAT 20.7.90 (210/89) and IDS Brief 433 Nov 1990, the employer wanted to change Mr Johnson's contract of employment so that half an hour's travelling at the start and end of the day would no longer be remunerated. He objected and was dismissed. The company made clear that they would re-engage him on the new terms but not on his original contract. The tribunal decided that it was unreasonable to refuse re-engagement at only slightly less favourable terms. However, the EAT ruled that the tribunal had paid insufficient attention to the reasonableness of Mr Johnson's refusal of those terms (applying the subjective test, see paras 19–23 and 19–10 to 19–13).

In *Smith v. NE Transport & Plant Hire Ltd* EAT 5.10.83 (402/83) IDS 264 Nov 1983, Mr Smith was dismissed from his job as an HGV driver. He was very soon re-employed after the company received representations on his behalf. However, he was given a different non-HGV lorry to drive. He refused and left. This was unreasonable and amounted to a failure to mitigate, even though he was not offered exactly the same job as he had before.

When the offer is made

19–28 A refusal of an offer of re-employment made immediately after dismissal is more likely to be unreasonable than one made months later, for example just prior to the hearing of the claim.

In *Martin v. Yeoman Aggregates Ltd* [1983] I.R.L.R. 49, Mr Martin was dismissed "in the heat of the moment". Within minutes the Director responsible for the dismissal realised that he had acted in breach of the disciplinary procedure and informed Mr Martin that he would be suspended. Mr Martin rejected this and pursued a claim to the tribunal. Although the EAT decided that there had been no dismissal. They also held, in the alternative, that he had failed to mitigate his loss by refusing to accept suspension in place of dismissal. He had "shut his mind" to a reasonable assessment as to whether or not he should accept or refuse.

An offer made just before a tribunal hearing, months after the dismissal may be regarded by the tribunal as a sham. Equally, by that time attitudes may well have hardened still further by the process of litigation, making it reasonable for the complainant to refuse such an offer. In *John Crowther & Sons (Milnsbridge) Ltd v. Livesey* 21.12.84 EAT 272/84 IRLIB 280, 7 May 1985.8, the offer of re-employment was made during a one month adjournment following a finding of unfair dismissal. Mr Livesey had not failed to mitigate his loss by refusing the offer. The tribunal took into account the timing of the offer.

Clarity of the Offer

19–29 In the *Livesey* case, the tribunal also took into account the fact that there was dispute between the parties as to what was offered and on what terms. Lack of clarity is likely to make it reasonable to turn down an offer.

Nature of the Dismissal

19–30 If the nature of the dismissal is such that the complainant could reasonably reach the view that he had lost all trust and confidence in the employer then it is likely to be reasonable to refuse an offer of re-employment or alternative employment. However, in a redundancy situation it may be unreasonable to refuse to consider offers of alternative employment subsequent to dismissal.

In *Gallear v. J.F. Watson & Son Ltd* [1979] I.R.L.R. 306, Mr Gallear, after being made redundant, turned down the chance to apply for two vacancies. The EAT agreed with the tribunal that he had failed to mitigate his loss. "He rightly felt aggrieved but, after all, his dismissal was on the grounds of redundancy and not on some misconceived notion of bad conduct or anything derogatory of that kind."

19–31 Where the circumstances of the dismissal have destroyed the employee's trust and confidence in management, a refusal to agree to an offer of re-employment will be reasonable. In *John Crowther & Sons (Milnsbridge) Ltd v. Livesey* 21.12.84 EAT 272/84 (see also para. 19–28), Mr Livesey had worked for the company for 44 years. New management took over. He had to have time off work because of rheumatoid arthritis. He received a verbal warning after one absence and then, during the next absence, was dismissed. The dismissal was handled in such a way as to shatter Mr Livesey's trust and confidence in the new management. It was reasonable for him to be suspicious of the genuineness of the offer. There was, accordingly, no failure to mitigate loss.

In *How v. Tesco Stores Ltd* [1974] I.R.L.R. 194, Mrs How was dismissed summarily without the company complying with an agreed disciplinary procedure and without her being given the chance to provide an explanation. She had taken 50 pence from a till, on the understanding it would be repaid, so as to contribute to a present for the store manager's new baby. She was a long serving and trusted employee. The tribunal held that there had been no failure to mitigate by refusing an offer of re-engagement. "The applicant could not reasonably have been expected to accept such offer of re-engagement."

Other factors influencing reasonableness in refusing offer of re-employment/ alternative employment

1. *Complainant has found other work*
   19–32 If the complainant has already found other work it is less likely to be unreasonable to refuse an offer of re-employment.
   See *MOD v. Cannock and others* [1994] I.R.L.R. 509. One of the "others" was Mrs Bolton-Braidwood. After her unlawful discharge from the armed forces she found a new career in the museum service. The EAT accepted that it was not unreasonable for her to decide to keep her existing career rather than apply to rejoin the armed forces (which she could have done but only for a relatively short period due to her age).

2. *Complainant planning to set up in business*
   If the complainant has taken significant steps in setting up a new business and if this is a reasonable way of attempting to mitigate loss, the rejection of a subsequent offer of re-employment may be reasonable.

19–33 However, in *Cocking v. Moulinex Swan Holdings Ltd* EAT 1233/94, Mr Cocking was offered re-engagement about three weeks after being made redundant. By that time he had made a commitment to set up in business with someone else. The EAT agreed with the tribunal that it was unreasonable to refuse the offer of re-engagement in such circumstances. The nature of the dismissal was not such as to make it impossible for Mr Cocking to work for the company again.

Preventing an Order for re-employment being complied with

19–34 Note that s.117(8) ERA provides that if the complainant has "unreasonably prevented" an order for either re-instatement or re-engagement from being complied with, the tribunal can take such conduct into account as a failure to mitigate loss when assessing compensation.

Consequences of a finding of failure to mitigate by not accepting re-employment

19–35 If the tribunal finds that the complainant was unreasonable in not accepting an offer of full re-instatement, the consequence would be an award of nil compensatory award. Had the complainant mitigated his loss in such a way he would have suffered no loss (other than conceivably incurring expenses as a result of dismissal prior to the offer of re-instatement, see *Sweetlove v. Redbridge & Waltham Forest Area Health Authority* [1979] I.R.L.R. 195 EAT—if re-instatement had been accepted all the employee's rights would have been restored including pension rights. Mr Sweetlove's unreasonable refusal to accept re-instatement deprived him of the right to claim any loss). Similarly by virtue of s.122(1) ERA, the tribunal has the power to reduce the basic award by up to a maximum of 100 per cent in such circumstances.

19–36 In a discrimination claim the same logic applies. Compensation for loss would be reduced to nil, although the chances of a tribunal finding that an employee who has suffered discrimination should reasonably have accepted an offer of re-instatement are perhaps less likely.

If the complainant unreasonably refuses an offer of re-employment at a lower salary or with fewer benefits then the tribunal may still award the compensation in respect of the difference in value between the old and new remuneration packages. However, if, for example, the tribunal decides that, had the employer followed a fair procedure in a redundancy or re-organisation situation, the complainant should have accepted such a post then there may be a nil compensatory award. Had the complainant mitigated his loss by accepting the re-engagement he would have suffered no loss when compared with what a fair procedure would have led to.

The duty to mitigate where complainant has applied for re-employment: Unfair Dismissal

19–37 If the complainant is seeking re-employment as the remedy for unfair dismissal can he argue that that is his proposed method of seeking to mitigate his loss and that he should not also be required to seek other work pending the decision of the tribunal? From the complainant's perspective it is inconsistent to be seeking re-employment but at the same time have to look for other work. Nonetheless, re-employment is ordered in a very small minority of cases and it is likely that a tribunal would conclude that it is unreasonable for the complainant to "put all his eggs in one basket".

19–38 The tribunal has to decide whether the steps taken by the particular complainant were reasonable. If the tribunal hearing on liability is listed reasonably soon after dismissal, and the particular facts of the case make re-employment a realistic option, then the tribunal might be satisfied that it was reasonable for the complainant to steadfastly pursue re-employment without simultaneously applying for other work.

In *Williams v. Lloyds Retailers Ltd* [1973] I.R.L.R. 262, the case came to hearing within about two months of the dismissal. After a finding of unfair dismissal the tribunal adjourned the hearing to allow the parties the chance to settle the claim on the basis of a recommendation for re-employment. No settlement was achieved and a further hearing was fixed at which the company argued that Mr Williams should have found work while he was awaiting the company's decision on possible re-engagement. "We do not agree. The delay in communicating the company's decision not to offer re-engagement to him was the fault of the company, and we do not think he was unreasonable in not finding another job in the meantime."

No duty to mitigate whilst pursuing internal appeal

19–39 If the dismissed employee lodges an appeal against dismissal to his former employer it is likely to be regarded as reasonable for him to wait until the result of that appeal is known before launching into the task of seeking new employment.

Offers of early retirement and other financial packages

19–40 In *Fyfe v. Scientific Furnishings Ltd* [1989] I.R.L.R. 331, Mr Fyfe was made redundant without notice. Later that day he was offered the alternative of an early retirement package which appeared to be much more generous than his entitlement to redundancy pay. After a couple of days, and some discussion with a chartered accountant friend, he decided to reject the offer of early retirement. The EAT, overturning the decision of the tribunal, decided that there had been no failure to mitigate. Looking at all the circumstances surrounding the offer—the employer's failure to set out the full implications of the offer and their failure to give sufficient time to consider it—the employers had not proved that Mr Fyfe had failed to mitigate his loss. The outcome of such arguments will, again, depend on all the facts.

19–41 An employer may also argue that an employee's refusal to accept a very generous *ex gratia* payment amounts to a failure to mitigate. A rejection of an offer of more than the statutory maximum compensatory award, in circumstances where the dismissed employee claims to have been unfairly dismissed and where there is no other claim which could increase compensation further, could lead to a finding of a failure to mitigate. However, an offer made on a without prejudice basis following issue of proceedings could not lead to such a finding.

The duty to mitigate and the search for new employment

19–42 Applying the principles outlined in paras 19–03 to 19–16 the following guidance emerges. The complainant cannot simply remain unemployed, allowing the loss to accumulate. Such loss would be avoidable and the complainant would have failed to mitigate.

However, the complainant is not obliged to apply for any sort of work irrespective of wage level or status as soon as he is dismissed. The tribunal decision in *A.G. Bracey Ltd v. Iles* [1973] I.R.L.R. 210 puts it clearly:

"It may not be reasonable to take the first job that comes along. It may be much more reasonable, in the interests of the employee and of the employer who has to pay compensation, that he should wait a little time. He must, of course, use the time well and seek a better paid job which will reduce his overall loss and the amount of compensation which the previous employer ultimately has to pay."

However, if this is not successful then a reasonable approach would be to scale down expectations and widen the range of jobs to apply for.

Wage below benefit level

19-43 Depending on the facts of the particular case it may even be reasonable to expect a complainant to accept work at a wage which is less than the state benefits he is receiving following dismissal. In *Daley v. Dorsett (Almar Dolls Ltd)* [1981] I.R.L.R. 385 EAT, May J. said that tribunals should be "very slow indeed in finding reasonable a decision of a dismissed employee not to accept subsequent employment because thereunder he would be receiving less than the unemployment benefit or any other benefit". However, this was at a time of high unemployment and, as we have seen, the test is a subjective one. What steps are reasonable for the particular complainant to take to mitigate their loss?

Labour Market

19-44 The state of the labour market is a relevant factor in determining what a reasonable approach would be to the search for new employment. If the job market is such that it is likely to be futile to wait for a similar vacancy to appear, then a reasonable approach would be to reduce expectations and apply for lower paid work or even be prepared to look elsewhere for employment.

Moving Home

19-45 In *Collen v. Lewis & Anor* COIT 1547/27 a teacher was unfairly dismissed from a school in London. Teaching jobs in London and the South East were scarce. The only offer of employment was for a job in Wales. This job was at a lower salary and did not have London weighting. The tribunal decided that it would have been reasonable to accept that job. She was awarded the net difference between the two salaries for a period of one year. Whether it would be reasonable for a particular complainant to move location again depends on their particular circumstances. Generally, it is more likely to be reasonable to expect someone on good pay of professional or managerial status to move than someone in unskilled work whose costs of moving may outweigh the benefits of increasing the chance of finding work on low pay.

Efforts to find work

19-46 The complainant must do more than sign on at a job centre to demonstrate reasonable efforts to mitigate his loss (see *Burns v. George Boyd (Engineering) Ltd* EAT 458/84).

In *Bristol Garage (Brighton) Ltd v. Lowen* [1979] I.R.L.R. 86 EAT, Mrs Lowen visited the Job Centre twice a week to look for jobs. She had also made three telephone applications for similar work and had then applied for a nursing job. The EAT was not satisfied that there was "material available to … conclude that there was a failure to mitigate". (Arnold J., who highlighted inadequate cross-examination of Mrs Lowen in the tribunal on the issue of mitigation, see also paras 19–05 to 19–06).

19–47 Steps that it might be reasonable for the complainant to take (depending on the circumstances) include contacting specialist employment agencies. In *Field v. Leslie & Godwin Ltd* [1972] I.R.L.R. 12, Mr Field was dismissed from his job as a placing broker. There were three recruitment agencies he could have gone to which specialised in that type of business. He had only contacted one, and that was only two days before the tribunal hearing. He had also failed to take up a reference which had been promised to him. This amounted to a failure to reasonably mitigate his loss. Compensation was limited to a period of four months—the length of time the tribunal believed it would have taken him to find alternative work had he taken proper steps.

Temporary Work

19–48 It may be reasonable for a complainant to take up temporary work to keep losses to a minimum but not if this prejudices the chances of being able to apply for better paid permanent work. In *Hardwick v. Leeds Area Health Authority* [1975] I.R.L.R. 319, the tribunal thought that Mrs Hardwick had failed to fully mitigate her loss by giving up part-time, temporary work involving considerable inconvenience in travelling on two buses to get to work. Her reason for giving this up was that the wages were insufficient with three children at school and a handicapped husband. Given that less than a month later she managed to obtain work at a higher rate of pay than the job she had been dismissed from, the tribunal decision appears harsh.

Giving up work following dismissal

19–49 In other cases tribunals have found that, on the particular facts, it was reasonable for the complainant to give up work he had taken on following the unfair dismissal. However, there must be a good reason for such a step.

In *Dundee Plant Co. Ltd v. Riddler* EAT 11.11.88 (377/88), Mr Riddler took up another job soon after dismissal at similar pay. He was, however, unhappy with the amount of travelling involved. He left within three months and obtained lesser paid work. On the particular facts Mr Riddler had acted reasonably. There was no failure to mitigate and he was entitled to compensation for ongoing losses based on the difference between his original wages and those in the lower paid job.

19–50 In *Wilson v. Gleneagles Bakery Ltd* EAT 28.4.88 (40/88), Ms Wilson got work as a hotel chambermaid just over a month after her dismissal. She left after only five days because, as someone of limited intelligence, she could not cope with the pace of work. The EAT concluded that she had acted reasonably. Her failure to cope with the job did not mean that she was acting unreasonably in leaving. Just as an unfairly dismissed employee is not obliged to take on any job irrespective of its suitability, someone who starts new employment but finds it unsuitable should not be treated less favourably (see also paras 10–37 to 10–59 for further discussion on the impact of new work in the context of the compensatory award for unfair dismissal).

Self employment/setting up in business

19–51 There is no reason, in principle, for a complainant to be obliged to seek to mitigate his loss by searching for employment. The duty is to act reasonably. Depending on the circumstances, it may be more appropriate to use one's skills in seeking to establish a business than in a fruitless search for employment. Age may well be a relevant factor.

In *Gardiner-Hill v. Roland Berger Technics Ltd* [1982] I.R.L.R. 498, Mr Gardiner-

Hill was a managing director until his unfair dismissal. He was 55 years old. The EAT held that it was reasonable for him to seek to exploit his experience in his own business. He had spent 80 per cent of his time in the seven months since dismissal in setting up his business rather than looking for other work. The EAT was satisfied he had acted prudently (see also paras 3–58 and 10–67 for award of compensation for costs of setting up new business).

19–52   The fact that a business set up by a dismissed employee subsequently fails does not of itself lead to the conclusion that the complainant has failed to mitigate his loss. If he has acted reasonably in the circumstances in choosing to mitigate his losses by setting up in business then there will be no failure to mitigate. In *Blick Vessels & Pipework Ltd v. Sharpe* 19.10.84. EAT 631/84 and 1RL1B 274 5/2/85, Mr Blick set up his own business but had to close it down ten months later because it was losing money. "We accept that he did his best, under circumstances which were far from propitious to mitigate his loss by running a business" concluded the tribunal. The EAT agreed.

Retraining/Further Education

19–53   It may be reasonable for a dismissed employee to pursue re-training or further education in order to make himself more employable. This argument has been accepted on many occasions by tribunals on the basis of the particular circumstances of the complainant. When considering possible steps a dismissed employee could take, the right approach is to put to one side the question of whether he can get compensation from his former employer and ask: "Acting purely in is own interests, has he acted reasonably by pursuing retraining/further education with a view to keeping his loss to a minimum?" (Sir John Donaldson in *Archbald Freightage Ltd v. Wilson* [1974] I.R.L.R. 10).

So in *Glen Henderson Ltd v. Nisbet* EAT 17.5.90 (34/90) and IDS Brief 423, June 1990, Ms Nisbet accepted advice from her Job Centre to go on a five-week business enterprise course with a view to becoming self-employed. The EAT accepted that this was a reasonable step to take and upheld the tribunal's decision to award compensation for the period of the course and for a year thereafter (calculated on the basis of the difference between her previous wage and her self employed earnings).

19–54   In *Mutton v. MOD* COIT 9/272/461, a pregnancy dismissal case, Mrs Mutton went to college to do A levels with a view to eventually qualifying as a teacher, which would have taken at least four years. She took this decision some four years after her unlawful discharge from the army, having already worked full time in two different jobs. Given Mrs Mutton's particular circumstances and the scale of the loss she had suffered as a result of the army's discrimination, this was a reasonable approach. "We find that the applicant is perfectly entitled to take any reasonable course for the future of herself and her family. What she has done is eminently reasonable, many would not have the guts or determination to do it." The EAT upheld the tribunal's reasoning (*MOD v. Mutton* [1996] I.C.R. 590).

This decision does, however, have to be seen in the context of the somewhat unusual circumstances of the loss Ms Mutton had suffered. She had lost the right to an engagement of twenty two years with good promotion prospects and an excellent pension. With her unlawful discharge she suffered a potentially large loss and therefore a decision to undertake more education and retrain as a teacher can be seen as a reasonable approach to minimising her long term loss (see also para. 19–06).

19–55   Generally, the longer the course and the less vocational it is in nature, the more likely it is that the tribunal will regard the decision to undertake such study as a *novus actus*, an intervening act which breaks the chain of causation (see paras 10–15 to 10–19 for further commentary in the context of unfair dismissal).

In *Simrad Ltd v. Scott* [1997] I.R.L.R. 147, Ms Scott got other low paid work following her dismissal. The job had no career prospects and eventually she decided to retrain as a nurse, embarking on a three-year course. The EAT took the view that her decision to embark on a new career was too remote to be directly linked to the dismissal and properly attributable to the conduct of her employers. Lord Johnston reached this view on the basis of s.123(1) ERA 96 which provides that the compensatory award can only compensate for loss attributable to action taken by the employer.

19–56 It is important to note that Lord Johnston stated that they did "not find it easy to determine whether or not, in the particular case, the decision to embark upon a nursing career is sufficiently directly linked to the original dismissal". They reached their view that it was too remote "with some hesitation". Note, however, that the decision is based on a finding that the loss was too remote, rather than a finding of a failure to mitigate (see paras 10–15 to 10–19 for commentary on the two concepts between these).

Clearly, therefore, a decision taken by a dismissed employee to undertake a course of retraining or education is capable of being seen as linked to the dismissal and then, if the decision is a reasonable one, taken with a view to limiting their loss, it would neither break the chain of causation nor amount to a failure to mitigate. As always, each case must be looked at on its own merits.

Sickness or incapacity following dismissal

19–57 What happens if the dismissed employee is sick or incapacitated in some way following dismissal making it more difficult for him to obtain other work? In assessing the compensatory award for unfair dismissal, compensation may be reduced on a "just and equitable" basis if the incapacity might have led in any event to a fair dismissal at a later stage (see paras 11–25 to 11–27). However, issues of mitigation may also arise if the employee signs on for sickness benefit reducing his chances of obtaining work. In *Wilson v. (1) Glenrose (Fish Merchants) Ltd (2) Chapman & ors* EAT 21.7.92 (444/91) IDS Brief 481, November 1992, Mr Wilson had suffered with back problems for some time before his dismissal. His efforts to find work following dismissal all foundered because of his health. After four weeks he got a medical certificate and went "on the sick". In the Job Centre's view, he was therefore no longer available for work. He did, however, apply for some jobs, albeit unsuccessfully. Overturning the tribunal's decision that compensation should stop from the point he went on to sickness benefit, the EAT said that the crucial question was whether he had acted reasonably in seeking to mitigate his loss by at least receiving sickness benefit.

Mitigation and the notice period: Unfair Dismissal

19–58 Where an employee is summarily dismissed but the dismissal is found to be unfair, it appears as if the normal rules on mitigation may not apply during the notice period. (see paras 10–38 to 10–42). It seems as if during this "special" period the dismissed employee may be under no duty to mitigate his loss. However, where there is a long notice period and the employee has good employment prospects it is likely that the tribunal would find that the duty to mitigate applied (see *Isleworth Studios v. Rickard* [1988] I.C.R. 432, see also para. 10–40).

Pregnancy Dismissal Cases

19–59   Reference has already been made to various cases which concerned women discharged from the armed forces on grounds of pregnancy (see paras 19–01 and 19–03 to 19–06). In the cases of *MOD v. Sullivan* [1994] I.R.C. 193 and *MOD v. Cannock and Ors* [1994] I.R.L.R. 509, the EAT considered the question of the duty to mitigate where a woman has given birth and would, if in employment, enjoy the benefit of maternity leave.

In *Cannock*, Morison J. gave general guidance on the application of the duty to mitigate in such cases (equally relevant in the case of a woman automatically unfairly dismissed on grounds of pregnancy under s.99 ERA):

> "Tribunals should approach the question of mitigation on the hypothesis that the applicant was fully fit for onerous employment duties six months after the birth of the first child. An applicant who has been dismissed by reason of pregnancy may have good reasons for not looking for other work, but that does not mean that she can 'stay at home with the child' and recover compensation. She is complaining of the loss of employment, often the loss of a career. After the six month period she is expected to be in the job market actually looking for work and applying for jobs, and if one is not, then however understandable her behaviour might be, she cannot recover damages for loss of employment thereafter."

19–60   This comment was made in a section of Morison J.'s judgement in which he gave *obiter* guidance to tribunals on a range of issues. It is therefore just that; guidance, and it may not be relevant depending on the facts of a particular case. Maximum statutory maternity leave is, of course, 29 weeks after the birth of the child, rather than 26 weeks, and if the employer's contractual scheme offers a longer period then it would be unreasonable to expect a woman to be actively looking for work during a period when she could still have been on such extended contractual leave.

In the *Sullivan* case the EAT took a similar view to that taken by Morison J. in *Cannock* and also found that a woman dismissed because of pregnancy was entitled to be compensated for six months from the date of birth of the child whilst she made a decision as to whether to return to work. Further loss would depend on the normal principles discussed in this chapter and elsewhere.

19–61   What compensation the complainant would recover for the period of six months following the birth of her child would depend on what she would have received during that period had she not been dismissed. If there is no contractual entitlement to pay during the maternity leave period, her loss would be limited to any loss of statutory maternity pay and the loss of any benefits to which she would have been entitled during the basic 14 week maternity leave period. (s.71 ERA provides for entitlement to the "benefit of the terms and conditions of employment which would have been applicable to her if she had not been absent" (this does not provide for an entitlement to remuneration) (s.71(2) ER)).

CHAPTER 20

Pension Loss

20–01 Whether an employee has been unfairly dismissed or dismissed (or resigned) in circumstances which amount to unlawful discrimination (sex, race or disability) the loss of pension benefits may be a very significant element in the assessment of loss. Likewise, a complainant who is found to have suffered discrimination in not being appointed to a post which benefited from a pension must also be compensated for that lost benefit. The problem is that the task of assessing the extent of pension loss is extremely difficult. Tribunals have been assisted in this task by the publication of guidelines prepared by three tribunal chairman in 1990, with a second edition published in 1991. These guidelines are contained within a booklet called "*Industrial Tribunals Compensation for Loss of Pension Rights*" which is reproduced in the Appendix O. The booklet is known as the "Blue Book". The status of these guidelines is explained at para. 20–08.

20–02 The chairmen in their introduction made the point that many people underestimate the value of an occupational pension which can be a "very significant" asset. The risk of advisors paying insufficient attention to the loss of such a benefit remains today. In a case where the complainant has found new work which does not benefit from a pension, the largest element of financial loss is likely to be the pension. As will be explained below, there are some cases where the guidelines may not be appropriate. This may be particularly so in discrimination cases, where a substantial loss has been suffered and where there is no statutory cap on compensation. The guidelines approach may not adequately compensate the complainant for the loss suffered in respect of pension benefits.

The Statutory Provisions

20–03 As explained above, pension loss is recoverable in both unfair dismissal and discrimination cases.

Unfair Dismissal

20–04 Section 123 ERA 1996 sets out the rules for the calculation of the compensatory award payable to someone who has been unfairly dismissed and who is not re-instated or re-employed (see Chapter 10). Section 123(1) states that the compensatory award shall be an amount which the tribunal considers just and equitable in all the circumstances having regard to the loss sustained (see para. 10–01). Section 123(2)(b) provides that that loss includes the "loss of any benefit which he might reasonably be expected to have had but for the dismissal". Entitlement to a pension is clearly such a benefit which is lost as a result of dismissal and is therefore to be taken into account in the assessment of the compensatory award.

Reinstatement and re-engagement

20–05 Note also that s.114(2) ERA provides that when a tribunal orders reinstatement, the tribunal should specify any amount payable by the employer in respect of any benefit which the complainant might reasonably be expected to have had but for the dismissal for the period between the date of termination of employment and the date of reinstatement. Such benefits again include any pension benefits to which the complainant was entitled. The order for reinstatement is an order that the employer shall treat the complainant "in all respects" as if he had not been dismissed (s.114(1) ERA). Therefore the pension position must be fully restored to what it would have been but for the dismissal (see paras 8–17 to 8–22 for commentary on re-instatement). Similarly, under s.115(2) ERA, where a tribunal orders re-engagement it must specify the terms on which re-engagement is to take place, including any amount payable by the employer in respect of any benefit which the complainant might reasonably be expected to have had but for the dismissal for the period between the date of termination of employment and the date of re-engagement.

Discrimination Cases

20–06   All three of the Discrimination Acts, the SDA, the RRA and the DDA, provide that compensation for unlawful discrimination shall be calculated in the same way as damages in tort (ss. 65 and 66 SDA, ss. 56 and 57 RRA, and s.8 DDA). This basis of calculating compensation includes compensation for financial loss suffered (see paras 13–56 to 13–57). It is clear that the loss of pension benefits is part of such financial loss.

Should the Chairmen's Guidelines be used?

20–07   It was because of the complexity of calculating the extent of pension loss that three tribunal chairmen prepared guidance on how to go about the task. Although it was originally drafted as an aid to assessment of compensation specifically in unfair dismissal cases, it has since been approved also as a basis for assessing pension loss in discrimination cases. (See *MOD v. Cannock and others* [1994] I.R.L.R. 509 EAT: "We recommend, in our general guidelines, that [tribunals] should calculate pension losses in accordance with the guidance [given by the tribunal chairmen]"). However, some important qualifications to the application of the guidance need to be stressed both generally and, in particular, in relation to discrimination cases.

Qualifications in application of Guidelines

A number of qualifications to the use of the Guidelines need to be stressed.
   20–08

1.   The guidance has no statutory basis. There is, therefore, no obligation on the tribunal to follow it in any particular case. If a complainant considers that the guidance understates the extent of the loss of pension benefits suffered, he can propose a different method of calculation to the tribunal. At paragraph 2.4 of the booklet it states: "It is always open to either or both parties to call actuarial evidence and it is hoped that the more general parts of this paper will assist chairmen in assessing such evidence where it is called." At paragraph 11.2 it states: "These recommendations are only guidelines. They will become tripwires if they are blindly applied without considering the facts of each case. Any party is free to canvass any method of assessment which he considers appropriate. We hope that this paper will be found useful as a starting point."

This important qualification to the application of the guidelines was recognised by the EAT in the unfair dismissal case of *Bingham v. Hobourn Engineering Ltd* [1992] I.R.L.R. 298. In that case, the EAT took the view that "the actuarial assumptions which are set out in ... the booklet were in fact in several important respects shown to be inaccurate. That of course is not a criticism of the booklet which ... has necessarily to be generalised." Two particular facts in the *Bingham* case made the Guidelines approach inappropriate. First, had Mr Bingham not been unfairly dismissed he would have had very limited promotion prospects. That, said the EAT "vitiates any assumption such as that which is found in appendix 3 of the Guidelines— 'Salaries are assumed to increase at seven per cent per annum' ".

20–09 Equally important was the fact that Mr Bingham actually managed to find new employment on a higher salary with pension benefits. The effect of the dismissal was, therefore, to enhance his income upon which his "final salary" pension would be based. Again, this was not in accordance with the actuarial assumptions used in the Tribunal Chairmen's Guidelines (see Appendix 3 to the booklet at Appendix O of this text).

Note, however, the case of *Tradewinds Airways Ltd v. Fletcher* [1981] I.R.L.R. 272, in which the EAT said that a figure for pension loss arrived at using a different method was so much higher than it would have been, using the guidance approach that "something must have gone wrong in the evaluation of the opinion of [the pension expert called by Mr Fletcher]". The EAT sent the issue back to the tribunal for reconsideration, although Bristow J. stressed that the tribunal may properly reach the same conclusion to accept Mr Fletcher's expert's evidence but only after they had heard evidence on both sides, which had been denied to them first time round.

2.   The guidance makes particular reference to the statutory basis for calculating loss in unfair dismissal cases. In the introduction it states: "The tribunal is not obliged, as a court is, to seek to calculate as precisely as possible the loss that the applicant has suffered, but to order a 'just and equitable' sum by way of compensation [see s.123(1) ERA]. This entitles the tribunal to use a rough and ready system if necessary *Manpower Ltd v. Hearne* [1983] I.R.L.R. 281."

20–10 This is not the case with assessment of compensation for discrimination. Here the tribunal is obliged to assess compensation as a court would when calculating damages in tort. Note also the principle which must be applied in sex discrimination cases, that compensation must be "full" (*Marshall (No.2)* [1993] I.R.L.R. 445 ECJ) in order to properly implement the requirements of the Equal Treatment Directive (see paras 11–26 to 11–31).

3.   The tribunal chairmen also specifically referred to the upper limit of compensation in unfair dismissal cases: "Industrial tribunals were established to provide an economical and expeditious means of resolving disputes. There is an upper limit on the amount of compensation which they can award in the case of unfair dismissal. Our task has been to set out guidelines for the assessment of compensation for loss of pension rights which are consistent with the constraints within which [a tribunal] operates." (para. 1.3 of the Guidelines).

20–11   Again, those constraints do not apply in discrimination cases. There is no upper limit. The tribunal's task must be to assess all loss as accurately as possible. The lifting of the lid on compensation in sex discrimination cases was acknowledged by Morison J. in *MOD v. Cannock and Others* [1994] I.R.L.R. 509 EAT as a potential justification for using a more accurate method of assessing pension loss than can be achieved using the guidelines method proposed by the Committee of Chairmen of Tribunals.

"There is an argument for saying that, because the limits on compensation have been removed in cases of unlawful sex discrimination, it would be more appropriate to measure pension loss by reference to prospective loss of benefit, rather than by the contribution method [proposed by the Chairmen of Tribunals in their guidance] which is a rough and ready method suitable and appropriate for the bulk of cases with which the [tribunals] have to deal" (Morison J.). The same argument, of course, also applies to cases of race and disability discrimination.

20–12   The question of which method should be used was also considered by the EAT in *MOD v. Mutton* [1996] I.C.R. 590. This was another of the pregnancy dismissal cases in which the tribunal had found that Mrs Mutton had, as a result of her unlawful discharge, lost the prospect of a long term career in the army. Expert evidence had been presented to the tribunal in support of Mrs Mutton's claim for compensation for pension loss based on the "value method" which involves an actuarial calculation of the value of the benefits lost. The MOD had argued that the tribunal should follow the guidelines method. The EAT upheld the tribunal's decision to use the "value method". Kay J. said that in Mrs Mutton's case there was a "volume of evidence emphasising the likelihood that she would have been an exceptional long term prospect in the Army, coupled with expert evidence produced on her behalf which the tribunal was entitled to and did prefer."

20–13   In summary, despite the qualifications referred to above, in the majority of cases it will be appropriate to use the guidelines method. This is particularly likely to be the case with unfair dismissal claims because of the statutory cap on compensation. When one takes into account the cost of instructing an actuary to prepare an expert report on pension loss and to give evidence it is unlikely, in most cases, to be cost effective. In discrimination cases, with no cap on compensation, the judgement as to whether it is worth a complainant instructing an actuary is more difficult. If the complainant has lost the benefit of a "final salary" pension and is unlikely to find employment with similar pension rights for a long time then it may be a worthwhile investment to call such expert evidence and to seek to persuade the tribunal to assess pension loss using the value method (see para. 20–06).

TYPES OF PENSION

20–14   In order to go about the task of assessing pension loss it is important to have a basic understanding of the different types of pension.

State Pension Provision

20–15   The state pension has two elements:

1.   *The Basic Pension*
     This is payable to all persons over state pension age provided certain contribution requirements are met.

2.   *SERPS*
     This element is earnings related and varies depending on the person's earnings upon which full National Insurance contributions have been paid since April 1978.

Contracting Out

20–16   Employers can contract out of SERPS in respect of employees who are members of occupational pension schemes, provided the scheme meets specified criteria. If an employee has, throughout his working life, been in a contracted out scheme, he will receive the Basic Pension from the State plus a pension from the contracted out scheme. Employees themselves can also contract out of SERPS or opt out of their employer's pension scheme and arrange, instead, their own personal scheme. See paras 20–26 to 20–27 for guidance on the position of a complainant who was not in an occupational pension scheme but only benefited from the two elements of the state pension.

Occupational Pension Schemes

20–17   There are two main types of occupational scheme: final salary and money purchase.

Final Salary Schemes

Here the pension is based on a proportion of salary at retirement age and length of service during which the employee has been in the scheme. Many schemes are based on 1/60th of salary at retirement age for every year of service.

> *Example*
> **20–18**   Employee joins the company's pension scheme in 1978 and retires in 1998. The scheme provides for 1/60th of final salary for each year in the scheme. His salary on retirement is £30,000. His pension is therefore 20/60 × £30,000 = £10,000.

With final salary schemes the employer guarantees that he will make sufficient contributions to the scheme to ensure that it is well enough funded to provide a pension, based on final salary, for employees in the scheme. This means that the amount paid in may vary from time to time depending on how healthy the fund is. If it is very well funded at a particular time the employer may be able to enjoy a "contributions holiday" for a while—in other words paying nothing into the scheme. The employee, generally, will make contributions out of his salary at a fixed percentage of salary throughout his employment.

20–19   The "Blue Book" suggests that a good scheme will be based on an average contribution of 15 per cent of the payroll of those employees in the scheme. If it is a contributory scheme (*i.e.* with contributions from employees) this could be made up of 10 per cent from the employer and five per cent from the employees. Note that because the pension is based on final salary and years of service, the pension may not be proportional to contributions paid into the scheme. The employer's contributions are not earmarked for any particular employee. The money simply goes into the general pot. Publicly funded schemes for the civil service and armed forces can be treated in the same way as other final salary schemes. Although there is no specific pension fund, notional contributions are fixed by the scheme's actuary and are available, if requested.

Money Purchase Schemes

20–20 These schemes are totally different. The pension is related to the contributions paid in by employer and employee. The contributions paid by both employer and employee are earmarked for that particular employee. How much pension the employee receives will depend on how much has been accumulated as a result of the contributions paid into the scheme over the years being invested by the fund managers. The position is very similar if the employer agrees to make specified payments into a personal pension scheme.

The Effect of Dismissal in respect of Occupational Pension Schemes

1.   Money Purchase Schemes

20–21 If the dismissed employee was a member of a money purchase scheme the position is reasonably straightforward when it comes to assessing loss. The contributions already made by the employer and employee remain invested for the employee's benefit. The effect of the dismissal is that the dismissed employee loses the contributions which the employer would have continued to make had he not been dismissed. If, for example, the dismissed employee gets another job with an equivalent pension six months later then his loss is the total value of the contributions which his former employer would have made over that six month period had he not been dismissed. There may be a penalty payable for leaving such a scheme early (because of the dismissal). Such a loss is clearly attributable to the dismissal and can easily be identified. It is therefore recoverable.

2.   Final Salary Schemes

20–22 The effect of the dismissal, if the employee was a member of a final salary pension scheme, is more complicated. If an employee who is a member of such a scheme is dismissed or resigns, he becomes entitled to a pension which is payable only when he reaches retirement age. This is known as a deferred pension. The problem is that the deferred pension is based on salary at the date of dismissal, or resignation. If, for example, he has been in the scheme for 15 years at the date of dismissal, he may become entitled to a deferred pension based on 15/60ths of his salary at the date of dismissal. If his salary at that time was £20,000, his deferred pension would be $15/60 \times £20,000 = £5,000$. Had he remained in his job for another fifteen years his salary might have increased to, say, £45,000. His pension then would have been $30/60 \times £45,000 = £22,500$. Half of this, some £11,250, would relate to the first fifteen years of service.

20–23 So even if he gets another job straight away with the same salary, the same future increases in salary and an identical pension scheme he has still suffered a loss of the difference between £11,250 and £5,000, *i.e.* £6,250 per year from the date of retirement until his death. This is described as the loss of enhancement of accrued rights. The position, in fact, is not so stark as a result of the Social Security Act 1990. Now such a deferred pension must be increased by five per cent per annum up to retirement or by the annual rate of inflation whichever is the lower. However, because an employee's salary would probably increase by more than five per cent per year or by more than the rate of inflation, this measure is not likely to extinguish the loss of enhancement of accrued rights suffered by someone dismissed who is a member of such a scheme.

CATEGORIES OF LOSS

20–24   The loss of pension benefits suffered by an unfairly dismissed employee, or an employee who leaves his employment as a result of unlawful discrimination can be put into three categories:

1.   loss of pension rights which would have accrued during the period between dismissal and the date of the remedy hearing;

2.   loss of future pension rights which would have accrued between the remedy hearing and retirement;

3.   loss of enhancement of the pension rights already accrued at the date of dismissal (see paras 20–23 and 20–51).

The Guidelines Approach to Assessing Categories of Loss

20–25   In this section we consider the guidance provided by the Blue Book on how to assess the different categories of loss in respect of each type of pension scheme.

No Occupational Pension Scheme

20–26   The guidelines in the Blue Book make the assumption that if the dismissed employee was not in an occupational pension scheme then no loss is suffered in respect of pension rights (see para. 3.4 of the Blue Book). However, it may be the case that the employee could subsequently have joined an occupational pension scheme had he not been dismissed. It is often the case that employees need a period of qualifying employment or need to attain a specified age before gaining access to the employer's pension scheme. The complainant may, therefore, be able to argue that he has suffered loss by being denied the opportunity of joining such a scheme.

20–27   In *Samuels v. Clifford Chance* EAT 559/90, there was a service qualification of five years before employees could join the company pension scheme. Ms Samuels was dismissed after two and a half years service. She claimed compensation for the lost opportunity of joining the scheme. The tribunal considered her evidence with regard to her future intentions prior to her dismissal. They also considered her curriculum vitae which showed that she had never stayed in any previous job for five years. The EAT supported the tribunal's conclusion not to award compensation for the lost opportunity of joining the pension scheme.

The correct approach in a discrimination claim is for the tribunal to assess the percentage chance that the dismissed employee would have stayed sufficiently long to qualify to join the pension scheme (using the same approach as with other forms of future financial loss, see paras 13–58 to 13–76). Any calculated loss is then multiplied by that percentage to determine compensation for such pension loss (see paras 20–32

20–45 for the assessment of future pension loss). In the unfair dismissal context, the tribunal might adopt a similar approach so as to determine what would be just and equitable to award for the lost chance of joining a pension scheme (s.123(1) ERA; see also paras 11–03 to 11–37).

Money Purchase Schemes

20–28 The calculation of pension loss in circumstances where the dismissed employee benefited from a money purchase scheme is reasonably straightforward. The first two charts set out in the Blue Book at Appendix O (Appendix 2 of the Blue Book) can be used to calculate loss on the basis of the guidance considered in this section. The Guidelines provide as follows:

1. Loss of pension rights from the date of dismissal to the date of hearing

20–29 As has been stated at para. 20–20, with a money purchase scheme the employer makes defined contributions into the scheme. The employer's contributions are normally clearly shown on the wages or salary slip. To calculate the pension loss up to the date of hearing one simply multiplies the weekly pension contributions from the employer by the number of weeks from dismissal to the date of hearing. The guidelines state that one must make an allowance "for any sums paid in lieu of notice". This is, of course, only the case if, as part of the payment in lieu of notice, a sum has been paid by the employer in lieu of the pension contributions he would have made during the notice period. A payment made by the employer only in lieu of wages during the notice period does not compensate for lost pension contributions.

> *Example*
> The dismissed employee earned £200 per week gross.
> The employer paid contributions of 10 per cent of gross salary into a money purchase scheme. This gives a weekly pension loss of £20. The hearing is 20 weeks after dismissal.
>
> Compensation for loss of pension rights from the date of dismissal to the date of hearing:
> £20 × 20 =   £400

20–30 Note that the employer's contributions of a specified percentage of gross salary may exclude variable elements of pay such as bonuses or commission or payments for overtime. One therefore needs to determine what is included within the employee's "pensionable pay". However, as stated at para. 20–29, the employer's contribution should be clearly identifiable from the pay slip.

Additional Note: New job prior to hearing date

20–31 If the complainant has already found a new job by the date of the tribunal hearing and that job enjoys the benefit of a pension then the tribunal should set off payments made by the new employer into the scheme. If, for example, the new employer pays the same percentage contribution based on an identical salary into the new scheme then there would be no continuing pension loss.

2. Loss of future pension rights

20–32 The guidelines recommend that in calculating the extent of loss of pension rights in respect of the period after the date of the hearing, one should again use the contributions which would have been made by the employer into the money purchase pension scheme as the basis of the calculation. Just as with calculating any other future financial loss, the tribunal has to indulge in a "highly speculative process" (para. 9.2 of Blue Book) in determining the period over which the complainant is likely to suffer the loss of those pension contributions. There are various scenarios to consider:

No new job at date of hearing

20–33 The tribunal will have to decide when it believes the complainant will find new employment. At paragraph 9.2 of the Blue Book it states:

> "If the Tribunal takes the view that the [complainant] is likely to obtain fresh employment in, say, one year or two years and that his earnings in that new employment are likely to be comparable, it is reasonable to assume that the pension scheme will also be comparable."

If this is the view the tribunal takes, then the future loss will be the total contributions the employer would have made into the pension scheme during the period up until the complainant would have obtained comparable work.

For example, if the weekly pension contributions by the employer totalled £20 prior to dismissal and the tribunal decides that the period of future loss (until the complainant gets other comparable work) is 52 weeks then the award for future pension loss will be:

$$52 \times 20 = £1,040$$

If the tribunal decides that there is likely to be a longer period of future loss then the multiplier/multiplicand approach may be used (see paras 13–86 to 13–92)

Additional Note: Loss of promotion

20–34 If the tribunal also concludes that the complainant would have been promoted had he not been dismissed, or would simply have received an annual pay rise, the employer's contribution used for calculating future pension loss must be based on the relevant percentage of that higher salary.

Percentage Reductions

20–35 Also, in both unfair dismissal and discrimination cases the tribunal might decide to apply a percentage reduction to compensation for financial loss ("just and equitable" and "contributory fault" reductions in calculating the compensatory award in unfair dismissal cases and "percentage chance" reductions in discrimination cases when assessing the chances of what would have happened but for the discriminatory act (see Chapter 11 in respect of unfair dismissal and paras 13–58 to 13–76 in respect of discrimination claims). Such a percentage reduction would apply equally to compensation for pension loss.

Qualifying period in new scheme

20–36   The guidelines point out that lengthy qualification periods (before a new employee can join a pension scheme) are now unusual (para. 9.3 of Blue Book). It may, therefore, be appropriate to disregard the effect of any qualifying period in any new job which the complainant might obtain and simply award compensation for the contributions the employer would have made up to the point at which the tribunal believes the complainant would have got comparable work. It is, of course, always open to a complainant to argue that he is unlikely to get a job with the benefit of a pension. It will then be up to the tribunal to consider the available evidence taking into account their own knowledge of the job market in order to reach a decision.

The employee has found new work but there is no pension scheme

20–37   If there is no pension scheme with the new employment the complainant has obtained then there will be a continuing loss of his previous employer's contributions week by week or month by month into the pension scheme. However, the new employer will be contributing to SERPS and those payments should be deducted from the lost pension contributions in order to calculate actual pension loss. If the SERPS contributions are not known then the guidelines recommend that the tribunal assumes that they amount to three per cent of the complainant's gross pay in his new job.

For example, if the employee is earning the same in his new job as he previously earned but does not have the benefit of an occupational pension which, in his old job was based on an employer contribution of 10 per cent of gross salary then the continuing pension loss will be 10%−3% (SERPS contribution) = 7% × gross salary.

20–38   Just as with other financial loss, tribunals, (particularly in unfair dismissal cases where compensation is such as to be just and equitable), are cautious about speculating too far into the future in the award for pension loss. However, if the facts justify it then the tribunal may be willing to make an award for future pension loss based on a long period of time.

In *Hearne v. Manpower Ltd* COIT 1353/213, the tribunal awarded compensation for the loss of employer's contributions into a pension scheme for a period of ten years in circumstances where Mr Hearne was likely to remain in the new job he had found which had no pension entitlement.

One may have a situation whereby the complainant has found new work on higher pay but without any pension scheme. The tribunal simply calculates whether the higher pay offsets the loss of employer pension contributions in order to determine whether there is any continuing loss.

New job with pension scheme

20–39   If the new employment has the benefit of a pension scheme then the tribunal will have to compare the value of the new employer's contributions as compared with those made by the previous employer in order to determine whether there is any continuing loss. This, of course, will depend both on the total pay upon which the pension calculation is based and the actual percentage contributed by the employer.

3.   Loss of enhancement of accrued pension rights

20–40   There is no loss of any enhancement of accrued pension rights in the case of money purchase schemes. Sums already paid into the scheme at the date of dismissal remain in the fund for the benefit of the complainant and will continue to grow in value. If the scheme requires a penalty to be paid for leaving it early (for example, as a result of dismissal) then the complainant can recover the penalty paid as part of his loss.

Final Salary Schemes

20–41 The guidelines approach in relation to final salary schemes is less satisfactory. The authors of the guidelines accepted that the approach was "not technically correct" (para. 8.3 Blue Book) but was the "fairest method" and has the benefit of simplicity. The three charts set out in the Blue Book at Appendix O, (Appendix 2 of the Blue Book) can be used to calculate loss on the basis of the guidance considered in this section. It works as follows:

1. Loss of pension rights from the date of dismissal to the date of hearing

20–42 With a final salary scheme, as we have seen, the employee gets a deferred pension on termination of employment. Had he remained in employment up to the date of the tribunal hearing and then been dismissed he would be entitled to a slightly higher deferred pension (para. 8.2 Blue Book). If he had, however, remained in employment (rather than being dismissed at the date of hearing) then "he would simply have gained additional service to put into the calculation of his final pension". (para. 8.2—Blue Book). The guidelines then propose that instead of looking at such "additional contingent benefits he would have gained" one should base the calculation on the "contributions ... the employer would have made to the pension fund" (para. 8.3 Blue Book). As has been noted at para. 20–19, payments made into the fund of a final salary scheme are not attributed to any particular employee in the scheme but go into the general pot in order to ensure there is sufficient in the fund to provide the guaranteed pensions based on final salary.

20–43 It has also been noted (para. 20–18) that the contributions made by the employer may vary from time to time depending on how healthy the fund is. Sometimes the employer may be able to enjoy a contributions holiday with no contributions being made for a period of time. However, the scheme's actuary will state in his annual report the "normal cost of the scheme to the employer" and this is usually given as a percentage of the total wage bill. If the scheme is based on "pensionable pay" which excludes variable elements such as bonus or overtime pay then the report will state the percentage of that pensionable pay which the employer normally pays into the fund. In order to calculate loss of pension rights from the date of dismissal to date of hearing the guidelines propose that this percentage is applied to the complainant's gross pensionable pay at the date of dismissal to determine the weekly loss. This is then multiplied by the number of weeks from dismissal to the date of hearing.

20–44 The guidelines state that if there is no evidence from the employer to show what is included within "pensionable pay", then the tribunal should simply assume that "pensionable pay is the same as actual gross pay". (para. 8.5 Blue Book). In circumstances where the percentage contribution made by the employer "cannot be easily ascertained or is currently anomalous (because of a contributions holiday)" the guidelines propose that the tribunal should use a figure of 10 per cent if it is a contributory scheme or 15 per cent if non-contributory (para. 8.6 Blue Book). Whether the scheme is contributory will be apparent from the wage slip—if it is, it will show an element of the employee's wage going into the pension fund.

Example

The complainant earned £200 gross per week. This is defined as his "pensionable pay". The employer contributes 10 per cent of the gross wage bill into the pension scheme. The employee contributes £10 per week (five per cent).

The complainant's continuing loss, using the guidelines method, is £20 per week, being the 10 per cent contribution of the employer multiplied by his gross weekly pay. This sum is then multiplied by the number of weeks from dismissal to the tribunal hearing to determine total loss for that period. Note that, just as with the calculation of past loss with a money purchase scheme, one has to take into account any new pensionable employment already obtained (see para. 20–31).

2. Loss of future pension rights

20–45 The guidelines suggest a similar approach to the assessment of future loss as with past loss. The employer's contributions to the pension fund are used as the basis for assessing future loss. As we have seen, unlike money purchase schemes, there is no specified contribution from the employer going into a fund directly for the benefit of the particular employee. However, just as with assessing past loss, one uses the percentage of the total pensionable wage bill going into the pension scheme as the contribution rate.

The same approach as with past loss is also used if the contribution rate cannot be readily ascertained (see para. 20–44). Then, in the same way as with money purchase schemes, one ascertains the weekly future pension loss by applying this percentage to the complainant's pensionable pay (see para. 20–33) and then multiply that weekly loss by the number of weeks of future loss identified by the tribunal (see para. 20–33).

No job at date of hearing

20–46 The loss would be for the period up to when the employee got another job with a comparable pension scheme. The guidelines make the point that the new job may have a qualification period before the complainant could join the new pension scheme. However, with final salary schemes, benefits "are often backdated once the qualification period has been met". (para. 9.4 Blue Book). The guidelines go on to state that "if the qualification period is two years or less and if, on the qualification period being met, the entitlement is backdated to the beginning of employment, there is no need to make any allowance for this period".

New employment with pension

20–47 If the complainant has got a new job, the tribunal will compare the pension benefits. So far as the new job is concerned, the notional employer's contribution will be applied to the complainant's pensionable pay. Then a comparison can be made with the value of the previous scheme so as to ascertain whether there is any continuing loss.

Example

In the previous job the complainant earned £200 per week. There was a final salary scheme with a notional employer's contribution of 10 per cent of salary (according to the actuary's report). This means that the weekly loss is £20. Then the complainant gets a new job on the same salary but with a contribution rate of eight per cent. This means that there is a continuing loss of two per cent of £200 per week, *i.e.* £4.

New job without pension

20–48 Just as with the loss of a money purchase scheme, one deducts the contribution into SERPS by the new employer from the percentage notional contribution rate in respect of the lost pension to calculate continuing loss.

Transfer of pension benefits

20–49 Section 2 of the Social Security Act 1985 introduced an entitlement for a person to require his former employer to transfer the value of the accrued pension to a similar scheme run by a new employer. The value of the pension benefits which are transferred is calculated in accordance with the Occupational Pension Schemes (Transfer Values) Regulations 1985 S.I. 1985 No.1931). These regulations came into force on January 1, 1986. The guidelines state: "Our understanding is that the transfer value is an actuarial figure which represents the present value of the deferred pension he can anticipate."

In *Freeman plc v. Flynn* [1984] I.R.L.R. 486, Mr Flynn had the benefit of a final salary pension until he was dismissed by Freeman plc. The dismissal was held to be unfair. In the tribunal's assessment of compensation they found that Mr Flynn had suffered nearly £10,000 of pension loss. A substantial element of that was in respect of the loss of pension rights to which he was entitled at the date of dismissal. The EAT, however, pointed out that those rights were "not wholly lost to him". The contributions to date entitled him to a deferred pension of £1,135 per year or "the right to transfer at value to a new employer's scheme".

20–50 With regard to future loss, the tribunal had awarded 15 months of lost wages on the assumption that he would then get employment. However, they also concluded that "it will take a further three years [after the expiration of the 15 months] before the applicant is in an equivalent pensionable position".

The EAT disagreed with this. The tribunal's decision involved an assumption that he would be back at work for a full three years without any pension entitlement. "This is one of the rare cases where we have found the conclusion startling enough to offend reason" (Waite J.). That element of loss was accordingly struck out. The EAT held that no loss had been suffered because he could transfer the pension benefit straight into the new scheme.

3.   Loss of enhancement of accrued pension rights

20–51 As explained at paras 20–22 to 20–23, a dismissed employee may suffer a loss of enhancement of the accrued pension rights where the pension is a final salary scheme. The loss is "the difference between the deferred pension he will receive and that part of the pension he would have received had he stayed with the company which is referable to his employment to date" (para. 10.3 of the Blue Book). There are, of course, many imponderables which make it difficult to assess this element of loss. For example, the more the complainant's salary would have gone up had he not been dismissed, the greater the difference will be between the deferred pension (which is based on salary at the date of dismissal) and the pension he would have got had he not been dismissed (based on that higher salary). Alternatively, he may have been dismissed fairly in any event soon after the unfair or discriminatory dismissal. In such a case, the loss of enhancement of accrued rights would be small.

No compensation at all

20–52   The guidelines state that in certain types of case "it would not be just and equitable to make any award of compensation in respect of loss of accrued pension rights". Note the use of the words "just and equitable". This is specifically relevant to the assessment of the compensatory award in unfair dismissal cases (s.123(1) ERA 96, see para. 10–01). As stated at paras 20–09 to 20–10 this test is not relevant in discrimination cases. Nevertheless, even in a discrimination case, the conclusion reached may be the same, simply on the basis that the tribunal concludes that no loss has been suffered under this head. The categories referred to are:

1. All public sector schemes (such schemes are inflation proof and so the usual problem with the deferred pension being based on a much lower salary at the date of dismissal does not apply, see para. 20–23).

2. Private sector schemes if the employee is within five years of retirement. The assumption here is that little loss of enhancement will occur during this period. However, this will not necessarily be the case if earnings are rising fast at that time.

3. Where the tribunal finds that the employment would have ended in any event within five year.

20–53   A pension based on a much higher final salary at retirement than the deferred pension could still result in a loss of accrued rights. Also, the cost of living increases could be running at more than the rate of five per cent by which deferred pensions are increased by virtue of the Social Security Act 1990.

Guidelines simplified actuarial method

20–54   Where the circumstances do not fall within any of these categories in which it can be assumed there will be no loss, some assessment needs to be carried out to determine the loss of enhancement of accrued rights. Generally, we are dealing here with private sector employees with more than five years to go until they retire. (Note, however, as explained at paras 20–52 to 20–53 there may be a good case for arguing that there is likely to be a loss of enhancement of accrued rights even if there is less than five years until retirement, and it is open to the complainant to argue this.) The Blue Book recommends use of a simplified actuarial calculation designed by the Government Actuary's Department.

20–55   The method takes account of the built-in indexation of the deferred pension (by five per cent or rate of inflation whichever is less) required by the Social Security Act 1990 (see para. 20–33). The assumptions used in this actuarial method are as follows:

1. The scheme provides for a widow or widower's pension at 50 per cent of the employee's pension.

2. No lump sum is available.

3. There is a three per cent increase per annum in most of the pension after retirement.

4. The scheme applies equally to men and women (which is in any event required to avoid discrimination) (para. 10–22 of the Blue Book).

20–56 In the Government Actuary's report contained in Appendix 3 of the Blue Book the assumption is also made that salaries increase by seven per cent per annum and that money can be invested at eight and a half per cent per annum on average. It is quite possible that some of these assumptions are not accurate for a particular scheme or at a particular time, in which case adjustments could be proposed to the tribunal, and it may be that actuarial evidence may need to be called for this purpose. The method works as follows:

One takes as a starting point the deferred pension to which the complainant is entitled. This can readily be obtained from the pension fund administrators. A multiplier is then applied to that deferred pension. The multiplier is based on the person's age and is simply obtained from a table of multipliers set out at Appendix 4 of the Blue Book (see Appendix O).

20–57 As can be seen, in order to determine the appropriate multiplier one needs the complainant's age and the normal retirement age under that pension scheme.

> *Example*
> Complainant aged 46 when dismissed. He is informed that his deferred pension entitlement is £5,000. His normal retirement age would have been 65. From the table of multipliers the appropriate multiplier is 1.4:
>   £5,000 × 1.4 =   £7,000

This figure of £7,000 is, however, only the starting point in determining the proper award for loss of enhancement of accrued pension rights. The assumption upon which the table of multipliers is based is that if the employee had not been dismissed he would have stayed in that employment until retirement age (subject to death or disability). That is often an unlikely scenario.

Reduction to take account of contingencies

20–58 The total obtained from the initial calculation (in the example above, £7,000) has to be reduced to take account of the chance that the complainant would have left his job in any event before retirement age. This could be as a result of a fair dismissal, possibly on the basis of redundancy, or simply because he chooses to leave. The extent to which this sum is reduced is a matter for the discretion of the tribunal. The percentage reduction is not based on the percentage chance that the complainant would have left his employment in any event before retirement. Whenever the complainant would have left had he not been dismissed, there is still likely to be some loss of enhancement of accrued rights (see explanation of how this loss occurs at paras 20–22 to 20–23). The tribunal has to assess the extent to which the loss of enhancement of the accrued rights would be reduced by departure from the scheme before retirement.

Relationship with percentage reductions for contributory fault: Unfair dismissal compensatory award

20–59 In an unfair dismissal claim, the tribunal may decide that the complainant has been unfairly dismissed but that he contributed to his dismissal by his own conduct (s.123(6) ERA 96, see paras 11–38 to 11–87). If the contributory fault is assessed at 50 per cent then his compensatory award is reduced by that amount. The complainant may have been a member of a final salary scheme and may suffer a loss of enhancement of his accrued pension rights. In calculating the award for this loss the tribunal may decide that there should be a percentage reduction to reflect the extent to which the loss of enhancment to accrued rights would be reduced by departure from the scheme before retirement.

The case of *TBA Industrial Products Ltd v. Locke* [1984] I.R.L.R. 48 is an example of this scenario. The tribunal decided to reduce the figure for loss of enhancement of accrued pension rights by 70 per cent because of the chance that Mr Locke would not have remained in the company's employment until the retirement age because of redundancy or because of his unsatisfactory work performance. His overall compensatory award (including the reduced compensation for pension loss) was reduced by 70 per cent to reflect his contributory fault. This approach was upheld by the EAT. This did not amount to him being penalised twice for poor performance. Although his poor performance was taken into account twice in assessing compensation, there were "two quite separate purposes. The [tribunal] first had to assess the present value of his future pension rights. In doing so they were bound to take account of the fact that he might never have enjoyed those pension rights by reason of his being fairly dismissed before his normal age of retirement. For this purpose they plainly had to consider the probability of his being so dismissed ... Having put a figure on the present value of his pension rights, to give effect to [what is now s.123(6)] they were bound to reduce the aggregate compensation to reflect the extent to which he contributed to his dismissal. These are two necessary steps in fixing compensation" (Brown-Wilkinson J.).

Guidance on applying reduction in award for loss of enhancement of accrued rights

20–60   Appendix 5 to the Blue Book sets out examples of how tribunals might exercise their discretion in deciding the extent of any reduction in the amount calculated to compensate for loss of enhancement of accrued rights. In one example, an employer dismisses two employees when he finds out they are planning to set up their own business. They are unfairly dismissed because they have not broken any term of the contract. However, the tribunal concludes that they would have left soon after anyway. Because of this it is unlikely that they have suffered any significant loss of their accrued pension rights. In other words, their deferred pension on dismissal is probably virtually identical to what it would have been at the point when they would have resigned had they not been dismissed. At the other end of the scale is an employee aged 53 who has been with the company for twenty-five years. The tribunal accepts that had he not been dismissed his intention was to stay until retirement. In such circumstances the tribunal might conclude that the chance of him leaving the company (apart from by death or disability) before retirement is small. Therefore any percentage reduction of the sum calculated for loss of enhancement of accrued pension rights would be "modest".

The Value Method

20–61   At paras 20–08 to 20–13 the question of whether the tribunal's guidelines should be used in any particular case is considered. If the conclusion is reached that the guideline approach is likely to seriously understate the extent of the pension loss then the complainant should instruct an actuary to prepare a report on the value of the lost pension rights. The actuary will require details of both the complainant's circumstances and the pension scheme itself. The report should be disclosed to the respondent well before the hearing so that he has an opportunity to challenge the evidence by obtaining his own report and by calling the actuary to give evidence. A failure to notify the respondent long enough before the hearing to enable him to respond is likely to lead to an adjournment and the risk of an order for costs wasted as a result. The complainant should ensure that the actuary is available to give evidence at the hearing.

Burden of Proof

20–62   In both unfair dismissal and discrimination cases the burden of proving pension loss, as with any other type of loss, lies with the complainant. However, particularly with unrepresented complainants, the tribunal should inquire into all possible heads of loss and should raise the issue of pension entitlement. That said, it is still then up to the complainant to prove the loss (see *Tidman v. Aveling Marshall Ltd* [1977] I.R.L.R. 218 EAT). This was an unfair dismissal case but the principle applies equally to discrimination cases. "The whole atmosphere of the [tribunal] work and the EAT work is far more generous to the unrepresented person or the person who is not represented by skilled legal advisers". Kilner-Brown J.

However, in *Cawthorn & Sinclair Ltd v. Hedger* [1974] I.C.R. 146, the NIRC was less sympathetic to Mr Hedger, who had been employed as Chief Accountant. The tribunal's award for pension loss was low but Sir Hugh Griffiths in the NIRC found that Mr Hedger had made "scant attempt to discharge the burden of proving pension loss". As Chief Accountant he ought to have understood the company's pension scheme. The EAT refused to disturb the tribunal's decision.

Pension Loss and Recoupment

20–63   In unfair dismissal cases, recoupment (which is considered fully at paras 16–18 to 16–30) does not apply to compensation for pension loss. The Schedule to the Employment Protection (Recoupment of Jobseeker's Allowance and Income Support) Regulations 1996, sets out the categories of payment to which the "prescribed element" is attributable. The prescribed element is that part of an award from which benefits can be deducted (Regulation 3 and the Schedule to the Regulations). In respect of the compensatory award the prescribed element is "compensation for loss of wages for the period before the conclusion of the tribunal proceedings". If the total loss is greater than the statutory maximum compensatory award it is important to calculate the full extent of pension loss. This is because the prescribed element must be reduced by the same proportion as the total loss in order to reduce the award to the statutory maximum. This could be to the complainant's benefit because it may mean that the prescribed element is reduced below the total amount of benefit received leaving more of the compensatory award payable to the complainant.

Pension Loss and Mitigation

20–64   The duty to mitigate one's loss applies as much to pension loss as to any other sort of loss (for full commentary on mitigation, see Chapter 19). However, in the case of *Bardsley v. Sturdy Finance Ltd* [1979] I.R.L.R. 65 EAT, Mr Bardsley opted to obtain a refund of his contributions rather than benefit on retirement from a deferred pension. A deferred pension is generally a better option, financially. However, Mr Bardsley "felt that he could make better use of the money by putting it into a business which he was then to set up. Without the money he would have had difficulty in starting his business". The EAT found there had been no failure to mitigate. There may be cases where an employee does act wholly unreasonably by opting to take out his contributions rather than accept a deferred pension, but the duty is on the respondent to prove a failure to mitigate. In this case the EAT agreed with the tribunal that there was no evidence to suggest that it was unreasonable for the employee to take a refund of his contributions.

CHAPTER 21

Redundancy Pay
(and Protective Award)

21–01 This chapter considers the tribunal's power to enforce an employee's entitlement to a redundancy payment. A full analysis of the circumstances in which an employee is entitled to a redundancy payment is beyond the scope of this book. However, the key principles relating to entitlement are summarised. The chapter covers the calculation of statutory redundancy pay and looks at the circumstances in which it can be reduced, either automatically because, for example, the employee is nearing retirement age or by virtue of the discretion of the tribunal. First some basic principles.

Entitlement to redundancy pay

21–02 The basic entitlement to a redundancy payment is contained in s.135 ERA. An employee is entitled to such a payment if:

(a) he is dismissed by reason of redundancy,

(b) he is eligible by reason of being laid off or kept on short time.

Service qualification

21–03 An employee only qualifies for a redundancy payment if he has been continuously employed for at least two years by the "relevant date" (s.155 ERA). Broadly, this is the date notice expires. However, if notice shorter than the statutory minimum notice has been given then continuous employment is effectively extended to the date the statutory minimum notice would have expired had it been given (s.145 ERA). If this "extension" takes an employee over the two year period then he is entitled to a redundancy payment. If the employee was employed on a fixed term contract which expires without being renewed, the relevant date is the date the contract expires (s.145(2)(c) ERA).

Continuous employment begins on 18th birthday

21–04 Note that for the purposes of determining entitlement to claim a redundancy payment and also for calculating the size of the payment, an employee's continuous employment is treated as beginning on his eighteenth birthday. No employment before that date counts (s.211(2) ERA).

Upper age limit

21–05 If the employee is over the age of 65 (or above the normal retiring age for that job if lower than 65) then he does not qualify for a redundancy payment (s.156 ERA).

Scaling down after 64th birthday

21–06 If an employee is made redundant when he is between the age of 64 and 65 then the statutory redundancy payment is reduced by 1/12th for each complete month of employment following the 64th birthday (s.162(4) ERA).

Example
X's 64th birthday is on December 14. He is made redundant with the relevant date being March 12 the following year. (This is the date the notice ends unless notice was shorter than the statutory minimum notice required, in which case the relevant date is the date such statutory minimum notice would have expired had it been given (s.145 ERA).)

X has worked for his employer for five years and earns more than the statutory maximum week's pay of £220 (see para. 21–09).

The statutory redundancy payment (before making the "age" reduction)
$1.5 \times 5 \times £220 = £1,650$

He has worked for two whole months following his 64th birthday. The normal redundancy payment is therefore reduced by 2/12ths.
$£1,650 \times 2/12 = £275$
$£1,650 - £275 = £1,375$

Calculation of redundancy payment

21–07 The calculation of the statutory redundancy payment is essentially the same as for the basic award for unfair dismissal, with the important proviso that only continuous employment from the eighteenth birthday counts for redundancy pay purposes (see para. 21–04). Calculation of the basic award is considered at Chapter 9. The ready reckoner set out at Appendix P provides a quick method of determining the figure by which a week's pay has to be multiplied to arrive at the statutory redundancy payment. The rules for calculating the statutory redundancy payment are set out in s.162 ERA.

Week's Pay

21–08 For the purposes of calculating the statutory redundancy payment, a week's pay is calculated using the statutory formula considered at Chapter 24. Broadly, it is based on gross contractual remuneration but special rules apply where working hours and pay vary from week to week or where pay varies according to the amount of work done (piece work or where pay includes a performance element, see paras 24–10 to 24–34).

Maximum Week's Pay

21–09 The same statutory maximum applies to a week's pay for the purposes of calculating the statutory redundancy pay as for calculating the basic award for unfair dismissal compensation (s.227 ERA). Currently, the maximum week's pay is £220 for any redundancy dismissal where the relevant date is on or after April 1, 1998 s.227(2) provides that the Secretary of State may vary this limit by Statutory Instrument.

Calculation date

21–10   In determining the week's pay in accordance with the guidance given at Chapter 24, the calculation date is worked out as follows (ss.226(5) and (6) ERA):

1. Where no notice has been given, or where the notice is shorter than the statutory minimum notice required, the calculation date is the date the termination takes effect (see ss.226(5)(b) and 145(5) ERA).

2. Where statutory minimum notice has been given the calculation date is the date such notice was given (s.226(6) ERA).

3. Where the employer gives longer notice than the statutory minimum notice required, the calculation date is the date statutory minimum notice would have been given in order to terminate the contract on the date the actual notice terminated. So, if the employer gives six weeks' notice to an employee who was entitled to four weeks' statutory minimum notice then you count back four weeks from the end of the six week notice to determine the calculation date (s226(6) ERA).

4. Where a woman has been refused the right to return after maternity leave (which amounts to a dismissal by virtue of s.137(1) ERA), the calculation date is the last day on which the woman worked before the start of her maternity leave (s.226(5)(a) ERA).

Maximum number of years which count

21–11   Note that, just as with the basic award, the maximum number of years which count in calculating the statutory redundancy payment is 20, counting backwards from termination of employment.

Reductions to Statutory Redundancy Pay

21–12   In some circumstances the statutory redundancy payment is automatically reduced by virtue of specific statutory provisions. Thus, the reduction can be calculated according to a formula provided by the ERA or statutory instrument and the employer accordingly pays the reduced sum to the employee. In other specific cases the tribunal has a discretion to reduce the statutory redundancy payment.

Automatic reductions

Age

21–13   Already considered at para. 21–06 is the automatic reduction in statutory redundancy pay for employees made redundant between their 64th and 65th birthday.

Pension cases

21–14   If the employee is entitled to a pension on termination of employment then the statutory redundancy payment may be reduced or extinguished. The basis upon which this reduction is calculated is provided by The Redundancy Payments (Pensions) Regulations 1965 (S.I. 1965 No.1932). The current statutory provision which allows the Secretary of State to make such regulations is s.158 ERA. Schedule 2, paragraph 2(1) to the ERA provides that regulations made under legislation repealed by the ERA have effect as if made under the ERA. This means that the 1965 regulations remain effective. Broadly, the larger the pension entitlement the more the redundancy payment will be reduced and if, in accordance with the formula provided by the 1965 Regulations, an immediate pension entitlement is at least one third of the employee's annual pay, then the redundancy payment will be extinguished in full.

Discretionary reductions

21–15 First of all, it should be noted that there are circumstances in which an employee may not be entitled to any redundancy payment where he is guilty of gross misconduct, even though a redundancy situation exists. s.140(1) ERA provides that an employee is not entitled to a redundancy payment "by reason of dismissal where his employer, being entitled to terminate his contract of employment without notice by reason of the employee's conduct, terminates it" either:

(a) without notice,

(b) by giving notice shorter than the statutory minimum notice which would have been required had it not been for the employee's gross misconduct, or

(c) by giving notice which includes, or comes with, a written statement confirming that, because of the employee's gross misconduct, the employer would have been able to terminate the contract without notice.

21–16 This is, without doubt, a clumsily worded section which has been the subject of considerable case law. Clearly covered is the situation where the employer expressly terminates the contract of employment on grounds of both gross misconduct and redundancy. Also covered would be a situation where the employee is dismissed on grounds of redundancy and the employer subsequently discovers that the employee was guilty of gross misconduct prior to the service of notice of dismissal. Note, however, that it is not enough for the employer to show reasonable belief that the employee was guilty of gross misconduct. The test is an objective one. Was the conduct such as to entitle the employer to terminate the contract without notice? The burden is on the employer to show that the employee was guilty of conduct which was a significant breach going to the root of the contract or which showed that he no longer intended to be bound by one or more of the essential terms of the contract (see *Bonner v. H. Gilbert Ltd* [1989] I.R.L.R. 475 EAT).

21–17 We now consider the limited circumstances in which the tribunal has a discretion to award all or part of the statutory redundancy payment where the employee is guilty of gross misconduct. Section 140(3) ERA provides that where an employee has been served with notice terminating his employment, but is then dismissed for gross misconduct during the notice period, the tribunal may determine that the employer is liable to make a payment of all or part of the statutory redundancy payment if it appears to the tribunal "in the circumstances of the case, to be just and equitable that the employee should receive it". Note that, for this provision to apply, the termination of employment for gross misconduct must, strictly speaking, take effect during the "obligatory period of notice" (ss.140(3) and (4) and s.136 ERA). Where the notice already served by the employer is no longer than the statutory minimum notice required then the obligatory period of notice equals the actual notice given. If, however, longer notice was given, the dismissal for gross misconduct must take effect during the period ending on the actual date the original notice expired and then counting back from there the number of weeks of statutory minimum notice required.

21–18   If the dismissal falls outside this period then the provisions of s.140(3) ERA do not apply. Take, for example, an employee who has been served with six weeks' notice of termination of employment on grounds of redundancy in circumstances where he was entitled to statutory minimum notice of four weeks. If he is summarily dismissed for gross misconduct in the first two weeks of the six week notice, this falls outside the "obligatory period of notice" and therefore s.140(3) does not apply. There is no discretion for the tribunal to award all or part of the statutory redundancy payment. If, in such circumstances, the misconduct occurred after the service of the original six week notice (and was not just discovered after service of notice) then s.140(1) ERA does not apply so as to disqualify the employee from entitlement to a redundancy payment (it appears as if he would get his full entitlement). Note that under s.140(3) the tribunal can exercise its discretion to award the whole redundancy payment or such part as the tribunal "thinks fit" (s.140(4)(b) ERA).

21–19   In *Lignacite Products Ltd v. Krollman* [1979] I.R.L.R. 22 EAT, Mr Krollman was served with notice terminating his employment on grounds of redundancy. He had worked for the company for twenty four years. During his notice period he was convicted of theft from his employer and was summarily dismissed. The tribunal exercised its discretion under what is now s.140(3) ERA to order the respondent to pay Mr Krollman 60% of his redundancy payment. The respondent company appealed but the EAT upheld the tribunal's decision. Phillips J. pointed out that the amount awarded by the tribunal was "somewhat larger than we think we would have awarded ourselves, but not so much larger that we can interfere with it".

21–20   A decision of the tribunal, where it exercises its discretion, can only be overturned if they apply the wrong test or if they "arrive at a result which is so obviously wrong that the only reasonable conclusion must be that although they did not say so, they must have applied the wrong test" (Phillips J.) It was also the case that a "redundancy payment in part … is also earned by the previous service of the employee, in this case 24 years service". Clearly, relevant factors will be the length of the employee's service (as in Krollman) and the seriousness of the misconduct. Note that the same tribunal powers apply in cases of gross misconduct following an employee giving notice to his employer indicating his intention to claim a redundancy payment in respect of lay-off or short-time working (s.140(3)(b) ERA).

Leaving before the end of the notice period

21–21   In circumstances where an employer has served notice of termination of employment by reason of redundancy, the employee may be able to leave early and still retain his entitlement to a statutory redundancy payment. The objective of this option, which is provided for by s.136(3) ERA, is to facilitate access to new employment. If an employee, under notice of dismissal, manages to find new work, he should, if possible, be able to take it up without undue delay rather than risk losing it. The ERA, however, aims to balance the needs of the employee and the employer, who has served notice of termination. There may be good reason for the employer needing to retain the services of the employee during the notice period. This balance is achieved by requiring the employee, who wishes to leave early, to serve notice terminating his employment. The Act is silent as to the notice period required from the employee. It appears, from the EAT decision in *Ready Case Ltd v. Jackson* [1981] I.R.L.R. 312, that the employee can give less than the statutory minimum notice of one week. Note, however, that the employee can only give such notice during the obligatory period of notice. For commentary on how this is defined see paras 21–17 to 21–18.

21–22   On receipt of such notice from the employee, and before it expires, the employer can serve a counter-notice on the employee (s.142(1) ERA). Such notice must be in writing. The notice can require the employee to withdraw his notice and to continue to work until the original notice served by the employer has expired. The employer's counter-notice must also state that if the employee does not continue to work, the employer will contest any liability to pay him a redundancy payment (s.142(2) ERA). If the employee does not comply with the employer's notice requiring him to stay, he may indeed lose his entitlement to a redundancy payment. However, the issue may be referred to a tribunal, which may decide that the employer is liable to pay either the whole of the redundancy payment otherwise due or "such part of that redundancy payment as the tribunal thinks fit" (ss.142(3) and (4)). In reaching its decision the tribunal must have regard to:

(a)   the reasons why the employee wants to leave early, and

(b)   the employer's reasons for wanting him to stay.

In this way the tribunal balances the claims of each party in determining what proportion, if any, of the redundancy payment should be paid to the employee.

Redundancy pay and strike action

21–23   Special rules also apply in circumstances where the employee goes on strike during the period of notice served by the employer by reason of redundancy (or after the employee has given notice indicating his intention to claim a redundancy payment in respect of lay-off or short-time). Note, first of all, that if an employer terminates employment as a result of the employee taking strike action (limited to a strike in respect of terms and conditions of employment—s.235(5) ERA) the employee will not be entitled to a redundancy payment provided the employer acts in accordance with the requirements of s.140(1) ERA relating to service of notice (see paras 21–15 to 21–16 and Simmons v. Hoover Ltd [1976] I.R.L.R. 266).

Strike following notice of termination

21–24   The position is different, however, where the employee goes on strike after having been given notice by reason of redundancy. In such circumstances, the right to a redundancy payment is not lost if the employer dismisses the employee because of taking part in the strike (see s.140(2) ERA). Note that the employee must have gone on strike during the obligatory period of notice for this provision to apply (ss.140(2) and (4) ERA, see paras 21–17 to 21–18 for commentary on the obligatory period of notice).

Notice of extension

21–25   The employer does have the right to serve a "notice of extension" on an employee who has taken part in a strike after having received notice of termination of employment by reason of redundancy (s.143(1) ERA). The notice of extension must be in writing. It requests the employee to agree to extend the contract of employment to make up for the days lost as a result of strike action. It must also:

- state the reasons for making the request, and

- inform the employee that if he does not agree to the proposed extension, the employer will contest any liability to pay redundancy pay, unless the employer is satisfied that as a result of sickness or injury or some other reason the employee is unable to comply, or, even if he is able to comply, it is reasonable in the circumstances not to do so (s.143(2) ERA).

So, if the employee does not comply with such a request, the possible outcomes are as follows:

1. The employer may simply agree to pay the redundancy pay (s.143(4) ERA), this then would be the end of the matter, or

2. If the employer refuses to pay the redundancy payment then the employee can refer the matter to the tribunal (s.143(5) ERA).

21–26   The tribunal then has a discretion to determine that the employer is, after all, liable to pay all or part of the redundancy payment (s.143(5) and (6) ERA). If it appears to the tribunal that the employee was unable to comply with the request to extend the contract of employment, or it was reasonable in the circumstances for him not to comply with it, then the tribunal may decide that the employer is liable to pay either the whole redundancy payment or "such part of that . . . payment as the tribunal thinks fit". Note that, unless the employee manages to persuade the tribunal to exercise its discretion to award some or all of the redundancy payment, he loses his entitlement even if he has turned up for work for part of the extended period. That does not amount to compliance with the notice of extension (s.143(3) ERA).

References to tribunal

21–27   Note that the power to refer questions to a tribunal relating to the right of an employee to a redundancy payment or relating to the amount of such a payment is provided by s.163 ERA. Section 163(2) ERA provides for a presumption that the reason for the dismissal was redundancy for the purposes of such references to the tribunal, unless the contrary is proved.

Remedies for Failure to Inform and Consult in Redundancy and Business Transfer Situations

21–28   An employer is under an obligation to inform and consult elected representatives or representatives of a recognised independent trade union in certain redundancy situations and also where there is a business transfer. Failure to comply with these duties can result in potentially substantial awards being made against the employer. This section summarises the main duties and sets out the rules relating to the awards which can be made by the tribunal.

Redundancy Consultation (s.188 TULR(C)A)

21–29   If the employer proposes to dismiss as redundant 20 or more employees at one establishment within a period of 90 days or less the employer must inform and consult either elected representatives of those who may be dismissed or representatives of a recognised independent trade union (s.188(1) and s.188(1B) TULR(C)A). If the employees concerned have elected such representatives but where there is also a recognised trade union the employer can choose which to consult. Note that for the purposes of this duty to consult, "redundancy" has a wider meaning than that which applies to the entitlement to statutory redundancy pay. If the dismissal of an employee is for a reason(s) not related to the individual concerned then the employee is taken to be dismissed as redundant (s.195(1) TULR(C)A). So, for example, if the reason for the dismissal relates to a business reorganisation or where the employer dismisses employees who refuse to agree to a cut in pay then the consultation obligations apply (provided there is a proposal to dismiss 20 or more employees within a 90 day period for this reason).

Timing of consultation

21–30 The consultation must start "in good time" and in any event—

(a) where the employer is proposing to dismiss 100 or more employees at least 90 days

(b) otherwise, at least 30 days

before the first of the dismissals take effect (s.188(1A) TULR(C)A).

Duty to provide information

In order to facilitate consultation the employer must disclose, in writing, to each representative the following information:

(a) the reasons for the proposals

(b) the number and descriptions of employees whom it is proposed to make redundant

(c) the total number of employees of any such description employed at that establishment

(d) the proposed method of selecting the employees who may be dismissed

(e) the proposed method of carrying out the dismissals, with due regard to any agreed procedure, including the period over which the dismissals are to take effect

(f) the proposed method of calculating the amount of any redundancy payments to be made (over and above statutory redundancy pay) (s.188(4) TULR(C)A).

What must the consultation cover?

21–31 The employer must consult about ways of—

(a) avoiding the dismissals

(b) reducing the number of employees to be dismissed, and

(c) mitigating the consequences of the dismissals (s.188(2) TULR(C)A).

Access to employees

The representatives must have access to the employees concerned and they must be given appropriate office space and facilities (s.188(5A) TULR(C)A).

Special circumstances

If special circumstances mean that it is not reasonably practicable to inform or consult as early as required then the employer must do what he can to comply (taking all such steps as are reasonably practicable to do so) (s.188(7) TULR(C)A). In circumstances where the employer first of all has to invite the employees to elect representatives before the consultation can start then provided he has done this long enough before the consultation has to start to allow them to elect representatives in time then, even if the elections take longer than expected, he will be taken to have complied with his duties under this provision if he informs and consults as soon as is reasonably practicable following the elections (s.188(7A) TULR(C)A).

Complaint to tribunal

21–32 If the employer fails to comply with *any* of these obligations then a complaint can be made to the tribunal. Note that there are strict limitations as to who can make the complaint (s.189(1) TULR(C)A). The complaint can be made by the trade union or any elected representative as appropriate. It is only where the employer has failed to allow for representatives to be elected that one of the employees actually made (or likely to be made) redundant can complain. The complaint must be presented within three months starting with the date of the last dismissal (or before that dismissal) (s.189(5) TULR(C)A). The same limited discretion to allow late complaints applies as with unfair dismissal (the reasonably practicable test).

Remedy

If the tribunal finds the complaint well founded it shall make a declaration to that effect and *may* also make a protective award (s.189(2) TULR(C)A).

Protective Award

21–33 The protective award is made in respect of employees who have either been dismissed or whom it is proposed to dismiss as redundant. The award orders the employer to pay remuneration for the *protected period* (s.189(3) TULR(C)A). The protected period starts on the date on which the first dismissals take effect or the date of the award, whichever is earlier and is of such length as the tribunal determines to be just and equitable in all the circumstances having regard to the seriousness of the employer's default (in complying with the duties under s.188 TULR(C)A). The maximum protected period is 90 days (where 100 or more employees are proposed to be made redundant in a 90 day period) and thirty days in any other case (s.189(4) TULR(C)A).

Entitlement to protective award

Although it is normally only the elected representatives or the trade union who can present a complaint to the tribunal, the award results in every employee made redundant (or whom it is proposed to make redundant) being entitled to be paid remuneration for the protected period (s.190(1) TULR(C)A).

Rate of remuneration

The rate of remuneration is a week's pay for each week of the period with proportionate reductions for part of a week. There is no limit to a week's pay (see Chapter 24 for calculation of a week's pay) (s.190(2) TULR(C)A). The calculation date is the date the protective award was made or if the employee has already been dismissed, the same calculation date used for calculating redundancy pay (s.190(5) TULR(C)A).

An employee is not entitled to remuneration under a protective award for any period during which he is employed by his employer unless he is entitled to be paid for that period by virtue of the contract of employment or by virtue of ss.87–91 ERA (see paras 25–38 to 25–39) (s.190(4) TULR(C)A). Note, however, that entitlement is in addition to any pay under the contract of employment. If the employee dies during the protected period the entitlement ends on that date (s.190(6) TULR(C)A).

Length of the protected period

21–34   Note that the length of the protected period (up to the maximum permitted) depends on what period the tribunal considers to be just and equitable in all the circumstances having regard to the employer's default (s.189(4)(b) TULR(C)A). In determining the length of the protected period the tribunal should not aim to penalise the employer. Instead, the aim of the award is to compensate the employee (see *Take Fashions Ltd v. Amalgamated Society of Textile Workers and kindred Trades* [1977] I.R.L.R. 309 EAT). In that case the EAT held that in exercising its discretion the tribunal had to consider two different criteria:

(1)   How much of the required period of consultation has been lost
(2)   The seriousness of the employer's default as it affects the employees concerned.

In *Spillers-French (Holding) Ltd v. Union of Shop, Distributive and Allied Workers* [1979] I.R.L.R. 339, the EAT held that employees were not being compensated merely for financial loss suffered as a result of the employer dismissing them earlier than he should have done. They were also being compensated for the loss of the opportunities which may emerge from a consultation process. "The consultation may result in new ideas being ventilated which avoid the redundancy situation altogether" (Slynn J). Consultation may also result in fewer redundancies than might otherwise have been the case.

Clearly the starting point for deciding the length of the protective period should be the extent to which the employer has curtailed the consultation period, so that if the consultation started two weeks later than it should have done then the tribunal may determine that the protective period should be two weeks long. However, other factors such as the likelihood of the consultation leading to another outcome or fewer redundancies should be taken into account. The EAT in the *Spillers-French* case also said that any earnings received by an employee following dismissal could not be taken as discharging the employer's liabilities. If the employer has failed to consult for the proper period for reasons over which it had no control, this may be a reason for reducing the protected period (see *Transport and General Workers' Union v. Gainsborough Distributors (UK) Ltd* [1978] I.R.L.R. 460) but this is only one factor. Overall, the period must be just and equitable in all the circumstances.

Note the recent case of *GMB & AEEU v. Campbell's UK Ltd*, Carlisle Tribunal 1.5.98, Case Nos. 26787/96 and 40769/96 in which the company informed the workforce that the factory was going to close prior to entering consultation with the trade unions. This did not meet the statutory criteria of what the consultation should cover. Consultations had to cover the possibilities of avoiding redundancies or reducing the number. What consultation there was, was a sham. With regard to the decision to close the factory there had been no consultation at all. The tribunal accordingly concluded that the protected period should be the maximum of 90 days.

Termination of employment during protected period

21–35 Special rules apply where the contract of employment is terminated during the protected period. So, if the employee is fairly dismissed for a non-redundancy reason (such as for misconduct) or if the employee unreasonably resigns during the protected period then he is not entitled to remuneration for the further period he would have been employed but for such a dismissal or resignation. Note, however, that if, for example, the employee unreasonably resigns a week before his employment was due to end then he is not entitled to remuneration under the protective award for that last week but if the protected period covers a further period of perhaps one week then he will be entitled to remuneration for that week (s.191(1) TULR(C)A).

Special rules also apply where the employer offers to renew the contract of employment or to re-engage the employee (with the renewal or re-engagement taking effect during the protected period). The offer of renewal must result in the employee being employed on terms and conditions which do not differ from his original contract (and employed in the same capacity and at the same place). The offer of re-engagement must amount to an offer of suitable alternative employment (s.191(2) TULR(C)A). If these conditions apply and if the employee unreasonably refuses such an offer, he is not entitled to remuneration under the protective award in respect of the period during which, but for that refusal, he would have been employed. In reality, this is likely to extinguish the award (s.191(3) TULR(C)A).

If the employee accepts suitable alternative employment or if his contract is renewed then he has a minimum of a four week trial period (s.191(4) and (5) TULR(C)A). If during that period the employee resigns then he remains entitled under the protective award unless he acted unreasonably by resigning (s.191(7) TULR(C)A). If the employer dismisses the employee during the trial period for a reason connected with or arising out of the change to the renewed or new contract then again the employee remains entitled under the protective award (s.191(7) TULR(C)A). If the employee remains employed throughout the trial period he remains entitled to the protective award.

Complaint by employee to tribunal

21–36 If the employee does not receive the full amount of remuneration he is due by virtue of the protective award he can complain to the tribunal (s.192(1) TULR(C)A). The normal three month time limit applies, running from the last date (if more than one) when the employer failed to pay remuneration. The same limited discretion applies to late complaints as applies in unfair dismissal cases (the reasonably practicable test) (s.192(2) TULR(C)A). If the tribunal finds the complaint well-founded it shall order the employer to pay the complainant the amount of remuneration which it finds due (s.192(3) TULR(C)A).

Transfer of Undertakings: Consultation (Transfer of Undertakings (Protection of Employment) Regulations 1981 (TUPE Regs))

There is also a duty to inform and consult either elected representatives or representatives of a recognised independent trade union in connection with the transfer of an undertaking within the terms of the Transfer of Undertakings (Protection of Employment) Regulations 1981. Both the transferee and the transferor are required to consult with representatives of any employees who may be affected by the transfer or may be affected by measures taken in connection with it (Reg 10(1) TUPE Regs).

Information

Long enough before the transfer to enable consultation to take place, the representatives must be informed of the following in writing:

(a) the fact that the transfer is to take place, when it is to take place and the reasons for it

(b) the legal, economic and social implications of the transfer for the affected employees

(c) the measures which the employer envisages he will, in connection with the transfer, take in relation to those employees, or confirmation that he does not propose to take any such measures

(d) the transferor must also inform representatives of his employees of the measures which the transferee envisages he will take or confirm that he does not envisage taking any measures.

(Reg 10(2) TUPE Regs).

There is an obligation on the transferee to give the necesssary information to the transferor to enable him to perform this duty (Reg 10(3) TUPE Regs).

Consultation

21–37 If the employer of any affected employees envisages that he will be taking measures in relation to those employees, he must consult their representatives. Consultation must be with a view to seeking their agreement to the measures to be taken (Reg 10(5) TUPE Regs).

During the consultations the employer shall:

(a) consider representations made by the representatives
(b) reply to those representations and, if he rejects any of those representations, state his reasons (Reg 10(6) TUPE Regs).

Access to employees

The representatives must be given access to the affected employees. They must have appropriate office space and other facilities (Reg 10(6A) TUPE Regs).

Special circumstances

21–38 If there are special circumstances which make it not reasonably practicable for the employer to perform the duty of informing and consulting then he shall "take all such steps towards performing that duty as are reasonably practicable in the circumstances" (Reg 10(7) TUPE Regs). If the employer has invited affected employees to elect representatives and the invitation was issued long enough before the point at which the employer had to give information to those representatives, then the employer shall be treated as complying with the requirements of the Regulations even if the elections take longer than expected and provided he provides the information (and if necessary consults) as soon as reasonably practicable after the election of representatives (Reg 10(8) TUPE Regs).

Complaint tribunal

Either an elected representative or the trade union can complain to the tribunal if the employer has failed to comply with the information and consultation requirements (Reg 11(1) TUPE Regs). If no representatives have been elected then an affected employee can present a complaint. If, following such a complaint, the transferor claims that the transferee prevented him from complying with the requirement to inform representatives of any measures which the transferee envisaged taking then he must give the transferee notice of his intention to put this to the tribunal. This makes the transferee a party to the proceedings (Reg 11(3) TUPE Regs).

Remedy

21–39 If the tribunal finds a complaint well-founded it shall make a declaration to that effect and may:

(a) order the employer to pay compensation to affected employees, or

(b) if the complaint relates to the transferor's failure to perform the duty to notify representatives of measures the transferee envisaged taking and the tribunal accepts that this was due to the fault of the transferee, then the transferee may be ordered to pay compensation to affected employees.

(Reg 11(4) TUPE Regs)

Compensation shall be such sum as the tribunal considers just and equitable having regard to the failure of the employer to comply with this duty subject to a maximum of four weeks' pay (Reg 11(11) TUPE Regs). For the calculation of a "week's pay" see Chapter 24. The calculation date (for calculating the week's pay) in relation to an employee who was dismissed by reason of redundancy shall be the same calculation date as is used to calculate the redundancy payment. If the employee is dismissed for any other reason the calculation date is the effective date of the termination. In any other case the calculation date is the date of the transfer (Reg 11(12) TUPE Regs).

Complaint by employee

If an employee does not receive compensation following an order made by the tribunal then he himself may present a complaint to the tribunal (Reg 11(5) TUPE Regs). If the tribunal finds the complaint well-founded it shall order the employer to pay the complainant the amount of compensation which it finds due to him (Reg 11(6) TUPE Regs).

Time Limits

Where a representative of the trade union claims that the employer has failed to comply with any of the information and consultation duties then the complaint must be either before the transfer or within three months of that date. Where an employee claims that he has not received payment due under a tribunal order then the complaint must be within three months of the order. The same limited discretion to accept late complaints applies as is the case with unfair dismissal (the reasonably practicable test) (Reg 11(8) TUPE Regs).

CHAPTER 22

Rights During Employment

22–01   This chapter considers a wide range of rights during employment and the remedies available where those rights have not been observed by the employer.

ACTION SHORT OF DISMISSAL/DETRIMENT

22–02   As the number and range of rights during employment has grown, so have the corresponding schemes of protection. A right for an employee, such as the right to stand for election to become an employee representative for information and consultation purposes in a redundancy situation, is of limited value unless there is a scheme of protection for that employee in exercising that right. So for a range of different rights in employment, primarily set out in the ERA and the TULR(C)A, the employee has a right not to suffer a detriment—such as demotion, transfer, disciplinary action, blocking promotion, preventing access to training or a cut in pay or benefits—for exercising those rights. These are just some of the more common examples of detriments which an employee may suffer. Note that the detriment in respect of the rights set out in the ERA may amount to an action by the employer on a deliberate failure to act. Protection is also given to employees in respect of trade union membership or activities (s.146 TULR(C)A). Employees are given the right not to have "action short of dismissal" taken against them. In this context, however, a failure to act or an omission by the employer does not constitute "action" (see *Associated Newspapers Ltd v. Wilson; Associated British Ports v. Palmer* [1995] I.R.L.R. 258 HL).

22–03   For every situation in which there is a right not to suffer a detriment or action short of dismissal, there is also a corresponding right not to be dismissed for exercising the particular employment right. These rights not to suffer a detriment/action short of dismissal (and the equivalent unfair dismissal rights) are available from day one of entering a contract of employment. There is no qualifying period. This section will consider the remedies available to an employee who suffers a detriment/action short of dismissal as a result of exercising an employment right. First, set out below is a summary of the employment rights for which protection against suffering a detriment/action short of dismissal is available.

	Employment Right	Statutory Provision
1.	Health & safety cases such as:	s.44 ERA
	carrying out health and safety duties having been designated to do so;	s.44(1)(a) ERA
	performing activities as a health & safety representative;	s.44(1)(b) ERA
	Taking part in consultation on health & safety issues.	s.44(1)(ba) ERA
	(The full range of situations where the employee has protection in health and safety cases is listed in s.44 ERA)	

2.	Sunday shop workers—refusing to do shop work on a Sunday, etc.	s.45 ERA
3.	Performing or proposing to perform functions as an occupational pension scheme trustee.	s.46 ERA
4.	Performing or proposing to perform functions as an employee representative in connection with redundancy consultation or consultation in a transfer of undertakings situation or as a candidate in an election to become such a representative.	s.47 ERA
5.	Rights under Working Time Regulations 1998.	Regulation 31 Working Time Regulations and s.45A ERA.
6.	Worker making a protected disclosure (Public Interest Disclosure Act 1998, effective from 1st January 1999). (Note that a broad definition of worker under s.43K ERA who has his contract terminated can pursue a complaint that he has suffered a detriment. In such a case the maximum compensation is that to which he would have been entitled had he been an employee unfairly dismissed (s.49(6) ERA)).	s.47B ERA

The Remedy Section for the above rights is: **s.49 ERA**

7.	Right to be or seek to become a trade union member. Right to take part in trade union activities. Right not to be a trade union member. Right not to make payments if not a trade union member.	s.146 TULR(C)A

The Remedy Section for the above is: **s.149 TULR(C)A.**

Third party joined in action: trade union cases

22–04   Note that by virtue of s.150 TULR(C)A, a trade union or other third party can be joined in proceedings if either party claims that the employer was induced to take action to compel the employee to be or become a trade union member by that third party.

Remedy

22–05   In all these cases, the remedy can include both financial compensation for loss suffered and compensation for injured feelings.

Employment Rights Act Cases

22–06   First, s.48 ERA provides that an employee can present a complaint to the tribunal that he has been subjected to a detriment in contravention of any of the provisions referred to in 1–5 above. s.48(2) ERA puts the burden on the employer to show the ground on which any act or deliberate failure to act was done.

Time Limit

22–07 A complaint must be presented within three months of the date of the act/failure to act. If there is a series of acts or failures the complaint must be within three months of the last of them (s.48(3) ERA). The same "not reasonably practicable" extension as applies to unfair dismissal claims applies here. In other words, the three months time limit is strict and it will be difficult to persuade a tribunal to accept a late application (see, generally, case law relating to unfair dismissal).

Remedies: statutory provisions

22–08 Section 49 ERA then provides that where the tribunal finds any such complaints well-founded the tribunal:

(a) shall make a declaration to that effect, and

(b) may make an award of compensation to be paid by the employer to the complainant in respect of the act or failure to act to which the complaint relates (s.49(1) ERA).

The amount of compensation awarded "shall be such as the tribunal considers just and equitable in all the circumstances having regard to:

(a) the infringement to which the complaint relates, and

(b) any loss which is attributable to the act, or failure to act, which infringed the complainant's right" (s.49(2) ERA).

The loss includes:
22–09

"(a) expenses reasonably incurred by the complainant in consequence of the act or failure to act, to which the complaint relates, and

(c) loss of any benefit which he might reasonably be expected to have had but for that act or failure to act" (s.49(3) ERA).

Section 49(4) confirms that the common law duty to mitigate applies (see Chapter 19). Section 49(5) provides that "where the tribunal finds that the act, or failure to act, to which the complaint relates was to any extent caused or contributed to by action of the complainant", it shall reduce compensation by such proportion as it considers just and equitable having regard to that finding.

Trade Union Cases (TULR(C)A)

22–10 The provisions of s.149 TULR(C)A in respect of the trade union rights referred to at para. 22–03 are not any different in substance. Note, however, that compensation cannot take account of pressure on the employer by some form of industrial action or the threat of such action (s.149(5) TULR(C)A), although, as referred to at para. 22–04, a third party such as a trade union can be joined as a respondent and can be ordered to pay all or part of the compensation. Section 149(5)

TULR(C)A confirms that the common law duty to mitigate loss applies (see Chapter 19). Section 149(6) TULR(C)A also provides that "where the tribunal finds that the action complained of was to any extent caused or contributed to by action of the complainant, it shall reduce the amount of the compensation by such proportions as it considers just and equitable, having regard to that finding".

Commentary on compensation

22–11   Note that the tribunal has a discretion to award compensation. It is not obliged to do so (s.149(1) TULR(C)A and s.49(1) ERA). If the tribunal decides to award compensation it is then for the tribunal to decide how much is "just and equitable" having regard to both the infringement and to loss suffered.

Financial Loss

22–12   Given that the tribunal has a discretion with regard to the amount of compensation to award based on their judgement of what is "just and equitable", it seems that a similar approach should be taken as when assessing the compensatory award for unfair dismissal (s.123(1) ERA). This is no accurate science but the discretion should be exercised judicially (see Chapter 10 in relation to the compensatory award). The following case is an example of an award for financial loss.

O'Shea v. Department of Trade COIT 814/99. Mr O'Shea lost out on promotion because of his trade union activities. It would be a year before another opportunity would arise. He was awarded the net difference between his salary and that he would have received in the "promotion job" for a year.

22–13   This was then reduced by an amount Mr O'Shea would have received for doing a temporary job at a higher salary which he refused to do because he had not been promoted. This amounted to a failure to mitigate. If the tribunal concludes that, had the employee not been victimised for exercising one of these statutory rights, there was, for example, a 50 per cent chance that he would have been promoted, then the tribunal can award 50 per cent of the loss suffered by not being promoted. (See commentary on the percentage chance approach in the discrimination context at paras 13–58 to 13–76 and 13–75 to 13–76 in particular in relation to the lost chance of promotion).

In *Cleveland Ambulance NHS Trust v. Blane* [1997] I.R.L.R. 332, the EAT upheld an award of 25 per cent of the difference in pay between Mr Blane's salary and the salary for a job he may have got had he not been victimised for his trade union membership. The tribunal had "adopted the right approach by assessing the loss of a chance" (Clark J.).

Non-financial loss

22–14   It seems clear that compensation for suffering a detriment/action short of dismissal in any of the examples at para. 22–03 above can include compensation for non-financial loss.

The EAT, in the 1977 case of *Brassington v. Cauldon Wholesale Ltd* [1977] I.R.L.R. 479, stated that the comparable provision in the Employment Protection Act 1975 was not limited to pecuniary loss resulting from the infringement complained of. The EAT also confirmed that the statutory provisions did not give the tribunal a right to impose a "quasi-fine" on the employer. The discretionary power allowed the tribunal to award compensation for injury sustained by the employee. The employee must, however, show that he has suffered some sort of injury in order to be so compensated. This case concerned action short of dismissal taken because of union membership. Bristow J. stated "such action might be very easily shown to have caused injury to the individual other than injury to his pocket. The stress engendered by such a situation might easily cause injury to health". Bristow J. also acknowledged that compensation may be awarded because an employee's "deep and sincere wish to join a union ...... had been frustrated".

22–15 In *Cleveland Ambulance NHS Trust v. Blane* [1997] I.R.L.R. 332, another case involving action short of dismissal in respect of trade union membership, the EAT upheld an award of £1,000 for injury to feelings. Clark J. considered the statutory provisions and concluded that the words in s.149(2) TULR(C)A (and in s.49 ERA) "having regard to the infringement complained of and" gave the tribunal the "power to award compensation over and above pure pecuniary loss" (see para. 22–08 for statutory wording.) For full consideration of compensation for injury to feelings in the context of unlawful discrimination see paras 13–96 to 13–183 (including case digest at paras 13–137 to 13–183).

REMEDIES FOR BREACH OF OTHER EMPLOYMENT RIGHTS

22–16 This section considers a number of other employment rights conferred on an employee by the ERA and the TULR(C)A and examines which remedies are available should the employer breach those rights.

Time off work

22–17 The ERA and TULR(C)A give a range of rights to time off work for various reasons. For each right there is an associated entitlement to compensation for non-compliance with the statutory obligation on the part of the employer. The rules are summarised below.

Unpaid Time Off

Time off for public duties (Section 50 ERA)

22–18 An employee is entitled to take time off work for performing a number of public duties. So, for example, employees who are justices of the peace or members of a local authority, police authority, a statutory tribunal or are members of a board of prison visitors (for full list see s.50(2) ERA) have a right to time off work to perform the functions of that office such as attending meetings or carrying out functions approved by that body. The entitlement is to reasonable time off (s.50(4) ERA). Further guidance on what this means is provided by this sub-section. If the employer fails to permit an employee to take time off he can present a complaint to the tribunal(s.51 ERA). The complaint must be presented within three months of the date the failure occurred. The same strict rule applies to late applications as with unfair dismissal.

Remedy

22–19 If the tribunal finds such a complaint well-founded, the tribunal:

1. shall make a declaration to that effect

2. may make an award of compensation to be paid by the employer to the employee (s.51(3) ERA).

Compensation shall be such as the tribunal considers just and equitable in all the circumstances, having regard to:

(a) the employer's default in failing to permit time off, and

(b) any loss sustained by the employee which is attributable to the matters to which the complaint relates (s.51(4) ERA).

22–20 Note the similarity in the statutory framework for compensation to that which applies where the employee has suffered a detriment or action short of dismissal in certain defined circumstances (see para. 22–08). This statutory framework seems to give the tribunal the power to award compensation not only for financial loss but for injured feelings (see paras 22–14 to 22–15). It is perhaps more often the case that where an employee has been refused time off he simply wants to establish his right to time off rather than pursue a claim for compensation. However power is there, in appropriate circumstances, to make such awards. Note that there is no right to be paid for time off for public duties.

In *Emmerson v. Commissioners of Inland Revenue* [1977] I.R.L.R. 458, the tribunal made a declaration to the effect that Mr Emmerson's claim that he had been refused reasonable time off for the performance of his public duties was well-founded. He had been allowed eighteen days off per year to perform his public duties as a member of Portsmouth Council. When he became leader of the opposition he had additional duties. He claimed that eighteen days were not enough. Although the tribunal thought that it would be reasonable to allow up to thirty days off per year in such circumstances, they left it to the parties to negotiate the exact number of extra days leave. No claim was made for compensation and no award was made.

22–21 In *Ratcliffe v. Dorset County Council* [1978] I.R.L.R. 191, the tribunal pointed out that they had no power to make a direction as to the amount of time which should be allowed off. Mr Ratcliffe had not claimed compensation. Consequently, the only formal outcome was for the tribunal to make a declaration that the complaint was well-founded. Nonetheless, the tribunal was prepared to give a view of what would be reasonable in the circumstances.

The tribunal is not permitted to impose any conditions as to whether or not time off should be paid. In *Corner v. Buckinghamshire County Council* [1978] I.R.L.R. 320, the EAT overturned a decision by the tribunal to impose such a condition. "It is not for the tribunal to, as it were, re-write the terms of service between the employer and the employee. They may be able to consider whether the conditions are reasonable in deciding whether there has been a refusal [to allow reasonable time off] but in our judgment beyond that, they are not empowered to go" (Slynn J.)

Time off for trade union activities Section 170 TULR(C)A

22–22 An employee who is a member of an independent trade union which is recognised by the employer (in respect of that group of workers) has a right to time off work for the purpose of taking part in:

(a) activities of the union, and

(b)   any activities in relation to which the employee is acting as a representative of the union (s.170(1) TULR(C)A).

This right does not cover industrial action (s.170(2) TULR(C)A). The entitlement is to reasonable time off work (s.170(3) TULR(C)A). There is no entitlement to pay for this time off work. The Code of Practice on "Time Off" provides guidance on the set of activities which are covered. A complaint must be presented to the tribunal within three months of the date the failure to provide time off occurred. The same rules on late applications apply as with unfair dismissal complaints (s.171 TULR(C)A).

Remedy

22–23   Section 172 TULR(C)A provides that where the tribunal finds a complaint well-founded:

(a)   it shall make a declaration, and

(b)   may make an award of compensation to be paid by the employer to the employee.

Compensation is to be assessed in the same way where there has been a breach of the right to time off for public duties (see para. 22–19). Further, the same limitations apply to the powers available to the tribunal (see paras 22–20 to 22–21).

Paid Time Off

Right to time off for pension scheme trustees Section 58 ERA

22–24   An employee who is a trustee of an occupational pension scheme has a right to time off:

(a)   to perform his duties as a trustee

(b)   for training to help him perform those duties

(s.58(1) ERA).

The entitlement is to reasonable time off (s.58(2) ERA).

Section 59 ERA provides a right to be paid for taking such time off work. Where remuneration does not vary with the amount of work done, the entitlement is to be paid as if the employee had been at work (s.59(2) ERA). If remuneration varies according to the amount of work done, the employee must be paid "average hourly earnings" (s.59(3) ERA). "Average hourly earnings" is defined in s.59(4) ERA as the average hourly earnings of the employee concerned or "if no fair estimate can be made of those earnings, the average hourly earnings for work of that description of persons in comparable employment with the same employer or, if there are no such persons, a figure of average hourly earnings which is reasonable in the circumstances". If the employee is entitled to more than such average hourly earnings for this time off by virtue of his contract of employment then he is entitled to the sum due under his contract (s.59(5) ERA). Note that the rules on a "week's pay" do not apply to this entitlement. The normal three-month time limit applies for presenting a complaint to the tribunal (s.50(2) ERA).

Remedies

22–25   If the employee has been given time off but has not been paid in accordance with s.59 ERA then the tribunal "shall order the employer to pay the amount which it finds to be due" (s.60(5) ERA). If the employee has not been given time off as required by s.58 ERA and the tribunal finds the employee's complaint well-founded, the tribunal:

(a)   shall make a declaration to that effect, and

(b)   may make an award of compensation to be paid by the employer to the employee (s.60(3) ERA).

Compensation is to be assessed in the same way as where there has been a breach of the right to time off for public duties and the right to time off for trade union activities (see paras 22–19 to 22–23 and 22–11 to 22–15). The same limitations apply to the powers available to the tribunal (see paras 22–20 to 22–21).

Right to time off for employee representatives and Health and Safety representatives Section 61 ERA

22–26   *Regulation 7, Health and Safety (Consultation with Employees) Regulations 1996 Regulation 4, Safety Representatives and Safety Committees Regulations 1977*

We have witnessed the development, over the last few years, of a number of circumstances in which an employer is obliged to consult with elected representatives of employees in non-union workplaces. This development had its roots in a decision of the European Court that where collective consultation was required as a result of the implementation of European Directives, it was not sufficient to restrict consultation to circumstances where there was a recognised independent trade union (see *EC Commission v. UK Case C-382/92 and 383/92* [1994] I.R.L.R. 392).

22–27   These cases concerned consultation obligations in relation to redundancies and business transfers. Now, in non-unionised workplaces, there are obligations to inform and consult elected representatives in redundancy situations (s.188 TULR(C)A); in connection with business transfers (Regulation 10, Transfer of Undertakings (Protection of Employment) Regulations 1987); and in relation to health and safety (Health and Safety (Consultation with Employees) Regulations 1996). In all of these cases, the elected representatives are given a right to time off with pay to perform their duties. Those who stand as candidates for election are also given the right to reasonable time off for that purpose. Similar rights apply in relation to safety representatives appointed by a recognised trade union under the "Safety Representatives and Safety Committees Regulations 1977". The right to time off is contained in the following provisions:

Elected representatives in relation to redundancies and business transfers (as is reasonable to perform functions and stand as a candidate)	s.61 ERA
Representatives of employee safety (as is necessary for performing functions or training and as is reasonable to stand as a candidate)	Reg. 7, Health and Safety (Consultation with Employees) Regulations, 1996

Union safety representatives (as is necessary to perform functions and for training)	Reg. 4, Safety Representatives and Safety Committees Regulations, 1977

Pay for Time Off

Representatives: Redundancies and business transfers

22–28   Section 62 ERA sets out the rules for entitlement to pay for time off for representatives in respect of redundancies and business transfers. A representative is to be paid the appropriate hourly rate (s.62(1) ERA). This is defined in s.62(2) and (3) and is based on the week's pay which is considered at Chapter 24. Where the employee works normal working hours the week's pay is divided by normal working hours in a week for that employee under the contract in force on the day time off is taken (s.62(2) ERA). If the number of normal working hours differs from week to week (or a longer period) the calculation is as follows:

One week's pay divided by:

(a)   the average number of normal working hours over twelve weeks ending with the last complete week before the day time of was taken, or

(b)   if the employee has been employed for less than twelve weeks, a number which fairly represents the number of normal working hours in a week, having regard to "the average number of normal working hours in a week which the employee could expect in accordance with his contract and the average number of normal working hours of other employees engaged in relevant comparable employment with the same employer" (s.62(4) ERA).

If any amount so calculated is less than the employee is entitled to for that time off under his contract of employment then he is entitled to receive the sum provided for by the contract (s.62(5) ERA).

Representatives of employee safety

22–29   Schedule 1 to the Health and Safety, (Consultation with Employees), Regulations 1996 (S.I. 1996 No 1513) sets out the rules on entitlement to pay for time off for representatives of employee safety. The calculation of pay is the same as for trustees of pension schemes (see para. 22–24).

Union Safety Representatives

22–30   The Schedule to the Safety Representatives and Safety Committees Regulations 1977 (S.I. 1977 No 500) sets out the rules on entitlement to pay for union safety representatives. The calculation is again the same as for trustees of pension schemes (see para. 22–24).

Remedies

22–31   In all the above cases the representative can complain to the tribunal if his rights to paid time off have been infringed. The normal three-month time limit applies for presenting a complaint to the tribunal (s.63(2) ERA, paragraph 3 of Schedule 2 to the 1996 Regulations and Regulation 11, 1977 Regulations). If the representative has been given time off but has not been paid in accordance with the statutory rules (see paras 22–28 to 22–30) the tribunal shall order the employer to pay the employee the amount which it finds due to him. (See: s.63(5) ERA (representatives / candidates for redundancy and business transfer consultation); Paragraph 5 of Schedule 2 to Health and Safety etc. Regulations 1996 (representatives / candidates of employee safety); and Regulation 11(4) Safety Representatives and Safety Committees Regulations 1977 (union safety representatives). If the right to time off is denied then the tribunal has power to award compensation but the rules are not the same in each case. The position is as follows:

Representatives/candidates: redundancies and business transfers

22–32 Section 63(4) ERA provides that if the complaint is that the employer has unreasonably refused to permit the employee to take time off, the tribunal shall order the employer to pay to the employee an amount equal to the remuneration to which he would have been entitled if the employer had allowed him to take time off. The effect of this is that if, for example, an elected representative has asked for two hours off work to perform his functions as a representative and has been refused, he will be paid normally by his employer for working those hours. He can then complain to the tribunal that the refusal was unreasonable. If the tribunal upholds this complaint then the employer will be ordered to pay the employee remuneration for those two hours, calculated using the statutory formula set out in s.62 ERA (see para. 22–28). The employee is, consequently, paid double for those two hours. This is the penalty paid by the employer for the refusal of time off. If the employee has not been paid the full amount for time off to which he is entitled, then the tribunal shall order the employer to pay the full amount due (s.63(5) ERA).

Representatives/candidates of employee safety

22–33 The Health and Safety (Consultation with Employees) Regulations 1996 provide that compensation *may* be awarded where time off has been refused. Here, therefore, the tribunal has a discretion to award compensation, rather than a duty (as is the case with representatives in connection with redundancies and business transfers, see para. 22–32). Paragraph 4 of Schedule 2 to the 1996 Regulations states that where the tribunal finds a complaint that the employer has refused time off in accordance with the regulations well-founded, the tribunal:

(a)   shall make a declaration to that effect, and

(b)   may award compensation.

This must be of an amount which the tribunal finds just and equitable in all the circumstances, having regard to the employer's default to permit time off and to any loss sustained by the complainant which is attributable to the matter complained of (see paras 22–11 to 22–15 for commentary on similar framework in respect of compensation for suffering a detriment). The same limitations also apply, so far as the declaration is concerned, as are considered in relation to time off for public duties. The declaration can merely state that the right to time off has been infringed. It cannot make conditions for the granting of future time off.

Paragraph 5 of schedule 2 of the 1996 Regulations provides that where a tribunal finds that an employer has failed to pay a complainant the whole or part of the amount due (see para. 22–29) the tribunal shall order the employer to pay the complainant the amount due. (This covers the situation where time off is granted but the employer fails to pay all or part of the amount due).

Union Safety Representatives

22–34 The same compensation rules apply in the case of union safety representatives who have been denied time off as apply in the case of representatives of employee safety (see para. 22–33). If the tribunal upholds the employee's complaint, Regulation 11(3) of the Safety Representatives and Safety Committee Regulations 1977 provides that the tribunal shall make a declaration to that effect and *may* award compensation (see paras 22–11 to 22–15 for guidance on the same rules on assessment of compensation in relation to suffering a detriment).

Regulation 11(4) of the 1997 Regulations provides that where the tribunal finds that the employer has failed to pay a complainant the whole or part of the amount due (where the employee has had time off but has not been paid the full amount due under the Regulations (see para. 22–30)) the tribunal shall order the employer to pay the amount due.

Time Off for Trade Union Duties Section 168 TULR(C)A

22–35 Section 168(1) TULR(C)A provides a right for an employee who is an official of an independent trade union recognised by the employer to take time off work in order to carry out his duties in connection with collective bargaining and associated matters (which have been agreed with the employer). There is also a right to time off for training for such purposes (s.168(2) TULR(C)A). The right is to reasonable time off (s.168(3) TULR(C)A. The official is entitled to pay for such time off by virtue of s.169 TULR(C)A. Pay is calculated in the same way as with time off for pension trustees (see para. 22–24), representatives of employee safety (see para. 22–29) and union safety representatives (see para. 22–30).

Remedies

22–36 The remedies for failure by the employer to provide time off or to pay the employee for such time off are the same as those available to pension trustees (see para. 22–25), representatives of employee safety (see para. 22–33) and union safety representatives (see para. 22–34) (s.172 TULR(C)A).

Time off to look for work: redundancy situations Section 52 ERA

22–37 Employees who have been given notice of termination because of redundancy are entitled to reasonable time of work during the notice period to look for new employment or to make arrangements for training (s.52(1) ERA). To qualify for this right, the employee must have been employed for two years by the date notice expires or, if the notice is shorter than the statutory minimum notice, by the date that such notice would have expired (s.52(2) ERA). The entitlement is to be paid for such time off and the calculation of pay is the same as for employee representatives in connection with redundancy and business transfers (s.53 ERA, see para. 22–28). There is, however, one exception. Where the number of normal working hours differs from week to week the twelve week period over which the average number of normal working hours is calculated ends with the last complete week before the day on which the notice was given.

Remedy

22–38 Section 54(1) ERA provides that an employee can complain to the tribunal if he has either been denied time off or if he has not been paid the full amount due for such time off. The normal three month rule applies for presenting the complaint to the tribunal (s.54(2) ERA). If the tribunal finds the complaint well-founded, it shall make a declaration to that effect and "order the employer to pay to the employee the amount it finds due to him" (s.54(3) ERA) The amount "due to him" where the employee has been refused time off is the amount he would have been entitled to had he been given time off in accordance with s.52 ERA. So the employee, in such circumstances, gets his pay under the contract of employment for working during that time and receives pay again for that time by way of an award made by the tribunal. This is the same remedy as is provided for elected representatives in respect of redundancies and business transfers who are denied time off work (see para. 22–32). However, in the case of time off to look for work and arrange training, the maximum the tribunal can award is 40 per cent of a week's pay of that employee (s.54(4) ERA). Note that there is no ceiling to the week's pay for these purposes (see Chapter 24 for commentary on a "week's pay"). The same limitations apply to the declaration which the tribunal can make as apply in the case of the denial of time off for public duties (see paras 22–20 to 22–21 for commentary).

Time off for ante-natal care

22–39 A pregnant employee is entitled to time off work for ante-natal care (s.55(1) ERA). To exercise the right, the employee must produce a certificate from a registered medical practitioner, registered midwife or registered health visitor confirming the pregnancy, and an appointment card (s.55(2) ERA). This does not apply to the first such appointment. The entitlement is to pay for this time off work (s.56(1) ERA) and the remuneration due is calculated in the same was as for elected representatives in respect of redundancies and business transfers (see para. 22–28 for commentary).

Remedies

22–40 The employee can present a complaint to the tribunal if she has been denied time off or if she has not been paid in full for such time off (s.57(1)ERA). The normal three month rule applies for presenting the complaint to the tribunal (s.57(2) ERA). If the tribunal finds the complaint well-founded, it shall make a declaration to that effect (s.57(3) ERA). The same limitations apply in respect of the declaration as were considered in relation to the denial of time off for public duties (see paras 22–20 to 22–21). If the complaint is that the employer has unreasonably refused time off, the tribunal shall order the employer to pay to the pregnant employee the amount she would have been entitled to had she been granted her entitlement to time off in accordance with s.56 ERA (s.57(4) ERA).

22–41 In this way the employer effectively pays double wages for the time she should have been allowed off (see para. 22–32 for commentary on a similar provision in respect of elected representatives in connection with redundancies and business transfers). It is not permissible for the employer to give time off and then require the pregnant employee to work additional hours, even if she is paid at a higher rate for such hours. If the woman has to have time off for an ante-natal appointment she is entitled to be paid for that time unless the tribunal concludes that it was reasonable for the employer to refuse the request for time off. This may be the case with a part time worker who may be able to organise the appointment to avoid working time. If the employee complains to the tribunal that she has not been paid (in whole or in part) the amount to which she is entitled in respect of time off for ante-natal care, and the tribunal finds the complaint well founded, it shall order the employer to pay the employee the amount due (s.57(5) ERA).

Suspension from work on medical grounds and on maternity grounds Sections 64 and 66 ERA

22–42   In certain circumstances an employee may be suspended from work on medical grounds. Such circumstances are referred to in s.64 ERA. If the employee is so suspended, he is entitled to remuneration for up to twenty six weeks (s.64(1) ERA). To qualify for this entitlement the employee must have been employed for at least one month by the date the suspension begins. If the employee is engaged on a fixed term contract of not more than three months, or is working under a contract to perform a specific task not expected to last more than three months, then he will not qualify unless he has actually been continuously employed for more than three months ending on the date the suspension starts (s.65 ERA). If the employee is incapable of work because of "disease or bodily or mental disablement" he will not be entitled to remuneration although the contract of employment may always provide for sick pay in such circumstances (s.65(3) ERA). (The provision is intended to assist employees who are capable of working but cannot be permitted to do so because of health risks).

22–43   Further, the employee will not be entitled to remuneration if he has unreasonably refused an offer of suitable alternative work or if he does not comply with reasonable requirements imposed by the employer to ensure his services are available (s.65(4) ERA). There are also circumstances in which an employee may be suspended from work on maternity grounds. Broadly, such suspension occurs when the woman is exposed to risk by continuing to perform her duties and it has not proved possible to avoid the risk by adjusting her working conditions or hours and it is not possible to offer temporary alternative work. These rules were introduced as a result of the Pregnant Workers Directive No.92/85/EEC. The rules are now contained in the Management of Health and Safety at Work Regulations 1992 (Regulation 13A). Section 66 ERA provides guidance on the meaning of suspension on maternity grounds and s.68 ERA confirms that the woman is entitled to remuneration while she is suspended. The entitlement applies without any qualifying period of employment. The woman is not entitled to remuneration if she has unreasonably refused an offer of suitable alternative work (s.68(2)).

Calculation of remuneration

22–44   The calculation of remuneration in respect of suspension on both medical grounds and on maternity grounds is based on a week's pay (s.69 ERA) (see Chapter 24 for commentary on calculation of a week's pay). There is no statutory maximum week's pay for these purposes. If the employee is entitled to more than the statutory calculation of a week's pay by virtue of her contract of employment, she is entitled to the amount due under the contract (s.69(2)).

Complaint and remedy

22–45   Section 70 ERA provides a right to complain to the tribunal if the employer has failed to pay the employee's full entitlement to remuneration. The normal three month rule applies for presenting the complaint to the tribunal (s.70(2) ERA). If the tribunal finds the complaint well-founded, the tribunal should order the employer to pay the amount of remuneration due to the employee based on the calculation of remuneration provided for in s.69 ERA (see para. 22–44).

Right to offer of alternative work Section 67 ERA

22–46 Before an employer suspends an employee on maternity grounds the employer must consider whether there is suitable alternative work available (s.67(1) ERA). The terms and conditions must not be "substantially less favourable" than those applying to her normal work (s.67(2) ERA).

Complaint and Remedy

22–47 An employee may complain to the tribunal that her employer has failed to offer such work (s.70(4) ERA). If the tribunal finds the complaint is well-founded, the tribunal may make an award of compensation (s.70(6) ERA). The normal three month rule applies for presenting the complaint to the tribunal (s.70(5) ERA). The compensation shall be such as the tribunal considers just and equitable in all the circumstances, having regard to:

(a)   the infringement of the employee's right,

(b)   any loss sustained by the employee which is attributable to the failure to offer such work (s.70(7) ERA).

Note that this framework for compensation is the same as applies with many other rights during employment. See commentary on the assessment of such compensation at paras 22–11 to 22–15.

Entitlement under Working Time Regulations

22–48 The Working Time Regulations 1998 provide various entitlements to workers and if the employer fails to permit a worker to exercise any of those rights he may make a complaint to the tribunal and may recover compensation. The rights concerned are summarised as follows:
The right to—

(i)   daily rest (Regulation 10)

(ii)   weekly rest period (Regulation 11)

(iii)   rest breaks during a working day (Regulation 12)

(iv)   annual leave (Regulation 13)

(v)   compensatory rest (Regulation 24)

(vi)   payment in lieu of leave on termination of employment (Regulation 14)

(vii)   pay for periods of leave (Regulation 16).

Where any of the above rights have been infringed, the worker can complain to the tribunal by virtue of Regulation 30, Working Time Regulations, 1998. The normal three month time limit applies with the "reasonably practicable" test for late applications as applies to unfair dismissal claims (Regulation 30(2)). If the tribunal finds the complaint well-founded, the tribunal:

(a)   shall make a declaration to that effect, and

(b)   may make an award of compensation to be paid by the employer (Regulation 30(3) Working Time Regs).

22–49   The amount of compensation is such as the tribunal considers just and equitable in all the circumstances having regard to:

(a)   the employer's default in refusing to permit the worker to exercise his right, and

(b)   any loss sustained by the worker which is attributable to the matter complained of (Regulation 30(4)).

This is the same framework for assessment of compensation as with many other rights during employment. Commentary on assessment of compensation using this framework is considered at paras 22–11 to 22–15. The same limits to the tribunal's powers with regard to the making of a declaration also apply as with other cases (see paras 22–20 to 22–21 for commentary). Where the employer has failed to pay holiday pay for holiday which the worker takes as his entitlement under the regulations (see Regulation 16 for holiday pay rules) or where the employer has failed to pay holiday pay on termination of employment (see Regulation 14), the tribunal shall order the employer to pay the worker the amount it finds due. Holiday pay is based on the calculation of a "week's pay" (see ss221 to 224 ERA and Chapter 24). There is no statutory maximum to the week's pay. The calculation date for assessing the week's pay is the first day of the period of leave (Regulation 16(3)(C)) (see also para. 25–47 in respect of contractual claims relating to entitlement to holiday pay on termination of employment).

Entitlement to Itemised Pay Statement

22–50   Employees are entitled to a written itemised pay statement at or before the date of payment of wages or salary (s.8 ERA). The statement must contain details of:

1.   the gross amount of wages/salary;

2.   the amounts of any variable or fixed deductions from the gross sum and the purpose of such deduction;

3.   the net wage/salary payable;

4.   where different parts of the net sum are paid in different ways, the amount and method of payment of each part-payment.

Complaint and remedy

22–51   If the employer fails to give such a statement (or if it does not contain the required information) the employee may complain to the tribunal (s.11 ERA). The normal three month time limit applies for presenting the complaint to the tribunal (s.11(4) ERA). If the tribunal finds that the employer has failed to provide the statement in accordance with s.8 it must make a declaration to that effect. If the tribunal finds that the pay statement does not contain particulars of a deduction which has been made and if such unnotified deductions have been made from pay in the period of thirteen weeks preceding the application to the tribunal (whether or not those deductions have been made in breach of the contract of employment) the tribunal may order the employer to pay to the employee a sum not exceeding the aggregate of the unnotified deductions (s.12(4) ERA).

22–52   Note that these powers are separate and distinct from the powers of the tribunal in respect of unlawful deductions from pay. The power contained in these provisions is triggered by a failure of the employer to give particulars of a deduction from pay on the pay statement. The deduction may or may not also be an unlawful deduction (see paras 22–58 to 22–67 for commentary on the tribunal's powers in respect of unlawful deductions). Note that the power to award compensation under s.12 ERA is at the discretion of the tribunal. The cases summarised below demonstrate the exercise of this discretion.

In *Milsom v. Leicestershire County Council* [1978] I.R.L.R. 433, Mr Milsom was asked for repayment of £111.68, which had been provided for examination fees and other associated expenses, when he resigned from his employment. Mr Milsom disputed the matter and said he would not agree to the sum being deducted from his salary. Soon after, the respondents issued a pay statement showing a deduction of £111.68. The column which specified the nature of the deduction simply referred to Code No. 70. The key to the code on the reverse side of the statement showed that Code No. 70 covered "miscellaneous deduction/payment". The tribunal held that this did not comply with the requirements of what is now s.8 ERA. The statement did not give sufficient particulars of the purposes of the deduction.

22–53   The tribunal had the power to order compensation of up to £111.68, being the total amount of the deduction, but exercised its discretion to award compensation of just £25. The complainant had suffered no financial loss (the County Court had already decided that the deduction was authorised by the contract of employment). He had, however, "probably been caused some financial embarrassment by having the whole sum deducted in one fell swoop. Moreover, he had specifically requested that the respondents should not make any deductions from his salary and it was therefore surprising that the respondents did so when they knew the matter was disputed". The tribunal remarked that the power to order compensation amounted to a penalty imposed on the employer for failing to comply with the statutory requirements.

In *Scott v. Creager* [1979] I.R.L.R. 162 EAT, Miss Scott was employed by Mr Creager, a dentist, for 12 weeks and 3 days. At the start of her employment she asked for a gross wage of £40 per week. The respondent said he would pay her £30 net per week. The issue was never resolved but throughout her period of employment she received £30 per week. She was not given any pay statements showing deductions from pay.

22–54   The tribunal held that the respondent had been in breach of what is now S8 ERA. The tribunal also found that she was contractually entitled to £40 gross per week. The total shortfall between the gross wage entitlement and the net wages received came to £144.09. Of this sum £99.18 was in respect of tax and National Insurance. The remaining £53.91 was an actual shortfall in her net wages. The tribunal exercised its discretion to award compensation of £53.91 although they could have awarded the total shortfall of £144.09 (because it had not been detailed on any pay statement). The EAT upheld the tribunal's decision. There was nothing perverse in restricting the award to the sum to which she was contractually entitled. The tribunal had properly taken into account the fact that the respondent was a "busy professional man", that the Act requiring the itemised statement was new, that the respondent had no experience of it and that the respondent had already been penalised by having to pay legal expenses and spend time in litigation. The provision amounted to a potential penalty on the respondent. It was reasonable to take these factors into account.

Written particulars of terms of employment

22–55 Employers are required to give new employees a written statement of particulars of employment within two months of the start of employment (s.1 ERA). The statement must contain a number of key particulars which are set out in s.1 ERA. Section 4 ERA provides that if there is any change in any of the matters covered by the s.1 statement, the employer must give the employee a written statement of the change at the earliest opportunity and, in any event, not later than one month after the change (s.4(3) ERA). The entitlement to a written statement does not apply where the employee is working wholly or mainly outside Great Britain, unless the employee ordinarily works in Great Britain for the same employer or the law governing this contract of employment is the law of England and Wales or Scotland (s.196 ERA). Also excluded are employees whose employment continues for less than one month. Supplementary provisions are contained in ss. 1–7 and ss. 196, 199 and 209.

Complaint and remedy

22–56 If the employer does not give an employee a statement at the start of employment (s.1 ERA) or a statement of any change in particulars (s.4 ERA), he can complain to the tribunal (s.11(1) ERA). The reference to the tribunal is to determine "what particulars ought to have been included or referred to in a statement so as to comply with the requirements" of s.1 or s.4 ERA (s.11(1) ERA). Also, if a statement under s.1 ERA or s.4 ERA has been given to the employee but there is a dispute as to the particulars which ought to have been included or referred to, either the employer or the employee may refer the matter to the tribunal (s.11(2) ERA). Any such reference must be made before the end of three months following termination of employment. Where no statement has been given which complies with s.1 ERA or s.4 ERA, the tribunal then determines the particulars which ought to have been included or referred to (s.12(1) ERA).

22–57 Where either the employer or the employee has referred a question to the tribunal relating to a statement which has been given to the employee, the tribunal can either:

(a) confirm the particulars as included or referred to in the statement given by the employer, or

(b) amend the particulars, or

(c) substitute other particulars for them.

The tribunal acts as it considers appropriate (s.12(2) ERA).

This is the extent of the tribunal's power. It determines what should be in the statement and that then becomes the statement as if it had been given by the employer. There is no power to award compensation to the employee for breach of these statutory obligations. However, once the tribunal has determined the particulars, an employee could rely on that determination to enforce his rights under the contract in subsequent proceedings in the tribunal or in the County Court.

Unlawful deductions from wages

22–58 An employer may not make a deduction from wages of a worker employed by him unless:

(a) the deduction is required or authorised to be made either by virtue of a legal requirement or under the worker's contract, or

(b) the worker has previously signified in writing his agreement to the deduction being made (s.13(1) ERA).

Note that the definition of "worker" is wider than that of "employee". Section 230(3) ERA states that a worker includes those working under a contract of employment but also includes someone who works under "any other contract, whether express or implied and (if it is express) whether oral or in writing, whereby the individual undertakes to do or perform personally any work or services for another party to the contract whose status is not by virtue of the contract that of a client or customer of any profession or business undertaking carried on by the individual". This definition equates to the wider definition of those protected in the employment field under the SDA, RRA and the DDA.

22–59   Non-payment of wages amounts to a deduction (see s.13(3) and the decision in *Delaney v. Staples* [1991] I.R.L.R. 112 CA which was upheld on different grounds in the House of Lords [1992] I.R.L.R. 191. For details of what payments are included within the definition of "wages" see paras 3–07 to 3–08. Note that "wages" does not include "pay in lieu of notice"—see *Delaney v. Staples* [1991] I.R.L.R. 112 CA. Where the sum of wages due is totally extinguished by a deduction made by the employer, this still amounts to a deduction which will be unlawful unless it meets the conditions set out in s.13 ERA (*Alsop v. Star Vehicle Contracts Ltd* [1990] I.R.L.R. 83).

22–60   Unilateral withdrawal of shift premiums without written consent (*Bruce v. Wiggins Teape (Stationery) Ltd* [1994] I.R.L.R. 536 EAT), the phasing out of a contractual pay supplement (*McCree v. Tower Hamlets London Borough Council* [1992] I.R.L.R. 56) and a unilateral cut in salary following disciplinary proceedings in breach of contract (*Morgan v. West Glamorgan County Council* [1995] I.R.L.R. 68 EAT) have all been held to amount to unlawful deductions from wages. Also, in *Kent Management Services Ltd v. Butterfield* [1992] I.R.L.R. 394, the EAT held that a discretionary commission payment was "wages" for the purposes of what is now s.13 ERA and that, therefore, the non-payment of part of that commission on termination of employment amounted to an unlawful deduction from wages. It was a sum normally paid "in connection with his employment" and "it was within the reasonable contemplation of both parties that in ordinary circumstances ... it was payable" (Wood J.). The unilateral reduction by the employer of the amount of tips paid to staff may also be an unlawful deduction wages (see *Saavedra v. Aceground Ltd* [1995] I.R.L.R. 198 EAT. The restaurant had decided to keep a proportion of the amount raised as tips to make up for a drop in revenue. This was an unlawful deduction.

Non-payment of wages and holiday pay on termination of employment

22–61   In the context of a termination of employment, an employee may pursue a claim for unlawful deduction from wages where accrued holiday pay has not been paid. Note that the Apportionment Act 1870 (s.2) has been interpreted as providing for pay to be allotted on the basis of calendar days of the year not working days. Therefore a day's holiday pay due is calculated by dividing annual salary by 365, not by the number of working days in the year. The contract of employment can, however, override this by an express provision (see *Thames Water Utilities v. Reynolds* [1996] I.R.L.R. 186 EAT). Also, non-payment of a commission payment which has been earned but was not due to be paid until after termination of employment, can come within the scope of s.13 ERA (see *Blackstone Franks Investment Ltd v. Robertson, The Times*, November 12, 1996, EAT).

In *Chiltern House Ltd v. Chambers* [1990] I.R.L.R. 88 EAT, an employee left without giving the contractual notice required. The employer withheld wages already earned. This was an unlawful deduction. If an employer wants to be able to withhold wages in such circumstances, he has to provide for it in the contract of employment.

Agreement must predate event giving rise to deduction

22–62   Note also that s.13(6) ERA provides that a written agreement authorising a deduction will only be valid if it has been signed by the worker before the event giving rise to the deduction. So, for example, if an employer agrees to pay for an examination on the basis that the sum be repaid if the worker leaves within a stated period of time, the agreement authorising a deduction from wages must be signed by the worker before the sum has been paid by the employer for the examination, not just before the deduction is made (see *Discount Tobacco and Confectionery Ltd v. Williamson* [1993] I.R.L.R. 327, EAT where deductions in respect of stock shortages were unlawful because the employee's agreement to the deductions was signed after the stock shortages had occurred).

Excepted deductions

22–63   Section 14 ERA sets out exceptions to the scope of s.13 ERA. In particular, where the deduction amounts to a reimbursement of a previous overpayment of wages there will be no breach of s.13 ERA (s.14(1) ERA). Also excluded are deductions required to be made and handed over to a public authority such as the Child Support Agency, deductions by virtue of the contract or other agreement with the worker whereby the sum concerned is paid to some other third party, deductions made in consequence of the worker taking part in a strike or other industrial action and deductions made to satisfy a Court or tribunal order.

Payments to employer

22–64   Section 15 ERA provides for restriction on the circumstances in which an employer can require a sum of money to be paid to him by an employee. The provisions are in similar terms to the restrictions on making deductions from wages.

Retail employment

22–65   Special rules apply to payments by employees in respect of cash shortages in the retail sector (see ss.17–21 ERA). The provisions impose a limit of 10 per cent of gross wages which can be payable by the worker to the employer in respect of cash shortages.

Complaints and remedies

22–66   A worker can complain to the tribunal that his employer has made an unlawful deduction from wages (or that his employer has received a payment from him in contravention of s.15 ERA or, in the retail sector, that the employer has recovered more than the amount allowed). Normally a complaint must be brought within three months of the deduction. Where a complaint relates to a series of deductions the complaint must be within three months of the last of the deductions (similar rules apply in the case of unlawful payments, s.23 ERA) (see para. 25–17 in respect of the time limit for contractual claims).

If the tribunal finds the complaint well-founded it shall make a declaration to that effect and shall order the employer to pay to the worker the amount of any deduction made or to repay to the worker the amount of any payment received in contravention of s.15 ERA. Similar orders can be made in respect of the provisions relating to the retail sector (s.24 ERA). If part of the sum deducted or paid was in fact a lawful deduction or payment then only the unlawful balance shall be ordered to be repaid to the employee (see s.25(1) and (2) ERA).

22–67 Note that if the employer is found to have made an unlawful deduction in circumstances where he is properly due payment of a sum from the worker, he loses the right to recover the amount he had unlawfully deducted (s.25(4) ERA). A similar provision applies in relation to unlawful deductions or payments for cash shortages or stock deficiencies in the retail sector (s.25(5) ERA). Note that these provisions do not affect the jurisdiction of the tribunal to consider a reference by an employee under s.11 ERA in respect of a failure by the employer to detail deductions from wages on the pay statement (s.26 ERA). However, the employee cannot double recover by pursuing complaints under both s.11 and s.23 ERA (see paras 22–50 to 22–54 in respect of s.11 ERA).

Guarantee Payment

22–67 An employee is entitled to a guarantee payment by virtue of s.28 ERA for days when he would normally be required to work but when no work is provided because of a reduction in the need for work of the sort the employee is employed to do or because of any other occurrence which affects normal working. The entitlement depends on one month's continuous employment up to the day before the day for which the guarantee payment is claimed (s.29(1) ERA).

There is no entitlement for an employee employed on a contract for a fixed term of three months or less or employed under a contract to perform a specific task which is not expected to last for more than three months unless he has actually been continuously employed for more than three months (up to the day before the day for which the guarantee payment is claimed (s.29(2) ERA). There is also no entitlement if the workless day results from a strike, lockout or other industrial action involving an employee of that employer (or associated employer) (s.29(3) ERA).

There is no entitlement if the employer has offered suitable alternative work (which may not be work which the employee is employed to do under his contract of employment) and the employee has unreasonably refused the offer (s.29(4) ERA).

There is no entitlement if the employee has failed to comply with reasonable requirements of his employer aimed at ensuring that his services are available (s.29(5) ERA). Finally, the employee must be required by the contract of employment to work normal working hours on the day in question (s.30(1) ERA). If there are no normal working hours for that day there is no entitlement.

Calculation of Guarantee Payment

22–68 Calculation of the guarantee payment is in accordance with s.30 ERA and with the limits set by s.31 ERA. The calculation is beyond the scope of this book. Note, though, that there is a limit, which is currently £15.35, to a guarantee payment in respect of any day (s.31(1) ERA). The right to a guarantee payment does not affect any contractual entitlement to pay but any guarantee payment made goes towards discharging that liability. Likewise, any contractual pay received goes towards discharging the liability of the employer to pay a guarantee payment (s.32 ERA).

Complaint to the Tribunal

22–69   An employee may complain to the tribunal that his employer has failed to pay all or part of a guarantee payment due (s.34(1) ERA). The normal three-month time limit applies with the same limited discretion for late applications as applies in unfair dismissal claims (s.34(2) ERA).

Remedy

22–70   Where the tribunal finds the complaint well founded it shall order the employer to pay to the employee the amount of the guarantee payment it finds due to him (s.34(3) ERA).

CHAPTER 23

Right to Written Reasons for Termination of Employment

23–01 An employee has the right to a written statement giving particulars of the reasons for dismissal (s.92(1) ERA). This right applies where the employer has either given notice of termination or has terminated the contract of employment without notice or where a fixed term contract has expired without being renewed.

Service qualification

23–02 An employee is only entitled to this right to a written statement if he has been employed for at least two years on the "effective date of termination" (s.92(3) ERA) (note pregnancy/maternity exception at para. 23–05).

Effective date of termination

23–03 The effective date of termination (EDT) is determined as follows:
If notice of termination of employment has been given, the EDT is the date the notice expires unless that notice is shorter than the statutory minimum notice required, in which case the EDT is the date the statutory minimum notice would have expired (s.92(6)(a), s.92(7) and s.92(8) ERA).
If no notice of termination of employment has been given, the EDT is the date the termination takes effect, provided the employer was entitled to summarily dismiss the employee. Otherwise, the EDT is the date the statutory minimum notice would have expired had it been given (s.92(6)(b), s.92(7) and s.92(8) ERA).
In circumstances where a fixed term contract has expired and has not been renewed, the EDT is the date the contract expires (s.92(6)(c) ERA).

Employee must request written reasons

23–04 The entitlement is triggered by a request from the employee (s.92(2) ERA). The request need not be in writing but it is wise to make a written request so as to avoid evidential problems. Once the request has been made, the employer must respond within 14 days (s.92(2) ERA).

Pregnancy/maternity cases

23–05 Note that in circumstances where a woman is dismissed at any time while she is pregnant, or after childbirth, where her maternity leave ends by reason of dismissal, the woman is entitled to a written statement giving particulars of the reasons for dismissal without having to make a request and irrespective of how long she has been employed (s.92(4) ERA).

Excluded employees

23–06   There is no entitlement if, under the contract of employment, the employee ordinarily works outside Great Britain (s.196(2) and s.196(3) ERA). For other excluded classes of employee see s.199(2) ERA (Mariners) and s.200 ERA (Police Officers).

Complaint and remedy

23–07   An employee can make a complaint to the tribunal on the ground that the employer has "unreasonably failed to provide a written statement under s.92" or on the ground that the particulars of reasons given in purported compliance with s.92 are inadequate or untrue (s.93(1) ERA).

If the tribunal finds the complaint well-founded the tribunal:

(a)   may make a declaration as to what it finds the employer's reasons were for dismissing the employee, and

(b)   shall make an award requiring the employer to pay to the employee a sum equal to two weeks' pay (s.93(2) ERA).

Note that the tribunal has a discretion as to whether it makes a declaration of what it finds to be the reasons for the dismissal. However, the award of compensation of two weeks' pay is mandatory if it finds the complaint well-founded. There is no discretion to award a lower sum. A week's pay is calculated in accordance with the statutory criteria considered at Chapter 24. There is no cap to the week's pay for these purposes.

Calculation Date

23–08   The calculation date for calculating the week's pay is the date notice of termination of employment was given. If no notice was given then the calculation date is the date the dismissal took effect (s.226(2) and s.97(1) ERA).

CHAPTER 24

A Week's Pay

24–01 A number of remedies in the tribunal involve the calculation of the week's pay of the complainant. This chapter explains how the week's pay is calculated. First, set out below is a list of remedies or entitlements for which a calculation of the week's pay is required. Also provided are cross references to the commentary elsewhere in the text and the main statutory provision concerned.

	Paragraph	**Statutory Provision**
Unfair Dismissal		
Basic Award	9–02 to 9–08	s.119 ERA
Additional Award	8–39 to 8–41	s.117 ERA
Special Award	8–51 to 8–54	s.125 ERA
Reduction/increase in compensatory award where appeal denied or not pursued	10–10 and 11–01	s.13 ER(DR)A & s.127(A) ERA
Statutory Redundancy Pay	21–08 to 21–09	s.135 & s.162 ERA
Protective Award: Failure to inform and consult appropriate representatives in redundancy situation	21–28	s.189 & s.190 TULR(C)A
Compensation: Failure to inform and consult appropriate representatives with regard to transfer of undertaking	21–28	Reg. 11 TUPE Regs. 1981
Failure to give written statement of reasons for dismissal	23–07	s.93 ERA
Rights during employment Guarantee payment	22–68	s.28 & s.30 ERA
Right to time off to look for work or arrange training: redundancy dismissal	22–37 to 22–38	s.52 & s.53 ERA
Right to time off for ante-natal care	22–39 to 22–41	s.55 & s.56 ERA
Right to time off for employee representatives (redundancies/TUPE)	22–28	s.61 & s.62
Right to pay during statutory notice period of absent for various reasons	25–38 to 25–39 and Chapter 25 in general	s.87, s.88, s.89 ERA

| Right to pay whilst suspended from work on maternity grounds | 22–42 to 22–45 | s.68 & s.69 ERA |
| Right to pay whilst suspended from work on medical grounds | 22–42 to 22–45 | s.64 ERA |

Note that in the case of the right to have time off for carrying out trade union duties (s.168 and s.169 TULR(C)A) the right of representatives of employee safety to have time off (Health and Safety (Consultation with Employees) Regulations 1996) the rules on the calculation of a week's pay under ERA do not apply. Both TULR(C)A and the 1996 Regulations set out their own rules on calculating remuneration to which those having time off are entitled (s.169 TULR(C)A and Schedule 1 to the 1996 Regulations, see paras 22–35 to 22–36 and 22–29 for commentary. See also Chapter 22 generally for other similar cases).

Statutory Maximum

24–02   For the purposes of calculating the basic award and the additional award for unfair dismissal (but not the special award), and statutory redundancy pay there is a statutory maximum to the week's pay. This is currently £220 (see paras 9–08 and 8–40 in respect of the basic and additional awards; see para. 8–54 in respect of special award; see para. 21–09 for redundancy pay). The statutory maximum also applies to guaranteed debts in insolvency situations (see ss.182–188 ERA).

Statutory provisions relating to week's pay

24–03   The rules for calculating a week's pay are set out in Part XIV, Chapter II, ERA (ss.220–229). Different rules apply depending on whether the employee has normal working hours or, alternatively, works variable hours, or works on a piece rate basis or has irregular shift patterns.

CALCULATION DATE

24–04   Before considering the different methods of calculating a week's pay it is important to determine the correct date for calculating the week's pay.

Basic Award

24–05   For the purposes of calculating the basic award for unfair dismissal the rules determining the calculation date are explained at para. 9–09.

Redundancy Pay

24–06   The calculation date for the purposes of ascertaining a week's pay in order to calculate statutory redundancy pay is explained at para. 21–10.

Special Award/Additional Award

24–07   The same rules apply to determine the calculation date in respect of both the additional award and the special award (see paras 8–41 and 8–54).

Rights during employment

24–08 In respect of those rights during employment referred to above at para. 24–03, the calculation date is as follows:

Guarantee Payment: s.30 ERA

(a) Where the employee's contract has been varied or a new contract entered into in connection with a period of short-time working the calculation date is the last day on which the original contract was in force, and

(b) Otherwise, the day in respect of which the guarantee payment is payable (s.225(1) ERA)

Pay for time off to look for work or arrange training: redundancy dismissal: ss.52, 53 ERA

The calculation date is the day on which the employer's notice was given. (s.225(2) ERA).

Paid time off for ante-natal care: ss.55, 56 ERA

The calculation date is the day on which time off was taken or on which it is alleged the time off should have been permitted (s.225(3) ERA).

Paid time off for employee representatives: ss.61, 62 ERA

The calculation date is the day on which the time off was taken or on which it is alleged the time off should have been permitted (s.225(4) ERA).

Paid suspension on maternity or medical grounds: ss.64–69 ERA

The calculation date is the day before that on which the suspension begins (s.225(5) ERA). However, if the day before suspension on maternity grounds begins/falls within the maternity leave period or the further period up to the day on which the employee exercises the right to return, the calculation date is the day before maternity leave started (s.225(5)(b)).

Failure to give written notice of reasons for dismissal

24–10 The calculation date is explained at para. 23–08.

Entitlement to pay during notice period

The calculation date is the day immediately preceding the first day of the period of notice required by s.86 ERA (s.226(1) ERA) (see paras 25–38 to 25–39).

Week's Pay: Normal working hours: Flat rate

Section 221(2) ERA provides that "if the employee's remuneration for employment in normal working hours (whether by the hour or week or other period) does not vary with the amount of work done in the period, the amount of a week's pay is the amount which is payable by the employer under the contract of employment in force on the calculation date if the employee works throughout his normal working hours in a week". This sub-section sets out the most straightforward situation: normal working hours with pay that does not vary. In such a case, the week's pay is the amount payable under the contract of employment on the calculation date.

24–11 Note that what the contract of employment provides is the critical issue. In *Truelove v. Matthew Hall Mechanical Services Ltd* [1968] 3 I.T.R. 65, Mr Truelove was required to work 54 hours per week. An analysis of his actual working pattern showed that he never worked that many hours. "The fact that he regularly worked less than the agreed hours without objection by the employer does not, except perhaps in exceptional cases, imply that there has been a variation of a contract. At any time the employer may start to insist that the agreed hours be worked ... Unless there was a variation by conduct the fewer hours worked do not affect the contract." The tribunal therefore decided that Mr Truelove's redundancy pay should be based on a week's pay calculated using the hours required by the contract, not those hours actually worked.

Example of calculation of week's pay

Normal working hours, constant pay

Employee works 37.5 hours per week, every week.
He earns £12,000 per annum.
Week's pay = £12,000 divided by 52 = £230.76.

Varied contract

24–12 Note that if there is evidence that the contract has actually been varied by the conduct of the parties or by express agreement and that, in fact, the current contract provides for a lower—or a higher—number of normal working hours than that set out in the original written contract, then the varied contract will provide the basis for determining normal working hours and hence the calculation of the week's pay.

This was the case in *Armstrong Whitworth Rolls Ltd v. Mustard* [1971] 1 All E.R. 598. Mr Mustard's original contract provided for a 40 hour week. However, after some 10 years he was told that because a colleague had left he would have to work 12 hour shifts, five days a week, totalling 60 hours. He worked those hours for another seven years until his redundancy. The High Court (hearing an appeal from the tribunal) held that although there was no express mutual agreement to vary the terms of the contract, it was impliedly varied by the conduct of the parties.

Temporary variations: Short time working

24–13 Where employees have agreed to go onto short-time working and they are made redundant during that period, the crucial question is whether there has been a variation to the contract so that the week's pay would be calculated on the basis of a lower number of hours. If this were to be the case then the statutory redundancy payment could be significantly reduced. Generally, the tribunal will have to consider the evidence to determine whether there has been a variation to the contract. Tribunals are reluctant to reach this conclusion but in such cases it is worthwhile for the employees, or their union, to reach express agreement at the start of the short-time working that this is a temporary arrangement which does not vary the contract of employment and that any redundancy payment will be calculated on the basis of normal working hours prior to the short-time working.

24–14 In *Friend v. PMA Holdings Ltd* [1976] I.C.R. 330, a number of upholstery workers agreed to work reduced hours because of the impact of the three-day week and a shortage of work. They would be paid for the work they actually did. The tribunal ruled that there had been a variation to the contract and that the redundancy payments were correctly calculated on the basis of the actual hours worked. The EAT disagreed, allowing the employees' appeal. The change to reduced hours had been a *de facto* arrangement adopted in an emergency. There had been no new agreement reached without normal working hours. Redundancy pay should accordingly be calculated on the basis of the normal working week prior to the short-time working as provided for in the contract.

Unclear provisions of contract

24–15   There may, of course, be no written contract, in which case it is up to the tribunal to construe the contract after hearing evidence from the parties. There may be a statement of written particulars of employment such as that required by s.1 ERA. However, such a statement is not conclusive evidence of the terms of the contract. It provides strong prima facie evidence of the terms but it may be possible to satisfy a tribunal that the actual agreed terms of the contract are different (see *Parkes Classic Confectionery v. Ashcroft* [1973] 8 I.T.R. 43).

If the contract states nothing about "normal working hours" the court may be able to infer the terms from the conduct of the parties. In *Dean v. Eastbourne Fishermen's and Boatmen's Protection Society and Club Ltd* [1977] I.C.R. 556, there was no written contract. The EAT had to determine the terms of the contract from what could be implied from the action of the parties. They looked at the actual hours of work over the period of his employment.

Normal working hour where overtime is worked

24–16   The straightforward position of an employee working fixed hours at a constant rate of pay becomes more complicated when overtime is also worked. The important question is whether the hours of overtime worked can be included in normal working hours for the purposes of calculating a week's pay. The starting point is to consider the statutory provision which sets out the rules. s.234(1) ERA states that "where an employee is entitled to overtime pay when employed for more than a fixed number of hours in a week or other period, there are for the purposes of this Act normal working hours". So the mere fact of overtime does not prevent there being "normal working hours". Subsection 2 provides that in most circumstances the normal working hours in such a case will be the fixed number of hours.

24–17   So, for example, if a worker is required by his contract to work 40 hours per week but regularly works a variable amount of overtime, as and when required by the employer, the normal working hours will be 40. That is the fixed number of hours.

In the case of *Fox v. C. Wright (Farmers) Ltd* [1978] I.C.R. 98 EAT, Mr Fox was not required by his contract to work a specified number of hours a week. He worked as many hours as the job demanded—often as many as 50 or 60 hours a week. His employment came within the terms of the Agricultural Wages Order 1976. This did not provide for a minimum number of hours work but it did state that he was entitled to an overtime rate for any hours which exceeded 40 hours a week. The EAT agreed with the tribunal that although the employee was not obliged to work a minimum number of hours a week, he was entitled to overtime pay for hours over and above 40 per week and that 40 hours amounted to the "fixed" hours referred to in what is now s.234(1) ERA and that therefore he had "normal hours of work". The redundancy pay was calculated on the basis of pay for those 40 hours.

24–18   Mr Fox had argued that there were no fixed hours and, therefore, no normal hours of work. If this had been the case the rules on variable hours would have applied (see paras 24–31 to 24–33) and he would have been able to include overtime pay in the calculation of the week's pay. The decision is open to criticism. In reality, it is hard to claim that someone in Mr Fox's position is working normal working hours and the Agriculture Wages Order did not specify normal working hours. It simply confirmed the point beyond which overtime rates were payable.

Fixed period of obligatory overtime

24–19   Overtime hours will, however, be included within "normal working hours" if they are "fixed" by the contract and consequently the employer is obliged to provide them and the employee is required to work them. Section 234(3) ERA states that

> "where the contract of employment fixes the number, or minimum number, of hours of employment in a week or other period (whether or not it also provides for the reduction of that number or minimum in certain circumstances) and that number or minimum number of hours exceeds the number of hours without overtime, the normal working hours are that number or minimum number of hours (and not the number of hours without overtime)".

Example
The contract of employment states that the employee is entitled to £4 per hour for 40 hours per week. It also provides that the employee is required (and is entitled) to work a further eight hours each week for which he is guaranteed pay at the rate of £6 per hour. The normal working hours in this case would be 48 hours.

24–20   These provisions were considered by the Court of Appeal in the case of *Tarmac Roadstone Holdings Ltd v. Peacock and ors* [1973] I.C.R. 273. The Court of Appeal ruled that the employees could not have their overtime counted in for the purpose of redundancy payments unless a fixed amount of overtime had been agreed as obligatory on both sides and made a term of the contract. Mr Peacock's contract required him to work 40 hours per week and gave the employer the right to require him to work additional hours for which he would be paid at an enhanced rate. However, he had no right to work such additional hours (although he frequently worked as many as 57 hours a week). Lord Denning confirmed the position by stating that: "Where the obligation to do overtime is not obligatory on both sides, but only obligatory on the workman—so that the employer has an option whether to demand it or not—then that overtime does not come within the "normal hours worked" as defined by statute".

This analysis of the statutory provisions was approved and followed in the subsequent Court of Appeal decision in *Lotus Cars Ltd v. Sutcliffe and Stratton* [1982] I.R.L.R. 381. In this case, although the staff handbook provided for an additional five hours' work per week on top of the "basic working week" of 40 hours, this was not guaranteed by the company and therefore could not be included in the "normal working hours".

Week's Pay: Normal working hours: piece-workers/variable rate

24–21   The ERA does not make reference to piece work but s.221(3) ERA deals with employees who have normal working hours but whose remuneration varies with the amount of work done. Section 221(4) states that such remuneration may include any commission or similar payment. This means that employees who receive a variable bonus on top of a flat rate of pay fall within this category and their week's pay must be calculated in accordance with the rules set out below (see *Jones v. Shellabear Price Ltd* [1967] 2 I.T.R. 36).

Also in *Keywest Club Ltd (t/a Veeraswamys Restaurant) v. Choudhury and others* [1988] I.R.L.R. 51, Mr Choudhury was made redundant from his job as a waiter. The restaurant operated a system whereby all service charges received were put into a fund and distributed amongst the waiters. The EAT held that in respect of Mr Choudhury and other waiters, each meal they served increased the service charge fund and therefore his remuneration. The increase in his remuneration attributable to each meal could not be calculated. Nonetheless, his remuneration varied depending on the amount of work done and, therefore, his redundancy pay fell to be calculated under this category of case.

Twelve-week period

24–22   The sub-section provides for an average hourly rate to be determined by looking at the remuneration received over a 12 week period ending on the calculation date (see paras 24–04 to 24–10) if the calculation date is the last day of the week, or ending with the last complete week before the calculation date if the calculation date is on any other day of the week (for weekly paid employees the last day of the week is the day they get paid, for others it is a Saturday (s.235(1) ERA)). Note that if during the 12 week period there were one or more weeks when there was "no remuneration payable by the employer to the employee", that week is disregarded and earlier weeks are added so as to bring the number of weeks back up to 12 (s.223(2) ERA, see paras 24–29 to 24–30 for commentary on a comparable provision relating to circumstances where there are no "normal working hours"). A guaranteed payment made by an employer when there was no work available would be ignored in such a calculation. This is not paid in respect of work actually done. (See *Adams and ors v. John Wright & Sons (Blackwall) Ltd* [1972] I.C.R. 463 NIRC).

24–23   However, weeks with very low pay for actual work done all count. The employee is counted as working if he has to attend the employer's premises and is on call and under the employer's direction for any work that should be done (see *Mercer v. Associated Electrical Industries Ltd* [1968] I.T.R. 188). In this case, Mr Mercer was paid on a different basis for such periods. Those weeks were taken into account in determining average remuneration over the twelve week period.

Calculating total hours over 12 weeks

Having determined the 12 week period (taking into account any weeks when no pay was due to the employee) the next task is to add up all hours actually worked during that period. This includes all overtime hours (s.223 ERA).

Calculate total remuneration for hours worked

Once the total number of hours has been ascertained, one then calculates total remuneration payable for those hours (s.223 ERA).

24–24   The House of Lords in the case of *British Coal Corporation v. Cheesbrough* [1990] I.R.L.R. 148, has confirmed that, in respect of overtime hours, any enhanced rate is deducted when determining total remuneration for hours worked during the 12 week period. This is the case whether overtime is voluntary or compulsory and guaranteed. So, for example, if a total of 20 hours' overtime has been worked over the 12 week period at a premium rate of 1.5 times the normal hourly rate of £4, overtime pay would have totalled £120 for that period. However, for the purposes of calculating the week's pay, although those 20 overtime hours are included, the enhanced rate of an extra 50 per cent of normal hourly pay is deducted so that the calculation for those overtime hours will be 20 × £4 = £80.

Shift premiums or bonuses payable during normal working hours are, however, included in the total calculation.

Calculating the average hourly rate

24–25 Having ascertained total remuneration for the 12 week period (including shift premiums or bonuses, but excluding the enhanced element of overtime pay) this is then divided by the total number of hours worked including all overtime hours. This gives an average hourly rate of remuneration (s.221(3) ERA).

Week's Pay

The week's pay can then be determined by multiplying this average hourly rate of remuneration by the number of normal working hours. As noted at paras 24–16 to 24–20 this includes overtime if obligatory for both employer and employee, but excludes voluntary overtime or overtime which is not guaranteed.

Summary: Normal working: piece workers/variable rate

24–26

1. Decide calculation date (see paras 24–04 to 24–10).

2. Does calculation date fall at the end of the week (see para. 24–22)? For weekly paid this means pay day. For others, Saturday (see s.235(1) ERA).

3. If yes, work back 12 weeks from calculation date (see para. 24–22).

4. If no, work back 12 weeks from the end of the week prior to the calculation date (see para. 24–22).

5. Are there any weeks during the 12 weeks when no remuneration was payable to employee?

6. If yes, add an earlier week to compensate. So, if there was one week when no remuneration was payable, ignore that week and include 13th week working back.

7. Calculate total hours actually worked during the 12 week period including all overtime.

8. Calculate total remuneration for those hours excluding enhanced element of overtime pay (so if time and a half is paid for overtime, exclude the additional 50 per cent of hourly pay rate). Include shift bonuses and premiums (see para. 24–24).

9. Divide this total remuneration by the total number of hours worked (see 7, above). This gives the average hourly rate.

10. Multiply this average hourly rate by normal working hours, which excludes overtime unless it is guaranteed by employer and obligatory for employee. This gives the week's pay (see para. 24–25).

Normal Working Hours: Rota workers

24–27   Many employees work on some sort of shift system which results in them working different hours in one week compared to the next. It may be that during Week 1 they are working days then in Week 2 they work nights. The rate of pay may be different for the night and day shift. This category of employee falls within s.222 ERA for the purposes of calculating a week's pay. Section 222(1) ERA applies if

> "the employee is required under the contract of employment in force on the calculation date to work normal working hours on days of the week, or at times of the day, which differ from week to week or over a longer period so that the remuneration payable for, or apportionable to, any week varies according to the incidence of those days or times".

24–28   Note that the Section applies if remuneration payable varies along with the changes to the hours worked. So, in the example given above, if the rate of pay for the night shift worked every second week is higher than for the day shift worked in alternate weeks, then this Section clearly applies. This is the case even if the employer and employee, by arrangement, average out pay so that the employee receives the same amount each week. It is the actual entitlement which counts. If, however, the contract provides for the same rate of pay for such a shift arrangement, irrespective of which shift the employee happens to be working in any particular week, then they are taken to be working normal working hours at a flat rate and the rules set out at paras 24–10 to 24–20 apply. Also falling within the scope of s.222 ERA are those workers whose pay varies both on the basis of the varying normal working hours (shift arrangement) and whose pay varies with the amount of work done (piece rate or performance bonus, etc.).

Method of calculation

24–29   Section 222(2) ERA provides that the amount of week's pay "is the amount of remuneration for the average number of weekly normal working hours at the average hourly rate of remuneration". Section 222(3) states that "the average number of weekly hours is calculated by dividing by twelve the total number of the employee's normal working hours during the relevant period of twelve weeks, and the average hourly rate of remuneration is the average hourly rate of remuneration payable by the employer to the employee in respect of the relevant twelve week period." The 12 week period ends on the "calculation date" (see paras 24–04 to 24–10) if the calculation date is the last day of the week (meaning the pay day for weekly paid staff or Saturday for others). If the calculation date does not fall on a pay day then the 12 weeks end with the previous week. (s.222(4) ERA)

24–30   Note that the same provision for excluding weeks from the 12 weeks during which there is no remuneration payable to the employee applies as with piece workers (see paras 24–22 to 24–10).

Summary: Normal working hours: Shift workers

1. Decide calculation date (see paras 24–04 to 24–10).

2. Does calculation date fall at the end of the week? (see paras 24–22 and 24–29) For weekly paid staff this means pay day; for others, Saturday.

3. If yes, work back twelve weeks from calculation date (see para. 24–29).

4. If no, work back from 12 weeks from the end of the week prior to the calculation date.

5. Calculate total normal working hours over 12 week period. This excludes overtime unless it is guaranteed by the employer and obligatory for the employee.

6. Divide this total by 12 to ascertain average number of weekly hours.

7. Calculate total remuneration for the 12 week period excluding enhanced element of overtime pay. Include shift bonuses and premiums. (This is the same as for piece rate workers, see para. 24–24).

8. Calculate the total number of hours worked (this includes all overtime worked).

9. Divide total remuneration for 12 week period (see 7 above) by total number of hours worked. This gives the average hourly rate.

10. Multiply this average hourly rate by the average number of weekly hours (see 6 above).

Week's Pay: No normal working hours

24–31 If an employee does not have normal working hours under his contract of employment as described above, then different rules apply. The rules are set out in s.224 ERA. Sub-section 2 states:

"The amount of a week's pay is the amount of the employee's average weekly remuneration in the period of twelve weeks ending:

(a) where the calculation date is the last day of the week, with that week and
(b) otherwise, with the last complete week before the calculation date.

(See paras 24–04 to 24–10 for commentary on the calculation date).

For weekly paid employees the last day of the week is the day they get paid. For others, it is a Saturday (s.235(1) ERA). Sub-section 3 provides an adjustment to this calculation where in one of the 12 weeks used for calculating average weekly remuneration, the employee was not entitled to receive any remuneration. If this is the case, earlier weeks (before the start of the 12 week period) are brought into the equation so as to ensure that 12 weeks, when the employee received remuneration, are counted. The week (or weeks) when the employee was not entitled to receive any pay is left out of the equation.

24–32 For a week with no pay to be disregarded in this way, it must be a week for which no pay is legally payable to the employee. If it is simply a case of the employer having failed to pay what is due, that week is taken into account and the wages due from the employer are included in the calculation. This analysis was confirmed by the EAT in *Secretary of State for Employment v. Crane* [1988] I.R.L.R. 238. The circumstances in which no pay is legally payable for a particular week may be that, under the contract, the employer was not required to pay remuneration for whatever reason or because the employee had agreed to forego pay or because there was no work to be done and, in such circumstances, the contract allowed the employer not to pay any remuneration.

Overtime and other payments included

24-33   If the tribunal concludes that an employee did not have normal working hours then overtime pay over the 12 week period would be included. Other payments to the employee may also be included unless they are repayments of expenses with no "profit" element. Remuneration has the same meaning as with all other calculations of a week's pay (see paras 24–36 to 24–48). Set out below is an example of the calculation of the week's pay where there are no normal working hours.

> *Example*
> Total gross remuneration received
> over 12 weeks preceding calculation date   £3,000
> Week's pay   =   £3,000 ÷ 12
>   =   £250.00

(Note, however, the statutory maximum provisions—see para. 24–02).

Summary: No normal working hours

1. Decide calculation date (see paras 24–04 to 24–10).

2. Does calculation date fall at the end of the week (see para. 24–31)? For weekly paid employees this means pay day; for others, Saturday (s.235(1) ERA).

3. If yes, work back 12 weeks from calculation date (see paras 24–31 to 24–32).

4. If no, work back 12 weeks from the end of the week prior to the calculation date (see para. 24–31).

5. Are there any weeks during the 12 week period when no remuneration was payable to employee (see para. 24–31)?

6. If yes, add on earlier week to compensate (see paras 24–22 to 24–23 for the same calculation).

7. Calculate the total remuneration for 12 weeks and divide by 12.

New employees

24-34   Note that special rules apply to new employees who have not yet worked for 12 weeks. Section 228 ERA provides that in any case where normally a calculation has to be made over 12 weeks (see paras 24–21 to 24–33) in such circumstances the amount of the week's pay is "the amount which fairly represents a week's pay". In making this assessment, Subsection 2 provides that the tribunal "shall apply as nearly as may be such of the preceding provisions of this chapter as it considers appropriate". This would suggest that if, for example, the employee had worked nine weeks, the average remuneration should be calculated over that period. The tribunal may have regard to the following considerations as it thinks fit:

(a) Remuneration already received by the employee in this employment.

(b) The amount offered to the employee as remuneration for this employment.

(c) The remuneration received by others in comparable employment with the same employer.

(d) The remuneration received by others in comparable employment with other employers.

(Section 228(3) ERA)

TUPE Transfers

24–35 Where, within the 12 weeks preceding the calculation date there has been a transfer of an undertaking, the tribunal can take into account earnings with the previous employer so as to determine average remuneration over the twelve week period (s.229(1) ERA) (see paras 24–21 to 24–33 for circumstances in which this applies). Continuity may also be preserved where the employee transfers from one associated employer to another. In such a case the same rule applies.

Remuneration

24–36 Determining what is included in the term "remuneration" is crucial to the calculation of a week's pay. Unfortunately, it is not defined in the ERA. However, clear principles have emerged from case law and these are explained in this section.

Gross remuneration

24–37 It is the gross amount paid under the contract of employment, before deduction of tax and national insurance, which is used as the basis for determining the week's pay. This was confirmed by the EAT in *Secretary of State for Employment v. John Woodrow & Sons (Builders) Ltd* [1983] I.R.L.R. 11).

Guidance on "Remuneration"

24–38 Remuneration should be taken to have the same meaning for all categories of employees considered in this chapter (see *S & U Stores Ltd v. Wilkes* [1974] I.R.L.R. 283 NIRC). In the *S & U Stores* case, Sir John Donaldson described the test for determining the "average weekly rate of remuneration":

1. Any sum which is paid as a wage or salary.

2. Any sum or part of a sum which, although described as expenses, actually "represents a profit or surplus in the hands of the employee".

3. The value of any benefit in kind (e.g. free accommodation) is excluded.

4. Also excluded is cash paid by someone other than the employer.

Clearly, these categories include all monetary payments to the employee provided for by the contract of employment.

24–39 Note that s.221(2) ERA (which relates to employees on normal working hours whose remuneration does not vary) states that "a week's pay is the amount which is payable by the employer under the contract of employment". In *Donelan v. (1) Kerrby Constructions Ltd and (2) Secretary of State for Employment* [1983] I.R.L.R. 191, the EAT drew attention to this provision. Further, Brown-Wilkinson J. said that, even though the provision dealing with a week's pay for those on piece rates and others whose pay varies with the amount of work done (s.221(3) ERA) does not refer to the contract of employment, "it has not been disputed before us that 'remuneration' for the purposes of subsection (3) has to be remuneration payable by the employer under the contract of employment".

Discretionary Payments

24–40   It seems then that payments which are discretionary in nature and to which the employee cannot be said to be "entitled" are not part of remuneration.

In *A & B Marcusfield Ltd v. A Melhuish* [1977] I.R.L.R. 484, Miss Melhuish took over the operation of a machine from her employer due to his ill health. They agreed an extra payment of £10 per week for doing this. The arrangement carried on for five months until she was made redundant. The EAT pointed to the regularity of the payment as being the determining factor making the £10 part of remuneration for the purposes of calculating the statutory redundancy payment. This might suggest that a regularly paid discretionary bonus could count as remuneration. However, Arnold J. seemed to characterise the situation as a variation to the contract agreed between Miss Melhuish and her employer. He described this sort of situation as "a regular payment and a regular receipt of the amount in question as part of the contractual arrangements between the two for the time being in force, even if they are a departure from the regular, basic contract". This case then does not amount to any authority for including genuinely discretionary payments as part of remuneration. Whilst Miss Melhuish was operating the machine she was "entitled" to the payment and therefore it was right to include it as remuneration.

Tips and Gratuities

24–41   Tips added voluntarily by customers to cheque and credit card payments to the restaurant owner and then shared out and distributed to waiters are included in remuneration. This was the decision of the Court of Appeal in *Nerva and ors v. RL & G Ltd* [1996] I.R.L.R. 461 HC (the case concerned minimum wage legislation.)

The payments were made by the employer (after receiving them from customers) to the employee and there was a "specific contractual obligation ... that the employer would pay, in addition to basic pay, as part of the weekly pay a share of the amount of the difference between the bill and the amount on cheques and the amount inserted by the customer on the credit card slip" (Douglas Brown J.). A distinction was drawn between such payments and cash tips paid directly by a customer to a waiter which does not count as remuneration. The earlier case of *Palmanor Ltd (t/a Chaplins Night Club) v. Cedron* [1978] I.R.L.R. 303 confirmed that tips paid direct by the customer to the waiter were not counted as remuneration.

A fixed service charge distributed amongst employees after being collected in a "tronc" or pool was held to be remuneration in *Tsoukka v. Potomac Restaurants Ltd* [1968] 3 I.T.R. 259.

Retrospective Increases in Pay

24–42   It sometimes happens that, after an employee has been dismissed, the category of employees of which he was part is awarded a pay increase backdated to a date prior to the date of dismissal. Although there have been contradictory decisions as to whether such a backdated increase can be taken into account in determining remuneration for the purposes of either the dismissed employee's redundancy pay or basic award, the correct view seems to be that it should not. The EAT considered the point in *Leyland Vehicles Ltd v. Reston* [1981] I.R.L.R. 19. The relevant issue was the amount of remuneration payable under the contract of employment on the calculation date (see paras 24–04 to 24–10). On this date there had been no increase and it should not, therefore, be taken into account.

Total Pay

24–43 It is clear that, however the payments from the employer to the employee are described, the tribunal will look at the reality of the situation to determine what should be included in remuneration (see *Ogden v. Ardphalt Asphalt Ltd* [1977] 1 All E.R. 267).

Commission and bonus payments

24–44 Shift bonuses to which the employee is entitled are included in remuneration (see *Mole Mining Ltd v. Jenkins* [1972] I.C.R. 282 NIRC). Similarly, the following are also included if, under the contract of employment, the employee is "entitled" to them:

1. Monthly departmental bonus (see *Gilham v. Bletchley Timber Co. Ltd* COIT 1678/160)

2. Site bonus paid by a sub-contractor to his employees even if sub-contractor is reimbursed by main contractor. (See *Donelan v. Kerrby Constructions Ltd and Secretary of State for Employment* [1983] I.R.L.R. 191. In this case the EAT said that, as a general rule, where the employee of a sub-contractor receives a site bonus by virtue of an agreement between the main contractor and the union, a term can be implied into his contract of employment that whilst the site bonus is payable by the main contractor, the sub-contractor will pay the agreed bonus to his employee.)

3. Commission—a commission payable annually will be apportioned as if accruing by equal weekly instalments and will be included as remuneration. In *J & S Bickley Ltd v. Washer* [1977] I.C.R. 425 EAT, Mr Washer was entitled to an annual commission based on sales. The agreed commission was two per cent for orders of £3,000 for the year; four per cent for orders of £40,000. There was a monthly payment on account of such commission of 50 per cent.

    The employer argued that, for the purposes of determining remuneration for the 12 weeks prior to dismissal, the tribunal should look at actual orders during that period. However, trade varied seasonably and this would have given a low figure for remuneration. The EAT agreed with the tribunal that as the contract of employment provided for an annual bonus it was right to apportion it equally week by week.

Expenses

24–45 As has been noted at para. 24–38, *S & U Stores Ltd v. Wilkes* [1974] I.R.L.R. 283 NIRC, referred to any element of expenses which actually "represents a profit or surplus in the hands of the employee" as being part of remuneration (provided, of course, that it meets the contractual test—that the employee was entitled to the sum). So where the contract described a sum as payable for "expenses" but it bears no relation to the amount actually incurred then the tribunal can seek to determine the "profit" element.

In *Davies v. Mee Mulrey Ltd* COIT 917/170, Mr Davies had declared the "profit" element to the Inland Revenue. That element was included in remuneration. In *London Borough of Southwark v. O'Brien* [1996] I.R.L.R. 420, Mr O'Brien pursued a claim for unlawful deduction from wages when a mileage allowance was withdrawn. The allowance was more than Mr O'Brien incurred in expenses. The EAT therefore concluded that at least part of it was profit and, therefore, remuneration.

24–46 It may be the case, however, that an inflated sum is regularly paid for expenses as a way of evading tax on wages. If this is the case then the contract of employment itself will be illegal and, therefore, not one that the tribunal can enforce. This was the case in *Tomlinson v. Dick Evans U Drive Ltd* [1978] I.R.L.R. 77 EAT. A payment of £15 per week out of petty cash in return for bogus vouchers for collection and delivery charges was, in reality, a payment of wages and should have been taxed through PAYE. Where, however, the payment made relates directly to expenses incurred then it will not count as remuneration.

Payment in kind

24–47 Payments in kind such as the provision of a company car or free accommodation are not remuneration. (See *Skillen v. Eastwoods Froy Ltd* [1967] 2 I.T.R. 112—company car not remuneration; and *Lyford v. Turquand* [1966] 1 I.T.R. 554—free accommodation not remuneration).

Payments other than from the employer

24–48 As was noted at para. 24–38 the case of *S & U Stores Ltd v. Wilkes* [1974] I.R.L.R. 283 NIRC confirmed that payments received from someone other than the employer are not to be regarded as remuneration. (Note, however, the position with regard to tips described at para. 24–41). So, for example, the Easter offering paid by the congregation would not be remuneration for a clergyman (Sir John Donaldson in *S & U Stores v. Wilkes*); neither would state benefits count as remuneration.

CHAPTER 25

Contractual Claims in the Tribunal

25–01   For 20 years a statutory provision existed which provided for the extension of the jurisdiction of the tribunal to cover contractual claims relating to employment (s.131) EP(C)A). However, it was only in July 1994 that this power was eventually exercised by way of the Employment Tribunals Extension of Jurisdiction (England and Wales) Order 1994 (S.I. 1994 No.1623) and its Scottish equivalent (S.I. 1994 No.1624) (the 1994 Order). These Orders, however, set limits to the jurisdiction of the tribunal. These are considered at paras 25–03 to 25–04.

CURRENT STATUTORY FRAMEWORK

25–02   The power to extend the jurisdiction of the tribunal in respect of contractual claims is now provided by s.3 ETA 1996 (Employment Tribunals Act 1996). The power is exercisable by the Lord Chancellor (or the Lord Advocate in Scotland) and is in respect of:

(a)   claims for damages for breach of a contract of employment or other contract connected with employment. Note that this includes claims in respect of a breach of:

   (i)   a term implied into the contract by or under any enactment or otherwise.
   (ii)   a term of a contract modified by or under any enactment or otherwise.
   (iii)   a term which is not contained in the contract but is incorporated into it by another term of the contract.

(b)   claims for a sum due under such a contract.

(c)   claims for the recovery of a sum in pursuance of any enactment relating to the terms or performance of such a contract.

It must be a claim that a court in England and Wales or Scotland would have jurisdiction to hear (s.3(2) ETA and article 3(a) 1994 Order). Note that the reference in (a) above to "other contract connected with employment" does not appear to extend jurisdiction to self employed contracts. Section 42 ETA states that in that Act, "employment" means employment under a contract of employment. There is, therefore, no equivalent extended definition of employment as is found in the Discrimination Acts. What this expression is intended to cover is not clear. There may be circumstances in which the parties to a contract of employment enter what amounts to a collateral contract separate from the main contract of employment. Such a contract may, however, be "connected with employment" and therefore within this definition. See also paras 25–14 to 25–15 in respect of claims to enforce compromise agreements entered into on termination of employment. It has been held that compromise agreements are contracts "connected with employment".

Exceptions and Limitations

25–03 Both s.3 ETA and the 1994 Orders provide exceptions to the jurisdiction of the tribunal to hear contractual claims in the employment context. The 1994 Orders also set a financial limit to such claims. The exceptions are as follows:

1. Claims for damages or for a sum due in respect of personal injuries (s.3(3) ETA). Such claims must still be brought in the County or High Court.

2. The claim cannot be brought in the tribunal unless it "arises or is outstanding on the termination of ... employment" (see paras 25–12 to 25–13 in respect of claims relating to the termination of a contract of employment before the employee starts work). Therefore, any contractual claim which an existing employee wishes to bring must be pursued in the County or High Court unless the claim also amounts to an unlawful deduction from wages in which case the tribunal will have jurisdiction (see paras 22–58 to 22–67). See also Chapter 22 generally for the range of claims which can be brought in the tribunal during employment. An employee who has, for example, suffered unlawful action short of dismissal or a detriment during employment (see paras 22–02 to 22–15 in particular) may also have a breach of contract claim if that action or detriment amounts to a breach of contract. However, such a breach of contract claim must be pursued in the County or High Court if the employee continues in employment.

3. Article 5 of the 1994 Order lists further claims which cannot be pursued in the tribunal. They are claims for breach of a contractual term of any of the following descriptions:

   (a) a term requiring the employer to provide living accommodation for the employee or imposing an obligation on the employer or employee in connection with such accommodation,
   (b) a term relating to intellectual property (including copyright, rights in performances, moral rights, design rights, registered designs, patents and trade marks),
   (c) a term imposing an obligation of confidence,
   (d) covenants in restraint of trade.

Financial Limit

25–04 Article 10 of the 1994 Order imposes a limit of £25,000 on the award a tribunal can make, however many claims are brought in respect of the contract of employment. This is the total that the tribunal can order. Note at para. 25.16 that the employer can effectively bring a counterclaim alleging a breach of contract by the employee or claiming a sum due under the contract from the employee. This limit of £25,000 applies equally to the amount the tribunal can order the employee to pay in respect of such a counterclaim.

In circumstances where an employee claims he has been unfairly dismissed but also claims that the employer has acted in breach of contract or owes the employee a sum by virtue of the contract of employment, then it would be wise for the employee to pursue both an unfair dismissal claim and a contractual claim under this extended jurisdiction. The employee will not be able to recover twice for the same loss but, with the compensatory award for unfair dismissal limited to £12,000, a contractual claim may provide a basis for fuller recovery of the loss suffered. So, for example, an employee unfairly dismissed with a substantial period of a fixed term left unexpired, may be able to claim the sum due in respect of the unexpired contract by way of a breach of contract claim up to a limit of £25,000 and then claim up to £12,000 for further loss suffered by way of the compensatory award for unfair dismissal. In this way compensation for loss could total £37,000 (see also commentary at para. 25–73).

Tactical Considerations

25–05   A wrongfully dismissed employee has the choice of whether to pursue his claim in the tribunal or in the County or High Court. Several factors should be considered in deciding the most appropriate venue. These are summarised below:

Legal Aid

25–06   Legal Aid is not available for claims in the tribunal, although the complainant may be eligible for preliminary advice and assistance under the Green Form Scheme. This, however, does not cover representation at the tribunal hearing. In the County or High Court the plaintiff may be able to obtain legal aid depending on the strength of the claim and his financial position. This may be an important consideration.

Costs

25–07   As a general rule, costs are not awarded in tribunal claims. Commentary on the rules relating to costs in the tribunal is at Chapter 17. In the County and High Courts, costs will generally be awarded to a winning plaintiff unless the claim comes within the limits for arbitration. However, the potential disadvantage is that if the claim is lost the plaintiff will have to pay the defendant's costs.

Interest

25–08   Interest from the date of the breach of contract cannot be awarded in the tribunal. Interest is only available on late payment of damages. See Chapter 18 for commentary. In the County or High Court interest generally is awarded. If the claim is substantial this could add a significant sum to the amount awarded. Set against this is the fact that a tribunal hearing is likely to take place much sooner than an equivalent claim in the County or High Court.

Court Fee

25–09   A minor point to note is that no fee is payable to issue a claim in the tribunal. This is not the case in the County or High Court although the fee, is, of course, recovered if the claim is successful.

Procedural Points

25–10   The tribunal procedure is more "user friendly" for an unrepresented complainant than the County or High Court. The claim is also likely to be heard sooner in the tribunal. Further, if the complainant is also pursuing an unfair dismissal or discrimination claim there is a strong case for pursuing all claims in the same forum. This indeed was the main purpose of extending the tribunal's jurisdiction (see comments of Keene J in Sarker v. South Tees Acute Hospital NHS Trust [1997] I.R.L.R. 328 at para. 25–13). However, note that a tribunal claim has to be brought within three months of the termination of employment (see para. 25–17) whereas a County or High Court claim can be brought within six years of the breach of contract.

Maximum Award

25–11 As noted at para. 25–04, the maximum amount a tribunal can award for a contractual claim is £25,000. If, therefore, the claim is for more than this, the employee is likely to favour the County or High Court.

To summarise, the most significant point is likely to be the size of the claim. If the claim is modest in size the tribunal is likely to be the best option. If the claim is substantial, then the case for pursuing the claim in the County or High Court becomes much stronger, particularly because of the availability of interest on the sum awarded and because of the £25,000 limit on awards in the tribunal. Note that if the tribunal makes findings in a contractual claim those findings will be binding on the County or High Court. Further if a complainant seeks to pursue a claim in the county court which has already been decided in the tribunal, the claim will be struck out. This is the principle of *res judicata*.

Claims in respect of termination of contract of employment before employee starts.

25–12 The EAT has held that the extended jurisdiction applies to claims brought in circumstances where a completed contract of employment is terminated before the employee actually starts work (*Sarker v. South Tees Acute Hospital NHS Trust* [1997] I.R.L.R. 328). As has already been noted at para. 25–03 the extended jurisdiction is limited to circumstances where the claim arises or is outstanding on the termination of the employee's employment (article 3(c) 1994 Regulations). The EAT in Sarker held that the phrase "the termination of the employee's employment" was intended to refer to the termination of the contract of employment. In reaching this conclusion Keene J. pointed to the approach widely used in employment legislation. For example, the definition of "employee" in what is now s.230 ERA includes an individual "who has entered into ... a contract of employment". This is an additional category to others who work under a contract of employment.

25–13 It is also the case that, for the purposes of unfair dismissal protection, s.95(1)(a) ERA provides that an employee is dismissed if the "contract under which he is employed is terminated by the employer". This, therefore, enables an individual to claim unfair dismissal if the contract of employment is terminated for an inadmissible reason before they start work. An obvious example of this is where an employer discovers that a woman, who has entered a contract of employment but has not yet started work, is pregnant. As a result she is not taken on. She would be able to claim automatic unfair dismissal. If, said Keene J., such a woman could claim unfair dismissal she should also be able to claim damages for breach of contract before the same tribunal. In expressing this view, Keene J. looked to the purpose of the 1994 Order which was "to avoid the situation where an employee (or for that matter an employer) is forced to use both a tribunal and a court of law to have all his or her claims determined".

Enforcing a compromise agreement using the tribunal's extended jurisdiction

25–14 We have already noted at para. 25–02 that the extended jurisdiction allowing the tribunal to hear contract claims applies to claims for damages or for sums due under a contract of employment or other contract connected with employment (s.3(2) ETA). In the case of *Rock-It Cargo Ltd v. Green* [1997] I.R.L.R. 581, the EAT held that a compromise agreement was a contract connected with employment. Mrs Green had entered a compromise agreement with her employers on the termination of her employment. Under this agreement she was to receive one payment of £5,000 at the end of July 1996 when she ceased work. She would then remain on unpaid leave up to September 30 when her employment would terminate. At that time she would receive a further £10,000. The agreement also included a confidentiality clause. The employer alleged that Mrs Green had breached this clause during August or September and refused to pay the sum of £10,000 at the end of September. Mrs Green issued tribunal proceedings claiming that the failure to pay this sum resulted in the compromise agreement being set aside enabling her to bring an unfair dismissal claim or, in the alternative, that she could recover the sum of £10,000 due under the compromise agreement by way of tribunal proceedings.

25–15 The EAT's conclusion was that the compromise agreement met the statutory requirements set out in s.203 ERA and was therefore effective and binding. No unfair dismissal proceedings could be brought. However, because the compromise agreement was a contract connected with employment (meeting the test for the extended jurisdiction in s.3(2) ETA) and because the claim was one arising or outstanding on the termination of employment (meeting the requirement of article 3(c) of the 1994 Order), the tribunal did have jurisdiction to hear her claim for recovery of the £10,000 due under the compromise agreement. Kirkwood J. did make the point that the employer could raise the alleged breach of the confidentiality clause by way of defence to the claim.

Counterclaim by employer

25–16 Note that, unlike any other area of the tribunal's jurisdiction, in the case of contractual claims, the employer may also claim against the employee (article 4, 1994 Order). However, such a claim may only be brought in response to a contract claim made by the employee by virtue of the 1994 Order. In other words, the employer has a right to bring what amounts to a counterclaim against the employee. Such a counterclaim is subject to the same limitations and exceptions as apply to a claim brought by the employee (see paras 25–03 to 25–04). Note that the same financial limit also applies.

Limitation Period

25–17 Effectively the same rule applies to contract claims as with unfair dismissal (see article 7, 1994 Order). The claim must be brought within three months beginning with the effective date of termination of the contract or, where there is no effective date of termination, within three months beginning with the last day of work. The same strict test as with unfair dismissal applies with regard to late claims. Such a claim will only be heard if the tribunal is satisfied that it was not reasonably practicable for the complaint to be presented within the three month period. Even then a claim will only be allowed "within such further period as the tribunal considers reasonable" (article 7(c) 1994 Order).

Note that these rules may allow a period of more than three months to bring a claim from the date of the breach of contract where the claim relates to a breach which occurred prior to the termination of employment. Such a claim would come within the jurisdiction of the tribunal if it was outstanding on the termination of employment (article 3(c) 1994 Order). So, for example, if a breach of contract occurs two months before the termination of employment, the employee has, effectively, five months from the date of the breach to bring the claim in the tribunal. Contrast this with the rules relating to unlawful deductions from wages. Here, the three month period runs from the date the wages were paid from which the deduction was made (s.23(2) ERA). Such a claim which is outstanding on termination of employment may have to be brought very quickly to get it in within the three month period from the date the unlawful deduction was made from wages (see also para. 22–66).

Time limit for employer's counterclaim

25–18 The rules relating to the time limit for the employer's counterclaim are as follows: First, the counterclaim can only be brought whilst the employee's claim is before the tribunal and has not been settled or withdrawn (article 8(a) 1994 Order). Secondly, it must be presented within six weeks, starting with the day the employer received a copy of the originating application in respect of the contract claim from the tribunal (Article 8(c)(1) 1994 Order). Again, there is the same power to extend the period of time for the employer to counterclaim as applies to the claim brought by the employee (the reasonably practicable test) (see para. 25–17) (article 8(c)(ii) 1994 Order).

Appeals

25–19 A drafting flaw in s.21 ETA was identified by the EAT in the case of *Pendragon plc v. Jackson* [1998] I.R.L.R. 17 which meant that the EAT had no jurisdiction to hear appeals in respect of decisions of the tribunal hearing claims brought by virtue of the extended contract jurisdiction. The problem has been remedied by paragraph 17(1) of Schedule 1 to the Employment Rights (Disputes Resolution) Act 1998 which restores the missing right of appeal. The EAT had in the meantime issued a practice direction on November 24, 1997 which stated that until the new legislation was in force introducing the right of appeal, no appeals would be listed. Paragraph 17(1) of Schedule 1 to the 1998 Act came into force with retrospective effect on Royal Assent.

Remedy

25–20 Note that the only remedies which can be pursued in a contract claim in the tribunal are financial. Section 3(2) ETA provides for the extension of the tribunal's jurisdiction covering:

(a)   a claim for damages for breach of contract,

(b)   a claim for a sum due under the contract, and

(c)   a claim for the recovery of a sum in pursuance of any enactment relating to the terms or performance of the contract.

(See para. 25–02 for further commentary.)

MEASURE OF DAMAGES: BREACH OF CONTRACT

25–21   This section considers the law relating to the measure of damages for breach of contract in respect of the sort of claims which can be brought in the tribunal by virtue of its extended jurisdiction.

Common law applies

25–22   The first point to make is that, subject to the financial limit on awards referred to in para. 25–11, the tribunal applies the normal common law principles relating to the measure of damages for breach of contract. Damages for breach of contract are designed to put the complainant/plaintiff into the position he would have been in had the parties performed their obligations under the contract. A duty to mitigate loss suffered as a result of the breach applies. See Chapter 19 for full commentary on mitigation and paras 25–64 to 25–70 for commentary on points specific to mitigation in breach of contract cases. The most common breach of contract claim brought in the tribunal under the extended jurisdiction is for wrongful dismissal. If the employer acts in breach of the contract of employment in terminating that contract without the required notice then, if the employee has suffered loss as a result, he may bring a claim for wrongful dismissal.

PERIOD OF LOSS

Failure to give employee notice required by the contract

25–23   Damages will cover the period from the date of dismissal up to the point at which the contract could lawfully have been terminated by the employer. The starting point is that the employee is entitled to the notice of termination provided for in the contract of employment (unless, of course, he is dismissed for gross misconduct which entitles the employer to terminate the contract summarily). However, s.86 ERA provides for statutory minimum periods of notice to be incorporated into contracts of employment of employees who have been continuously employed for at least one month. The statutory minimum periods are as follows:

Period of continuous employment	Statutory Minimum Notice
1 month up to 2 years.	1 week
2 years up to 12 years.	1 week for each year served
12 years or more.	12 weeks

The employee is required to give one week's notice as a statutory minimum.

25–24   If the period of notice set out in the contract of employment is less than the statutory minimum then the statutory minimum applies. In such circumstances, any measure of damages for a breach of the contract is based on that statutory minimum period of notice. If the contract contains no notice period then a reasonable period of notice will be implied by the tribunal based on the nature of the work, status, whether the employee is weekly or monthly paid, etc. If such a reasonable period of notice is longer than the statutory minimum then that reasonable period applies and any damages for breach of contract for failing to give adequate notice will be based on that period.

Failure to follow contractual procedure

25–25   Many employees enjoy the protection of a contractual disciplinary procedure which imposes requirements on the employer which must be followed before any disciplinary action is taken. If the employer dismisses an employee without complying with such a contractual procedure he acts in breach of contract and the employee can pursue a claim for damages. The same principle would apply to any other sort of contractual procedure. The contract of employment may, contain, for example, a procedure for dealing with poor performance issues or sickness absence cases. Increasingly, however, employers are expressly stating that all such procedures fall outside the contract of employment and are there for guidance only.

It is clearly important to check whether an employee has been dismissed in breach of a contractual procedure. If this is the case it may provide a remedy for an employee who does not have sufficient continuity of service to be able to claim unfair dismissal. However, case law demonstrates that the period of loss for which such an employee can be compensated is limited to the period of time it would have taken for the employer to properly complete the contractual procedure. In assessing damages, it is not possible to speculate as to the chance that the employee would not have been dismissed had the employer followed the contractual procedure.

25–26   This was the conclusion reached by the EAT in the recent case of *Janciuk v. Winerite Ltd* [1998] I.R.L.R. 63 in which Mr Janciuk had been summarily dismissed. He claimed that he was contractually entitled to the benefit of disciplinary procedure and that if the procedure had been followed, there was a chance that he would not have been dismissed. The President of the EAT, Morison, J. stated the principles as follows:

> "When, for the purposes of calculating compensation, the court considers what would have been the loss had the contract been performed, the court assumes that the contract breaker would have performed the contract in a way most favourable to himself. This principle prevents the employee from recovering a windfall payment. If there were two lawful ways of performing the contract, the employee will be compensated on the basis that the employer will have chosen to perform the contract in the way which was least burdensome to him: *Lavarack v. Woods of Colchester* [1967] 1 Q.B. 278. Therefore, in a simple wrongful dismissal case the court does not ask what might have happened had the employer known that he had no right to determine the contract summarily, and then calculate compensation on a loss of a chance basis, the assumption is that the employer would have chosen to have terminated the contract lawfully at the very moment that he had brought (or sought to bring) the contract to an end unlawfully in breach of contract."

Where the contract requires an employer to follow a disciplinary procedure before notice of termination can be given but the employer fails to do so, the measure of damages "is based upon an assessment of the time which, had the procedure been followed, the employee's employment would have continued. Again, that does not require an analysis of the chances that had the procedure been followed the employee might never have been dismissed." Applying the principle in *Lavarack v. Woods of Colchester*, "the assumption that must be made is that the employer would have dismissed the employee at the first available moment open to him, namely after the procedure had been exhausted."

25–27   The EAT was dismissive of the appellant's attempts to introduce the loss of a chance (that he would not have been dismissed) into the calculation of damages. This, said Morison, J. was "a heresy and it represents a misunderstanding of the process involved in quantifying a dismissed employee's damages for breach of contract". It was an attempt to "overlay contractual questions with concepts of fairness which, in our view, do not apply". The logic of this reasoning has, however, been the subject of criticism. Damages for breach of contract are intended to put the employee into the position he would have been in had the parties performed their obligations under the contract. So, if the employer properly implements a contractual disciplinary procedure, one possible outcome could be that the employee is not dismissed— otherwise the procedure is necessarily a sham. There is a persuasive argument that, as damages are designed to put the employee in the position he would have been in but for the employer's breach, damages for a breach of contract by an employer by failing to follow a contractual disciplinary procedure should reflect the chance that the employee would not have been dismissed. There seems no reason, in principle, why a percentage chance approach could not be applied in the assessment of damages for breach of contract just as it is, for example, in sex and race and disability discrimination where common law rules for the assessment of damages in tort are applied (see paras 13–58 to 13–76).

25–28 Note also the case of *Clark v. BET plc and anor* [1997] I.R.L.R. 348 considered at para. 25–44. That case concerned the question of whether damages for breach of contract should take into account an increase in salary which the contract stated "shall be reviewed and be increased annually ... by such amount as the board shall in its absolute discretion decide." The High Court decided that there was a contractual right to an increase in salary and that it was only the amount of that increase that was within the discretion of the board. Mr Justice Timothy Walker stated: "if the board had capriciously or in bad faith exercised its discretion so as to determine the increase and therefore pay Mr Clark no increase at all, that would be a breach of contract". Accordingly, the court awarded damages on the basis of a 10 per cent increase in salary each year (based largely on the evidence of previous increases). By analogy, it could be said that if an employer implemented a contractual disciplinary procedure and then "capriciously or in bad faith" exercised its discretion to dismiss, whatever the findings of the disciplinary hearing, that also, surely, could be a breach of contract.

Loss of the chance to claim unfair dismissal

25–29 Another issue which has recently been the subject of litigation, is the measure of damages for breach of contract in circumstances where the employee is wrongfully dismissed just before he qualifies for the right to claim unfair dismissal. Whatever the qualifying period for claiming unfair dismissal, there will always be the tendency for the employees to suffer the fate of being dismissed just before they qualify. First, it is important to remember that if an employee is dismissed without notice, in circumstances where there has been no gross misconduct justifying summary dismissal, then the statutory minimum notice must be added on after the actual date of termination in order to identify the "effective date of termination" for the purposes of calculating the period of continuous employment. So, if the employee is summarily dismissed after one year and fifty-one-and-a-half weeks then one week statutory minimum notice is added (unless he is guilty of gross misconduct) and he therefore has two years' continuous employment enabling him to claim unfair dismissal (ss.97(2) and 108 ERA).

Now consider the situation in which an employee is entitled to one month's contractual notice. He is summarily dismissed three weeks before he would have achieved two years' continuous employment. He does not benefit from the addition of one week's statutory minimum notice because he still falls short of the two years' employment required in order to claim unfair dismissal. His only alternative claim, therefore, is for breach of contract. The question is, can the measure of damages include the loss of the chance to claim unfair dismissal which is a direct result of the employer's breach of contract?

25–30 This was the issue considered in the case of *Morran v. Glasgow Council of Tenants Associations and ors*, Court of Session [1998] I.R.L.R. 67. Mr Morran started his employment with GCTA on October 8, 1991. He was summarily dismissed on September 16, 1993, some three weeks short of two years' continuous employment. He therefore had no right to pursue a claim for unfair dismissal. His contract of employment provided for a notice period of one month but also stated that he could be summarily dismissed for gross misconduct and, in other circumstances, a "payment in lieu of notice may be made". Mr Morran received no pay in lieu of notice. His claim for breach of contract for failing to give him his contractual notice of four weeks asserted that he was entitled to be compensated for the lost chance of being able to claim unfair dismissal. This, he said, entitled him to claim for continuing losses which would have been awarded by way of the compensatory award for unfair dismissal. He further argued that the option of summary dismissal with a payment in lieu of notice had not been followed and that, therefore, he was entitled to rely on the "primary" obligation of giving him four weeks' notice. That had been breached by the employer and he should be fully compensated for that.

25–31 The Court of Session in Scotland disagreed. They relied on the decision in *Lavarack v. Woods of Colchester Ltd* [1967] 1 Q.B. 278 (see also para. 25–26). In an action for breach of contract the plaintiff/complainant is "entitled to recover damages which will put him in the position in which he would have been if the [defendant/respondent] had fulfilled their obligation in the way which would have been less burdensome to them" (The Lord President). In this case, the least burdensome way for the company to fulfil its obligation under the contract would have been to dismiss Mr Morran and make a payment in lieu of notice. "If that is so, then the [plaintiff/complainant] is entitled to damages calculated on the basis that the [defendant/respondent] would have been entitled to dismiss him, but would have been obliged to make a payment in lieu of notice." He could, therefore, only seek to recover pay in lieu of notice and could not recover damages in respect of the loss of the right to claim unfair dismissal.

The Court of Session left open the question of whether the outcome would have been different had the contract of employment not included the right to make a payment in lieu of notice. If this was the case and the employee has been dismissed summarily in breach of contract and has thereby lost the chance to claim unfair dismissal, there may be an argument that damages could take into account the loss of the chance to claim unfair dismissal. How such compensation would then be calculated is open to doubt. The tribunal could proceed to assess the chance of an unfair dismissal claim succeeding, something tribunals are, of course, well versed in handling. Alternatively, it has been argued that the tribunal could simply award a nominal sum for the loss of this statutory right (see IDS Brief 607 commentary on *Morran v. Glasgow Council of Tenants Associations and ors*).

25–32 Note, also, that a number of appeal decisions in England have included *obiter* support for the argument that compensation for breach of contract might include the loss of the right to complain of unfair dismissal. For example, in *Robert Cort & Son Ltd v. Charman* [1981] I.R.L.R. 437 EAT, Browne Williamson J. made the following *obiter* remarks after concluding on the facts that the employee did not have sufficient continuous service to claim unfair dismissal. "However, he may have another remedy. The dismissal without notice seems to us to be a clear breach of contract. The measure of damages for such breach may not be limited to one month's wages [the notice period] but may also include the loss of the right to compensation for unfair dismissal which he would have had if the correct notice had been given."

In summary, therefore, where an employee loses the right to claim unfair dismissal because he is dismissed in breach of contract by not receiving his contractual notice entitlement and where there is no contractual right for the employer to make a payment in lieu of notice, the employee may be able to recover compensation for the lost chance of claiming unfair dismissal. However, there is, as yet, no decision directly on this point, only *obiter* support. Where, in the above scenario, the employer has the right to make a payment in lieu of notice, the following appears to apply. If he makes a payment in lieu of notice there is no breach of contract and, therefore, no claim in any event. If he fails to make such a payment, the compensation is limited to the pay in lieu due under the contract because this is the least "burdensome" way that the employer could have complied with the contract.

Loss of chance to obtain redundancy payment

25–33 If the employee is wrongfully dismissed and thereby loses the chance of receiving a redundancy payment because it is likely that he would have been made redundant during the contractual notice period then he can claim, as part of his damages, the lost redundancy payment. In the case of *Basnett v. J. & A. Jackson Ltd* [1976] I.R.L.R. 154 HCQB, Mr Basnett was actually made redundant two years into a five-year fixed term contract. He recovered damages for breach of the fixed term contract. The High Court held that account should be taken of the additional redundancy payment he would have received had the contract been allowed to run its course and had he been made redundant on the expiry of the contract. However, the court also decided that there was only a 50 per cent chance of him being made redundant on the expiry of the term and so awarded 50 per cent of the additional redundancy payment which he would have received at that time.

Stigma damages and the manner of dismissal

25–34 The well established view has been that an employee dismissed in breach of contract cannot recover compensation, in respect of that breach, for the manner of the dismissal. This equates to the position with regard to compensation for unfair dismissal (see para. 10–10). This rule was confirmed in the case of *Bliss v. South East Thames Regional Health Authority* [1987] I.C.R. 700 CA in which Dillon L.J. stated "the general rule laid down by the House of Lords in *Addis v. Gramophone Co. Ltd* [1909] A.C. 488 is that where damages fall to be assessed for breach of contract rather than in tort it is not permissible to award general damages for frustration, mental distress, injured feelings or annoyance occasioned by the breach". Dillon L.J. accepted that there were exceptions to this general rule. He referred to the case of *Jarvis v. Swan Tours Ltd* [1973] Q.B. 233 which concerned a spoilt holiday. This related to a contract which was itself intended to provide peace of mind or freedom from distress. This was not the case with employment contracts. Dillon L.J. also made reference to the case of *Cox v. Philips Industries Ltd* [1976] I.C.R. 138 in which Lawson J. had taken the view that damages for distress, vexation and frustration, including consequent ill-health, could be recovered for breach of a contract of employment if it was in the contemplation of the parties that the breach would cause such distress, etc. Dillon

L.J. rejected this approach, stating: "I do not think that that general approach is open to this court unless and until the House of Lords has reconsidered its decision in the *Addis* case". Consideration of this issue is, therefore, awaited from the House of Lords. Until then, the rule is: no general damages for breach of contract in the employment context.

25-35 A potentially important development, however, occurred with the House of Lords decision in the case of *Malik and anor v. Bank of Credit and Commerce International S.A. (in compulsory liquidation* [1997] I.C.R. 606. This well known case concerned BCCI, which had for some years been carrying on its business fraudulently. Mr Malik was made redundant by the provisional liquidators in October 1991. He was unable to obtain other employment in the financial services industry. He alleged that this was the result of the stigma attaching to him as a former member of staff at the bank, even though he was not himself guilty of any wrong doing. The House of Lords held that there was an implied obligation on the employer not to carry on business in a dishonest or corrupt manner. This obligation stems from the term of trust and confidence implied into every contract of employment which imposes mutual obligations on the parties. So far as the employer is concerned, it imposes an obligation that it shall not "without reasonable and proper cause, conduct itself in a manner calculated and likely to destroy or seriously damage the relationship of confidence and trust between employer and employee" (see *Woods v. W.M. Car Services (Peterborough) Ltd* [1981] I.C.R. 666, Browne-Wilkinson J.). This clause, it was noted, had been developed since the *Addis* decision in 1909. If it is reasonably foreseeable that corrupt practices will lead to a serious possibility that an employee's future employment prospects would be handicapped, damages were recoverable for any continuing financial losses sustained. Having established that such losses are potentially recoverable, it is important to consider the potential implications of this decision.

25-36 Lord Steyn, in the *Malik* case, sought to limit the potential impact of the judgement by pointing out first that in order to establish a breach of the implied term of trust and confidence there has to be "no reasonable or proper cause" for the employer's conduct and such conduct must be calculated to destroy or seriously damage the relationship of trust and confidence. Secondly, he pointed to the problems of recovering damages for injury to his employment prospects: "The Law Commission has pointed out that loss of reputation is inherently difficult to prove (Consultation Paper No. 132 on Aggravated, Exemplary and Restituionary Damages). It is, therefore, improbable that many employees would be able to prove 'stigma compensation'. The limiting principles of causation, remoteness and mitigation present formidable practical obstacles to such claims succeeding".

It is possible, however, to see how the principle established in the *Malik* case could be extended in the employment context. Take, for example, an employee wrongly accused of an act of serious dishonesty. The employer acts in breach of the implied term of trust and confidence if he dismisses the employee without any investigation or any real evidence that he is guilty of that offence. If, as a result of that dismissal, the employee is stigmatised so that he is unable to get alternative employment there may be a basis for him claiming continuing financial loss resulting from the employer's breach of contract. Such claims could be pursued in the tribunal by virtue of the extended jurisdiction subject to a cap of £25,000 (see para. 25-11).

Apprentices

25-37 Note that the extended jurisdiction applies to contracts of apprenticeship. Section 3 ETA refers to claims for damages for breaches of contracts of employment.

"Contract of employment" is defined in s.42 ETA as "a contract of service or apprenticeship ..." In such cases, the damages period may go beyond the normal rule. In the case of *Dunk v. George Waller & Son Ltd* [1970] 2 Q.B. 163, the plaintiff had his apprenticeship prematurely terminated. He claimed damages for breach of contract. The Court of Appeal held that the contract of apprenticeship was an agreement of a special character and, as a result of the breach by the company, he was entitled to damages for his loss of earnings and of training during the rest of the term of the apprenticeship agreement and also for diminution of his future prospects. He was awarded lost wages for a period of two years after the end of the apprenticeship period. There seems no reason why such an award cannot now be made by the tribunal using the extended jurisdiction.

Statutory Minimum Damages

25–38   There is one important respect in which statute intervenes in the question of the measure of damages for breach of contract and the measure of sums due under the contract. Sections 87 to 91 of the ERA set out rights an employee has during a period of notice. These provisions only apply if the employer has been employed for at least one month (s.87 ERA). It makes no difference whether it is the employee or employer who serves notice (s.87(1) and (2) ERA). The rights provided by these sections apply to the periods of statutory minimum notice (s.87(3) ERA) (see para. 25–23). Indeed, if the employer's contractual notice is at least one week longer than statutory minimum notice then the provisions of these sections do not apply at all (s.87(4) ERA).

The rules then deal with the rights of employees depending on whether they have normal working hours. The purpose of the provisions is to provide a basic entitlement to pay for the notice period. If the employee has normal working hours under his contract of employment in force during the notice period and he is ready and willing to work but no work is provided, or he is incapable of work because of sickness or injury or, in the case of a woman, she is absent from work because of pregnancy or childbirth, or the employee is absent on contractually provided holiday, then the employer is liable to pay a sum calculated as follows: the sum must be not less than the amount of remuneration for the particular part of the working week covered by the circumstances referred to above (such as absence on sick leave) "calculated at the average hourly rate of remuneration produced by dividing a week's pay by the number of normal working hours" (s.88(1) ERA). (See Chapter 24, and para. 24–10 for calculation date, for commentary on week's pay.)

25–39   Set against the amount calculated in this way are any payments made to the employee by the employer covering that part of the notice period—such as sick pay, SSP, maternity pay, SMP or holiday pay (s.88(2) ERA). Also, sums paid by way of incapacity benefit or industrial injury benefit are deducted (s.90 ERA). This section could come into play, for example, where an employee has been on sick leave for a long time and has exhausted his entitlement to any company sick pay and to SSP. Nothing further is due under the contract of employment and if the employer was then to serve statutory minimum notice the employee would be entitled to nothing during the notice period but for the provisions of s.88. This section then entitles the employee to recover pay during the notice period according to the statutory formula described above. If no pay is received then the employee can claim either an unlawful deduction from wages or bring a claim for a sum due under the contract.

In the case of employees without normal working hours, the rules in s.89 ERA apply. The provisions are similar. The employee is entitled to a week's pay (as calculated in respect of employees without normal working hours—see paras 24–31 to 24–33) for each week of the notice period (s.89(1) ERA). Liability is conditional on the employee being "ready and willing to do work of a reasonable nature and amount to earn the week's pay" (s.89(2) ERA). However, this proviso is not applicable in the case of absence from work because of sickness, injury, pregnancy, childbirth or contractually provided holidays (s.89(3) ERA). The same rules apply to sums paid by the employer which are set off against the employer's liability. Note also that any sums paid by way of incapacity benefit or industrial injury benefit are deduced (s.90 ERA).

Exceptions to liability

25–40 These special statutory provisions do not give an entitlement to pay for time off. In respect of any time off, other statutory provisions apply to determine entitlement to pay (see Chapter 22) (s.91(1) ERA). The employee is not entitled to be paid by virtue of these provisions if, after he gives notice, he takes part in a strike during the notice period (s.91(2) ERA).

Failure to give notice

25–41 If the employer fails to give statutory minimum notice then the employee can claim the sums he would have been entitled to by virtue of these special provisions, during the notice period, as damages for breach of contract by the employer (s.91(5) ERA). This claim can, of course, be brought in the tribunal under the extended jurisdiction. Note that the duty to mitigate applies in respect of such a claim and any sums earned during the damages period are therefore taken into account in assessing the damages (*Westwood v. Secretary of State for Employment* [1984] I.R.L.R. 209 HL, see also commentary at para. 25–68).

ELEMENTS OF LOSS: WRONGFUL DISMISSAL

25–42 In broad terms, the extent of the loss recoverable for breach of contract is based on the sums due under the contract. In other words, the employee can recover the net value of contractual pay and benefits for the period of loss (see paras 25–23 to 25–37 for commentary on the period of loss). It is the net value of pay and benefits because this is what puts the employee back into the position he would have been in but for the breach. Discretionary payments or benefits are not recoverable.

Salary or wages: Grossing up

25–43 At paras 6–67 to 6–72 there is commentary on the principle of grossing up net pay in order to establish the amount of damages payable to an employee for breach of contract or as a result of a discrimination claim. This principle is important in cases where the damages are themselves taxable because they exceed the exempt amount which is currently £30,000 (see s.148 ICTA and paras 6–42 to 6–43). The damages after they are taxed have to reflect the loss due to the complainant. However, in contractual claims in the tribunal the statutory maximum limit on compensation is £25,000. This means that, generally, damages within this limit will not be taxable. No grossing up would therefore be required. The tribunal can simply assess compensation for wrongful dismissal by deducting tax and N.I. from the gross salary and benefits. Note that if compensation is awarded for both unfair dismissal and for a contractual claim then the £30,000 exempt amount could be exceeded and a grossing up exercise would become necessary.

Increase in salary/wages

25–44 If the employee would have been contractually entitled to an increase in salary or wage during the period of loss, such an increase is taken into account in the assessment of damages. This may be the case, for example, where there is a nationally negotiated pay round and where the contract of employment provides that the employee's pay increases in accordance with the outcome of those negotiations.

The recent High Court decision in *Clark v. BET plc and anor* [1997] I.R.L.R. 348 provides an interesting interpretation of a contractual provision on salary review. The contract provided that "the executive's salary shall be reviewed annually and be increased by such amount if any as the board shall in its absolute discretion decide". Mr Clark was dismissed without receiving the three years notice to which he was entitled under his contract. He claimed damages for breach of contract. The High Court held that the contractual provision on salary review amounted to a contractual obligation on the employers to provide an annual upward adjustment. The salary "shall be reviewed and increased". The absolute discretion referred to in the clause only relates to the extent of the increase. Further, "if the board had capriciously or in bad faith exercised its discretion so as to determine the increase at nil and therefore pay Mr Clark no increase at all, that would have been a breach of contract" (Walker J). The court looked at the increases Mr Clark had actually received annually prior to his dismissal. Between 1991 and 1996 the increases had been about 10 per cent. Mr Clark's successor had received increases well in excess of 10 per cent for the previous five years with Rentokil (who had acquired BET). Other comparable employees had received at least 10 per cent as an annual increase. The court therefore awarded damages based on Mr Clark's salary increasing by 10 per cent per year. (Note the contrast of this decision with *Janciuk v. Winerite Ltd* [1998] I.R.L.R. 63 considered at paras 25–25 to 25–28).

The important point to note is that it is a question of interpretation of the contract to determine whether it provides a contractual right to a pay increase.

Backdated pay increase

25–45 If the contract provides that a pay increase will be backdated, then a subsequent increase, awarded after termination of employment which is backdated to cover the period of loss, will be taken into account on the basis of the principle that damages for breach of contract are to put the employee into the position he would have been in had the employer performed his obligations under the contract.

Holiday Pay

25–46 If, on termination of employment, the employee has accrued but untaken holiday entitlement then he may be entitled, by virtue of his contract of employment, to receive payment in respect of that untaken holiday. Whether there may be such an entitlement is considered at paras 3–19 and 25–48 to 25–50. Note, however, that such holiday pay comes within the definition of wages for the purposes of the provisions relating to unlawful deductions from wages in the ERA (see s.27(1)(a) ERA). This means that non payment in respect of accrued holiday entitlement in circumstances where the contract of employment provides for such payment on termination of employment, will amount to an unlawful deduction from wages. In such circumstances the employee could either pursue a claim under s.23 ERA asserting that his employer has made an unlawful deduction from wages or use the extended jurisdiction of the tribunal to bring a claim for a sum due under the contract. The best course of action from the employee's point of view is the former because the employer will have no right to bring any sort of counterclaim by way of those proceedings. As we have noted at para. 25–16, the employer can, however, bring what is effectively a counterclaim in response to a contractual claim issued by the employee by virtue of the tribunal's extended jurisdiction.

25–47   Note, however, that if the employee has been wrongfully dismissed, he may have lost further accrual of holiday entitlement during what would have been the full period of contractual notice or the remainder of a fixed term contract. If the contract provides for payment in respect of accrued holiday on termination of employment then the employee will have suffered the loss of this accrual during the notice period. He will be able to include a claim for the loss of that holiday pay in a damages claim for breach of contract. In these circumstances there is no alternative option of a claim for unlawful deduction from wages. The claim is for damages for breach of contract. Such damages are not wages for the purposes of the ERA provisions on the right not to suffer unlawful deductions. Note also the new right to three weeks paid holiday per year (rising to four weeks from November 23, 1999) contained in the Working Time Regulations, 1998 (Regulation 13). Regulation 14 provides for a right to pro rata accrued holiday pay on termination of employment. Regulation 30(1)(b) provides a right to complain to the tribunal if it is not paid (see paras 22–48 to 22–49 for commentary).

Is the employee entitled to pay in respect of accrued but untaken holiday on termination of employment?

25–48   The question of whether the employee is entitled, under his contract of employment, to pay in respect of accrued but untaken holiday on termination of employment is crucial both for the purposes of determining whether the employee may have a claim for unlawful deduction of wages (see paras 22–58 to 22–67) and whether a wrongfully dismissed employee can recover damages for breach of contract in respect of holiday which would have accrued during the damages period (see para. 25–47). Many contracts of employment specifically provide for pay in lieu of accrued but untaken holiday entitlement on termination. Often this is subject to an exception that no such payment will be made if the employee is dismissed for gross misconduct (however note the entitlement to accrued holiday pay on termination provided by regulation 14 Working Time Regulations 1998 (see paras 22–48 to 22–49). If nothing is stated in the contract then it may be that the parties have verbally agreed to such a term. Alternatively, it may be possible to imply the term by virtue of the fact that the employer has always, in the past, made such payments. In other words, the term is implied by custom and practice. What if there is nothing in any written or verbal contract and nothing can be implied from past conduct? Well, it seems that the tribunal is unlikely to imply such a term on the basis that it is necessary to give business efficacy to the contract.

25–49   In *Morley v. Heritage plc* [1993] I.R.L.R. 400 the Court of Appeal upheld the decision of the County Court that Mr Morley, who was chief financial director of the defendant company, was not contractually entitled to accrued holiday pay on termination of employment. Mr Morley's contract of employment said nothing about any right to accrued holiday pay on termination. Further, the contract stated: "This agreement records the entire agreement between the parties at the date hereof ...".

The Court of Appeal rejected the contention on behalf of the plaintiff that it was necessary to imply such a term to give business efficacy to the contract: "I hope I show no disrespect to this particular submission when I say no more than in my view it is quite unsustainable. The contract works perfectly well without any such implication" (Sir Christopher Slade).

It should be noted that the Court of Appeal's decision was, of course, in relation to one particular contract. Rose L.J. specifically referred to "this contract for this group financial director ...". He then concluded: "The business efficacy of this contact does not require the implication of any such term". Nonetheless, it is hard to imagine circumstances in which a different contract might require such a term to give it business efficacy. As Rose L.J. remarked in the *Morley* case: "it is likely to be much more difficult to say that a term affecting the relationship of the parties on termination of the contract between them is necessary in order to give business efficacy to the contract which has hitherto existed". Note also that the Court of Appeal rejected the contention that a term had to be implied into the contract providing for holiday pay on termination in order to satisfy the requirements of what is now s.1 ERA. Section 1(4)(d)(i) requires that the statement of main terms shall contain details of any terms and conditions relating to "entitlement to holidays, ... and holiday pay". This provision "does no more than recognise that a contract can include such a provision" (Rose L.J.), it does not require it to be included.

25–50 A decision of the EAT a year after the *Morley* case appears to be inconsistent with the Court of Appeal's reasoning. In the case of *Janes Solicitors v. Lamb-Simpson* EAT 323/94, the EAT did imply a term into the employee's contract for a payment to be made on termination of employment in respect of accrued holiday pay. This was an unwritten contract and the EAT considered that such a term could be implied to give the contract business efficacy. Although the nature of the contract was different from that in the *Morley* case, there seems to be a compelling case for the same logic of the Court of Appeal to apply. How can it be said that the contract was unworkable without such a clause?

Calculation of holiday pay where payment is due under the contract

25–51 Whether the complainant is pursuing a contractual claim, making use of the tribunal's extended jurisdiction, or, alternatively, is claiming an unlawful deduction from wages in respect of non payment for holiday already accrued at the date of termination of the contract, it is important to determine the basis of calculation of holiday pay.

This was the question which the EAT considered in the case of *Thames Water Utilities v. Reynolds* [1996] I.R.L.R. 186. When Mr Reynolds was made redundant, he had accrued eight days' holiday which he had not taken in that holiday year. The employer calculated the sum due by dividing Mr Reynolds' annual salary by 365 to get salary for one day and then multiplying that sum by 8. This approach was accepted by the EAT (overturning the decision of the tribunal that there had been an unlawful deduction from wages). The tribunal had ruled that annual salary should be divided by the number of working days in a year—260—and then multiplied by 8. The EAT referred to s.2 of the Apportionment Act 1870. This provided that "all ... periodical payments in the nature of income ... shall ... be considered as accruing from day to day and shall be apportionable in respect of time accordingly". The expression "day to day" means calendar days, not working days.

It should be noted that s.7 of the Apportionment Act provides: "The provisions of this Act shall not extend to any case in which it is or shall be expressly stipulated that no apportionment shall take place". Therefore the provisions of the Act can be expressly excluded. The contract of employment can provide for a different basis for calculating holiday pay and if it does, the Apportionment Act is irrelevant.

Checklist of treatment of benefits, perks, etc., provided by contract of employment

25–52   Set out below is a checklist of other benefits, perks, etc. and how they should be treated.

Commission payments, bonuses

25–53   Commission payments and bonuses are only recoverable if they were a contractual entitlement. Discretionary payments are excluded (see *Lavarack v. Woods of Colchester Ltd* [1967] 1 Q.B. 278 CA). In that case, the Court of Appeal had to consider whether Mr Lavarack could recover compensation for wrongful dismissal in respect of a bonus which was not contractual. It was held that he was not. The company was "under no contractual obligation to him to continue the [bonus] scheme and in fact it was discontinued". If the bonus is contractual, the tribunal has to assess the net amount the employee would have received during the period of loss. In *Clark v. BET plc & anor* the court assessed the bonus Mr Clark would have received at 50 per cent of his salary. This was based on looking at the bonus received by comparable employees and Mr Clark's successor. It was also based on a "rough and ready assumption" as to where Mr Clark would have fitted into the hierarchy.

Fringe benefits

25–54   The following are examples of fringe benefits which may be provided for by the contract of employment. Remember, they will not be recoverable in a wrongful dismissal claim if they are discretionary in nature.

> Car
>
> Private mileage
>
> Private health care (BUPA, PPP etc)
>
> Life insurance
>
> Free or subsidised accommodation
>
> Free or subsidised meals
>
> Payment of telephone accounts
>
> Staff discount schemes

The tribunal has to assess the net value of any such benefit. The crucial question is: What would it cost the employee to replace the benefit himself on the open market? It makes no difference that the employer might have been able to purchase a benefit, such as a particular kind of insurance, at a low rate for all its employees. In putting the wrongfully dismissed employee back in the position he would have been in had the employer performed his obligations under the contract he would have to go out and purchase replacement insurance himself. Note, also, that it is only that element of the "benefit" that really is an additional benefit to the employee which will be compensated. So, for example, it is the private use of a company car and the private mileage paid which can be compensated (see paras 3–32 to 3–47 for commentary on the assessment of the value of such perks in the context of unfair dismissal compensation and Appendix L for AA and RAC guidance on the cost of motoring).

Gratuities

25–55   Again, the tribunal will assess the value of tips or gratuities to which the complainant was contractually entitled and which he would have received but for the wrongful dismissal. In *Manubens v. Leon* [1919] 1 K.B. 208, there was an implied term of the contract that the plaintiff should be allowed to receive tips from customers. Lush J. held that it was within the contemplation of the parties to the contract that the plaintiff would receive tips. The plaintiff was, accordingly, entitled to include the loss of such tips in his claim for damages for wrongful dismissal.

Expenses

25–56   Genuine repayment of expenses incurred does not amount to a benefit and, therefore, will not be taken into account in the assessment of damages for wrongful dismissal. However, if there is an element of sums paid in respect of expenses which amounts to a "profit" for the employee then this element may be taken into account. If it is described as "expenses" in order to avoid tax then the contract will be illegal and will not be enforced by the court. However, if the employee pays tax on the "profit" element then there will be no illegality and this element can be included in the assessment of damages (see paras 24–45 to 24–46 for further commentary on the treatment of expenses in the context of determining a week's pay for redundancy pay calculations, etc.).

Pension Rights

25–57   Provided the employee was entitled to pension benefits as a contractual right, he will be able to recover compensation for the loss of those benefits during the period of loss. This may be a valuable benefit. For full commentary on the calculation of pension loss see Chapter 20. Note that when applying the guidance at paragraphs 20–41 to 20–61 on assessing pension loss where the employee was a member of a final salary scheme the loss will be the difference in the value of the deferred pension he actually receives based on service up to the date of the wrongful dismissal and the deferred pension he would have received had he been dismissed on contractual notice (or at the end of a fixed term). With regard to the contributions the employee made out of his salary or wage into the pension fund, these should be deducted from pay in the assessment of damages for wrongful dismissal in circumstances where the period of non contribution has resulted in no reduction in his pension entitlement (see *Dews v. National Board* [1987] I.R.L.R. 330 HL).

Profit related pay/profit sharing

25–58   Any scheme which provides additional pay or shares to the employee based on level of profit can be taken into account in the calculation of damages for wrongful dismissal, provided the scheme is contractual. The tribunal has to assess the value of the benefit lost as a result of the wrongful dismissal during the period of loss.

Share Options

25–59   First, note that, as with all the other benefits considered above, the loss of a share option clearly cannot be compensated for if it is not a contractual entitlement. However, even if there is a contractual entitlement, the position depends on the terms of the contract.

In *Micklefield v. SAC Technology* [1990] I.R.L.R. 218, Mr Micklefield was in a share option scheme. However, a term of the scheme provided that: "If an option-holder ceases to be employed within the SAC Technology Group for whatever reason whatsoever, then the option granted to him shall lapse and not be exercisable". The scheme also provided that: "If any option-holder ceases to be an executive for any reason he shall not be entitled, and by applying for an option an executive shall be deemed irrevocably to have waived any entitlement, by way of compensation for loss of office or otherwise howsoever to any sum or other benefit to compensate him for the loss of any rights under the Scheme." Sixteen days before he was entitled to exercise his option Mr Micklefield wrote to the directors seeking to exercise it. Eight days later he was summarily dismissed, in breach of contract, and informed that the option had accordingly lapsed.

The High Court held that Mr Micklefield was not entitled to recover damages for loss of the option. The exemption clause in the contract was effective. It was clear and decisive and was not void under the Unfair Contract Terms Act, 1977. The case fell within an exclusion to the Act contained in paragraph 1(e) of Schedule 1 ("any contract so far as it relates to the creation or transfer of securities or of any right or interest in securities"). In order for a contract to come within paragraph 1(e) it did not have to be a contract specifically for the creation or transfer of securities. It was wider than that and "is worded to apply to *any* contract *so far as* it relates to the creation or transfer of securities" (Deputy Judge Mowbray). So far as Mr Micklefield's contract of employment related to his option to acquire shares, it was excluded from the Act by paragraph 1(e) of the schedule.

25–60   The water has been muddied somewhat by a subsequent Scottish decision in the case of *Chapman v. Aberdeen Construction Group plc* [1991] I.R.L.R. 505. In this case, an exclusion clause in a share option scheme was held to be void by virtue of the Unfair Contract Terms Act, 1977. Mr Chapman had been summarily dismissed from his post as executive director of Aberdeen Construction Group on July 8, 1987. He brought a claim for wrongful dismissal on the basis that he was entitled under his contract to six months' notice. As part of his claim he argued that he had lost the benefit of a right to exercise options he had been granted under the company's share option scheme. The rules of the scheme provided that the option could not be exercised until three years after they had been granted. At the date of his summary dismissal the three year period had not yet expired. However, had he been given his contractual notice he would have been able to exercise his option. The company's defence was based on an exclusion clause in the share option scheme which stated that: "It shall be a condition of the scheme that in the event of the dismissal of a participant from employment he shall not become entitled to any damages or compensation or any additional damages or compensation by reason of any alteration of his rights or expectations under the scheme".

Now, under the Unfair Contract Terms Act 1977, there are special provisions applying to Scotland. In particular, s.23 states that "any term of any contract shall be void which purports to exclude or restrict or has the effect of excluding or restricting (a) the exercise by a party to any other contract, of any right or remedy which arises in respect of that other contract in consequence of breach of duty, or of obligation, liability for which could not by virtue of the provisions of this Part of this Act be excluded or restricted by a term of that other contract; (b) the application of the provisions of this Part of this Act in respect of that or any other contract." The side note for this section in the Act states "Evasion by means of secondary contract". The Court of Session held that the purpose of s.23 was to prevent rights in a primary contract—in this case the contract of employment—being limited or extinguished by a provision in a secondary contract—the contract granting the share option under the scheme—which could not have been achieved had the provisions been incorporated into the primary contract. Section 17, which is another of the special provisions applying to Scotland, excludes terms in contracts of employment (along with a range of other contracts) which seek to exclude or limit liability for breach of contract unless it is fair and reasonable to incorporate such terms in the contract. The effect of this provision is that if the exclusion clause had been inserted into the contract of employment itself it would have been void (unless it was fair and reasonable).

25–61   The Court of Session held that the exclusion clause in the secondary contract did attempt to remove a remedy arising under the contract of employment itself because its aim was to restrict the employer's liability to pay damages for breach of the contract of employment. The exclusion clause did, therefore, come within s.23 and was void by virtue of that section. It would not have been fair and reasonable to include such a clause in the primary employment contract and s.23 accordingly prevented it from being included in a secondary contract. What, then, might be the effect of the reasoning in the *Chapman* case on the position in England and Wales?

First, the specific exclusion of the provisions of the Act in Schedule 1, paragraph 1(e)—contracts so far as they relate to the creation or transfer of securities or of any right or interest in securities—does not apply in Scotland. This provision, as we have seen from the *Micklefield* decision (see para. 25–39), excludes the Act in relation to such provisions in an employment contract.

25–62   It has been argued that the Schedule 1, paragraph 1(e) provision does not apply to secondary contracts in England and Wales and that, accordingly, if an unreasonable exclusion clause was contained in a secondary contract (in the form of a separate contract for the grant of the share option) it could be struck down by virtue of s.10 which relates to such secondary contracts (see IDS Employment Law Handbook Series 2, No. 15, Chapter 8 and I.R.L.R. Highlights, December 1991, Volume 20, Number 12). However, the wording of s.10, which renders void certain terms in secondary contracts, specifically relates back to the primary contract. It prevents a party to one contract (such as the contract of employment) evading the restrictions imposed by the Act by stating that that party cannot seek to achieve the same end by way of term in a secondary contract. The wording of s.10 is as follows:

> "A person is not bound by any contract term prejudicing or taking away rights of his which arise under, or in connection with the performance of, another contract, so far as those rights extend to the enforcement of another's liability which this Part of this Act prevents that other from excluding or restricting".

Since that Part of the Act does *not* prevent the exclusion or restricting of liability in any contract, so far as it relates to the creation or transfer of securities or of any right or interest in securities (by virtue of Schedule 1, paragraph 1(e), it is suggested that s.10 does not come into play and that, so far as England and Wales are concerned, an exclusion clause in a secondary contract would not be made void by the UCTA. All of this does not affect the right to damages where a contractual share option is lost as a result of a wrongful dismissal, where there is no exclusion clause in the share option rules in the event of dismissal.

Valuing the loss of share option

25–63   If this is the case then the tribunal will have to consider how best to value the lost share option. No guidelines exist to assist in this task. The tribunal could seek to ascertain what "profit" the employee would have made had he purchased the shares as soon as the option was exercisable and sold them straight away at market value. However, the wrongfully dismissed employee may argue that he would not have sold them immediately and that by keeping hold of them they would have become worth more. Alternatively, the tribunal could use pricing models which have been developed to value options in the options market. How valuable such models are in relation to executive share schemes where the shares are not traded is open to doubt. One such model is known as Black-Scholes.

MITIGATION

25–64   The same common law duty to mitigate applies in respect of a claim for wrongful dismissal as with unfair dismissal and discrimination claims. Mitigation is considered fully at Chapter 19. We will consider a number of specific issues relating to mitigation where the claim is for wrongful dismissal, but first we look at claims where no duty to mitigate applies.

Claims for sums due under the contract: No duty to mitigate

25–65   It is important to note that the duty to mitigate applies when an employee is pursuing a claim for damages for breach of contract. So, if the employer terminates the contract with no notice in circumstances where there has been no gross misconduct then this is a breach of the contract, unless the contract allows for such a termination with a payment in lieu of notice. If there is no such provision in the contract, then the employee can pursue a claim for wrongful dismissal—alleging breach of contract by the employer—but the duty to mitigate will apply. In other words, he has to show that he has taken reasonable steps to find other work, which may be either employed or self-employed. If, however, the contract provides for summary dismissal with a payment in lieu of notice, and the employer dismisses the employee without notice and without payment in lieu of notice, does the duty to mitigate apply?

In *Abrahams v. Performing Rights Society* [1995] I.R.L.R. 486 CA, the Court of Appeal decided that, in such circumstances, the dismissal was not wrongful because the contract specifically allowed the employer to dismiss the employee without notice. This was a lawful dismissal. However, the provision in the contract for pay in lieu of notice gave rise to a contractual entitlement. If a contractual payment in lieu of notice is not made then the employee's claim is for a contractual sum due and no question of mitigation arises. In the *Abrahams* case, Mr Abrahams was summarily dismissed with no pay in lieu with two years to run on his contract. The contract provided for the right to make a payment in lieu of notice and so Mr Abrahams was entitled to the full sum of two years' pay with no obligation to set off against it any new earnings.

25–66   Note also the recent case of *Hutchings v. Coinseed Ltd* [1998] I.R.L.R. 190 in which Ms Hutchings resigned from her employment giving one month's notice. The employer confirmed that they did not want her to work her notice and would pay her in lieu at the end of the notice period. Ms Hutchings immediately started a new job with a competitor at a higher salary. Coinseed Ltd then refused to pay the salary for the notice period and she sued them. The Court of Appeal held that there had been no repudiatory breach of contract by Ms Hutchings. Starting the new job was not in breach of her obligations to her employer at that time because the employer had specifically released her from any requirement to do any further work. Accordingly, Ms Hutchings was entitled to be paid her salary for the notice period. Note that because the salary claim was for monies due under her contract of employment, no duty to mitigate applied and the fact that she had received salary from her new job during this period was irrelevant and should not be taken into account.

Cases involving liquidated damages

25–67 If a contract of employment contains a provision which states that, in the event of a breach, the guilty party will pay a specified sum to the other party, the sum due is categorised as liquidated damages. If the employer dismisses an employee in breach of contract so as to trigger a liquidated damages claim then, again, it appears as if the employee will be entitled to the full sum without being subject to any duty to mitigate his loss. This was the *obiter* view of Hutchinson L.J. in *Abrahams v. Performing Rights Society* [1995] I.R.L.R. 486 CA: "It seems to me that, as a matter of principle, where there is a liquidated damage clause which is valid—*i.e.* cannot be impugned as a penalty—there is no room for arguments on mitigation of damages— a concept relevant only in cases where damages are at large."

Wrongful dismissal

25–68 As we have already noted, full commentary on the duty of mitigation is at Chapter 19. However, there are some specific points in relation to mitigation in wrongful dismissal claims which should be considered.

Statutory Notice and the duty to mitigate

In the case of unfair dismissal claims, special rules apply to the statutory notice period. During this period, no duty to mitigate applies. This is fully considered at paras 10– 38 to 10–42. In the case of a wrongful dismissal claim no such special rule applies. The duty to mitigate applies throughout the period of damages—the period of notice the employee was entitled to under his contract of employment or the unexpired part of a fixed term contract (see *Westwood v. Secretary of State for Employment* [1984] I.R.L.R. 209 HL). This means that sums received during the damages period, by way of either new earnings or benefits, are deducted from the net wages which the employee would have received had he not been wrongfully dismissed. Also, if the tribunal considers that the employee has failed to properly mitigate his loss during the damages period then damages will be reduced so that the employee recovers the loss he would have suffered had he properly mitigated his loss.

In *Westwood* the House of Lords ruled that benefits received by the employee should be deducted in the assessment of damages. Note, however, that the House of Lords held that it would not be right to deduct the full amount of benefits received. In that case, Mr Westwood remained unemployed following the end of the twelve- week period covered by his claim. The net result of his wrongful dismissal was that he received his unemployment benefit (now Jobseekers Allowance) twelve weeks earlier than he would otherwise have done. But, of course, his entitlement also expired twelve weeks earlier. So far as unemployment benefit is concerned, he did not receive any payment which he would not have received had he been lawfully dismissed—he simply received it twelve weeks earlier. He did, however, receive the lower sum of supplementary benefit (now Income Support) during the twelve-week damages period. This he would not have received but for the wrongful dismissal and, accordingly, it should be deducted from the damages rather than the additional unemployment benefit.

Is the employee under a duty to claim benefits during damages period?

25–69 As noted at para. 25–68, benefits received by the employee during the damages period will be deducted from the loss claimed from the employer in order to assess the level of damages. What happens though, if the employee fails to claim benefits to which he would be entitled during the damages period? Does this amount to a failure to properly mitigate loss? The answer is that it might, depending on whether the employee acted reasonably in deciding not to claim benefit.

In *Secretary of State for Employment v. Stewart* [1996] I.R.L.R. 334, EAT, Mr Stewart was dismissed when his employer went into receivership. He did not claim unemployment benefit to start with but did apply to the Secretary of State for Employment under what is now s.182 ERA for compensation for not having been given notice to pay in lieu of notice. The Secretary of State agreed to the claim but deducted £151.40, being the amount of unemployment benefit he would have received had he claimed it. Mr Stewart challenged this decision in the tribunal and won. The Secretary of State appealed to the EAT. There it was held that, in assessing the amount due by virtue of s.182 ERA, account had to be taken not only of any sum which the employee actually received such as unemployment benefit but any sum which might have been received by the employee if reasonable steps had been taken by him.

25–70 The EAT did, however, point out that it might be reasonable for an employee who is pursuing a claim to the Secretary of State for pay in lieu of notice not to claim unemployment benefit for that period. Reference was made to Regulation 7(1)(d) of the Social Security (Unemployment, Sickness and Invalidity Benefit) Regulations 1983. This prevents an employee from obtaining unemployment benefit for the period in relation to which he received pay in lieu of notice or compensation for payment in lieu. The Secretary of State produced evidence that this was not followed in practice. Nonetheless, a dismissed employee may be confused about his entitlement. He may be advised that he cannot recover unemployment benefit for the period for which he is claiming pay in lieu. In such circumstances it may well be reasonable not claiming unemployment benefit.

Although this case relates to the question of how the duty to mitigate applies in circumstances where the employee is claiming pay in lieu of notice from the Secretary of State, by analogy the position is likely to be the same in the case of an employee pursuing a wrongful dismissal claim against his former employer. Indeed, in the EAT, counsel for the Secretary of State argued the case on the basis that common law rules applied to applications under s.182 ERA. Counsel submitted that "the Secretary of State was treated as if he were discharging a liability of the employer, and that the debt so discharged was … a debt to be ascertained on common law principles" (Lord Coulsfield). This argument was accepted by the EAT.

Recoupment rules do not apply

25–71 Note that, unlike unfair dismissal compensation, damages for wrongful dismissal are not subject to the rules of recoupment. Because the value of benefits paid are deducted from the amount claimed against the employer rather than benefits being repaid to the Secretary of State by way of recoupment, the employer ends up paying out less than he would had the same loss been recovered by way of unfair dismissal compensation. See paras 16–18 to 16–30 for commentary on recoupment.

Redundancy Pay

25–72 If an employee is wrongfully dismissed but at the same time receives a redundancy payment, does this have to be deducted from damages for such wrongful dismissal? The general rule is that redundancy pay is not deducted from damages for wrongful dismissal.

This was confirmed by the House of Lords in *Wilson v. National Coal Board* [1981] S.L.T. 67. Redundancy pay is a collateral benefit as defined in the case of *Parry v. Cleaver* [1970]. A.C.1. It is paid as compensation for loss of employment and has nothing to do with losses which flow from a wrongful dismissal. However, the *Wilson* case recognised that there were exceptional cases where a redundancy payment should be set off against damages for wrongful dismissal. If it is the case that the redundancy payment would not have been received but the wrongful dismissal, then this would be the sort of exceptional case acknowledged in *Wilson*.

In *Baldwin v. British Coal Corporation* [1995] I.R.L.R. 139 HC QB, Mr Baldwin accepted voluntary redundancy. Special terms had been available which gave redundant employees an additional lump sum of £5,000. The problem was that these terms were about to expire. In order to ensure that Mr Baldwin (and others) benefited from these terms, the respondents terminated his employment without giving him his full notice entitlement. He received no pay in lieu of notice. Mr Baldwin pursued a wrongful dismissal claim, alleging that he was unaware that he would not get pay in lieu.

The High Court held that there had been no breach of contract by the respondents. Mr Baldwin had either agreed to early termination in order to benefit from the £5,000 payment or alternatively, he had waived his right to notice. No damages were therefore due to him. The High Court also went on to state that, even if the early termination had been a breach of the contract, the special £5,000 lump sum redundancy payment had to be credited against his damages because it was one of those exceptional cases described in *Wilson* on the basis that he would not have received it but for the breach of contract.

The case of *Basnett v. J. & A. Jackson Ltd* [1976] ICR 63 QBD, is an example of the normal rule that the redundancy payment is not to be set off against damages for wrongful dismissal.

Unfair dismissal compensation

25–73 Unfair dismissal compensation is, generally, made up of the basic and compensatory awards (for other possible awards see Chapter 8 and para. 10–10). The basic award compensates the unfairly dismissed employee for loss of job security and reflects the age and length of service of the employee as well as his earnings (see Chapter 9). In the same way as redundancy pay is not generally set off against damages for wrongful dismissal, neither should the basic award.

In *Shove v. Downs Surgical plc* [1984] I.R.L.R. 17 HC, Mr Shove pursued a claim for damages for breach of contract. Mr Shove had been dismissed with just over three weeks' notice despite his contract providing for a notice period of 30 calendar months. Sheen J. made the point that Mr Shove would still have been entitled to the basic award had the notice been 30 months rather than three weeks. "Accordingly, it would not be correct to make any deduction from the damages to which the plaintiff is entitled by reason of the fact that the tribunal will award him a basic award." On the other hand, the compensatory award, which compensates the complainant for loss suffered as a result of the unfair dismissal, will be set off against damages for wrongful dismissal in so far as it covers the same period of loss. The complainant cannot recover the same loss twice.

25-74   A complainant who has been both unfairly and wrongfully dismissed, and who has suffered substantial financial loss, would be wise to pursue both an unfair dismissal claim and a claim for breach of contract using the tribunal's extended jurisdiction (see paras 25–05 to 25–11 for commentary on choice of venue for wrongful dismissal claim). By pursuing both claims, the complainant may be able to persuade the tribunal to award loss for the period of notice as damages for wrongful dismissal, subject to the statutory maximum award of £25,000, and then further financial loss by way of the compensatory award for unfair dismissal, subject to the statutory cap, which is currently £12,000. Note that damages for wrongful dismissal cannot be reduced on the basis of contributory fault or because it would be just and equitable to do so. If there has been a breach of contract the common law basis for assessment of damages applies—to put the parties back in the position they would have been in had the parties performed their obligations under the contract. By contrast, the compensatory award for unfair dismissal can be reduced for these reasons (see Chapter 11).

The impact of the compensatory award on the assessment of damages for wrongful dismissal was considered by the Court of Appeal in the case of *O'Laoire v. Jackel International Ltd* [1991] I.R.L.R. 170 CA. Mr O'Laoire was employed as deputy managing director by the respondent company. Having been told that he would become managing director when the incumbent retired, he was then informed that this would not happen and was subsequently dismissed without notice. His contractual notice entitlement was six months. Mr O'Laoire pursued a claim for unfair dismissal in the tribunal and a wrongful dismissal claim in the High Court. The tribunal found that he had been unfairly dismissed and assessed his loss at £100,700.00. The period of loss went well beyond the contractual notice period. However, the statutory maximum then was £8,000 and this is what he was awarded.

25-75   In his High Court action, the company succeeded in their argument that the compensatory award should be set off against damages for wrongful dismissal. However, the Court of Appeal overturned this decision. The compensatory award could only be set off against damages if it could be proved that the plaintiff would be obtaining compensation under two heads for the same loss. That could not be the case. In reducing the compensatory award from £100,700 to the then statutory maximum of £8,000 the tribunal could not allocate the £8,000 to any particular period of loss. Accordingly, the defendant company could not show that the £8,000 already awarded by the tribunal or any part of it was attributable to loss of earnings during the six-month notice period. It should not, therefore, be set off against damages for wrongful dismissal. This decision also accorded with the justice of the case in the view of the Vice Chancellor, Sir Nicholas Browne-Wilkinson. Had the defendant company given Mr O'Laoire his proper notice, but still unfairly dismissed him, he would have been paid his salary for the notice period, or pay in lieu, and would have received the maximum compensatory award of £8,000. "In my judgement, the defendants' breach in failing to pay the plaintiff his salary during the notice period cannot put them in a better position than they would have been in had they performed the contract properly."

Pensions and monies received under insurance scheme

25-76   If, following a wrongful dismissal, the dismissed employee becomes entitled to payments from a pension scheme such payments are not to be deducted from his claim for damages for wrongful dismissal. Nor will payments received as a result of insurance such as a mortgage protection policy, be deductible. The position seems to be the same as with the assessment of compensation in discrimination and unfair dismissal cases.

In *Hopkins v. Norcross plc* [1994] I.R.L.R. 18 CA, Mr Hopkins was wrongfully dismissed two years short of the normal retiring age of 60 as defined by his employer's pension scheme. His contract of employment provided that he was to be employed up to the age of 60. Nonetheless, under the pension scheme he became entitled to an immediate pension following his dismissal. Mr Hopkins brought a claim for wrongful dismissal. The issue which was considered by the Court of Appeal was whether the pension payments had to be deducted in the assessment of damages. It was argued by the company that the case was distinguishable from *Parry v. Cleaver* [1970] A.C. 1 HL, where the House of Lords held that pension payments are not deductible from damages for loss of earnings in personal injury cases. The Court of Appeal rejected this proposition: "The fact that this was a claim for wrongful dismissal rather than personal injury was no basis for drawing a distinction." Counsel for the company submitted that the assessment of damages for breach of contract was different from that applying to tort. "I can see no ground for supposing that that is a relevant distinction. There is a faint suggestion in the American re-statement that the rule for damages in contract might be different from that in tort in this context; but I can see no authority for that proposition in English law, and no grounds for supposing that it is the case" (Staughton L.J.). For further commentary see paras 16–13 to 16–17.

Similarly, the state pension received by an employee wrongfully dismissed who is over state retirement age should not be deducted in the assessment of damages. This is received as an entitlement.

Reduction for accelerated payment

25–77   Just as with the receipt of compensation for unfair dismissal or for unlawful discrimination, payment of damages for wrongful dismissal can result in accelerated payment to the dismissed employee. Generally, where the damages claim relates to a wrongfully dismissed employee who has lost the benefit of contractual notice of a few weeks or even a few months, by the time the tribunal hears the claim the damages period will already have passed and therefore no issue of accelerated payment arises. If, however, the employee has lost the benefit of a long notice period, such as a year, or a substantial part of a fixed term contract, then some account may have to be taken of the fact that the employee is receiving damages earlier than he would have received his pay and benefits during the notice period or the remainder of the fixed term.

In *Shove v. Downs Surgical plc* [1984] I.R.L.R. 17 HC, Mr Shove was wrongfully dismissed with just over three weeks' notice when he was entitled under his contract to 30 calendar months' notice. The case came before the High Court some 20 months after his dismissal. In these circumstances, with more than seven months of the damages period still in the future, the parties agreed that the damages should be discounted by seven per cent to take account of accelerated payment "and other contingencies".

Note the reference to other contingencies. It may be that the employee would in any event have resigned (the notice period may be shorter for the employee) or he may have died before the end of the notice period. This may be reflected in a reduction to compensation. The court may use the percentage chance approach considered in relation to discrimination compensation at paras 15–58 to 15–76. However, in a wrongful dismissal case the damages period will rarely be long enough to justify the use of a multiplier to calculate future loss. For guidance on this approach, see paras 13–86 to 13–92.

CHAPTER 26

Fairness at Work and other Developments

26–01 The long awaited Fairness at Work White Paper was published in May 1998. The White Paper contained three sets of proposals. These were described as "New Rights for Individuals", "Collective Rights" and "Family Friendly Policies". In the section dealing with rights for individuals, two key proposals were included relating to unfair dismissal.

Qualifying period for employment

26–02 First, it is proposed that the qualifying period of employment be reduced from two years to one year. This would reinstate the rule which applied up until 1985. At the same time, the case of *Secretary of State for Employment ex p. Seymour-Smith* [1995] I.R.L.R. 464 has been referred to the European Court on the question of whether the two year qualifying period is contrary to the Equal Treatment Directive 76/207 because it has a disproportionate affect on women, fewer of whom remain in employment for two years. At the time of going to print, the Advocate General's Opinion had been published. Unfortunately, this shed little light on the issue and appeared to be based on a misunderstanding of UK law. Although the Advocate General decided that the two-year rule was unlawful, his unsound reasoning leaves open the question of whether the full court will follow his Opinion.

Removal of the cap on compensation

26–03 The more controversial proposal in the White Paper is the removal of the cap on compensation for unfair dismissal. This is what the White Paper says:

> "Tribunals must be seen to be fair to both parties. Where a tribunal finds that individuals have been unfairly dismissed, they should receive a proper remedy. Tribunals issue very few re-employment orders, so the amount of compensation for unfair dismissal is very important. Although many awards are well below the current limit on compensation, which the Government has recently increased, the existence of a limit prevents some individuals from being fully compensated for their loss. The likelihood of proper compensation being awarded should also encourage employers to put proper voluntary systems in place. The current cap on compensation for unfair dismissal, which has steadily fallen in real terms, provides no such incentive. The Government therefore proposes to abolish the maximum limit on such awards. Abolition in sex discrimination claims has not led to a significant rise in the number of cases and although race discrimination cases have risen, these are relatively few in number."

Since the publication of the White Paper, employers' organisations such as the CBI have argued against the lifting of the cap on compensation. At the time of going to print press reports suggest that the Government might have second thoughts.

One alternative option would be for the statutory maximum sum to be raised substantially. The CBI, in its submission to the DTI on the White Paper, has proposed that the cap be lifted to £40,000. This would still significantly benefit many of those who currently fail to obtain an adequate remedy because their compensation is capped. It is worth noting that since the publication of the White Paper, Margaret Beckett M.P. has been replaced by Peter Mandelson M.P. as Secretary of State at the Department of Trade and Industry. This change may result in a more pro-business emphasis in the final legislation. This solution would, however, maintain the inconsistency between the treatment of compensation for unfair dismissal on the one hand and unlawful discrimination, where no statutory cap exists on the other.

26–04 If the Government's proposals to remove the statutory maximum compensatory award proceeds, it is likely to be the summer of 1999 at the earliest before it is implemented. The Government has indicated that such a change would be dealt with by way of primary legislation along with all the other reforms proposed in the Fairness at Work White Paper. If the cap on the compensatory award is lifted, one result is likely to be that highly paid executives whose contracts are terminated could decide that it is worthwhile pursuing a claim for unfair dismissal. At present it is unlikely to be worth such employees pursuing a tribunal claim with the maximum capped at £12,000. A wrongful dismissal action in the County or High Court is likely to be the most attractive route at present. If, however, the cap is lifted the possibility of unlimited compensation going beyond the period of loss in a wrongful dismissal action may make the tribunal unfair dismissal route very attractive.

It is important to note that the lifting of the cap (or raising it substantially) will not mean that the assessment of compensation for unfair dismissal will necessarily equate to the assessment of compensation for unlawful discrimination. Unlawful sex, race or disability discrimination results in compensation assessed in the same way as damages in tort. The complainant must be put in the position he would have been in but for the unlawful conduct (see para. 13–24). However, with unfair dismissal, the compensatory award is such amount as the tribunal considers "just and equitable in all the circumstances" having regard to loss sustained. There is no proposal to change this statutory formula for the assessment of compensation once the cap is lifted. The "just and equitable" test will still apply. What is uncertain is how tribunals will apply this test with the cap lifted or substantially raised. We already know of tribunals' reluctance to award future loss covering more than a year. Assessment of compensation which is "just and equitable" is not an exact science. How this will work with unlimited compensation is at present unclear.

26–05 It should also be noted that lifting of the cap on compensation for unlawful discrimination has not resulted in a vast number of high awards. The Ministry of Defence pregnancy dismissal cases led to a number of substantial awards but the circumstances of these were highly unusual, given that many of the women involved had lost years of fixed period engagements with very generous pension benefits. Since these cases there has been a number of significant awards, but still a large number of cases where the award is less than £12,000, the statutory cap for unfair dismissal. What is harder to estimate is the impact of the lifting of the cap on the level of settlements achieved before the case gets to the tribunal. Fear of a substantial award in the tribunal is bound to encourage employers to contemplate settlement at higher levels than previously. It could also lead to a further growth in the use of compromise agreements to protect the employer from a potentially substantial claim. From the employee's point of view, there will be a more difficult judgement to make on whether to accept the offer of a compromise agreement. Good advice will be very important. Another consequence of raising or removal of the cap on unfair dismissal compensation would be an increased emphasis on the duty to mitigate loss. Evidence of efforts to mitigate loss became a central feature of many of the MOD pregnancy dismissal cases (see Chapter 19 for commentary).

Limits on additional and special awards

26–06 The Fairness at Work White Paper also raises the possibility of the limits of additional and special awards for unfair dismissal being removed. For commentary on these awards see paras 8–39 to 8–61. The White Paper states:

> "There are minimum and maximum limits on both additional and special awards. It is therefore possible to receive an award without having suffered any loss. On the other hand, the upper limit may act as a deterrent to someone exercising a legitimate role or right. This issue has surfaced recently in the context of the Public Interest Disclosure [Act] which is aimed at protecting "whistle-blowers".
>
> A majority of the respondents to the consultation exercise on [that Act] including the CBI and the TUC, took the view that there should be no limit on compensation awarded under [that Act]. The Government's view is that it would wish the compensation to be in line with other employment rights. The Government has therefore proposed that awards made under the Public Interest Disclosure [Act] should attract a higher special award [as opposed to an additional award]. An alternative approach to special awards would be to allow tribunals to award aggravated damages in these limited circumstances. The Government would welcome views."

Index-linking limits on compensation

26–07 Other limits on compensation, such as for the basic award and redundancy pay (by way of a limit to a week's pay used in the calculation), are currently reviewed annually. The Fairness at Work White Paper proposed the index-linking of such limits, subject to a maximum rate. This, obviously, would not apply to the compensatory award limit if it is lifted as proposed.

Voluntary arbitration

26–08 Note also the imminent introduction of a new voluntary arbitration scheme for unfair dismissal cases. The legislative basis for the new scheme is the Employment Rights (Dispute Resolution) Act 1998. It is proposed to be introduced in the spring of 1999. The Fairness at Work White Paper commented that the Government "hopes that the voluntary arbitration alternative provided by ACAS will create a change of culture so that individuals who have been dismissed unfairly are more likely to get their jobs back". How successful this scheme will be is unclear. There will be no appeal against the outcome of the arbitration.

Appendices

APPENDIX A

Non-statutory lump sum redundancy payments   SP1/94

(The Revenue's practice has been revised following the decision of the House of Lords in *Mairs v. Haughey* [1993] S.T.C. 569, and this statement replaces the Statement of Practice 1/81).

1.   Section 579(1) and section 580(3) Income and Corporation Taxes Act 1988 (ICTA) provide that statutory redundancy payments shall be exempt from income tax under Schedule E, with the exception of any liability under section 148 of that Act.

2.   Lump sum payments made under a non-statutory scheme, in addition to, or instead of statutory redundancy pay, will also be liable to income tax only under section 148 ICTA provided they are genuinely made solely on account of redundancy as defined in section 81 Employment Protection (Consolidation) Act 1978. This will be so whether the scheme is a standing one which forms part of the terms on which the employees give their services or whether it is an ad hoc scheme devised to meet a specific situation such as the imminent closure of a particular factory.

3.   However, payments made under a non-statutory scheme which are not genuinely made to compensate for loss of employment through redundancy may be liable to tax in full. In particular, payments which are, in reality, a form of terminal bonus will be chargeable to income tax under Schedule E as emoluments from the employment under section 19(1)1 ICTA. Payments made for meeting production targets or doing extra work in the period leading up to redundancy are examples of such terminal bonuses. Payments conditional on continued service in the employment for a time will also represent terminal bonuses if calculated by reference to any additional period served following issue of the redundancy notice.

4.   The Revenue is concerned to distinguish between payments under non-statutory schemes which are genuinely made to compensate for loss of employment through redundancy and payments which are made as a reward for services in the employment or more generally for having acted as or having been an employee. As arrangements for redundancy can often be complex and provide for a variety of payments, it follows that each scheme must be considered on its own facts. The Revenue's practice, in these circumstances, is to allow employers to submit proposed schemes to their Inspectors of Taxes for advance clearance.

5.   An employer or any other person operating a redundancy scheme, who wishes to be satisfied that lump sum payments under a scheme will be accepted as liable to tax only under section 148 ICTA should submit the full facts to the Inspector for consideration. Applications for clearance should be made in writing and should be accompanied by the scheme document together with the text of any intended letter to employees which explains its terms.

APPENDIX B

Ex gratia awards made on termination of an office or employment by retirement or death
SP13/91

(1) An ex-gratia payment made on or in connection with an employee's death or retirement from an office or employment is a "relevant benefit" as defined in section 612 ICTA 1988. (But this term does not include payments made solely because of death or disablement by accident or severance payments on redundancy or loss of office.)

(2) An ex-gratia payment is made under a retirement benefits scheme if the decision to make the payment involves an arrangement. Self evidently, there will be an "arrangement" if the payment flows from any prior formal or informal understanding with the employee. But the term "arrangement" in this context goes wider and includes any system, plan, pattern or policy connected with the payment of a gratuity. Some examples are:

a. a decision at a meeting to make an ex-gratia payment on an employee's retirement; or

b. where, say, a personnel manager makes an ex-gratia payment under a delegated authority or on the basis of some outline structure or policy; or

c. where it is common practice for an employer to make an ex-gratia payment to a particular class of employee.

(3) There may be some exceptional situations where a gratuity is not paid under an "arrangement". The position in individual cases can be determined only on their facts. If an employer is unsure whether a gratuity is paid under an arrangement advice may be sought from the Superannuation Funds Office at Lynwood Road, Thames Ditton, Surrey, KT7 0DP. Any such request should give full details of the circumstances in which the gratuity is to be paid.

(4) The following paragraphs explain the tax treatment of these ex-gratia arrangements. All statutory references are to the Income and Corporation Taxes Act 1988.

Pensions

(5) An ex-gratia pension to an employee or the employee's spouse or dependant will be chargeable to income tax under Schedule E whether or not paid under a tax approved scheme.

Lump sums

(6) Lump sum relevant benefits are not taxable when paid under an approved scheme. In the past, approval has been given only to contractual schemes. But approval may now be given to certain ex-gratia lump sum payments in the circumstances described in paragraph (7); or payments may be treated as from an approved scheme where paragraph (8) applies.

(7) An employer may apply for tax approval of an arrangement to pay an ex-gratia lump sum relevant benefit. In order to qualify for approval, the payment must:

(a) be the only lump sum relevant benefit potentially payable in respect of the employment; in other words the employee should not be a member of either of the following—

   (i) a retirement benefits scheme that is either approved or is being considered for approval; or

   (ii) a Relevant Statutory Scheme (as defined in Section 611(A), **unless** the payment is made on retirement and the scheme provides benefits only on death in service; and

(b) satisfy the normal requirements for tax approval of a retirement benefits scheme (which are described in the booklet Practice Notes on Approval of Occupational Pension Schemes (IR 12)). These include a limit on the amount of lump sum payable. On retirement, for example, the limit is 3/80ths of final salary for each year of service with an employer (up to 40 years), while on death it is normally two times salary, though it can be as high as four times salary.

Details on how to apply for approval may be obtained from the Superannuation Funds Office. Where a payment is made before confirmation of approval is received the employer should deduct tax in accordance with the PAYE system. If and when approval is granted the employee will be able to claim repayment of the tax deducted.

(8) In addition, the Inland Revenue will accept that an arrangement to pay a single ex-gratia lump sum relevant benefit to a particular employee need not be submitted for approval where:

(a) the condition at paragraph (7)(a) above is satisfied, and

(b)   the total of all lump sum payments from all associated employers (as defined in Section 590A(3)) made in connection with the retirement or death does not exceed one-twelfth of the earnings cap prescribed under Section 590C for the year of assessment in which the payments are made. For the year ended 5 April 1994 the limit is £6,250 (£6,250 for 1992/93 and £5,950 for 1991/92).

In these cases the payments will be treated as from an approved retirement benefits scheme. They will therefore not be chargeable to income tax and so need not be reported by an employer to its tax office.

(9)   An ex-gratia lump sum relevant benefit not falling within paragraphs (7) or (8) above, will constitute a non-approved retirement benefits scheme. It will be charged to tax under Schedule E (under either Section 19(1)1 or Section 596(A) on the recipient for the year of assessment in which the payment is made. When making such payments an employer should deduct tax in accordance with the PAYE system.

Payments for redundancy or termination of employment caused by accident
(10)   An ex-gratia payment made to an employee on severance of an employment due to redundancy or loss of office, or because of death of disability due to an accident, is not affected by this Statement of Practice where the arrangements for making the payment are designed solely to meet such a situation. Nor will the tax treatment of any such payment be affected by the payment of early retirement benefits under other arrangements (such as the employer's approved pension scheme). The taxation of such lump sum payments is not therefore effected by this Statement of Practice. In particular, genuine redundancy payments within the terms of Statement of Practice 1/1981 will continue to be taxed under Section 148 (subject to the exemptions in Section 188).

Inland Revenue Press Release, October 31, 1991

Ex-gratia payments on retirement or death: statement of practice

The Inland Revenue have today issued a statement of practice (SP13/91) explaining a change of practice on ex-gratia payments made on retirement or death.

The statement explains that *pensions* payable under ex-gratia arrangements are always taxable; but in certain circumstances *lump sum* payments may be made tax-free. The tax treatment described in the statement will be applied to payments made after today. A copy of the statement is [reproduced below].

NOTES
1   In the past most ex-gratia lump sum payments made on termination of an office or employment have been regarded as chargeable to income tax under TA 1988 s.148 (subject to the exemptions in TA 1988 s.188) the "golden handshake" rules, under which the first £30,000 of any payment is exempt from tax.
2   Even where payments were made because of the retirement or death of an employee they were not treated as being within the separate tax rules for payments by pension schemes. But legal advice has been received that this treatment was incorrect. In March the Superannuation Funds Office (who administer the pension scheme tax approval rules) issued a memorandum amending their published guidance accordingly [Joint Office Memorandum 104].
3   The statement of practice explains which ex-gratia payments are subject to the pension scheme tax rules, and sets out the procedures employers should follow in respect of them. In brief, ex-gratia payments made on retirement or death will in future normally come within the pension scheme tax rules. Such payments are chargeable to income tax, except *lump sum* payments from an *approved* scheme which are tax-free.
4   In the future, the Superannuation Funds Office will be prepared to approve ex-gratia schemes—until now only contractual schemes have been approved. Where a scheme is approved, the change of practice means that lump sum payments will be tax-free instead of taxable under the "golden handshake" rules. But where a scheme is not approved, lump sum payments will be taxable in full, and not qualify for the £30,000 exemption under the "golden handshake" rules.
5   The tax treatment of ex-gratia termination payments made *other than* on retirement or death is unchanged. Unless such payments are taxable as pay, they will continue to be taxable under the "golden handshake" rules.

6   When making taxable lump sum payments of any kind an employer should deduct tax under the PAYE system. Employees should consult their PAYE tax office if they are in any doubt about the deduction of tax from any particular lump sum payment.

Appendix C

Inland Revenue Correspondence

Reproduced from ICAEW, Faculty of Taxation Technical Release TR851

Letter from the Inland Revenue
"The Statement (SP13/91) follows an announcement made in March by the Superannuation Funds Office in Memorandum 104. This explained that an arrangement to pay ex-gratia relevant benefits to an employee would constitute a retirement benefits scheme. As a result such payments fall within the pension scheme tax rules instead of the 'golden and shake' rules as has hitherto been the case.

It is, however, important to be clear that the only ex-gratia payments affected are those which come within the definition of relevant benefits in Section 612(1) Taxes Act 1988. In broad terms this covers pensions, lump sums, gratuities and similar benefits which are, or will be, given:
- where a person retires or dies;
- in anticipation of retirement;
- after a person has retired or died (if the reason for payment is in recognition of past service); or
- as compensation for any change in the conditions of a continuing employment (as distinct from compensation on *loss* of employment).

Disability benefits (whether regular payments or lump sums) are, however, not relevant benefits if they are payable solely because of an employee's death or disablement by accident. For this purpose an accident does not have to be workplace related. For example, an ex-gratia lump sum payable because of an employer's death while travelling would not be a relevant benefit. Such a payment will continue to be chargeable to income tax under Section 148 Taxes Act 1988 (subject to the exemptions in Section 188).

Although the list of relevant benefits is wide ranging, what is beyond doubt is that it does not cover severance payments on genuine redundancy or loss of office. In this regard we would not distinguish between directors or senior executives and other employees. In each case, provided the reason for the ex-gratia payment is to compensate for loss of employment the payments will *not* be relevant benefits.

In considering this issue we will be looking only at the reason for the ex-gratia payment; no account will normally be taken of payments under other arrangements. For example, if, on being made redundant, the employee is given early retirement benefits from an approved pension scheme, that will not affect the nature of the ex-gratia redundancy payments.

Having described those ex-gratia payments which are outside the Statement of Practice, it may be worthwhile to explain which payments are within its scope. They obviously must be relevant benefits—and so will not have been paid as a result of redundancy or loss of office. The most common situations will be:
- ex-gratia payments made on retirement or death by an employer who has no tax-approved pension scheme;
- ex-gratia payments made on retirement or death to an employee who is also entitled to benefits under a tax-approved pension scheme (this will probably be the case where the benefits are taken at the scheme's specified retirement age or on voluntary early retirement);
- other ex-gratia payments (not being for reasons of redundancy or compensation for loss of office) which are made in anticipation of retirement.

It is likely that the last of these situations could be in point where an ex-gratia payment was made shortly before the employee was planning to retire. It is an area where we would need to look very carefully at the facts before deciding on what the appropriate tax treatment might be.

The Statement of Practice modifies the guidance given in memorandum 104. It explains that the Superannuation Funds Office are now prepared to consider approving an arrangement to pay ex-gratia lump sum relevant benefits where no tax approved pension arrangements exist for the employee.

But tax approval of such an arrangement is not considered appropriate where the employee is already a member of a tax approved pension plan. Nonetheless, where the benefits under the approved plan fall short of the normal tax approval limits, the employer could (instead of making an ex-gratia payment to the employee or his dependants) pay a special contribution to the approved scheme so that the benefit it pays may be increased (within the tax approval limits).

Paragraph 8 of the Statement of Practice describes a work saving measure for employers who make small (about £6,000 in the current tax year) ex-gratia payments on their employees' retirement or death. The main condition is normally that the employee should not have been a member of the employer's tax approved occupational pension scheme. In such cases, the lump sums may be paid tax-free without applying for formal approval of the arrangement.

I hope you find this further explanation helpful; its contents may be circulated to your members. The Superannuation Funds Office will shortly be issuing further guidance on the procedures for applying for approval of arrangements for paying ex-gratia lump sum relevant benefits."

"From the Law Society
When Statement of Practice SP 13/91 was issued in October 1991, it was read by members of the Law Society's Revenue Law Committee with interest although we had at that time no particular points to raise.

Having considered the matter further, we do feel that there is a case for a more general rule to be applied where payment is made to an employee on—
(a) his or her resignation in circumstances which amount to constructive dismissal, and
(b) his or her resignation before normal retirement age where the employee intends to seek other full-time employment.
We are aware that you have expressed the view that the tax treatment of any payment made would depend upon the precise circumstances of each case and an application to the appropriate tax office would have to be made in order to obtain a ruling.

Our view is that payment of a lump sum in such circumstances should fall within the 'golden handshake' provisions. We believe that it would be very helpful if a test, based upon motive and circumstances could be developed in order to eliminate unnecessary uncertainties in this area.

From the Inland Revenue
I do not think that it is possible to give hard and fast rules of universal application in the second instance you cite; that of an employee resigning with the intention of seeking further employment. Whether an individual continues to work, or makes him or herself available for work, after employment is terminated is simply a factor which we may take account of in determining whether or not termination of the employment was a 'retirement'.

It is, like the age of the individual concerned, something to be weighed in making an overall assessment of the circumstances in which termination of employment occurred and the reason why the ex gratia payment was made. An ex gratia payment made to a man moving on to further full-time employment in his middle years will obviously not be made 'on or in anticipation of retirement'. However, an ex gratia payment to a man of older years who has no other full-time employment in prospect could fall on the other side of the line.

As to the other point that you raised, I think it fair to say that, provided the situation has not been contrived for the purpose of obtaining favourable tax treatment, then termination of employment in circumstances which amount to unfair dismissal, whether that comes about because the employee is sacked or is forced to resign, will not constitute 'retirement' for the purposes of Statement of Practice SP 13/91. This situation would be covered by para 10 of the Statement of Practice, ie, the payment made to the employee comes to him as compensation for loss of office and not on or in anticipation of retirement. Subject, therefore, to the Revenue being satisfied that the lump sum payment was indeed made for unfair dismissal and not merely given that label for tax purposes. I can confirm that the 'golden handshake' provisions would apply thereto: *Law Society's Gazette,* 7 October 1992 p 42".

Letter from Faculty of Taxation, ICAEW
"It is appreciated that each case must to an extend depend on its facts, but we seek clarification as to whether the Revenue would normally seek to contend that a payment is made in connection with an employee's retirement in any of the following circumstances:
(*a*)   A person who has worked for the company for 20 years leaves at age 45 to take a senior executive position in another company.
(*b*)   A long-service employee leaves to take a senior executive position in another company at the age of 60.
(*c*)   A division of the company is sold and the 55 year old manager responsible for running it leaves to take a job with the purchaser.
(*d*)   A person in his 50's has a heart attack and is advised by his doctor to leave and seek a less stressful position.
(*e*)   An employee aged 35 is involved in an accident and suffers disabilities that make him unable to continue with his job.
(*f*)   An employee aged 50 leaves to take a job nearer home to be able to nurse her aged parents.

Revenue response
We would not accept that the issue last year of SP13/91 and Memorandum 111 has created uncertainty about the tax treatment of ex gratia payments made on the termination of a person's employment. Whether, in a particular case, the termination of employment constitutes 'retirement' must depend on the facts of the case, as you acknowledge. So am afraid the Statement of Practice and Memorandum could not lay down an exhaustive list of criteria which would define 'retirement'. But we do believe they provide useful guidelines on our approach in this difficult area of the law.

We can provide some indication of how we would view each of the hypothetical scenarios you postulate though, again, with the caveat that actual cases would need to be decided on their own facts. All statutory references are to the Income and Corporation Taxes Act 1988.

(*a*)   A senior executive changing jobs at age 45, obviously as part of his or her normal working career, is not retirement. Any payment would fall within section 148.
(*b*)   This is a borderline case which would depend very much on the precise circumstances. But, given the age, this might well be regarded as retirement, despite the new appointment. Any payment might well fall within section 596A.
(*c*)   The action of the employee does not look to be consistent with retirement but with maximising his opportunities to continue working until normal retirement age. So any payment would fall within section 148.
(*d*)   The circumstances set out may well be viewed as retirement. But if the ex gratia payment made is purely consolation for the loss of health which results in the premature termination of employment, it would not be regarded as made in connection with retirement. So section 148 would apply.
(*e*)   As paragraph 10 of SP13/81 indicates, a lump sum paid on retirement solely by reason of disability from an accident is excluded from the definition of a 'relevant benefit' in section 612. Section 148 would apply.
(*f*)   This again is a borderline area. The example described probably would not be regarded as retirement bearing in mind the age of the employee, and the fact that she obtained further work. But the decision might well go the other way of the employee left to nurse a relative without seeking a further job, especially if she was nearer the normal retirement age for her job."

Appendix D

Section 313 ICTA: termination payments made in settlement of employment claims [4 April 1996] SP3/96

1.   Section 313 Income and Corporation Taxes Act 1988 imposes a charge under Schedule E on payments made to individuals for undertakings, given in connection with an employment, which restrict their conduct or activities.

2.   A financial settlement relating to the termination of an employment may contain terms whereby the employee agrees to accept the termination package in full and final settlement of his or her claims relating to the employment, and/or may expressly provide that the employee should not commence or, if already commenced, should discontinue legal proceedings in respect of those claims. These may relate to claims at common law arising from the contract of employment or to claims arising under employment protection or other legislation. The settlement, therefore, seeks to avoid legal dispute or proceedings, for example before a court or an industrial tribunal, in connection with those rights. The termination settlement may also reaffirm undertakings about the individual's conduct or activity after termination which formed part of the terms on which the employment was taken up.

The Inland Revenue will accept that no chargeable value will be attributed under Section 313(2) to such undertakings by an employee or former employee.

3.   But this does not affect the application of Section 313 to sums that are attributable to other restrictive undertakings which individuals give in relation to an employment, whether these undertakings are contained in a job termination settlement or otherwise.

APPENDIX E

Extra statutory concessions: termination payments and legal costs A81

1. In taking legal action to recover compensation for loss of employment, employees may succeed in recovering from the former employer some or all of their legal costs. This may occur either because the employee is successful in the Court action or because a settlement is reached which provides that costs be reimbursed.

2. In the Inland Revenue's view any payments made by way of recovery of costs are assessable to income tax as is the compensation to which the former employer has agreed or is obliged to pay. The charge to tax arises under Section 148 Income and Corporation Taxes Act 1988. This applies to payments made directly or indirectly in connection with the termination of the holding of an office or of employment.

3. No deduction is strictly allowable for the legal costs which the former employee or office holder may incur in pursuing the former employer for wrongful dismissal.

4. However, the Board of Inland Revenue have decided that *in the following circumstances* tax will not be charged on payments of costs to the former employee or office holder.

5. In cases where the dispute is settled without recourse to the Courts, no charge will be imposed on payments made by the former employer—
- direct to the former employee's solicitor **and**
- in full or partial discharge of the solicitor's bill of costs incurred by the employee only in connection with the termination of his or her employment **and**
  under a specific term in the settlement agreement providing for that payment.

6. In cases where the dispute goes to Court, no charge will be imposed on payments of costs made by the former employer, even where these are made direct to the employee, in accordance with a Court order (whether this is made following judgment or compromise of the action).

7. This concession applies only to legal costs. It does not apply to other professional costs e.g. accountancy fees nor to legal costs incurred over and above the amount which the former employer may pay in the circumstances mentioned. Inspectors of Taxes may ask to see documentary evidence in support of a claim that a payment by a former employer meets the necessary requirements as outlined above.

Appendix F

Extract from the Law Society Gazette, November 3, 1993 relating to taxation of legal costs

"The Revenue has subsequently confirmed in correspondence that the requirement for the costs to be incurred 'only' in connection with the termination of employment does not mean that the solicitors' bill must relate exclusively to costs so incurred but the concession would only apply to those costs and it follows that accordingly, they should be clearly identifiable in the solicitors' bill".

Letter from the Inland Revenue to the Faculty of Taxation, ICAEW, December 1993
"I confirm that the Concession applies only to legal costs which the employee recovers from the employer. (There is, of course, no question of any parallel relief for costs, legal or otherwise, which an employee has to bear himself.) When the legislation under which termination payments are charged to tax was in its infancy, doubts were expressed as to whether awards of such costs by Courts were within the scope of the legislation. A practice of not charging tax on awards of costs built up and was later extended to reimbursement of legal costs of a similar nature where the matter did not reach Court. (We were subsequently advised that reimbursed costs were strictly taxable and the published Concession is recognition that not taxing them is a departure from the statutory position.)

The Concession is not directed at the expenses which an employee may incur in negotiating the amount of compensation for the loss of his or her employment. They have never qualified for relief. Rather, the object of the Concession is to enable us to continue not to tax sums recovered in respect of substantial expenses that may be incurred when enforcement of the claims through the Courts has to be considered. Advice on the enforcement of a legal claim will properly be the province of a solicitor rather than an accountant or other professional. However, we would accept that where, exceptionally, the employee's solicitor found it necessary to consult other professionals for the specific claim, the cost to the solicitor would represent a disbursement and would, therefore, as legal costs, be within the Concession. Similarly if a dispute proceeded to Court, we would accept that any part of the Court proceedings, which included the expenses of expert professional witnesses were legal costs and, therefore, within the Concession."

APPENDIX G

Contributions to retirement benefit schemes on termination of employment [10 March 1981]
SP2/81

1. Where, as part of an arrangement relating to the termination of an employment, an agreement is reached between the parties for the employer to make a special contribution into an approved retirement benefit scheme or an approved personal pension scheme in order to provide benefits for the employee, the Inland Revenue will not seek to charge such a payment under s.148 ICTA 1988 (s.187 ICTA 1970) provided that the retirement benefits are within the limits and in the form described by the rules of the scheme.

2. Similarly, they will not seek to charge the payment under s.148 ICTA 1988 (s.187 ICTA 1970) where the employer purchases an annuity for his former employee from a Life Office, so long as the transaction is approved under Chapter 1, Part 14, ICTA 1988.

Notes—The text of SP 2/81 above is as it appears in IR131 (1996).

Appendix H

Payments on account of disability resulting in cessation of employment
[3 November 1981]   **SP10/81**

1. Section 148 ICTA 1988 provides for the taxation of those payments on retirement or removal from an office or employment which otherwise are not chargeable to tax. Section 188(1)(a) excludes from the ambit of Section 148 any payment "made on account of injury to or disability of the holder of an office or employment".

2. The practice of the Inland Revenue has in the past been governed by the view that "disability" used in juxtaposition with the word "injury" meant a loss of physical or mental health with which a person was afflicted suddenly at a particular time and which rendered him physically or mentally incapable of carrying out the duties which he had previously performed. A gradual decline in physical or mental disability caused by chronic illness culminating in incapacity to perform the duties of an office or employment was not regarded as "disability".

3. As a result of a decision given by the Special Commissioners on 6 January 1981 the Revenue reconsidered its practice and now accepts that "disability" covers not only a condition resulting from a sudden affliction but also continuing incapacity to perform the duties of an office or employment arising out of the culmination of a process of deterioration of physical or mental health caused by chronic illness.

Notes—The text of SP 10/81 above is as it appears in IR131 (1996).

APPENDIX I

Inland Revenue: Technical Guidance
[ICAEW Technical Release TR 830, April 1991]

TR 818 issued in October 1990 set out the text of a letter dated 18 October 1990 from the Inland Revenue regarding their practice in responding to requests for information or guidance. The following sets out extracts from subsequent correspondence clarifying certain aspects of this practice.

Extracts of a letter from the Institute to the Inland Revenue
Committee members and others have questioned the extent to which, in practice, there will continue to be some limitation on the guidance available. Perhaps I can explain this by an analysis of the new arrangements as I understand them.
Barry Pollard's letter of 26 April 1986 said:

> "our Technical Division will, as regards enquiries from tax practitioners, in future be able to respond only to those involving recent legislation and changes in practice."

Your letter refers to:

> "requests for guidance on the Revenue's interpretation of ... recent legislation, statements of practice and other published information, but also in cases where there is a major public interest in developments in an industry or in the financial sector but, where the operation of the law is uncertain."

It goes on to refer to the continuing practice to be adopted by local inspectors as regards particular cases and states that neither Head Office nor local inspectors will advise on the arrangement of a person's own affairs.

Finally, the letter refers to the need to have regard to the principles set out by *Bingham* LJ and sets out the information which the enquirer must make available.

Our first concern is that the first part of your letter quoted above (up to "published information") effectively restates the area in which Barry Pollard said that guidance would be continued: the second part ("but also ... uncertain") represents the relaxation now made. This second part is, however, limited to those areas in which there is a "major public interest" in an industry or in the financial sector. On reconsideration, we have difficulty in seeing precisely what you have in mind here, and in particular whether this will in fact represent a meaningful extension to the assistance the Revenue currently lives. We should appreciate your comments.

Our second area of concern is the extent to which the pre 1986 practice is further limited by the need to have regard to the "Bingham principles" if the enquirer wishes to rely on the Revenue guidance (which will naturally always be the case). We do not dissent from conditions (a) to (d) (which I think are intended to summarise these principles as set out on p. 110 of the judgment), but the need to give the tax district and reference seems to make it clear that all enquiries are limited to specific cases rather than points of general application, even if they are of "major public interest".

There is, of course, what appears to be a relaxation in the paragraph towards the end of your letter which states "There may occasionally be cases ... is otherwise concerned". It seems that in such cases, as implied in the last sentence, the information outlined above would not be required, since the response is to be informal and non-binding. This seems to be more in the nature of the pre-1986 practice, although it appears to be confined to an interpretation of new legislation with the expectation that it is limited to views sought by representative bodies, although we are not aware that there has been any reluctance by the Revenue in this respect since 1986.

It is, incidentally, not clear whether "new legislation" means the most recent Finance Act or whether it extends to earlier, but recent, legislation, and whether the paragraph is intended to apply only infrequently as implied by the words "There may occasionally be cases...".

I would agree that guidance of this kind should not be regarded as tantamount to legislation, or even a Statement of Practice, and it may seem inappropriate to subject it to the above analysis, but it is a matter of considerable importance to our members.

Extract of a reply from the Inland Revenue
I have delayed my response to your letter of 8 January until I could obtain comments from my colleagues on their expertise so far in handling, enquiries for guidance since my letter to you (and the other representative bodies) of 24 October. I am glad to say that they reported little difficulty so far. In one respect their responses were varied as I had expected. As I said in my letter, we had found that some parts of Head Office had found it possible to give guidance on a less restrictive basis than Barry Pollard had foreshadowed in April 1986. So while in many areas the practice set out in my letter has led to an extension of the types of case in which guidance has been given, in other areas it has led to little change. But what it does mean is first, that there should now be a consistent approach across Head Office, and second that practitioners and their representative bodies should know what the position is.

I find it difficult to explain what I meant by "a major public interest in developments in an industry or in the financial sector" without repeating those words: broadly, however, while I would expect it to exclude most transactions which any company was contemplating, I would expect it to include an industrial or financial development likely to be of importance to the country generally, going well beyond the circumstances of the particular company in question; in appropriate circumstances it might cover matters such as developments in the oil industry with consequences for the development of the North Sea; novel and major engineering projects; the application of the capital allowances legislation to projects involving leading-edge technology; and of course major issues arising from Government policy. But of course in any individual case the interpretation of my letter must be left to the individual who is responsible for handling the matter: it is, I think, self evident that not every transaction in the area covered by this list would be likely to be of major public interest, but equally nor anything not listed above be necessarily excluded. And, as I made clear, we are not covering tax dodges, nor are we setting out to offer an alternative service to that provided by your members in giving guidance (let alone advising) on matters which should be within their competence or that of their legal advisers.

As to your second point, in the large majority of cases what practitioners want is guidance on our understanding of the application of the law in its relation to a specific case. To say anything in such circumstances without knowing which was the case involved would be rash to say the least. If we are going to go wider and give general guidance on certain types of transaction, then a statement of practice would probably be appropriate so that our view of the law would be available to every practitioner and not just to one who wrote and asked for it. When consultation seems appropriate there is of course a wide range of options between the extremes of formality and informality: as you say, these are matters which we are well used to discussing with the representative bodies rather than with individual practitioners.

On your final point I would expect most enquiries from representative bodies to relate to the most recent Finance Act but if issues remain unclear there is no hard and fast rule which would prevent a view being expressed on earlier legislation.

There is perhaps one point which I might mention myself while I am writing. That is that some of our people have found that quite a lot of their time is being taken up in dealing with these issues on the telephone. While in some cases practitioners (particularly those who are less used to our ways) may find it helpful to have a brief discussion on the telephone to find out how best to go about seeking a request for guidance, for the most part these are I think issues which can only be satisfactorily handled in writing.

APPENDIX J

Taxation of ex-gratia payments
[ICAEW Technical Release TR 851, November 1991]

This guidance note sets out the text of correspondence received from the Inland Revenue regarding the taxation of ex-gratia payments.

Part 1 relates to Statement of Practice SP 13/91 issued on 31 October 1991, while Part 2 deals with the transfer of a company car as part of an ex-gratia severance package.

Part 1

The Statement follows an announcement made in March by the Superannuation Funds Office in Memorandum 104. This explained that an arrangement to pay ex-gratia relevant benefits to an employee would constitute a retirement benefits scheme. As a result such payments fell within the pension scheme tax rules instead of the "golden handshake" rules as has hitherto been the case.

It is, however, important to be clear that the only ex-gratia payments affected are those which come within the definition of relevant benefits in ICTA 1988, s.612(1). In broad terms this covers pensions, lump sums, gratuities and similar benefits which are, or will be, given:

- where a person retires or dies;
- in anticipation of retirement;
- after a person has retired or died (if the reason for payment is in recognition of past service); or
- as compensation for any change in the conditions of a continuing employment (as distinct from compensation on *loss* of employment).

Disability benefits (whether regular payments or lump sums) are, however, not relevant benefits if they are payable solely because of an employee's death or disablement by accident. For this purpose an accident does not have to be workplace related. For example, an ex-gratia lump sum payable because of an employee's death while travelling would not be a relevant benefit.

Such a payment will continue to be chargeable to income tax under ICTA 1988, s.148 (subject to the exemptions in s.188).

Although the list of relevant benefits is wide ranging, what is beyond doubt is that it does not cover severance payments on genuine redundancy or loss of office. In this regard we would not distinguish between directors or senior executives and other employees. In each case, provided the reason for the ex-gratia payment is to compensate for loss of employment the payments will *not* be relevant benefits.

In considering this issue we will be looking only at the reason for the ex-gratia payment; no account will normally be taken of payments under other arrangements. For example, if, on being made redundant, the employee is given early retirement benefits from an approved pension scheme, that will not affect the nature of the ex-gratia redundancy payments.

Having described those ex-gratia payments which are outside the Statement of Practice, it may be worthwhile to explain which payments are within its scope. They obviously must be relevant benefits—and so will not have been paid as a result of redundancy or loss of office. The most common situations will be:

- ex-gratia payments made on retirement or death by an employer who has no tax-approved pension scheme;
- ex-gratia payments made on retirement or death to an employee who is also entitled to benefits under a tax-approved pension scheme (this will probably be the case where the benefits are taken at the scheme's specified retirement age or on voluntary early retirement);
- other ex-gratia payments (not being for reasons of redundancy or compensation for loss of office) which are made in anticipation of retirement.

It is likely that the last of these situations could be in point where an ex-gratia payment was made shortly before the employee was planning to retire. It is an area where we would need to look very carefully at the facts before deciding on what the appropriate tax treatment might be.

The Statement of Practice modifies the guidance given in Memorandum 104. It explains that the Superannuation Funds Office are now prepared to consider approving an arrangement to pay ex-gratia lump sum relevant benefits where no tax approved pension arrangements exist for the employee.

But tax approval of such an arrangement is not considered appropriate where the employee is already a member of a tax approved pension plan. Nonetheless, where the benefits under the approved plan fall short of the normal tax approval limits, the employer could (instead of making an ex-gratia payment to the employee or his dependants) pay a special contribution to the approved scheme so that the benefits it pays may be increased (within the tax approval limits).

Paragraph 8 of the Statement of Practice describes a work saving measure for employers who made small (about £6,000 in the current tax year) ex-gratia payments on their employees' retirement or death. The main condition is normally that the employee should not have been a member of the employer's tax approved occupational pension scheme. In such cases, the lump sums may be paid tax-free without applying for formal approval of the arrangements.

I hope you find this further explanation helpful; its contents may be circulated to your members. The Superannuation Funds Office will shortly be issuing further guidance on the procedures for applying for approval of arrangements for paying ex-gratia lump sum relevant benefits.

Part 2

The following guidance has also been given by the Inland Revenue in connection with the transfer of a company car as part of an ex-gratia severance package.

Where an employee or office holder receives a company car as part of an ex-gratia severance package on retirement or removal from an office or employment, both the cash and the car fall within ICTA 1988, s.148. The car is "valuable consideration other than money" under s.148(3) and its value is therefore aggregated with the cash payment when applying the £30,000 exemption in s.188(4).

But s.148 applies only to payments which are not otherwise chargeable to tax, and there are two circumstances in which liability could arise without the benefit of the £30,000 exemption.

First, the gift of a car would attract liability under ICTA 1988, s.19 where it was a reward for past services even though the recipient may have no entitlement to receive it on termination of his office or employment. The criteria for determining whether a s.19 charge arises on the value of such a gift would follow long established Sch. E principles and would be identical to those applicable to a cash payment made in similar circumstances.

Second, the gift of a car would attract liability under ICTA 1988, s.596A where it was received under a non-approved retirement benefits scheme set up to provide "relevant benefits". The criteria set out above for determining whether ex-gratia payments constitute "relevant benefits" would also be used to determine whether s.596A should apply to the gift of a car.

APPENDIX K

Payments in Lieu of Notice
—extract from Inland Revenue Tax Bulletin Issue 24

There has been increasing interest in the Revenue's views about the tax treatment of payments in lieu of notice ("PILONS"). This article describes our established practice and comments on some current issues.

Background
In recent years PILONS have increasingly been included in employees' contractual arrangements. This is because employees have wanted to formalise their employment rights, and also because employers have wanted to retain the effect of restrictive covenants. These covenants might be lost where the terms of a contract of employment are breached on summary dismissal. This process has heightened interest in the taxation treatment of PILONS.

Nature of the Payment
"Payment in lieu of notice" is not a tax term and the expression covers payments made in a wide range of circumstances. Compare, for example, a payment made on a summary dismissal, where contractual arrangements oblige an employer to make a PILON if due notice is not given, with a payment made where the contractual arrangements provide only for notice of termination. In the second situation, the employer breaches the contractual arrangements and a payment made in compensation for that breach is not an emolument from the employment within Section 19 Income and Corporation Taxes Act (ICTA) 1988. But in the first situation, the contract of employment is terminated in accordance with its terms and the payment is an emolument within Section 19 ICTA 1988. Both payments will however be labelled PILONS.

Sometimes a payment is described as "in lieu of notice" where notice is in fact given but not worked—this is sometimes called gardening leave. In such circumstances the employee is employed until the end of the notice period but is not required to provide services during that period. Gardening leave payments are payments of emoluments from the employment and are taxable as such under Section 19 ICTA 1988.

So establishing the correct section of charge for tax purposes involves an analysis of the specific characteristics of the particular payment. This is followed by applying the principles of taxation appropriate to those characteristics.

Where that process shows that a PILON is an emolument from an office or employment, it is taxable under Section 19 ICTA. Section 148 ICTA 1988 is relevant only where Section 19 ICTA 1988 does not apply.

Emoluments from the Employment
An emolument is within Section 19 ICTA 1988 if it is an emolument from the employment. The fact that a payment is made under contractual arrangements is not of itself conclusive for taxation purposes in this context. In general, contractual sums are emoluments from employment, but that principle is subject to exceptions (most obviously, for example, pensions).

The Courts have held that certain contractual payments on termination are emoluments from employment and we see contractual PILONS as within that line of cases. But a payment for the loss of some personal right, or for complete abrogation of contractual terms, is not from the employment. In our view contractual PILONS are not of those types.

For tax purposes, emoluments by definition include wages. It has been suggested that, since for some purposes it has been held that a PILON is not wages (whether or not it is paid under contractual arrangements), it cannot be within Section 19 ICTA 1988.

However, what constitutes wages under employment law is not the same as what constitutes emoluments under tax law. The former depends on the provision of services whereas tax case law shows that the latter includes payments which are not strictly a reward for services, for example, compensation paid for the loss of the protection of certain employment law rights.

This point demonstrates that it may be inappropriate to use cases on the construction of one piece of legislation in the construction of the same or similar words in different legislation.

Contractual PILONS and Breach of Contract
Where contractual arrangements provide that a PILON is to be paid as an alternative to notice, the contract is terminated in accordance with its terms where there is summary dismissal. Compensation will be a matter of contractual entitlement rather than liquidated damages and the payment is chargeable under Section 19 ICTA 1988.

Some taxpayers have suggested that such a provision for a PILON merely quantifies the sum of damages payable following any failure to give due notice of termination. Employment law in this area indicates that, because the contract itself provides for the PILON, its character is not damages for breach of contract.

Employer and employee may agree at the time of terminating the employment that it is to be terminated without proper notice but on the making of a PILON. Provided that there was no existing understanding in respect of that payment which could be viewed as a contractual provision or amendment, its source lies only in the agreement to terminate the employment. It does not lie in any bargain struck between the parties governing the employment relationship and its termination. The payment is not an emolument from the employment and so it is properly taxed under Section 148 ICTA 1988.

Where contractual arrangements do not provide for a PILON and there is no other agreement of the sort mentioned in the previous paragraph, failure to give due notice is a breach of contract by the employer. A payment made for such a breach represents liquidated damages and is not an emolument from the employment within Section 19 ICTA 1988. As a payment in connection with the termination of the employment, it is chargeable under Section 148 ICTA 1988 subject to the exemptions and reliefs in Section 188 ICTA 1988.

Scope of Contractual Arrangements
In establishing whether contractual arrangements provide for a PILON, it is necessary to consider all relevant terms and conditions which have governed the employment relationship. For example, rules dealing with PILONS which are expressed only in a Staff Handbook or wage agreement may nonetheless be part of the contractual arrangements. Similarly, where there have been oral agreements about the employment relationship these may also constitute part of the contractual arrangements.

Even where there is no such contractual arrangement, an employer may regularly make a PILON instead of giving whatever notice is due. It is then possible that an implied contractual term of service may come into being, and where it does the payment is also properly regarded as made under contractual arrangements. All the facts of an individual case, including the employee's knowledge of an established practice, would need to be considered in deciding whether this was so.

Reserved Rights and Discretion
Some contractual arrangements give the employer a reserved right, or discretion—as opposed to imposing an obligation—to make a PILON where due notice is not given on termination of employment. Where an employer exercises such a reserved right or discretion, we regard the contract as being terminated in accordance with its terms under the agreed contractual arrangements for the provision of services generally.

The existence of such a reserved right or discretion is not therefore a determining factor for tax purposes, any more than it is where a bonus of remuneration is payable subject to an employer's discretion.

Section 49 Employment Protection (Consolidation) Act 1978
It has been suggested that Section 49 Employment Protection (Consolidation) Act 1978 may result in a contractual PILON being properly analysed as a payment of damages for breach of contract.

Section 49(1) specifies the minimum statutory notice period to which an employee is entitled. This period, when it exceeds the contractual notice entitlement of the employee, effectively supplants the contractual term.

It has been argued that any provision for a contractual PILON which purports to permit termination on notice shorter than that statutory notice period may then be void. However, the Courts have rejected the contention that failure to give the statutory notice period necessarily constitutes a breach of contract. Section 49(3) expressly allows contracting parties to accept a PILON and in that event the payment is not made in breach of the contractual terms.

Payment Context

A PILON is often paid in association with other sums of money or benefits when an employment is terminated. What determines its taxation treatment is not the context in which a sum is paid, but the characteristics of the payment. In particular, the fact that a PILON is paid in the context of redundancy does not affect its character and the way in which it is taxed.

We accept that payments for redundancy, within the meaning of Section 81 Employment Protection (Consolidation) Act 1978, fall outside Section 19 ICTA 1988 as a matter of law (see Statement of Practice 1/94). We include "bumped redundancies" as within this statement—that is, where a reduced need for employees leads to dismissal of employees whose functions are not specifically disappearing.

In our view a PILON is not a payment for redundancy. It does not share the qualities which characterise such a payment, such as, for example, the variation in amount related to service, the concept of compensation for a stake in the employment and the distress element of the employee being out of work in circumstances beyond their control. Such characteristics are special and have their roots in the fact that redundancy is a creation of statute.

Another aspect of the context of a payment is its timing. The fact that a payment is made after termination is simply one factor in considering whether it is from an employment and assessable under Section 19 ICTA 1988. It is not in itself a determining factor.

Summary

The Revenue's approach to PILONS will continue to be based on the principles outlined in this article.

Appendix L

AA and RAC Motoring Costs

1. RAC Illustrative Vehicle Running Costs—Petrol Engines

Copyright RAC Motoring Services, 1998. Further advice on other motoring related concerns is always available to RAC members from the National Technical Centre on 0990 313131.

The RAC National Technical Centre in conjunction with Emmerson Hill Associates (Vehicle Management Consultants) have compiled the following Illustrative Vehicle Running Costs. The figures represent a guide to the cost of running, from new, a *Privately Owned* motor car for a period of three years with an annual mileage of 12,000 miles.

	Up to 1000cc	1400cc	1600cc	1800cc	2000cc	2500cc
Insurance Grouping	3	5	7	10	11	15
Assumed Fuel Consumption*	47.5	41.0	37.0	35.0	32.5	27.5
Typical Cost Delivered New	7500	11000	13750	15400	16850	25000
Average Value @ 3 yrs	3550	5050	5800	6800	7450	11750
Projected Depreciation	3950	5950	7950	8600	9400	13250
Finance @ 24.0% Flat	1800	2840	3300	3696	4044	6000
Fuel cost 36,000 miles**	2387	2768	3065	3240	3489	4124
Servicing & Maintenance	550	595	650	685	840	1275
Tyres/replacement parts	320	350	370	395	470	665
Insurance premiums 3 yrs	990	1080	1395	1800	2235	2955
Excise Licence 3 yrs	450	450	450	450	450	450
RAC Membership 3 yrs***	423	423	423	423	423	423
Projected Total Cost	10870	14254	17603	19289	21351	29142
Annual Cost	3623	4751	5867	6429	7117	9714
Cost Per Mile	30.2p	39.6p	48.9p	53.6p	59.3p	80.9p

*Utilising the new EC93/116 combined figure.
**UNLEADED FUEL costed @ £3.15/gallon or 69.4p/litre.
***RAC Membership allows for REFLEX by Direct Debit with joint membership, and allowance for cars which have RAC Membership included by certain Manufacturers during the 1st year.

Illustrative Vehicle Running Costs—Diesel Engines

The RAC National Technical Centre in conjunction with Emmerson Hill Associates (Vehicle Management Consultants) have compiled the following Illustrative Vehicle Running Costs. The figures represent a guide to the cost of running, from new, a *Privately Owned* motor car for a period of three years, with an annual mileage of 12,000 miles.

	Up to 1500cc	1501–2000cc	over 2000cc
Insurance Grouping	5	8	13
Assumed Fuel Consumption*	53	46	38
Typical Cost Delivered New	9450	15050	23650
Average Value @ 3 yrs	4750	6850	10950
Projected Depreciation	4700	8200	12700
Finance @ 24.0% Flat	2268	3612	5676
Fuel cost 36,000 miles**	2174	2504	3032
Servicing & Maintenance	520	635	1215
Typres/replacement parts	300	395	540
Insurance premiums 3 yrs	1080	1620	2565
Excise Licence 3 yrs	450	450	450
RAC Membership 3 yrs***	423	423	423
Projected Total Cost	11916	17839	26601
Annual Cost	3971	5946	8867
Cost Per Mile	33.1p	49.5p	73.9p

*Utilising the new EC93/116 combined figure.
**DIESEL FUEL costed @ £3.20/gallon or 70.5p/litre.
***RAC Membership allows for REFLEX by Direct Debit with joint membership, and an allowance is made for cars that have RAC Membership included by certain Manufacturers during the 1st year.

Fuel Reimbursement Costs

Emmerson H Associates, Vehicle Management Consultants, have calculated a reasonable Fuel Reimbursement Cost that by taking the current price of fuel and dividing it by an average of the *Urban* fuel consumption figures for a sample 'basket' of cars in each engine size band, then adding 0.5p/mile for top up oil between services. Using this method, with pump prices for Unleaded petrol @ £3.15/gallon (69.4p/litre) and Diesel @ £3.20/gallon (70.5p/litre).

Unleaded @ £3.15/gallon (69.4p/l)

up to 1400cc/33.6 mpg = 9.9p
up to 2000cc/30.7 mpg = 10.7p
over 2000cc/19.5 mpg = 16.6p

Diesel @ £3.20/gallon (70.5p/l)

up to 1500cc/53 mpg = 6.5p
1501–2000cc/42 mpg = 8.2p
over 2000cc/31 mpg = 10.8p

Adjustments can be made to these figures by using 0.15p per 1p/litre movement up or down.

2. AA Technical Information—Motoring Costs 1997

The Automobile Association,
Norfolk House,
Priestly Road,
Basingstoke,
Hampshire
RG 24 9NY

A general guide to the costs of owning and running a car for the private motorist

Reproduced here with the kind permission of the Automobile Association.

The costs of motoring

How much does it cost to run your car?

A simple question, but a vital one for today's way of life. This guide to the costs of motoring—which has become a popular reference for all those who need to know the expenses involved in buying and running a car—can help you to find the answer.

The AA classifies the costs of motoring under two headings:

– running costs;
– standing charges.

Running costs

These are the actual costs of using the car, including petrol, oil, tyres, routine servicing and repairs and replacements. Here we have taken into account the fact that most new cars are protected by manufacturers' warranties, which cover the costs of repairs and replacements in the first year.

We have also considered the impact of extended warranties, which are increasingly popular among new car buyers and will further affect Running Costs. And, of course, each individual driver has his or her unique driving style, which also affects the costs of using the car.

With so many variables to consider, it is impossible to quote precise figures. However, the figures quoted here and the comprehensive notes which accompany them serve as a guide to help the **private motorist** estimate the cost of owning and using a car today.

Standing charges

These are the basic costs of owning a car for use on public roads. Standing Charges have to be paid whether the car is used or not. As such they include road tax, insurance and, we recommend, AA membership. A figure is also quoted for depreciation, ie, the gradual loss in value of the car. This figure is affected by the mileage of the vehicle and we have taken this into consideration in compiling our guide estimates.

What should my employer pay me for using my own car on business?

This will be a matter for negotiation between you and your Employer. Our figures are not a recommendation as everyone's circumstances are slightly different, but they can be useful in the negotiation process.

Do I need to pay tax on my reimbursement allowance?

Employees are liable to tax on any "profit" they make from the reimbursement rate. To avoid complicated administration the Inland Revenue operates a simplied arrangement known as the Fixed Profit Car Scheme (FPCS). Where the reimbursement rate exceeds the FPCS allowance, tax will be payable on the extra amount. More information can be obtained from your PAYE Tax Office.

Petrol Cars

	Up to 1100	1101 to 1400	1401 to 2000	2001 to 3000	3001 to 4500
		Engine Capacity (cc)			
Standing Charges per annum (£)					
(a) Road Tax	145.00	145.00	145.00	145.00	145.00
(b) Insurance	249.57	322.68	389.26	601.21	621.09
(c) Depreciation (based on 10,000 miles per annum)	984.40	1449.99	2050.25	3778.38	5086.42
(d) Subscription	70.00	70.00	70.00	70.00	70.00
TOTAL £	1448.97	1987.67	2654.51	4594.59	5922.51
Standing Charges per mile (in pence)					
5,000	28.98	39.76	53.08	91.88	118.44
10,000	14.49	19.88	26.54	45.94	59.22
15,000	10.97	15.18	20.43	35.67	46.27
20,000	10.20	14.29	19.42	34.31	44.87
25,000	9.73	13.75	18.82	33.49	44.04
30,000	8.11	11.46	15.68	27.91	36.70
Running Costs per mile (in pence)					
(e) Petrol*	6.90	7.89	9.21	12.55	13.81
(f) Oil	0.30	0.31	0.32	0.39	0.63
(g) Tyres	0.69	0.90	1.10	2.11	2.72
(h) Servicing	0.85	0.85	0.85	1.33	1.88
(i) Repairs & Replacements	3.02	3.45	3.50	5.37	5.53
TOTAL PENCE	11.76	13.40	14.98	21.75	24.57

*Unleaded petrol at 60.8 pence per litre.

| For every penny more or less add or subtract: | 0.11 | 0.13 | 0.15 | 0.21 | 0.23 |

TOTAL OF STANDING AND RUNNING COSTS (IN PENCE)
BASED ON ANNUAL MILEAGE OF:

	Engine Capacity (cc)				
	Up to 1100	1101 to 1400	1401 to 2000	2001 to 3000	3001 to 4500
5,000 miles	40.74	53.16	68.06	113.63	143.01
10,000 miles	26.25	33.28	41.52	67.69	83.79
15,000 miles	22.73	28.58	35.41	57.42	70.84
20,000 miles	21.96	27.69	34.40	56.06	69.44
25,000 miles	21.49	27.15	33.80	55.24	68.61
30,000 miles	19.87	24.86	30.66	49.66	61.27

Additional Notes—Petrol cars

(a) Road Tax.
(b) *Insurance* This is the average cost for fully comprehensive policy with a 60% no claims allowance.
(c) *Depreciation* All cars will depreciate at different rates, depending on make, model, age, mileage, condition etc. For the purpose of this publication an average annual depreciation figure is calculated and is based on the average cost of a new car within the various engine capacity groups. In the case of secondhand cars the depreciation should be assessed individually.
(d) AA Membership Subscription including Relay.
(e) *Petrol* Based on the average price of a litre of petrol at the time of publication. The cost per mile figure is calculated from what we consider to be a reasonable fuel consumption for the various engine groups.
(f) *Engine Oil* Allowance is made for normal oil consumption and routine oil changes.
(g) *Tyres* Estimated tyre life of 30,000 miles.
(h) *Servicing* Routine servicing as recommended by the vehicle manufacturers. In the case of older motor cars the servicing costs may be more.
(i) *Repairs and Replacements* An allowance is made for routine repairs and replacements which are likely to be needed due to normal wear and tear. However it is unrealistic for us to allow for any major repairs, which will only occur as a result of unexpected mechanical or electrical failures. For this reason only the owner of the vehicle can assess the true cost of this item, as repair costs will vary, even when comparing identical cars.

Diesel Cars

	New Purchase Price (£)			
	Up to £10,000	£10,001 to £15,000	£15,001 to £20,000	OVER £20,001
(a) Road Tax	145.00	145.00	145.00	145.00
(b) Insurance	249.57	322.68	389.26	601.21
(c) Depreciation (based on 10,000 miles per annum)	1121.85	1608.39	2154.25	3128.38
(d) Subscription	70.00	70.00	70.00	70.00
TOTAL £	1586.42	2146.07	2758.51	3944.59
Standing Charges per mile (in pence)				
5,000	31.72	42.92	55.16	78.88
10,000	15.86	21.46	27.58	39.44
15,000	12.07	16.45	21.26	30.47
20,000	9.05	12.34	15.95	22.85
25,000	8.04	11.44	15.20	22.28
30,000	7.53	10.37	13.50	19.41
Running Costs per mile (in pence)				
(e) Diesel*	6.23	7.01	7.38	9.34
(f) Oil	0.45	0.45	0.58	0.72

(g) Tyres		0.69	0.90	1.10	2.11
(h) Servicing		0.92	0.92	1.15	1.39
(i) Repairs & Replacements		3.02	3.45	3.50	5.37
	TOTAL PENCE	11.31	12.73	13.71	18.93

*Diesel at 61.7 pence per litre.

For every penny more or less add or subtract: 0.10   0.11   0.12   0.15

TOTAL OF STANDING AND RUNNING COSTS (IN PENCE)
BASED ON ANNUAL MILEAGE OF:

New Purchase Price (£)

	Up to £10,000	£10,001 to £15,000	£15,001 to £20,000	OVER £20,001
5,000 miles	43.03	55.65	68.87	97.81
10,000 miles	27.17	34.19	41.29	58.37
15,000 miles	23.38	29.18	34.97	49.40
20,000 miles	20.36	25.07	29.66	41.78
25,000 miles	19.35	24.17	28.91	41.21
30,000 miles	18.84	23.10	27.21	38.34

Additional Notes—Diesel cars

Please note

Due to the increasing popularity of diesel engined cars and the common use of turbo charges, it is felt that engine size does not adequately reflect the class of car. New purchase price has therefore been used for classification.

(a) Road Tax.

(b) *Insurance* This is the average cost for fully comprehensive policy with a 60% no claims allowance.

(c) *Depreciation* All cars will depreciate at different rates, depending on make, model, age, mileage, condition etc. For the purpose of this publication an average annual depreciation figure is calculated and is based on the average cost of a new car within the various classification groups. In the case of secondhand cars the depreciation should be assessed individually.

(d) AA Membership Subscription including Relay.

(e) *Diesel* Based on the average price of a litre of diesel at the time of publication. The cost per mile figure is calculated from what we consider to be a reasonable fuel consumption for vehicles in the various classification groups.

(f) *Engine Oil* Allowance is made for normal oil consumption and routine oil changes.

(g) *Tyres* Estimated tyre life of 30,000 miles.

(h) *Servicing* Routine servicing as recommended by the vehicle manufacturers. In the case of older motor cars the servicing costs may be more.

(i) *Repairs and Replacements* An allowance is made for routine repairs and replacements which are likely to be needed due to normal wear and tear. However it is unrealistic for us to allow for any major repairs, which will only occur as a result of unexpected mechanical or electrical failure. For this reason only the owner of the vehicle can assess the true cost of this item, as repair costs will vary, even when comparing identical cars.

Mopeds, Motorcycles and Scooters

Standing Charges per annum
(£)

	Engine Capacity (cc)						
	50*	50*	125	250	500	750	1000+
(a) Road Tax	15.00	15.00	15.00	35.00	60.00	60.00	60.00
(b) Insurance	100.94	110.93	241.90	510.59	650.00	963.77	1142.68
(c) Depreciation	141.19	205.69	334.54	458.07	570.46	1025.49	1231.35
(d) Helmet/Clothing	100.00	100.00	200.00	200.00	200.00	200.00	200.00

(e) Subscription		37.00	37.00	37.00	37.00	37.00	37.00	37.00
	TOTAL £	394.13	468.62	828.44	1240.66	1517.46	2286.26	2671.03

Standing Charges per mile (in pence)

5,000		7.88	9.38	16.56	24.82	30.34	45.72	53.42
10,000		3.94	4.69	8.28	12.41	15.17	22.86	26.71
15,000		2.63	3.13	5.52	8.27	10.11	15.24	17.81
20,000		1.97	2.34	4.14	6.20	7.58	11.43	13.35

Running Costs per mile (in pence)

(f) Petrol**		2.76	3.07	3.68	4.60	5.52	6.14	6.90
(g) Oil		0.35	0.46	0.64	0.68	0.71	0.90	0.90
(h) Tyres		0.53	0.62	1.07	1.54	2.07	2.52	2.85
(i) Servicing		1.47	1.96	2.52	2.52	2.83	3.19	3.19
(j) Repairs & Replacements		0.68	0.86	1.03	1.28	1.71	2.57	3.42
TOTAL PENCE		5.79	6.97	8.94	10.62	12.84	15.32	17.26

**Unleaded petrol at 60.8 pence per litre
For every penny more or less add or subtract:

		0.04	0.05	0.06	0.08	0.09	0.10	0.11

*50cc Class: The two figures represent, respectively, the lowest priced commuter mopeds and the more sophisticated motorcycles and mopeds up to 50cc.

TOTAL OF STANDING AND RUNNING COSTS (IN PENCE)
BASED ON ANNUAL MILEAGE OF:

	Engine Capacity (cc)						
	50*	50*	125	250	500	750	1000+
5,000 miles	13.67	16.35	25.50	35.44	43.18	61.04	70.68
10,000 miles	9.73	11.66	17.22	23.03	28.01	38.18	43.97
15,000 miles	8.42	10.10	14.46	18.89	22.95	30.56	35.07
20,000 miles	7.76	9.31	13.08	16.82	20.42	26.75	30.61

Additional notes—mopeds, motorcycles and scooters

(a) Road Tax.

(b) *Insurance* Average rates for a Third Party Fire & Theft policy: No allowance has been made for no-claims discount.

(c) *Depreciation* Based on average new motorcycle prices.

(d) *Helmet/Clothing* Allowance made for the purchase of helmet and protective clothing and assuming a service life of 3 years.

(e) AA Membership Subscription.

(f) *Petrol* Based on the average price of a litre of petrol at the time of publication. The cost per mile figure is calculated from what we consider to be a reasonable fuel consumption for the various engine groups.

(g) *Engine Oil* Allowance is made for normal oil consumption and routine oil changes.

(h) *Tyres* Service life is adjusted according to the type of motorcycle.

(i) *Servicing* Routine servicing as recommended by the manufacturer.

(j) *Repairs and Replacements* Allowance is made for repairs and replacements, but this figure can only be accurately assessed by the individual owner, as repair costs will vary even with identical motorcycles.

APPENDIX M

Nelson Jones Table

Reproduced by permission of the Law Society Gazette

	1980	1981	1982	1983	1984	1985	1986	1987	1988	1989
January	208.58	193.58	180.87	167.21	154.59	142.47	130.47	118.68	106.91	96.05
February	207.31	192.52	179.60	166.11	153.53	141.45	129.45	117.64	105.97	94.94
March	206.13	191.56	178.45	165.11	152.54	140.53	128.53	116.70	105.10	93.95
April	204.86	190.50	177.26	164.01	151.48	139.51	127.51	115.66	104.17	92.84
May	203.63	189.48	176.11	162.98	150.50	138.52	126.52	114.69	103.26	91.77
June	202.36	188.41	174.92	161.92	149.48	137.50	125.50	113.69	102.45	90.67
July	201.13	187.39	173.77	160.89	148.50	136.52	124.52	112.73	101.67	89.60
August	199.86	186.32	172.66	159.83	147.48	135.50	123.50	111.73	100.87	88.50
September	198.58	185.26	171.56	158.77	146.47	134.48	122.52	110.73	99.93	87.39
October	197.36	184.24	170.49	157.74	145.48	133.49	121.58	109.77	99.03	86.32
November	196.08	183.17	169.39	156.68	144.47	132.47	120.60	108.77	98.09	85.22
December	194.86	182.15	168.32	155.65	143.48	131.49	119.65	107.84	97.09	84.05

	1990	1991	1992	1993	1994	1995	1996	1997	1998
January	82.84	68.59	56.47	46.20	38.01	30.01	22.01	13.98	5.98
February	81.63	67.38	55.60	45.33	37.33	29.33	21.33	13.30	5.30
March	80.53	66.28	54.79	44.71	36.71	28.71	20.69	12.69	4.69
April	79.32	65.07	53.92	44.03	36.03	28.03	20.01	12.01	4.01
May	78.15	64.09	53.08	43.38	35.38	27.38	19.35	11.35	3.35
June	76.94	63.07	52.21	42.70	34.70	26.70	18.67	10.67	2.67
July	75.77	62.08	51.36	42.04	34.04	26.04	18.02	10.02	2.02
August	74.56	61.06	50.49	41.36	33.36	25.36	17.34	9.34	1.34
September	73.35	60.04	49.62	40.68	32.68	24.68	16.66	8.66	0.65
October	72.18	59.06	48.78	40.02	32.02	24.02	16.00	8.00	
November	70.97	58.19	47.91	39.34	31.34	23.34	15.32	7.32	
December	69.80	57.35	47.07	38.68	30.68	22.68	14.66	6.66	

Accumulated total of days October 1998–March 1999

31 October 1998	31
30 November 1998	61
31 December 1998	92
31 January 1999	123
28 February 1999	151
31 March 1999	182

Ogden Tables

Multipliers for loss of earnings to pension age 65 (males)

Age at date of trial	Multiplier calculated with allowance for population mortality and rate of interest of								Age at date of trial
	1.5%	2.0%	2.5%	3.0%	3.5%	4.0%	4.5%	5.0%	
16	33.3	30.1	27.4	25.0	23.0	21.2	19.6	18.2	16
17	32.8	29.8	27.1	24.8	22.8	21.0	19.4	18.1	17
18	32.4	29.4	26.8	24.5	22.6	20.8	19.3	18.0	18
19	31.9	29.0	26.5	24.3	22.4	20.7	19.2	17.9	19
20	31.4	28.6	26.1	24.0	22.1	20.5	19.0	17.7	20
21	30.9	28.2	25.8	23.7	21.9	20.3	18.9	17.6	21
22	30.3	27.7	25.5	23.5	21.7	20.1	18.7	17.5	22
23	29.8	27.3	25.1	23.2	21.5	19.9	18.6	17.4	23
24	29.3	26.9	24.7	22.9	21.2	19.7	18.4	17.2	24
25	28.7	26.4	24.4	22.6	20.9	19.5	18.2	17.1	25
26	28.2	26.0	24.0	22.2	20.7	19.3	18.0	16.0	26
27	27.6	25.5	23.6	21.9	20.4	19.1	17.8	16.7	27
28	27.1	25.0	23.2	21.6	20.1	18.8	17.6	16.6	28
29	26.5	24.5	22.8	21.2	19.8	18.6	17.4	16.4	29
30	25.9	24.0	22.4	20.9	19.5	18.3	17.2	16.2	30
31	25.3	23.5	21.9	20.5	19.2	18.0	17.0	16.0	31
32	24.7	23.0	21.5	20.1	18.9	17.7	16.7	15.8	32
33	24.1	22.5	21.0	19.7	18.5	17.5	16.5	15.6	33
34	23.4	21.9	20.6	19.3	18.2	17.1	16.2	15.3	34
35	22.8	21.4	20.1	18.9	17.8	16.8	15.9	15.1	35
36	22.2	20.8	19.6	18.5	17.4	16.5	15.6	14.8	36
37	21.5	20.3	19.1	18.0	17.1	16.2	15.3	14.6	37
38	20.9	19.7	18.6	17.6	16.7	15.8	15.0	14.3	38
39	20.2	19.1	18.1	17.1	16.3	15.4	14.7	14.0	39
40	19.5	18.5	17.5	16.7	15.8	15.1	14.4	13.7	40
41	18.9	17.9	17.0	16.2	15.4	14.7	14.0	13.4	41
42	18.2	17.3	16.4	15.7	15.0	14.3	13.7	13.1	42
43	17.5	16.7	15.9	15.2	14.5	13.9	13.3	12.7	43
44	16.8	16.0	15.3	14.6	14.0	13.4	12.9	12.4	44
45	16.1	15.4	14.7	14.1	13.5	13.0	12.5	12.0	45
46	15.4	14.7	14.1	13.6	13.0	12.5	12.1	11.6	46
47	14.6	14.1	13.5	13.0	12.5	12.1	11.6	11.2	47
48	13.9	13.4	12.9	12.4	12.0	11.6	11.2	10.8	48
49	13.2	12.7	12.3	11.9	11.5	11.1	10.7	10.4	49
50	12.4	12.0	11.6	11.3	10.9	10.6	10.2	9.9	50
51	11.7	11.3	11.0	10.6	10.3	10.0	9.7	9.5	51
52	10.9	10.6	10.3	10.0	9.7	9.5	9.2	9.0	52
53	10.2	9.9	9.6	9.4	9.1	8.9	8.7	8.5	53
54	9.4	9.2	9.0	8.7	8.5	8.3	8.1	7.9	54
55	8.6	8.4	8.3	8.1	7.9	7.7	7.6	7.4	55
56	7.9	7.7	7.5	7.4	7.2	7.1	7.0	6.8	56
57	7.1	6.9	6.8	6.7	6.6	6.4	6.3	6.2	57
58	6.2	6.1	6.0	5.9	5.9	5.8	5.7	5.6	58

59	5.4	5.3	5.3	5.2	5.1	5.1	5.0	4.9	59
60	4.6	4.5	4.5	4.4	4.4	4.3	4.3	4.2	60
61	3.7	3.7	3.6	3.6	3.6	3.5	3.5	3.5	61
62	2.8	2.8	2.8	2.8	2.8	2.7	2.7	2.7	62
63	1.9	1.9	1.9	1.9	1.9	1.9	1.9	1.9	63
64	1.0	1.0	1.0	1.0	1.0	1.0	1.0	1.0	64

Multipliers for loss of earnings to pension age 65 (females)

Age at date of trial	Multiplier calculated with allowance for population mortality and rate of interest of								Age at date of trial
	1.5%	2.0%	2.5%	3.0%	3.5%	4.0%	4.5%	5.0%	
16	33.9	30.7	27.8	25.4	23.3	21.4	19.8	18.4	16
17	33.4	30.3	27.5	25.1	23.1	21.3	19.7	18.3	17
18	32.9	29.9	27.2	24.9	22.9	21.1	19.5	18.2	18
19	32.4	29.5	26.9	24.6	22.7	20.9	19.4	18.1	19
20	31.9	29.1	26.6	24.4	22.4	20.8	19.3	17.9	20
21	31.4	28.6	26.2	24.1	22.2	20.6	19.1	17.8	21
22	30.9	28.2	25.9	23.8	22.0	20.4	19.0	17.7	22
23	30.4	27.8	25.5	23.5	21.8	20.2	18.8	17.6	23
24	29.8	27.3	25.1	23.2	21.5	20.0	18.6	17.4	24
25	29.3	26.9	24.8	22.9	21.2	19.8	18.4	17.3	25
26	28.7	26.4	24.4	22.6	21.0	19.5	18.3	17.1	26
27	28.2	26.0	24.0	22.3	20.7	19.3	18.1	17.0	27
28	27.6	25.5	23.6	21.9	20.4	19.1	17.9	16.8	28
29	27.0	25.0	23.2	21.6	20.1	18.8	17.7	16.6	29
30	26.4	24.5	22.8	21.2	19.8	18.6	17.4	16.4	30
31	25.8	24.0	22.3	20.8	19.5	18.3	17.2	16.2	31
32	25.2	23.5	21.9	20.5	19.2	18.0	17.0	16.0	32
33	24.6	22.9	21.4	20.1	18.9	17.7	16.7	15.8	33
34	24.0	22.4	21.0	19.7	18.5	17.4	16.5	15.6	34
35	23.3	21.8	20.5	19.3	18.2	17.1	16.2	15.3	35
36	22.7	21.3	20.0	18.8	17.8	16.8	15.9	15.1	36
37	22.0	20.7	19.5	18.4	17.4	16.5	15.6	14.8	37
38	21.4	20.2	19.0	18.0	17.0	16.1	15.3	14.6	38
39	20.7	19.6	18.5	17.5	16.6	15.8	15.0	14.3	39
40	20.1	19.0	18.0	17.0	16.2	15.4	14.7	14.0	40
41	19.4	18.4	17.4	16.6	15.8	15.0	14.3	13.7	41
42	18.7	17.7	16.9	16.1	15.3	14.6	14.0	13.4	42
43	18.0	17.1	16.3	15.6	14.9	14.2	13.6	13.0	43
44	17.3	16.5	15.7	15.0	14.4	13.8	13.2	12.7	44
45	16.6	15.8	15.1	14.5	13.9	13.3	12.8	12.3	45
46	15.8	15.2	14.5	14.0	13.4	12.9	12.4	11.9	46
47	15.1	14.5	13.9	13.4	12.9	12.4	12.0	11.5	47
48	14.4	13.8	13.3	12.8	12.4	11.9	11.5	11.1	48
49	13.6	13.1	12.7	12.2	11.8	11.4	11.0	10.7	49
50	12.9	12.4	12.0	11.6	11.2	10.9	10.5	10.2	50
51	12.1	11.7	11.3	11.0	10.7	10.3	10.0	9.8	51
52	11.3	11.0	10.7	10.4	10.1	9.8	9.5	9.3	52
53	10.5	10.2	10.0	9.7	9.4	9.2	9.0	8.7	53
54	9.7	9.5	9.3	9.0	8.8	8.6	8.4	8.2	54
55	8.9	8.7	8.5	8.3	8.1	8.0	7.8	7.6	55
56	8.1	7.9	7.8	7.6	7.5	7.3	7.2	7.0	56
57	7.3	7.1	7.0	6.9	6.8	6.6	6.5	6.4	57
58	6.4	6.3	6.2	6.1	6.0	5.9	5.8	5.7	58
59	5.6	5.5	5.4	5.3	5.3	5.2	5.1	5.1	59
60	4.7	4.6	4.6	4.5	4.5	4.4	4.4	4.3	60
61	3.8	3.8	3.7	3.7	3.7	3.6	3.6	3.6	61
62	2.9	2.9	2.8	2.8	2.8	2.8	2.8	2.7	62
63	1.9	1.9	1.9	1.9	1.9	1.9	1.9	1.9	63
64	1.0	1.0	1.0	1.0	1.0	1.0	1.0	1.0	64

Multipliers for loss of earnings to pension age 60 (males)

Age at date of trial	Multiplier calculated with allowance for population mortality and rate of interest of								Age at date of trial
	1.5%	2.0%	2.5%	3.0%	3.5%	4.0%	4.5%	5.0%	
16	31.3	28.5	26.1	24.0	22.1	20.5	19.0	17.8	16
17	30.8	28.1	25.8	23.7	21.9	20.3	18.9	17.6	17
18	30.3	27.7	25.4	23.4	21.7	20.1	18.7	17.5	18
19	29.8	27.3	25.1	23.2	21.5	19.9	18.6	17.4	19
20	29.2	26.8	24.7	22.9	21.2	19.7	18.4	17.2	20
21	28.7	26.4	24.4	22.6	21.0	19.5	18.2	17.1	21
22	28.1	25.9	24.0	22.2	20.7	19.3	18.1	16.9	22
23	27.6	25.5	23.6	21.9	20.4	19.1	17.9	16.8	23
24	27.0	25.0	23.2	21.6	20.1	18.8	17.7	16.6	24
25	26.4	24.5	22.8	21.2	19.8	18.6	17.4	16.4	25
26	25.8	24.0	22.3	20.9	19.5	18.3	17.2	16.2	26
27	25.2	23.5	21.9	20.5	19.2	18.0	17.0	16.0	27
28	24.6	23.0	21.5	20.1	18.9	17.8	16.7	15.8	28
29	24.0	22.4	21.0	19.7	18.5	17.5	16.5	15.6	29
30	23.4	21.9	20.5	19.3	18.2	17.2	16.2	15.4	30
31	22.7	21.3	20.1	18.9	17.8	16.8	15.9	15.1	31
32	22.1	20.8	19.6	18.5	17.4	16.5	15.7	14.9	32
33	21.4	20.2	19.1	18.0	17.0	16.2	15.3	14.6	33
34	20.8	19.6	18.5	17.6	16.6	15.8	15.0	14.3	34
35	20.1	19.0	18.0	17.1	16.2	15.4	14.7	14.0	35
36	19.4	18.4	17.5	16.6	15.8	15.1	14.4	13.7	36
37	18.7	17.8	16.9	16.1	15.3	14.7	14.0	13.4	37
38	18.0	17.2	16.3	15.6	14.9	14.2	13.6	13.1	38
39	17.3	16.5	15.8	15.1	14.4	13.8	13.2	12.7	39
40	16.6	15.9	15.2	14.5	13.9	13.4	12.8	12.3	40
41	15.9	15.2	14.6	14.0	13.4	12.9	12.4	12.0	41
42	15.1	14.5	13.9	13.4	12.9	12.4	12.0	11.5	42
43	14.4	13.8	13.3	12.8	12.4	11.9	11.5	11.1	43
44	13.6	13.1	12.7	12.2	11.8	11.4	11.0	10.7	44
45	12.9	12.4	12.0	11.6	11.2	10.9	10.6	10.2	45
46	12.1	11.7	11.3	11.0	10.7	10.3	10.0	9.7	46
47	11.3	11.0	10.6	10.3	10.1	9.8	9.5	9.2	47
48	10.5	10.2	9.9	9.7	9.4	9.2	8.9	8.7	48
49	9.7	9.5	9.2	9.0	8.8	8.6	8.4	8.2	49
50	8.9	8.7	8.5	8.3	8.1	7.9	7.8	7.6	50
51	8.1	7.9	7.7	7.6	7.4	7.3	7.1	7.0	51
52	7.2	7.1	7.0	6.9	6.7	6.6	6.5	6.4	52
53	6.4	6.3	6.2	6.1	6.0	5.9	5.8	5.7	53
54	5.5	5.5	5.4	5.3	5.2	5.2	5.1	5.0	54
55	4.7	4.6	4.6	4.5	4.5	4.4	4.4	4.3	55
56	3.8	3.7	3.7	3.7	3.6	3.6	3.6	3.5	56
57	2.9	2.9	2.8	2.8	2.8	2.8	2.8	2.7	57
58	1.9	1.9	1.9	1.9	1.9	1.9	1.9	1.9	58
59	1.0	1.0	1.0	1.0	1.0	1.0	1.0	1.0	59

Multipliers for loss of earnings to pension age 60 (females)

Age at date of trial	Multiplier calculated with allowance for population mortality and rate of interest of								Age at date of trial
	1.5%	2.0%	2.5%	3.0%	3.5%	4.0%	4.5%	5.0%	
16	31.7	28.9	26.4	24.3	22.4	20.7	19.2	17.9	16
17	31.2	28.5	26.1	24.0	22.1	20.5	19.1	17.8	17
18	30.7	28.0	25.7	23.7	21.9	20.3	18.9	17.7	18
19	30.1	27.6	25.4	23.4	21.7	20.1	18.8	17.5	19
20	29.6	27.2	25.0	23.1	21.4	19.9	18.6	17.4	20
21	29.0	26.7	24.6	22.8	21.2	19.7	18.4	17.2	21
22	28.5	26.2	24.2	22.5	20.9	19.5	18.2	17.1	22
23	27.9	25.8	23.8	22.1	20.6	19.2	18.0	16.9	23
24	27.3	25.3	23.4	21.8	20.3	19.0	17.8	16.7	24
25	26.7	24.8	23.0	21.4	20.0	18.7	17.6	16.6	25
26	26.1	24.3	22.6	21.1	19.7	18.5	17.4	16.4	26
27	25.5	23.8	22.1	20.7	19.4	18.2	17.1	16.2	27
28	24.9	23.2	21.7	20.3	19.1	17.9	16.9	16.0	28
29	24.3	22.7	21.2	19.9	18.7	17.6	16.6	15.7	29
30	23.7	22.1	20.8	19.5	18.4	17.3	16.4	15.5	30
31	23.0	21.6	20.3	19.1	18.0	17.0	16.1	15.3	31
32	22.4	21.0	19.8	18.7	17.6	16.7	15.8	15.0	32
33	21.7	20.4	19.3	18.2	17.2	16.3	15.5	14.7	33
34	21.1	19.9	18.8	17.8	16.8	16.0	15.2	14.5	34
35	20.4	19.3	18.2	17.3	16.4	15.6	14.9	14.2	35
36	19.7	18.7	17.7	16.8	16.0	15.2	14.5	13.9	36
37	19.0	18.0	17.1	16.3	15.5	14.8	14.2	13.5	37
38	18.3	17.4	16.6	15.8	15.1	14.4	13.8	13.2	38
39	17.6	16.8	16.0	15.3	14.6	14.0	13.4	12.9	39
40	16.9	16.1	15.4	14.7	14.1	13.5	13.0	12.5	40
41	16.1	15.4	14.8	14.2	13.6	13.1	12.6	12.1	41
42	15.4	14.8	14.2	13.6	13.1	12.6	12.1	11.7	42
43	14.6	14.1	13.5	13.0	12.6	12.1	11.7	11.3	43
44	13.9	13.4	12.9	12.4	12.0	11.6	11.2	10.8	44
45	13.1	12.6	12.2	11.8	11.4	11.1	10.7	10.4	45
46	12.3	11.9	11.5	11.2	10.8	10.5	10.2	9.9	46
47	11.5	11.2	10.8	10.5	10.2	9.9	9.7	9.4	47
48	10.7	10.4	10.1	9.9	9.6	9.3	9.1	8.9	48
49	9.9	9.6	9.4	9.2	8.9	8.7	8.5	8.3	49
50	9.1	8.9	8.6	8.5	8.3	8.1	7.9	7.7	50
51	8.2	8.0	7.9	7.7	7.6	7.4	7.3	7.1	51
52	7.4	7.2	7.1	7.0	6.8	6.7	6.6	6.5	52
53	6.5	6.4	6.3	6.2	6.1	6.0	5.9	5.8	53
54	5.6	5.5	5.5	5.4	5.3	5.2	5.2	5.1	54
55	4.7	4.7	4.6	4.6	4.5	4.5	4.4	4.4	55
56	3.8	3.8	3.8	3.7	3.7	3.6	3.6	3.6	56
57	2.9	2.9	2.9	2.8	2.8	2.8	2.8	2.8	57
58	2.0	1.9	1.9	1.9	1.9	1.9	1.9	1.9	58
59	1.0	1.0	1.0	1.0	1.0	1.0	1.0	1.0	59

APPENDIX O

Industrial Tribunals

Compensation for loss of pension rights

Guidelines prepared by a committee of chairmen of Industrial Tribunals in consultation with the Government Actuary's Department, Second Edition

A Paper prepared in consultation with the Government Actuary's Department by a Committee of Chairmen of Industrial Tribunals appointed by the President of the Industrial Tribunals (England and Wales)

TABLE OF CONTENTS

1 Introduction

1.1 Compensation for loss of pension rights following a finding of unfair dismissal in a Industrial Tribunal is just a part of the whole issue of compensation for loss of employment. The starting point is s.74 of the Employment Protection (Consolidation) Act 1978 which provides:

> "The amount of the compensatory award shall be such amount as the tribunal considers just and equitable in all the circumstances having regard to the loss sustained by the complainant in consequence of the dismissal in so far as that loss is attributable to action taken by the employer"

1.2 The Tribunal is not obliged, as a court is, to seek to calculate as precisely as possible the loss that the Applicant has suffered, but to order a "just and equitable" sum by way of compensation. This entitles the Tribunal to use a rough and ready system if necessary, Manpower Ltd v. Hearne [1983] I.R.L.R. 281.

1.3 Industrial Tribunals were established to provide an economical and expeditious means of resolving disputes. There is an upper limit on the amount of compensation which they can award in the case of unfair dismissal. Our task has been to set out guidelines for the assessment of compensation for loss of pension rights which are consistent with the constraints within which an Industrial Tribunal operates.

1.4 We believe that many people underestimate the value of an occupational pension. It can be a very significant financial asset, worth at least as much as the family home. This is illustrated in the examples in Appendix 5, part 1.

1.5 The Social Security Acts of 1985 and 1990 have improved the position of employees who leave prior to retirement. This applies to those who leave voluntarily as well as to those who are dismissed. An employee whose employment is terminated on or after 1 January 1991 has his or her pension entitlement indexed (up to retirement) to the Retail Price Index or 5% per annum whichever is the lower. This is a considerable improvement since before 1 January 1985 an employee's pension entitlement was "frozen" at the level which pertained when the employment was terminated. However, even for an employee whose pension entitlement is "index-linked" in accordance with the 1990 Act, the loss on leaving employment can be considerable if he or she has a number of years before retirement age."

2   Our approach

2.1   As will appear from this paper, the whole subject of pensions and the losses which may arise on dismissal is a complex one. In our view it is vital that the method used to calculate loss of pension rights should be readily comprehensible and acceptable to ordinary litigants. Where there is a conflict between technical purity and comprehensibility we make no apology for choosing comprehensibility. This is not an actuarial paper and does not pretend to be. It has, however, received the approval of the Employment Appeals Tribunal in general terms in Benson v. Dairy Crest Ltd (EAT/192/89).

2.2   Pension provision is but one of the financial advantages of employment. The benefit an employee derives, or the cost that the employer has to incur to fund that provision, may well vary according to a variety of factors. In times of high inflation the employee with a public sector index-linked inflation-proofed pension may well enjoy a coveted position which may not be matched by any privately funded scheme. In times when inflation is low and yet interest rate yields are high, or where equities have made substantial gains, an index-linked pension may not be as attractive as a privately funded scheme. Pension fund managers in the late 1970s were worried whether they could continue to fund any post retirement increases without enormous increases in the contributions made by the employers. By the mid 1980s certain pension funds were so well funded that employers were having pension contribution "holidays" to prevent the fund becoming overfunded.

2.3   In these circumstances because there are so many variable factors it is impossible to foresee with any great precision exactly what the financial consequences may be for an employee who is unfairly dismissed and therefore loses certain entitlements to a pension. Our guidelines therefore have to be broadly based and we have consciously ignored certain factors in the interest of simplicity.

2.4   These recommendations are put forward to assist tribunals who find themselves without adequate evidence to reach a conclusion on loss of pension rights without applying some kind of formula. Nevertheless we are very much aware that the recommendations, particularly in respect of loss of enhancement of accrued pension rights, are based on assumptions which may not apply to the particular case in question. Accurate assessments in any particular case can only be reached with the assistance of actuarial evidence. It is always open to either or both parties to call actuarial evidence and it is hoped that the more general parts of this paper will assist Industrial Tribunal in assessing such evidence where it is called.

3   State Pension Provision

3.1   The retirement pension payable by the State can be made up of the Basic Pension, a Graduated Pension and an Additional Pension payable pursuant to the State Earning Related Pension Scheme:—

The Basic Pension

This pension is much the same as the old flat rate National Insurance pension. Provided that certain contribution requirements have been completed the Basic Pension is payable to all persons over State pension age.

Graduated Pension

This pension is based on the amount of graduated National Insurance contributions paid by an employee in the period between April 1961 and April 1975. The amount of an individual's Graduated Pension varies according to the number of units of Graduated Pension contributions paid by him.

The State Earnings-Related Pension Scheme ("SERPS")

This pension is earnings related and varies according to an individual's earnings in respect of which he has paid full National Insurance contributions as an employee since April 1978. This is the so called "Additional Pension".

Contracting Out

3.2   Since its introduction it has been possible for employers to contract out of SERPS those employees who are members of a final salary scheme which satisfies certain criteria. National Insurance contributions payable in respect of employees who are members of an occupational pension scheme which is contracted out are paid at a lower rate than that payable for employees not in such a scheme. A final salary scheme which is contracted out must provide a Guaranteed Minimum Pension ("GMP") as a substitute for the Additional Pension which would otherwise be provided by the State. The GMP is broadly equivalent to the Additional Pension paid under SERPS and is the minimum amount of occupational pension which must be paid from a contracted out scheme. Often a contracted out scheme provides benefits which are higher than and additional to the GMP. An employee who has served all his pensionable service under a contracted out scheme will receive the Basic Pension paid by the State as well as a pension pursuant to the contracted out scheme. When the State pension is paid the Basic Pension and Additional Pension have an inflation protection element built into them. For an employee who is still employed the GMP increases with wage inflation. For the tax year 1988–1989 and later years after retirement the GMP element of the retired employee's pension will be increased in line with price inflation subject to an upper limit of 3% per annum.

3.3   From April 1988 it has been possible for money purchase schemes to be contracted out of SERPS by employers. Since the 1st July 1988 employees have been able to make their own pension arrangements and opt out of SERPS or their employer's pension schemes. In this case both the employer and the employee pay the full rate National Insurance contributions and part of these (grossed up at the appropriate tax rate) is paid by the Department of Social Security into the employee's personal pension scheme. If an employee has not been in a contracted out pension scheme for the two calendar years before commencing his personal pension scheme, an additional 2% of relevant earnings is paid into the pension plan by the Department during the period to April 1993 as an incentive to the employee to set up the scheme.

3.4   In line with our general conclusions set out below we recommend that the assumption is made there is no loss of pension rights in respect of a dismissed employee who is not in an occupational pension scheme.

4   Occupational Pension Schemes

4.1   Occupational pension schemes come into two main categories: final salary and money purchase.

Final salary schemes

4.2   These are schemes where the amount of pension paid is based not on the contributions made by the employer or the employee, but on a proportion of the salary of the employee when he retires (e.g. 1/60th of his final salary for each year of service). This proportion depends on the number of years he has been in the company pension scheme.

Example 1:—

A joined the company scheme in 1970. He retires in 1990 on a salary of £20,000 p.a. The scheme is based on 1/60th of his final salary for each year. Therefore his annual pension will be 20/60ths of his final salary i.e. £6,667.

We have used males as examples throughout this paper but all examples apply equally to females.

4.3   In about 80% of cases the employee makes a contribution of a fixed percentage of his income into the fund throughout his employment. The employer usually agrees to make contributions to the fund at least matching those made by the employees as a whole. There is usually little difficulty in establishing the contributions currently made by the employer as a percentage of the total pay-roll but this may vary from year to year depending on how well the pension fund is keeping up with the demands that are likely to be made on it. Sometimes there will be contribution "holidays". Where there is a lack of accurate evidence or where the current contribution position is anomalous we are advised that on average the overall contribution for a good scheme is 15% of the pay-roll made up in a contributory scheme as to 10% from employers and 5% from employees. It is important to note that the employer's contribution is not ear-marked for the pension of any individual employee and that the pension an employee actually receives will not necessarily be proportional to his and the company's contributions.

4.4   On the face of it non-funded schemes (particularly publicly financed schemes like the civil service pension) might seem to be different from normal final salary schemes because, as there is no fund, there are no contributions as such. However, although the pension is paid out of the Consolidated Fund and not out of any specific ear-marked fund, the notional contributions are fixed by the scheme's actuary and should be easily obtainable. These non-funded schemes, therefore, can be treated in the same way as any other final salary scheme. Most publicly financed schemes, however, do have a special advantage, which is unusual in other schemes, in that they are index linked to the cost of living index (though not to average increases in earnings) both from the date of leaving until retirement and after retirement and without any top limit.

4.5   Not all final salary schemes are the same. Not all schemes use the same fraction. Some schemes use the best of the employee's last few years as final salary; others may use the average of the last few years. However, the essence of a final salary scheme is that the employee's pension is based on his earnings and service and not directly on what he or his employers have contributed to the fund.

4.6   "Additional Voluntary Contributions" (AVCs) have existed for many years but the Social Security Act 1986 has now made it compulsory for employers to allow them to be made. Additional voluntary contributions usually operate on a money purchase basis, even where the main scheme is a final salary scheme. As such they should be treated in the same way as company money purchase schemes (see 4.8 below). However, some schemes (mainly public sector) allow employees to buy extra years. If this has been done the additional years already bought will be put into the equation as if the employee had actually worked those extra years.

4.7   AVC contributions are made by the employee alone. They, therefore, have no significant bearing when future loss of pension rights comes to be considered. Such "AVCs" should be distinguished from the new "free-standing additional voluntary contributions" introduced in

October 1987 which are in effect separate money purchase plans and should be dealt with as personalised money purchase plans.

Money Purchase Schemes

4.8   **Company Money Purchase Schemes:—**

These are quite different from final salary schemes. The pension payable is directly related to the contributions made by the employer and the employee to the fund over the years. In the past they have made inadequate allowance for inflation and have become unpopular, but there is a move back to them, because they enable the employer as well as the employee to know exactly how much the scheme will cost them each year and to budget accordingly whereas a final salary scheme may be an open-ended commitment.

Example 2:—

A joined the company in 1970. He retires in 1990. Over the 20 years he and his employers have contributed £20,000 to the scheme, but let us say that contributions are now worth £50,000. For this, on current annuity rates, he gets a pension of about £6,667 per annum. The amount of the pension, of course, varies not only according to the success of the investment policy but also with the age and even the sex of the annuitant and the interest rates current at the date of his retirement.

4.9   **Personalised plans,** including personalised life insurance backed schemes:—

These are the plans introduced for employees by the Social Security Act 1985 and include the "free standing additional voluntary contribution" plans. They are similar to plans that have been available to self-employed persons since 1956. The idea, very simply, is that the employee and the employer or either of them make contributions to a private pension policy with an insurance company or other pensions provider of the employee's choice. On retirement the employee then receives an annuity based on the value of his personalised fund. The main difference between these plans and company money purchase schemes is that it is the employee and not the employer who decides where the money is to be invested. They can now also be used to contract out of SERPS.

4.10   Free standing additional voluntary contributions are a form of personalised plan designed as a private top up for employees in company pension schemes.

4.11   **Life Assurance Cover**

Many pension schemes provide, or have associated with them, schemes which provide life assurance benefits for their members. In appropriate cases it may be just and equitable to compensate former employees for the loss of the benefit of belonging to such schemes.

5   Early leavers

5.1   Anyone who leaves pensionable employment before retirement is known as an "early leaver". A person who is unfairly dismissed is one example. The effect of leaving early will depend on whether the scheme is a final salary or a money purchase scheme.

5.2   Where the scheme is a money purchase scheme, whether company or personalised, the fund contributed to the date of leaving by employer and employee remains invested for the employee's benefit. Accordingly what the employee loses on dismissal is the prospective value of the further contributions that his employer would have made. As far as his own future contributions are concerned there is no loss since he can use the money to pay into a different scheme.

5.3   In addition a person dismissed who is a member of a money purchase scheme may be required to pay a penalty for leaving the scheme early. This is also a loss directly attributable to the dismissal, but it is easily quantifiable. Apart from this he does not lose any part of the current value of contributions already made by his employer and himself.

5.4   In a final salary scheme the position is much more complicated. By being dismissed the employee loses the prospective right to a pension based on his final salary. In most cases that come before the Tribunal, however, he will be entitled to a deferred pension. It is the difference between this deferred pension (including any cost of living increases and other benefits) and the pension and other benefits that he would have received had he not been unfairly dismissed that constitutes his loss.

6 Deferred pension

6.1 When a person who is a member of a final salary scheme is dismissed or leaves for any other reason he is entitled to a pension payable at what would have been his retirement date as an annuity for the rest of his life. This is referred to in this paper as a "deferred pension".

6.2 In the most common form of this scheme an employee when he retires receives 1/60th of his final salary for each year he has worked for the employer. For the employee retiring at age 60 there is a maximum of 40/60ths. Frequently part of this pension is commuted to provide a lump sum.

6.3 The early leaver receives a deferred pension representing 1/60th of his final salary for each year he has worked for the employer (providing he has 2 years' service as nearly all applicants to the tribunal must have). The problem was that until the Social Security Act 1985 came into force the final salary which used to be used for calculating this figure was his salary at the date he left. This is likely to be much less than the final salary would have been had he remained with the company until retirement or indeed until the next pay rise.

Example 3 (Pre-1985):—

A worked for his employers for 15 years; he left on 1 December 1983 with a final salary of £10,000. His basic deferred pension is 15/60th of £10,000 = £2,500 p.a.

Example 4:—

Instead of leaving he stays with the company for another 15 years when he retires with a final salary of £25,000 (an increase of not much more than 5% a year). His pension is £12,500 a year, of which £6,250 is referable to his first 15 years service.

6.4 By leaving early he has lost £3,750 a year from retirement to his death. This is the case even on the assumption that he obtains fresh employment with identical salary and identical increases and with an identical pension scheme. There will be a corresponding reduction in any lump sum on retirement and any widow's or widower's benefit.

6.5 In order to alleviate this unfairness the Social Security Act 1990 provides that the deferred pension increases by 5% per annum up to retirement or by the annual price rises if lower than 5%.

Example 5:—

B left on 1 January 1991 after 15 years service at the age of 50 years with a final salary of £10,000 a year. His deferred pension is still £2,500, but it goes up by 5% each year until it vests (that is comes into payment) unless price inflation is less than 5%.

6.6 What he has lost, however, is not simply a question of finding the difference between example 4 and example 5, because he might well not have stayed with the company until retirement even if he had not left at 50 years of age. He might have left or been sacked or the company might have gone into liquidation. Equally he might have ended up as managing director with a salary of £100,000 a year and a pension of £50,000 a year. Alternatively he might move to a new job where his pension can be transferred in such a way as to preserve his years of service. Who knows? Nevertheless his real loss on leaving could be substantial.

6.7 A fresh element was introduced by s.2 of the Social Security Act 1985, which entitles a person to require his ex-employee to transfer the value of his accrued pension either to a similar scheme run by a new employer or personally to make other arrangements meeting the prescribed requirements (Para 13(2) of Sch. 1A to the Social Security Pensions Act 1975 as amended by the 1985 Act).

6.8 The transfer value is calculated in accordance with the Occupational Pension Schemes (Transfer Values) Regulations 1985 S.I. 1985/1931 which came into force on 1 January 1986. These refer in turn to "Retirement Benefit Schemes—Transfer values (GN11) issued by the Institute of Actuaries and the Faculty of Actuaries and issued on 18 December 1985". We have inspected this document. It gives the actuary a certain amount of discretion and, anyway, the pension fund trustees may, if they wish, be more generous to early leavers than the law requires e.g. they may allow them to participate in excess profits or (most importantly) may allow the whole of the accrued pension to increase in line with the cost of living and not just the post 1985 element. However, our understanding is that the transfer value is an actuarial figure which represent the present value of the deferred pension he can anticipate.

6.9   In theory, he should be no better or worse off by taking the transfer value and re-investing it than if he chooses to leave the deferred pension in the fund. However, it does create the additional possibility that the employee will find a better private pension fund to put his money into or that the transfer values will be assessed on a generous basis.

6.10   A common fallacy is the belief that an employee does not lose financially if his pension is transferred from his old employer's pension fund to his new employer's pension fund. In fact this transfer value will usually be assessed on the limited commitment in example 5 and will not take account of the additional benefits he might have received if he had stayed on as in example 4. The position is explained further in paragraph 10.11.

7 The Problems

7.1 It is impossible to know what would have happened to the employee had he not been dismissed. It is the attempt to find a way of assessing what is "just and equitable" compensation for loss of that contingent interest which is the subject of this paper.

7.2 About half of all employees are in occupational pension schemes. The pension losses suffered by an employee who is unfairly dismissed come into three main categories

(1) Loss of pension rights which would have accrued during the period between dismissal and the hearing,

(2) Loss of future pension rights which would have accrued between the date of hearing and the date of retirement and

(3) Loss of enhancement of the pension rights which had already accrued at the date of his dismissal ("accrued pension rights").

7.3 Industrial Tribunals have to deal with cases which cover a wide range of employers who vary in their administrative and financial resources and the sophistication of their management. It is inevitable, therefore, that there should be a wide variety of pension provision resulting in variations in the losses suffered by employees on dismissal. We are only dealing with the mainstream schemes.

7.4 It is unlikely that in most cases the parties will come equipped with the necessary information to calculate loss of pension rights. The best course seems to be to assess in the first place the basic and the compensatory award without taking account of loss of pension rights. As is explained below it may also be possible, with only very limited information about the pension scheme, to calculate the loss of pension rights between the date of dismissal and the date of hearing and also future loss of pension rights.

7.5 Once these figures are calculated, it is necessary to consider next whether, for the various reasons set out below, there is no loss of accrued pension rights or even that it is not so important to consider this issue because the statutory limit for compensation has been reached.

7.6 If there is a loss which has to be assessed, the matter can, if necessary, be put back to a later date to enable a sum representing loss of accrued pension rights to be agreed or failing agreement to be determined at a further hearing. Even where the statutory limit has been reached it may be necessary to make some assessment of the full value of compensation in order to calculate the pro rata deduction under the Recoupment Regulations.

8   Loss of pension rights from the date of dismissal to the date of hearing

8.1   This is dealt with first because it is the simplest and most precisely quantifiable of the different types of loss of pension rights. Had the applicant remained in employment between the date of his dismissal and the hearing he would have gained the right to additional pension benefits. Equally he would have made additional contributions to the pension fund and his employer may well have also made contributions to the pension fund because of his continued employment.

8.2   In the case of a money purchase scheme it is easy to calculate the money value of the additional benefits he would have received in respect of the employer's contributions. In a final salary scheme this is not possible. Had he remained in the scheme until the date of the hearing and then left he would have qualified for a slightly higher deferred pension, but had he still been in employment at the date of the hearing then he would simply have gained additional service to put into the calculation of his final pension.

8.3   We consider that the fairest method, though not technically correct, is to look not at the additional contingent benefits he would have gained, but at the contributions which his employer would have made to the pension fund. If this is done it is not necessary to consider refinements such as widow's benefits or inflation-proofing after retirement since the better the scheme the more money will have to go into it. This is the approach which was recommended in the 1980 Government Actuary's paper which is referred to in Section 10.

8.4   When calculating loss of earnings during this period it is necessary to work out the weekly loss and multiply it by the number of weeks between the applicant's dismissal and the hearing (allowing for any sums paid in lieu of notice). Our recommendation for calculating the loss of pension rights during this period is simply to include a sum to represent what the employer would have contributed nationally towards the applicant's pension had he still been employed. Of course in the case of a final salary scheme this is not strictly a correct method of assessing the applicant's loss since the benefit that would have accrued to the applicant by remaining in employment does not necessarily correspond to this figure, but it would, we believe, be regarded as fair by both applicants and respondents. It is not, in our view, inconsistent with Dews v. N.C.B. [1987] I.C.R. 602 where the Plaintiff remained in the Defendants' employment and where he suffered no loss of pension rights as a result of the absence of contributions during his period off work.

8.5   In a typical final salary pension scheme the employer does not make a specific contribution to each person's pension, but make a contribution to the general pension fund which is related to the total wage bill or to some part of the wages bill, such as basic wages excluding commission and/or overtime. The normal cost of the scheme to the employer is usually given as a percentage in the actuary's report. This percentage should be applied to the applicant's gross pensionable pay to produce a weekly figure for loss of pension rights. "Pensionable pay" is that part of the applicant's pay which is used for calculating his pension. It may be all of his pay, or his basic pay or some other figure. In the absence of evidence from the employer it should be assumed against him that pensionable pay is the same as actual gross pay.

8.6   If the percentage contributed by the employer cannot be easily ascertained or is currently anomalous (e.g. because of a "contributions holiday") apply the figure of 10% (or 15% for a non-contributory scheme) to his pensionable pay. Whether a scheme is contributory or not can usually be determined by inspection of a wages slip. Applying this percentage to the applicant's gross pensionable pay is, in our view, the fairest and simplest way of calculating his continuing loss of pension rights.

Example 6:—

A earns £150 a week gross, which is his pensionable pay. He contributes £7.50 a week to the pension fund. His employers contribute 10% of the gross wage bill to the pension fund. A's continuing loss of pension rights is £15 a week.

8.7   Although to this extent pension provision is being treated as part of the applicant's weekly loss, it is not part of his pay and the Recoupment Regulations do not apply to the pension element.

8.8   Where there is a company money purchase scheme or where the employer is contributing to a personalised plan or a money purchase top up then assessing the contribution that the employer would have made is both the simplest and the most accurate way of assessing the employee's loss. The same system, therefore, can be applied using the percentage contributed by the employer towards the pension on a weekly basis.

9   Loss of future pension rights

9.1   The Applicant's loss on dismissal may include the loss of benefits he would have gained under his employer's pension scheme if he had continued in the employment beyond the date of the hearing. As with Section 8, our recommendation is to treat these additional pension rights as being equivalent to the contributions that the employer would have made to the pension fund in respect of his employment. For the purpose of calculating compensation, this employer's contribution can then be treated as if it was additional earnings which the employee would have received but for the dismissal. If the employer's contributions are taken as the basis of assessment it is not necessary to go into the details of the precise benefits under the scheme (e.g. widow's pension, disability payments etc).

9.2   Sometimes the Applicant has not found other employment by the date of the hearing. In this situation the Tribunal is engaged in the highly speculative process of deciding when he is likely to find other employment and how much he is likely to earn if and when he does. Forecasting the likely pension, if any, in such employment is just one part of this highly speculative process which includes whether the Applicant would have left his job anyway and whether he would have been promoted if he had not been dismissed. If the Tribunal takes the view that the Applicant is likely to obtain fresh employment in, say, one year or two years and that his earnings in that new employment are likely to be comparable, it is reasonable to assume that the pension scheme will also be comparable.

9.3   It is unlikely today that there will be a substantial qualification period before an employee can benefit from a new employer's pension scheme. Therefore if the Tribunal's decision is that his new employment terms are likely to be comparable, then the calculation is simply the multiplicand, being his previous net earnings including the pension contributions, with a multiplier of the time during which it is determined that he is likely to be unemployed.

9.4   Even if there is a qualification period, benefits are often back-dated once the qualification period has been met. An assumption of five years before any benefits would accrue from a new pension scheme has been held to be far too long, Freemans v. Flynn [1984] I.C.R. 874. We consider that if the qualification period is two years or less and if, on the qualification period being met, the entitlement is back-dated to the beginning of employment there is no need to make any allowance for this period. After all, the usual assumption of any award for loss of future earnings where the applicant has got a new job, is that he is no more likely to lose that job than if he had stayed with the respondent.

9.5   If the Applicant has found other employment the Tribunal has to compare the remuneration from that employment against the remuneration from his previous employment. This comparison will include the respective pension provisions just as much as the pay and such fringe benefits as the use of a company car.

9.6   If the new employment has no pension scheme then any continuing loss of earnings will be increased by the value of his previous employer's pension contribution assessed as a weekly or other periodic sum. However, in this event the employee will be in the State Earnings Related Scheme (SERPS). Therefore the contribution made to SERPS by the new employer should be deducted. If the SERPS contribution is not known it can be assumed that the new employer is contributing 3% of the employee's gross pay to SERPS.

9.7   If the new employment does have a pension scheme then the Tribunal will have to weigh up this scheme against the old one. Again a good rule of thumb is to compare the employer's contribution under the new scheme with the employer's contribution under the old scheme. The difference can be regarded as the weekly loss of future pension rights under the new scheme and can be used as a multiplicand to which the Tribunal can apply an appropriate multiplier.

9.8   Where the scheme is a company money purchase scheme or where the employer is contributing a personalised plan the same method can be used with greater certainty since the contributions which would have been made by the employer amount, in effect, to a payment by the employer into an investment fund for the employee's benefit.

10   Loss of enhancement of accrued pensions rights

10.1   Apart from the additional rights the Applicant would have been gaining had he still been employed, he may also have lost the benefit of further enhancement of the rights which have already accrued. In some cases he may forfeit his accrued rights.

10.2   Where the scheme is a money purchase scheme the sums accrued at the date of leaving continue to be invested just as they would have been had the employee remained with the company though sometimes employees have to pay a penalty on leaving money purchase schemes. Such penalties do not usually create great difficulties since the amount of compensation referable to the loss of accrued rights will simply be the amount of the penalty.

10.3   Where, however, the scheme is a final salary scheme it is obvious that even the post-1990 provision can involve loss representing the difference between the deferred pension he will receive and that part of the pension he would have received had he stayed with the company which is referable to his employment to date. There is a good chance that the applicant's salary would have increased at more than 5% or the annual price rise whichever is the lower and furthermore the employee might well anticipate promotion. On the other hand he may have lost his job before long anyway. He may find a fresh lease of life in new employment or self-employment. Assessing this loss is undoubtedly the most difficult aspect of compensation for loss of pension rights.

10.4   In 1980, long before there was any statutory dynamism in deferred pensions, the Government Actuary's Department produced a paper. This was intended to provide a simple system of calculating the difference between the value of the deferred pension to which the applicant was actually entitled and what he would have received in respect of service to date if he had not been dismissed (described in the 1980 paper as "the accrued pension"). In most cases it recommended an actuarial method. As explained above this involved balancing a mass of uncertainties, such as anticipated wage rises and mobility of labour of employees at different ages. It sought to produce a "rough and ready" formula. It also dealt with loss during the period of unemployment and with new employment without occupational pension rights.

10.5   Everyone, including the Government Actuary's Department, agrees that the 1980 Government Actuary's paper now requires revision. Firstly the assumptions for salary rises and mobility of labour are not necessarily the same now as they were when the paper was written. Secondly the problems of assessing the withdrawal rate accurately in any particular case are enormous and any alteration in the withdrawal rate applied can make a great difference to the sum assessed. We consider that this is a matter which should be assessed by the Tribunal on the facts of each individual case and therefore it is not appropriate to use generalised withdrawal rates. Thirdly it did not deal satisfactorily with the fact that some pensions are index-linked in payment, nor could it deal with the effect of the dynamism subsequently built into deferred pensions by the Social Security Acts 1985 and 1990. The Government Actuary's Department sought to deal with these points by adding notes to the tables (Table 1 Notes 3 and 4). However, the suggestion that compensation be reduced by half for each of these factors is undoubtedly a rough and ready approach.

10.6   We are also very much aware that Tribunals and parties have found the method difficult and rather daunting to operate, partly at least because the concepts it enshrines are not easy to understand. The reported cases have borne this out.

10.7   In trying to resolve this problem we have considered three possible approaches. We have concluded that none of these is appropriate to all circumstances but each can be of value in particular categories of case. Of course it is always open to an applicant to argue that a different approach should be adopted by the Tribunal in calculating the compensation to be awarded.

(a) No compensation at all

10.8   We consider that in respect of certain categories of cases it would be just and equitable not to make any award of compensation in respect of loss of accrued pension rights.

10.9   These categories are:—

   (1) All public sector schemes

(2) Private sector schemes where the applicant is near retirement (e.g. has five years or less until retirement).

10.10   The reason for this recommendation is that the uncertainties are such that the best "rough and ready" approach is to regard the cost of living increases as broadly in line with forecast improvements. This approach assumes the increases which the state regards as reasonable for persons who have left the company of their own accord, usually to better themselves, or for people who have already retired, are equally reasonable for a person who has been unfairly dismissed.

10.11   The problem with this approach is that in fact the evidence suggests that earnings rise faster than prices and therefore a cost of living inflation proofing does not correspond to anticipated increases in salary. Furthermore even cost of living inflation may well exceed 5% per annum.

10.12   We recommend that this approach should be used in cases where the applicant is fairly near to his anticipated retirement date e.g. within 5 years of retirement, because the difference between cost of living increases and anticipated increases in earnings has less cumulative effect over this shorter period.

10.13   We also recommend that there should be no compensation for loss of enhancement of accrued pension rights for all Applicants who are dismissed from the public service whose pensions are index-linked without the 5% limit. The justification for this approach is that their pensions are completely inflation-proofed albeit only against increases in the cost of living.

10.14   Where the Tribunal finds as a fact that the employment would have terminated in any event within a period of up to a year it would not be appropriate to order any compensation for loss of accrued pension rights.

(b) The Government Actuary's New Table

10.15   Where the Applicant was in the private sector and had more than 5 years to retirement we recommend a different approach. Whilst preparing this paper we have had detailed consultations with Derek Renn of the Government Actuary's Department and he has put forward a simplified actuarial method set out in Appendix 3 and the table of multipliers in Appendix 4.

10.16   His approach is actually similar to that in the 1980 Paper. It takes as the starting point that deferred pension to which the applicant is entitled (without any allowance for anticipated cost of living increases or other benefits) and then applies a multiplier based on the applicant's age. The figure resulting from this calculation is the starting point for working out the award for loss of enhancement of accrued benefit rights.

10.17   To calculate this figure, therefore, all that is needed is the deferred annual pension (see Section 6), the applicant's age and the anticipated age at retirement. It is entirely an arithmetical calculation. The table assumes that the Applicant would not have left his employment before retirement for reasons other than death or disability.

10.18   The figure obtained by applying the multiplier should be reduced if appropriate by a percentage representing the likelihood that the applicant would have lost his job before retirement even if he had not been unfairly dismissed for other reasons such as a fair dismissal, redundancy, leaving voluntarily etc. The earlier paper set out a table of such deductions called the "withdrawal factor", but we have come to the conclusion that any such figures are inappropriate and that it is best to leave this percentage to the discretion of the Tribunal.

10.19   The appropriate reduction is not the same as the percentage likelihood that the successful Applicant would have left his employment anyway before retirement. Even if he remained only for a few years more his accrued pension would still have been enhanced. However, we consider that a Tribunal can make a reasonable assessment of the appropriate reduction without guidance tables.

10.20   Appendix 2 Table 3 is a flow chart which should be of assistance in calculating the figure. Some examples of the general principles in assessing the withdrawal reduction are given in Appendix 5 part 2.

10.21   The rationale of this scheme is that the amount a person will lose over the years can be seen as a proportion of the value of his pension and can be related to his age. Generally the younger he is the greater the loss.

10.22   Because of the simplification on which we have insisted Appendix 4 makes various assumptions. It assumes that:—

(1) There is a widow or widower's pension at 50% of the members' rate.

(2) There will be no lump sum.

(3) There is a 3% per annum increase in most of the pension after retirement.

(4) It applies equally to men and women.

10.23   The effect of inflation and taxation, have been taken into account in the assumptions used in the table in Appendix 4. The actuarial basis is set out in Appendix 3.

10.24   Assumptions of this nature are the only way in which the kind of simple table set out in Appendix 4 can be put into effect. However, both the assumptions are liable to change fairly rapidly and we feel that the table and the assumptions on which it is based should be considered every year.

10.25   We have come to the conclusion that despite these crude assumptions it is the best system that can be devised in most circumstances. We therefore recommend it for use. If either party considers that it is inapplicable in any particular case he can put forward his arguments. The point is that it provides a starting point which can be used in the absence of more detailed evidence and modified as necessary.

(c) The Contribution Rate Method

10.26   The other method suggested is the contributions method. This involves adding up the contributions made by the employer and the employee to the pension fund and thereby assessing the value of the applicant's accrued pension. If what he has actually received is a deferred pension it is then necessary to work out the cash value of that deferred pension, by assessing its transfer value in accordance with the 1985 Act.

10.27   Despite its superficial attraction, however, this is an even more difficult calculation than the actuarial method in the 1980 Government Actuary's paper and is much more complex than the formula we recommend. The amount contributed by the employer to the pension scheme will vary from year to year and a complex calculation is needed to work out the current value of a contribution of say £5 a week made 15 years ago.

10.28   We have tried to simplify this method by using the contribution rate method which works on the basis of the current rate of contributions. However, after consultation with interested bodies we have come to the conclusion that it is less accurate than our formula and, furthermore, adds a further and unnecessary complication to the task facing the Tribunal. We do not, therefore, recommend that this method be used in unfair dismissal cases. However, if evidence is adduced that the difference between the contributions made and the transfer value is far greater than the loss assessed in accordance with the tables the Tribunal may decide to take this into account in assessing a fair and equitable award.

10.29   None of the other methods suggested to us of calculating loss under this section provide, in our view, a simpler or fairer solution.

11   General Conclusions

11.1   It is important to note that where the compensation exceeds the statutory limit even without consideration of loss of pension rights, the importance of calculating the sum involved diminishes. However, it must be remembered that the Recoupment Regulations (r. 5(2)) provide for a pro rata deduction from the sum repayable to the Department of Employment where the award of compensation would have exceeded the limit. Therefore, though the assessment is less important, it is still necessary to assess a figure where the Recoupment Regulations (r. 5(2)) provide for a pro rata deduction from the sum repayable to the Department of Employment where the award of compensation would have exceeded the limit. Therefore, though the assessment is less important, it is still necessary to assess a figure where the Recoupment Regulations apply, to enable the Tribunal to assess how much to reduce the sum repayable to the Department of Employment.

11.2   These recommendations are only guidelines. They will become tripwires if they are blindly applied without considering the facts of each case. Any party is free to canvass any method of assessment which he considers appropriate. We hope that this paper will be found useful as a starting point.

11.3   Appendices 1 and 2 set out respectively a practical guide and a flow chart for applying our recommendations. Appendix 3 is the Government Actuary's paper on which our conclusions as to loss of enhancement of accrued pension rights are based. Appendix 4 contains the table of multipliers and Appendix 5 gives examples showing in Part 1 the importance of assessing pension loss and in Part 2 problems connected with the likelihood of withdrawal.

Prepared by

Colin Sara	*Full-time chairman*	*Bristol*
David Pugsley	*Full-time chairman*	*Birmingham*
Douglas Crump	*Part-time chairman*	*Birmingham*

Appendix   1

1   Loss of pension rights from date of dismissal to the hearing
Unless there are arguments to the contrary we consider that the following formula should apply:—

(a)   Ascertain the employer's contribution as a percentage of the Applicant's pay. It may be necessary to adjust this figure if exceptional circumstances pertain; if for example the pension fund is over-funded and the employer is having a pension contribution holiday. If the pension is a non-contributory one which is not funded e.g. a civil service pension, then it may be necessary to impute a notional employer's contribution.

(b)   If the figure for the employer's contribution is not readily forthcoming then assume that the employer's contribution is 10% (15% in the case of non-contributory schemes).

(c)   Treat the employer's contribution as a weekly loss, in the same manner as a weekly loss of earnings.

2   Loss of future pension rights
Use the same rate of contributions as for 1 and the same multiplier as for assessment of future loss of earnings.

3   Loss of enhancement of accrued pension rights
Assume no loss of enhancement of accrued pension benefit unless the contrary is proved in:—

(a)   Schemes in which pension benefits are referable to contributions made and not final salary (i.e. company money purchase schemes, personalised plans etc).

(b)   Public sector schemes—funded and non-funded.

(c)   Private sector final salary schemes where the applicant has less than 5 years until retirement.

Loss of enhancement of accrued benefit in final salary schemes (where condition 5 c(i) and c(ii) do not apply):

(1)   Ascertain the deferred pension he will receive (ignoring any anticipated increases or additional benefits).

(2)   Ascertain the applicant's present age and his anticipated age of retirement.

(3)   Apply the appropriate multiplier as set out in the table in Appendix 4.

(4)   Reduce the resulting figure by a reasonable percentage for the likelihood of withdrawal (i.e. that he would have left before retirement for reasons other than death or disability).

Appendix 2   Table 1

Flow chart for calculation of loss of pension rights from date of dismissal to the hearing

1. Ascertain the employee's gross weekly
    pensionable pay

2. Ascertain the employer's normal
    contribution as a % of the pay-roll

3. If the figure for the employer's
    contribution is not readily forthcoming
    then assume that the employer's
    contribution is 10% (15% for non-
    contributory schemes)

    Weekly continuing pension loss

4. Multiply by number of weeks between
    effective date of termination and date
    of hearing

                                        AWARD

£
£
X

Appendix 2   Table 2

Flow chart for calculation of loss of future pension rights

1. Ascertain the employee's gross weekly
    pensionable pay

2. Ascertain the employer's normal
    contribution as a % of the pay-roll

3. If the figure for the employer's
    contribution is not readily forthcoming
    then assume that the employer's
    contribution is 10% (15% for non-
    contributory schemes)

    Weekly continuing pension loss

4. Multiply by number of weeks allowed
    for future loss of earnings whether total
    or partial

                                        AWARD

£

£

X

Appendix 2   Table 3

Flow chart for calculation of loss of enhancement of accrued pension rights

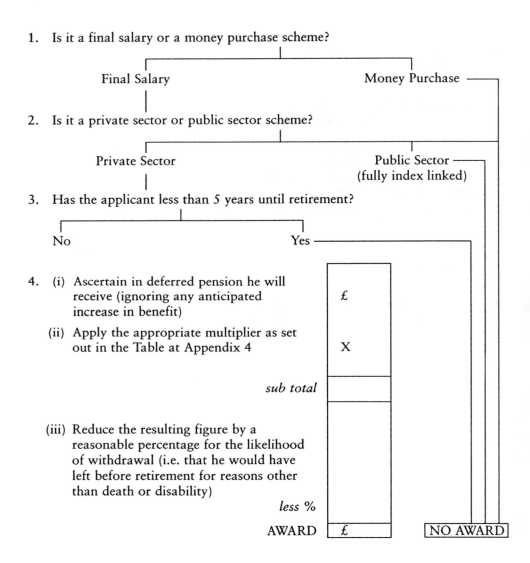

1.   Is it a final salary or a money purchase scheme?

      Final Salary   Money Purchase

2.   Is it a private sector or public sector scheme?

      Private Sector   Public Sector
                             (fully index linked)

3.   Has the applicant less than 5 years until retirement?

    No   Yes

4.   (i)   Ascertain in deferred pension he will
         receive (ignoring any anticipated   £
         increase in benefit)

   (ii)   Apply the appropriate multiplier as set
         out in the Table at Appendix 4   X

                              sub total

  (iii)   Reduce the resulting figure by a
         reasonable percentage for the likelihood
         of withdrawal (i.e. that he would have
         left before retirement for reasons other
         than death or disability)
                              less %

                 AWARD £   NO AWARD

Appendix 3

Assessing loss of occupational pension scheme rights following a finding of unfair dismissal by an industrial tribunal

The Government Actuary's 1980 paper under the above title was intended to provide chairmen of Industrial Tribunals with a simple system of assessing the loss in respect of service before dismissal by calculating the difference between the value of the deferred pension to which the applicant remained entitled and what he would have received had he not been dismissed. It is acknowledged that the formula is now less satisfactory because of the recent legislation aimed at preserving at least some of all pension entitlement, for which only very approximate adjustments were proposed in the notes issued in 1980 and 1987.

This paper puts forward a revised system to take account of the legislation, together with an approximate simple formula which may be useful to chairmen in the absence of expert evidence. The formula relates to a pension derived from final salary at exit, continuing (at one-half rate) to a dependant.

If a member of a final salary pension scheme withdraws, he loses potential benefits in respect of his past service to the extent that the accrued benefits are not fully indexed in line with salaries (including an allowance for possible future promotion) until normal retirement age.

The value of each pension unit depends on many factors, in particular:—

- sex, attained age, normal retirement age
- estimates of future rates of salary progression and promotion, of inflation (prices and/or pensions) and of interest on investments

as well as of estimates of rates of withdrawal (dismissal, redundancy, resignation, transfer), death (in service and after retirement) retirement (age and ill-health) and for (dependants' benefits) age and death rates of dependants and the proportion of staff leaving an eligible dependant on their own death.

The 1980 tables were constructed on simplified assumptions, assuming that money could be invested to earn an average of 9 per cent per annum. For continuing beliefs (based on final salary with a half-rate pension continuing to a dependant wife (but not husband)), salary was assumed to increase at $7\frac{1}{2}\%$ per annum and pension at 3% per annum.

Frozen (deferred) benefits were assumed to increase at 3% per annum after dismissal. Mortality was assumed to be similar to that experienced by a large public sector scheme, and ill-health retirement benefits were assumed to be worth as much as those on normal retirement. No allowance was made for exits except by death; chairmen were expected to assess for themselves the reduction for the possibility of withdrawal (by resignation etc. but *not* unfair dismissal) before normal pension age.

The revised tables shown below in this paper assume that money can be invested to earn 8% per annum on average. Salaries are assumed to increase at 7% per annum and pensions to increase by 3% per annum. Mortality is assumed to be similar to that estimated to apply to current insured pensioners.

Transfer values of pension rights are calculated on different assumptions from those used in valuing benefits to continuing staff. A transfer value passes between pension schemes in cash form, so the sending scheme has to realise assets at current market rates, not the long-term average assessment. Further, there is a change in benefit expectations: the salary linkage is broken, and there are often differences in death and ill-health benefits between schemes (especially enhancement on early exit).

Consequently it can be inequitable to value benefit loss by deducting the transfer value from a standard table of continuing benefit values. It may be fairer to use a standard table representing the loss of benefit on dismissal allowing for standard deferred benefits, including the guaranteed minimum pension (GMP) required by legislation for contracted-out schemes. This GMP is assumed in the table to increase by 7% per annum to State Pension age but only to the extent of post March 1988 service will it increase (by 3% per annum) thereafter.

The maximum required by legislation is for 5% increases in frozen pensions up to normal pension age. A pensions increase of 3% per annum is also assumed to apply to any balance of pension over the GMP.

This requires each pension to be divided into 3 parts namely the continuing benefit value, pre and post 1988 GMP and any balance above GMP and a different factor applied to each part. Tables are given at the end of this Appendix.

To simplify procedures, a single factor has been found (varying with age) (Appendix 4) to apply to the accrued pension to estimate the loss of pension rights assuming:—

    (i)   accrued pension for past service equals that preserved on dismissal;

    (ii) GMP represents two-thirds of the total pension and will be revalued at least to the same extent as any balance. (At present the post-1988 service need not be separated).

These fractions will change with time.

Appendix 4 may be compared with the difference between the columns of the 1980 paper. For men retiring at 65 the figures are:—

Age last birthday	Under 30	40	45	50	55	60	64
1980 values	4.3	4.2	3.9	3.4	2.7	1.6	0.2
1991 values	1.5	1.5	1.4	1.3	1.2	0.8	0.2

All estimates of loss need to be reduced by an individual assessment of the likelihood of withdrawal from the pension fund other than on account of unfair dismissal.

It has been suggested that the value of continuing benefits in a good (sixtieths) scheme can be estimated at 15% or so of the product of pensionable salary and service. As the tables show, this factor is a reasonable one at certain ages only. The pension multiplier for men retiring at 65 is about 10.5 (corresponding to $17\frac{1}{2}\%$) shortly before that age but only 5.5 (corresponding to 9%) at age 25. It must be emphasised that pensionable salary may not be the same as total salary.

Table 1 to Appendix 3

Value of pension of 1 per annum

(1)   Salary linked until vesting then 3% pension increase

(2)   Salary linked until vesting then NO pension increase

(3)   5% increase until vesting then 3% pension increase

FEMALES NORMAL
RETIREMENT
AGE 60

AGE LAST BIRTHDAY	(1)	(2)	(3)
Under 30	7.5	5.8	3.7
30–34	8.2	6.4	4.7
35–39	8.8	6.9	5.6
40	9.3	7.3	6.4
41	9.4	7.4	6.6
42	9.5	7.5	6.8
43	9.7	7.6	7.0
44	9.8	7.7	7.3
45	10.0	7.8	7.5
46	10.1	7.9	7.8
47	10.3	8.0	8.1
48	10.5	8.1	8.4
49	10.6	8.3	8.7
50	10.8	8.4	9.0
51	11.0	8.5	9.3
52	11.2	8.6	9.7
53	11.4	8.8	10.0
54	11.6	9.0	10.4
55	11.8	9.2	10.8
56	12.0	9.4	11.2
57	12.2	9.5	11.6
58	12.4	9.7	12.1
59	12.7	9.9	12.6

Table 2 to Appendix 3

Value of pension of 1 per annum

(1) Salary linked until vesting then 3% pension increase

(2) Salary linked until vesting then NO pension increase

(3) 5% increase until vesting then 3% pension increase

FEMALES NORMAL
RETIREMENT
AGE 65

AGE LAST BIRTHDAY	(1)	(2)	(3)
Under 30	6.0	4.8	2.7
30–34	6.7	5.4	3.5
35–39	7.2	5.8	4.2
40	7.5	6.1	4.7
41	7.6	6.2	4.8
42	7.7	6.3	5.0
43	7.8	6.4	5.2
44	8.0	6.4	5.4
45	8.1	6.5	5.6
46	8.2	6.6	5.8
47	8.3	6.7	6.0
48	8.5	6.8	6.2
49	8.6	6.9	6.4
50	8.7	7.0	6.6
51	8.9	7.1	6.8
52	9.0	7.3	7.0
53	9.2	7.4	7.3
54	9.3	7.5	7.6
55	9.5	7.6	7.9
56	9.6	7.7	8.2
57	9.8	7.9	8.5
58	10.0	8.0	8.8
59	10.2	8.2	9.2
60	10.4	8.3	9.6
61	10.6	8.5	10.0
62	10.8	8.7	10.4
63	11.1	8.9	10.8
64	11.3	9.1	11.2

Table 3 to Appendix 3

Value of pension of 1 per annum

(1) Salary linked until vesting then 3% pension increase		MALES NORMAL
(2) Salary linked until vesting then NO pension increase		RETIREMENT
(3) 5% increase until vesting then 3% pension increase		AGE 60

AGE LAST BIRTHDAY	(1)	(2)	(3)
Under 30	7.0	5.4	3.6
30–34	7.7	6.1	4.5
35–39	8.3	6.5	5.4
40	8.7	6.8	6.0
41	8.8	6.9	6.2
42	9.0	7.0	6.4
43	9.1	7.1	6.6
44	9.3	7.3	6.9
45	9.4	7.4	7.1
46	9.6	7.5	7.3
47	9.7	7.6	7.6
48	9.9	7.7	7.9
49	10.0	7.8	8.2
50	10.2	8.0	8.5
51	10.4	8.1	8.8
52	10.6	8.3	9.1
53	10.7	8.4	9.5
54	10.9	8.5	9.9
55	11.2	8.6	10.3
56	11.4	8.8	10.7
57	11.6	9.0	11.1
58	11.9	9.2	11.5
59	12.1	9.5	12.0

Table 4 to Appendix 3

Value of pension of 1 per annum

(1) Salary linked until vesting then 3% pension increase
(2) Salary linked until vesting then NO pension increase
(3) 5% increase until vesting then 3% pension increase

MALES NORMAL
RETIREMENT
AGE 65

AGE LAST BIRTHDAY	(1)	(2)	(3)
Under 30	5.7	4.8	3.0
30–34	6.3	5.1	3.5
35–39	6.8	5.5	4.0
40	7.1	5.6	4.5
41	7.2	5.7	4.7
42	7.3	5.8	4.9
43	7.4	6.0	5.0
44	7.5	6.1	5.2
45	7.6	6.2	5.4
46	7.8	6.3	5.5
47	7.9	6.4	5.7
48	8.0	6.5	5.9
49	8.1	6.6	6.1
50	8.3	6.7	6.3
51	8.4	6.8	6.5
52	8.5	6.9	6.8
53	8.7	7.0	7.0
54	8.8	7.1	7.2
55	8.9	7.2	7.5
56	9.1	7.4	7.8
57	9.3	7.5	8.1
58	9.4	7.6	8.4
59	9.6	7.7	8.7
60	9.8	7.9	9.1
61	10.1	8.1	9.5
62	10.3	8.3	10.0
63	10.6	8.5	10.4
64	10.9	8.7	10.8

Appendix   4   **1991 Edition**

Tables of multipliers to be applied to the deferred annual pension to assess compensation for loss of enhancement of accrued pension rights.

Age last birthday at dismissal	Normal retirement age 60	Normal retirement age 65
Under 35	1.9	1.5
35–44	1.8	1.5
45–49	1.7	1.4
50	1.6	1.4
51	1.5	1.4
52	1.4	1.3
53	1.3	1.3
54	1.1	1.3
55	1.0	1.2
56	0.8	1.2
57	0.6	1.1
58	0.3	1.0
59	0.1	0.9
60	NIL	0.8
61		0.6
62		0.4
63		0.3
64		0.2

Appendix 5 – Examples

Part One – Illustrations of the value of an occupational pension

An occupation pension can be a very significant financial asset. This can be illustrated by comparing the position of twin sisters: Betty a civil servant and Beryl who has throughout worked as a music teacher on a self-employed basis. Both retire when they are 60, having worked for the same number of years and with the same final salary of £10,000 per annum.

Betty has an occupational pension which provides her with the maximum permitted pension; namely a lump sum of $1\frac{1}{2}$ times her final salary and an index linked pension of half her final salary. She therefore receives £15,000 as a lump sum and a pension of £5,000 per year and is secure in the belief that her pension will rise with inflation. In addition she is entitled to the basic state pension.

Beryl being self-employed was not covered by an occupational scheme and had made no private pension provision. All she receives is the same basic state pension as her sister. To buy an annuity to provide her with a pension of £5,000 would, depending on interest rates which pertain at the time, cost her between £40,000 and £60,000. If she were to attempt to protect herself against her pension being eroded by inflation she would have to pay much more and even then she would be unlikely to be able to purchase an annuity which was completely inflation proofed rather than providing yearly increases at predetermined rates.

Assume Betty and Beryl have a rich aunt who is in the last stages of a terminal illness and is revising her will on the basis she wishes to see both her nieces equally well provided for in their old age. If she were to lay these facts before a professional adviser and ask how much it would cost to place Beryl in the same position as Betty the advice would be that given the incidence of inflation, the legacy to Beryl would probably need to be £75,000 to £100,000 more than to Betty to ensure that they were both placed in comparable positions.

Although actuaries can advise companies or particular individuals on the cost of providing pensions no actuary can define with precision the exact value that the recipient of a pension will derive from the pension scheme. The fact that Beryl would need £75,000 to £100,000 to place her in a comparable position to her sister, Betty, does not mean that Betty is necessarily going to receive that sum from her pension fund. She may die next year in which case the cost to the pension scheme is minimal; she may live to be 100 in which case the total cost of her pension will be enormous.

Part Two – Likelihood of withdrawal

(1)   A & B are planning to set up their own business. X their employer finds out about this and dismisses them forthwith. The Tribunal find that the dismissal is unfair since neither A nor B were in breach of any contractual obligation and neither had the opportunity of giving any explanation of their actions before they were dismissed. However it is accepted that they were intending to set up their own business and would have left X's employment in any event. By the time of the hearing their new business is trading. Since they would have left X's employment anyway there is no significant loss on enhancement of accrued pension rights arising from the dismissal.

(2)   C has been unfairly dismissed. He had been a salesman with the respondent company for 3 years. He is 28 years of age. The Tribunal conclude that given his age and the general mobility of salesmen, which has been illustrated by his own career pattern, he would have left of his own accord within 12 months. The Tribunal follow the recommendation (made in paragraph 10.14) and award no compensation for the loss of enhancement of accrued pension rights.

(3)   D had been employed for 15 years when he was dismissed. He is 52 years of age and had been earning £14,000 a year. The Tribunal accept his evidence that he had no intention of leaving the respondent company. However D admits that it was unlikely he would have continued to work to 65, the normal retirement age of that company's scheme. His wife (who is older than he is) is a doctor and earns much more than he does. D accepts that he would probably have resigned when his wife retired as they would have been financially secure and they intended to join their only child who lives in Australia. On the evidence

before it, the Tribunal conclude that there would have been little prospect of D leaving his employment for five years but thereafter there was an increasing likelihood of his leaving so that there was a near certainty he would have left within 10 years. In assessing the prospects of withdrawal the Tribunal has to give weight to these two findings of fact.

(4) E has been with the company for twenty-five years. He is 53 years of age. The Tribunal accept his evidence that it was his intention to stay with the company for the rest of his working life. A Tribunal might well conclude that the percentage chance of his having left the company (other than by death or disability) before retirement was small. Consequently any reduction from the sum produced by the application of the formula should be modest.

APPENDIX P
Ready Reckoner for Redundancy Payments

To use the Table—read off employee's age and number of complete years service. Any week which began before the employee attained the age of 18 does not count. The Table will then show how many weeks' pay the employee is entitled to. The Table may also be used to calculate the basic award for unfair dismissal purposes, but in that case service before the age of 18 does count. Table follows overleaf.

For an employee aged between 64 and 65, the cash amount due is to be reduced by one-twelfth for every complete month by which the age exceeds 64.

AGE (years)	SERVICE (years) 2	3	4	5	6	7	8	9	10	11	12	13	14	15	16	17	18	19	20
20	1	1	1	1	—														
21	1	1½	1½	1½	1½	—													
22	1	1½	2	2	2	2	—												
23	1½	2	2½	3	3	3	3	—											
24	2	2½	3	3½	4	4	4	4	—										
25	2	3	3½	4	4½	5	5	5	5	—									
26	2	3	4	4½	5	5½	6	6	6	6	—								
27	2	3	4	5	5½	6	6½	7	7	7	7	—							
28	2	3	4	5	6	6½	7	7½	8	8	8	8	—						
29	2	3	4	5	6	7	7½	8	8½	9	9	9	9	—					
30	2	3	4	5	6	7	8	8½	9	9½	10	10	10	10	—				
31	2	3	4	5	6	7	8	9	9½	10	10½	11	11	11	11	—			
32	2	3	4	5	6	7	8	9	10	10½	11	11½	12	12	12	12	—		
33	2	3	4	5	6	7	8	9	10	11	11½	12	12½	13	13	13	13	—	
34	2	3	4	5	6	7	8	9	10	11	12	12½	13	13½	14	14	14	14	—
35	2	3	4	5	6	7	8	9	10	11	12	13	13½	14	14½	15	15	15	15
36	2	3	4	5	6	7	8	9	10	11	12	13	14	14½	15	15½	16	16	16
37	2	3	4	5	6	7	8	9	10	11	12	13	14	15	15½	16	16½	17	17
38	2	3	4	5	6	7	8	9	10	11	12	13	14	15	16	16½	17	17½	18
39	2	3	4	5	6	7	8	9	10	11	12	13	14	15	16	17	17½	18	18½
40	2	3	4	5	6	7	8	9	10	11	12	13	14	15	16	17	18	18½	19
41	2	3	4	5	6	7	8	9	10	11	12	13	14	15	16	17	18	19	19½
42	2½	3½	4½	5½	6½	7½	8½	9½	10½	11½	12½	13½	14½	15½	16½	17½	18½	19½	20½
43	3	4	5	6	7	8	9	10	11	12	13	14	15	16	17	18	19	20	21
44	3	4½	5½	6½	7½	8½	9½	10½	11½	12½	13½	14½	15½	16½	17½	18½	19½	20½	21½
45	3	4½	6	7	8	9	10	11	12	13	14	15	16	17	18	19	20	21	22
46	3	4½	6	7½	8½	9½	10½	11½	12½	13½	14½	15½	16½	17½	18½	19½	20½	21½	22½
47	3	4½	6	7½	9	10	11	12	13	14	15	16	17	18	19	20	21	22	23
48	3	4½	6	7½	9	10½	11½	12½	13½	14½	15½	16½	17½	18½	19½	20½	21½	22½	23½
49	3	4½	6	7½	9	10½	12	13	14	15	16	17	18	19	20	21	22	23	24
50	3	4½	6	7½	9	10½	12	13½	14½	15½	16½	17½	18½	19½	20½	21½	22½	23½	24½
51	3	4½	6	7½	9	10½	12	13½	15	16	17	18	19	20	21	22	23	24	25
52	3	4½	6	7½	9	10½	12	13½	15	16½	17½	18½	19½	20½	21½	22½	23½	24½	25½
53	3	4½	6	7½	9	10½	12	13½	15	16½	18	19	20	21	22	23	24	25	26
54	3	4½	6	7½	9	10½	12	13½	15	16½	18	19½	20½	21½	22½	23½	24½	25½	26½
55	3	4½	6	7½	9	10½	12	13½	15	16½	18	19½	21	22	23	24	25	26	27

AGE (years)	SERVICE (years)																		
	2	3	4	5	6	7	8	9	10	11	12	13	14	15	16	17	18	19	20
56	3	$4\frac{1}{2}$	6	$7\frac{1}{2}$	9	$10\frac{1}{2}$	12	$13\frac{1}{2}$	15	$16\frac{1}{2}$	18	$19\frac{1}{2}$	21	$22\frac{1}{2}$	$23\frac{1}{2}$	$24\frac{1}{2}$	$25\frac{1}{2}$	$26\frac{1}{2}$	$27\frac{1}{2}$
57	3	$4\frac{1}{2}$	6	$7\frac{1}{2}$	9	$10\frac{1}{2}$	12	$13\frac{1}{2}$	15	$16\frac{1}{2}$	18	$19\frac{1}{2}$	21	$22\frac{1}{2}$	24	25	26	27	28
58	3	$4\frac{1}{2}$	6	$7\frac{1}{2}$	9	$10\frac{1}{2}$	12	$13\frac{1}{2}$	15	$16\frac{1}{2}$	18	$19\frac{1}{2}$	21	$22\frac{1}{2}$	24	$25\frac{1}{2}$	$26\frac{1}{2}$	$27\frac{1}{2}$	$28\frac{1}{2}$
59	3	$4\frac{1}{2}$	6	$7\frac{1}{2}$	9	$10\frac{1}{2}$	12	$13\frac{1}{2}$	15	$16\frac{1}{2}$	18	$19\frac{1}{2}$	21	$22\frac{1}{2}$	24	$25\frac{1}{2}$	27	28	29
60	3	$4\frac{1}{2}$	6	$7\frac{1}{2}$	9	$10\frac{1}{2}$	12	$13\frac{1}{2}$	15	$16\frac{1}{2}$	18	$19\frac{1}{2}$	21	$22\frac{1}{2}$	24	$25\frac{1}{2}$	27	$28\frac{1}{2}$	$29\frac{1}{2}$
61	3	$4\frac{1}{2}$	6	$7\frac{1}{2}$	9	$10\frac{1}{2}$	12	$13\frac{1}{2}$	15	$16\frac{1}{2}$	18	$19\frac{1}{2}$	21	$22\frac{1}{2}$	24	$25\frac{1}{2}$	27	$28\frac{1}{2}$	30
62	3	$4\frac{1}{2}$	6	$7\frac{1}{2}$	9	$10\frac{1}{2}$	12	$13\frac{1}{2}$	15	$16\frac{1}{2}$	18	$19\frac{1}{2}$	21	$22\frac{1}{2}$	24	$25\frac{1}{2}$	27	$28\frac{1}{2}$	30
63	3	$4\frac{1}{2}$	6	$7\frac{1}{2}$	9	$10\frac{1}{2}$	12	$13\frac{1}{2}$	15	$16\frac{1}{2}$	18	$19\frac{1}{2}$	21	$22\frac{1}{2}$	24	$25\frac{1}{2}$	27	$28\frac{1}{2}$	30
64	3	$4\frac{1}{2}$	6	$7\frac{1}{2}$	9	$10\frac{1}{2}$	12	$13\frac{1}{2}$	15	$16\frac{1}{2}$	18	$19\frac{1}{2}$	21	$22\frac{1}{2}$	24	$25\frac{1}{2}$	27	$28\frac{1}{2}$	30

(Crown Copyright reproduced by permission of the Controller of Her Majesty's Stationery Office from "Ready Reckoner for Redundancy Payments" (RPL 2)).

Index